IN THE LOOP

IN THE LOOP

A Political and Economic History of San Antonio

DAVID R. JOHNSON

Maverick Books
Trinity University Press
SAN ANTONIO

Maverick Books, an imprint of
Trinity University Press
San Antonio, Texas 78212

Book design by BookMatters
Cover design by Rebecca Lown

San Antonio map, chapter 1, created by Ivan Ventura in consultation with Ian Caine and Rebecca Walter

ISBN 978-1-59534-922-4 hardcover
ISBN 978-1-59534-923-1 ebook

Trinity University Press strives to produce its books using methods and materials in an environmentally sensitive manner. We favor working with manufacturers that practice sustainable management of all natural resources, produce paper using recycled stock, and manage forests with the best possible practices for people, biodiversity, and sustainability. The press is a member of the Green Press Initiative, a nonprofit program dedicated to supporting publishers in their efforts to reduce their impacts on endangered forests, climate change, and forest-dependent communities.

The paper used in this publication meets the minimum requirements of the American National Standard for Information Sciences—Permanence of Paper for Printed Library Materials, ansi 39.48-1992.

CIP data on file at the Library of Congress

30 29 28 27 26 | 5 4 3 2

To Elizabeth Sureau Thomas
Our own native Texan
And to her native Texans
Zach, Graham, Dean, and Eila

CONTENTS

Introduction

When I first began to explore San Antonio's past in the late 1970s, I was intrigued by the contradiction between the city's size and its small-town "feel." It was a large city, but it did not act like one. It lacked the brash aggressiveness of Chicago, a much larger city, and the cosmopolitan sophistication of New Orleans, a smaller city, where I had previously lived. Business leaders were obviously proud of San Antonio, but they did not seem particularly interested in being actively involved in promoting its development. Local politics, on the other hand, roiled with passionate conflicts about North Side development and West Side service deficiencies, suggesting serious disagreements about the state of the city.

The contrast between complacency and conflict would eventually provide clues about San Antonio's development as I began to seek answers to the question of why the city had grown so large without acquiring the amenities and resources that its size implied it should have. My search for the sources of the ideas and events that created San Antonio took me much farther back in time than I had originally expected. I eventually discovered that I had accidentally arrived at a particularly decisive moment in the community's history, and understanding just how important that moment was required a detailed exploration of its rich and complicated past to explain how and why the city grew the way it did.

San Antonio's growth is of course part of a larger story of America's cities. At a basic level, growth requires that a city continuously attract more residents. Attractiveness is a complicated issue, but jobs are at its heart. San Antonio, and Texas, joined the Union at a point when the national economy had begun to industrialize, which created a demand for huge numbers of factory workers who had to be fed. That led to the need to increase food production; farming became more mechanized, and the efficiency of machinery freed increasing numbers of farm workers to join the march into cities in search of work. Some cities assumed roles as organizers, collectors, and distributors for the industrial economy. And those local economies that created the most jobs attracted more of those mobile Americans and immigrants than their competitors, causing those cities to grow at astonishing rates. Chicago, for instance, doubled its population every ten years until 1890, when it became home to a million people.

Industrialization was a national phenomenon that prompted the development of specialized regions. Texas integrated into the national industrial economy by becoming an important source of raw materials and food to feed both machines and workers living elsewhere. Its role as a large wholesale center encouraged urban growth but also limited the kinds of work opportunities that its cities could offer prior to World War II. Dallas, Houston, and San Antonio competed to become the dominant wholesaling center in the state, while Galveston tried, but failed, to become a major port.

National economic trends continued to shape Texas's urban development through the twentieth century, with the most dramatic effects emerging with the onset of World War II. Supplying the weapons to fight the war created a huge demand for workers that encouraged massive population movements toward new job opportunities. The evolution of sophisticated weaponry also stimulated technological and scientific revolution that launched a shift toward service industries that relied heavily on university research for their success after 1945. World War II also transformed the federal government into a major influence in the national economy. The government's needs and policies dramatically affected the development of Texas cities, creating unprecedented opportunities for growth.

The national economy provided the basic framework for Texas cities to compete among themselves for the honor of becoming the state's largest city. Local residents, however, had to make their own decisions about how best to take advantage of the opportunities that the national economy offered. Some residents could establish businesses whose labor needs would increase jobs; they could also organize their hinterlands to exercise control over raw materials and food destined for the national market. They needed help, however, with the elusive task of making their city more attractive to potential residents, especially wealthy investors or middle-class citizens who expected certain urban amenities if they were going to move to town. Businessmen could deal with some aspects of attractiveness on their own, but others required help from local government. Improvements in the physical appearance of cities through such innovations as better street paving, and in public health with the introduction of water and sewer systems, were proliferating in the late nineteenth century, and the need for such improvements only increased with population growth in the twentieth century.

Such improvements required public funding, which meant that government had an essential role in the competition between cities. Theoretically an alliance between businessmen and politicians was an inevitable necessity. In fact, such alliances were so common that they became a trait of American culture labeled "boosterism." Booster coalitions worked to improve their city's competitive advantage by increasing its attractiveness. National political and economic developments, such as the proliferation of defense plants in World War II, helped their efforts, but oftentimes boosters had to focus on keeping up with their competition in providing modern conveniences. In San Antonio, however, boosters were rare, and their rarity became an important reason for the ways in which the city developed. By the 1970s San Antonio was a large, relatively successful city with an economy deeply dependent on the military. The lack of economic diversity affected basic city services, public policies discriminated against minority residents, and low-income residents had little money to support a broad range of amenities that made city life enjoyable for wealthier individuals.

Many cities at the time found themselves in similar circumstances, but San Antonio was more fortunate than most in finding solutions, or the beginnings of solutions, to its problems. Political turmoil provided an opportunity for new directions in public policies, and new leadership organized a booster coalition that sought quite literally to develop a more dynamic economy and, by extension, a more dynamic city. The emergence of that coalition was an extraordinary event in San Antonio's history, with consequences that helped create a very different city. I hope that telling the story of San Antonio's development from its origins will provide an understanding of what they have achieved.

ONE

The Birth of Boosterism

1718–1844

On March 9, 1844, James Dunn, coroner for Bexar County, stood on the steps of the old colonial courthouse in San Antonio's Main Plaza to auction a house and lot located just a few yards away at the plaza's northwest corner. It was a prime piece of property, eleven by fifty-two yards fronting on Main (later Commerce) Street, in the center of town. The property had become available for sale because its owner, Juan Seguín, defaulted on a loan from the mercantile firm of George T. Howard and Duncan C. Ogden, which sued to recover its money. Shortly after Dunn opened the bidding, Samuel A. Maverick offered what turned out to be the winning bid: $533.33.[1]

Although superficially just another routine foreclosure to settle legal obligations between businessmen, this sale was instead a defiant act of faith in the town's future. But San Antonio had been an isolated frontier community for more than a hundred years. Considering its imperfect location, small size, and lack of local economic opportunities, it should not, in theory, have survived at all.[2] Its survival had depended on its role as a political outpost for Spanish imperial and then, after 1824, Mexican national interests. That role disappeared in 1836 with Texas's successful revolt against the Mexican government. For the next nine years San Antonians had practically no opportunities for economic development despite the wishful thinking of their leaders. When Maverick risked his capital on Seguín's empty house, San Antonio was teetering on the brink of extinction. This dire state was not simply due to the political and military turmoil of the Texas Republic. Problems with the town's location, with attracting settlers, and with the vagaries of Spanish imperial and Mexican national policies had severely hindered urban development for more than a hundred years.

Competition between the Spanish, French, and English colonial empires encouraged the creation of settlements to assert control over frontier areas. French incursions into Florida in the mid-sixteenth century, in particular, precipitated a long, albeit episodic, struggle with Spain for control of the Gulf Coast. That struggle grew more serious when the French founded Mobile (1698) and New Orleans (1718). With the French so solidly established on their border, Spanish imperial officials decided that they needed to enhance their frontier defenses in Texas to protect the heartland of their empire.[3]

They adopted, at least on paper, a systematic approach to defending Texas. During the planning stages of this ambitious project several expeditions in the late seventeenth and early eighteenth centuries had identified possible sites for towns. Recognizing that the size of the province required multiple settlements, planners incorporated information from those expeditions into their plans and designed a rudimentary urban system for Texas. In effect, these imperial officials became San Antonio's first boosters because they needed urban development to help defend their frontier.

In 1717 they first built a mission in far northeastern Texas, close to Natchitoches, a French outpost, as a boundary marker for their presumed border with their rival. Named Los Adaes, the mission collapsed in a face of a French military probe in 1719 and had to be reestablished in 1721—this time with a presidio to provide protection. In the meantime a small group of soldiers and missionaries founded a presidio and the Mission San Antonio de Valero in late April 1718, on a site with an abundant water supply some 180 miles from the Texas coast. Finally, to protect the coastline, a military detachment established a presidio at La Bahía on the site of an abandoned French fort on what is modern-day Matagorda Bay in April 1721.[4]

This rudimentary provincial urban system suffered from a number of important problems. Its remoteness from the imperial center at Mexico City challenged common sense regarding town development, which depended on increasing population and expanding markets for success. New Spain, however, had a shortage of people willing to leave the relative comforts of established communities to live on a remote frontier. And unfortunately the closest markets were in Louisiana, but the Spanish viceroy prohibited trading with the French, complicating the task of building local economies. The sheer size of Texas also created a serious obstacle to development. Shipping local products to distant markets, friendly or otherwise, would be a major challenge because the costs of overland transportation might exceed potential profits. Security for urban development would prove equally challenging. The French military probe against Los Adaes demonstrated the reality of how fragile this planned urban system really was, and the Apaches and Comanches posed a similar threat to San Antonio.

Spanish planners showed some awareness of these difficulties in developing a strategic plan that the viceroy had approved in 1714. They proposed a rudimentary road system to connect the settlements and adopted a methodical approach to local development at least in San Antonio. Franciscan priests would create the preconditions for urban development by first converting the local Native Americans to Christianity and then transforming them into a pliable workforce. Since that process would take some time—the planners estimated ten years—the army would provide protection to the missionaries with troops living in an adjacent presidio. Following pacification of the natives, the viceroy would initiate the second phase by recruiting settlers for San Antonio who would have ready access to a docile workforce to help them with city-building. According to the plan, the town could then evolve from the mission and presidio complexes into a civilian political center that would cement Spanish control over their vast northern province.[5]

The planners also relied on the powers of New Spain's central government in Mexico City to place these fledgling urban outposts on life support. Imperial politics dictated that these tiny settlements must survive, so the viceroy issued orders for subsidies. At least on paper, his plan had a tidy solution to each new settlement's isolation that relied on the military to create the basis for a local economy. In San Antonio, for instance, the soldiers would guarantee its security and their monthly payroll would inject cash into the economy when they bought foodstuffs from local farmers. Civilian settlers, who accompanied the military contingent that founded San Antonio, received a salary, livestock, and supplies from the viceroy to sustain them while they adapted the land to commercial farming.[6] In effect, viceregal planning assumed these communities could survive their initial period of development by creating hermetically sealed local economies that relied on imperial subsidies as a substitute for a trade network. On paper, it was a reasonable idea for dealing with a complicated problem that would work as long as the subsidies arrived in a timely fashion—and the French and hostile Native Americans remained cooperative.

Years of planning, however, quickly came to naught. Los Adaes was so remote from Spanish support that its residents, from necessity, quickly developed trade with the nearby French outpost in order to survive. Since Spanish laws forbade such trade, the settlers technically had created an economy based on smuggling. Ignoring that, or perhaps hoping to shame the Los Adaesans into respectability, the viceroy named their settlement the capital of the province of Texas in 1729. La Bahía's presidio, followed by its mission, changed locations at least twice, moving inland despite its obligation to defend the bay and exact customs charges from the occasional trade ship. San Antonio's small garrison could not subdue the Apaches and Comanches, who raided the community with relative impunity in the early decades of its existence.[7] In these conditions, San Antonio could not attract many residents. Its location far from the principal Spanish settlements to the south, and the inability to generate local economic activity on any significant scale, meant that San Antonio existed in a sort of limbo.

The Spanish viceroy had not, however, forgotten his imperial plan for Texas. Assuming that the missionaries had accomplished their responsibility for converting local Native Americans into a pliable workforce by the late 1720s, he organized a search for additional settlers willing to locate in San Antonio. To attract volunteers, and to implement Spanish policies that required civilian settlements to have an elite who was loyal to and protective of imperial interests, the viceroy offered social promotions to anyone willing to undertake the long journey. Even that did not entice a large number of volunteers, but fifty-five freshly minted hidalgos from the Canary Islands accepted the offer and walked into San Antonio in March 1731.

The new arrivals found conditions somewhat less than advertised. In addition to the primitive living conditions, they discovered that the promised labor force did not exist. Franciscans at the five missions adamantly refused to allow their Native American converts to work for the new arrivals, just as they had rejected demands from the military commander for help in constructing the presidio's buildings. As a result, the presidio remained unfortified. And instead of providing access to a pliable workforce, the Canary Islanders found that the missionaries had created a separate self-contained series of communities with significant economic assets of land and livestock that sold their surplus to the garrison, the only available market for local products. The Franciscans had become the beneficiaries of the viceroy's plan for a hermetically sealed economy, which affronted the Canary Islanders who had assumed they would have that role.[8]

Not surprisingly, relations between civilians, priests, and soldiers in San Antonio became strained and remained so for many years. In the meantime the imperial government launched yet another ambitious settlement effort, focusing this time on the region along the Rio Grande to found towns such as Laredo (1755) to "thicken" the nascent urban system of Texas. Unfortunately the government also encouraged the creation of numerous latifundia that engaged in large-scale cattle raising. As in California, these large ranches needed few employees and produced most of their own necessities, thus stunting market opportunities for either the newly founded towns or older settlements such as San Antonio.[9]

Imperial politics took a dramatic turn in 1763 when the British victory over France in the Seven Years' War forced the French to cede Louisiana to Spain. Rethinking their plans for Texas, the viceroy made a series of decisions that increased San Antonio's population to about two thousand residents. First he decided to abandon Los Adaes and resettle its residents in San Antonio. He also named San Antonio as the new capital of the province in 1772. Some of the Los Adaesans returned to East Texas in the 1770s to resettle at Nacogdoches, the site of the initial missions in that area, but many others became permanent residents of San Antonio. Their arrival created the largest single increase in the town's population in the colonial period.[10]

Although these imperial changes did not solve San Antonio's basic problems, particularly the need for better political relations and economic ties with Mexico City, they did encourage the emergence of local boosterism as some residents sought to reorganize and diversify the local economy. Seeking farms to support themselves, the Los Adaesans petitioned the crown for land, apparently because the Canary Islanders could not or would not accommodate their needs. Crown officials responded by ordering secularization of Mission San Antonio de Valero in 1779, although local authorities ignored the order while the padres fought secularization for years. They were, though, in an increasingly precarious position. Disease had inflicted such a toll on the missionaries' charges that the missions could not sustain themselves. And the padres' continuing unpopularity among other residents undermined their previously formidable position in the community, allowing secularizing to begin in 1793.

Secularization transferred valuable economic resources from the padres to the civilian population by giving them access to farmland east of the San

Antonio River for the first time. Many of the Los Adaesans, for example, settled on land north of the Alamo. In addition, the garrison finally acquired its presidio when the local commander moved his men into the Alamo.[11]

While the conflict over control of mission resources worked toward a resolution, other San Antonians began efforts to rid themselves of their hermetically sealed economy through local initiatives. Imitating the missionaries, a few residents had begun ranching operations along the river between San Antonio and La Bahía by the 1760s, an effort that dovetailed nicely with the sudden addition of Louisiana—and New Orleans—to the Spanish empire. Some San Antonians responded by organizing an occasional cattle drive to that city, which created what became a long-standing relationship with the distant market.

Other residents took it upon themselves to negotiate treaties with the Comanches, which not only improved the community's safety but also encouraged regular trade with them. The Comanches over time became accustomed to visiting town to acquire trade goods and to pay local artisans for such things as gun repairs. Although the monetary value of their business remains elusive, it justified the construction of a rather large building in the loop of the river—a sort of early tourist hotel—that housed tribesmen during their visits to town.[12]

The individuals who participated in these early ventures did not constitute a separate mercantile community. Instead they represented the first generation of native San Antonians who had learned from practical experience the limitations of depending on a distant and often indifferent imperial government for their economic well-being. They had recognized that Spain's acquisition of Louisiana presented an opportunity to export cattle, a plentiful local product, to create trade links with New Orleans. Although their activities did not cause additional population growth, that initiative, combined with their trade with the Comanches and other tribes, had nonetheless begun to extend San Antonio's influence over its potential hinterland. These initiatives encouraged some residents to assume a more active role in their community's future development.

Despite these nascent efforts, San Antonio survived primarily because of its function as a provincial political center. That role justified the presence of important colonial officials who lent prestige to the town as well as opportunities for the local elite to lobby them for imperial favors that would improve San Antonio's economic prospects. In addition, that role made the town the province's major military center, and the garrison continued to be the principal source of income for local farmers. Officials, though, responded infrequently to pleas to ease imperial restrictions on trade and frequently failed to pay the garrison's payroll, undermining the soldiers' ability to perform their economic role in the community. Even more importantly, when Napoleon forced the Spanish to return Louisiana to France, and then sold the territory to the Americans in 1803, Spain ended trade with New Orleans, further retarding local development efforts.

By the early nineteenth century a long history of neglect punctuated with periods of flawed centralized planning efforts to create an urban system in Texas helped transform San Antonio into a hotbed of opposition to imperial rule. A failed revolt from 1811 to 1813 resulted in a severe repression that included many executions and exile for a number of prominent local leaders. San Antonians supported Mexican independence in 1821 in the hope that a federal system for the new nation would create more local autonomy to promote economic development. In general, however, the central government continued the imperial practice of managing the province from afar in ways that did not encourage local initiatives.[13]

With federal policies hindering development opportunities in central Texas, some San Antonians had turned to smuggling as a source of income. Government controls of tobacco sales, for instance, provided a classic opportunity for illegal trading. Demand for tobacco in Mexico created an illegal market in which smugglers could provide customers with more ready access at prices lower than the regulated market. Given its legal status, the role of smuggling in San Antonio's economy is impossible to measure, but government protests over smuggling indicate that it had become a common feature of the feeble trade network as early as the 1820s.[14]

On the other hand, both the San Antonio ayuntamiento (city council) and the Mexican government agreed that increasing the population of Texas was crucial to its future development. Since Mexican frontier settlements had found it difficult to attract native residents and American settlers were already expressing considerable interest in the province, the Mexican government authorized the empresario program in a controlled (at least officially) experiment in population growth in March 1824. The enabling legislation stipulated that American immigrants had to accept Catholicism, live in designated areas, and eschew slavery, but they would otherwise be free to develop their colonies. Conceptually this was a bold, calculated risk that attempted to balance the need for significant population growth in Texas against the possibility that these settlers might eventually pose a threat to Mexican territorial integrity.[15]

Stephen F. Austin was the most successful of the empresarios because he made a careful survey of possible sites and in 1826 selected an area along the shallow rivers that emptied into the Gulf of Mexico, where there was good land for cotton cultivation. Shortly thereafter cotton became a major export. That failed to solve San Antonio's development problems, however, because the town had no economic ties to the emerging cotton economy on the coast.[16]

Although supportive of the empresario system despite its minimal local impact, the town's leaders continued to press for their own development program. They repeatedly petitioned the central government for help in promoting the local economy. Although not indifferent to their pleas for help, the central government became increasingly concerned about the numbers of Americans moving into Texas and sought ways to regulate these immigrants—a policy shift that threatened the underlying assumption that population growth was the key to future prosperity for the region. In a move that alarmed San Antonians, the government retracted its approval for a port of entry on Matagorda Bay in 1827 and required all trade to pass through a port Stephen Austin had created on Galveston Island.[17]

Better control over imports helped the Mexican government, but it also dampened local urban development by creating the basis for a rival urban center. In the aftermath of the failed rebellion against Spanish rule in 1813, some of the survivors had fled to New Orleans. While in exile, they became acquainted with various businessmen keen to develop trade with Texas, some of whom expressed their intention to move to San Antonio. José Cassiano, an Italian by birth who had considerable experience in commercial activities, was one of these businessmen who did move to town, where he quickly became one of its most important merchants because of his access to credit and trade goods in New Orleans. Some exiles who returned home to San Antonio also received appointments as tax or trade officials that gave them opportunities to promote San Antonio's economy. During the 1820s Tejanos like Ramón Músquiz, José and Ángel Navarro, Juan M.

de Veramendi, and Erasmo and Juan Seguín emerged as public officials and businessmen who consistently promoted economic development. While not numerous—San Antonio was after all still a small town—they had inherited from their late eighteenth-century predecessors the belief that local effort had an important role to play in their town's growth.[18]

None of these initiatives, though, created enough economic activity to alter San Antonio's fundamental problems with isolation. Goods from New Orleans trade trickled into town, with long periods between shipments, and transportation costs inflated their prices so that few local residents could afford them. Peaceful relations with the Comanches continued to generate some trade, but they remained rather self-reliant, which limited their need for the town's services. Most San Antonio residents earned their living through subsistence farming, producing only enough for themselves and their families, with an occasional small surplus that they could exchange with their neighbors.

These circumstances limited the possibilities for more dynamic expansion. When Colonel Juan Almonte conducted an official survey of San Antonio's prospects in 1834, he concluded that "extensive undertakings cannot be entered upon in Bexar, as there is no individual capital exceeding $10,000. All the provisions raised by the local inhabitants are consumed in the district.... The whole export trade is confined to 8,000 to 10,000 skins of various kinds, and the imports to a few articles from New Orleans, which are exchanged in San Antonio for peltry or currency."[19]

Absent significant alternatives, the town continued to rely heavily on the local garrison, whose payroll remained the most important source of circulating currency until the Texas Revolution. When the Mexican Revolution dramatically disrupted delivery of that payroll in 1821, the Tejano elite demonstrated their recognition of its importance, and their own commitment to their hometown, by creating the National Bank of Texas. For the next two years the bank performed only one function: issuing to the soldiers scrip that served as local currency until the new Mexican government could resume cash deliveries. Once the financial institution had served its purpose, its creators dissolved the bank. In effect, a local initiative in the midst of a national crisis preserved the town's most valuable economic asset.[20]

Despite such efforts, the absence of reliable opportunities for development caused a steady decline in San Antonio's population. By 1836 towns closer to the coast, and closer to the American colonies, had begun to develop more rapidly than San Antonio. San Felipe de Austin, founded as the capital of Austin's grant, was three times larger than San Antonio, and La Bahía—now Goliad—had grown significantly because of the American presence. Nacogdoches also prospered in this period, continuing to be a lucrative hub for smuggling. A small urban system without many economic links to San Antonio had emerged in East Texas. The town was increasingly less central to the focus of urban development in Texas and was therefore in danger of becoming irrelevant.[21]

San Antonio's small, but ambitious business elite seemed not to notice the town's declining fortunes, perhaps because the community remained the province's capital. These leaders' frustrations with the central government's refusal to grant them greater economic autonomy, however, made San Antonio a center of opposition to the Mexican government's drift toward greater centralization in the early 1830s. Several members of the business community eventually became staunch supporters of independence from Mexico, participating in crucial events that led to the revolution of 1836.

Frustrations over economic issues did not by themselves drive some Tejanos toward independence. Support for independence within San Antonio may well have evolved as a natural corollary to the emergence of a Tejano identity. San Antonio's isolation created a peculiar situation in which its residents, despite their Mexican origins, had forged a sense of communal distinctiveness within that heritage.[22]

That sense of difference created a cultural context for the local elite's interest in their town's development. Like their American city-booster counterparts, they were committed to growing their hometown. Inspired by that vision, the elite had learned how to use their social status in provincial Mexican politics to lobby for changes in laws and government policies that could potentially enhance San Antonio's opportunities for growth. Considering that centralized government planning had created the rationale for San Antonio in the first place and had then become an obstacle to local development efforts, their focus on altering the political framework for economic development made sense.

Choosing to support independence, of course, constituted the ultimate change in the political framework. With independence the town would lose the military garrison that had sustained the local economy for so long. San Antonio would have to create city-building services in a new political culture that valued individual and local initiatives over imperial or national control of economic development. In addition, new towns like Galveston and Houston were eager to compete with San Antonio to dominate the would-be republic's economy. Local initiatives to promote growth mattered more than they ever had prior to 1836.[23] The rapid growth of the American population in East Texas, and the emergence of a more vigorous urban system temptingly just beyond San Antonio's reach, gave some assurances that independence from Mexico could work to the Tejano town's advantage. In order to succeed, though, the local elite needed to establish a coalition with Americans so they could continue their development activities in the aftermath of the revolution.

Here history seemed to be on their side. They had supported American colonization prior to 1836, some of their most prominent members had been personally involved in earlier revolts, and they already had working relationships with some Americans due to their efforts to create ties to the New Orleans market.

And, as a practical matter, these Tejanos had a great deal to offer prospective partners in urban development. They had firm control over San Antonio's major assets, including its political system, its social networks, and its economic resources. Furthermore, at a time when Americans would still be a minority in town, they would need the cooperation of the elites as they integrated into this old, established community. In fact, Americans would in some cases display an understanding of those advantages by marrying into San Antonio's elite families.

Equally important, San Antonio, unlike Houston or Galveston, neither of which had existed prior to 1836, had cultural characteristics that could potentially affect future development initiatives. The Spanish approach to the role and scope of public authority in cities had been an integral part of the fabric of town life prior to 1836. The Laws of the Indies granted to municipal government control over two key city-building resources: land and water. In effect, those two resources had been public, not private, property since 1718. For more than a hundred years San Antonio's Tejano elite had relied on their power over those resources to shape the local environment in particular ways.

Imperial town planning laws stipulated that every town should have a grid pattern that would create an orderly community physically arranged to reflect the political and social order of Spanish society. The laws required that all the buildings intended to display and enforce public authority—a main church, government buildings, and residences of local officials—should be arranged around a central plaza, creating a religious and political (but not economic) focal point for the community.

Conforming to these strictures took several years, as the components that formed San Antonio came together slowly. Initially the military commander had placed his garrison on a site close to the source of the San Antonio River; Franciscans located the Mission San Antonio de Valero at the source of San Pedro Creek. When, for various reasons, these original sites proved unsatisfactory in the early 1720s, the commander moved the presidio downstream to the west side of a great bend in the river while the mission moved to the east bank. Facing each other across the river, both institutions now bracketed the area that would become the civilian center of the settlement.[24]

When the Canary Islanders arrived in 1731, they established the villa San Fernando de Bexar between those two institutions. This arrangement finally completed the original, loosely formed grid for the town. This piecemeal development caused some alterations in the basic plan the Laws of the Indies mandated. When the Canary Islanders built their church in the middle of the area the presidio and the new civilians occupied, they created two public squares rather than the single one required by law. The military compound would become the Plaza de las Armas while the other would be the Plaza de las Islas. Instead of a unified design that emphasized military, government, and church control over the community, the two-plaza design isolated the military portion of the community. Since the Canary Islanders controlled both the church and the town's government, that outcome may well have been an intentional effort to declare who was really in charge of San Antonio.[25]

Once settled, the Canary Islanders also organized the first ayuntamiento and assumed control of the town's public lands. Since Mission Valero owned the east bank of the river at the time and a second mission, San Juan, had chosen a site close to the river on the west bank well south of the Plaza de las Islas, the ayuntamiento initially controlled most of the west bank of the settlement as well as a large territory surrounding the town that the original grant defined as San Antonio's hinterland. The islanders used their control over the city council to regulate land use in and outside of town. Residents had to petition the council to buy town lots and ranchland, and the islanders tended to reserve the best lots for themselves, which created a rudimentary elite neighborhood north of the Plaza de las Islas. By the early nineteenth century the council had redesigned the original oblong shape of that plaza into a more orderly square and was also approving the construction of modest residences among the military buildings at the western end of the Plaza de las Armas. Both activities illustrated the ways local elites sometimes used the political authority they enjoyed in the Spanish colonial system to adapt its planning mandates to their own needs.[26]

Since San Antonio did not experience vigorous economic or population growth at any time prior to 1836, its physical design changed little over the ensuing decades. Residents constructed housing that accommodated the climate and their minimal resources. The elite built occasionally with stone, though more often with adobe. Most residents made do with humble jacals of wood reinforced with mud. Security considerations dictated that the residents concentrate together, and there seems to have been little segregation of economic and residential functions into separate areas of the town. Jacals intermingled with adobe and stone houses; civilians built homes in the Plaza de las Armas, ignoring its military role; and merchants typically did not have separate stores, usually operating their businesses out of their homes.[27]

Public control of land, despite its modest results, had been a long tradition by the time of the republic, and since the Texas constitution confirmed Mexican legal practices, the town of San Antonio continued to own a large amount of the land American city-builders needed for their own plans. The Tejano elite understood the legal and cultural relationships between the public ownership of community land and a resident's private rights to use his or her land productively within that matrix.

Americans, though, did not appreciate the idea of public ownership of urban land. Their culture defined land as a private, not public, asset. That assumption created much of the dynamism that characterized mid-nineteenth-century urban development in the United States. In San Antonio that assumption would complicate city-building once Americans assumed control of the town.

By this point, city-builders across the United States had pioneered antebellum American territorial and economic expansion, creating opportunities for enormous personal and community wealth to be made in the process. With large numbers of people tramping over the Appalachians in search of opportunity, aggressive competition between seaboard cities seeking to dominate emerging western markets, and a generous national policy regarding the sale of western lands, potential city-builders had a supportive environment for risking their capital.[28]

Speculators working ahead of actual settlers determined the location for a town and platted the site using a simple grid pattern. Unlike the Spanish use of the grid to design towns, these speculators paid as little attention as possible to such issues as the location of public buildings. Individual speculators, not some governmental authority, selected a town site and applied the grid template to it because the grid's regularity allowed them to carve its standardized blocks into the largest possible number of lots. For them, the design of these grids maximized sales, not town planning.[29]

With tens of thousands of Americans moving westward, speculators easily found a pool of eager customers for each of their towns' lots. Businessmen and workers bought lots and moved into the towns to begin the more arduous task of actually building a city. This process produced cities like Cincinnati, Chicago, and Memphis, while hundreds of smaller towns sprung up seemingly overnight. Successful cities—and not all were successful—provided examples of what could be accomplished in the West's virgin lands, creating high expectations among those seeking to identify and profit from the next great urban project.[30]

Much of that development rested on two assumptions: that the national government had an obligation to make public lands available to its citizens as quickly and as cheaply as possible, and that the acquisition of public land imposed no obligation to consider public needs on the buyers. Development also rested on the presumption that there were no prior restraints or claims on western lands. Yet in central Texas, San Antonio's Tejano residents did in fact have a valid prior claim on the community's land as well as a cultural tradition that government had the right to regulate its use. Negotiating a resolution of the differences between these two conflicting cultural approaches to land ownership would become a major issue in the town after 1836.

Whatever plans the newcomers might have to transform San Antonio into an American city, they would have to deal with an important legacy of the Tejano era: the acequia system. Spanish planners had expected San Antonio to become an agricultural center in addition to serving military and religious functions. Accomplishing that required extensive modifications of the existing waterways. The San Antonio River originated slightly more than three miles north of town, and San Pedro Creek sprang from springs located roughly two miles southwest of the river's source. Running roughly parallel to each other in a south-southeasterly direction, they provided dual axes defining a potentially rich watershed for agriculture. Residents, however, needed to divert that water onto their particular farms.

The Spanish had become expert in the art of constructing irrigation systems long before their conquest of Central and South America. They built acequias, which relied on gravity to move water, by astute analysis of the contours of a locality's land. Irrigation "ditches" therefore tended to wander across a landscape to take advantage of those contours. Despite their rather unimpressive physical appearance—narrow and fairly shallow—acequias required considerable engineering skill to ensure the continuous movement of water.[31]

Missionaries at San Antonio de Valero and San José (founded in 1720) organized the first efforts to create an acequia system. The first ditch, begun east of the San Antonio River in the 1720s, began near the source of the river and wound southward to create a subset of acequias that could irrigate most of their lands. When the other missions moved south of town in the 1730s, they constructed their own acequias. On the west side, settlers tapped San Pedro Springs in 1748 to provide water for the Acequia Madre, which ran southward between the river and the creek, passed through town, and connected with the river about three miles south. The Acequia Madre supplied civilian residents with drinking water and irrigated the original farming area just south of town. As the civilian population slowly expanded on the west side, the city council added the Alazán and Upper Labor Acequias to serve new farms.[32]

By the late eighteenth century the acequia system defined the settled area of the town more effectively than its rudimentary grid design. Water access determined the shape and orientation of land allocations. In the Tejano era, narrow rectangles of farmland stretched between water sources, with their length depending on the distance required for a particular farm to access water on one side and release it on the other. Since water followed the slope of the terrain, farm lot boundaries slanted on a northwest-southeast axis on both banks of the river on the north side. Farm boundaries south of the plazas on either side of the river had various orientations to accommodate the peculiarities of the terrain.

The town's residents occupied a narrow band of land less than a mile wide and approximately six miles long centered on the river. Each resident had contractually defined water rights for their individual grant of farmland. Those contracts gave explicit directions as to how much water each farmer could access on a routine basis by opening and closing his sluice gates. Access also created responsibilities. Landowners had to maintain their own portions of the irrigation system by keeping them clear of obstructions and undertaking repairs at their own expense. Thus the acequia system created both individual opportunities for self-sufficiency and a commitment to sustaining the community. Without this system even the subsistence farming that dominated the local economy would have been impossible.

Acequias were so effective in San Antonio that they supplied the community's water needs until the late nineteenth century. Managing this system as the population grew would become a major political issue in the decades after 1836 as the ditches increasingly took on the burden of being the community's sanitation system in addition to the source of its drinking water and continuing agricultural activity. In addition, this finely tuned irrigation system would complicate American efforts to redesign the urban landscape. None of the farm lots conformed to a standard grid, which would pose seemingly endless problems to creating a street grid to facilitate property sales and developing a downtown.

The Tejano elite possessed valuable experience managing the peculiarities of the town's landscape and legal system. In the early years of the republic, some Americans recognized the value of that experience and sought ways to access it. A few Americans, for instance, married into San Antonio's elite families, giving them familial connections that automatically entitled them to leadership roles in the community. Tejanos also received valuable support from the republic's legislature for their effort to create other ties to the Americans in 1837, when a new city charter required council minutes to be recorded in both English and Spanish. Francisco Ruiz, another Tejano with a history of supporting San Antonio's development, happened to be serving in the Texas Senate in 1837, and may have had a hand in establishing this requirement.[33]

However promising these marriages and legislative arrangements might have been, nothing was more important to the Tejano elites' hope to become an integral part of a new booster coalition than concrete economic and political cooperation with their new American neighbors. Given antebellum American views on ethnic groups, it is rather surprising that a bicultural booster coalition sprouted quite quickly.

Land, the most basic resource for developing a city by attracting new residents, created the glue that bound this coalition together. Having won independence, the new republic's leaders needed to establish a legal framework for land ownership, which they did in the constitution of 1836. Every adult male resident of the republic who had not left to avoid military service or who had not assisted Mexico's efforts to suppress the rebellion received a headright equivalent to 4,605 acres at no cost except for the need to pay surveyor and legal fees. These headrights did not identify a specific parcel of land. Each recipient had to locate and file their own claim, which theoretically meant any owner of a headright could claim 4,605 acres anywhere in the republic, with the exception of lands that had been acquired by private individuals prior to 1836 under the terms of Spanish laws.[34]

Superficially this constitutional provision appeared to be a generous gift to the republic's citizens. In practice, the headright system created a speculator's market in certificates. Most of the republic's residents were impoverished, illiterate Tejanos and American immigrants who did not have the capital necessary to develop raw land. Few of them even had the cash to pay surveyors and lawyers to locate land for them and register their claims. For these people, the certificates offered an opportunity to raise a little cash—a scarce commodity in post-revolution Texas—by selling their grants to the nearest (but not necessarily the highest) bidder.

These grants established the framework for a potentially massive transfer of public lands to private ownership in the shortest time possible. Speculators were not slow to notice. In scenes reminiscent of Chicago's heyday as a speculator's heaven, investors poured into the republic's towns. Unimproved town lots in Houston sold for $4,000 to $5,000 each at the height of the boom in 1837, and the city's population increased dramatically.

Land speculators also appeared quickly in San Antonio. Although some of these individuals lacked long-term commitments to San Antonio's development, the sheer number of speculators in such a small community gave them a dominant role in efforts to boost the town. They all had a common interest in acquiring and selling a lot of land as quickly as possible. Longtime residents such as José Navarro, Rafael de la Garza, Juan Seguín, and another dozen of their compatriots joined forces with longtime American residents like Nathaniel Lewis, John Smith, and Erastus (Deaf) Smith to form one group of speculators. A second group of more recent arrivals included Samuel Maverick, John James, Ludovic Colquhoun, William Jaques, and nearly seventy other newcomers from outside of Texas. In all, eighty-seven men participated in the local headright certificate market, buying exclusively from lower-class Tejanos who, at least from the available evidence, eagerly sought buyers for their claims.[35]

John Smith was the crucial bridge across the town's ethnic boundary. He had lived in San Antonio for many years, had married into the Tejano elite, and spoke fluent Spanish. He was also a lawyer and, prior to 1836, had been a land surveyor, which gave him both practical knowledge of the area surrounding San Antonio and a reputation among Tejano residents as a man they could trust. As an adopted son of the Tejano elite, he had the ability to help forge interethnic bonds in transforming the town in this new phase of city-building.[36]

Smith launched an effort to utilize the town's economic and political resources to support his and his associates' speculative ventures. He allied himself with Joseph Baker to control the processes critical to land sales. Baker had emigrated from his native Maine to Texas in 1831 and had initially settled in San Felipe de Austin, where he became secretary of the city council in 1835. After a brief venture in publishing a newspaper, he joined the Texas army and fought at San Jacinto. Moving to Austin, he became a municipal judge and an official state translator in 1836. Then in a move that probably could only occur in a fluid frontier society, Baker was elected as the first chief justice of the Bexar County court in December 1836.[37]

There is no record of how or why Baker and Smith joined forces, but when the court opened for business in 1837, Smith appeared as its first chief clerk. As the key officials of the court, Baker and Smith supervised the entire process of land speculation. County courts had assumed de facto oversight of land transactions while the legislature struggled to establish a general land office. Anyone who sold a headright needed to register the sale with the court, and the registration process required the assistance of a lawyer. The lawyers who served this need included José Navarro, Juan Seguín, and Nathaniel Lewis, members or associates of the old Tejano elite. Other lawyers like William Daingerfield and John McCreary were new arrivals. In effect, the court created a social and political environment for interethnic mingling in the context of a mutual interest in acquiring and selling land to increase personal fortunes while attracting settlers to central Texas.[38]

Smith also served three terms as San Antonio's mayor between 1837 and 1844, becoming the first of several mayors who combined politics with land speculation. Daingerfield and Samuel Maverick served one term each, and Juan Seguín also served one term. While Americans usually controlled the mayoralty, Tejanos dominated the city council during the republic era. Although control of the council no doubt reflected the fact that most voters were Tejanos who would vote for ethnic representatives, a bicultural political and economic coalition of the community's elite did emerge.[39]

Control of local government gave this coalition opportunities to improve the town's public services to encourage growth that would enhance the value of the speculators' land. The town's 1837 charter, however, had hamstrung improvement projects by mandating an "equitable and moderate" property tax as the sole source of public revenue. At that point, the Tejano elite owned most of the taxable assets and their control of the council allowed them to adopt eminently reasonable tax rates. Their American partners had no interest in high taxes either, but this left the coalition with the problem of paying for potentially expensive public improvements.

In these circumstances the town's ownership of its land under the original Spanish grant offered a useful, and fateful, solution. The coalition requested a new city charter from the republic's legislature, which obliged in January 1842. Nestled among the mostly minor changes was a new authority to sell public lands to pay for urban improvements. The council promptly authorized a sale to raise money for a bridge across the river at Main (Commerce) Street.[40]

Superficially a rather routine change, this authority in fact had profound implications. First it created a mechanism for transferring town land to private hands. Previously most speculators had dealt in headrights for land located beyond the town's public holdings. Now they gained access to land that theoretically had greater potential to appreciate in value. The first sale amounted to only twenty-three lots, but all the buyers were members of the Smith coalition, including Maverick, Bryan Callaghan, Ludovic Colquhoun, and William Jaques. Maverick was especially active, beginning to assemble an impressive amount of land around and north of the Alamo.

Broader concerns about urban development intermingled with personal advantage in changing the charter. Considering the coalition's control of the city council, it would probably have been fairly easy for individual speculators to obtain its consent to purchase town lots just as Tejano residents had done for many decades. That approach, though, would not necessarily create a fund for public works. By identifying a specific purpose for the sale of town lots in the charter, the coalition reserved the sale proceeds for urban improvements. And by requiring public auctions, they also established a mechanism for funding those projects. Originally, then, these sales supported public projects to make San Antonio more attractive to potential residents.

This approach to funding improvements would eventually have unintended consequences. With a separate source for funding public projects, the property tax in effect became the account for ordinary expenses such as governmental salaries and other routine items. This strategy ensured that property taxes remained low, which meant residents came to expect a low tax rate. By the 1850s the standard rate was one-fourth of 1 percent per $100 of assessed value. What would happen if population growth increased a demand for city services that exceeded the revenues from land sales, and taxpayers, habituated to the low property tax rate, balked at any increases? The land speculators had in effect created a context for a political culture to evolve that believed that taxes could and should remain low in perpetuity.[41]

Such problems were not necessarily obvious in 1842, and speculators mixed business and politics quite freely in their efforts to attract settlers and investors to San Antonio. Baker and Smith advertised as land agents in a Houston newspaper and recruited local clients routinely.[42]

Smith's influence also gave him opportunities to attract additional outside capital to his land purchasing. Enoch Jones, a wealthy Saint Louis merchant, visited San Antonio in 1837 to assess investment possibilities. Perhaps impressed by Smith's multiple public and private roles in the land market,

Jones entered into a formal partnership with him to invest in land. Jones represented a rare breed of investor for San Antonio at this point: an outsider with considerable venture capital willing to risk some of his fortune in the town.[43]

Although Smith and his colleagues had made a promising start on building a typical booster coalition, events beyond their control conspired to undermine their efforts. Within a year the panic of 1837 undermined the republic's principal policy for attracting large numbers of settlers. The national depression discouraged westward migration, depriving speculators of potential customers. In 1837, for instance, William Richardson paid $46,350 for more than 250,000 acres of land (eighteen cents an acre). Two years later he sold a portion of his holdings for an $8,200 loss. Samuel Maverick's wife, Mary, noted that her husband "has been investing everything in land and is still dabbling in headrights & land, but he could not sell what he bought for much more than half its cost."[44]

In the meantime the town maintained a faint economic pulse. Isolated as it was from the evolving urban economies along the coast, San Antonio's natural market remained northern Mexico. Given the distances involved and slowness of ox and mule carts, trade with Mexico remained sporadic. Mexican wagon trains made only annual pilgrimages to town. Local businessmen like Nat Lewis and John Twohig had "agencies" along the Rio Grande that served as transfer points for smuggling goods into Mexico. These tenuous arrangements generated enough profit, however, to sustain economic life without creating the basis for vigorous expansion that would allow San Antonio to compete effectively with Houston or Galveston.[45]

With the collapse of the boomlet, most of San Antonio's speculators simply disappeared. A few like Smith, James, and Maverick remained optimistic that they would still prevail—a useful, indeed essential characteristic of boosters who often had to rely on blind faith rather than rational economic analysis to succeed. Members of the Tejano elite probably remained optimistic because they had no other choice. Both sides of the potential ethnic divide continued to cooperate for their mutual benefit. Class appeared about to trump ethnicity in the conduct of the city's business, but this nascent coalition needed time to develop lasting relationships to become permanent. Whether their coalition could prosper, however, depended on political circumstances beyond their control.

Conflicting cultural traditions, local ethnic tensions, and continuing hostilities between Mexico and the Texas Republic doomed efforts to perpetuate an interethnic booster coalition in San Antonio. Juan Sequín became the lightning rod that attracted all the social tensions the coalition failed to manage.

A member of one of San Antonio's most prestigious families, Seguín had long been a leader in community affairs and an avid supporter of American immigration into Texas. He had a remarkable record of service to his hometown during the Texas Revolution. Not only did he support independence and lead troops against Santa Anna at San Jacinto, he also literally saved San Antonio from destruction. In March 1837 General Felix Huston, concerned about the possibility of new Mexican military threats, ordered the town to be evacuated and razed. Seguín, serving as the town's military commander, successfully appealed Huston's order to Sam Houston. After serving in the Texas Senate from 1838 to 1840, Seguín returned to San Antonio to become mayor in early 1841. His service to the new republic, his long friendships with Stephen F. Austin and Sam Houston, and his interest in San Antonio's development made him John Smith's essential counterpart in the critical mediation of Tejano-American relationships.[46]

Despite his impressive status and accomplishments, Seguín, and his fellow Tejanos, faced long odds in their efforts to sustain the bicultural speculator coalition. Texas's precarious relations with Mexico created a volatile sense of insecurity. Many Americans refused to believe that Tejanos could be loyal to the republic, and fundamental cultural hostilities lurked beneath the surface of ethnic relations, threatening to erupt at any time. These problems created a volatile social context in which particular incidents could easily confirm American suspicions of their new neighbors.[47]

Unfortunately for Seguín, such an incident arose early in his mayoral term. James Goodman, claiming that the president of the Texas Republic had given him Military Plaza in payment of a debt owed to him, erected a fence around it to assert his ownership. This was a bizarre claim since the president did not have the arbitrary authority to assign ownership of particular pieces of public land to settle his private debts (if such existed). As mayor, Seguín had to direct the legal process that rejected Goodman's claim. Goodman promptly became his vocal and bitter enemy and joined with some other residents nursing slights to oppose him politically.[48]

Such incidents occurred in a cultural context in San Antonio that could easily impede mutual understanding and provide men such as Goodman with grist for their political mills. Tejano culture defined a way of life that most Americans found puzzling, if not offensive. As a Catholic community, the town organized its public social rituals and work routines according to a calendar dedicated to religious and political observances. Mexican Independence Day, saints' days, and major holidays such as Easter or Christmas were occasions for major public events featuring parades, games, music, and dancing. These were opportunities for the community to celebrate and affirm its identity, while individuals could display culturally important skills such as fine horsemanship or grace in performing the fandango that won their neighbors' admiration. These festivities centered on San Fernando Cathedral in Main Plaza, which made the plaza the symbolic social and political, as well as physical, heart of the town's Tejano culture.[49]

Goodman had in effect been claiming ownership of half that heart. Fighting in and around San Antonio during the Texas War for Independence had caused a great deal of physical destruction, but the functions of the two plazas remained intact in the minds and practices of the Tejano population. In effect, Goodman's claim asserted an American intention to seize control of the town's major public spaces and to reuse them in accordance with American approaches to city-building. While a rather futile and even silly effort, Goodman's claim illustrated the potential threat that ignorance born of cultural differences posed to the Tejano elites' hopes for an ethnically integrated approach to urban development.

The next crisis profoundly damaged ethnic relations. Mexican forces had been gathering for possible action against the Texas Republic, and their commanders had identified San Antonio as the most likely target for their campaigns. Seguín's own Mexican sources kept him informed about these military preparations, and he attempted to warn his American friends about the impending threat. At an emotional meeting Seguín had called to discuss that threat, a young man accused Seguín of being insincere in his concern for his American neighbors. Provoked by this affront to his honor, Seguín impulsively resigned as mayor despite vociferous support for him by others at the meeting.[50]

General Ráfael Vásquez seized the defenseless town in March 1842. Once in control, Vásquez publicly claimed that Seguín sympathized with Mexico, probably in an effort to discredit him because Seguín had been assisting political allies in Mexico opposed to the current regime. When Vásquez withdrew, Seguín confronted an angry mob led by Goodman that accused him of spying for Mexico. François Guilbeau, a recent French immigrant, dispersed the mob while John Twohig and Cornelius Van Ness offered Seguín the protection of their homes.[51]

This incident simultaneously demonstrated how volatile ethnic relations were in San Antonio in the midst of a continuing state of war between Mexico and Texas as well as the solidity of the bonds that existed between the Tejano and American elites. Guilbeau had migrated with his father to San Antonio in 1838 and established a bakery near Military Plaza. As a fledgling businessman (who would later play an important role in establishing a network of overland trade routes to Mexico and the Gulf Coast), Guilbeau had already begun to integrate into the local elite. Twohig, an Irish Catholic, had been in town for many years and had become a popular merchant. Van Ness was a member of Bexar County's legislative delegation. In assisting Seguín, they displayed a public willingness to defend one of their own against popular prejudice at a point when such help could have been personally dangerous to them. In effect, they were showing class solidarity with a valued member of the local elite.[52]

Seguín, however, apparently believed he and his family faced a continuing threat of violence. He left town for Mexico, which of course only confirmed in the minds of his enemies that he was a spy.[53]

In exile in northern Mexico Seguín faced suspicion about his loyalty to Mexico because of his actions during the Texas Revolution. When General Adrián Woll decided to launch a second invasion aimed at San Antonio in September 1842, he forced Seguín to choose between demonstrating his loyalty or facing prosecution for his role in the 1836 rebellion. Seguín chose to save his family and agreed to lead a company of troops in Woll's invasion, which provided further evidence to Americans that he was, after all, a traitor despite his numerous contributions to Texas independence. Following the invasions, he remained in exile for another decade before returning to his hometown.[54]

Woll's invasion was particularly traumatic for both San Antonio and its American residents. The general arrested fifty-two Americans, including John Twohig, Samuel A. Maverick, Duncan C. Ogden, and Wilson J. Riddle, whom he incarcerated in Perote prison in Mexico. Most of those men spent the next two years there while diplomats negotiated their piecemeal release. In addition, Woll seized most of San Antonio's archives and convinced many Tejanos to return to Mexico. In a single stroke he had deprived the town of most of its written historical memory, reduced its population to perhaps seven hundred residents, and deprived the fledgling American business community of its leadership.[55]

The second invasion created the immediate context for the sale of Seguín's house. His debt arose from his efforts to support an effort by Mexican federalists to defeat a centralist faction in the ongoing struggle over the political framework of the Mexican government. He had borrowed $3,000 from Howard and Ogden for that purpose and then attempted to pay the loan by organizing a smuggling expedition into Mexico. Ogden accompanied Seguín to the Rio Grande to arrange the details of the smuggling operation. The expedition apparently failed, however, leaving Seguín vulnerable to having his note called.[56]

He might have been able to rely on his membership in San Antonio's elite to find ways to extend his loan except for the timing of the dual invasions of 1842, which destroyed his credibility. Howard had to consider the likelihood of regaining the firm's money. Ogden was at this point in Perote prison and did not regain his freedom until early 1844. He probably had little say in the firm's decision to call for the payment of Seguín's loan that year. Howard, as the sole partner able to act for the firm, made his decision in the context of a town in dire social and political distress. Increased social tension and economic uncertainty following the invasions created a context in which the American minority, deprived of its leaders, facing the task of rebuilding in a town that was culturally foreign to them, was probably in no mood to give a self-exiled participant in the last invasion a break on his debts.

The potential for Tejano and American elites to engage in mutually beneficial city-building activities in the early days of the republic fell victim to events beyond their control. Nascent local alliances needed time to develop and that depended on a secure environment for economic development in San Antonio and East Texas. Regional issues such as the political tensions between the republic and Mexico undermined the possibility of such alliances. San Antonio's relative proximity to Mexico, and its role in the Texas Revolution, made it a target, as the double invasions in 1842 abundantly demonstrated. The combination of political uncertainty and invasion did not encourage the growth of local commerce, and the absence of prosperity added an asperity to ethnic relations that thwarted the Tejano elites' goals.

Despite elite Tejanos' support for the empresario system, their participation in the revolution, and their efforts to develop a bicultural business coalition in San Antonio, the political hostilities between competing Mexican and American empires allowed Americans suspicious of Tejanos' loyalties to transform their ethnicity into a liability. The sale of Seguín's home symbolized the coalition's failure, but not the death of boosterism itself. Indeed Maverick's decision to buy Seguín's house demonstrated that the belief in San Antonio's future greatness persisted despite all the dire evidence of a hopeless future.

TWO

Boosterism Derailed

1845–1861

San Antonians faced a bleak future in the wake of the 1842 invasions. With the town's population plummeting below a thousand residents, its economy in ruins, and its ethnic relations tense, the community was on the cusp of disintegration. Miraculously, though, San Antonio become a miniature boomtown by 1847. National ambitions and war fueled this miracle, giving boosters such as Maverick a much more favorable environment for promoting urban development.

This stroke of fortune arose as a result of the problems being faced by the Texas Republic and the territorial ambitions of the United States. The republic's size, small population, political bickering, and a national depression threatened its viability. A generous policy that essentially gave public lands to anyone interested in claiming them had not prompted a huge population boom because settlers seeking opportunities in the West preferred more secure areas than Texas.

All of the republic's towns suffered as a result. Despite their extravagant booster rhetoric, neither Houston nor Galveston was setting any growth records. Southerners did establish more plantations in the fertile coastal areas, and both towns were well positioned to benefit financially from increases in cotton production. On the other hand, plantations did not stimulate large increases in the white population, and they tended to be self-sufficient, reducing the need for urban services other than those related to marketing the annual cotton harvest.

If the republic's underlying economic and demographic trends boded ill for the future, its political situation only made matters worse. Tax revenues, when they could be collected, were inadequate to finance essential government services, particularly defense. Santa Anna's twin invasions in 1842 dramatically exposed the republic's military weaknesses. On the diplomatic front, the republic faced a delicate challenge of not becoming a pawn of England or France in their competition for influence in the region.

The possibility of annexation to the United States, which many Texans had expected in 1836, took on more urgency as the republic's problems multiplied. Annexationists such as Samuel Maverick, who had personal experience with Mexico's military threat and its prisons, became increasingly influential in the legislature, especially following the invasions.[1]

Fortunately for Texans, President James Polk, among others, favored annexation as quickly as possible despite significant opposition in Congress. Polk's bellicose expansionist policies coincided with Texas's needs to make annexation possible despite Mexico's strident protests, and the republic gladly dissolved itself in 1846 to join the Union.

The Mexican-American War that followed resurrected San Antonio. The town's rudimentary road network offered the U.S. Army secure communications and a supply route to support military operations in northern Mexico. By concentrating troops, equipment, and supplies in and around San Antonio, the army created a typically overheated wartime economy that attracted several hundred people. Transforming the army into a long-term economic asset, however, depended on national policies, not local interests.

Fortunately, national military policy included plans for defending the Texas frontier after the war, which became the key to making the army an economic force in San Antonio. Even before the war ended, the army began to turn its attention to plans for pacifying that frontier. In 1847 Lt. Edward Everett received orders to repair the Alamo mission, which the army intended to rent from the Catholic Archdiocese of San Antonio for a permanent depot that would funnel federal funds into the town every year. From the military's perspective, San Antonio had a number of attractions. Its size, built environment, and natural assets combined with its role as a communications hub to make it an excellent depot site. The town was large enough to provide a good labor pool for the army's needs; many of its buildings would make suitable officer and troop quarters; and its abundant water and vacant land could accommodate large numbers of horses, mules, and cattle. All of these advantages would translate into significant amounts of federal money for the local economy from soldiers' pay, property rentals, and contracts for providing and transporting army supplies.[2]

Although the arrival of U.S. troops recalled the days when Spain's garrison had been the mainstay of the local economy, the American military had the ability to make much more substantive contributions to urban development. Washington, D.C., was not the center of the antebellum national urban network, but it proved to be a more than adequate substitute for Mexico City. Through no effort on its own, San Antonio had become connected to a dynamic political center that would consistently and more effectively support its local economy than Spain or Mexico had. Unlike other American cities such as Cincinnati, Detroit, and Chicago, which derived temporary benefits from military installations, San Antonio would see the army become a more significant and permanent source of urban development.[3]

The army was initially so critical because its presence temporarily negated San Antonio's geographical isolation and the high costs of transportation associated with that isolation, making the town competitive with Houston and Galveston for the first time. Congress would fund the policy of pacifying the frontier regardless of such costs, allowing the army's needs for local goods and services to become the basis for the town's development. In effect, the army transformed San Antonio from a subsistence economy to a service center securely linked to the national military supply network.[4]

For their part, San Antonians were not slow to recognize the implications of federal largesse for city-building. In February 1846 the city council offered the army one hundred acres of land at San Pedro Springs, north of the city, for a post. Their resolution justifying this offer was a masterful expression of booster rhetoric, asserting that a military post would "greatly tend to enhancing the value of Real Estate, the increase of Population, and the best interest of this city."[5] Perhaps inadvertently, the council's rationale captured the order of its members' priorities in city-building. On the other hand, their reference to "the best interest of this city" indicated that some residents had begun to consider ways to attract public support for an ambitious booster program. And recognizing that the army would be around for some time, some boosters began to explore ways it could assist urban development in San Antonio's still formless hinterland (the territory surrounding the city that is its primary market area).

San Antonio had few roads connecting it to the Houston and Galveston markets, improved routes to Mexico would be useful in the long run, and routes into the vastness of central and western Texas would enhance the town's influence in its as yet unorganized and underpopulated market area. There had already been some minor but encouraging progress in that regard before the war. French settlers had founded San Antonio's first satellite community, Castroville, in 1844. German settlers established New Braunfels, fifteen miles to the north, in 1845 and had plans under way for Fredericksburg, farther to the northwest. Since hinterland population growth was critical to San Antonio's development, local boosters hoped that increased frontier security and better roads linking new settlements to San Antonio would provoke a flood of settlers.

The army could provide invaluable help with those tasks as the war wound down. Although the army had no authority to engage in urban development directly, it did need good roads linking all the forts and other installations that it planned to build, and of course all those posts needed to be connected to San Antonio. Military necessity easily justified the use of the army's surveyors and engineers to identify and build a communications network that served both the army and the city's needs. And boosters such as Samuel Maverick, who were interested in locating the most promising land in the surrounding territory, rode with the army's surveying parties.

By partnering with the army, local boosters promoted development in San Antonio's territory at a fairly impressive pace. Surveying parties between 1848 and 1854 identified routes to San Antonio from the coast at Matagorda Bay that would improve the delivery of army supplies arriving at Indianola; other surveyors marked out future roads into central Texas, to the Rio Grande, and to El Paso.[6]

Army surveying expeditions thus helped define San Antonio's market area. Essentially, boosters claimed the area from Indianola on the coast to El Paso on the west, with a northern border running just below Austin and a southern border on the Rio Grande. Army posts served to some extent as boundary markers, with most of these installations sitting on land rented from San Antonians. In Kinney County, north of San Antonio, the army leased land from Samuel Maverick to build Fort Clark. To the west, John James provided the land for Fort Davis; to the south, John Twohig owned the property for Fort Duncan, which created the nucleus for Eagle Pass. Farther west, Fort Bliss protected El Paso and depended on San Antonio merchants for its supplies, as did all of these posts.

The army's assistance and protection also encouraged speculative town platting in this evolving hinterland. Oscar Brackett platted Brackettville near Fort Clark, and James founded Bandera. Both towns reflected a heightened sense of optimism about population growth outside of San Antonio and a greater willingness to take risks in their investments. James even created a miniature military-industrial complex, building a saw mill at Bandera that sold lumber for many of the forts under construction in the area.[7]

Participating in these surveys gave some San Antonians an expansive view of the possibilities for growing their city. By 1850 a small group of boosters had developed an ambitious program that sought simultaneously to solve permanently the problem of the town's geographical isolation, to reshape its physical form, to stimulate local manufacturing, and to improve its infrastructure. Each of their ideas faced its own challenges, but each concept was critical to successful city-building.

The program they envisioned was a daring and complicated entrepreneurial approach to urban development.[8] It would require far more coordination by a collective leadership to manage private and public resources than the land speculators of the late 1830s had displayed.[9] It also involved taking calculated risks in order to transform San Antonio into a major city in exchange for being in the best position to benefit from its growth.

Nothing better demonstrated this new taste for risk than their proposal to end San Antonio's isolation by building a railroad to the coast. Railroad projects elsewhere in Texas may have spurred them into action. Houston had begun experimenting with short lines into its cotton hinterland as a new service to planters and others who needed improved means of transporting crops to market. Individually unimpressive, these lines nonetheless gradually organized Houston's outskirts into a more integrated market, increasing profits for its merchant community. San Antonians may well have believed that they needed to build their own railroad, not only to end their isolation but also to compete effectively with a major rival.[10]

Twenty-two business and community leaders joined together to petition the state legislature for a railroad charter in fall 1850. Nine of those petitioners, including Maverick, Enoch Jones, and Bryan Callaghan, had been associated with the original group of land speculators. Newcomers to this coalition included a greater variety of individuals than had characterized the previous group. John O. Meusebach, for example, had worked to settle

German immigrants at New Braunfels and Fredericksburg, while Robert Neighbors had organized El Paso County and was working for the state as its foremost Indian agent.[11]

Seven men quickly emerged as the core of this coalition: Thomas J. Devine, John J. Giddings, François Guilbeau, John James, Enoch Jones, Samuel Maverick, and Isaiah A. Paschal. These men worked more consistently on the railroad and other projects than their other colleagues, they used political office to advance the coalition's agenda, and they were its most active speculators.[12] Although a small group, they managed to reflect some of the diversity of San Antonio's population. Devine and James were Nova Scotians of Irish parentage, Guilbeau was French by birth, Jones hailed originally from Ohio, and Maverick and Paschal were native southerners.

Members of the Tejano elite were notably absent from this booster coalition. This is somewhat puzzling considering the history of interethnic cooperation in the republic era. Social ties that had developed within the town's tiny upper class seem to have persisted despite the problems of the early 1840s. Intermarriage (typically of Tejano women to American males) within the elite remained relatively common. Guilbeau and Callaghan, for example, had married into prominent Tejano families. Less formal relationships also persisted; Maverick apparently maintained a close friendship with José Cassiano.[13]

Elite Tejanos did, however, participate in the real estate market that blossomed in San Antonio following annexation. Cassiano averaged one transaction a month from 1845 to 1850, selling primarily to other Tejanos. While Cassiano seems to have taken advantage of rising demand for land, José Navarro established more direct ties to the booster coalition by selling two leagues of land to Enoch Jones for the railroad project in 1851.[14] Elite Tejanos, in sum, controlled economic assets that would be useful to, and benefit from, the booster coalition.

The Mexican-American War and the unresolved ethnic tensions of the late republic period, on the other hand, probably made public membership in the coalition unwise. Ethnic relations were still a work in progress. Since the coalition members would be seeking public assistance for their program, it was possible that these boosters did not want ethnic issues disrupting the coalition.

In truth, the boosters faced serious challenges to the success of their program from the outset. Oddly enough for a group hoping to promote San Antonio's development, the boosters attracted no significant support from businessmen. Indeed, the most important local merchants apparently had no interest in organized development. Edward Dwyer, one of the wealthiest merchants in town and a former mayor, remained aloof. Nathaniel Lewis and John Twohig, the two most prominent businessmen from the Tejano era, initially lent their names to the railroad charter but never participated in the coalition's activities. Bryan Callaghan also dropped out after two years.

The absence of such prominent men from a booster coalition is peculiar, but perhaps also understandable given their particular business interests.[15] Lewis, Twohig, and others like John Groesbeeck had developed lucrative relationships with the army just as the booster coalition formed. Army contracts paid very well, with some firms realizing profits between $30,000 and $50,000 a year (equivalent to $784,000 and $1.3 million, respectively, in modern dollars).[16] Such a steady and large source of revenue could have dampened interest in speculative development initiatives, leading to a complaint that "our wealthy men, some of whom revel in ingots, are wickedly supine and inert."[17] There may well have been an underlying irony to the military's dominance of the local economy. It controlled the town's only secure source of large profits, but its overwhelming dominance meant boosters would be hard-pressed to convince already wealthy freight contractors that untested, risky, and costly ideas for developing the city were worth the effort.[18]

In addition, the merchant community lacked internal stability and cohesion. San Antonio's wartime prosperity attracted the attention of ambitious men, but that did not necessarily mean all those who came would stay. Nor did it mean that those who stayed would succeed. Of the fifty-three men who identified themselves as merchants in the 1850 census, twenty-seven would not establish mercantile houses in the coming decade, demonstrating how fortune did not necessarily smile on good intentions.[19] Additions to the town's ethnic diversity also created problems. Germans, who would later dominate mercantile activity, were only just arriving. At this point they were artisans and keepers of small shops who lacked familiarity with, or sympathy for, booster ideas about economic development. August Nette, a druggist, and Charles Hummel, a gunsmith, were the only prominent German businessmen in town, and both remained independent of the booster coalition.[20]

These circumstances forced the boosters to rely on their personal social and political resources to implement their program. Fortunately for them, at least at the outset, the core group had considerable local influence.[21] In the late 1840s no one in San Antonio had more influence than Samuel Maverick. As the son of a wealthy Charleston planter, Maverick had the money to buy enormous amounts of raw Texas land, allowing him to become one of the largest, if not the largest, landowners in San Antonio by the late 1840s. He was also a hero of the Texas Revolution and the republic. After participating in the early battles of the Texas Revolution in San Antonio, he had only missed martyrdom at the Alamo because its defenders had elected him to the convention that declared Texas independence, where he had signed the republic's Declaration of Independence. During the republic's brief life he had served as San Antonio's mayor and as the county's representative to the legislature.

None of Maverick's booster colleagues could match his prestige. Bryan Callaghan's influence derived from his success as a merchant and his political experience as a former mayor and alderman. John James's reputation rested on his skills and honesty as the land surveyor who had reidentified the town's boundaries after the documents describing them had disappeared during the 1842 invasions. Thomas Devine and Isaiah Paschal had used their legal skills to successfully defend San Antonio's public lands in a major lawsuit that arose from James's work. Enoch Jones, having made a fortune in various businesses prior to moving to San Antonio, managed large land holdings and was developing into one of the most important ranchers in the town's outskirts. François Guilbeau had abandoned baking to become a major merchant and promoter of a road network tying San Antonio to communities in its developing surrounding towns as well as to Mexico.

With the exception of John Giddings, of whom little is known, the core group of boosters was made up of lawyers and land speculators whose important services to San Antonio prior to 1849 were inextricably intertwined with their personal ambitions for wealth—which was typical of frontier boosters throughout the West at the time.[22]

Money for their program, on the other hand, was more of a problem. While fairly successful people in the community, none of these men had the personal wealth or financial connections to attract, for instance, capital to build a railroad. At first glance, these deficiencies made that idea seem completely ridiculous, but in fact a template for doing so already existed. State governments had adopted the practice of granting railroad charters that authorized investors to sell bonds in the nation's capital markets, especially Boston and New York City, to raise cash for construction costs. Railroad promoters also received land grants from states whose sale created another source of cash. Finally, legislatures also authorized towns and cities along a proposed route to sell bonds to raise cash for a railroad.[23] These practices, then, gave local boosters some tools to use in raising money for the proposed San Antonio and Mexican Gulf Railroad (SA&MG).

Infrastructure development would also require money. Many of the key components of urban life—schools, parks, bridges, markets, paved streets—were notable by their absence. Boosters like Maverick and Callaghan, who had memories of using local government to enhance public services in the early 1840s, would probably have wanted to revive that effort. Others, familiar with far more developed cities like Charleston, New York, and New Orleans, would presumably support a comprehensive effort to enhance their town's attractiveness as a place for doing business. Given the scope of the boosters' urban amenities program, it is clear that they planned to give the city council a major role in economic development.

One key idea in the boosters' program would have to rely on the local market for its success. These men apparently understood the importance of factories for simultaneously reducing San Antonio's reliance on expensive imports, diversifying the economy, expanding employment opportunities, and creating local wealth. Import replacement was a standard technique for developing a local urban economy, but a reliable source of power was critical to successful industrialization. Rivers had been a source of mechanical power for mills, and San Antonio appeared to have a major asset for creating local manufacturing capacity with its own river. As early as 1845 a visitor observed that the San Antonio River appeared to offer an inexhaustible source of power for mills.[24]

The boosters also benefited initially from fortunate timing. Organized political parties had not yet developed locally to contest elections, probably because most American residents maintained a nominal commitment to the Democratic Party and the Whigs had too few adherents to make any difference. Furthermore, differences over social and cultural issues that could spur efforts to organize voters had not yet provoked enough tension to precipitate political factions.[25] Practically speaking, that meant there were not yet any definitions of the public good or the appropriate uses of public power that contradicted the boosters' assumptions.

Finally, San Antonio was still a small town that lacked the complexity of much more successful cities in the late antebellum era. Mushrooming new cities like Chicago or San Francisco and older, larger places like New York or Philadelphia contained a greater variety of social and economic groups competing for control over the public agenda. San Antonio's small size in 1850 (about four thousand residents) made it easier for the boosters to dominate local politics. As the only organized interest group in town, they easily assumed control of city government in 1849, winning seven of twelve council seats and the mayor's race. They would control local government in all but one of the next five years.[26]

Unfortunately these boosters squandered their opportunity to build a better city. Displaying an astonishing ineptitude, they plunged into a briar patch of blatant greed, financial mismanagement, and self-destructive policies that destroyed their program.

First, they intermingled their roles as private land speculators and public officials, triggering considerable suspicion about their motives and their program. Twice in 1849, twice in 1850, and again in 1851 the booster-dominated council authorized the sale of public land on the west side of town to pay for such improvements as a new courthouse and jail. Several coalition members participated in these sales. Then, late in 1851, the Texas Supreme Court sided with the city in a lawsuit over San Antonio's boundaries that had been in the courts since 1845.[27] Suddenly the city once again held clear title over a great deal of potentially valuable land.

The booster-dominated city council promptly made arrangements for a large public land auction in November 1852. In preparation for this event, the council ordered the first survey of the town under American auspices. Predictably, the surveyor sought to create a grid over the city's lands in an attempt to reshape the old Tejano town into an American city. But that old town survived because Texas and U.S. laws protected the property rights of landowners within the former town boundaries. Lots within those boundaries retained their peculiar shapes and orientations in the center of what would become the downtown. The boosters' failure to replace the Tejano town with a fully gridded American city created an awkward impediment to the physical evolution of the downtown area.

Ignoring the anomalies of their new city plan, the boosters adopted exceedingly generous terms for the public auction of city lands. Previously, successful bidders had to make a deposit of one-third of the sale price and pay the remaining two-thirds in two installments within a year. For the 1852 auction, the council changed the terms to only one-fifth down and the remainder due in fifty years.[28] Buyers of course had to pay interest on their notes, but these terms were exceedingly generous. The city sold four hundred tracts totaling thirteen thousand acres for just over $53,000. At an average price of $4 per acre, speculators paid $400 for one hundred acres with a mere $80 down payment, had fifty years to pay a $320 balance, and in the meantime could dispose of the land as they saw fit. Purchasing patterns were also interesting. Of the twenty-seven men who placed winning bids on those tracts, twelve (44 percent) were members, associates, or relatives of the booster coalition. And those twenty-seven individuals bought 57 percent of all the land in the sale.[29]

Most of that land was west of the San Antonio River, revealing where the boosters expected the town's growth to occur. The east side received little attention. Only half of those who bought land on the west side also acquired property east of the river, and then they bought very little. Their lack of interest seems to have given newer residents who were not members of the coalition opportunities to speculate in a minor way.

The sale was a public relations disaster for the boosters. Rumors and complaints of numerous irregularities during the auction forced the council to appoint a special committee in February 1853 to revise the sale process. The committee's recommendations amounted to an admission that the council had not acted responsibly in selling the lots. Other problems quickly added fuel to public anger. In April the council ordered its secretary to review the 1852 sales because no one could figure out how much public land had been purchased or even the exact locations of all the lots that had been sold. The council had to order a new survey to rectify all the errors.[30]

In the meantime Thomas and James Devine managed to confirm public suspicions about the land auctions in concrete, and indeed spectacular, displays of arrogance and insider dealing. Prior to the November auction,

Thomas Devine, to whom the city owed fees for his work on the lawsuit over city lands, had agreed to exchange his fees for the right to claim any plots of land he desired that remained unsold after the public auction. Reasonably enough, the value of the lots he selected could not exceed the total amount of the fee the city owed him. When Devine selected his lots, though, he chose land that had not been offered at the 1852 sale. In other words, he selected desirable lots without having to compete for them in an open auction. Then in April 1853 James Devine, acting on his own authority as mayor, sold his brother fifty-three town lots for $10,360. The money went into the town's treasury, but rumors of Thomas's selection methods after the public auction, and the rather unusual spectacle of the mayor selling public property to his brother without first consulting the city council, caused enough of an uproar to force an investigation.

A special committee issued a report that repudiated the actions of both men, nullified James's sale of city lots to Thomas, and recommended the city sue Thomas to recover the land he had appropriated in 1852. He won the initial legal battle in district court but lost five years later when the city appealed to the Texas Supreme Court.[31]

In sum, these auctions exposed the council (and by implication the booster coalition that controlled it) to suspicions of incompetence if not outright malfeasance in its stewardship of the community's most valuable asset. Political turmoil over the council's handling of these auctions created a contentious backdrop to the boosters' efforts to implement their program. Anger over favoritism to speculators and insider dealing would inspire growing opposition to the boosters and contribute to an emerging debate about the appropriate role of local government in urban development.

The railroad project provided additional opportunities to discuss those issues. As a member of the legislature when the boosters applied for their charter to build the San Antonio and Mexican Gulf Railroad's charter, Maverick had inserted a clause requiring that two-thirds of the voters in a community had to approve governmental contributions to such projects. The legislature also capped such assistance at $50,000. In sponsoring that provision Maverick was implicitly recognizing the critical role that community consensus played in such ambitious projects. He would, before long, have reason to regret that proviso.[32]

When the legislature approved the charter in September 1850, the city council asked for voter support for the railroad in the December elections. Community support at this point—well before the scandals over the sale of public lands—was impressive. By a vote of 253 to 3, voters approved $50,000 in railroad bonds. The Bexar County court also received approval for an additional $50,000 with only nine negative votes.[33]

Having secured public support for the railroad, the council appointed a committee that included Alderman Maverick, who was then serving as president of the SA&MG's board of directors, to assess the value of all city property for the purpose of establishing collateral for the bonds. The city and the county then issued their respective bonds within a couple of months.[34] In the meantime the SA&MG directors opened subscription books to sell stock to local residents and began soliciting additional support from towns along the proposed route to the coast. By June a local newspaper announced the directors had received enough pledges of support to begin construction.[35]

Despite this auspicious start, the SA&MG directors quickly found themselves in difficulty. In the first sign of significant internal problems, only nine of the original twenty-two directors attended the meeting to elect a new board in October 1851. This absence turned out to be permanent for all but one of them, implying a serious fragmentation of private support for the single most important project of the boosters' program.[36]

The remaining directors coped with these losses by recruiting new men to the coalition. George T. Howard, one of the most successful freighters in town, and Charles Riotte, a recent immigrant from Germany, joined the board. Riotte's election may indicate the boosters' interest in creating support for the railroad among German residents, a group not previously represented.[37]

San Antonio's mayor and the chief justice of the county court also became permanent board members at this point. With their $50,000 investments, the city and county each controlled five hundred voting shares of stock. While they could technically claim that it was their duty to represent their respective constituencies, their presence could easily create the impression that the relationship between public officials and railroad directors was altogether too cozy, a charge that would become more believable when the directors voted to hold their annual meeting in the mayor's office starting in fall 1852.[38]

Political problems were not long in coming under these circumstances. As early as June 1851, an anonymous letter appeared in a newspaper attacking the city's administration. "Bexar" asserted that "unfortunately for the common interests of our city, its councils [*sic*] have been clogged by men, who when they are called upon in duty to act against the interest of some of their particular friends, disregard their oath of office, and strenuously oppose every thing [*sic*] affecting the private interests of some of their friends." The writer linked this apparent reference to the problems associated with the sale of public land to questions about the railroad, saying, "When appropriations of $500 are made to survey a particular line for the rail road [*sic*], they [the citizenry] wish to be satisfied that there is not private individual interest at the bottom; and if so, the expenses should be paid by the parties interested out of their own purses."[39]

Frustrated over the presumed nefarious motives of those who controlled the city's administration, "Bexar" argued that the council should focus on infrastructure improvements such as a new courthouse, more bridges, and better streets. Reflecting public opinion elsewhere around the country at the time, the letter writer was arguing that city support for a railroad promoted by boosters did not meet the definition of that common good.

Distrust of the SA&MG directors increased in spring 1852 when the council created a railroad tax to pay for the bonds. That ordinance, which established a tax of one-fifth of 1 percent of assessed property, raised a storm of protest. Property owners apparently believed that this tax, added to the existing property tax of one-fourth of 1 percent, could not be borne.

The uproar over the new tax indicated that the public supported the railroad in principle, but not enough to pay taxes for it, especially after observing the behavior of the coalition's land speculators who populated both the council and the board. The boosters' political base was eroding.[40]

Announcing the obvious, the council issued a public declaration that "great dissatisfaction exists among the people with regard to the direct taxation" to support the city's railroad bonds. Unwilling to repudiate the tax (which would have seriously affected the bonds' market value), the council instead announced that payment of the railroad tax would entitle each taxpayer to stock in the railroad at the rate of one share of stock for every $100 in taxes. This incongruous legerdemain failed to impress the voters, who simply refused to pay the railroad tax. A controversy over supporting the railroad had produced a tax revolt.[41]

At this point the booster coalition suffered another blow when Volney Howard, who had supported the boosters as owner of the *San Antonio Western Texan*, sold his newspaper to John H. Lyons and John McDonald. The new owners promptly shifted editorial policy against the railroad, commenting that "we will not disguise the fact that we yet have a shade of doubt about securing the road."[42] Normally city newspapers adhere to booster programs as an article of faith; to have one of two local papers expressing doubts about so important a project was not helpful.

Nonetheless, the boosters staggered on into 1853, a year of penultimate disaster. Money problems became acute at this point. Neither the city nor the county's bonds had attracted investors, depriving the railroad of cash. Several directors had donated land to the project in exchange for stock, but the board could not sell the land without a completed track. Stockholders were routinely reneging on annual installments for stock they had pledged to buy, contributing to an emerging financial crisis. Strapped for cash, the directors sought help from New York investors, but they declined to underwrite the SA&MG's costs.[43]

Some $300,000 in paper pledges had in effect turned to dust. Without cash the directors could not find a contractor, and without some construction under way, public support within San Antonio and also within the city's hinterland eroded even further. The directors had mismanaged their relations with several towns about as badly as they had handled local doubts about the railroad. Assuming (rightly) that San Antonio was the major city supporting this railroad, the directors paid little attention to the ambitions of other towns along its route. Indianola, on Matagorda Bay, had competed relatively well against Galveston as an alternate port, and its residents had close ties to San Antonio. Expecting to be the terminus of the SA&MG, they resented the way San Antonians demanded subsidies for the railroad while refusing to include them in planning activities. When the directors chose Saluria, an unoccupied town site owned by land speculators, as the road's terminus in late 1852, Indianola's citizens voted to withdraw their support for the SA&MG and to build their own railroad.[44]

Indianola's defection was another disaster for the railroad project. Without the community's support, and that of Victoria, which also withdrew from the project, the directors no longer had even the pretense of a market area that the SA&MG would serve. The whole point of the SA&MG was to end San Antonio's isolation. Accomplishing that goal required linking

Indianola, Victoria, and San Antonio together as a system that would simultaneously reduce transportation costs and attract settlers to the essentially unpopulated prairie between San Antonio and the coast. In planning to build across undeveloped frontier lands, the SA&MG directors were attempting something no other city had yet succeeded in doing, and their insensitivity to the civic hopes of smaller towns complicated their effort enormously, if not fatally.

Facing bankruptcy, the directors returned to the now well-worn path of public relations disasters. In April 1853 they gave Enoch Jones and Thomas Devine the contract to construct the line; they also agreed to turn over all the financial assets of the SA&MG to Jones and Devine for their use in paying for construction costs. At this point, Jones was president of the board of directors and Devine's legal battles with the city council over his land speculations were ongoing. Neither man had the personal resources to build the SA&MG, but in demanding all the company's assets as collateral for taking on the road's construction they had essentially seized control of the railroad project. Nothing could be better calculated to produce the suggestion of insider dealing than this arrangement.[45]

A fierce public reaction compelled the directors to defend themselves. They appointed a committee of board members (Maverick, Isaiah Paschal, and Robert Campbell) who reviewed the problems that led to the contract, and not surprisingly, concluded that it had been the only reasonable way to construct the railroad line. In defending the decision, the committee also made public the underlying causes of the directors' plight. Asserting that the railroad had been sponsored by "a few public spirited" people in 1850 because "all at that time admitted the importance and even necessity of the Road," the committee complained that "many of our most wealthy citizens refused to embark their means in an enterprise which they regarded as extremely doubtful if not hopeless. Thus the burden of the enterprise, upon the more public spirited of our fellow citizens, was greatly increased."[46]

Self-serving as these plans may have been, they nonetheless revealed how little support the booster coalition enjoyed among the city's elite. Too many businessmen had interpreted the army's increasingly important contributions to the local economy as a personal, rather than communitywide, opportunity to prosper. Some, who operated freighting companies that received profitable government contracts, may even have regarded a railroad as a threat to their newfound prosperity. A railroad, after all, would carry cargo at much cheaper rates and much more quickly than they could.[47] Whatever their reasoning, the booster coalition's incompetent management of the SA&MG had now obscured the larger issue of the need to end the town's isolation.

Bryan Callaghan, one of the charter members of the SA&MG who had lost interest in the project by 1851, now delivered a fatal blow to the enterprise when he returned to the city council in 1853. He claimed that the referendum authorizing the council to issue bonds was invalid because less than two-thirds of the *eligible* voters had cast ballots. His motives may have been entirely personal. As a consequence of the Texas Supreme Court's ruling, the council had been confronted with the problem of residents who had built on land that now belonged to the town. Several prominent businessmen, including Callaghan, Nat Lewis, José Cassiano, and George Howard, had constructed stores on the south side of the Military and Main Plazas on land the council now claimed, and they refused to vacate those premises. The council sued to recover these lands in 1852, alienating important members of the business community, who would hardly look favorably on the coalition's city-building activities.[48]

Callaghan's attack, coming as it did at the time when he was struggling to keep valuable land, suggests that he was retaliating against the booster coalition, which controlled the council. And with the public reaction to the shenanigans of the SA&MG's directors, he could easily mask a personal agenda with an attack grounded in serious legal issues. Maverick's attempt to create community support for the railroad by inserting that requirement into the charter now created a huge problem. In what may have been rather tense discussions, the council reviewed the evidence and concluded that Callaghan was correct. With no legal basis for continuing its financial support, the council suspended the railroad tax.[49]

The booster coalition maneuvered to overturn this disaster when a new council met in January, briefly winning a vote to reinstate the railroad tax. Public reaction to their victory was apparently immediate and ferocious. Six days after that vote, the council met again because "a large majority of the Tax Payers are dissatisfied with paying Taxes until the work is commenced" and again suspended the tax.[50] The coalition's maneuvers had created yet another tax revolt. Its hopes to end San Antonio's isolation had collapsed under the weight of its own mismanagement of the railroad project.

Despite their troubles with the SA&MG, members of the coalition pursued other elements of their program. Their interest in manufacturing, for instance, prompted seven of the original SA&MG Railroad directors, including Maverick, to join with five other men to apply for a state charter for the Bexar Manufacturing Company in 1850, the same year they obtained the railroad charter.[51]

All they needed, in theory, was a reliable source of raw materials for this company to meet local demand for ordinary household items such as mattresses and blankets. John James was already investing in sheep by the early 1850s, and he was not alone in his interest in wool production. Turning that wool into consumer products probably did not seem too farfetched an idea, but it foundered on the rock of cost. Shortly after producing the first batch of mattresses, the mill's manager had to defend the prices of his products to irate customers accustomed to cheaper imports. He assured the public that prices would decline as production and sales increased and pleaded for patience and support for this venture. Apparently he received neither; the mill discontinued operations almost immediately.[52]

J. H. Beck, another of the original SA&MG directors, tried to redeem this situation by announcing in 1851 that he would build a cotton mill within a year. Cotton was not a major crop in the burgeoning hinterland, but farmers had assured Beck, or so he said, that they would plant cotton if he first built the mill so that they would have a market for it. Albert Lockwood, an ally of the boosters, imported cotton seeds and advertised for volunteers to experiment with the staple, possibly in cooperation with Beck. His mill went the way of the woolen factory within a year.[53] Despite the boosters' innovative thinking about manufacturing, local investors do not seem to have been willing to risk their capital in supporting either mill because of the difficulties inherent in such start-up ventures.

These failures did not dampen booster enthusiasm for the *idea* that the river would one day transform San Antonio into a major manufacturing center. James Newcomb, editor of a new newspaper, the *Alamo Star*, ignored the implications of these failures and proclaimed that the river "possesses the greatest water power in the world, and on its banks will one day be a second Lowell or Manchester."[54] Newcomb was not alone in his optimism;

newspaper editors would remain fixated on the river's manufacturing potential for several decades.

In the meantime even as opposition to their control of local government continued to grow, the boosters turned to their agenda for improving urban amenities to make San Antonio more attractive to potential residents and, perhaps, investors.[55] The aldermen made their most concerted attempt to create an infrastructure commensurate with the boosters' dreams from November 1853 through January 1854. In November the council's Committee on Public Improvements recommended a comprehensive plan for two market buildings, a hospital, a poorhouse, numerous stone bridges, extensions and widening of existing streets, street grading, and "the enclosing and ornamenting of Military Plaza and planting with grass and trees." The total price amounted to an estimated $12,000.[56]

Securing money to cover the cost of these improvements would be a problem. The council's decision to adopt more favorable terms for the 1852 land auction dramatically reduced the amount of revenue to fund their improvement program. If the 1842 sale terms had been in force, the council would have had more than $36,000 (the initial payment plus one installment) on hand. Instead there was approximately $5,000 available. Buyers had paid their one-fifth down payment, amounting to a little more than $10,000, but half of that money went to legal fees related to the city's lands. If the boosters had not changed the terms for the land sale, they would have had more than enough cash on hand to pay for their improvement program, but their policy on public land auctions had cost them the money to fund their urban amenities agenda.

Attempting to compensate for that horrendous financial mismanagement, the Committee on Public Improvements recommended that the Finance Committee issue enough city script to pay for the entire program. That script had begun circulating about a year earlier to pay the city's bills because too many citizens were not paying their property taxes. Since the council could not redeem its script at par, asking local contractors to accept it in payment for their work amounted to asking them to subsidize the amenities program.[57]

The records do not reveal public reactions to this program, but it is noteworthy that the council for 1854 retained only two members of the booster coalition. In addition, at its January meeting the Ways and Means

Committee submitted a sobering report that read: "Your committee does not forget the financial condition of the city and the scarcity of available means." With that cautionary note, the report recommended a much less ambitious program that focused only on street improvements and building bridges. Even with that limited agenda, the committee selected only those projects that "appear to be the most urgent." The savings were considerable. An estimate that constructing a new bridge over the river at Commerce Street would cost $9,000 because of the need to raise the west bank six feet to be level with the east bank prompted the Ways and Means Committee to budget only $35 for repairs to the existing bridge.

With its stronger sense of fiscal responsibility evident, the committee also proposed a bizarre solution to the problem of paying for its minimalist approach: "Your committee begs leave to suggest the levying of a tax of one day's work from every grown male resident in money or labor for the carrying out of the above mentioned works." Despite the inventive approach to funding issues for public projects, even this drastically reduced program failed to pass the council.[58]

The boosters' decision in 1842 to fund public improvements separately through public land sales had returned to haunt them. Proposals to fund such projects with city script or taxpayer labor resulted in a desperate search for ways to avoid the property tax as a source of revenue. At this point voters had become extremely attached to their low tax rates, which would increase if the council began relying on the property tax to fund improvements.

As the boosters' comprehensive improvement plans disintegrated due to the consequences of their managerial mistakes and fiscal policies, national politics and ethnic tensions combined to create yet more problems for them. Illinois senator Stephen A. Douglas introduced his Kansas-Nebraska Act in January 1854. His proposal reignited the debate over slavery, dealt a death blow to the Whigs, and provoked the rise of the Republican Party. San Antonio's newspapers tended to support Douglas's bill for its potential to expand slavery into new territory even though the community's own slave population was small.

Douglas's proposal was not the only issue affecting politics. Nativism, which became an important national issue in the 1840s, had created serious problems for Mexican Americans in Texas. Organized prejudice against other ethnic groups appeared in the mid-1850s, when some German immigrants' ideas about slavery suddenly made their ethnicity a source of great concern among proponents of slavery. A few Germans in the new Hill Country towns north of San Antonio were highly educated professionals with strong commitments to nineteenth-century European liberalism. While their liberalism preached small government and low taxes as articles of faith, it also espoused other ideas that fit less easily into local American boosters' ideas about the intersections between public and private efforts to build San Antonio. Concerned about the national debate over slavery, the area's German residents organized a convention in San Antonio in May 1854 in response to a national meeting of German Americans in Louisville in which the participants had urged their countrymen across the nation to join in a united effort to affect national politics.

The timing could not have been worse for them. Douglas had guided his bill through the Senate in March; the House would pass it in late May, and President Franklin Pierce would sign it at the end of May, provoking a national political storm that did not admit much rational discussion. When the Germans convening in San Antonio issued a statement outlining their political principles, the document provoked a volcanic eruption of anti-German rhetoric.

Most of the angry response focused on the language on slavery in the Germans' platform, which declared it "an evil" and urged the federal government to assist any state that decided to abolish the peculiar institution. Although the Germans' statement was only a single recommendation among many others that dealt with a variety of other topics, slave owners around the state responded with such fury that German community leaders in the Hill Country towns and elsewhere promptly disowned the document and vowed undying loyalty to the South's commitment to slavery.[59]

In the meantime, however, there were several other provisions in the Germans' document likely to create problems for local American boosters. Among them were statements that "the soil should not be an article of speculation," that public land should only be sold to "actual settlers," and that uncultivated land should be taxed at a higher rate "in order to check land speculation." In addition, the authors of the statement declared "religion is a private matter," which required the abolition of all religious oaths, the repeal of all Sunday laws and thanksgiving days, and the removal of religious instruction from public schools. Finally, the document called for the repeal of all temperance laws.[60]

These ideas reflected the responses of immigrants throughout the nation to their experiences, particularly in the larger cities where controversies over religious instruction in public education and cultural differences over the consumption of alcohol had generated a great deal of social turmoil. Closer to home, the boosters' ethnic and religious diversity had created a potentially important political liability. As if he did not already have enough problems, Thomas Devine's Irish Catholicism now could be added to the catalogue of his sins. François Guilbeau's French Catholicism may have been considered a bit exotic, but nativist anti-Catholicism was not notable for making fine distinctions. In addition to these issues, local supporters of slavery might now have some problems with Isaiah and George Paschal, both of whom espoused strong views on the virtues of the Union at a time when southern loyalties were shifting toward secession.[61]

As the boosters' mistakes multiplied, these deficiencies provided additional ammunition for opponents to successfully challenge their political domination of San Antonio. Nativism first appeared as a political tool of the boosters' opponents in January 1853, when some outgoing aldermen claimed that two of their successors, Charles Riotte and Jean LaCoste, were not citizens.[62] That protest failed, but nativism as a political issue reappeared in the fall. When the SA&MG directors blithely reelected Devine to another term on the board in October 1853, the county court convened a special session to order their chief justice, John McLeod, to rescind his vote for Devine. In justifying their action, the judges condemned the board's blatant favoritism in giving him and Enoch Jones the contract to build the railroad and then told McLeod that it was wrong to vote for a director "who is not a citizen of the United States."[63] Thus the only extant nativist statements concerning citizenship, which was a core issue in the national debate over immigration, focused attention on the legal status of key members of the booster coalition.

By 1854 these concerns had coalesced into an assumption that a "railroad contract party" controlled local politics to its own benefit, as McLeod discovered in his bid for reelection as chief justice. Criticism of his record focused on his role as a director for the SA&MG Railroad. In a letter protesting these attacks, McLeod complained that an anonymous group had been attacking the board for the past year: "They have, I am sorry to say, carried their view out to perfection so far as the city of San Antonio is concerned, in the shameless repudiation of the city's legally authorized subscription" to the railroad. He accused this group of now attempting to force the county to revoke its support as well.[64] McLeod won reelection, but his opponents responded to their defeat with righteous anger that summarized anti-booster frustrations: "If they are willing to cast their votes for men who have not only violated the trust imposed on them, and squandered the money wrung from the hard earnings of the people, but [also] insulted them when asked what they had done with it, let it be so."[65] The boosters' failures were becoming serious political liabilities.

It was in this context that the German elite's proclamation of its political principles affected the booster coalition's future. The public denouncement of land speculation and urge for higher taxes on undeveloped land would hardly please the coalition's land speculators. Furthermore, the proclamation was not simply a theoretical criticism of the boosters; it was a personal betrayal.

In October 1853 the SA&MG stockholders had elected directors for 1854, including Charles N. Riotte and H. S. Osswald. Riotte had been an active board member since 1851; Osswald was new. Both men served as crucial links to their increasingly important ethnic community in town and in the hinterland. It would therefore have come as a shock to the boosters when Riotte and Osswald participated in the German convention. Riotte, perhaps anticipating his colleagues' reaction to his political beliefs, resigned before the convention met.[66] Osswald, however, did not; even worse, from the boosters' perspective, he served as a vice president of the meeting and signed the public proclamation of principles. Having even one of its directors publicly endorsing such peculiar views on land speculation and slavery probably upset other coalition members and added to the distrust of the coalition among southerners. Needless to say, neither Riotte nor Osswald was reelected to the board in October 1854.

By 1854 opposition to the boosters and growing distrust of ethnic loyalties coalesced into the establishment of a Know-Nothing Party. It is impossible to know how many San Antonians had become disenchanted with the boosters at this point, but the *Ledger* helpfully printed a list of the leaders of the Know-Nothings on August 1, 1855. Most of these individuals are noteworthy primarily for their obscurity. Only J. N. Fisk, John H. Lyons, John McDonald, and James Sweet had significant political experience. As newspaper editors, Lyons and McDonald had a history of opposing the boosters. Nor did the group's members feature major business interests; in fact, twenty-one of these men had no identifiable occupations. Lawyers, most prominently John Wilcox, prevailed among those who did have some professional affiliation.

The Know-Nothings were not completely bereft of resources. In the mid-1850s several of them became land speculators, but their lower rates of participation in the land market compared to the boosters' hints at an inability to compete with that group of speculators.[67] Rising prices may also have affected their ability to rival the booster coalition. Land that sold for $4 an acre had increased to $150 or more. In general the Know-Nothings' investments in land increased significantly at just the point when the booster coalition's reputation had reached its nadir. While individuals probably had a variety of motives for affiliating with the Know-Nothings, it is also likely that the organization represented a new group of people who were struggling to establish themselves in town. Maverick's coalition in effect had become the establishment, but it had also become a target of public wrath for its handling of crucial urban development issues, creating an opportunity for newer residents unaffiliated with the boosters to assert a claim on public offices.

The boosters paid the price for their mismanagement in the December 1854 municipal elections. In the absence of political wards, candidates for all offices ran at-large, which placed a premium on block voting organized around a candidate's personal reputation. Previously the booster coalition had been extremely successful in this system, but in this election the Know-Nothings showed they had learned that lesson well. In the mayoral contest, Know-Nothing James Sweet won handily over a complete nonentity, which in itself indicated disarray in booster coalition since it had previously supported community notables for mayor. Twenty-one men competed for eight city council seats. Know-Nothings won four, benefiting from block voting in which there was a mere fifteen-vote difference between their highest- and lowest-winning candidates. German voters, perhaps with an eye to their public repute at this point, rejected Osswald and settled on August Nette and A. Diffenbaugh as their representatives. The remaining two council positions went to Charles F. King, a former mayor and popular businessman, and J. G. Viall, whose election was the sole consolation for the booster coalition since he sat on the board of the SA&MG.

Nativist and reputational considerations apparently influenced other races. José Navarro's son Ángel received a stunningly low fifty-seven votes in losing his bid to the council, implying a rebuke to an iconic figure in the Tejano community. And Maverick suffered a humiliating defeat in his bid to become the city treasurer, losing to Know-Nothing John H. Lyons by a two-to-one margin. This may well have been a stinging rebuke for Maverick, who was one of the most distinguished politicians in Texas and the primary force behind the booster coalition.[68]

With half the council and the mayoralty in their control, the Know-Nothings wasted little time enacting their cultural agenda. They banned fandangos, a major cultural pastime among Tejanos; passed an ordinance to prohibit gambling; and raised the license fee for retail liquor stores to a prohibitive $300 a year.[69] Banning dancing, drinking, and betting all in one fell swoop may have been satisfying to their sense of rectitude, but it did not endear the nativists to Tejanos, Germans, and even many Americans who would shortly have the opportunity to express their opinions on this agenda.

Interestingly, other members of the Know-Nothing coalition supported urban development, which may well have been a reflexive tendency among the coalition's land speculators but also a trait that imperiled their hold on public office. They sought to solve the problems with financing public improvements by, of all things, raising taxes. In fact, they tripled the property tax.[70] Whatever voters may have thought of the Know-Nothings' campaign to purify local society, they had clear opinions on taxation. By increasing the tax rate so dramatically, the new party seriously damaged its credibility with voters within two months of assuming office.

The party also waivered significantly from its cultural agenda when an opportunity arose to promote development. In March 1855 William Menger petitioned the council "to establish a Brewery" and asked for tax relief from the license fee. As a German immigrant requesting a tax break to make an alcoholic beverage when nativists had just increased that fee in an effort to curtail alcoholic consumption, Menger seems to have chosen infelicitous timing. But the council promptly obliged, reducing the new license fee by two-thirds and giving Menger the first tax abatement for manufacturing purposes in San Antonio's history.[71]

Why the council did so remains a mystery. There are, however, some circumstances that hint at an explanation. Menger, a cooper by training, had arrived in town in 1847, married a widow who owned the boardinghouse where he lived, and prospered as the town grew. In the mid-1850s the Mengers built a larger boardinghouse just south of the army depot on Alamo Plaza. With thirsty customers literally next door, Menger probably did not need to ponder his next business idea for long before deciding to attach a brewery next to his boardinghouse (which would be rebuilt into the town's most lavish hotel in 1859).[72] For the Know-Nothing–dominated council, encouraging business development around the most important economic asset in town may well have been reason enough to rethink their licensing policy.

On the other hand, the party's maladroit behavior regarding taxation and Tejano culture encouraged local Democrats to organize themselves for the first time. The elite leadership among southern whites and Tejanos combined their organizational skills and ethnic ties within their respective communities to create a political coalition that also included German Catholics in order to take advantage of the Know-Nothings' mistakes. By midsummer 1855, the Know-Nothing candidates for state offices in the summer elections were in the awkward position of campaigning for Tejano votes by claiming they had nothing against Catholics. The Democrats in the meantime had founded a Spanish-language newspaper, *Los Bejareños*, to convey their agenda to Tejanos and had enlisted José Navarro in a publicity campaign denouncing Know-Nothings as bigots. In August the Know-Nothing Party suffered a crushing defeat across the state, prompting an eruption of vituperative anti-Catholic rhetoric in the party's state newspaper that did not resonate well in San Antonio. By December the Know-Nothings were facing extinction.[73]

James Devine returned to the mayor's office in January 1856, as the Democrats swept the city elections. A new council committee quickly reported that the previous administration's tripling of the property tax had been completely unnecessary and recommended reducing the rate to one-half of 1 percent per $100 of assessed valuation—oddly enough, not the previous one-quarter of 1 percent.[74]

This election marked the emergence of an organized Democratic Party, which was not only ready to defend southern culture, but also created a permanent political alliance between southern and Tejano community leaders that remained intact until the mid-twentieth century. It did not, however, resurrect the booster coalition. The Democrats had won partly because most voters had little commitment to the Know-Nothings' cultural agenda, and primarily because they had revealed too much commitment to taxation as a means of funding public improvements. Having rejected the railroad tax, a comprehensive public improvement plan, and now the attempted increase in their property taxes, voters had in effect defined limits on the use of the public's purse for ambitious schemes to improve their town.

The booster coalition apparently understood both the voters' message and its implications for their program. Seeking to bypass public resistance to their ambitions, Maverick guided a new city charter through the legislature in July 1856. This charter, appropriately enough, reads as though the legislature had adopted the booster coalition's entire agenda. It authorized a hospital, poorhouse, workhouse, or house of correction, and, in a separate section devoted entirely to "opening and improving streets," it granted the council the power to create a special tax to pay the costs of paving and improving the town's avenues. The council also received authority to issue bonds without any limits on the total amount of such obligations, although the voters had to approve each issue by a two-thirds majority of those voting. Shifting to bonds as a source of revenue for urban amenities indicated that the boosters had recognized that public land sales could no longer provide revenue for that purpose. Indeed, the last such sales occurred in 1860.

Other sections of the charter seemed designed to deal with other obstacles to booster success. The legislature mandated the creation of political wards for the first time and extended the mayor's and aldermen's terms of office from one to two years. Maverick and his associates may have sought greater stability in local government with these changes in anticipation of working within the newly energized Democratic Party, whose candidates had swept the December 1855 city elections.

Finally, the charter reduced the town's boundaries to a square league (thirty-six square miles), with the square defined as three miles in any direction from San Fernando Cathedral. There is no contemporary explanation for this boundary change, although it may have been related to the unhappiness of land speculators over the loss of some of their properties after the 1851 court ruling. John James had recently sued to recover the value of lands included in the court decision, and shrinking the city's limits may well have opened the way for him to press his claim.[75]

If the boosters thought a new charter would assist their campaign to improve the town, they were to be disappointed. Only one current SA&MG director, Isaiah Paschal, won a seat on the council, a far cry from the days when a majority of aldermen had simultaneously been board members. On the other hand, the nominating committee had chosen two Germans for their ticket in a sign of the rising importance of that ethnic group in town, and both won. Since German voters would be among those most wary of the tax implications of urban development programs, their victory did not bode well for Maverick's coalition. Indeed the composition of councils until 1861 indicates that a new cohort of businessmen was beginning to flex its muscles, though this group offered the public no vision of how to develop the city, perhaps in deference to the dominance of the anti-tax, anti-improvement consensus that had emerged by the mid-1850s.

By 1856, then, Maverick's coalition had failed to accomplish any of its ambitious goals. Yet San Antonio had prospered. The population more than doubled during the 1850s. More remarkably, San Antonio became the largest city in the state in 1860, triumphing over its arch rivals Houston and Galveston.[76]

Ironically, San Antonians owed this achievement to their city's location. It was a better site than either Houston or Galveston for implementing the nation's military strategy of establishing frontier security to encourage settlement. Military protection inadvertently stimulated urban development at this point in the evolution of Texas cities. San Antonio had no functional hinterland in the 1840s, but federal forts created one for the town. German immigrants, attracted by glowing promises of fertile farmland, arrived in impressive numbers beginning in the late 1840s. Small farming towns sprouted in the Texas Hill Country just north of San Antonio, and farm goods in need of a market began to flow into town.

Population growth in San Antonio's market area encouraged commercial development in San Antonio. At least thirty-five businessmen established profitable importing companies to serve this emerging market, creating a symbiotic relationship with its surrounding territory for the first time.[77]

German farm productivity and continuing population growth increased the amount of goods needing transit to and processing in San Antonio. Several settlers decided to found their own businesses, relying on their ethnic ties to attract hinterland customers. In effect, the German settlements began contributing business talent to the growth of San Antonio. With the advantage of a shared language and culture, these new merchants gradually assumed a prominent position in the local economy.[78]

Military contracts poured unprecedented amounts of money into San Antonio, creating multiplier effects essential to local growth. Neither Houston nor Galveston had any comparable single source of development dollars. Between 1852 and 1858 the military spent more than $1.5 million (equivalent to $39 million today) for contracts, goods, and other services in San Antonio.[79] Military supplies had to be imported to the depot and then disseminated to the garrisons, creating a great demand for long-distance hauling. That demand, and the cost of hauling bulk goods over long distances, generated lucrative contracts. A single shipment of military equipment from Baltimore to the Texas forts in the 1850s cost $90,000 in transit fees. San Antonio's freighters did not, of course, collect all of that money, but freighting became the city's core service because it generated larger profits than any other economic activity.[80]

The army's presence also began to affect the town's physical development. When Maj. E. B. Babbitt, the depot commander, decided that Military Plaza would not serve his future needs, he relocated to the abandoned Alamo mission in 1849. Since few homes, and even fewer businesses, existed east of the river at that time, Babbitt may have believed that the army would have enough space to expand to meet its future needs.

Major Babbitt failed to understand that in moving the depot he was expanding the location of economic opportunity in San Antonio. New businesses dependent on the army for their livelihood sprouted around the depot, displacing lower-class Tejanos who had been living in jacals near the Alamo. Babbitt's move would also transform Commerce Street. In 1849 it was only a footpath lined with jacals and adobe houses from Main Plaza to the river. Commerce became the principal street linking the old heart of the city to this new economic magnet by the early 1860s. As early as 1852 a local newspaper editor noted the shift, remarking that "the eastern part of the city . . . is improving more rapidly than any other."[81]

With the proliferation of businesses in the growing town, the demand for commercial space increased considerably throughout the 1850s. The council responded to that demand by enlarging both Military and Main Plaza, razing the jacals that lower-class Tejanos had constructed in those public squares. Displaced by the emerging business district, poor Tejanos moved west, across San Pedro Creek into the colonial-era districts of Laredito and Chihuahua, where, simultaneously, a small vice district began to emerge.[82]

Residential development on the east side of town followed a different path. Local speculators platted land immediately north of the depot for a development dubbed Alamo City (later changed to Irish Flat). West of Alamo City, and north of the river's not-yet-famous bend, other speculators laid out a second residential subdivision that would evolve, after the Civil War, into Travis Park. Shortly before 1860 some members of the local elite began to build Saint Mark's Episcopal Church on the park's north side, creating a magnet for fashionable residential development. These developments signaled a general shift in San Antonio's most desirable residential development to the east, away from the original settlement west of the river.[83]

Growth also created some problems. The streets on Main and Military Plazas followed a rough grid pattern, but there was no organized approach to surveying and opening avenues anywhere else. Acequias, the river, and the creek still defined the spaces for streets, and, since the town had few bridges, those watercourses prevented what streets there were from forming an efficient system for moving people or goods around town. Since the streets were unpaved, they became impassable when it rained and intolerable because of dust when it did not.

The boosters' plans for urban amenities and a new grid remained just that—plans. A dearth of schools, parks, or other amenities did not bother soldiers who limited their expectations of town services to housing and entertainment. The army was making major economic contributions to San Antonio's development, but it was not a source of pressure to improve urban services and the quality of town life.

Relying on the army for its prosperity carried certain risks that few residents recognized at the time. Elsewhere army installations were useful but temporary spurs to local urban development as city leaders worked to diversify their local economies. They could do so because their cities' locations were strategically important for other reasons than military defense.

Cincinnati, Detroit, Chicago, and San Francisco, all of which initially had small military centers, were located along major migration and economic development routes for western settlement in the antebellum era.[84] Texas's small cities were peripheral to those routes. As peripheral sites, San Antonio, Houston, and Galveston needed investors willing to take major risks to overcome the communities' locational disadvantages in order to take better advantage of the evolving national market system.

The ambitious scope of the boosters' plans implied an instinctive understanding that San Antonio needed to distinguish itself from its rivals while local development initiatives could still play a dominant role in promoting growth. Even in a peripheral area such as antebellum Texas, a town's size mattered. Maverick and his colleagues sought to use the most advanced technology of their day, the railroad, to overcome their town's geographical isolation and to transform it into a magnet of population growth. If they could have made San Antonio into a significantly larger place than Houston or Galveston, they would have established a basic growth dynamic that could have changed the importance of their town's location.

With the collapse of their coalition, however, San Antonio's potential for attracting a significantly larger population than its rivals ended. In 1860 the margin of victory over Galveston, a mere nine hundred more residents, did not constitute a significant advantage in the absence of ways to sustain economic diversification.[85]

The failure of Maverick's coalition therefore had important consequences for future development. On a personal level, land speculation did not prove to be a path to great riches. Although San Antonio's population doubled in the 1850s, demand for land did not exceed the supply because the Midwest was the preferred destination for migrants at the time. Real estate prices therefore remained low. When Maverick died in 1870, his estate included 385,000 acres of land valued at thirty cents an acre.[86] That estate was sufficient to make him a wealthy Texan, as were other coalition members, such as James and Jones, who converted portions of their land into working ranches for cattle or sheep and sold town lots to generate revenue. But none of them could match the wealth that midwestern urban speculators acquired through their booster activities.[87]

For San Antonio more generally, the failure of Maverick's coalition meant that the community had lost its risk-takers, individuals willing to define a common vision for community development and able to organize their colleagues into coalitions to implement that vision. None of those who had signed the SA&MG Railroad charter in 1850 would persist as boosters beyond 1860. Instead, as a result of its own mistakes, Maverick's coalition left a legacy of limits. From the boosters' perspective, their program had offered San Antonians an opportunity to develop the town's social, economic, and physical infrastructure to create the basis for future vigorous, diversified growth. Local merchants observing the failure of the boosters' program in the context of growing prosperity based on the military depot would naturally conclude that neither collective effort nor diversification was necessary. Geographical isolation remained a problem, but a developing hinterland and the army's needs generated demand for goods and services that masked the underlying structural weaknesses of the local economy.

For the voters, watching the boosters' gyrations as they struggled with unavoidable mistakes as well as poor political judgments, failure guaranteed low taxes. By the mid-1850s the town's residents had come to a consensus, forged by repeated tax revolts in response to the boosters' ineptitude, that the legitimate purposes of government did not include an aggressive investment in public improvements. Maverick and his colleagues had recognized that consensus and sought to cope with it in a new charter that relied on bonds to fund projects. Their solution, however, had an Achilles' heel in that it required a public referendum to issue bonds. Since the bonds had to be based on the town's capacity to pay interest and principal, which could only come from increased taxes on property, voters would prove reluctant to grant such permission.

Voters' resistance to increasing property taxes also extended to a refusal to pay other taxes, further eroding the town's revenue base. The behavior of some of San Antonio's leading citizens provided precedents for ordinary citizens to follow. In 1850 several prominent businessmen, including Bryan Callaghan, François Guilbeau, William Vance, and Nat Lewis, refused to cooperate in the assessment of their property or to pay taxes. Tax resistance by such prominent individuals probably encouraged ordinary residents to ignore their tax bills, as well. In 1851 the council ordered the city collector to call on residents to pay their 1849 and 1850 taxes, indicating that nonpayment was becoming a habit that forced the council to issue city script to meet its obligations.[88] The council could have authorized lawsuits to recover back taxes, but in the 1850s the aldermen chose not to do so. Penury rather than civic-mindedness was becoming part of San Antonio's civic culture.

In the end neither the business community nor the majority of ordinary San Antonians united behind the boosters' attempts to develop their city. The boosters' determined and successful efforts to buy large tracts of land in both the town and its hinterland on favorable terms that they had manipulated undermined public support for their urban development program. When they compounded that mistake with mismanagement of the railroad as well as of public improvements, they created the conditions for their own failure. But they also influenced the basic values and beliefs of many voters and businessmen, who now shared a belief that local improvements had no obvious connections to population growth or economic development. The emergence of that belief as a kind of local political environment that amounted to a cultural consensus would shape and complicate the future development of San Antonio for more than a hundred years.[89]

THREE

Reconstructing Consensus

1861–1880

Any postmortem on the demise of Maverick's booster coalition might reasonably conclude that it died of self-inflicted wounds. The coroner presiding at such a postmortem could have listed several such wounds, including overly ambitious goals, poor timing, greed, and egregiously inept political skills. Boosters across nineteenth-century urban America inflicted similar wounds on themselves, which caused their efforts to fail, as well. Failure, though, did not breed discouragement because boosters drew their strength from their faith in the future greatness of their cities. They lived in an era of extraordinary city-building when places such as Chicago and San Francisco mushroomed into urban powerhouses. With such examples to inspire them, boosters in countless other smaller cities could logically argue that their hometowns had the potential for equally explosive growth. Believing in San Antonio's destiny as a great city had fueled Maverick's coalition, and that belief had not died with its defeat.

In general San Antonians shared the boosters' belief in their city's destiny, but their reactions to Maverick's coalition, and their practical experience, convinced them that neither privately organized city-building nor public investments in development was necessary for achieving that vision. The coalition's collapse had not prevented San Antonio from becoming the largest city in Texas by 1860. With daily evidence of rapid growth and prosperity all around them, San Antonians naturally neglected to consider their city's flaws. Compared to Houston and Galveston, San Antonio was precariously dependent on a single "industry" for its prosperity, its merchant community was smaller and less wealthy, its rural surroundings were not organized to contribute to the city's development, and a larger proportion of its population was poor and unskilled.[1]

Becoming the state's largest city tended to obscure those problems, leaving San Antonians convinced that they already had the formula for continuing success. The Civil War and Reconstruction would, however, create social and political divisions within the community that undermined that consensus. And an unexpected resurgence of organized boosterism would further complicate the community's struggle to reconstruct and enforce its approach to "inevitable" growth.

Texas's secession cost the city its core economic asset and fractured the community. With the army's departure in February 1861, San Antonio lost not only its role as the lynchpin of the state's frontier defense system, but also all the federal cash it received via payrolls, transportation contracts, and rent money. And the city's hinterland once again became a dangerous place for settlers. Hostile tribes quickly noticed the withdrawal of federal garrisons, and the state government lacked the financial resources to man those forts effectively. Deep rural development basically halted for the duration of the war. The abrupt disappearance of federal largesse combined with a shrinking population in the hinterland to undermine many local businesses.[2]

The North's military strategy also harmed the local economy. Initially the North's blockade of Southern ports was more a nuisance than a serious threat to San Antonio's economy, but when federal troops eventually occupied Indianola, Galveston, and New Orleans, San Antonio lost its connections to shipping services and market centers. As a result, many local importers closed down during the war.

Economic opportunities did not disappear entirely. San Antonio's road network to Mexico proved strategically important in Texas's international cotton trade. The Union's blockade throttled coastal trade north of the Rio Grande, but smuggling flourished. Matamoros, and to a lesser extent Laredo and Eagle Pass, quickly became international ports for cotton. Local ranchers also found a temporary market for their beef by trailing herds into Louisiana (the Union seizure of New Orleans in 1862 and the closure of the Mississippi River after the fall of Vicksburg in 1863 essentially ended this trade). San Antonio did manage to produce small quantities of shoes, clothing, and powder for the Confederate forces, but those activities did not compensate for the other economic losses.

A few San Antonians were able to find opportunities in an otherwise dismal economic environment. James Sweet, Jacques LaCoste, Wharton A. Bennett, A. S. Kottwitz, and François Guilbeau, either in partnerships or individually, created a lucrative cotton trade into Mexico. George

Brackenridge, a future San Antonian, worked with Charles Stillman, founder of Brownsville, Texas, and a major merchant in southern Texas, who gave him unrivaled access to Southern cotton and Northern markets. All these men made fortunes in the cotton trade, taking payment in gold, which they deposited in English banks and other secure places. At the war's end, they would control a significant amount of scarce local capital.[3]

San Antonio's population also grew, although it is impossible to say how much of that growth occurred during the war itself. It is likely that refugees from Indian attacks along the frontier settled in town, and work opportunities at a tannery and powder mill—neither of which survived the war—attracted some new residents. Hauling cotton into Mexico no doubt provided jobs for freighters suffering from the collapse of access to the coast and New Orleans.

On the whole, however, the local businessmen failed to find an adequate substitute for the U.S. Army's prewar role in subsidizing economic development. Many established businesses languished or disappeared, especially if they had been dependent on federal contracts or had relied on hinterland customers for their livelihood. The newly minted Confederacy did not contribute much to the city's sagging economy. Inflation undermined the value of Confederate money as well as public faith in it, complicating the task of reorienting the local economy to the marketing system of a new nation. Indeed, the uncertainties of a future for the Confederacy, especially after 1863, did not bode well for local development.

Secession also undermined local social and political relationships that had developed in response to Maverick's boosters and the Know-Nothing episode in the mid-1850s. At the time, the city's ethnic groups had managed, in the absence of any alternative, to merge their disparate interests into a unified Democratic Party. With secession and war, however, that bargain of convenience fell apart, creating a challenging problem for white Southerners who controlled the party and who believed they needed a united community to rally around the Confederate cause.

Tejano residents did not pose any problems. Despite their steady decline into minority status during the 1850s, Tejanos never wavered in their commitment to Southern Democratic values that they had forged especially in response to the Know-Nothings. Several prominent Tejanos, including

Manuel Yturria II, Joseph M. Peñaloza, Ángel and Eugenio Navarro, and Erasmo J. Chavez, commanded regiments composed of Tejano volunteers. Other Tejanos served in regiments led by San Antonians like Trevanion T. Teel. Fighting for the Confederacy may not have earned Tejanos much in the way of concrete rewards—most were and remained laborers—but their loyalty ensured that their leaders would retain their political influence in the Democratic Party after 1865.[4]

Germans, on the other hand, had more complicated responses to secession. Northeast of San Antonio, New Braunfels's Germans became staunchly Confederate while their countrymen to the northwest in Fredericksburg remained predominately pro-Union. Some pro-Union Germans simply decamped for Mexico either to wait out the war or eventually to enlist in Northern army units. In San Antonio, Unionists included Forty-Eighters such as Edward Degener and August Siemering, who had participated in the infamous 1854 German convention. Small businessmen like John Kampmann, August Nette, and Louis Zork, on the other hand, supported secession. Kampmann would even raise his own company to fight for the Confederacy.[5]

These intra-ethnic divisions troubled San Antonio's Confederates. Although Germans were only 19 percent of the city's population in 1860, many Confederates apparently assumed that they figured prominently among the 46 percent of the local electorate who voted against secession. Memories of the 1854 German convention's condemnation of slavery no doubt played a large role in that assumption. Leading Confederates worried that German support for the Union in San Antonio, as well as in some areas of the Hill Country, would disrupt the war effort.[6]

Unionism in San Antonio also attracted support among non-Germans, which exacerbated the concerns of local Confederates. In the fall 1860 national election, Isaiah Paschal, Nat Lewis, and Gustav Schleicher founded a Union organization. James P. Newcomb, a former Know-Nothing and editor of the *Alamo Express*, publicized their arguments against secession. Their attempt to promote public discussions of ways to reconstruct the Union almost provoked a riot in Main Plaza in April 1861. When a mob prevented Paschal from speaking, Newcomb indulged his penchant for purple prose in several editorials that denounced secession and Jefferson Davis in language that alarmed loyal Confederates. While Newcomb was visiting a friend, a mob burned his newspaper office and destroyed the press. Newcomb left town the next day and spent the war in California.[7]

Newcomb's vitriolic editorials, the presence of an organized pro-Union faction, and concerns about German loyalty created a volatile environment of suspicion and uncertainty. Samuel Maverick and Thomas Devine called a public meeting on June 24, 1861, to "do something for the common defense" of the Confederacy. That meeting voted to create the Southern Defence [*sic*] Aid Society to solicit voluntary donations for the Confederate war effort. Several community leaders joined the society, including William Groesbeeck, son of one of San Antonio's wealthiest military contractors, and John James, longtime land speculator. James R. Sweet, four-time (and current) mayor, became the society's president. Devine served as vice president while Maverick became treasurer.

The ethnic composition of the society's officers and directors indicates that Maverick and his allies sought to neutralize German Unionists. Charles Hummel, Louis Zork, and John Kampmann, all loyal Confederates, served on key committees. Gustav Schleicher publicly endorsed the society, which would have conveyed a message to other Unionists that the time for opposition had ended.

Other measures for implementing the society's goals implied the same message. The town's leading citizens received instructions to "use your endeavors to obtain subscriptions in your immediate vicinity, or elsewhere," which empowered them to carry the society's message into every neighborhood. Each solicitor would be well-placed to gauge support and to identify resistance to the Confederacy across the city in the reactions they observed to requests for donations. Maverick and Devine had in effect created a volunteer organization to suppress dissent and rally support for the Confederacy.[8]

Despite these efforts, resistance continued. Some local merchants either refused to accept Confederate currency or discounted its face value. Military recruiters had problems finding volunteers. Placards in German mysteriously appeared one morning in late March 1862 denouncing Confederate money and announcing a revolution was at hand.

Continued resistance efforts prompted harsh countermeasures. Asa Mitchell, a charter member of the society, led a vigilante terror campaign against Unionists during spring 1862.[9] Gen. Hamilton Bee, Texas's military commander, declared martial law on April 28. Although there is no evidence that the society requested his help, its leaders organized a public meeting, also on April 28, that adopted resolutions supporting martial law and threatening death to anyone who undermined the Southern currency.[10]

General Bee also ordered James Duff, another charter member of the society and commander of Duff's Partisan Rangers, to Fredericksburg in May. Fredericksburg had become notorious for its resistance to the Confederacy, and Duff conducted a harsh campaign of intimidation, destroying some property and arresting several people for disloyalty. Gen. Paul Hebert, who succeeded Bee, created a military commission in San Antonio to try Duff's prisoners. The society seized on the commission as a way to deal with local dissenters, filing complaints against business associates and residents for undermining the currency, evading military service, and disseminating abolitionist tracts.[11]

In the meantime, Duff's campaign around Fredericksburg prompted approximately seventy Union sympathizers to leave for Mexico in August 1862. Warned of this escape attempt by an informer, Duff led a force of nearly one hundred San Antonians, who surprised the men on the Nueces River on August 10, killing thirty-two in what amounted to a massacre. After shooting the wounded and prisoners, Duff's force returned to Fredericksburg, where (by his account) they hanged some fifty men and killed an undetermined number of others he labeled as bushwhackers.[12]

Upon their return to San Antonio, Duff's Partisan Rangers turned over a letter to the military commission they had found on a corpse after the massacre. It was addressed to Edward Degener, a prominent German Forty-Eighter, staunch Unionist, and father of the dead man. The grieving father (who had lost a second son in the same massacre) was promptly convicted of disloyalty for having corresponded with his son and for having prior knowledge of the planned escape to Mexico.[13]

Although Jefferson Davis abolished the commission, Duff's campaign left bitter memories and at best imposed sullen compliance among Unionists. The result was an uneasy stalemate. Maverick and Devine continued to preside over public meetings that sought to force men to declare an oath of allegiance to the Confederacy and to enlist in the army.[14] Their efforts to shame resistors into compliance by exhortation seem to have had limited effect.

As the Confederacy collapsed in spring 1865, Devine and Maverick defiantly organized the Southern Rights Association of Bexar County in April. Maverick published the association's manifesto, which declared that "we are able to carry on the war for years to come and are firm in the intention to do so."[15] The association's members had reason to be defiant. As the organizers of the Southern Defence Aid Society, they had worked hard to promote Confederate unity. Had the South won, their prosecution of neighbors for disloyalty as well as their complicity in vigilante activities and the attacks on Fredericksburg would have been justified as necessary to that victory.

But the South had lost. Unionists would naturally dispute the idea that former Confederates should continue to lead the community. From their perspective, Maverick and his associates had committed treason, and the Unionists would seek to exclude them from political power as well as from community development as much as possible.

Many German San Antonians also had problems with a return to the antebellum status quo. As newcomers to town whose numbers were steadily increasing, German residents were in the early stages of acculturating to American society. The challenges they faced in adjusting to a new culture naturally heightened their ethnic self-consciousness and cohesion. During the 1850s they organized the Casino Club, the German-English School, and a number of singing societies to perpetuate German culture and language. Those who had established businesses prior to 1865 tended to own small shops such as book, candy, and drug stores that served their ethnic community. A few German artisans established a broader customer base by using their skills in making jewelry and guns, but in general German craftsmen and merchants had not yet begun to develop relationships with the other ethnic groups in town.[16] For many Germans, Duff's brutality and the prosecution of individuals like Edward Degener probably enhanced their ethnic sensitivities and disinclined them to support former Confederates as community leaders.

Unreconciled Confederates, triumphant Unionists, and ethnocentric Germans frayed the social relationships and authority of the city's traditional leaders. And without those relationships, individuals who might have personal status and influence within the Confederate, Unionist, or German factions could not bridge the differences among them to coordinate urban development.[17]

Two events in 1866 demonstrated the extent of these divisions. In October Gustav Schleicher, John Kampmann, John Withers, Thomas Williams, and A. G. Dickinson organized the Commercial Club "for social purposes, [and] for the encouragement of literary and commercial pursuits." If the sponsors' backgrounds are any guide, the club represented their attempt to bridge ethnic and political divisions between Southerners, Unionists, and Germans by establishing a meeting place for rebuilding relationships. Good intentions were insufficient grounds for success at this point, however, and the club remained inert for several years.[18]

City elections in December illuminated the stark ethnic and political divisions that the Commercial Club's sponsors were seeking to heal. Former Confederates and their Tejano supporters swept all but one of the citywide offices. Gustav Friesleben, the lone German candidate to win election (as city surveyor), had close ties to the Southern loyalists. Ethnicity and residence played a major role in determining the election results. In 1866 the vast majority of Germans lived east of the river; a similarly large majority of Mexican Americans resided west of it. More Southerners lived on the west than on the east side of town. West Side residents voted in each citywide race for the eventual winner by a margin of two to one; East Side residents voted against the winning candidate by the same margin. Even Friesleben failed to alter that pattern and had to rely on overwhelming support from West Side voters to win. Apparently ethnic loyalty among the Germans did not extend to forgiving a fellow countryman for his wartime Confederate sympathies. Indeed the election revealed extraordinary political discipline on both sides; the former Confederates only triumphed because their West Side supporters outnumbered their East Side German opponents.[19]

Such sharp divisions complicated efforts to recover from the effects of the war. The city and its government were not in good shape. Concerned about the postwar situation, Democrat Jeremiah Dashiell, editor of the *Herald*, demanded public improvements so that San Antonio "would begin to put on the appearance of a city, and no longer look like a mere one-horse town."[20] Such a plea from a former Confederate represented a timid reemergence of urban pride, but the city was broke. The council had invested its revenues in now worthless Confederate bonds, and a cholera epidemic that erupted in 1866 strained its meager resources beyond the breaking point.

Ignoring Dashiell's plea, the council ordered large-scale cuts in public services and halted all public improvement projects in September 1867.[21]

Gen. Joseph J. Reynolds, military commander of the District of Texas, inadvertently encouraged the reemergence of organized boosterism in the midst of this mess when he removed all Democratic city officeholders in November 1867. Reynolds naturally turned to the nascent Republican Party for replacements, appointing, among others, James P. Newcomb as an alderman.

Newcomb quickly emerged as the leader of a new booster coalition. Prior to his hasty departure from San Antonio in 1861, he had been a staunch advocate of economic development and a railroad to the coast. He had also been a leading Know-Nothing whose anti-Catholic editorials probably infuriated the large number of Catholics within the Germans community. Returning from California in 1867, he became a major Republican leader in Texas, serving on the city council from 1867 to 1870, in the 1868 State Constitutional Convention, and as secretary of state in the last Republican Reconstruction administration. He also purchased an interest in a new newspaper, the *San Antonio Express*, from its founder, August Siemering, a prominent Unionist. There was no one else in either the Republican or Democratic Parties who combined an interest in actively promoting development with the ability to implement it. As an editor, Newcomb could now publicize his ideas about urban development while simultaneously, as an alderman, shepherding them through the council.[22]

Newcomb's strategy for transforming San Antonio into a major city replicated ideas circulating in the broader booster community of his era. In editorials that appeared just prior to General Reynolds's dissolution of the city's government, Newcomb defined an ambitious program of improving the city's attractiveness to businessmen via infrastructure improvements, linking the town to national markets with a railroad, and diversifying the economy with factories. Opining that the streets were not designed to facilitate the movement of goods and people throughout the town or to cope with growth, he remarked: "Any person who will take the pains to walk over the city will see that the whole street plan is on the most parsimonious and mean order.... These streets may serve well enough for present uses, but a few years may bring us railroads, population and a business which will require wide streets." He also described the streets as unattractive and unfriendly to pedestrians: "Every street in the city should be widened so as to allow of ample sidewalks, and room to plant trees for shade."[23]

Observing that "San Antonio has always been and is now almost entirely a city inhabited by consumers," who only "eat and sell," Newcomb also urged San Antonians to manufacture products for export to regional and national markets. Since exports could not reach those markets without transportation links, Newcomb argued that "the first grand movement in the right direction is the building of a railroad to the Gulf and then the establishment of a direct line of steamers to New Orleans, New York, and Boston." Samuel Maverick could not have said it any better himself.[24]

The timing of Newcomb's prescription for San Antonio's development may not have been purely serendipitous. Businessmen in Dallas and Houston were also searching for ways to revive the fortunes of their cities, and, unlike San Antonians, they were determined to use the powers of local government to promote growth. In 1866 they presided over public meetings in both cities that established community support for their plans for economic development.[25] By eliminating development as a controversial topic in local politics, those businessmen gained valuable time to create partnerships with their governments to work on economic issues. Their unity would in time create competitive advantages for these cities in the race for regional dominance.

A variety of contingencies related to San Antonio's development prior to the late 1860s probably precluded a similar approach to development in San Antonio. Newcomb's personal history as a Know-Nothing and an intemperate Unionist would not have been the best credentials for calling a public meeting to endorse his booster agenda in late 1867. At this point there would have been too few San Antonians who respected his credentials enough to support him. Nor could he have called upon anyone from the defunct Maverick coalition to cosponsor a community discussion of his program. Resurrecting memories of past failures by calling a meeting to discuss a booster initiative would probably not have elicited much interest in a city still bitterly divided by the war and, now, military Reconstruction.

For whatever reasons, Newcomb initially chose to convince San Antonians to adopt his program through editorial exhortations, rhetorically asking his readers: "How can the prosperity of the city be increased? Certainly not by supinely waiting until chance effects the work."[26] However, in the absence of a community-wide consensus similar to that enjoyed in Dallas or Houston, florid rhetoric could not overcome the divisions over the booster initiative in San Antonio's local politics.

The only men Newcomb could rely on to support his program were fellow Republicans. Fortunately for Newcomb, several of them were important leaders of the German community, including August Siemering, Edward Degener, and Wilhelm C. A. Thielepape. Siemering, a former resident of Fredericksburg, had chaired the infamous 1854 German convention in San Antonio. His pro-Union, antislavery views earned him a forced enlistment in the Confederate army. After the war he founded the *Frei Presse* and the *San Antonio Express* to preach Republicanism and promote San Antonio's development.

Edward Degener participated in the abortive 1848 revolution in Germany before migrating to Texas with several other refugees who settled the town of Sisterdale. Initially a farmer, he moved to San Antonio and became a wholesale grocer without, apparently, any great success. His primary passion was politics, no doubt motivated in part by the deaths of his two sons at the Nueces River massacre. Degener served in the state constitutional conventions of 1866 and 1868, won election to Congress (1870–71), and then spent six years on the city council.

Thielepape was a university-trained engineer who emigrated to Indianola, where he engaged in railroad surveying work. Moving to San Antonio in 1854, he worked as an architect, designed a building for the Casino Club, and helped organize the German-English School. Self-exiled during the war, Thielepape returned to San Antonio in time to help raise the Union flag over the Alamo on July 21, 1865. That probably did not endear him to local Confederates, but it may have helped convince General Reynolds to appoint him mayor in November 1867.[27]

However able they may have been, these men lacked practical experience in creating citywide economic development coalitions. And, like Maverick's coalition, Newcomb failed to attract important businessmen to his program. His team consisted of "new men" who had no prior personal records of significant contributions to local civic and economic affairs. They had only two assets: their belief in organized urban development, and political power. For the next five years they would control the city council, first as military and then as gubernatorial appointees. Whether that would suffice depended a great deal on their skill and luck in negotiating a local minefield of political, racial, and ethnic conflict.

Luck, however, would be in short supply. When General Reynolds transferred political power to the Republicans, Democrats promptly accused them of planning to force whites to accept social equality with blacks. This accusation resonated with many white San Antonians who were disturbed by a dramatic growth in the local black population following the war. Although slaves had lived in the town since the eighteenth century, only 594 blacks (7 percent of the total population) lived in San Antonio in 1860. Following the war's end, the black population more than doubled to become 15 percent of the city's population by 1870. Black residents' increased numbers and dispersal throughout San Antonio made them more visible to white residents.[28] White rage at the prospect of black participation in government prompted the organization of a branch of the Ku Klux Klan in early 1868. The Klan paraded through the business district that spring and launched a terror campaign against blacks and their supporters during the fall elections.[29]

Democratic accusations that Republicans intended to impose social equality for blacks bothered some, but not all, Germans, and their hostility toward Southern Democrats seems momentarily to have offset any misgivings about racial equality.[30] That ambivalence created the opportunity for Republicans to cultivate German support, but the party also needed to tread a delicate line between Newcomb's activist plans for urban development and German opposition to using local government to promote that growth.

Complicating matters, the unpopularity of military rule deprived the new Republican regime of legitimacy in the eyes of many voters. In these circumstances, the Republicans made little progress with Newcomb's idea that the council should control the city's evolving physical spaces. Business opposition to that idea crossed political boundaries. A Democratic council had encountered opposition to the idea from Louis Zork in 1867 when it attempted to enforce an ordinance regulating setbacks along Commerce Street, which was rapidly becoming the most important business avenue in town. Although the council rejected Zork's petition, the city apparently did not enforce the ordinance. When the Republicans attempted to do so in early 1869, Edward Steves and John Kampmann demanded compensation from the city and won their claim in a jury trial. In effect, the business community rejected the idea that the council controlled the evolution of public space, creating an enormous obstacle to enhancing San Antonio's physical attractiveness.[31]

Funding problems also inhibited the Republicans' public improvement plans. The city was essentially bankrupt when Thielepape became mayor. In the first three years of Republican rule, barely half of the taxpayers settled their bills with the city. General Reynolds refused to help the council with this problem, and probably aggravated it by denying the city's request to prosecute ratepayers for nonpayment. Strapped for cash, the council struggled to meet ordinary expenses and shelved Newcomb's program.[32]

Another key project in Newcomb's program, building a railroad to the coast, ran afoul of the city's failure to retire the bonds it had sold to support the SA&MG Railroad. Creditors appeared in court beginning in 1867 to demand their principal and interest, prompting the Democratic council to hire Isaiah Paschal to defend the city against these claims. That strategy only delayed settlements, and by November 1868 the council had lost so many cases that it had to reintroduce a railroad tax to pay court judgments against the city. When continuing legal defeats forced the council to renew this tax, it became an annual reminder of the folly of the city government for investing in public improvements in general and railroads in particular.[33]

With an exquisite sense of timing, the depot commander dropped a major crisis into the ongoing struggles with taxes and railroad bonds. In February 1868 Gen. John Mason told Thielepape and the aldermen that New Braunfels had offered him a free site for a military headquarters and depot. He demanded that the council give him enough land to consolidate the depot and housing for his officers and men in one place and also to provide assurances that San Antonio would soon have a rail connection to the coast.[34]

Losing the army depot at this point would have been disastrous for the economy. Its reappearance in San Antonio had been essential to economic revival in 1865, both locally and in the hinterland. Federal troops quickly resumed their protection of outlying settlements and reestablished their central role in the local economy by contracting for goods, services, and food. Over the next decade the army would spend $2 million (in 1870 dollars) for freighting contracts alone, to say nothing of tens of thousands of dollars on forage, livestock, and wages.[35]

With the army once again the most important source of cash, businessmen of all political persuasions were not shy about claiming their share. Jeremiah Y. Dashiell, editor of the *Herald* and a rabid Democrat, for instance, contracted to supply the army with beef, while other Democrats like Robert Eager and the firm of Hardin B. Adams and E. D. L. Wickes won freighting contracts to supply various garrisons.[36]

And for the first time the army's cash subsidized new initiatives. George Brackenridge, backed by his former associates in cotton smuggling, obtained a charter for the First National Bank of San Antonio. Since the National Banking Act of 1863 required all federal funds to be deposited in national banks, Brackenridge immediately acquired a monopoly over the deposit and distribution of army cash when he opened for business in 1866.

His timing could not have been better because ranchers in southern Texas were just organizing the first cattle drives in response to national demand for beef. Cattle had multiplied spectacularly during the early 1860s, creating a vast pool of animals worth only $3 a head locally but $20 to $30 each at the railheads in Kansas. San Antonio's position at the apex of southern Texas's cattle country made it the natural starting point for the Chisholm Trail, the most important route to market until the late 1870s. Driving a herd north required loans for wages, equipment, and provisions, which trail drivers could repay when they sold the cattle at the railhead. Brackenridge's control over federal deposits placed him in the best position to loan money he had earned from managing the army's funds to the cattlemen. In effect, Brackenridge leveraged federal money to finance a major new business for the city. He was not the only banker in town—three private banks emerged by 1870—but he was the only one with access to a large, reliable source of funds.[37]

Cattle were not the only raw material attracting attention in national markets. Central Texas had been an important wool-producing area prior to the Civil War, and after 1865, with the army making that area safe once again, sheep ranching enjoyed spectacular growth as ranchers expanded their flocks in response to demand for wool in New England's textile mills. In the absence of a railroad, overland freighting was the only alternative for moving wool to market, and San Antonio's array of experienced freighting companies and its road network managed to make the city a central gathering and distribution point for sheep ranchers.[38]

By 1868 army cash, national demand for cattle and wool, and a reviving hinterland had begun to transform San Antonio's business district. Military Plaza was becoming the town's wholesaling center. Next door, in Main Plaza, merchants began specializing in retail ranch equipment sales. Hotels, saloons, restaurants, vaudeville theaters, gambling halls, and brothels intermingled around both plazas.[39] San Antonio had unwittingly become a business-tourist center, although these overwhelmingly male visitors probably did not come to town to see the Alamo.

Increasing prosperity helped create a modest recovery in the real estate market by the late 1860s, financed in part by army cash. Harden B. Adams and Edwin de Lacy Wickes, partners in a freighting business they founded in 1868, became the army's principal contractors for long-distance hauling. Investing their profits in local real estate beginning in 1870, they competed with Samuel Maverick Jr., John Kampmann, and Albert Steves to acquire land in the more desirable areas of town, particularly in the business district and on the east side of the river. Together, these five men accounted for 62 percent of all land purchases during the 1870s. With a steady source of federal funds at their disposal, Adams and Wickes became the largest land speculators in town.[40]

With prosperity returning and a real estate boomlet under way, the council quickly agreed to some of General Mason's demands, offering a new site for the headquarters and depot without specifying where that would be.[41] Thielepape, however, discovered that local landowners, especially those around the Alamo, had little interest in cooperating with him to find a site. They feared that if the army left, their property values would decline. Others who made a living from renting housing to the army also opposed moving the depot out of Alamo Plaza.[42]

Perhaps hoping to encourage action, General Mason announced in 1869 that the army headquarters (but not the depot) would move to Austin. His announcement forced a singular act of cooperation between political opponents. Thielepape negotiated with Samuel Maverick, who had recently denounced local Republicans for being in league with "that arch traitor from hell," Thaddeus Stevens, for land just north of Alamo Plaza as a site for a new depot. Disliking both the small amount of land Maverick offered and its location, the army rejected the offer.[43]

TABLE 1 Real Estate Transactions, 1860–80

Year	Number of Transactions	Percent Change	Year	Number of Transactions	Percent Change
1860	706	—	1871	609	-7
1861	288	-59	1872	620	2
1862	256	-11	1873	544	-12
1863	213	-17	1874	556	2
1864	156	-27	1875	557	—
1865	333	113	1876	763	37
1866	533	60	1877	912	20
1867	369	-31	1878	882	-3
1868	482	31	1879	812	-8
1869	542	12	1880	793	-2
1870	652	20			

Source: City Council Minutes, January of each year.

In the meantime General Mason's demand for rail connections to the coast prompted the formation of the Bexar Railroad Association. The association surprisingly decided that completing construction of the defunct SA&MG offered the best hope for satisfying Mason's demand. François Guilbeau, an original supporter of the SA&MG, traveled to New Orleans as the association's representative to talk with Charles Morgan about reviving it. Morgan had created a virtual monopoly on Gulf shipping and was seeking ways to undermine the Galveston Wharf and Cotton Press Company, which charged him (and everyone else) excessively high fees to use its docks. Since a railroad terminating on the coast south of Galveston would suit Morgan's interests, he offered to contribute $250,000 toward completion of the SA&MG if San Antonio would match his offer.

Guilbeau reported Morgan's offer to the association, which "concluded nothing could be done until after reconstruction." That odd explanation may have been part of a strategy to pressure the army into agreeing to a petition Democrats were circulating that demanded removal of all Republicans in local government in exchange for support for a railroad. Despite the army's threat to leave because there was no railroad, political animosity was trumping economic necessity among many San Antonians. Whatever its reasoning, the association's decision doomed the SA&MG. The federal government foreclosed on the railroad in 1870, and Morgan bought its assets.[44]

The Republicans, however, began an effort to salvage their political fortunes. Newcomb became secretary of state and president of the Union League in May 1870.[45] These positions gave him opportunities to help reorganize radical Republican voters, especially African Americans, across the state and to promote his development program for San Antonio. However, Newcomb's enhanced political stature did not increase his political acumen. Indeed, he now maneuvered to enact what would become the greatest folly of his short political career.

Perhaps recalling how Maverick's coalition had sought to overcome local opposition to its program by altering the city's charter in 1856, Newcomb resurrected the same ploy. In January 1868 Thielepape had appointed Newcomb and two aldermen to a charter revision committee. When the committee completed its work early in 1870, Newcomb circulated it privately among several aldermen instead of submitting it for formal council approval. When Thielepape told him that those favored few endorsed the draft, Newcomb arranged for legislative approval.[46]

The new charter transformed local government into a major engine for economic development. It gave the council "exclusive control and power over the streets" and the authority to "direct the location and regulate the management and construction of... manufacturing establishments." It also swept away taxpayer resistance to public improvements by correcting the Maverick coalition's mistake of requiring voter consent to bond issues. The council could now issue as much as $50,000 in bonds each year without a referendum. Moreover, the council received the authority to levy a special property tax of one-half of 1 percent to retire each bond issue.

Perhaps anticipating a jaundiced reaction to his inventive approach to funding public improvements, Newcomb inserted an equally remarkable innovation to counteract potential opposition. His charter prohibited the council from loaning money to private corporations or railroads unless the city owned them (which was unlikely).[47]

The defunct SA&MG's tortured history may explain this strange restriction. Court judgments forcing the city to redeem its SA&MG bonds with a railroad tax were a major political liability—ironically for Republicans rather than the Democrats who had issued the original bonds.[48] Newcomb may have been attempting to defuse public anger over that legal obligation by guaranteeing that such a situation would never recur. Unintentionally, though, he made a critical concession to the community's fundamental opposition to local government's participation in urban development.

Newcomb's charter restriction was also potentially damaging to efforts to deal with the military's insistence on a railroad, especially because the community's leadership was still unwilling to satisfy that demand. More broadly, Newcomb's restriction made little sense from the perspective of normal nineteenth-century boosterism. Cities across the United States were actively pursuing rail connections by contributing cash and land to railroad promoters. Newcomb was handing Dallas and Houston yet another competitive advantage in the race for regional dominance.

Oddly enough, many San Antonians were not grateful for Newcomb's efforts. Instead they were enraged by the absence of any public notice or discussion of a new charter and by its provisions for funding public improvements. Newcomb's political ineptitude made him a divisive figure among Republicans. More importantly, he provoked a furious effort to resurrect the antebellum consensus against any government role in development, thereby giving his opponents in both parties a common cause that eventually trumped their partisan differences.

The *Herald* began that campaign by focusing on the charter's most vulnerable innovation: its provisions on taxation. The newspaper urged everyone to attend a hastily called public meeting to discuss whether "the people of a republican government should have something to say in the adoption of a city charter that imposes city officials upon them without their votes of consent, and who are authorized to tax them to such extent that many of them may see their goods and chattels, lands and tenements sold from under them, and their families starve for bread."[49]

A broad array of community leaders from both sides of the river attended the meeting, including prominent men from the American, Mexican American, and French communities. Most ominously for Newcomb's Republican coalition, a majority of the attendees were German business leaders. Until this point local Germans had not made much progress in healing their internal divisions or their relations with other San Antonians. But Confederate supporters like Louis Zork and John H. Kampmann, who had absented themselves from public political events after 1865, attended this protest against the charter and had important roles in its proceedings.[50]

While not all Unionist German leaders were ready to embrace former Confederates within their community (Edward Degener, for instance, did not attend this meeting), Newcomb had given all Germans reason to rethink their commitment to Republicanism. Their views on limited government and low taxes were beginning to overshadow their unhappiness about their treatment during the war. But they were also not yet prepared to embrace the Democrats, and not simply because of the war. Maverick's prewar booster coalition, after all, had pursued a public improvements program as aggressive as Newcomb's. From that perspective, Democrats were no better than Republicans, leaving the Germans in something of a quandary about how to deploy their political clout.

Members of Newcomb's booster coalition displayed an astonishing indifference to the political storm swirling around them. The *Express* editor matter-of-factly said, "We do not deny that the taxes are high, but we maintain and believe we have shown clearly that the necessities of the State demand the enforcement of the measures for which these taxes have been levied."[51] Linking the "necessities of the State" to high taxes neatly captured the essence of Newcomb's approach to city-building, but it also gave Germans who resented higher taxes to fund government activism further food for thought.

The council served them more to chew on when it returned to its public improvement agenda, authorizing street improvements and bridges and offering land to the federal government and the state for a courthouse and a penitentiary. Late in 1871 councilmembers capped a year of numerous if scattered improvements by approving a memorial from Mayor Thielepape to develop "a general system of drainage and repairing all streets," signaling the intent to expand the scope of their activities.[52]

Seeking to resolve the army's demands for a new depot site after it rejected Maverick's offer, Thielepape also made his own contribution to the council's growing reputation for ineptitude by asking Anthony Dignowity, a major East Side land speculator, for help. Dignowity agreed to sell the city a mere twenty-eight acres—considerably less than Maverick had offered—for an extortionate price of $8,000 in silver coin. Astonishingly Thielepape agreed to the terms, perhaps because it was more important to demonstrate a serious effort to meet the army's demand for a new site than to quibble over money. Since the city treasury did not have the funds, Thielepape resorted to appointing an alderman to solicit donations.[53]

In the meantime a group of Republicans including Newcomb and Siemering tried to deal with the army's demand for a railroad. They announced their intention to build the Indianola, San Antonio, and El Paso Railroad in April 1871. Whether this group could in fact succeed remained to be seen, especially with a board of directors composed entirely of Republicans who lacked the financial resources for constructing a railroad.[54]

While Newcomb dabbled with his railroad project, some of his putative allies began searching for new leadership. Conservative German politicians began experimenting with ways to gain control of the city council to squelch its booster projects. They created bitter ethnic and racial tensions by insisting that all candidates for local office should be German. In defense of this strategy they argued, for example, that African Americans should vote for German candidates because the Army of the Potomac's XI Corps, half of whose regiments were German immigrants, had fought for them in the Civil War. This strategy offended Mexican Americans, who complained that the Germans refused to support candidates from their community. All of this heightened antagonism among the party's major constituencies, and its massive defeat in fall 1871 state and congressional elections, did not improve its prospects for unity.[55]

Perhaps in response to this intraparty bickering, Thielepape and his aldermen, five of eight of whom were German, maneuvered to distance themselves from Newcomb by challenging his control of political appointments. When both sides appealed to Governor Davis to settle this dispute, Siemering pointedly notified Davis that his countrymen would continue to support him "if the Governor will let us settle our little local affairs." Davis, who was desperate for local support in his doomed battle to preserve Republican unity in state government at this point, heeded the message and backed Thielepape, which badly damaged Newcomb's political authority in San Antonio.[56]

With his supporters reporting that "there is something radically wrong here in the organization of the Republican party.... All pander to the German and Rebel interest,"[57] Newcomb struggled to reassert his power. The council provided him with the opportunity in January 1872, when it voted to accept an offer from George W. Brackenridge to sell his home and property at the head of the river to the city. In the 1850s Mayor James Sweet had bought that land from the city, converting its water source into private property. Brackenridge acquired the land in 1869 and was willing to part with it on generous terms: $50,000 paid out over fifty years at 8 percent interest. He even added another two hundred acres of contiguous land to the package as an added inducement.[58]

Superficially, regaining control over the city's water supply seemed reasonable, but Brackenridge had only paid $4,500 for the land. Those who regarded his profit margin as excessive created a political storm over his offer. With his Republican opponents on the defensive, Newcomb had an opportunity to use public indignation to reassert his leadership and to salvage his booster program for the city.

Local Republican politics mirrored that disarray within the state party by 1871, and Newcomb had made significant contributions to that chaos with his egregiously high-handed behavior and aggressive booster program. His role as the leader of the Radical Republicans, which meant that he favored civil rights for blacks, also made him vulnerable to his opponents. Many, if not most, San Antonians had little interest in helping blacks with their struggles to succeed.

Newcomb, though, still had considerable political influence as a major ally of Gov. Edmund Davis and as secretary of state. In addition, the legislature had given the governor the power to appoint mayors and aldermen in November 1871, shortly after Newcomb lost his battle with the city council over patronage. The stage was set for a possible political comeback, but he needed new allies to replace those he had lost in the patronage fight. His search for new supporters, though, displayed an ineptness that would undermine his chances for success and contribute to a different political outcome than he had intended.

With the prospect of finding influential allies within his own party becoming problematic, Newcomb decided on a bipartisan approach to resurrecting his political fortunes by inviting John Kampmann to collaborate with him in reconstructing local government.[59] Newcomb may have felt comfortable with this choice because of Kampmann's recent activities. Kampmann had publicly expressed his opposition to Brackenridge's offer, and he had recently become a director for a street railway company that Newcomb and several other Republicans had organized in May 1871. Kampmann had also helped the lobbying campaign to retain the army depot by hosting a large banquet when Gen. Philip Sheridan visited San Antonio to assess that situation.[60]

Julius Van Slyck, editor of the *Express,* had praised Kampmann lavishly for sponsoring that banquet, describing him as "our patriotic, public spirited and genial fellow citizen . . . who is capable of contributing largely to the energy and enterprise of our city."[61] Van Slyck's rhetorical flourishes symbolically acknowledged that Kampmann had become one of the few people in the city at this point who had a broad network of associates that crossed political and ethnic boundaries. His service on the Confederate Defence Aid Society and in the Third Texas Infantry connected him to die-hard Democrats; as an architect and builder, he had constructed the homes of many prominent businessmen. He had personal and business relationships with men like Edward Steves who were new to town and in the process of making their fortunes, and he employed large numbers of Mexican Americans in his woodworking factory and architecture firm, giving him access to their community leaders. His personal business history also gave him great credibility—he was a self-made man in a culture that esteemed economic success. Kampmann, in sum, had become a man who could make things happen.[62]

With Kampmann's help, Newcomb launched his counteroffensive. Posing as a champion of democracy, he pointed out to Governor Davis that all the current councilmen lived east of the river, depriving the West Side of representation. Newcomb conveniently ignored the fact that this imbalance derived from the refusal of West Side Democrats to serve as aldermen, forcing the appointment of East Side residents to represent West Side wards.

Newcomb asked the governor to replace the current mayor and aldermen with men who Newcomb and his allies chose for him. Davis accepted his suggestions, and the new council promptly voted to rescind the city's agreement to buy the head of the river property.[63] But Davis also scheduled charter and general elections for late 1872 that would prove disastrous for Newcomb. Newcomb's maneuvers to recapture control of San Antonio's government would in fact set the stage for his demise as a major political leader.

Perhaps because his duties as secretary of state kept him in Austin much of the time, Newcomb had failed to notice that in response to an improving economy businessmen were working to heal the divisiveness stemming from the Civil War by developing a nonpartisan approach to local politics.

In May 1871 thirty-four men from politically and ethnically diverse backgrounds had resurrected the San Antonio Commercial Club that Kampmann had helped found in 1866. That group included men whose careers had begun in the 1850s, individuals who made fortunes during the war, and postwar newcomers. The club also recruited nearly twenty army officers, creating closer ties with the military at a critical point in the city's negotiations to retain its economic anchor. While not encompassing the entire business community, the club did recruit 198 members during the summer.[64]

Another group of Germans and Southerners, some of whom belonged to the Commercial Club, also founded a Board of Trade in fall 1872. While officially an organization devoted to the "promotion of Trade and... advancement of the Commercial and Manufacturing Interests of San Antonio," its initial bylaws did not create any committees for achieving those goals. Instead the board's founders designed it to arbitrate disputes between members. President Charles Merritt, a grocer, could appoint committees on arbitration and appeal as needed, and the committees' findings would be binding on the parties to a dispute.[65] Kampmann was therefore associated with those businessmen who were becoming more interested in healing, not perpetuating, the ethnic and political bitterness that had divided the city since the Civil War. And Newcomb failed to understand this change.

Growing cooperation between these German and Southern businessmen and politicians eroded their commitment to intensely partisan politics. A rebellion within the national Republican Party against President Grant in 1872 provided ideal political cover for these men to experiment with local nonpartisan cooperation. Calling themselves Liberal Republicans, these rebels to the party overall nominated Horace Greeley in May 1872 to oppose Grant and campaigned for an end to Reconstruction. The national Democratic Party then joined the Republican dissenters. By October San Antonio's Democrats and Germans had organized Greeley and Brown Clubs in every ward and had selected a balanced slate of Southern Democratic and German candidates for office. That same month German voters announced their political independence in a separate citywide convention that denounced "strict party discipline" and endorsed the entire Greeley/Brown slate. Fayette Walker, a major African American politician, criticized "radical demagogism" and announced his support for the Greeley/Brown ticket as well. The coalition then won control of the mayor's office and the city council.[66]

Amid all the electioneering, Newcomb's Indianola, San Antonio, and El Paso Railroad had dropped from sight, leaving city fathers with the awkward task of explaining to the depot commander how San Antonio would acquire rail connections to the coast. Gen. Philip Sheridan was apparently not amused. The International and Great Northern Railroad had reached Dallas during 1872. He recommended that the depot move to Fort Worth, which was now much closer to an existing railroad. In December the secretary of the army agreed. San Antonio seemed about to lose its basic economic-development tool.[67]

That threat focused the community's attention on finding a quick but believable solution. With their control of city government secure, the Southern/German coalition could now appeal to the Board of Trade for help in January 1873. The board promptly recommended negotiating with Thomas Pierce, a Boston capitalist living in New Orleans who was building a railroad across Texas from Galveston.

Despite the board's help, local businessmen were not united in support of a railroad. Resistance in fact remained pervasive, perhaps because many businessmen feared that a railroad would eliminate their lucrative federal contracts for transporting the army's goods and also increase competition among businessmen. San Antonio's isolation seems to have bred an insularity that made some merchants resist changes that would promote economic development. When the decision to move the depot became public knowledge, an anonymous writer to the *Express* commented that "a merchant lately remarked that there were too many here, engaged in business, who were opposed to a railroad from any direction, fearing the competition to which it would give rise."[68] The author of a guidebook, who was trying to promote San Antonio's investment possibilities, noted the same phenomenon: "It is exceedingly difficult to arrive at anything like correct data regarding the commercial standing of San Antonio, for the reason that no statistics are kept, and that much of the business is in the hands of those who are averse to giving information, thinking that it will induce competition."[69]

These attitudes added to the challenge of attracting a railroad to town, and Pierce did not help matters when he demanded a $500,000 subsidy from San Antonio. That created a conundrum. The city's charter now prohibited the council from investing public funds in a private corporation. Fortunately there was a loophole. State laws permitted localities to support railroads, which allowed the Bexar County commissioners to arrange for a subsidy with voter approval. Rural Bexareños apparently thought well enough of Pierce's proposal to help pass a referendum in July 1873 that approved bonds for his subsidy, although his railroad had to arrive in San Antonio within two years or the deal would be null and void.[70] These efforts, supplemented by a lobbying campaign in Washington, persuaded the secretary of the army to suspend plans to move the depot.[71]

Having resolved that immediate economic crisis, San Antonians now could return to continuing battle over the proper role of government in urban improvements. An attempt to replace Newcomb's 1870 charter provided an opportunity to restore that consensus. Following their electoral triumph, the council responded to popular demand by appointing a citizens' charter revision committee. Its draft charter revealed considerable hostility to government. One clause eliminated alderman salaries in an attempt to transform political office holding into a form of community service rather than a viable career choice. Even more pointedly, the draft prohibited the city from borrowing money for any reason without prior voter consent.[72]

Governor Davis eventually refused to approve a new charter when some local Democrats attempted to use it for personal advantage. Thomas Devine and François Guilbeau reportedly had helped the citizens' committee redraw the city's West Side boundary to exclude property they owned there from taxation. That maneuver embarrassed and compromised the revision effort.[73]

As the proposed charter wended its way toward Davis's veto, the council lurched unexpectedly into boosterism. The *Express,* probably unintentionally, foreshadowed the aldermen's thinking when it urged them to adopt a systematic approach to urban improvements, commenting, "Without *system,* money will be wasted."[74] As if on cue, the council promptly asked Mayor Francis Giraud to appoint a special committee to create a general plan for public improvements. That committee issued its report in July 1873, recommending a "general system of paving," four new major streets to improve traffic circulation, new bridges, a flood control plan, and the construction of a city water works. With regard to a water works, the committee thought a private company could construct it, but "it would probably be more advantageous to the City to own the works."[75] Newcomb himself could not have authored a more comprehensive booster vision for urban improvements. Campaigning as advocates of minimalist government had obviously not inoculated the winning candidates against the temptations of office.

While waiting for that report, the council continued to struggle with the practical challenges of governing without revenue. They were discovering that their authority under the 1870 charter to issue bonds without voter approval did not mean that the voters would dutifully pay their taxes to fund those bonds. During the spring and summer aldermen had to grant the mayor authority to borrow money to pay routine expenses. In a sign of how pervasive and stubborn nonpayment had become, the aldermen ordered their attorney to canvas assessment records from 1864 to 1872 for delinquents.[76] Tax avoidance had become endemic, forcing the council to repeat the cycle of issuing new debt the following year.[77]

Despite these revenue problems, the newly elected Democrats and Liberal Republicans began issuing bonds for improvements that they distributed equitably among neighborhoods on both sides of the river (which ignored the comprehensive approach to infrastructure development favored in their own special committee's report). It apparently did not occur to the aldermen that they should find ways to pay for these improvements since they had neglected to adopt a budget or to track expenses for them.[78]

If the aldermen expected all of their neighbors to approve of their approach to improvements, they were to be sadly disappointed. The council's actions discredited the Democratic/Liberal Republicans coalition because it had not replaced the much-hated 1870 charter and had adopted an improvement program that increased the city's debt.

Remarkably, the Democrats sought reelection on this record, unintentionally transforming the 1875 election into a referendum on both governmental activism and partisanship as the organizing principles for local politics. They may have misinterpreted their brief alliance with the Liberal Republicans as a sign that the Germans had returned to their prewar Democratic loyalties. If so, that was a mistake, because they instead turned to the Independent Party, which introduced its candidates for office in January

1875 by announcing that "party politics... *rightly have nothing to do with administering the affairs of our city.*"[79]

Superficially, the Independent Party was a continuation of the partnership between Democrats and Liberal Republicans. But it was in fact a genuinely new phenomenon that reflected the business community's search for civic harmony. Its candidates were men who had not previously sought political office and shared a genuine commitment to fiscal conservatism. Furthermore, these were individuals who retained their loyalty to the official Democratic and Republican Parties in elections for county, state, and national elections, but who were determined to suspend that loyalty in city government. They made that clear with the name of their new party; "independent" was a declaration that civic affairs should be exempt from partisanship.

James H. French, who became the Independent Party's mayoral candidate, exemplified its approach to city politics. A Virginian by birth, French had moved to San Antonio as a teenager in 1851 and established a grocery business in 1859. During the war he helped organize the Southern Defence Aid Society and served in administrative positions in the Confederate army. During Reconstruction, he served on the executive committee of Southern Life Insurance and the Board of Trade (whose focus on reconciling differences among businessmen may have given him valuable experience as a mediator). French had never held public office, but his business connections initially gave him a broad base of support among important Democrats and Republicans. His connections included army contractor Hardin B. Adams, Republican banker George W. Brackenridge, Democrat and land developer Sam Maverick Jr., and the city's most important businessman, John Kampmann. French's daughter Olive had married a son of Thomas J. Devine, giving him a social relationship to another iconic conservative Democrat and major landowner.[80]

Unfortunately neither French nor anyone associated with him left any records that would help explain how or why he was able to become the most remarkable politician of his generation. He gave the city its first "modern" (for its day) administration, bludgeoned the council into fiscally responsible policies, played an important role in securing a railroad for San Antonio, made nonpartisanship a permanent feature of city politics, and campaigned

TABLE 2 Percentage of Vote for James French for Mayor, 1875

West Side Wards		*East Side Wards*	
First	*Second*	*Third*	*Fourth*
29	48	68	59

Source: Calculated from City Council Minutes, January 15, 1875.

tirelessly for civic improvements. And while compiling this record he became San Antonio's first political boss.

German voting power was crucial to French's career and to the success of nonpartisanship. Indeed it may well have been the Germans' unhappiness with both the Democratic and Republican Parties and their desire to dominate local politics to ensure that their views on government prevailed that transformed them into the most important source of support for nonpartisanship.

The Germans provided the crucial votes for French's first election victory in 1875. Since that election was the first confrontation between politics-as-usual and nonpartisanship, the regular Democratic Party (but not the Republicans) presented their own complete slate of candidates, no doubt expecting to crush the Independents. The results were mixed. French's ticket won most of the citywide offices while the Democrats captured the council. Voting patterns revealed that nonpartisanship was essentially an East Side phenomenon at this point. The predominantly Mexican American West Side opposed the Independent ticket, but higher voter turnout combined with an overwhelming preference for the Independents on the East Side to give French his victory.

That split indicated that French and his allies had work to do in order to transform nonpartisanship into a permanent fixture in city elections. Although the details of how French managed to convince West Side voters to adopt nonpartisanship remain obscure, his coalition apparently achieved its goal by creating the city's first political "machine." Within two years they had made enough progress that one editor commented that "the election of Mayor French… appears to have killed the parties.… It is regarded by Republicans as well as Democrats that there will virtually be no party lines…

at the next election."[81] The leaders of both parties were unhappy about this situation but admitted they could do nothing about it, especially because the Independents (whose formal party name changed with every election) became such an effective organization:

TABLE 3 Percentage of Vote for Mayor French, 1877–83

	West Side Wards		*East Side Wards*	
Year	*First*	*Second*	*Third*	*Fourth*
1877	38	51	73	67
1879	66	67	53	69
1881	59	68	45	52
1883	74	67	49	40

French initially used his popularity to modernize the city's government. He dealt with the city's deplorable financial condition by preparing an annual budget (which his predecessors had failed to do), insisted on identifying sources to fund budget proposals, and used his veto power to enforce budgetary discipline when the aldermen strayed from fiscal probity. French also insisted that the council adopt standard parliamentary procedures for enacting ordinances to enforce orderly debate over alderman proposals. These and other reforms during his decade in office ended the chaos that had characterized city government prior to 1875. French consistently demonstrated that he was a superb administrator and a sound fiscal conservative.[82]

He also presided over the resolution of the army's need for a larger facility and a railroad. Lawsuits over land titles that Thielepape bought for a new depot in 1871 finally concluded in 1875. The council authorized French to deed the land to the military in April for the nominal sum of $1. General Sheridan, eyeing the building progress of Thomas Pierce's Galveston, Harrisburg, and San Antonio Railroad, recommended construction of a new depot.[83]

Pierce, though, failed to meet the deadline for collecting his subsidy, which created an awkward situation. Secretary of War W. W. Belknap had not yet formally approved Sheridan's recommendation. When construction brought the railroad to within twenty-eight miles of town in late 1875, Pierce ordered a halt and demanded a new subsidy to finish those last few miles. With the prospects for obtaining Belknap's approval of the city's core economic asset hanging by a thread, many local businessmen displayed their usual disinterest in a railroad. An anonymous writer complained that "the wealthy property owners of San Antonio evince but little public spirit" and attributed their indifference to a belief that a railroad "would injure our business."[84] Indeed only Kampmann had donated land to the GH&SA in 1874, while other major land speculators and community leaders had ignored the railroad entirely.[85]

A handful of men finally did respond to this crisis. Returning again to the county for help, French, Newcomb, Kampmann, Steves, Brackenridge, and a few others organized an impromptu campaign to issue bonds to meet Pierce's demand for $300,000. Searching for every vote, they created an ad hoc committee in late January 1876 that included representatives from all of San Antonio's ethnic and racial communities. Fayette Walker urged African Americans to support the bonds, Juan Cardenas and Manuel Serna argued the case among Mexican Americans, and August Siemering appealed to his countrymen. Irish, French, and American speakers rounded out the committee's roster.[86]

It worked—barely. In a dramatic demonstration of just how divided San Antonians were over the railroad, 5,330 voters went to the polls and gave the bond issue a miniscule plurality of twenty-eight votes.[87] Ten days after this victory Belknap agreed to keep the depot in San Antonio, clearing the way for the development of Fort Sam Houston two miles northeast of downtown, in an area temporarily devoid of urban development.[88] Pierce finished laying track, and San Antonians celebrated the arrival of their first railroad in February 1877.[89]

In the nineteenth century acquiring a railroad normally produced a spurt of economic development accompanied by a spasm of booster rhetoric. San Antonio was no exception, with one editor proclaiming: "With her railroad in operation, San Antonio can now take a position in the great family of first-class cities of the American continent, and move grandly on to . . . greatness and prosperity."[90] Real estate transactions, which had been declining in the early 1870s, spiked 37 percent in 1876 and reached a historic high in 1877, as speculators anticipated an influx of residents seeking homes.[91]

On the other hand, the railroad's arrival coincided with a nadir in organized boosterism. Newcomb's booster efforts had ground to a halt with his political demise, and there had been no effort to revive it prior to 1877. That was rather awkward since it meant San Antonians were not well prepared to take advantage of their new economic asset. Mayor French tried to remedy that situation. Shortly before the railroad arrived, he devoted his annual message to emphasizing its potential importance to the city.

Declaring that completion of the railroad meant "we will cease to be a frontier town," French urged his listeners to adopt "more modern means and methods" to give San Antonio "a forward and progressive impetus." Attempting to deflect concerns about the cost of urban amenities, he argued that "wise economy would dictate the adoption at this time of a system of public improvements commensurate with the needs and requirements of our City, the wants of a higher civilization, and the greater development of our resources." He defined the key "wants" as better streets, sidewalks, and a drainage system.[92]

However prosaic his list might appear, French recognized that San Antonio needed to become a more attractive city. Most streets were unpaved; depending on the weather, the plazas were either dust bowls or mudholes. Other towns across the nation had similar issues, but French was attempting to distinguish San Antonio from them with physical amenities that would impress visitors and entice investors.[93] In effect, he was also arguing that local government not only needed to provide those amenities, it also had a role in urban development.[94]

A financial crisis in spring 1877 no doubt blunted the immediate impact of the railroad's arrival and also distracted attention from the fact that French had just committed heresy. Fiscal conservatism and its corollary, government inaction, were the bedrock beliefs of his coalition, and French had seemingly abandoned political orthodoxy to recommend government activism. Although he had already established a commitment to fiscal conservatism, he had now revealed a booster streak that seemed to contradict his own fundamental principles. French, however, had his own ideas about how to pay for improvements while maintaining fiscal discipline: "I am... firmly convinced that sound discretion would dictate that future generations should be required to pay a portion at least of the cost of improvements permanent in their character," by which he meant the city should borrow money to fund his program.[95]

French apparently spent the remainder of 1877 working with the council and others to create a systematic plan for improving the city's physical attractiveness and diversifying its economy. These discussions may have involved James Newcomb, who would win a place on the new city council in January 1878.[96] Aside from any practical help Newcomb could render French, his return to public office probably created suspicions about the origins of French's heretical views in the ensuing public debate over enhancing the city's attractiveness.

When finally launched in early 1878, French's plan proposed various public improvements that would make his administration a key player in development. He and the aldermen assumed a considerable political risk when they relied on the still extant 1870 charter to commit $50,000 to funding his plan without voter approval.[97] Newcomb's boosterism may have been dead, but French had now resurrected the corpse.

Curiously the local press almost simultaneously launched a campaign to promote manufacturing as a way to diversify the economy. The editors of both newspapers wrote editorials arguing for converting the river into an industrial corridor, claiming, with classic booster hyperbole, that doing so would transform San Antonio into "the principal manufacturing city of the Lone Star State."[98] Arguing that "to build up a great and prosperous city... we must have manufactories," Frank Grice of the *Express* claimed that "we have the material right from the fields and the flocks, the [water] power to run machinery, the labor as cheap as can be obtained anywhere, a healthy climate and a great market to be provided for."[99]

This press campaign for industrial development required assistance from the mayor and council because the 1870 charter delegated considerable authority over the location and regulation of industrial activities to them. Grice made that point explicit when he opined: "We must have action and that must be concerted. The council should start the ball rolling by giving the matter an official recognition. See... whether the city can afford to make any special grants, give immunity from taxation for a number of years, or offer anything calculated to attract manufacturers."[100]

On the other hand, neither the press nor the government could implement such an ambitious program without help from the business community, and that quickly turned into a major problem. Grice attempted to recruit businessmen for a comprehensive booster coalition by inviting them to drop by his office and offer ideas for potential factories. Few did, forcing him to issue a rather plaintive plea: "We must trust our representative men will take hold of this matter. . . . Who will lead in the movement?"[101]

Rejecting that plea for help, the city's leading businessmen instead organized a public meeting on November 27, 1878, to discuss ways to throttle this latest booster outburst. Charles Merritt, president of the Board of Trade, and major landowners like John Kampmann and Thomas J. Devine, among others, helped organize the Taxpayers' Association. They also drafted its statement of purpose, which declared the right of taxpayers "to define the policy of any future city government in regard to expenditures."[102] A majority of the association's prominent men were Germans, but it drew members from all the city's neighborhoods without regard to ethnic or political differences. The association in effect reaffirmed the voting public's, and especially the Germans', commitment to keeping government out of urban development.

As if to remove any doubts as to its opposition, the association announced it would nominate a candidate to replace French in the next election. Its campaign platform would advocate shrinking the city's boundaries to reduce the costs of expanding services to new areas of town (which were minimal at this point) and curtailing the council's bonding authority to reduce the tax burden.[103] Its spokesmen also launched personal attacks on French, declaring him incapable of leadership because he had failed as a businessman.

French thwarted the association's attempt to remove him from office, but the spring of 1879 turned into a debacle for the boosters nonetheless. By April they had assembled several proposals for woolen and paper mills into an attractive package to stimulate manufacturing. One unnamed outside investor even promised to import skilled labor for his factory. Grice wrote editorials stressing how this package would provide employment opportunities for local residents and also increase city tax revenues.[104] But for reasons they never explained, the boosters insisted on harnessing the "unlimited" power of the river rather than relying on steam power to run factories.[105] That insistence ran afoul of two major community concerns about the river.

First, the river's propensity to flood made many residents wary of any proposal that could impede its flow. The millraces of flour mills already along the river had been blamed for aggravating its flooding problem, leading to an ordinance banning water mills on the river within the city's limits in June 1878. That ordinance now became the flash point between supporters and opponents of the booster program.

Boosters reacted to this concern with a maladroit political maneuver. Shortly after their manufacturing program became public, the city engineer and the council's Public Improvements Committee issued reports supporting the program. This was no surprise since James Newcomb was chair of the committee and wrote its report. He assured the public that "rigid enforcement [of the 1878 ordinance] would result in great damage to the future prosperity of our city." He then proceeded to inform his audience it was the "duty of the city to aid and encourage such enterprises" as mills. Furthermore, the proposed dams would "not act as a serious impediment to the free flow of the river."[106]

With memories of Newcomb's prior booster record in their minds, it is doubtful that his opponents found this report very credible. They proceeded to organize a committee of East Side residents who steered the debate into the other objection to creating a manufacturing corridor along the river. Many East Siders had riparian rights to river water in their property deeds (which had originated in the city's Spanish colonial era) and relied on those rights for their gardens and domestic needs. Factories along the river would, in their opinion, impede the river's flow and deprive them of their legal rights. When their committee made formal complaint about the boosters' proposal to the council, it issued an ordinance that authorized citizens with riparian rights to sue anyone who diverted water from the river.[107] That ended the boosters' hopes for a coordinated effort to attract manufacturing to the city.

As the boosters' opponents worked to defeat the proposal for factories, they simultaneously attacked Newcomb's 1870 charter. When French won reelection in January 1879, the Taxpayers' Association announced that it would concentrate its efforts on lobbying the legislature for a charter amendment that would limit the council's bonding capacity to $10,000 a year. The legislature agreed to that amendment in April and solidified the association's political clout by adding a requirement that two-thirds of the voters had to approve any proposed bond issue. Given the political realities at this point, such a super majority was exceedingly unlikely.[108] Indeed, the Taxpayers' Association emphatically demonstrated that point in September 1879, when French scheduled a bond election to widen a single street downtown. Few voters turned out, but those who did trounced the proposal. The East Side wards rejected the proposal by a margin of 92 percent.[109]

The changes to the charter wrecked the city's credit in the bond markets and forced the council to abandon public improvements because there was no source of revenue to fund them. San Antonio businessmen, with the support of a majority of the voting public, had eliminated local government as a resource for promoting economic development.

While perhaps extreme in their views, San Antonians were not unique in their resistance to tax-funded public improvements. Nineteenth-century city residents typically approached urban services and amenities in a piecemeal fashion, believing that local government should only provide urban amenities when residents petitioned the city council for them. But meteoric growth in northern cities like Chicago quickly forced city councils to develop ways to finance city services and assist economic development without raising the ire of taxpayers.[110]

The growth rate of smaller cities like San Antonio did not create enough stress on the local infrastructure to convince businessmen to support major public service improvements. Superficially, population growth looked impressive; the population had increased by roughly 50 percent each decade from 1850 to 1870, and then by 68 percent in the 1870s, but the city had only twenty thousand residents by 1880. An aerial rendering of San Antonio in 1873 depicted a rather bucolic, low-density urban scene. Even allowing for a certain amount of booster editing of the city's appearance, its homes and businesses were well dispersed over the landscape.[111] In the absence of practical experience with massive growth, neither businessmen nor ordinary residents valued investments in urban amenities as a key to personal and community prosperity.

San Antonio's geographical location may also have reinforced the effects of parochialism on the city's development. Unlike its regional rivals, San Antonio had no serious challenger for control of its immediate hinterland. Houston and Galveston, of course, had fought each other for prominence since 1836. Dallas, itself a late bloomer, would acquire a serious competitor when Fort Worth suddenly blossomed after 1880. Simultaneously inspired and threatened by their nearby "urban twin," businessmen in those four cities adopted more aggressive, riskier attitudes toward city-building that included relatively impressive investments in public improvements. In 1880, per capita debt for such improvements amounted to \$91 in Houston, \$46 in Galveston, and \$29 in Dallas. San Antonio's per capita debt was a mere \$7.56.[112]

Not even the arrival of the city's first railroad, typically a major stimulus to booster campaigns for public improvements, could salvage Newcomb's or French's efforts to enhance San Antonio's attractiveness to new residents and investors. They, like Maverick, believed that local government played a critical role in promoting urban development; their opponents believed otherwise. With the Taxpayers' Association's victory, San Antonians had resurrected the lessons of the 1850s, leaving urban development to the business community. The key issue now was how that community would respond.

MAIN PLAZA

Heart of the Booster City

Booster ambitions for transforming San Antonio into a major American city depended on economic development and population growth. Ignoring the fact that they had no control over national trends that affected their local ambitions, the boosters relied on "improvements" to attract residents and businessmen to town. The word encompassed a variety of specific efforts, including a deliberate attempt to create a "modern" city that reflected contemporary assumptions about the organization and appearance of a successful American city.

Unlike most Western cities, though, San Antonio already had a well-established urban form and architecture. The acequia system that watered farmland created a distinctive urban form that violated every booster assumption about the proper shape of a modern city. One-story adobe houses and businesses that dominated local building styles also failed to meet their definition of modernity. San Antonio, in sum, needed fundamental changes in its architecture and design in order to grow.

The boosters tackled the design problem by imposing a grid—the universally accepted shape for American cities—over the agricultural town in 1855. The grid extended well beyond the settled area of the village, which facilitated land speculation and development beyond the community's boundaries, two advantages that were essential to the boosters' plans.

A grid, though, was only a necessary first step in the boosters' plans for transforming San Antonio into a modern city. The next step would take far longer to achieve because it required private property owners to introduce, one building at a time, modern architectural motifs into the business and residential areas of town.

Main Plaza was a major location for focus on that effort. Most of the town's population had lived around Military and Main Plazas, and Main Plaza (as the Plaza de las Islas) had been the more prestigious of the two.

In the antebellum period, Military Plaza became the town's wholesale market area, which gave it a certain seediness that served to enhance the respectability of Main Plaza. And until the 1870s Alamo Plaza was a military base that attracted its own rather dingy set of commercial buildings (with the exception of the Menger Hotel). Many of the town's earliest merchants who opened businesses in the original adobe buildings around Main Plaza gradually modernized its appearance. American wooden framed buildings (not particularly suited to the climate but definitely more prestigious than adobe) infiltrated the plaza beginning in 1847 with the Plaza Hotel.

Reconfiguring San Fernando Cathedral became one of the boosters' most important statements in their quest for modernity. The Church would remain the heart of the Hispanic community, but its French Gothic exterior, finished in 1873, reflected the boosters' insistence on making Main Plaza a showcase of their intention to portray San Antonio as an attractive city. All the plaza lacked was green space, a problem that the boosters solved by replacing the dusty, sunbaked, unpaved open space with a carefully designed park in the early 1880s. By the mid-1890s Victorian respectability combined with booster ambitions to banish the plaza's Spanish heritage, and transform Main Plaza into a commercial center for tourists and the city's rapidly growing Anglo population.

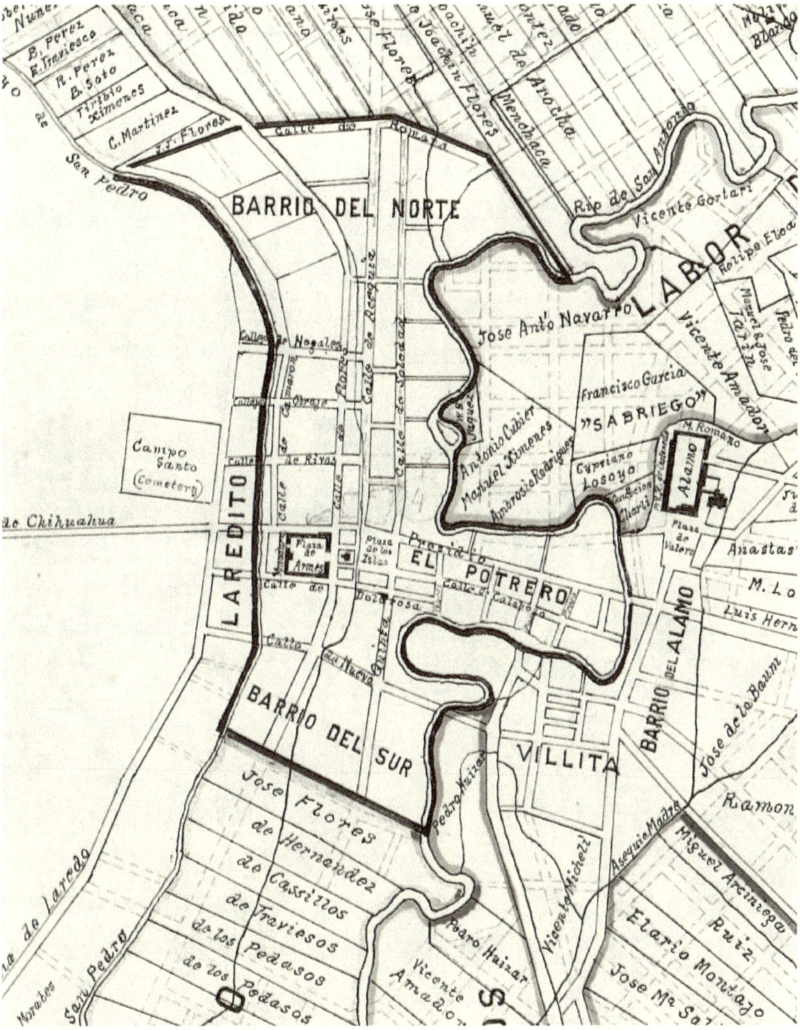

Early San Antonio agriculture relied on access to the river via a system of acequias, engineered irrigation ditches. Each farm's property lines radiated diagonally to the San Antonio River to facilitate the distribution of water by the acequia system as illustrated in this 1837 San Antonio map.

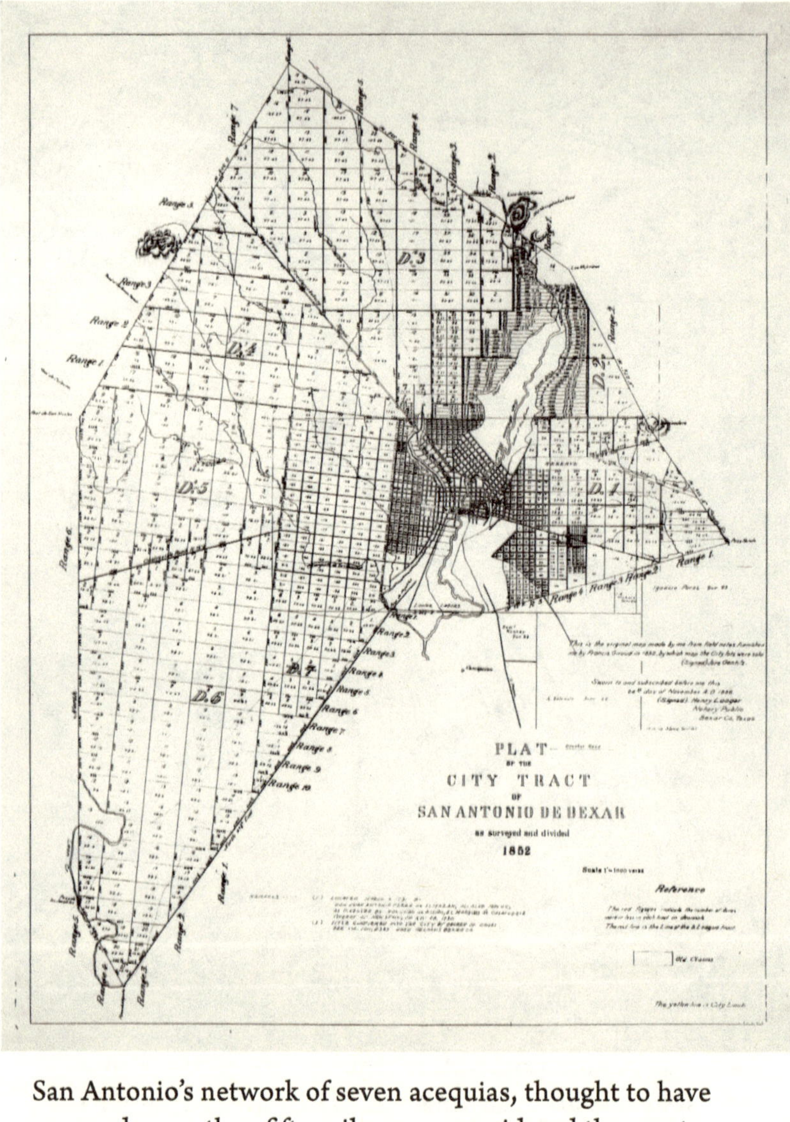

San Antonio's network of seven acequias, thought to have spanned more than fifty miles, was considered the most extensive system in Texas. But by the mid-nineteenth century, city planners sought to impose a standard grid onto San Antonio, resulting in vertical and horizontal boundaries that clashed with the natural flow of water, as illustrated by this 1852 city map.

Traditional adobe structures, such as these in the northwest corner of the square, dominated local architecture until the Civil War.

Mission-style architecture of the original San Fernando Cathedral on the west side of Main Plaza, circa 1866.

Efforts to align the San Antonio cityscape with more accepted visions of the modern city resulted in a revamped San Fernando Cathedral sporting a French Gothic exterior alongside new wooden structures on Main Plaza in 1889. One of the new structures is the White Elephant Saloon to the far right.

Main Plaza's redesigned garden landscape in 1895 accentuated the old-world elegance of the San Fernando Cathedral, with the city hall cropping up in the background.

FOUR

Ignoring Opportunities

1879–1895

In the late 1870s San Antonians were ill-prepared to embrace the opportunities for city-building that their new railroad offered. Drawing on their knowledge of their community's previous development, they strongly believed that growth was inevitable and, therefore, that organized local efforts to promote it were unnecessary.[1]

That sense of inevitability had become ingrained in businessmen through their experiences with the army in the 1850s. Its mission to pacify the frontier amounted to a massive federal subsidy for the local economy that resumed immediately with the end of the Civil War. Army freighting needs after 1865, for instance, averaged $200,000 a year (equivalent to $4 million today). As one observer noted, "The amount of money circulated in the city and its vicinity by the government is immense."[2] Since the city had no rivals for that subsidy, businessmen could afford to become complacent about the fundamental soundness of the city's economy. In this situation there was no need to learn how to cooperate with one another to promote growth. Instead they had focused on the opportunities the subsidy provided for developing their own businesses.

After 1877, however, the railroad created opportunities to diversify the local economy by manufacturing consumer goods for local and regional markets. Economic diversification was critical to San Antonio's ability to compete effectively in an increasingly dynamic national economy that the railroads were creating.[3] Dallas businessmen, for instance, were converting cotton seeds into animal feed and establishing farm machinery companies to serve their hinterland. San Antonio had become an important wholesale center for wool and cattle, but those products were not as valuable as finished goods that increased employment opportunities and created financial resources for further urban development. Local boosters therefore faced a conundrum: the victory of the Taxpayers' Association reaffirmed the wisdom of an approach to city-building that was hostile to the possibilities for urban development in this new economic environment.

Many San Antonians would not recognize that such a conundrum existed. German voters, for instance, would continue to believe that government had no legitimate role in city-building and that businessmen could grow the city without public assistance or organized effort. Several businessmen and landowners agreed with those ideas and ignored the implications of the railroad's arrival. Other community leaders did understand those implications, but they faced the difficult tasks of dealing with an established cultural consensus about city-building.

Further complicating matters, those leaders interested in a new strategy had to develop a clear understanding of San Antonio's strengths and weaknesses, experiment with effective ways to promote growth, and persevere when their ideas sometimes failed (as some inevitably would). All of these tasks had one thing in common: they required a commitment to systematic cooperation in city-building, which had been missing in the business community since the 1850s.[4] Creating a culture of cooperation and a more diverse economy would in fact prove to be their most formidable challenges.

While Newcomb's boosters fought their losing battle to industrialize the river, Thomas Pierce offered his own version of organized boosterism by implementing a package of promotional initiatives. He founded a land investment company to attract capital to western Texas, created an immigration agency to recruit new residents, launched an advertising campaign to extol the virtues and potential of the city and its hinterland, and considered personal investments in hotel and factory construction.[5]

Pierce's efforts produced visible results that ironically reinforced local beliefs in the inevitability of growth. Real estate transactions increased 19 percent in one year and housing construction soared. In all of 1877 the city had approved 135 building permits; in the first five months of 1878 it approved 223. All this construction was transforming some areas of town. East Side alderman William Prescott noted that Avenue C (running northeast out of the downtown) "has become one of the principal thoroughfares in the City since the advent of the Railroad."[6] A Mr. Freyman started a textile factory with thirty-five employees who made pants in three hours, "showing to what advantage our cheap labor may be employed." George Milburn, president of the Milburn Wagon Company of Toledo, Ohio, opened a "branch house" in San Antonio and hinted that he would transfer his headquarters operations to town, as well. And there were rumors that a cotton and woolen factory, as well as a meatpacking plant using refrigerated cars to reach northern markets, would open soon.[7]

Local leaders, though, needed to build on Peirce's early successes if they expected to encourage sustained economic development. His interest in town promotion was, after all, tied to his ambition to build a transcontinental railroad, and as his tracks extended farther west he would inevitably shift his promotional efforts beyond San Antonio. Furthermore, he was not a permanent resident, which meant that he could not provide sustained leadership for his own initial efforts to develop the city. Such leadership would have to come from local business and political leaders who, if they chose to become involved in city-building, would have to overcome the community's long-standing hostility to boosterism.

Some initial reactions to the railroad demonstrated the depth of that challenge. Many San Antonians were not pleased with their new railroad and declared that its arrival meant "the necessary ruin of the city."[8] That startling assessment arose from their discovery that the state's emerging rail network was eroding San Antonio's "natural" hinterland. Specifically, construction of the International and Great Northern Railroad from Dallas to San Antonio in the mid-1870s had created opportunities for small cities along its route to poach on San Antonio's territory. As the I&GN reached towns like Austin, their citizens quickly approved building feeder lines to rural markets in central Texas, which meant that "much trade that *belonged* to San Antonio, particularly in the grocery line, from the country about Fredericksburg and in the west, was now going to Austin."[9]

Even worse, such competition had begun to affect the army's role in San Antonio's economy. Fort Worth and Corpus Christi, among others, were using the same poaching technique to divert army contracts for freight hauling to them. One local freighter estimated that three-fourths of "all government freight that previously came to San Antonio for distribution" now went to those towns.[10]

Such poaching prompted a frenzy of injured complacency misdirected at Pierce. Many businessmen blamed him for setting freight rates that discriminated against San Antonio when in fact the emerging rail network simply created competitive advantages for towns that now had efficient and inexpensive rail service to previously isolated areas of the state.[11]

The perception that Pierce was the source of these problems created a momentary interest in risk-taking. Several businessmen proposed building a competing railroad to the coast. That would be built eventually, but outrage at Peirce's rates dissipated rapidly because the cost of a railroad frightened the protesters more than the threat of losing hinterland customers to rival cities. Seeking solace in illogic, they argued that the arrival of the International and Great Northern Railroad—whose construction was causing the disruptions in the city's market area—would force Pierce to lower his rates.[12]

But the underlying challenges to the city's future persisted, especially when the army's role in the local economy rapidly deteriorated once it had completed its mission to conquer the Comanches and Apaches in the late 1870s. With that victory freighting contracts, the core of the army's economic subsidy, disappeared, as did many local freight companies that included several owned by Mexican Americans.[13]

Local contractors would continue to earn income from the construction of Fort Sam Houston facilities, and the fort's role as a military headquarters and training center meant cash from its monthly payroll would still contribute to the local economy. Neither of these sources of income, however, matched the previous impact of the army's now defunct freight business because most Americans in the late nineteenth century had little interest in supporting the military. Congress kept force levels low and budgets tight. Construction activity at the fort was therefore erratic from year to year, and the small number of military personnel limited the size of its payroll. Although the fort would continue to be an important resource, San Antonio could no longer rely on federal money as the bedrock of its economy.[14]

The implications of losing their core "industry" apparently dawned slowly on some local leaders who finally launched two dramatically different experiments in cooperative development and economic diversification in 1881. On March 1 a small group of individuals met in the wool brokerage offices of Chabot, Moss & Co. to form a merchants' exchange. Stephen Gould, their new secretary, attributed the exchange's origins to the effects of railroads on the city's hinterland, which had "left business here in a chaotic mass ready at any time to be diverted to other channels under the magic touch of some commercial king or railroad magnate." The city "therefore required an internal organization of local forces to resolve this chaos into a commercial phalanx of such proportions as to compel our rivals to keep within their own legitimate limits."[15]

Exchanges were commercial organizations that helped cities extend their influence over hinterlands by offering rural customers essential services. Gould wanted initially to apply that model to wool growers around San Antonio who had been sending their dirty and unsorted clips to northeastern textile plants. Those practices earned Texas wool a bad reputation in the industry that resulted in low prices for the clips. Gould sought to correct those problems and simultaneously to make the surrounding rural areas a productive source of organized urban development. He wanted to offer growers grading, cleaning, and bagging services while also collecting information on the biannual clips. The exchange would in effect centralize wool marketing by making it convenient for buyers to use that information and its connections with the growers in making their purchases. With the exchange guaranteeing the quality of clips to the buyers, they would be willing to offer growers better prices. Local businessmen would benefit from the opportunities to expand the range of services they offered hinterland producers as Gould incorporated other raw materials into the exchange's operations.[16]

Gould had only recently moved to San Antonio. A Rhode Islander by birth, he was a thirty-four-year-old lawyer who opened a land office and business loans agency during the original burst of development following the GH&SA's arrival.[17] He took an expansive view of his duties with the exchange, transforming himself into an eloquent booster who wrote several promotional articles extolling his new hometown's undoubted advantages and brilliant future prospects. While he wrote in the perfervid style of boosters everywhere, he also displayed a firm grasp of the essentials of urban economics and the realities of San Antonio's circumstances. He may not have been the only businessman who was thinking strategically about San Antonio's development, but he was at this point the only one in a position to implement his ideas.

Despite Gould's best efforts, though, the exchange failed within three years. It lacked broad support within the business community, perhaps because its cooperative approach to organizing the hinterland threatened long-established individual relationships between ranchers and brokers. Thomas Frost, for instance, had arrived in San Antonio shortly after 1865 and had become the town's largest wool broker by creating a large network of ranchers who dealt with him directly.[18] Frost did not, however, become a member of the exchange.

Most of the exchange's members were not in fact directly involved in the wool business. John Kampmann was the most prestigious of a small group of supporters who included merchants like A. B. Frank, Charles Hugo, and Frederick Gross, who all served as officers of the exchange. Interestingly, neither Chabot nor Moss was an officer or director. In effect, the exchange's members lacked the personal relationships with ranchers that could have helped establish the organization's credibility.

Lack of expertise was not the only problem for the exchange. Sheep ranchers were not accustomed to paying for the kinds of services that it offered. They therefore complained about charges for bagging their wool for market, apparently preferring to perform that work themselves. That undermined the grading system, making their wool less competitive, but their concern that San Antonio was making too much money from their labor trumped that consideration. Gould's inability to generate revenue undermined his ability to provide the exchange's few members with a return on their investment, which encouraged them not to renew their memberships. By 1884 Gould was casting about with schemes to raise revenue to continue its operations.[19]

He need not have bothered because the directors voted that year to disband the exchange, prompting the editor of a new newspaper, the *Light*, to attribute its failure to "the merchants and property owners" who "utterly refuse to support it." The editor acidly concluded that "the merchants of San Antonio had better hide their heads in . . . shame and admit the enterprise of smaller cities with less advantages entirely outstrip that of the Alamo City."[20]

This failure severely damaged nascent efforts to develop a creative, cooperative approach to city-building. With the exchange's demise, businessmen lost the ability to gather systematic statistical information that was essential for exploring development opportunities.[21] They also lost an opportunity to learn how to manage an enterprise larger than any of their individual businesses, which might have made them more comfortable with taking risks to promote economic diversity.[22]

As the exchange's effort to reorganize the city's relationship with its hinterland unraveled, another group of businessmen attempted to solve the problem of insufficient capital for local development, which was a serious issue in all western communities at the time. They decided to focus on convincing capitalists to move to town. Pierce provided them with the raw materials for this effort. Like other railroad builders, he recruited groups of potential residents and investors who toured towns along his expanding rail route to encourage them to relocate, which would enhance his railroad's business prospects.

The size of these groups could be impressive. In the early days of Pierce's promotional efforts, a single train could deliver as many as nine hundred excursionists to town.[23] The problem with excursionists, though, was convincing them to stay. They needed to be cultivated, and local businessmen did not initially have a strategy for doing that. When the editor of the *Herald* learned, for instance, that a large number of Galveston residents would be visiting in late May 1878, he complained that the welcome program was long on entertainment and short on substance. He lectured his readers that "it is a well-known fact that there are in Galveston at this time a very large class of people who are possessed of moderate capital for which there is offered not adequate return on investments in that city." Arguing that "we should strive to impress them so favorably that they will be induced to make this city their home," he instructed his readers to show these visitors "what our capabilities are," which he defined as "everything which will go to show the superiority of San Antonio over other points in the South and West as a home for enterprising men with capital."[24]

Cultivating potential investors required time and reasonably tangible investment possibilities. With regard to potential investments, the failure to create an industrial corridor on the river was not a particularly good advertisement of the community's eagerness to diversify the economy. Ignoring the implications of that example for their plans, several major businessmen founded the San Antonio Club in December 1881 to cultivate outside investors. The club would introduce "the stranger, the capitalist, the tourist, the business man from abroad to . . . those whom he is most desirous of meeting," in order to "build up and add to the material progress and development of the city."[25]

Unlike the Merchant's Exchange, the club immediately attracted eighty-two members from the city's social and economic elite, a number that increased to 196 by 1887. E. D. L. Wickes, H. B. Adams (who were the two largest landowners in town), John Kampmann, Thomas J. Devine, George Brackenridge, and August Belknap (who had built the city's first streetcar line) helped organize it. Realizing that one or two pleasant social evenings might be insufficient to impress a touring capitalist, the directors also created a nonresident membership category so that they could continue to cultivate these prospects once they returned home.

Cultivating prospects also required an appropriate setting. President Wickes rented space on Alamo Plaza and raised $6,000 (nearly $150,000 in modern dollars) from his members to furnish the club's new headquarters. By the mid-1880s the members decided that they needed even more elegant quarters. They contributed to the plaza's modernization by building an opera house and moving the club to its upper floor.[26]

Despite their high hopes, the results were decidedly disappointing. Although the number of nonresident members grew to 236 by 1887, only two of them had had moved to town by 1892, and neither had established a new business.[27] Such a dismal rate of success indicates that entertaining out-of-town guests had limitations as a development strategy.[28] Implicitly admitting defeat, the club's directors abandoned their efforts to recruit outside investors and transformed the organization into an elite social club offering elaborate formal dances and dinners to its local members.

Investors, though, were only one rather specialized group within the rising tide of tourists in the late nineteenth century, most of whom did not have the kind of resources that merited an invitation to the San Antonio Club. They did, however, come in large enough numbers to attract attention.[29] Indeed, by 1885 an anonymous letter writer opined that the city was attracting 25,000 tourists a year.[30] The accuracy of that number is highly debatable, but it probably reflected a sense of awe over the visibly increasing numbers of tourists walking San Antonio's streets and spending money. Here, quite unexpectedly, was another, potentially very large group of strangers who could contribute to the city's development.

Initially many of these tourists came seeking better health. Tuberculosis was a major killer in the nineteenth century whose cause and treatment were medical mysteries. Doctors believed that the right climate would cure consumption and advised their clients to travel to recover. According to Augustus Belknap, prior to 1877 "San Antonio had but one claim to outside notice as being a delightful health resort for invalids," but the absence of inexpensive and comfortable transportation had severely restricted their numbers.[31] The GH&SA's arrival solved that problem, especially when Pierce hired M. Whildin to write a pamphlet describing the attractions of West Texas. Whildin stressed, among other things, that San Antonio was "specifically addressed to invalids, convalescents, and persons of delicate organization." He assured his readers that such sufferers would find the air in San Antonio "almost a specific for consumption and diseases of the throat."[32]

Consumptives were to some extent surrogates for healthy capitalists who were so much harder to recruit, as the San Antonio Club had learned. Poor consumptives could not afford to travel; by definition a touring consumptive had money. And they came prepared for an extended stay because their doctors instructed them to breathe enough pure air over a long enough period of time to cure them. They were therefore welcomed everywhere, not just in San Antonio, as a potential source of talent and capital that would be useful to local development—assuming, of course, that they did not die.[33]

With Pierce's initial help, San Antonio quickly became a major destination for consumptives. By late spring 1878, the city, in the judgment of one observer, had "become the popular resort of invalids from other parts of the country."[34] Many other western cities eagerly sought to become the nation's capital of consumption, but the presence of so many visitors coughing their way through the city seemed to convince San Antonians that their town had already claimed that prize.

Healthy tourists also arrived in steady, but uncounted, numbers. An urban middle class with money and time to travel was becoming more numerous and more conscious of America's national culture and history. Picturesque history, especially when it involved heroes and romantic settings, stimulated a desire to travel; inexpensive railroad fares provided the opportunity.[35]

Whildin included these potential tourists in his pamphlet promoting San Antonio. He flatly declared that "the city of San Antonio is the most unique city on the American continent. In more than one respect it presents an epitome of the history of civilization." Appealing to his audience's interest in heroism, he asserted that "every stone of this beautiful city has been consecrated with the blood of a patriot. San Antonio has for a century been the battle ground of human liberty." Novelist and travel writer Harriet Spofford also extolled the picturesque peculiarities of the city's "strange and foreign sights" that could be encountered in the "sinuosities of the countless streets" that "afford a good deal of interest and add much variety and vivacity to life for the invalids . . . seeking health."[36]

San Antonio's tourist attractions posed an interesting challenge to the city's business leaders. On the one hand, their desire to attract businesses to town required evidence of an increasingly prosperous and progressive metropolis. On the other, most tourists expected to see an old Spanish city with picturesque ruins, narrow, winding, enchanting streets, and an "exotic" ethnic culture. That combination made the town's existing physical appearance and social composition economic assets that needed to be preserved.

Initially the evolution of the city's physical landscape helped reconcile conflicts between the need to preserve and the need to modernize. San Antonio at this point was a compact city less than four square miles in size. Most of its built landscape was west of the river, in or around Main and Military Plazas; by comparison, the east side of town was much less developed. The river also acted as a social boundary, with the vast majority of the city's impoverished Mexican population living on the West Side while a similarly large majority of relatively wealthier Germans lived on the East Side. In effect, the decision to locate the colonial-era villa west of the river had eventually, and inadvertently, transformed the original settlement area into the "picturesque" and "exotic" San Antonio that attracted tourists in the late nineteenth century.[37]

With the surge in tourism after 1877, poor Tejano neighborhoods and food vendors became important economic assets. Keenly aware of tourists' expectations, the local press moved swiftly to assure them that "the customs of the Mexican people remain unchanged, and there are thousands of Mexicans still here who maintain an independent little community of their own."[38] Other western cities would also attempt to entice tourists to them by offering their versions of picturesque ethnic neighborhoods, foods, and customs, though San Antonio seems inadvertently to have been something of a pioneer in that strategy.[39]

The business community's concern with preserving Tejano culture was selective. Anglo San Antonians shared white Americans' beliefs about ethnic and racial minorities, although there were some interesting local variations to the ways in which they acted on their prejudices. Elite Anglo San Antonians, for instance, generally relied on political convenience and class distinctions in defining their attitudes toward local Tejanos, a tradition that began with Anglo settlers like James Bowie marrying the daughters of Canary Island descendants in the 1830s. Even as the number of Mexican Americans compared to Germans and other groups declined throughout the post–Civil War era, the city's business and political leadership found it useful to continue their alliances with those Canary Islanders. Democrats typically worked with them to influence the votes of poorer Tejanos.

Relationships rooted in mutual class interests also encouraged Anglo San Antonians to incorporate some aspects of Mexican culture into their lives. Families like the Mavericks could sponsor dinner parties where Mexican cuisine and the fandango were the featured attractions. Even if not a single participant in these social events was Mexican, the local elite could believe they had a genuine affection for Tejano culture, however narrowly defined. In the broader public arena, whites supported Mexican Americans' and African Americans' parades and festivals that celebrated their individual cultures.[40]

Commentary on poor blacks or Mexican Americans, on the other hand, combined racism with paternalism: "I fail to see what is the matter with them that provokes such malice among a certain class. Of course, the poorer Mexicans may be greasers, etc., but... when people don't have money they can't possibly live and dress well, not without resort to thieving and chicanery.... It is our business to elevate others and bring them to our standard, and not for us to come down to their level."[41] Elevating poor Mexicans apparently required suppressing their expressions of popular culture. The fandango, for instance, was acceptable in the drawing rooms of the elite, but not in the public places where the poor gathered for entertainment. Victorian tourists might be put off by encountering rambunctious lower-class versions of Mexican culture.[42]

While the West Side Tejano community evolved into a tourist site, the East Side, broadly defined as the residential and commercial areas east of Military Plaza, emerged as the preferred location for creating a modern urban landscape that might impress potential investors.[43]

In the mid-1870s the East Side was fallow ground for cultivating that landscape. Main Plaza was a large, unadorned dirt patch surrounded by a mixture of businesses that served the needs of both body and soul: clothing, hardware, and leather goods stores; a hotel; San Fernando Cathedral; and saloons and the Vaudeville Theater, all of which offered gambling and prostitution as additional attractions.[44]

Commerce and Market, the two principal business streets, were unpaved and lined with a mixture of single- and two-story adobe or wood-framed commercial and residential buildings dating in many cases to the colonial era. Mostly modest houses, a few stores, and more adobe remnants lined several side streets. Houston Street was at this point the least developed commercial street with occasional frame buildings serving as army barracks and residences like the Maverick homestead at the corner of Houston and Alamo Plaza.

Alamo Plaza's assortment of businesses reflected its role as the army's depot. A bedraggled collection of single-story saloons, hardware and leather goods dealers, clothiers, and barbers catered to the needs of army personnel. A large mule corral and a lumber yard also lent a certain ambiance to the plaza, as did one of the city's low-slung meat markets squatting pungently in its center. The Menger Hotel and the nearby Gallagher Building, which served as the city's post office, were the largest and most elegant buildings on the plaza. Clouds of dust from traffic drifted about in dry weather, while rain produced a mud lake due to poor drainage that earned the plaza its nickname, the Frog Pond.[45]

In sum, San Antonio was still very much a rough-hewn frontier town. Visible signs of a modern city, as exemplified by commercial and residential buildings designed by architects familiar with the latest styles and constructed with the most elegant and expensive materials, were almost nonexistent.

All of that was about to change rather dramatically. The state's urban population nearly doubled during the 1880s. Dallas and Fort Worth enjoyed spectacular growth while Houston and San Antonio merely did well. By 1890 Dallas could claim to be the state's largest city with 38,000 residents, but San Antonio was a close second at 37,600. Although none of the state's towns was particularly impressive compared to many eastern and midwestern cities, the surge in population nevertheless had important local consequences.

San Antonio's growth in fact fueled a major reorganization of its social geography. Most of its new residents were native-born Americans who helped make Anglos the city's dominant ethnic group. They all needed living space, and those among them who could afford it would demonstrate a desire to live in new homes in suburban areas. "Suburbs" at this point simply meant subdivisions located on vacant land within the city. Developers began platting subdivisions in the late 1880s, and since most of the land within San Antonio's formal political boundaries was vacant, subdivisions quickly sprouted in every direction.[46]

Distinctions among subdivisions appeared fairly quickly. Prior to the GH&SA's arrival, San Antonians had not yet distanced themselves from one another on the basis of class and income. Wealthier residents lived among middle- and lower-class neighbors, and there was "no one street or section of the city especially devoted to fine residences."[47] But San Antonio's newest residents seem to have imported a preference for greater social and income segregation, perhaps reflecting national trends in late nineteenth-century class and ethnic biases. The army's departure from Alamo Plaza and the simultaneous completion of San Antonio's first streetcar line in mid-1878 coincidentally combined to meet the housing preferences of many newcomers and, simultaneously, to make the East Side the center of efforts to build the modern city that businessmen wanted in order to promote development.

The streetcar and a major renovation of urban space in Alamo Plaza provided mutually reinforcing solutions to those (compatible) goals. Augustus Belknap, a former New York City hardware merchant who arrived in town in 1877, built the city's first line from San Pedro Springs to the plaza. Located one and a half miles north of town, the springs was an extremely popular public park with several attractions, including a small zoo; a racetrack; a beer garden; and boating, swimming, and fishing attractions. With a proven outdoor entertainment center as its destination, the car line would have a steady stream of riders and would increase land values along its route and near the springs. Belknap opened for business in June 1878, and in his first month of operations his mule-drawn cars carried more than twenty-two thousand passengers, which was not a bad start considering that San Antonio had only slightly more than twenty thousand residents in 1880.[48]

The convenience and speed with which his passengers could commute between home, work, and shopping made real estate along his route more attractive (and valuable) than land elsewhere. The price of lots along San Pedro Avenue, for instance, increased from $90 to $1,000 from the late 1870s to the mid-1880s. Almost all the additional routes he built in the 1880s served new residential areas north of Commerce Street.[49] In effect, Belknap's streetcar lines inserted a new geographical entity into the traditional east-west socioeconomic division of San Antonio. Technically, the residents that his lines served lived on the west side of the river; but their social, economic, and political composition would eventually coalesce to create the "North Side," which would become a colloquialism referring to the city's most powerful residents.

Belknap's mule cars also transformed commercial development. Many businessmen bought lots along Houston Street from the Vance and Maverick families, who owned most of that land, to be closer to potential customers in the new northern subdivisions. Retail and office buildings began to appear along Houston in increasing numbers throughout the 1880s, transforming it into a major competitor to Commerce Street merchants.[50]

With the army gone and the terminus of Belknap's car line in place, Alamo Plaza's real estate was ripe for redevelopment. Honoré Grenêt, a member of the city's small French population, understood the retail implications of having a reliable stream of middle-class suburban customers disembarking in the plaza. He bought the convent next to the Alamo church from the Catholic Archdiocese for $19,000 in January 1878 and spent the next two years constructing a large combined dry goods, grocery, clothing, and liquor store over the convent.[51]

Grenêt's store reflected the business community's disregard for the city's picturesque or historical attractions if they happened to be in the wrong place. Businessmen had no problems with the city's other four missions, squatting in isolated, decaying splendor along the river well south of town. The Alamo, however, sat squarely in the middle of what now had become the prime site for portraying San Antonio as a modern metropolis. Local opinion of the structure's usefulness as a tourist attraction therefore lagged far behind its national reputation as a hallowed embodiment of heroism. A Saint Louis visitor commented that the Alamo's condition "ought to bring a blush of shame to the cheek, not only of every San Antonian, but of every man and woman who calls Texas home.... It stands a reproach and a shame to the dollar-grasping spirit that could so degrade a building that in any other land [would] be preserved with religious care."[52]

Although Grenêt blushed slightly by adding imitation fort crenellations along the top of his store as an apparent allusion to the Alamo's history, he made no other concessions to its cultural symbolism. Other businessmen displayed even less restraint, opening stores and other buildings in the latest architectural styles that in less than ten years transformed the plaza into a haven for middle- and upper-class shopping and the center of the city's cultural and organizational life—although the Frog Pond still challenged the unwary pedestrian.[53]

Modernization and the needs of tourists also affected the redevelopment of Main Plaza. One editor's complaint that the "the meager accommodations and lack of comforts in the past have tended to injure our city" implied that tourism could wither in the absence of enough modern conveniences.[54] With the scarcity of good hotels in town, Main Plaza attracted construction because of its prime location. By 1884 three new hotels offering up-to-date conveniences straddled the plaza's southwest corner.[55]

"Comforts," though, was an expansive idea that included more than clean beds and bountiful meals. The plaza was not particularly comfortable for Victorian tourists. A volatile mix of liquor, gambling, raucous dancing, and chorus girls dominated its nightlife, encouraging fights, occasional shootings, and other unseemly behavior. The Vaudeville Theater, located on the plaza's northeast corner, earned that location a nickname as the Fatal Corner because of its numerous gunfights. Local businessmen had long tolerated such behavior and regarded at least some of this entertainment as highly respectable. When the three-story White Elephant Saloon replaced an old hotel on the plaza in 1883, a local editor commented: "It is without a doubt the finest and most convenient saloon south of Chicago and San Antonians are in ecstasy about its beauty. It is worthy of a visit."[56]

Despite the ecstasy, the plaza's days as an entertainment center for males were numbered. In 1882 Ben Thompson, a famous Texas gunfighter, killed Jack Harris in the Vaudeville Theater. Acquitted of murder because Harris, who owned the theater, was holding a shotgun at the time, Thompson returned to the scene of his triumph in 1884. Harris's friends, possibly affronted by his audacity, promptly shot him to death. Such violence contradicted the picturesque image that attracted tourists, especially when San Antonio found itself on the front page of the *New York Times* because of

Thompson. Billy Sims, Harris's business partner, renamed the theater the Fashion and moved it to Military Plaza shortly after Thompson died, initiating a general shift of vice activity into Military Plaza. Two years later a fire destroyed the original theater and the White Elephant closed its doors. A reputable clothing store expanded into the vacated saloon, and the Elite Restaurant and Hotel replaced the theater.[57] Literally and symbolically, the plaza's redevelopment created a more comfortable ambience for tourists while pushing the boundary between the picturesque and modern city landscapes farther west.

San Antonians had made considerable progress in accommodating tourists' needs by the end of the 1880s. An original inventory of five hotels, thirty-eight boardinghouses, and twelve restaurants had expanded to eight hotels, eighty-nine boardinghouses, and forty restaurants by 1888.[58] Collectively, hoteliers, boardinghouse owners, and restaurateurs had become one of the largest groups of businessmen in San Antonio. The city had unexpectedly developed a home-grown "industry" that admittedly did not produce finished goods, but it did import money into the economy and create jobs.[59] Although these proprietors were not yet organized into a coherent group with a deliberate strategy for promoting their industry, they now had a vested interest in its expansion.[60]

Progress in serving tourists contrasted sharply with anemic efforts in other areas, although there were two notable exceptions. Beer had quickly become a major import after the GH&SA's arrival, especially when the only local brewery closed in 1879. In its first year of operations, Pierce's railroad shipped thirty-five refrigerated carloads of beer a month into town from Saint Louis.[61] Adolphus Busch, who was aggressively expanding his operations into Texas, decided that San Antonio's location, its large German population, and its river would make an excellent site for a branch plant despite inadequate local sources of barley or hops in its hinterland. He bought land on the river for a future brewery in 1879.[62] It took him some time to find a local investor willing to partner with him, but in 1883 he contacted John Kampmann with an offer to provide expertise and equipment for a brewery if Kampmann would raise funds for a plant. Demonstrating that at least some businessmen could act promptly when they wanted to, Kampmann raised nearly $100,000 at just one meeting and organized the Lone Star Brewery.[63] With the help of Busch's deep pockets and aggressive marketing practices, the brewery made San Antonio a regional beer manufacturing center by the 1890s.

Carl Guenther's transformation of his small flour mill did not receive the kind of public attention that Busch's investment did, but he managed an even more impressive achievement through his own efforts. Since the city's rural surroundings could not supply him with the raw materials he needed, he arranged for their delivery from northern Texas and other wheat-farming areas. He solved the challenge of competing with well-established national milling firms by constantly investing in the latest technologies and by developing an aggressive and imaginative advertising campaign. In doing so, Guenther built Pioneer Flour Mills into a major export company with a national reputation by the 1890s.[64]

Guenther's achievement was far more impressive than Kampmann's because he had had to accept a much greater degree of risk to build his company. Kampmann raised capital for the brewery's building, but Busch bore the expense of providing the brewery with the latest technology and staff to operate it. But the mill and brewery demonstrated how to use the state's rail system to obtain raw materials and distribute their finished products. In effect, both illustrated how to create export industries that could diversify the economy, expand job opportunities, and increase local wealth.[65]

These examples did not, however, inspire emulation, which handicapped the development of a critical mass of industrial firms. A comment by the *Light*'s editor succinctly captured the business community's problem with economic diversification at this point in the city's evolution: "Our people are not a manufacturing people, and are not inclined to become so, having no experience."[66] Guenther and Kampmann provided practical examples of how to gain that experience, but their colleagues preferred to import capitalists (if they could be found) who could assume the risks of diversification for them. Despite the disappointing results of the San Antonio Club's efforts, they would increasingly rely on tourism to solve their diversification problems.

In the meantime, the economy began to suffer from the emergence of several problems in the late 1880s. The railroad boom gradually ground to a halt, and a severe drought made San Antonio look a lot less appealing to outsiders. Real estate sales reflected that problem, declining by 44 percent between 1883 and 1887. Tourism stagnated as Los Angelenos launched a successful advertising campaign to attract people to Southern California. Railroads such as the Southern Pacific eagerly supported that campaign, threatening to make San Antonio into a "way station" on the route to greener pastures. Wool sales remained strong, but cattle drives to northern rail hubs ended in 1885 with the closing of the open range era in ranching and bans on Texas cattle, which carried Texas fever, in several states. Cattle remained important to the local economy, but the end of the drives meant the industry needed to reorganize, which would take time.[67]

Other, perhaps more serious, problems were emerging in the city's hinterland. Railroad construction continued to reorganize the regional market. As a result, the city's antebellum claim to control more than half of the state had shrunk dramatically to a bare fifth of Texas, bounded by Eagle Pass to the west, five Hill Country counties to the north, Corpus Christi to the east, and the Rio Grande to the south. The largest part of that area, between San Antonio and the Rio Grande, was sparsely settled. Hill Country farmers had gradually abandoned experimenting with crop diversity to also focus on livestock. San Antonio's hinterland did not provide enough foodstuffs to feed its residents.[68] A shrinking hinterland with a small population and few resources was not a promising asset for the city.

With private efforts at city-building faltering, Mayor French decided it was time to reclaim a role for government in urban development. His timing indicates that the changing nature of his political base prompted him to make that attempt. French had never hesitated to express his support for public improvements that the Taxpayers' Association opposed. In January 1883 the association supported Fourth Ward alderman John Copeland for mayor. Copeland narrowly won the two East Side wards, where French's organization had been dominant since 1875. French owed his victory to West Side voters, who at this point included (especially in the Second Ward) many of the new middle- and upper-class residents of San Antonio. Presumably those voters had a more expansive view of the role of government in the city's development than the association. Less than a week after his reelection, French announced in his annual message that if the city's taxpayers would not support bond issues for public improvements, the council should pay for them through direct taxation. He then revealed the depth of his frustration with the Taxpayers' Association by saying that the average taxpayer did not understand the importance of improvements and informed the aldermen that "it is *our* duty to do, at all times, that which we think the public good demands."[69]

Support for French's activism was not strong on the city council, though, until two unexpected resignations brought streetcar magnate Augustus Belknap and John Bolton, a high-ranking civilian employee of the army, onto the council as, respectively, Second and Third Ward aldermen. With their support French launched a concerted effort to expand governmental control over the city's physical development.

Over the next eighteen months the council approved ordinances that attempted to create uniform street and sidewalk widths and alter the relationship of commercial buildings to streets by defining a standard distance between them. The council expected owners of buildings that intruded too closely to streets to move them back by tearing down their fronts, moving them back to conform to the new standard. In effect, these ordinances contributed to the campaign to create a modern urban landscape, an effort that would be more successful on the East Side where development around Alamo Plaza was still under way. Development around Main and Military Plazas was too advanced to change easily. Seeking to impose some order on suburbanization, the council required developers to submit plats for past and future subdivisions for approval. This phase of French's campaign concluded in September 1884 with adoption of a resolution ordering the city engineer to prepare a systematic plan for improvements that would guide council decisions thereafter.[70]

French also attempted to encourage economic diversification. In 1878 Frank Grice, editor of the *Express*, had suggested that the council should consider "whether the city can afford to make any special grants, give immunity from taxation for a number of years, or offer anything calculated to attract manufacturers."[71] Adolphus Busch's deal with Kampmann to build the Lone Star Brewery may well have revived that idea for French. In 1884 alderman John Bolton, with French's help, guided an ordinance through the council that granted a ten-year exemption from all except school taxes to any firm that invested at least $5,000 in a plant and equipment. It became effective March 1, 1885, and remained in force for three years.[72]

Whether or not a tax abatement would actually promote industrialization remained to be seen.[73] But it was at least a clever political gesture. It created a role for the council in economic development, which the Taxpayers'

Association opposed, by offering lower taxes to new industry, something to which the association could not object.

As his other initiatives wound their way through the council, French turned to his most ambitious and important goal. The state legislature had revised its statutes regarding the powers of cities under their charters, giving him an opportunity to modify the restrictions that the Taxpayers' Association had lobbied into the charter in 1879. In April 1884 the council created a committee of aldermen, citizens, and French, to write charter amendments that would "agree with" the new state regulations and contribute to "the wants of this growing city."[74]

This attempt at charter reform coincided with indications that the Taxpayers' Association's dominance of local politics had begun to waver. Population growth was increasing the number of shoppers, and the streetcar system was funneling a large number of those consumers into Houston Street, creating the need for Commerce Street merchants to find a way to compete more effectively for customers. Since neither street, nor for that matter any other street in the downtown, was paved, the Commerce Street merchants petitioned the council to make theirs the first business avenue with paving. This was a startling request given that the petitioners included some of the most important supporters of the Taxpayers' Association. The council swiftly approved the petition because it represented a breach in the previously adamant opposition to street improvements. First Ward alderman Joseph Dwyer noted the symbolic significance of the request, remarking that "if they succeed in the paving of Commerce Street it would open the gates for improvement in San Antonio."[75]

With that kind of encouragement, the charter committee wrote amendments designed to undermine the Taxpayers' Association. It restored the council's authority to issue $50,000 in bonds each year without a referendum. Voters still had to approve proposals for bonds in excess of that amount, but only by a plurality, not by two-thirds as the association had stipulated. In addition, there would be no limit on the total debt the council could incur in any year.

French also convinced his colleagues to restructure San Antonio's political landscape. The committee approved a proposal to divide the four wards into eight with one alderman for each ward. In addition, the proposal created four at-large aldermen. French had always opposed the council's preference for distributing public improvements equally among the wards, insisting that improvements had to be designed to benefit the entire city. In 1878, for example, his annual message had informed the aldermen of his preference for improvements that would reflect "a *system* of public improvements."[76] At the time, French's veto authority was his only tool for trying to direct the council's attention to his agenda. Rewriting the charter, however, presented him with an opportunity to create a group of at-large aldermen who would presumably provide reliable votes for a mayor who intended to direct a citywide approach to improvements.

Dividing the wards created another way to thwart the Taxpayers' Association. The new ward boundaries would take advantage of the growing tendency for San Antonio's middle- and upper-class residents to form neighborhoods based on income. On the West Side the new Third and Fourth Wards would create alderman positions that reflected the interests of the emerging North Side where San Antonio's newest business and professional men lived. East of the river, the boundaries of the new Fifth and Eighth Wards incorporated similar geographical concentrations of middle- and upper-class families. The Sixth and Seventh Wards would contain a majority of the German working-class voters who formed the core of Taxpayers' Association. In effect, French was maneuvering to increase representation on the council for the city's business and professional elite.

Last, the committee made several other changes that empowered the council to become an active participant in the effort to modernize the city. It gave the council authority to police undesirable public conduct by suppressing "vagrants, mendicants, street beggars, and prostitutes; [and] to restrain and control all gambling and publish the keepers of all games and gambling devices." In a move contrary to long-standing tradition, it also authorized the council to punish the owners or agents of lewd shows and to suppress "all such entertainments or establishments." Perhaps concerned that they may not have anticipated every contingency affecting governmental authority, the committee completed its draft charter with a provision that gave the council power to legislate any measures "necessary for the order or good government of the city; *or its trade, commerce and health.*"[77]

French's charter rivaled Newcomb's in its sweeping vision of government's role in urban development, which should have prompted a vigorous response from the Taxpayers' Association. The association's leadership, however, had drifted away from the original purity of its own vision for the city. The petition to pave Commerce Street demonstrated that, as did the behavior of other leaders. Alderman Arthur Lockwood, who had been a founding member of the Taxpayers' Association, served on the charter reform committee. He revealed how far he had drifted from the association's orthodoxy by commenting: "We will never be able to have a city of any importance unless we incur a debt. We must have the money if we expect to do anything in the direction of public improvements." Friedrich Groos, one of the prominent businessmen on the committee, concurred, according to an article in the *Express*: "If the money is wanted for needed public improvements, he would be favorably disposed towards the change."[78]

Ironically, French's mayoral career ended just as the state legislature approved his charter reforms in early 1885. Political factionalism, not the opposition of the Taxpayers' Association, was the cause of his demise. Nonpartisan city elections encouraged the creation of factions organized around individuals with political ambitions, especially within the dominant Democratic Party where the (reasonable) expectation of perpetual victory over the hated Republicans weakened organizational loyalty. By late 1884 French faced serious competition for the mayoralty from Bryan Callaghan Jr., who had spent the past several years building his own coalition.

Callaghan's father had been a successful businessman and mayor, who had married Concepción Rámon, a Canary Island descendant, in 1845. That success gave his son, who was born in 1852, the opportunities to spend five years studying in France and to earn a law degree from the University of Virginia in 1874. Returning to San Antonio to open a law office, Callaghan married into the influential Guilbeau family. Naturally gregarious, he was also a talented linguist who was fluent in Spanish, German, French, and English.[79]

Callaghan was also politically ambitious, launching what would become a forty-two-year career as one of San Antonio's most successful and important politicians by serving as First Ward alderman in 1880. Callaghan then devoted several years to building alliances with other major figures in the early stages of their careers, including José Cassiano, Thad W. Smith, and A. I. Lockwood, who were creating their own personal followings in the chaotic world of local Democratic politics. Cassiano and Smith were particularly important allies because the strength of their organizations enabled them to serve, respectively, as county tax collector and county clerk for more than twenty years, beginning in 1882. Since the city contained the largest number of county voters, each man had to build citywide coalitions that were excellent sources of support for Callaghan, who initially had only a localized following in the First Ward.[80]

While Callaghan was building his coalition, French was losing control of his. Copeland's 1883 campaign had cost French the East Side, and by late 1884 Callaghan had become the First Ward's most powerful politician. That left French with the Second Ward as a base of support. As the city's longest-serving mayor, French could count votes; he chose not to run again, settling for the nomination as the Second Ward's alderman (a race he could, and did, win).

Callaghan promptly assumed French's legacy by campaigning on a partisan, Democratic ticket as an advocate of active government. His platform, probably designed to broaden his appeal to Second Ward voters, proclaimed that the "vital interests of the city imperatively require that the policy of the incoming administration be a prudent and progressive one, and therefore we demand that there shall be inaugurated and completed a thorough system of drainage for the city and macadamizing or paving of streets and plazas."[81]

With two Taxpayers' Association candidates splitting the East Side vote between them, Callaghan won the 1885 mayoral election, but with no clear mandate for his platform. Officially, he won handily, with 2,222 of the 4,435 votes cast. By dissipating its voting strength between two candidates, the association probably missed an opportunity to defeat Callaghan. West Side voters gave Callaghan a 541 majority, which barely overcame his East Side opponents' combined majority of 519 votes. Callaghan's ties to the Canary Islander elite proved decisive in his victory. Poor residents in the First Ward, responding to Callaghan's own ties with them and to other ward leader allies like José Peñaloza and Cassiano, returned a huge majority for him. The Second Ward's San Pedro Club, a Canary Islander political organization led by José Morín, produced an equally impressive victory.[82]

Callaghan initially ignored the implications in that voting pattern. Announcing in his first mayoral address that "we must unite in our efforts… for the good of our city," he initially defined that "good" as a bond issue for a new city hall and scheduled an election for it for April.[83] The existing city hall, nicknamed the "Bat Cave," had been built in the northwest corner of Military Plaza in 1850, but its unanticipated role as home to a large colony of bats, and its physical deterioration, made the need for a new building self-evident—at least to Callaghan. The association, though, demonstrated that it was hardly a defunct political force. Callaghan's proposal lost decisively in every ward. His West Side supporters simply failed to turn out in the numbers his East Side opponents did.[84]

Such a decisive rebuke so soon after his successful mayoral election forced Callaghan to become more cautious about improvements. His only major first-term improvement proposal—$50,000 for street improvements—avoided a referendum because it stayed within the recently amended charter's new bonding limit. The aldermen supported it because Callaghan reverted to the custom of distributing improvements among all the wards, although ironically the East Side wards received twice as many projects as the West Side.[85]

But Callaghan had not lost his urge to improve. Biding his time until securing reelection in February 1887 (when the new ward system became effective), he promptly convinced the new aldermen to authorize a $150,000 bond issue for a new city hall. Again, the result was not exactly a mandate for improvements because of low turnout. West Side voters supported the proposal, with the Second (now Callaghan's political base) and Fourth Wards providing the largest majorities. East Side voters supplied 64 percent of the no votes, but their low turnout nullified their previous ability to defeat bond issues. The Taxpayers' Association remained as opposed as ever to improvements, but its members apparently failed to notice that French's charter amendments included a clause that changed the requirement for a two-thirds majority to a simple majority in bond elections. By staying away from the polls, they allowed a still weak movement for a more active government to win a rare victory.[86]

Having failed to defeat bonds for a city hall, East Siders demanded that it should be built in Alamo Plaza, where their efforts to modernize the city was well under way. Callaghan, who chaired a site selection committee, rejected that idea. Avoiding the obvious rejoinder that voters who had rejected the idea of a new city hall should not expect him to reward their opposition, Callaghan pointed out that no East Side landowner had offered to donate land to the city; they wanted to be paid, but the city needed free land to control costs. Seizing the symbolic high ground, Callaghan said he favored the "rule of even and symmetrical development . . . in helping the city's progress." Rather sanctimoniously he observed that "that the new federal building is to be erected on the east side of the river and there is much talk of putting the county courthouse there, too. Now, it is our duty in converting the people's money into public institutions to show no sectional partiality or class discrimination." Predicting that "depreciation of property and general shrinkage of values will of course follow" for the West Side if Alamo Plaza became the site, he concluded that "to prevent this and protect all the people alike we must look out a little for the west side of the river."[87]

By the west side Callaghan meant Military Plaza. The fact that the city already owned it lent plausibility to that idea. But the plaza, with its collection of wholesalers, chili queens, pawnbrokers, gamblers, and prostitutes, remained the only major unreconstructed public space in the city. Callaghan hastened the evolution of a modern downtown by transforming the plaza into a symbol of San Antonio's recent progress and future greatness. The city hall would also be an extravagant affirmation of government's role in city-building.

Remaking the plaza meant of course that its former uses and occupants had to move elsewhere, and Callaghan used the council's enhanced power to regulate urban space to relocate necessary but less desirable downtown activities. His general solution was simple: move everything west of San Pedro Creek. Wholesaling activities migrated west along Commerce Street to what became Haymarket Plaza. The council established boundaries for a West Side red-light district and banned public gambling houses anywhere east of the creek.[88]

Callaghan's determination to transform Military Plaza expanded the "respectable" space available to showcase San Antonio's claim to be a modern American city at the cost of eliminating a prime tourist location where visitors could sample Mexican culture, and especially its food and crafts. Male tourists, such as conventioneers and traveling salesmen, might venture into the new vice areas west of San Pedro Creek, but other tourists who sought out picturesque streets and quaint ethnic customs would not normally search for those experiences west of Military Plaza. Mexican American food and craft vendors had to move to Main Plaza and, especially, Alamo Plaza, where they could continue to sell their wares to tourists.

That was a fairly modest change in the spatial distribution of tourist facilities, but Callaghan's efforts at city-building had more dramatic consequences for the neighborhoods at the core of his political organization. By modernizing Military Plaza he essentially accelerated the evolution of a distinctive West Side, just as French's maneuvers to increase middle- and upper-class political power had contributed to the process of creating the North Side.

Local stereotypes about the social characteristics of desirable and undesirable neighborhoods were still in their formative years, but as the city's population grew the newer neighborhoods that attracted higher-income residents naturally acquired the reputation for being the best places to live. Although subdivisions appeared in every area of the city, changes in land use influenced the placement of those more desirable neighborhoods.

The placement of the railroads had perhaps the greatest impact on the future development of neighborhoods. Railroad tracks, marshalling yards, and depots not only needed a great deal of space, they also made the areas near them less desirable for residential development. Locating such facilities at the edge of the city made sense, and in fact Maverick's booster coalition had sensibly created a railroad reserve east of the river in the 1850s, anticipating (wrongly as it would turn out) that the West Side would become the most desirable part of San Antonio. The Galveston, Harrisburg, and San Antonio occupied that reserve. When the International and Great Northern Railroad arrived, the city council provided land for its facilities at the edge of the West Side's settled area. The GH&SA's tracks approached San Antonio from the east and then turned south at its depot to loop around the southern, undeveloped area within the city limits; the IGN approached from the north, and its tracks headed southwest from its West Side depot. When the San Antonio and Aransas Pass railroad arrived in the mid-1880s, coming into town from the southeast, the council located its depot west of the river, but at the southern edge of development. With the completion of these facilities, San Antonio's North Side was the only area that did not have to cope with the negative effects of railroad tracks on residential land values.

Although those effects were not an insurmountable obstacle to the location of middle- or upper-class subdivisions, developers created only two such residential areas on the West Side in the 1880s: Prospect Hill, along and south of West Commerce Street (ca. 1883), and West End, an elaborately planned community in the northwest section of the Second Ward (and subsequently the Third Ward) in 1888.[89]

As with most of the land within the city's official boundaries, the West Side consisted of mostly vacant land. Its settled portions were primarily south of West Commerce Street where the greatest number of Tejano residents lived; they were also disproportionately among the poorest San Antonians. Jacals, the local version of slum housing, dotted the landscape, especially along Alazán Creek and the Alazán Acequia, both of which bisected this quadrant of the city. Slaughter houses, which rivaled railroad tracks in their negative effect on the quality of residential development, had settled in this area by the early 1880s to provide city residents with their meat. Their presence probably encouraged local entrepreneurs to establish the Union Stock Yards adjacent to the IGN's tracks in the late 1880s.[90] Inadvertently the West Side south of West Commerce Street was becoming the favored location for necessary, but noisome, businesses and services.

Callaghan's success in moving the city's vice services across San Pedro Creek accelerated the emerging image of the West Side as an area of poverty and depravity. A newspaper editor captured that perception in denouncing "the illiterate Mexican vote across the San Pedro," asking his readers whether "the business interests, the educational process, the public health and the good government of this city [are] safe in the control of the vote '*over there*?'"[91] Although the phrase "West of the Creek" had not yet become a euphemism that summarized local attitudes toward the emerging slum district, the process of creating that district was well under way.

Having finally obtained voter consent for his signature civic project, Callaghan enjoyed several years of support for a limited campaign of public improvements. In 1889 he managed, again with dismal voter turnout, to win approval for his largest bond issue: $250,000 for various street improvements. By contrast, the business communities in Dallas and Galveston had amended their city charters to increase bonded indebtedness to more than $1 million, which allowed them to pursue improvements aggressively.[92] Main and Alamo Plazas were beautified, some downtown streets were paved, gravel appeared on forty miles of residential streets, and the city funded a new hospital. To some, the collective result was a marvel to behold and a boon to San Antonio's booster spirit: "It speaks well for the city and well for those who are pushing it."[93]

Boosterism seemed at last to have prevailed over the Taxpayers' Association. Indeed, the association apparently disappeared as an organization in the mid-1880s. But the sentiments that had created it in 1879 still resonated with many voters. Any proposal that might raise the tax rate could provoke considerable outrage. In 1890, when Callaghan strayed from a focus on modest improvements to propose a $2 million bond issue to buy the city's privately owned water works, voter turnout surged 247 percent and the proposal was overwhelmingly defeated. East Side voters, in a return to their glory days as the city's naysayers, cast 58 percent of the no votes.[94]

Callaghan's activism coincided with the emergence of yet another attempt to organize a systematic approach to economic development. Charles Dignowity, an important real estate speculator, had visited Dallas and Fort Worth in summer 1887. Both cities were growing at a faster rate than San Antonio, and he wondered why. During his visit he noticed that both had well-organized advertising campaigns to "boom" their attractiveness. Since San Antonio had nothing similar, he naturally concluded that advertising was essential to his hometown's future.[95]

Dignowity organized the Citizens' Association when he returned home.[96] He and his colleagues believed that a well-organized advertising campaign would enable San Antonio to compete more effectively with its rivals, particularly if they resolved some related problems that had hindered previous development efforts. Addressing long-standing complaints among boosters such as newspaper editors, Dignowity and his board of directors announced that they would organize an information bureau that would collect and publish systematic economic data for potential investors, they would lobby the railroads to cease discriminatory practices that discouraged tourism, and they would provide financial assistance to manufacturers seeking to locate in town.[97]

Last, reflecting the growing belief in tourism as crucial to the city's basic growth strategy, the association's directors pledged to work with the city's physicians in a campaign to "induce invalids and people of wealth to establish homes in our midst."[98] Like founders of the San Antonio Club, local doctors equated consumptives with wealthy tourists, arguing that a consumptive "brings his capital and invests in land and houses and thus adds to the material growth and prosperity of our country."[99] Their professional prestige made doctors valuable allies in the new association.

The value of that alliance became clear in the initial discussions over priorities when the traditional (albeit fitful) desire to encourage manufacturing conflicted with this renewed focus on tourism. When the chair of the manufacturing committee proposed creating a fund to assist outside investors to establish factories, Dignowity and Dr. Amos Graves countered with a request to support a "big" hotel effort. The association resolved that confrontation by sponsoring a public meeting "to consider the project of building a suitable hotel," a proposal that the meeting endorsed wholeheartedly. That decision made manufacturing a neglected priority in the association's agenda.[100] Hermann Kampmann, one of the association's directors, contributed to this budding priority by acquiring the Menger Hotel. As one of the city's wealthiest and most important men, his investment was a public statement of support for focusing on tourism as the key to development.

Despite its rather promising beginnings, though, the association did not attract much support within the broader business community. Its directors included ten men who had impressive financial resources and extensive experience. Most of the other directors came from the city's professions (lawyers, managers, editors of the city's newspapers, and real estate dealers). But with only four retail merchants and one stockman among the leadership, the association lacked representation from key constituencies like bankers and wool and cattle brokers.[101]

That became obvious when the association solicited funds for its advertising campaign. Initially the directors contributed approximately $4,200 to the fund, but efforts to raise more money apparently failed. In spring 1890 the association, which had been meeting less and less frequently, simply disappeared.[102] It left a legacy of ideas about where to focus on development opportunities, but once again the business community had shown itself unable to sustain an organized city-building effort.

Futility quickly became the principal theme of would-be boosters by the early 1890s. In December 1890 a short-lived commercial exchange resurrected a modified version of the Citizens' Association. The exchange printed brochures advertising San Antonio's virtues and hired three people to distribute them to pedestrians on the streets in Galveston and New Orleans during Mardi Gras; they also left brochures in passenger trains in both cities. Enthusiasm for this marketing idea failed to develop. The *Light*'s editor dryly noted that "the manner in which some of the very best men named in its directory stand aloof from its meetings and give no countenance to its work is not at all reassuring."[103]

Such meager efforts and caustic comments indicated that boosterism had fallen on hard times, as a surprising offer from a potential investor confirmed. Mayor Callaghan received a letter from a jeans manufacturer who offered to build a factory that would employ two hundred people "on certain conditions." It is unclear whether the exchange's advertising or the factory owner's knowledge of the tax-abatement ordinance that had been renewed in 1888 prompted this inquiry. Whatever its origins, the letter created chaos. Callaghan sent it to the Board of Trade, which the Citizens' Association had resurrected for the precise purpose of dealing with such offers. Denying they had any such responsibility, the board's directors decided that the commercial exchange ought to respond. The exchange's secretary returned the letter to the board, along with some choice words about its dereliction of duty. Having revealed the business community's complete inability to cope with an actual offer, the opportunity to attract a large factory disappeared.[104]

As private efforts to promote development again collapsed due to inadequate support from businessmen, public initiatives also wavered. Callaghan lacked French's interest in financial integrity, which resulted in spectacular cost overruns for his projects. He also adopted a laissez-faire approach to ordinary expenses, bankrupting the treasury by the time his fourth mayoral term began. Temporarily suspending common sense, Callaghan tried to solve his financial problems with what amounted to a public confession of incompetence, asking voters to endorse a $250,000 bond issue in April 1892 to pay for current city expenses. That provoked another significant defeat, with the difference this time that he lost the support of West Side voters as well as the East Side Germans, who gladly provided 68 percent of the no votes.[105]

Aside from the extraordinary nature of Callaghan's bond request, its timing was extremely problematic. The composition of the electorate changed dramatically during the 1880s. In 1878 only 23 percent of registered city voters were native-born Americans, while 27 percent were Germans and 25 percent were Mexican Americans or Mexican immigrants. By 1892 Americans had become 43 percent of registered voters, Germans had declined to 22 percent, and only 18 percent of voters were Mexican. With his political base in decline and his cavalier attitude toward financial integrity a matter of public record, Callaghan resigned as mayor in December to run for commissioner on the county court, where he could count on the support of José Cassiano and Thad Smith to continue his public career.[106]

Callaghan's departure left unresolved a major controversy that had been brewing for years. By the mid-1880s population growth had created tremendous stress on San Antonio's river and acequia system, which residents had traditionally used to dispose of household trash, garbage, and human waste. The severe drought from 1886 to 1888 enhanced public concerns about that habit by causing a dramatic drop in the river's water level, leaving raw sewage to rot on the waterway's banks.[107] In the absence of a sewer system, the city had no solution to this noxious mess. In what may have been a moment of sarcastic desperation, Alderman Bolton suggested legalizing the practice of dumping pollutants into the water system by repealing the city's sanitation laws.[108]

The drought ended, but the crisis did not. Population growth continued, especially on the north side of town, causing household effluents to overwhelm San Pedro Creek by 1892. And river water levels again declined when George Brackenridge bored artesian wells in 1891 and 1893 for his waterworks, drying up several springs that fed the river.[109]

By the early 1890s it was becoming abundantly clear that the city's historical reliance on its natural waterways to solve its sanitation needs was in deep trouble. Despite his fondness for public improvements, though, Callaghan was not an advocate for the creation of sewers. He had in fact helped defeat an 1884 bond referendum that failed because of opposition from the Taxpayers' Association. Early in his first term, he appointed a special citizens' committee dominated by members of the association to advise him about the necessity for a sewer system. The committee concluded that sewers were only a convenience, not a necessity.[110] Callaghan agreed and turned his attention to his own agenda of improvements.

Attorney George Paschal, a widely respected member of a family that had been deeply involved in local politics since the 1840s, succeeded Callaghan as mayor in February 1893. Paschal had to spend his first year restoring the city's finances, but once the budget was under control, he launched an extraordinarily adept campaign to win voter approval for the implementation of a sewer system.

Paschal presented his proposal not only as a solution to a serious health issue, but also as an important tool for promoting the city. He described sewers as "a matter of imperative necessity if we are in fact desirous of protecting the lives of our people," and as essential for providing "the comforts and conveniences which are considered absolutely necessary to any city desirous of calling itself a modern city." Maneuvering to neutralize tax-conscious opponents, Paschal risked his personal reputation by declaring: "I am fully aware that some are inclined to withhold their sanction for this measure out of fear that it will increase their taxes beyond due proportions. I am fully prepared to say that this system can be inaugurated without any increase in the present tax rate and without an increase in the present valuation of properties."

He did not, however, rely solely on rhetoric to win the bond referendum. When the council authorized a large bond issue ($500,000) in July 1894, he convinced the aldermen to schedule the referendum in a mere two weeks. Then he arranged for all city employees to have a day off to help campaign for the proposal.[111] Paschal also prepared replies to the opposition's attacks and visited every polling place on election day.[112]

Paschal's campaign succeeded. In what was the highest voter turnout in a decade, he carried every ward except the Seventh, the bastion of the former Taxpayers' Association. The emerging North Side was his key to victory. New members of San Antonio's expanding professional and managerial class, who were building homes in the northern suburbs, provided 56 percent of all the yeas for instituting sewers.[113]

With the leadership of French, Callaghan, and Paschal, local politicians managed to modify, but not eliminate, voter antipathy to using government as one tool to promote urban development. The Taxpayers' Association disappeared as a formal organization, but its beliefs persisted. In effect, politicians had earned a limited license to engage in modest public improvements, but voters retained a veto over any projects they deemed too ambitious (i.e., costly).

The business community, on the other hand, had not overcome its indifference to organized development, with the result that potentially important initiatives had collapsed from lack of support. Although tourism had emerged as a new industry, it evolved from the railroads' promotional efforts; local businessmen could not even organize themselves to support an independent advertising campaign to grow this industry, let alone attempt to "sell" San Antonio to potential investors. As far as they were concerned, the city's "natural advantages" would inevitably transform it into the state's dominant metropolis. Diversifying the economy therefore proceeded at a leisurely pace that relied on the vagaries of individual decisions.

The city's growth, however, had significantly increased the number of people who had not yet accepted the community's traditional attitudes regarding city-building; it remained to be seen whether they had an interest in changing, or the ability to change, those beliefs.

FIVE

Creating a Booster Machine

1895–1914

In January 1895 several men gathered together in a downtown office to found the Businessmen's Club of San Antonio. They were attorneys, bank cashiers, business managers, and realtors, and they were mostly young, mostly new to the city, and mostly residents of the growing North Side. Some of the sons of the ruling business elite, who apparently differed with their fathers about the value of boosterism, also joined this venture. As with previous attempts at organized development, the Businessmen's Club committed itself to building a great city.

Given the fact that boosterism had a legacy of failure dating back to Samuel Maverick, another attempt at organized development of San Antonio seemed a foolish venture. Making matters worse, their timing was odd. The city had not yet worked through all the consequences of the Depression of 1893, the worst of its kind in the late nineteenth century. Businessmen who survived the economic collapse would have little interest in supporting the ambitions of another manifestation of a generally unpopular approach to urban growth.

These boosters would, however, survive and eventually prosper because of two long-term national developments that affected Texas cities in the two decades prior to World War I. First Texas became a modestly attractive state for nearly a million Americans looking for opportunities to better themselves. Many of those migrants settled in the state's cities, which grew at respectable rates until the outbreak of World War I. In San Antonio these new residents provided a growing pool of potential supporters for the boosters' ambitious plans. Second, 1895 marked the beginning of progressivism in the United States. As a reform movement devoted in part to improving America's cities, progressivism's ideas would become a source of selective inspiration for local boosters.

Population growth and reform gave the boosters an opportunity to create an organized network of businessmen, urban professionals, and politicians that could alter local beliefs about the need for purposeful development. That was a daunting task though, and their success would depend on the choices they made as they worked to transform San Antonio into a city that could continue to attract new residents.

In preparation for dealing with that challenge, the Businessmen's Club adopted a fairly elaborate organization that included four executive officers and sixteen committees. James L. Slayden, a college-educated Kentucky native who moved to San Antonio from New Orleans in 1879 to establish a cotton brokerage business, became the club's first president. Edwin Chamberlain, who was the local agent for Mutual Life Insurance of New York, accepted the post of first vice president; August Briam, the secretary for the Hugo & Schmeltzer Department Store, was second vice president; H. L. Benson, a traveling salesman for Fargo Shoes, took on the role of club secretary; and N. S. Graham, an accountant for the Alamo National Bank, agreed to be treasurer.[1]

The club's committees reflected its ambition to deal with every aspect of urban development. Its most important committees were Manufacturing, Advertising, Commerce, Home Industries, Conventions, Public Improvements, and Real Estate. There were, however, hints that the club might have problems implementing its agenda. Only seventy people attended the initial meeting (although its members grew to more than four hundred within a few weeks). And, despite their intent to be comprehensive, the organizers found it necessary "to omit direct representation for many important interests."[2] That remark probably reflected the difficulty of overcoming the traditional indifference toward organized development among local businessmen.

In the absence of broad support within the business community—which accounts for the small membership—the club needed a strategy for developing San Antonio that matched its limited means. Quite naturally the club turned to San Antonio's most important claim to fame in 1895: tourism. The club announced in its first public notice of its goals that it would promote the city to investors through advertising "as the Best Climate and Health Resort in America."[3]

Conventioneers were not a promising source of investors who would move to San Antonio and use their capital to develop the economy, but they were a potential way to advertise its attractions. Beginning in the 1870s a few fraternal, veterans, and professional societies had chosen San Antonio as a site for their annual meetings even though there had been no organized effort to recruit them to town.[4] These had usually been small groups of visitors, but in 1888 the National Press Association chose San Antonio as the site for its convention provided that the city would offer a suitable venue and refreshments for its members. There was no venue able to accommodate the expected two thousand visitors, so the city council voted $1,500 to build a pavilion at San Pedro Springs if local businessmen would agree to cover other costs. The local breweries agreed to supply free beer, but there were no other offers of help. In the absence of business interest in supporting this convention, the council added more funds to its contribution to meet the National Press Association's requirements.[5]

That example may have inspired the Businessmen's Club to consider creative ways to attract conventions. Slayden's wife, Ellen, was a member of the Battle of Flowers Parade Association's executive committee in spring 1895, and he apparently prevailed on her to help him with a plan to entertain the Travelers Protective Association, which the club had persuaded to come to town in June. Slayden wanted the executive committee not only to agree to move the parade from April to June but also to allow the association's conventioneers to march in it.

Slayden was apparently trying to bolster San Antonio's attractiveness to conventions by offering visitors the opportunity to participate in what had become a signature event for the city. The Battle of Flowers parade, first held in 1891, had quickly become a major attraction. Mrs. John Frazer, the association's president, reluctantly agreed to this departure from tradition, which was to commemorate the Battle of San Jacinto. She lived to regret her decision; the change in the parade's date and the Travelers Protective Association's participation was not a success. There would be no further cooperation between the club and the association for some time.[6]

More bad news for the club's plans arrived in November when the West Texas Medical Association gave the city council a presentation on recent evidence that tuberculosis was contagious. The association recommended that the council adopt ordinances to prevent the spread of the disease among tourists and residents. San Antonio's doctors had long been vocal advocates for the city's beneficial climate for consumptives who had become the mainstay of the tourist industry. They reacted quickly, building an argument based on their analysis of mortality statistics that concluded that the association's concerns were "totally unwarranted."[7]

Unfortunately that conclusion was itself totally unwarranted. Since the discovery of germs through the work of Louis Pasteur and other researchers, the medical profession was in the midst of a scientific revolution that was transforming the treatment for a wide variety of contagious diseases. Tuberculosis was rapidly becoming "the white plague" and isolating victims from society was becoming the preferred treatment. Unfortunately for the club, its plan to advertise San Antonio as a major health resort was now in shambles.[8]

While the club considered what to do next to promote tourism, its executive committee made an extraordinary attempt to stimulate interest in diversifying the local economy by example. In February 1896 the committee bought land for a shoe factory, selecting a site three miles south of downtown that was convenient to the homes of unskilled workers. The committee also decided on the factory's size, recruited a manager, and required him to hire a minimum of 150 workers. Mayor Henry Elmendorf may have been the inspiration for this remarkable experiment. In February 1895 as the Businessmen's Club was getting organized, Elmendorf recommended that the city council develop policies to encourage manufacturing. Noting that San Antonio had raw materials "produced at our very doors," he said: "Let us legislate to offer every inducement for them [factories] to come here and locate among us. . . . We must become producers and exporters instead of non-producers and importers and keep up with the wheel of progress."[9]

The shoe factory demonstrated Elmendorf's point that readily available raw materials should stimulate the development of local manufacturing, but it became a singular experiment rather than an inspiration for others. Businessmen had been denying themselves opportunities to partner with government to promote development for decades now. Other cities were not so reluctant to do so. Atlanta, for instance, had a different tradition. During the 1893 depression Atlantans decided to sponsor an exposition to advertise the city's attractions, something they had done previously. The city council provided $75,000 to help fund it; businessmen created the Exposition Company and raised $134,000. And the city sent a delegation to Congress to lobby for additional funding that resulted in another $200,000. Then the company offered cash incentives for local builders to increase the number of Atlanta's hotel rooms, resulting in more than 1,500 additional rooms in time for the exposition, which opened in 1895.[10]

Such cooperation was alien to San Antonio's public culture. Indeed businessmen could not even support the club, which wobbled on the cusp of dissolution. In January 1897 its membership had fallen from more than four hundred to less than two hundred. Its officers prepared a resolution for the annual meeting that read: "it is clearly evident to us from the non-support we have received that the citizens of this town do not care to encourage an institution of this kind." They planned to hold a vote to dissolve the club.[11]

Club secretary L. C. Irvine had, however, appealed to several businessmen who were "prominent in local politics" for help prior to the meeting. They apparently came in droves. With only seven regular members present, the additional attendees turned the annual meeting into the largest meeting in the club's history. They had come to urge the club not to disband, which turned despair into hope. When the motion was made to disband, the members voted to postpone it and to instead launch a membership drive.[12]

A coincidence of timing had saved the club. Problems with Mayor Paschal's sewer system, still under construction after two years, unexpectedly spawned a reform movement that would transform itself into San Antonio's version of Progressive reform. In February 1896 the *San Antonio Light*'s editor, using classic Progressive rhetoric, had opined that the city "presents a ripe and inviting field for a Good Government Club" whose members would "repudiate and condemn bossism" and "fling away ambition" for political office for the sake of the community's well-being. Within days of this pronouncement a small group of businessmen that included recent club president James Slayden presented a petition to the city council asking its Public Improvements Committee to meet with a delegation of citizens to discuss "all matters pertaining to the public improvements of the city." When the council accepted the request, Slayden and his colleagues organized a mass meeting to select the delegation. In the discussions about nominations the attendees focused on one issue; the need for a professional expert to supervise the completion of the sewer system. They even had someone in mind. Samuel M. Gray was a civil engineer with a national reputation, and the meeting endorsed the idea that he alone should supervise the project.[13]

Such mass support for a major public improvement was unprecedented. It represented a fundamental change in local attitudes toward urban services among many, but not all, San Antonians. It did not necessarily follow, however, that the attitudes embodied by the now defunct Taxpayers' Association had disappeared. Instead the meeting revealed that newer residents, primarily from business and professional backgrounds, were aware of the importance of civil engineers in national reform and that they were willing to use their expertise to further their interest in improving San Antonio.[14] They would need to plunge into local politics themselves to deal with that opposition—and save boosterism in the process.

Disappointment over the council's response to their demands combined with other frustrating developments to convince the reformers to take the plunge. The council refused to give Samuel Gray control over sewer construction and took several months to renegotiate his contract. When the contractor abruptly resigned, the council dawdled over negotiating with a replacement.[15] And as the 1897 city elections drew near Mayor Elmendorf made it clear that he intended to seek reelection. Although Elmendorf was a widely respected businessman, his record as mayor had not inspired confidence among the reformers that he deserved reelection. In early January 1897 the *Express* reported that there was "a moment . . . to embrace all the elements which demand a change in city affairs, including the various ward reform and improvement clubs and a quiet businessmen's movement" under way. The *Light* indirectly endorsed these reformers as a booster movement by criticizing "the want of unity" that had been "a great hindrance to the progress and prosperity of San Antonio." It also denounced the "perverted ambition that prompts men to oppose all enterprises intended to increase the population and wealth of the city." The reformers presumably did not share that perversion.[16]

It was an impressive movement. The reformers had organized a citywide, ward-based Citizens Convention that attracted 1,646 delegates. Adopting classic Progressive rhetoric, the delegates denounced Elmendorf's record of "extravagant, wasteful and inefficient administration" and called for fiscal integrity, public improvements, and "retrenchment and reform in the public service." Seizing the moral high ground, they also called for "the people at large to unite with us in this movement in behalf of the public good."[17] Having adopted a platform, the convention nominated Augustus Lewy, a newcomer to San Antonio who had been a reform mayor in Temple, Texas, for mayor on the Citizens' Ticket.

The convention could claim to represent San Antonio's middle (and upper middle) class. Elite businessmen and the poor were conspicuous by their absence. On the other hand, the convention attracted 205 Mexican Americans (12 percent of the total), a surprising number considering that racial and ethnic tensions were becoming increasingly common. Almost half of those delegates, though, lived in the Third and Fourth Wards, the core of this reform movement's support. Like native-born middle-class white Americans, they were successful businessmen and professionals. Italians, who were the most recent arrivals, had 51 delegates representing them at the convention, indicating they were beginning to establish successful careers as well.[18]

If the number of delegates from each ward indicated enthusiasm for reform, then the Fourth Ward captures the prize for being most interested. It sent 366 delegates, far and away the largest number. Combined with the delegates from the Third Ward, they controlled 34 percent of the delegates overall. The Second Ward, which was becoming a slum, and the Eighth Ward, home of the city's business elite, sent the fewest delegates.

Some of the delegates inevitably were more interesting than others. James Slayden, Marshall Hicks, and Edwin Chamberlain, all founding members of the Businessmen's Club, attended the convention. The convention platform's support for public improvements essentially made organized boosterism an integral part of a reform movement that would eventually encompass broader concerns, such as civil service reform, the suppression of vice, new forms of urban government, and—Progressivism's bête noir—boss rule.

José Cassiano, Joseph Dwyer, and Thad W. Smith were also delegates, and their presence attracted considerable attention. They represented one half of the "Big Six" (the other half being Bryan Callaghan, John Campbell, and Nat Lewis). According to local lore, the Big Six epitomized bossism in San Antonio. Each member of the group had held either city or county office, mostly continuously, since the early 1880s. Over the course of their careers they had spent considerable time developing relationships with each other, evaluating each other's strengths and weaknesses, and testing everyone's ability to deliver votes.[19] Professional politicians, however, naturally raised suspicions among reformers who equated long public service with corrupt political practices. Their attendance at a reform convention was therefore rather peculiar.

Or perhaps not, at least from their perspective. The Big Six title itself spoke volumes about the nature of politics in a city where voters insisted on nonpartisan elections, and where the Democratic Party's overwhelming dominance undermined the need for a rigidly disciplined, hierarchical organization. Factionalism flourished in such circumstances, and the leaders of each faction had to continuously evaluate what their faction's best interests were in each election. That naturally led to alliances to protect and promote those interests; it also meant that alliances could shift from one election to another. Since the leaders habitually neglected to record their negotiations and share them with the public, it was natural to accuse them of corrupt bargains and attribute more political power to them than they might actually have.

The 1897 election illustrated the bewildering nature of this factionalism. Smith, Dwyer, and Cassiano, reputedly Callaghan's devoted colleagues, chose not to support him for mayor because he had been maneuvering to increase his power in county, as well as city, politics.[20] The reformers had shown considerable citywide skill in organizing their convention, and the number of delegates at the meeting was unprecedented. Faction leaders like Cassiano needed to pay attention to the reformers' rising political power. That sort of calculation ensured that professional politicians would become an integral part of the reform movement from the beginning.

Reformers would welcome their help because faction leaders had something important to offer them. In 1897, 57 percent of registered voters were native-born white Americans. That group included working-class German Americans, however, who lived primarily in the Sixth and Seventh Wards. As keepers of the Taxpayers' Association flame, they had a long history of defeating bond issues for public improvements. In this, their first election as a reform coalition, the Third and Fourth Wards had a combined advantage of 425 voter registrations over the combined votes of the German Americans.[21] But this election featured three mayoral candidates, two of whom would appeal to voters in the reform wards. If the reform agenda was to succeed with its booster projects, the reformers needed help from professional politicians who had relationships with ward leaders across the city.

Bryan Callaghan also understood the dynamics of the 1897 election. Although he was reputed to be the most powerful member of the Big Six, the defections of his three colleagues created problems for his ambition to become mayor again. In a three-way race, a plurality of votes would likely be sufficient to win. Recognizing how critical the German American vote would be, he announced he would not run unless unnamed representatives from the German American wards assured him of their support. He apparently received those assurances and proceeded to assemble his nonpartisan ticket.[22]

Callaghan calculated correctly. Although 59 percent of the voters preferred a reform candidate for mayor, they split between Lewy and Elmendorf, allowing Callaghan to win with a Lincolnesque plurality of 41 percent. German American voters made a significant contribution to that plurality; Callaghan won all but two of their East Side precincts. The division within the reform movement also cost them control of the city council. Marshall Hicks and three other reform candidates won seats, but Callaghan's ticket won the other eight.[23]

Defying expectations based on his reputation for budget-busting civic projects, Callaghan reclaimed the mayor's office on a platform that stressed frugality. He did promise to complete the sewer system using only local labor and to be fair in collecting taxes.[24] Those had been sore points for working-class San Antonians who were still suffering from the effects of the 1893 depression. But Callaghan's narrow agenda was essentially promising to reflect the beliefs of the old Taxpayers' Association.

That was not the sort of government that the reformers preferred, and it was quite possibly not the kind of approach that the city needed at this point in its development. San Antonio was arguably becoming large enough to require some attention to issues that had not been so pressing prior to the 1890s.

During the 1890s San Antonio became both a larger and less ethnically diverse city. The city grew from 37,673 residents in 1890 to 53,230 by 1900. Native white residents increased from 37 to 39 percent of the total population, but the proportion of Mexican and Mexican American citizens declined from 29 to 18 percent. Overall foreign-born immigrant voters also declined, from 24 to 17 percent of the electorate.[25]

These changes had important implications for the leaders of political factions. The influence of Mexican and Mexican American voters declined significantly; by 1897 they comprised only 8 percent of the electorate.[26]

Callaghan's public plea for support from East Side working-class German voters arose from the fact that the importance of his traditional base of support among Hispanics in the West Side wards had dramatically declined. Other faction leaders faced similar problems in calculating the strength of their voting blocs. In these circumstances, patronage jobs, which had been an important source of political influence, also declined in importance because city employees had fewer people in their neighborhoods whom they could inveigle to vote for their patrons.

Ironically Progressive reform had the potential to solve the patronage problems of faction leaders. The reformers' agenda included public improvements, which were the responsibility of city government. It is possible that politicians such as Cassiano and Smith had that in mind when they decided to support the reformers. But that, of course, meant that the reformers had to win.

Callaghan's victory stymied the reformers and dealt a blow to his political competitors. But population growth was creating stresses on new residents in particular because of where they chose to live. Those stresses would eventually combine with the reformers' own agenda to create a booster machine in local politics.

Suburban growth after the 1893 depression's effects dissipated became a major challenge to effective government and a major rationale for expanding the role of government. San Antonio's built area occupied only a fraction of the thirty-six square miles within its official boundaries. With an abundance of space available, subdivisions proliferated in every direction around the city. In the early years of all this suburbanization developers faced few, if any, restrictions about lot sizes, building materials, or city services. Developers did build with a particular market in mind, and that determined the quality of a subdivision's houses and its amenities. Working-class subdivisions tended to cluster south of Commerce Street on both sides of the San Antonio River; more expensive subdivisions, with occasional exceptions, were north of Commerce, again on both sides of the river.

Developers were a mixed lot in terms of their resources. A 1910 survey of subdivisions in the *Light* sought to impress its readers with the large number of subdivisions under construction, but it also inadvertently provided information illustrating a haphazard approach to development. The survey listed thirty-seven subdivisions with the capital available for improvements in each one for eight possible amenities that developers might provide. The amount of capital for improvements ranged from $300 to $100,000; the average was $10,775. With such a wide range of capital, the number of amenities varied considerably in the absence of any regulations that established minimum requirements. Sixty-five percent of these subdivisions had two or less amenities (fourteen had none). Even essential amenities were absent. Sixteen subdivisions had no source of water for their houses; thirty-three had no sewers or gas; thirty-two had no electricity; twenty-three had no streets.

By the standards of the times, the absence of amenities was normal. San Antonians, like most American city residents, were accustomed to low levels of public services. Despite all the effort Paschal and his successors invested in creating a sewer system, only 40 percent of the city's homeowners had paid the required fee for a connection to it by 1903. Many excused their failure to do so by saying they could not afford the fee, but it's more likely that they had not yet felt the need for a sewer connection—or the cost of installing indoor plumbing to use it. The old outhouse in the back corner of the yard was still just fine with them.[27] As for streets, this was still the era of horse power, and dirt was a better road surface for receiving the daily deposits from hundreds of horses than paving was. Water for domestic uses was essential, but except in the largest cities, obtaining it was largely left to the homeowner. A private company had a contract with the city to supply water to homeowners, but most San Antonians relied on other private companies, their own wells, or even private vendors who sold water by the barrel every day for their needs.

Population growth, however, strained the viability of traditional practices. And when developers petitioned the city council to annex their subdivisions, the problems inherent in those practices became a collective public problem. As technologies emerged to improve the quality of urban life, and as advances in medicine increasingly demonstrated the need for clean water and effective waste disposal, Progressive reformers campaigned to expand the role of local government in providing those public services.

In addition, ideas about the design of cities emerged from the Columbian Exposition in Chicago in 1893. A group of architects designed the exposition's White city, which defined clean, paved streets and attractive buildings as essential to urban life. Their ideas became the basis for the

City Beautiful Movement, which argued that these improvements defined a modern city.

Middle-class residents of the newly annexed areas, who were more likely to be aware of advances in public services, would become eager, and sometimes angry, supporters of a more active government. As early as 1894 the residents of West End, one of the more elaborately planned subdivisions for new middle-class residents, were carting their water "in barrels and buckets"; they had no police or fire protection, and they had no streets. Outraged that they were receiving no city services for which they were paying taxes, they petitioned the council for redress. Four years later they again petitioned for water mains, and again the council declined to act. Instead it pointed out that the private water company was responsible for water mains. By 1899 the absence of city services in subdivisions had become more widespread with population growth, prompting the *Light* to urge "fair and equitable recognition to our long neglected suburban districts" of their need for city services.[28]

Expanding city services was not a priority for Callaghan. Aside from his supporters' dislike of an active government, Callaghan lacked the means to repeat his previous extravagances because the city was bankrupt. He did manage to fulfill his campaign promise to complete the sewer system.[29] A new market house, which the city had needed for several years, only became possible when its supporters raised money for it through private contributions which Callaghan supplemented with a special tax.[30] Located on West Commerce Street at Paschal Square, the new market became the center for a wholesale district that reinforced the West Side's role as the repository for important, but otherwise undesirable urban activities.

Callaghan's opponents, on the other hand, spent two years promoting their reform agenda despite their minority status on the council. Marshall Hicks, who was preparing to challenge Callaghan in the next city election, was especially active in applying progressive reforms to San Antonio. In March 1897 he displayed an impressive knowledge about the importance of plumbing to public health, introducing a resolution to support the Texas Legislature's intent to regulate plumbers. He had read extensively on the topic and lectured the council on the importance of sanitary laws for promoting public and economic health. A year later the council passed an amendment that closed a loophole in the original sewer ordinance by requiring every house or building to be connected to the nearest sewer.[31]

Hicks also introduced ideas from the City Beautiful Movement into council deliberations. In October 1897 he argued for spending an equal amount of money in every ward to improve streets, which contradicted local wisdom that street improvements were a waste of scarce resources. Then in February 1898 he launched an effort lasting several months to protect the San Antonio River. Arguing that the river "has in the past been one of the chief attractions of our city," he contended that it had become so filthy as to create a threat to public health. He urged the council to return the river to "its former beauty and cleanliness." That prompted several efforts to restrict the discharge of sewers into the river, although Callaghan's councilmen defeated an attempt to authorize an artesian well to increase its flow.[32]

Last, Hicks and his supporters inveigled the council into a few gestures of support for the reformers' economic agenda. The Businessmen's Club had continued working to attract conventions to town, and Hicks, as a club member, may have been the inspiration for asking the council for official endorsements of its efforts. After an initial vague petition for help that the council ignored, someone convinced alderman W. L. Richter, a staunch Callaghan supporter, to introduce a successful council resolution inviting the United Commercial Travelers to hold their annual convention in San Antonio. A minor event at the time, this resolution created a precedent for helping convince potential conventioneers that the whole city, not just the Businessmen's Club, was committed to welcoming them. The next step was to add the personal touch from the mayor; in early 1899 the council officially asked Callaghan to send a personal telegram to the organizers of a convention, urging them to choose San Antonio.[33]

Despite his insouciant disregard for fiscal integrity in his first three terms as mayor, by 1897 Callaghan was becoming San Antonio's most skilled defender of the traditional consensus favoring low taxes, an inactive government, and minimal public improvements. German working-class voters in the Sixth and Seventh Wards usually provided the core voting support for that tradition because of their numbers. The Eighth Ward's German-born merchants who dominated the local economy at this point added their prestige and leadership too, sustaining it as well. G. A. Duerler, B. J. Mauermann, and Louis Mahncke, who belonged to that elite group, had accepted

Callaghan's invitation to join his ticket in 1897, and their role as candidates for alderman had been important to his victory. Callaghan had also been attentive to rising new talent within the German community, recruiting W. L. Richter to run successfully for alderman. Richter owned a popular bakery in the West Side Second Ward and was beginning a successful fifteen-year career as a ward boss.

The Progressive reformers drew their strength from newer residents. San Antonio's population increased by 41 percent during the 1890s. With so many voters who had not yet imbibed the traditional political culture's values moving into homes across the city, reformers had an opportunity to build a coalition that could challenge that culture. They did exactly that in 1897, losing only because of their internal divisions. Building on that initial effort, they retained their ward organizations, resolved their internal differences by focusing on Callaghan as the most significant obstacle to their goals, and prepared to win in 1899.

Marshall Hicks had emerged as the most obvious candidate capable of defeating Callaghan. His service as an alderman demonstrated both his enthusiasm for reform and his ambitions as a politician. A native of Rusk, Texas, he had graduated from Southwestern Presbyterian University in Clarksville, Tennessee, and had earned a law degree from the University of Texas in 1888. A lifelong Democrat, he showed an early interest in politics by winning election as a district attorney in Laredo at the age of twenty-six. Within a year of that victory he became a member of the Texas State Democratic Party's executive committee. Moving to San Antonio in 1895, he settled in the Fourth Ward where his previous record, party connections, and talent made him a natural choice to run for alderman in the first surge of reform in 1897. By July 1898, at the age of thirty-three, he had become an acknowledged leader of a faction within the Democratic Party and the chairman of the Bexar County delegation to the Democratic State Convention in Galveston that fall, an honor that reflected the popularity and respect he had earned among local professional politicians.[34]

The 1899 election would become just the first round in a long battle between competing visions of San Antonio's future. Styling themselves the Independent Citizens Organization, the reformers nominated Hicks for mayor and chose a slate of candidates who were political neophytes. Callaghan named his faction the People's Ticket and peppered his slate with seasoned veterans like Duerler, Mahncke, Richter, and Arthur Seeligson, although he also chose alderman candidates new to politics.[35]

Party platforms offered voters a stark choice between governing styles. Callaghan promised a "conservative business administration for the city," and denounced "extravagant expenditures," by which he meant his opponents' ambitious plans for public improvements. Echoing a now decades-old voter aversion to issuing bonds for improvements, he declared that "the people are opposed to it."[36] Confident in his assessment of the voters' allegiance to local traditional values, Callaghan offered no significant projects to enhance the quality of life in San Antonio.[37]

The reformers' platform was dramatically different, not simply in offering a list of standard Progressive reform promises such as civil service reform, but also in its commitment to boosterism as an approach to governing. John H. Clark, chairman of the Independent Citizens executive committee, attacked Callaghan as a political leader whose policies would fail to attract new residents and capitalists who would invest in the city's future. Clark declared that "the interests, the progress, and the prosperity of San Antonio are at stake."[38] The Progressives had in effect issued a direct challenge to the traditional governing consensus by defining boosterism as the principal focus of their political campaign.

Interest in the ensuing campaign was high; 86 percent of registered voters went to the polls on election day to give the Progressives a clear mandate for change. Callaghan suffered the worst defeat of his career, winning only the First, Second, and Eighth Wards, which were the core of his faction's voting strength. His People's Ticket won four seats on the city council and one city office. The independent ticket claimed eight council seats and six city offices. In the mayoral race, Hicks won 54 percent of the vote. The biggest surprise in the returns was Hicks's victory over Callaghan in the Sixth and Seventh Wards. He carried all six of their precincts, either by better organization or through alliances he had created with faction leaders in those wards in his capacity as a major Democratic Party leader.[39]

Hicks moved quickly to capitalize on this sweeping victory by setting an ambitious agenda for the city council. The heart of his message dealt with measures that borrowed ideas from the City Beautiful Movement to create a more attractive city. Quoting "the most distinguished authority on municipal government," he advised the council that "for a city like San Antonio, whose wealth may be said to largely consist of its climate and its historical attractions, to have poor streets is a policy suicidal in its effects." Beautiful streets, on the other hand, guaranteed prosperity: "With streets well-paved, well-lighted and well-cleaned . . . there could be attracted annually thousands of visitors who would infuse new blood into our city and place it in the first ranks of the health and pleasure resorts of the country."

Put simply, Hicks sought to make promoting tourism a major public policy for local government. To solidify that focus, Hicks urged the council to cooperate with all "fairs, celebrations, and conventions that tend to the upbuilding of the city and giving it fame abroad."[40]

Just what Hicks meant by cooperation was, probably by design, vague. The Businessmen's Club might seem an obvious partner for the council, but it was once again on the verge of dissolution. Its brief flirtation with the Battle of Flowers Association had ended badly, and the undesirability of consumptive tourists was becoming increasingly clear. Alternative strategies for prompting tourism were still in their infancy, although the club had made a promising start in attracting sportsmen to town with two conventions in 1896 and 1897. It had supplemented that effort by sponsoring shooting tournaments, and hunting and fishing would eventually become important tools for increasing the number of winter tourists. Its efforts to promote more manufacturing had been ineffective. A visiting travel writer, struggling to find something to impress his readers with regarding San Antonio's industrial potential, waxed eloquent about a new ostrich farm located near San Pedro Springs. He asserted that the United States was importing too many feathers, creating a golden opportunity to replace those imports with American-grown products.[41] His prediction would prove inaccurate, but in the meantime the club's efforts to establish an acceptable strategy for development that enjoyed broad community support was in disarray.

And so was the club. At its annual meeting the day after the Independent Citizens' nominating convention the club again considered disbanding; instead it created a committee to canvass for funds one more time. Four days later the committee reported that the business community had become receptive to their efforts and "appreciate the necessity of perpetuating the Business Men's Club for another year."[42] The fact that William Aubrey, its next president, nominated Hicks, its most prominent member, may explain this surge in support. Access to political power would prove to be an adequate substitute for a development strategy for the time being.

Mayor Hicks clearly intended to exercise power, but not in ways that would make many members of his reform coalition comfortable. The annual message establishing his priorities showed a willingness to borrow ideas from other kinds of Progressive reform besides the City Beautiful Movement. Financial issues, for instance, loomed large in his message. There was a major backlog of unpaid taxes stretching back several years and the city was essentially bankrupt. Hicks drew on Progressive ideas about the importance of expertise, efficiency, and retrenchment to deal with revenue problems and ineffective bureaucracy.[43]

On the other hand, Hicks was an active participant in a fragmented political culture in which power emerged from the ability to build coalitions and reward both partners and followers. Progressive reformers, who prided themselves in not being professional politicians, believed passionately in civil service reform. City workers should be honest, efficient, trained experts who qualified for their jobs by passing rigorous exams, not by knowing or campaigning for a professional politician. Callaghan and several other faction leaders, though, sustained their power by rewarding loyalty. As a faction leader Hicks intended to do just that.

He moved quickly to make appointments to various positions, including the police, shortly after assuming office. In late March, however, the council approved a procedural rule that implied that the aldermen had been unhappy with that traditional exercise of mayoral power. The rule required the mayor to submit recommendations for all appointments to the council for approval. But there were exceptions. Appointments to the fire department, street commissioner's department, street cleaning and sanitation department, and city hall clerkships were exempt from the rule. Those exemptions covered most of the jobs in city government, meaning that Hicks retained undisputed power to exercise his rights as a faction leader.[44] He did, however, pay a political price for his victory. The three aldermen from the Fifth, Sixth, and Seventh Wards became opponents of his political (but not his reform) policies.

Having settled that issue, Hicks and the council turned to their booster agenda. The dire financial situation took precedence since the city had to recover the ability to pay its employees and meet other obligations. Hicks brought in two auditors to review the records, a task complicated by the sudden death of the city collector. Records of cash receipts proved particularly challenging due to the absence of some key records. A search of the collector's office, though, uncovered the missing records hidden behind the steam radiator. It turned out that the collector had decided to divert interest payments on delinquent taxes to other, unspecified uses. After completing their review, the auditors submitted detailed recommendations, which the council adopted, for recording revenues and expenditures in a more orderly fashion.[45] Those changes coincided with a systematic effort to collect back taxes, which improved the city's financial situation.

Encouraged by that success, the council turned its attention to enhancing the city's attractiveness. This was a more ambitious goal than the reformers probably recognized because it required San Antonians to alter their traditional ways of using public spaces as well as their attitudes toward public improvements. Progressive reformers across the nation had to deal with that conflict in their campaigns to transform urban life; San Antonians just had their own particular version of it.

Population growth drove the confrontation between traditional and modern. San Antonio was a commercial, not a manufacturing, center, which meant that it was not affected by the massive economic and social changes that were transforming cities like Chicago and other northern cities. But its 40-plus percent increase in population in the 1890s was just the beginning of even more rapid growth in the next twenty years. Although Hicks and the Businessmen's Club focused on tourism as a growth strategy, they also needed to pay attention to the practical effects of all those new residents to maintain San Antonio's attractiveness as it grew.

The acequia system became an early victim of the stresses that growth caused. An intricate system that was a marvel of engineering, it was also a temptingly easy way to dispose of household garbage and other refuse. And since the main acequias with their numerous branches served the entire settled area of the city, most residents could use it as a disposal system. San Antonians had discovered those advantages as early as the 1840s. Excessive dumping had kept ditch commissioners busy removing obstructions for decades, but by 1899 rapid growth made that traditional practice a threat to public health. The new sewer system at last offered an alternative to the acequia's role as sewers. Hicks managed to convince the council to abolish the office of ditch commissioner, replacing it with a superintendent of street cleaning and sanitation. But the acequias remained popular. In July, a time when the decomposition of organic materials tended to reach its noisome peak, the city physician recommended closing and filling the Madre and Alamo ditches. Proceeding cautiously, the council instead had them cleaned and ordered the sanitary inspectors to make sure "no further pollution" occurred. Five months later the superintendent reported that cleanup had been a failure but noted that residents along the ditches adamantly opposed closing them. Two more years passed before the council managed to close and fill in both ditches after residents in the Eighth Ward, who exercised considerable political clout, finally had had enough of being the downstream recipients of their upstream neighbors' detritus. After that victory, the acequias in other areas of the city also disappeared.[46]

Rotting masses of household garbage were only one challenge to urban beauty. In December 1899 the council directed an assault on another blemish: the unsightly condition of downtown streets. In an elaborate amendment to the city's criminal code, the aldermen sought to impose new City Beautiful habits on downtown merchants. Property owners became responsible for cleaning and sweeping the sidewalks and streets adjoining their buildings every morning except Sunday. Owners of stables, yards, pens, and other enclosures had to sweep clean their properties three times a week. None of the resulting refuse and "filth" could be thrown into the streets; instead it was to be deposited in boxes and tubs for scavengers to collect.

A week later the council supplemented that ordinance with another one that provided trash cans and spittoons for public use and prohibited "throwing trash or spitting in public places."[47] Spitting in this case may have referred to consumptives, but tobacco juice was also a likely target. Chewing tobacco was a popular habit that required frequent spitting; its byproducts copiously dotted the streets and sidewalks.

Both regulations reflected the boosters' intent to deal with obstacles to an attractive city, but they also illustrate the limitations of their efforts. They were essentially relying on the power of laws to alter long-standing habits of degrading public spaces for private convenience. The rudimentary nature of the city's garbage and refuse collection, however, was a major problem that would take time to resolve. Enforcement was another problem. With only thirty-four officers the police force was not well-equipped to monitor obedience to these laws. Technology would offer some help though. A more efficient machine for making cigarettes, for instance, had been developed in the 1880s, and cigarettes would help promote greater cleanliness on public sidewalks. The automobile would prove to be even more important for improving street conditions. Internal combustion engines lacked the capacity to produce the manure that had plastered every street in every city for centuries.[48]

Paved streets offered another step toward an attractive city, and the boosters were convinced that paving was the correct path to that goal. State law, however, was a major obstacle to their plans. Prior to 1897 property owners controlled the process for street improvements. Since homeowners were required to pay two-thirds of the cost of improving their street, they were naturally reluctant to initiate upgrades. When they did so, however, the city paid the remaining one-third cost, which it recovered by assessing each homeowner a special tax. Over time many homeowners who did petition their city council for upgrades developed the habit of not paying the special tax, prompting lawsuits to force them to pay. In 1897 the Texas Supreme Court ruled that cities could not force the sale of a taxpayer's home for failing to pay the assessment. That ruling in effect required cities to pay the full cost of street improvements; since that was expensive, few Texas cities could do so.[49]

In this situation a bond issue for street improvements offered the only solution available to the reformers. But voter hostility to bonds was a notorious problem, and Hicks therefore spent a full year preparing his argument for this initiative. In March 1900 the council launched this campaign with an ordinance authorizing a bond election to approve $300,000 for street paving.

Limitations on bonded debt restricted the reformers' ambitions to something more modest than they might have wanted. San Antonio's city charter limited its bonded debt to $3 million and bond issues from previous administrations at this point totaled more than $2.5 million. Hicks and his aldermen had, though, thought carefully about the best use of their limited funds. They offered the public a clear plan that focused on permanent paving for downtown streets and macadamized paving for major streets in each ward. It was a plan with a "something for everyone" approach to enhance its chances at the polls.[50]

Hicks also devised a campaign strategy that argued the bond issue would not raise taxes and would reduce the city's operating costs. The sinking fund tax (not the property tax) would increase by a nickel, and the sizeable street maintenance fund would shrink because there would be less need for repetitive cleaning, brush removal (a problem in the subdivisions), and resurfacing. He also asked the Businessmen's Club to support the bond issue and to canvass voters.[51]

All his planning paid off. Voters approved the bond issue by a four to one majority, although the turnout was an abysmal 40 percent.[52] Unlike Mayor Paschal's personal triumph in persuading voters to endorse a major bond issue for sewers in 1895, Hicks's victory reflected an organized political effort to convince voters to support the agenda of San Antonio's Progressive reform movement. The low turnout, however, somewhat tempered the value of the lopsided vote as an indication that the reformers had indeed created a new attitude toward public improvements. Only subsequent events, including how well the reformers implemented their street paving plan, would confirm how strongly voters were willing to endorse the reform agenda.

Hicks and his aldermen worked hard to ensure success, relying on basic Progressive approaches to public improvements that stressed the importance of research, expertise, and competitive bidding on public contracts to guide them. Hicks led a delegation that included the city engineer and the chair of the Public Improvements Committee on a tour of several midwestern cities to investigate their experience with paving issues. The council adopted guidelines based on technical specifications to write a request for bids, which they advertised nationally, which attracted ten bids from companies located in New York, Louisiana, Texas, and Kansas. After a public ceremony to open the bids, the council evaluated each one to determine how well they met the budget and specifications. The winning bid came from Kansas City, which the council concluded was the only one that would enable it to pave all the streets proposed in the bond issue. The whole process was a case study of how Progressives approached the business of municipal affairs; the only remaining issue would be how well the contractor fulfilled his obligations under the contract.[53]

While the council devoted considerable time to paving, that was not the only major issue it attended to in 1900. Sanitation was also a concern because of public resistance to using the sewer system. Cost may have been one source of that resistance. There was a fee for connecting to a sewer line, but there was also the cost of installing indoor plumbing to use the connection. Privies were dirt cheap, and despite the potential threat they posed to a rapidly growing city's public health, they remained the preferred choice of homeowners and businesses.

The council first tried to deal with this issue with raw power. In May the aldermen proposed an ordinance to require all homeowners and businesses to connect to a sewer line, giving property owners several months to do so. After some deliberations, the Sewer Committee recommended against this draconian approach, prompting a rewrite of the original ordinance to instead require all new houses and businesses to connect to the nearest sewer line.[54]

Despite this more reasonable approach to modernizing the sanitation system, there was a major flaw in the council's ordinance. Paschal had designed the sewer system to serve residents living within the city's settled area as of 1895. Five years later the city's footprint was expanding as subdivisions proliferated in all directions. Some builders were constructing homes in existing neighborhoods that had sewer lines, but subdivision residents had no access to those. With Hicks's administration concentrating so intently on street improvements, there was as yet no solution to the question of how to expand the sewer system to the subdivisions.

An adequate water supply for the sewers as well as for domestic use posed another challenge for the council. In January 1900 George Brackenridge offered to sell his water company to the city. He had acquired it in 1879, when the original company went broke because San Antonians refused to pay a private organization for water when they had free access through the acequia system. Brackenridge acquired paying customers as population growth outran the ability of that system to meet the needs of residents.

Public ownership of municipal services was a major goal among many Progressives across the country, but San Antonians faced a major hurdle in the ensuing debate over Brackenridge's offer. The city's charter prohibited it from owning companies of any sort, which meant that the council would have to seek a charter amendment before it could consider his offer. After more than a year of dithering over that question, the aldermen voted against amending the charter.

In doing so the reformers revealed a blind spot in their understanding of how to create an attractive city. They were tightly focused on physical appearance in defining attractiveness, ignoring the reality that there were essential municipal services that had to support appearances. And there was a more immediate problem as well. The existing sewer system, however inadequate it was, needed a reliable supply of water. Population growth was beginning to stress the water company's ability to supply that need as well as the domestic needs of new residents.[55]

None of these issues posed any serious problem to Hicks's political dominance. Such opposition as there was managed to offer voters a feeble challenge to his independent ticket in 1901. He coasted to victory while his alderman candidates won eleven of twelve races, an achievement any respectable political boss would be proud of.[56]

The election did produce some surprises. Hicks announced that he would not run for mayor again in 1903 without explaining his decision. That was potentially problematic for the reform coalition, which would lose its most seasoned leader. On the other hand, the coalition seemed to strengthen its dominance by convincing alderman Richter to take its side. Richter had begun his career on Callaghan's ticket in 1897, but his instincts for self-preservation apparently led him to switch to the reform ticket. In any event his decision brought the Second Ward, traditionally a reliable Callaghan stronghold, into the reform fold. The reformers rewarded his new allegiance by selecting him as mayor pro tem, and Hicks appointed him chairman of the critically important Assessment Committee. Richter was suddenly in a position to enhance his popularity outside of his own ward by making sure that property owners across the city—and especially businessmen—enjoyed satisfyingly low tax assessments. Finally, Hicks used his patronage power to appoint Phil Wright as assistant fire chief. Fire (and police) personnel were particularly important figures in ward politics, and Wright apparently had shown enough talent in organizing voters to earn Hicks's gratitude. This would mark the beginning of Wright's more than thirty-year career as one of San Antonio's most important faction bosses.[57]

Hicks devoted more time to the booster agenda than to promoting reform in his second term. San Antonio had just become the largest city in Texas in the 1900 census. Achieving that distinction was the goal of every city booster in the state, and it significantly reinforced the tendency in Hicks's administration to favor efforts to improve San Antonio's physical attractiveness to ensure that the city retained that title. The council made its priorities clear by tabling a resolution to adopt an agenda for lowering taxes, reducing the budget, pursuing municipal ownership of public utilities, and advocating for women's suffrage by a vote of eight to three.[58]

Civil service reform did receive a nod though when the council approved an ordinance that required potential police officers to write a formal letter of application that included information on their current and previous employment, their age, residence, marital status, health statistics, and prior law enforcement experience. They also had to submit five letters of recommendation from "respectable" sponsors. Hicks was to review all applications for "mental, moral, and physical fitness" and submit his findings to the council, which would compile a final list from which he chose appointees. This was not an exemplary case study of civil service reform that was sweeping the country, but it was apparently what Hicks was willing to concede to the reformers within his coalition.[59]

Having dealt with that issue, the council tried to cope with the practical effects of continuing growth as best it could within the limitations of its budget. That was, though, a major constraint. When some residents of a West Side subdivision asked the council to macadamize its streets, the aldermen rejected their petition because "we have made it a rule not to grade or macadamize streets in the subdivisions of properties for private speculations." Since there is no record that the council had ever adopted such a rule, it appears to have been invented on the spot to deal with this request. On the other hand, the "rule" accurately reflected the council's dependence on developers to provide basic services in subdivisions. In reality, the city's budget could not have supported paving every subdivision's streets, so the "rule" quickly became a formal policy.[60]

The same reality applied to other city services in the absence of bond money to pay for improvements. Brackenridge's San Antonio Water Works contract with the city initially focused on supplying fire hydrants for the fire department. He gradually acquired residential customers as reliance on the acequia system faded, and by 1900 he had connections to perhaps half the homes in town. The city paid him $24,000 a year for that service, but there was no provision that required him to extend service to new customers at a time of rapid growth.[61]

Seeking a solution to that problem, the aldermen began negotiations with Brackenridge in November 1901 to extend water service to new areas, increase water pressure, and accept new rates. Finding a balance between the need for better service and Brackenridge's need to make a profit proved difficult, with negotiations finally ending in June 1902. Brackenridge agreed to provide 3,000 feet of extensions per year, build a new pumping station, and drill several artesian wells. But the extensions would be insufficient to keep up with growth and the cost of the new facilities threatened to eliminate his profits. Brackenridge solved those problems to his own satisfaction by selling the company to a Saint Louis firm in 1906.[62]

As the talks with Brackenridge moved toward an agreement, the aldermen began to plan their way into a political disaster. Of course, that was not their intention. It was, however, the consequence of a sudden failure to understand how various problems in Hicks's second term had affected voters' opinion about their competence.

In early June the council adopted a resolution asking Hicks to appoint a special committee to investigate "the necessity of sewer and other permanent improvements in various parts of the city." The timing of this request seemed appropriate because the street improvements authorized by the 1900 bond election were now complete, as were the negotiations with Brackenridge. Having spent most of their time since the 1901 election dealing with the consequences of growth, Hicks and his aldermen may have thought that the need for more improvements was obvious. It was therefore no surprise that the special committee concluded in early July that it was time for another bond election and presented their plan "to distribute improvements so as to do the greatest good to the greatest number of citizens."[63] The council promptly scheduled the election for the end of July.

Hicks and his aldermen apparently assumed that voter confidence in the booster-reform coalition remained high, which was partially justifiable in light of their easy victory in 1901. But a scandal had erupted in December involving street commissioner Scott's supervision of the contractor's work. A special committee investigated him and issued a preliminary judgment that he exhibited "an utter lack of business method and a casualessness [*sic*] as to compliance." That last point was particularly damning; the committee noted that the contractor's work was "now know[n] to be imperfect." A minority report from a committee member agreed with that assessment but recommended a more thorough investigation.

That recommendation prolonged the special committee's inquiry for another three months, during which it held public hearings, hired an outside expert, and heard from twenty-five witnesses. The parade of witnesses turned the proceedings into a trial of the boosters' competence to spend the bond money wisely. It did not help matters that the investigation found that macadamizing streets in neighborhoods had proven more costly than expected. The aldermen dealt with that problem by dropping some projects to finish paving other streets. In other words, promises to voters in some neighborhoods had not been kept.[64]

Having treated voters to a public indictment of their competence, the boosters performed another act of self-immolation just days after Hicks announced the date for the bond election. The committee in charge of planning the improvements discovered that the city lacked funds to pay its floating debt (a budget category that dealt with payments to local businessmen and other citizens for services they provided under contracts with the city). Aldermen had ignored budget guidelines to divert money for those payments to street improvements, leaving the city with a large debt. Asserting there had been no "reckless extravagance" in diverting those funds, the committee insisted that the council should add a second proposition to the pending bond election: a $100,000 bond to pay those debts.[65]

In these circumstances opponents of the bond proposals found it easy to organize. Within a matter of days they had created an executive committee to coordinate their efforts. Seventh Ward resident J. C. F. Kerr made the case against the bonds. He began by noting that his ward had received fewer improvements than others, but he quickly moved to a more general point: "We need more street improvements, but we need honest city government. We should not permit our needs to be used as a means of fast[en]ing upon the city an administration of those who 'live by politics.'" Kerr's remarks neatly summarize standard Progressive ideals such as efficiency, competence, and honesty in government as well as a commitment to another major Progressive belief, that politicians cannot be trusted to adopt those ideals.[66] He did not therefore agree with the traditional Seventh Ward residents' distaste for government activism. Instead he reflected Progressive reform's deep distrust of politicians, who happened to be the dominant members of the local booster-reform coalition.

That distrust apparently divided Hicks's reform coalition in the bond election. Voter turnout was, as usual, low on election day, but Hicks suffered a major defeat when seven of the eight wards voted against both propositions by substantial margins. Only the Fourth Ward's voters clung loyally to the flag of boosterism as it sank beneath the tidal wave of rejection.[67] The election marked the resurgence of the traditional opposition to government activism in urban development and weakened the influence of the boosters within Hicks's reform coalition.

Hicks further undermined the boosters when he won election as a state senator in fall 1902. With city elections scheduled for February 1903, he did not officially resign as mayor until January 12, causing a political uproar over his successor. Frederick Terrell and John Campbell emerged as the principal candidates and both portrayed themselves as reformers. Terrell had the better claim to that title. He had been born in Indiana in 1853 and had moved to San Antonio with his family in 1863. After earning a medical degree from Harvard in 1881, he had practiced medicine for nearly two decades before winning election to the city council as an independent candidate from the Fifth Ward in 1901. While not part of Hicks's coalition, his professional background and interest in civic affairs made him a reliable supporter of reform.

Campbell was an unusual candidate to lead a reform ticket. He had little in common with Terrell except the odd coincidences of sharing the same birth year and same year of arrival in San Antonio. As a young Irishman he hauled gravel for workers grading local streets while also developing a reputation as "an efficient cowboy" and a "practical cattleman." By 1878 his rather checkered career had earned him considerable popularity among San Antonio's Mexican residents, which was the basis for his election as the city's animal hide inspector. After devoting fourteen years to that work, during which he developed useful connections to important cattlemen in town, he won election as county sheriff. Campbell held that office until 1900, emerging as a major faction leader who earned a certain notoriety as a member of the Big Six, whose most famous member was Bryan Callaghan, by the late 1890s.[68]

In effect, the 1903 election featured a political neophyte battling a highly skilled "boss" who had a reputation for being "straightforward, honest and fearless." Perhaps more important, Campbell had "always been a popular man."[69] That popularity was especially noticeable in the Second Ward, home to the city's largest Mexican community. Campbell benefited from the fact that the long decline in the importance of the Mexican American vote halted after 1900. The Second Ward enjoyed a population increase of more than 100 percent between 1900 and 1910, once again making its votes an important influence in local elections. Campbell carried the Second Ward by a majority of 436 votes and won the Sixth and Seventh Wards by much smaller margins.[70]

His victories in those wards were crucial because he lost the Third and Fourth Wards, which were the core of Hicks's coalition, by a combined total of 558 votes. When the dust settled, Campbell won by a mere 208 votes. His victory may have been due to a split between reformers and boosters in Hicks's coalition. At least some of Campbell's supporters expected him to "run the city on business principles," which was a major Progressive reform goal.[71] And his platform pledged a "progressive city government" that would pursue municipal ownership of public utilities; enforcement of vice laws; appointment of men of "high grade, mentally and morally"; and "greater economy."[72] Despite his support for street improvement and parks, Campbell's platform tilted heavily toward reform goals that Hicks had ignored. That apparently made the boosters in the Third and Fourth Wards unhappy enough to make them vote against him.

Campbell's victory did not, however, mean that the boosters' campaign to create an attractive city was dead. Hicks used his position as a state senator to sponsor a new charter for San Antonio. He prepared a draft without consulting local officials, who scrambled to organize a citizens' committee to review it. While he left no public explanation of his goals in the charter, Hicks apparently drew on his experience as mayor to develop a way to cope with voter opposition to bond issues for improvements. The charter permitted the city council to create improvement districts authorized to issue bonds for streets, sewers, and other amenities.[73]

Having the authority to create improvement districts did not mean the council would do so. The city's tax rate of $1 for every $100 of assessed property, however, was not going to produce enough revenue to provide services to a population that would increase more than 80 percent between 1900 and 1910. Fourth Ward alderman John Kirkpatrick made that abundantly clear when he introduced a resolution acknowledging that the only way the city council could deal with all the requests for improvements that it had received was to create improvement districts. His colleagues agreed, setting the stage for an experiment in patchwork improvements to create an attractive city.[74]

Private citizens had to initiate these districts, and each district issued its own bonds for improvements the organizers chose. That guaranteed a patchwork approach to development since the districts did not have to coordinate their improvements among themselves. And because the districts did not share contiguous boundaries, there were gaps between improvements. Finally, these districts only appeared in areas where property values were high enough to support bonds. Since most neighborhoods lacked the tax base to create a district, this booster initiative would have limited impact on the whole city.

Not surprisingly, this idea proved popular among North Side wards. Residents there created eleven districts during Campbell's mayoralty, four of which were in the Fourth Ward.[75] The council did divide its own limited improvement funds among all the wards, but those were of limited use in dealing with the scope of the problems facing the city. The Second Ward, for example, was well on its way to becoming a major slum where the unregulated construction of "shacks" was creating health problems in the corrals (a collection of shacks around a shared privy that occasionally also had a common water source).[76]

Having resolved its improvement policy, the council turned to Campbell's reform promises to establish municipal ownership of public utilities, to introduce civil service requirements for public employees, and to create efficiency and economy in government. In September 1903 a council committee recommended public ownership of an electric light plant and then set an election date to obtain voter approval of $200,000 in bonds to build it. The aldermen apparently failed to gauge voter enthusiasm for this idea correctly. Although turnout was abysmally low, the proposal lost decisively in every ward. Civil service reform fared better, perhaps because it was far less expensive. The council spent much of 1904 working on a charter amendment to establish a board of fire and police commissioners of three members elected at large. Once the legislature approved the amendment, voters chose the commissioners in late 1905.[77]

Achieving economy and efficiency were two rather different issues. "Low" was more an ideological position than a precise calculation. In the years from 1899 to 1904 the tax rate amounted to $1 for every $100 of assessed valuation on property; it never changed, but the accusation that taxes were too high never changed either. The belief that taxes were too high fueled the perennial refusal to pay any taxes at all, making the effort to collect back taxes a standard feature of every administration stretching back to the 1850s. "Efficiency" was an equally vague term that affected the bureaucratic side of government. In the absence of any accepted standard about how many employees a city government needed to do its work, "efficiency" typically meant the belief that politicians gave too many of their friends jobs. The city council and the mayor assumed that patronage sustained their factions' loyalty and paid no attention to this aspect of efficiency.

But they did agree on the need to improve fiscal practices that would give them better control over budgets and department heads who spent money to provide various services to the public. By 1900 there was a growing recognition within the national Progressive movement that the administration of budgets and departments needed reform. The National Municipal League and the Census Bureau were developing models of urban administration that would have considerable influence in the nation's largest cities. In most cities, though, reformers were not as well informed about those models, leading them adopt less-systematic methods for implementing administrative reforms.[78] Campbell and his aldermen did apparently rely on information from national Progressivism to make important changes in their administrative practices.

They began with an ordinance in October 1903 to track expenses, requiring monthly reports from department heads about their expenses. In December they created an entirely new approach to budgets by moving the due date for property taxes back from September to May and by requiring all department heads to submit estimates of their projected costs for the new fiscal year. These were remarkable changes. Previously councils had prepared budgets every May without having any idea of how much revenue would be available or what their projected costs of running the government might be. In theory at least, they would now have the information they needed to prepare a realistic budget. To further increase their control over city finances, the aldermen ordered the city auditor to report monthly on all department expenditures and instructed all department heads to stay within their budgets.[79]

However important these measures may have been in establishing better oversight of the city budget, they were not the sort of reforms to earn the undying loyalty of Progressive voters. Civil service reform, though, could.

When Hicks guided the city charter through the legislature in 1903, he had authorized the creation of a Police and Fire Commission. Mayor Campbell, as an old-fashioned faction leader, probably opposed this idea until early 1905, when pending city elections changed his mind. His aldermen were getting restless under his leadership; in fact three of them would seek to replace him as mayor. Campbell proposed approval of a commission, and the council promptly obliged him. Campbell then nominated three men for the commission, which was to begin operation on June 1, 1905 (after the city elections).[80]

If Campbell had hoped to improve his prospects for reelection as mayor by endorsing civil service reform, he was to be sadly disappointed. Unhappiness over his leadership continued among the aldermen. His former colleagues in the Big Six probably had little interest in helping him either, particularly since there were rumors that Bryan Callaghan might run for mayor. In these circumstances he had little room to maneuver and announced he would not be a candidate.[81]

Whatever pleasure the reformers took from Campbell's decision was short-lived. They faced the practical problem that they lacked a citywide, organized faction to support them as the boosters had had during Hicks's career in city politics. In the absence of an existing "party" to stage a convention to nominate candidates, C. A. Goeth, the chairman of the Democratic City Committee, offered to organize a primary to select a mayoral candidate who could then assemble a ticket for the elections in May. Seeking to avoid that idea, a small group of Democrats tried to cobble together a "nonpartisan" ticket. They proposed an odd marriage between the reformers and Callaghan's faction, with Frederick Terrell as their mayoral candidate; they offered Callaghan the city attorney position. Since the proposed partners in this marriage of convenience harbored a visceral dislike of each other, it is not clear how this idea made any sense and it quickly expired.[82]

Goeth's offer remained the reformers' only recourse, and their various candidates entered the primary to fight among themselves in selecting a mayoral candidate while Callaghan went to work assembling his ticket, which he called the People's Party. His platform rephrased Thomas Jefferson's famous dictum in a clarion call to halt the activism of San Antonio's boosters and reassert the city's traditional political culture: "We believe the best governed people are those who are governed least." Callaghan did pledge to retain a long-standing tradition of supporting an eight-hour day and a daily wage of $1.50 for city workers. He also acknowledged the need to maintain and repair streets and plazas and to engage his version of permanent street improvements. It was, however, a remarkably short platform that ignored the needs of a growing city.[83]

Vories P. Brown won the opportunity to oppose Callaghan in the reformers' primary. A native of Ohio and a lawyer by training, he became a stockman when he moved to San Antonio. For several years he had been president of the San Antonio Fair Association and a member of the Bexar County Fair Board. He also served as an alderman in Campbell's administration. Although his background implied some interest in boosterism, he ran as a fervid moralist. His platform pledged to close all of San Antonio's gambling dens and wine rooms (where prostitutes plied their trade); all policy shops (a kind of lottery for the poor), slot machines, and vaudeville theaters (another venue for prostitution). And then for good measure he added prohibition to his goals.[84] It was an odd list considering that Brown did not propose shutting the brothels in the red light district, which was where most of those other noxious establishments were located. It was also odd because prohibition was an unpopular idea in San Antonio.

Brown had transformed his campaign into a crusade against vice, which was a major concern among Progressives, though not so much so among other voters. Indeed gambling and prostitution were also popular activities in most cities from the mid-nineteenth century to World War I. Their popularity made them important businesses not just in New York, Chicago, and San Francisco but also in innumerable smaller cities across the country. Professional gamblers and brothel madams met a demand for entertainment peculiarly tailored to the needs of single (or not) males who might be residents of a city, but also traveling salesmen, visiting businessmen, or conventioneers. Despite what Progressive moralists believed, vice was an integral part of every city's entertainment industry. And San Antonio was no exception.[85]

Organized vice districts developed in the late nineteenth century, but consuming alcohol had been a favorite pastime of Americans since the colonial era. Immigrants added their own cultural fondness for drinking to that long-established tradition. Social reformers starting in the 1830s became increasingly concerned about public drunkenness, launching what eventually became a national crusade to eliminate alcohol altogether. That was a difficult goal that created bitter political divisions by the 1890s, when prohibition became a major issue in Texas. Brown's decision to include prohibition in his platform meant that many businessmen, Mexican Americans, German Americans, and working-class whites would refuse to vote for him.

Further complicating matters, Brown's platform did little to attract booster voters. Their campaign to make San Antonio an attractive city focused on improving the city's physical appearance, not its moral fiber. Virtue was of course always desirable, but improved streets, so they believed, paved the way to becoming Texas's dominant city. They might privately share Brown's moral values, but they might also not be enthusiastic enough about his goals to help him win the election.

In these circumstances, Callaghan was probably fairly certain that he would return to the mayor's office. But he nevertheless took no chances, recruiting an impressive slate of candidates who had been deeply involved in local politics, and in supporting him, for decades. They included Ben Mauermann, Eli Arnaud, Ed Braden, John Bauer, John Hambleton, Arthur Lockwood, and Philip Shardein. Callaghan also reached out to rising new bosses, enticing William Richter from the reform ranks and J. Ray Lambert, a First Ward saloon keeper just launching what would become a successful political career.

Callaghan's superior organization and Brown's dedication to moral reform combined to produce one of the most lopsided electoral victories in San Antonio's history. With nineteen city offices at stake, the reformer managed to win one. Callaghan's slate did not simply win the other eighteen, they swamped the opposition. Brown lost to Callaghan by 1,008 votes, a margin the rest of Callaghan's team mostly matched for citywide offices. The alderman races were only slightly closer because the total vote in each ward was less than 1,000. Brown's followers salvaged their honor only in the Fourth Ward, where their candidate defeated Callaghan's choice by a respectable margin. On the other hand, Callaghan claimed 60 percent of the Fourth Ward's vote for mayor, which was astonishing considering the ward's pro-reform reputation.[86]

Callaghan's smashing victory appeared to spell the end of the boosters' efforts to change the city's traditional political culture, which in turn meant the end of their campaign to use government to create their version of an attractive city. Since that culture rejected systematic responses to the challenges of growth, and since San Antonio's population would more than triple between 1900 and 1920, there was now a strong possibility that the city would evolve in a singularly unattractive way—at least from the perspective of the boosters. Compounding their own problems, the boosters' once-formidable political organization had deteriorated badly by 1905. Nothing illustrated their decline more than the shift in support for Hicks and Callaghan in the Fourth Ward. In 1899 Hicks won 61 percent of the votes there; in 1905 Callaghan won 60 percent. The booster-reform coalition lacked the leadership and issues that could propel their faction to another victory.

Callaghan would dominate city politics for the next seven years because of the strength of his coalition and the struggle the boosters faced to rebuild their own organization. His clever paraphrase of Thomas Jefferson's famous dictum on limited government declared his allegiance to San Antonio's traditional political culture and its version of boosterism. The demand for limited government and low taxes did not necessarily translate into opposition to growth. Instead the advocates for those virtues believed that they were essential to future growth. In their view, limited government and low taxes defined an attractive city.

J. C. F. Kerr, a Seventh Ward resident, explained this approach to boosterism in July 1902, when he wrote to complain about the negative effects of bonds. In his view, issuing bonds would inevitably mean an increase in taxes that would drive away prospective investors. Recognizing that San Antonio was competing with other Texas cities for investors and new residents, he argued that the city's current tax rate was so high that it would cause them to go elsewhere.[87]

The fact that San Antonio had been growing for decades made this approach to boosterism hard to refute, especially in the absence of any widespread understanding of how and why cities grow. Hicks and his fellow boosters had been borrowing from national ideas that defined a city's attractiveness in terms of its physical appearance. Those ideas stressed, for example, the importance of wide, straight, paved, clean streets. But San Antonians, and for that matter most Americans living in cities, had not yet experienced the practical benefits of such improvements. They simply could not grasp how such expensive improvements were worth their cost. And without practical experience that could alter their opinions, most San Antonians would continue to resist the aspirations of Hicks's boosters.

Callaghan was therefore well positioned to govern for several years without serious opposition. He was an extremely able politician who understood his voters quite well. His political supporters would remain content with his rule as long as he kept taxes low and the size of his government small. Managing those goals turned out to be quite easy. Rapid population growth increased city revenues from property taxes quite dramatically from 1905 to 1912. City budgets increase from $450,000 to $1.2 million by 1912. Callaghan could have had even larger budgets, but he chose to reduce property taxes as the population increased, keeping them well under $1 for every $100 of assessed value.[88] In doing so, he deliberately limited the amount of money the city would have for dealing with the consequences of growth.

That did not matter because he had no program for developing the city that would require additional revenue. Instead he could adopt a piecemeal approach to solving problems as they arose without having to pay attention to the wider implications or consequences of temporary solutions.

Nothing illustrates his approach to dealing with rapid growth better than his policy for public improvements. Since he had pledged undying hostility to bonds, the city's current budget was the only source of public funds for improvements each year. And with the yearly increases in revenues there was certainly the possibility for allocating funds to improvements. Callaghan, however, did not dedicate revenue to specific improvements. He did have a contingency fund that averaged $68,500 (and in one year reached $100,000) that he controlled, but there is no record of what he did with that money. Essentially ignoring the budget as a tool for dealing with growth, Callaghan dealt with increasing demand for such key services as water, sewers, and streets by relying on a variety of private initiatives.

A private company, for instance, continued to be the primary source for supplying residents with water during Callaghan's mayoralty. Considering that the city's population increased by approximately 45,000 people during those years, it is surprising that the cost of the city's contract with George Brackenridge's company, and then its successor, never increased. The city did include in its contract with the company a requirement to install a minimum of 1,500 feet of new pipe each year, but since the price of the contract remained constant the company had no incentive to keep pace with demand

and the city had no way to force it to lay more than the minimum. Residents who wanted water therefore had to make their own arrangements. Some petitioned the city council for permission to connect with an existing water main. The council usually granted such requests with the proviso that the petitioner had to pay all the costs of the connection. Residents who had no access to a main either drilled their own well; contracted with one of the many other private water companies for service; or bought their water by the barrel from itinerant salesmen.

Those choices meant that large numbers of residents, especially in the emerging Second Ward slum, had inadequate supplies of water for their daily needs. For such residents the lack of water would eventually contribute to the worst health crisis in San Antonio's history. A more immediate problem was fire. The absence of water mains and hydrants meant that new subdivisions had no fire protection. Without water sources the fire department could not build new stations in the suburbs, and its protective coverage within older neighborhoods was not very comprehensive either. As a result, San Antonians paid the highest rates for fire insurance in Texas.[89]

Expanding the sewer system followed the same pattern. Four days after Callaghan formally assumed office, alderman Ed Braden submitted a resolution to the council stating that the city engineer would issue permits to "any citizen or contractor properly qualified" to lay "private sewer mains" when there were no city mains in the front or rear of a petitioner's house. A year later the council clarified procedures for sewer installation that required the city engineer to supervise each project, gave the city the right to make private sewers a part of the city's system, and established a limit on the amount a private home owner or contractor could charge for a connection to the new sewer. Oddly, though, the same resolution asserted that the city would not be obligated to provide water to flush private sewers.[90]

Callaghan took a personal interest in private sewers, at one point investigating their construction around town. He discovered that there were many that had not received council permission, prompting the aldermen to pass an ordinance banning the laying of sewers without their permission and requiring all contractors to submit detailed reports of their sewers.[91]

The council obviously sought to ensure proper supervision of sewer construction, but neither Callaghan nor the aldermen worried about sewer service in neighborhoods where residents could not afford the cost of constructing their own mini-system. Privies remained the only option for many working-class residents as well as the poor. Sewer construction in the Second Ward was virtually nonexistent except in the middle-class neighborhood of Prospect Hill. Sewer service also remained sporadic at best in subdivisions despite the fact that petitions for them became one of the most common features at council meetings. Relying on homeowners and subdivision developers to install sewers created a nightmare hodgepodge of different sizes of pipes, inadequate flushing, and numerous gaps in the overall sewer system.

In dealing with street development in subdivisions, and in some cases established neighborhoods, Callaghan continued Campbell's policy of relying on improvement districts. That quickly became a problem. Residents had organized ten districts prior to 1905, but created only seven more by 1912. The declining interest in IDs stemmed from a combination of Callaghan's behavior and their inherent limitations. When these districts first appeared, the residents controlled their own budgets, made their own choices about paving types, and supervised the work. Since the residents who organized a district assumed responsibility for paying off their district's bonds, this was eminently sensible. In 1907, however, the council appropriated $15,000 from Improvement District Number One's account and transferred the money to a street project outside of its boundaries. That remained a unique event, but it probably created uncertainty among the other districts about the security of their funds. Several months later Callaghan appointed a special committee to oversee a new district, effectively removing self-government from the districts. Callaghan had in effect seized control of the management of the districts' projects. Then in 1911 complaints emerged that bond money from at least one district had simply disappeared. Finally, when the residents of a Seventh Ward neighborhood tried to create a district they were unable to sell the bonds to finance their improvements. The assessed value of their properties did not impress investors as being enough to ensure payment to bond purchasers.[92]

Callaghan's treatment of the improvement districts probably stemmed from his political goals regarding streets. They had always been a prime source of patronage jobs, and the privatized districts impeded his ability to reward loyalists. On the other hand, he had consistently argued that street improvements should be paid for from current revenue. By 1909 he had devised a plan to sustain employment for low-level patronage appointees and to reduce contract costs for street paving. In July he began construction of a new municipally-owned utility: an asphalt plant. When workers finished the job in December, Callaghan decided to address the council about his vision for asphalt. Considering that complaints about dusty, dirty, unpassable, unpaved streets had been a routine part of living in San Antonio for years, Callaghan may well have believed this to be his great legacy to the city. He had never been a particularly eloquent speaker, but now he engaged in uncharacteristically grandiose oratory.

He began by introducing a resolution committing the council "to make successful the permanent improvement of every plaza and street in the City." That was itself a startling idea; no one—not even the boosters—had ever proposed such an ambitious goal. Furthermore, the enormity of his goal implied huge costs. But this was Callaghan talking, and he immediately dispelled any concerns about costs by reassuring his audience that "the expenditure should be as reasonable as possible." He then revealed his booster pride, saying that the plant "means that San Antonio will go to the front as the most beautiful city in the whole South."[93]

Despite his hopes, Callaghan's dream quickly dissolved into ridicule. The plant produced inferior asphalt that rapidly deteriorated once applied to the streets. By 1911 he had achieved the dubious distinction of having his paving material named after him. "Callaghan asphalt" became the catch phrase to describe the public's opinion of his plan.

The failure of Callaghan's plant was a small part of a larger problem with his, and his followers, vision for San Antonio. Relying overmuch on private initiatives to provide public services created uneven development; too few people had access to essential services. That undermined San Antonio's claims to be a modern, let alone an attractive, city. In early 1907 a visiting journalist named Frank Putnam captured the essence of the challenges facing the city. He had come because of San Antonio's status as Texas's largest city, but he was not impressed: "Broadly considered, as a social unit, San Antonio impresses the observer as a chaos of individualism." Its businesses and residential buildings were "scattered in a sort of hit-or-miss way" with "adobe huts" and fine homes "alternating in a bewildering fashion." Excessive individualism had, in his opinion, created a "heterogeneous no-arrangement of the town" that "indicates... the absence of a united civic spirit, which becomes more strongly apparent with each day that one remains on the ground." He blamed the town's appearance on its political system, saying it looked the way it did because of its devotion to the "old rule of the ward politician." Saving his most damning comment for last, Putnam concluded that "these conditions are due not to any lack of energy on the part of the people of San Antonio.... It is an indication of the lack of community spirit... that transforms a village."[94]

In blaming San Antonio's disheveled physical appearance on ward politicians Putnam was expressing a classic Progressive belief that their political system impeded the economic growth and development of cities. By the time of his visit, Progressives had developed a veritable library of works analyzing not just the faults of that ward system, but also offering an array of ideas for correcting them. University professors were proposing models for more efficient and effective government while other reformers were publishing guides to more attractive cities such as Charles M. Robinson's *Modern Civic Art, or, the City Made Beautiful* (1903). Closer to home, the hurricane that devastated Galveston in 1900 had prompted a new structure for city government called the commission. In 1901 a statewide convention had trumpeted the virtues of commission government to the state's Progressive reformers, and Houston, Dallas, Fort Worth, and El Paso had adopted it by 1907.[95]

All these developments created possibilities for choosing an issue that could reignite an organized reform movement that would create the "community spirit" Putnam believed to be essential to defining a city. Callaghan was a formidable opponent, however, and the choice of an issue for organizing opposition to his dominance would be critical. That task seemed even more hopeless after his victory in the 1909 mayoral election when he won an average of 96 percent of the votes in every ward. It helped that his only opponent was a Socialist, whose candidacy panicked every major politician in San Antonio into endorsing Callaghan.[96]

That artificial display of dominance dissipated within a year. On March 24, 1910, Thomas Conroy convened a meeting of thirteen men to create the Commission Government League. Despite its small size, the group represented a broad range of influence and experience in business and politics. Its members included James E. Webb, an attorney and president of the Guenther Hotel Company; Charles S. Fowler and Jay E. Adams, two of the most important realtors in town; Chester Terrell, a state representative; George Surkey, a former alderman in Hicks's mayoralty; and William Aubrey, who had nominated Hicks for mayor at the Independent Ticket convention in 1899 and was a past president of the Businessmen's Club. Conroy was a banker, an active member of the Businessmen's Club, and the founder in 1909 of the Publicity League for promoting tourism.[97]

Conroy had chosen an issue that would delight reformers and enrage Callaghan. Although the details of commission government varied from place to place, it basically promised to replace the existing system of ward-based politics with a radical model for governing based on such business principles as economy, efficiency, and expertise—all values dear to the Progressives. Voters would select commissioners in citywide elections. Each commissioner would supervise a specific city service, or set of related services such as fire and police; they would be experts in the delivery of such services; and they would hire employees based on their merit, not their political connections.

For reformers, there was little to dislike about commission government. Ward politicians, though, found it profoundly flawed. It eliminated aldermen and the ward system that elected them, which was of course immensely attractive to reformers. The aldermen and their supporters, however, would point out that it also eliminated representative democracy. Progressives, who tended to be suspicious about the influence of ethnic or racial minorities in city politics, did not mind that, but Callaghan, among others, found that deeply offensive.

Ward politicians would be at a great disadvantage in this fight because the ward system had fallen into great disrepute after years of stories regarding scandals, corruption, and general malfeasance in office. On the other hand, there had never been any great scandals about San Antonio's politicians, and the record of politicians in many other cities dealing with the effects of massive industrialization and urbanization had been far better than reformers were willing to admit. In the coming battle over the structure of government, though, Callaghan would struggle not just with the perception of incompetence that projects such as his asphalt plant created, but also with the consequences of his own missteps in combating the reformers.

Conroy proved to be an effective organizer and political tactician. In the five weeks following the March meeting he visited several Texas cities that had adopted commission government; opened a headquarters for the league on Houston Street; and had a committee write commission government into a draft for a new city charter. He then planned a public meeting for May 5 to launch an advertising and membership drive for the league. On May 2, however, Conroy cleverly forced the city council to declare its opposition to commission government. He submitted a petition asking the council to schedule a special election in June to gauge voter support for commission government. Callaghan denounced the idea as "ill-advised" and the council unanimously rejected the petition.[98]

Maneuvering the council into denying voters an opportunity to give their opinion on commission government probably increased public interest in the May 5 meeting. The mayors of Houston, Fort Worth, and Galveston extolled the virtues of commission government and several local notables endorsed it. To help those who missed the meeting, a letter to the editor by "Taxpayer" the next day attacked Callaghan for failing to improve San Antonio's streets. Interestingly, he argued that the problem with the current city administration was not dishonesty, but its use of unspecified "out dated methods" for dealing with improvements that commission government would replace with modern methods.[99]

By late May the league had begun to organize support in the ward precincts and was establishing a Citizens' League to contest upcoming legislative and county elections. Callaghan tried to slow the league's momentum—it had attracted four thousand members by July—by pointing out that cities that had adopted commission government had raised taxes and had issued large amounts of bonds to fund improvements. He also announced the creation of a committee of citizens to examine the merits of the current charter and to make recommendations for changes.[100]

Conroy outflanked Callaghan's efforts to slow the emerging revolt against ward-based government. The Texas Legislature was meeting in a special session during the summer, and a delegation from the league presented a draft new charter to the governor, who announced his support. Rep. Chester Terrell, a founding member of the league, then guided the draft through the legislature, which approved it on August 16.[101]

Since the charter required voter approval, a referendum on it was set for February 4, 1911. At this point the Commission Government League announced it would begin organizing for that election in October after its members had returned from their vacations. While the reformers took a break, Callaghan began to build a defense of the status quo by appointing a citizens committee to study the charter. He timed its report to coincide with the league's return to business. The committee condemned commission government for concentrating too much executive power in the hands of commissioners and strongly defended Callaghan's policy of voluntarism for public improvements, saying that provisions in the charter would "retard or stop a large part of the best improvements work to be accomplished in section[s] of the city where the property owners are willing to tax themselves for such improvements." In effect, the report sought to defend the existing political system as the best way to preserve the traditional culture's preference for low taxes, limited government, and minimal public improvements.[102]

The league reconvened to organize for the coming campaign on October 19. Judge James E. Webb stated the case for commission government. Webb cited Judge John F. Dillon, the most famous nineteenth-century authority on the legal status and powers of city government, who had, according to Webb, argued that the solution to the problems of cities was "a business administration by businessmen." Dillon's analysis had, in Webb's words, convinced local businessmen that "administration is a business affair and not a political affair." Webb's argument echoed national Progressive beliefs that city government was too important to be trusted to politicians. That was not, however, necessarily a universally held opinion. D. J. Woodward, who spoke after Webb, began by noting that "the absence of some of our businessmen is rather conspicuous, but we don't miss them." He was referring to the fact that the older business elite of San Antonio lent only tepid support at best to reform.[103]

Callaghan's political coalition faced some serious problems as the campaign for commission government heated up. He began this campaign handicapped by the fact that his generation of politicians was fading fast. Several of his key associates who were serving in his current administration had died. They included John Bauer, an alderman-at-large, in 1907; both Third Ward alderman John Hambleton and Sixth Ward alderman K. J. Carey in 1908; and Second Ward alderman Eli Arnaud in 1910. In a political culture as fractured as San Antonio's was, these were men who had developed relationships with and for Callaghan that extended back into the 1880s. Their loss likely disrupted Callaghan's ability to assess voter sentiment as the referendum campaign progressed. Complicating matters even more, Callaghan himself was not a well man. Beginning in June 1906 he was often absent from council meetings as he struggled with the onset of Bright's disease.[104]

While Callaghan struggled with the implications of those problems the league built a citywide coalition that appealed not just to white Progressives but also to some Mexican Americans and African Americans. Its formal membership reached 5,500 by December, and its campaign exerted intense pressure on the ward politicians by focusing on the supposed contrast between the deep flaws of ward politics versus the promise of a modern government.[105]

Faced with the extinction of a political system that had served him well, Callaghan manipulated the electoral process to bias the election's outcome in his favor. First, through his control of the council, he changed the balloting system. The council decreed that there had to be separate ballots, one for those who opposed commission government; another for those who supported it. This made it easy to observe the progress of voting on election day, giving Callaghan an opportunity to adjust the voting in precincts his organization controlled. Then he refused to appoint election judges recommended by the league in six precincts, three of which were in the Second Ward, his home base (all three produced lopsided votes against the charter).[106]

Confusion reigned on election day and for several days afterward. Newspapers reported conflicting accounts of the result, with stories announcing the charter's defeat but providing tallies that showed it had by a razor thin margin of 199 votes out of 14,547 cast. The council had not, however, completed its official review of the outcome. Callaghan appointed a committee composed of three stalwart supporters who concluded that the proposed charter had lost by 160 votes. Anticipating objections to the official count, Callaghan ordered the ballot boxes and tally sheets locked in a cell at the city jail and refused to open it.[107]

That rather astonishing performance provoked an immediate response. Augustus Jones, chairman of the Commission Government League, announced that it would field a ticket to oppose Callaghan in the city elections scheduled for late May. His executive committee created a Committee of One Thousand to organize a citywide base for the Citizens' Ticket and held a nominating convention in late March that selected Judge Webb to lead a full slate of candidates for the new party.[108]

Callaghan's behavior gave the Citizens' Ticket a natural issue to rouse voter ire. It would campaign for "clean government" to take advantage of that anger, but the party's organizers did not link purity with commission government. Instead the coalition that had campaigned so hard to change the structure of government dropped that issue to focus on booster goals for San Antonio. The shift in emphasis after having spent so much time and effort to structural reform apparently emerged from an implicit assumption among reformers that equated commission government with physical improvements. Shortly before the election, the *Light* had commented that "the lack of good streets seems to be one of the main reasons why the merchants of the city want commission government."[109]

Conflating the two would later prove problematic for reformers, but in the meantime Webb attacked Callaghan's record on street improvements while one of his supporters urged voters "to rise up and put this city in a position where it will never have any fear of opposition from Dallas, Fort Worth, or any other Texas city." Another speaker explained that San Antonio would defeat its rivals for the honor of becoming the largest city in the state with better streets, better pavements, more parks, a boulevard system, a convention hall, and a larger sewer system.[110]

While the reformers were creating future difficulties for themselves, Callaghan was conducting a thorough review of his coalition's prospects for the spring elections. He was not happy; rumors began circulating that some "old aldermen" might be replaced with "better vote getters" on his forthcoming ticket. There were also rumors that "the Mexican machine is divided," a reference to the coalitions in the Second and Third Wards that had supported Callaghan since the 1880s.[111] The reformers' choice of candidates lent some substance to that rumor. Jake Rubiola appeared on the Citizens' Ticket as its candidate for city tax assessor. He was a coleader with Andres Coy Jr. of a Third Ward political club. Since Coy had become a member of a reorganized Big Six county machine in 1908 that included Callaghan, it is unlikely that Rubiola did not consult Coy about his move to the reform ticket. Callaghan's problems may have tempted the Coy-Rubiola partnership to establish connections with the reformers as an insurance policy for their political careers.[112]

All the rumors combined with Rubiola's behavior indicated a further fraying among the coalitions that had made possible Callaghan's role as a major political leader for nearly three decades at this point. Jettisoning longtime ward leaders who were themselves suffering from a diminishing ability to manage voters might be an effective short-term strategy, but it implied that Callaghan himself was rapidly approaching an end to his own career.

Grim necessity did lead to a purge. Callaghan dropped four aldermen, the current tax assessor, and the city auditor from the slate for his People's Party in late March. Proud of his approach to public improvements, Callaghan chose to campaign on a pledge to continue his approach to boosterism. His platform stressed that his continuing leadership would keep San Antonio "abreast of the times and retain its foremost place among the cities of Texas."[113]

The election results revealed how evenly divided the voters were in choosing between the competing versions of boosterism. Victory margins were razor thin in citywide contests. In the mayor's race Callaghan emerged the victor by 185 votes (from a total of 12,443). Rubiola lost by only 97 votes (total of 12,545). Callaghan's candidates won three of the four alderman-at-large positions by an average of 96 votes; Albert Steves Jr. won the sole Citizen's Ticket victory there by a margin of five votes (total of 12,505).

Callaghan's People's Party did not, however, fare well in the ward aldermen contests, losing five of eight seats. The Fourth through Eighth Wards went to the reformers, although their average margin of victory was only 165 votes (vote totals ranged from about 1,200 to a little more than 2,000 depending on the ward).[114] The city council was now evenly divided (6–6); since the charter required eight aldermen to approve any financial matter, the reformers now had the ability to deprive Callaghan of his control over the budget.

Surveying the end of six years of undisputed power, Callaghan decided to muzzle the reform faction on the council as much as possible. He called a meeting of the council a week before the new government was to assume office to enact new rules and procedures. The lame duck council, loyal to the last, approved Callaghan's changes: seven aldermen would constitute a quorum; the mayor had the authority to "reserve order and decorum," which meant he had to recognize an alderman before he could speak; no alderman could speak more than ten minutes, and none could speak more than twice on any question; no speaker could use "unparliamentary language" and an alderman could be banished from a meeting for disorderly conduct (as defined by the mayor). Finally, a council committee needed only two members to constitute a quorum for conducting its business.

Having prepared for their arrival, Callaghan greeted the new aldermen with a speech in which he requested harmony in working together. More pointedly he said: "I have asked, and I ask now, your cooperation in making this administration succeed... I trust you will be aldermen of the City, not aldermen of any party. Only in this way can cooperation be assured."[115] It was a remarkable performance from someone who had lost the ability to dictate the agenda for the city's development.

Supporting Callaghan's administration was not the first priority of the Citizen's Party aldermen. They would spend the next six months bickering with Callaghan over budget issues. As his irritation grew, the mayor responded with increasingly arbitrary rulings, expulsions from council meetings, and, finally, ignoring rules when it suited him to contain the reform bloc's agenda. The reformers generally failed in their efforts, but occasionally their blocking tactics produced compromises of necessity. Normally the council had approved Callaghan's budgets without cavil in early June. After six weeks of failing to obtain the votes necessary to establish a budget, Callaghan granted a rare concession to his opponents and allocated a significant amount to widening streets. It was the first time such an item appeared in the budget, and it was an important victory in the reformers' desire to modernize the city's appearance with straighter streets. Downtown streets were notoriously quirky—Commerce Street still had seven different widths along its length from the river to Military Plaza for instance—and their cramped widths were especially problematic as automobile traffic began to appear in the city's center. (The council had passed its first automobile traffic ordinance in 1910 to deal with downtown congestion.)[116]

Council meetings remained contentious through spring 1912, reaching a new low in May when Callaghan managed to impose a new rule on the aldermanic rebels. It required an alderman who had been expelled "for cause" from a meeting to "purge himself from contempt" before he could resume his seat. The rule neglected to define what purging meant, but since Callaghan had sole authority to expel a member, the rule amounted to an attempt to drive his booster opponents out of the council.[117]

The onset of summer meant that the July elections for county offices were fast approaching. And the voting power of the Citizens' Ticket, as demonstrated in the 1911 city elections, hovered in the background as various factions considered their candidates and their prospects. Callaghan was assembling a county ticket to run under his People's Party label, which put pressure on faction leaders who had been allied with him for several years to calculate the risks of continuing to work with him. The state of Callaghan's health had to have figured into their calculations since he was now struggling daily with the effects of Bright's disease. In late June county clerk Frank Newton, district clerk Andres Coy Jr., and county sheriff John Tobin had decided to abandon him and join the Citizens' Ticket to enhance their prospects for reelection. Newton, Coy, and Tobin ranked among the most effective faction leaders in Callaghan's coalition, and their departure portended disaster for the People's Party.[118]

Callaghan died on July 8, throwing what remained of his coalition into a chaotic search for survival. The council hastily set a special election for mayor for July, and alderman William Richter, who had long served as mayor pro tem, announced that Callaghan would have wanted him to succeed him. That caused at least two other faction leaders to defect to the Citizens' Ticket, which would sweep the county elections in large part because of its opponents' disarray. In the meantime the reformers convinced Augustus Jones, a wealthy rancher and owner of the Saint Antony Hotel, to oppose Richter. Jones defeated Richter by 971 votes; the Fourth Ward provided 714 of those votes in what otherwise was a close election.[119]

With their victories in the county elections and the mayoral race the booster-reform coalition now appeared to be well-positioned to implement their full agenda. But Jones had inherited a badly divided council, and the next city elections would not be until May 1913. On his first day in office Jones chose to be cautious. He spoke to the need for better financial practices; said he would rely on the aldermen regarding public improvements; recommended public ownership of the water company; and said he wanted to survey the current state of sewers and streets before making any decisions.

Jones was equally cautious in mentioning commission government. Acknowledging that he had run on a platform promising adoption of commission government, he said that he would appoint a citizens' committee to solicit public ideas about it.[120] That was a subdued approach to such an important issue, but the bitterness of the campaign to adopt commission government in 1911 may have made the reformers wary of rushing ahead with their most important goal.

The new mayor was far less cautious in using his executive powers to dismiss several department heads, including the city marshal and the superintendent of the street cleaning department. These were important patronage positions, and Callaghan's aldermen may have taken a dim view of his haste. When Jones called a special council meeting a few days after his speech, those aldermen were nowhere to be found. Indeed their attendance at meetings became erratic, preventing quorums necessary to conduct any business.

Jones proved surprisingly adept in tempting the absent aldermen back to their duties. Within a month he had hired Louis Rubiola, son of Jake Rubiola, as superintendent of the street cleaning department. Jones was essentially signaling that defectors to the reformers' coalition would have access to patronage jobs. Old guard aldermen understood the importance of that to the future well-being of their factions, and their attendance at council meetings became more regular.[121]

In April 1913 their willingness to cooperate faced its severest test. Jones unexpectedly died just as the spring election session was getting under way. The council needed to elect a successor to serve until the end of May, and the reformers nominated Albert Steves Jr. After unsuccessfully trying to delay a vote, the old guard nominated William Richter. With an evenly divided council facing a choice between the old guard and its upstart challengers, someone had to break ranks. J. Ray Lambert, who had been one of Callaghan's most important supporters, voted for Steves.[122]

Lambert's vote presented the booster-reform coalition with an enormous, but challenging opportunity. Marshall Hicks had routinely worked with the leaders of political factions, making his supporters so comfortable with them that they supported John Campbell for mayor. But Callaghan had undermined that practice with his visceral dislike of Hicks's coalition. He profoundly disagreed with their ideas for improving San Antonio and assembled his own coalition to support his vision for San Antonio. And he had spent the last year of his life trying to suppress his opponents with increasingly harsh displays of raw power. If the ward politicians who supported him in that effort wanted to salvage their careers, they needed to cooperate with at least the booster faction within Hicks's coalition, whose focus on public improvements created opportunities for mutual aid.

There were good reasons for those boosters to seek accommodation as well. After two bitterly fought elections over commission government and the city elections in 1911, they probably understood how difficult it would be to rally a clear majority of voters to their side. With Callaghan's death, the defenders of San Antonio's traditional political culture had lost their most effective leader. But they remained a serious obstacle to reform, as they had demonstrated by defeating bond proposals in both Hicks's and Campbell's mayoralties. And, although the reformers had managed to win five of the eight ward alderman seats in 1911, their victories had been razor thin. Old-fashioned ward leaders who had reason to support the reform movement could be valuable allies in coming elections.

Managing voters who would continue to oppose government activism, however, addressed only one part of the challenge to any potential cooperation between boosters and ward politicians. Conroy's injection of commission government as a major issue in local politics created problems for boosters and ward healers alike. His idea obviously threatened ward politicians, but it also created practical problems for boosters trying to cope with voters who disliked their agenda. If they lost the skills that professional politicians could devote to winning elections, the boosters might also lose their ability to fund their improvement projects. Cooperation would be necessary on both sides to realize their separate but complementary agendas.

Reformers, in other words, had to be managed as skillfully as the voters who despised government activism. The battle over implementing commission government would therefore become the final obstacle to creating a booster political machine.

Clinton Brown inherited that challenge when he won the mayoral nomination of the Citizens' League in April 1913. An attorney who lived in the Fourth Ward, he was the son of a prominent banker and a graduate of the University of Texas. He had also become a practicing politician, having won election as county district attorney in 1910. The acknowledged leader of "the younger element" in the league, Brown sounded very much like Hicks with his emphasis on physical improvements: "The streets must be permanently paved for the better accommodation of commerce and the comfort of citizens; sanitary sewers and adequate storm drainage are absolutely necessary if the city is to retain its reputation for health." He did, though, embrace the league's broader platform pledging adoption of commission government, civil service, and cooperation with all "organizations instituted for the public good" (a vague reference to the numerous reform groups interested in specific reforms such as the suppression of vice and the City Beautiful Movement).[123]

A reporter wandering about at the league's convention noticed that "sprinkled about the hall and displaying equal interest and enthusiasm were men who constituted the brains and energy, and whose purse was open in behalf of former mayor Bryan Callaghan."[124] The league rewarded their enthusiasm by nominating Ray Lambert as an alderman-at-large and Francisco A. Chapa for alderman in the Third Ward. Chapa was a druggist who had built a career as an important Mexican American leader in the ward beginning in the mid-1890s.[125]

Joseph Ryan, city attorney during Callaghan's mayoralty, carried the tattered battle flag of what remained of his coalition in the ensuing election. Brown trounced him, winning 62 percent of the total vote, and the league's entire ticket won. Notably Brown defeated Ryan in Callaghan's perennial West Side stronghold composed of the First, Second, and Third Wards by almost a thousand votes—an indication of what the ward politicians could do for their budding partnership with the boosters.[126]

Brown chose to interpret the league's impressive victory as an endorsement of his focus on public improvements, particularly streets and sewers. He toured Fort Worth, Dallas, and Kansas City to study the effects of recent state legislative laws that allowed cities to assign two-thirds of the cost of street paving to the property owners with the local government paying the remaining third. This approach retained a strong element of voluntarism in that the residents had to petition for improvements and had to have a role in the decision making regarding types of pavement. Brown prepared a careful and elaborate proposal for the most ambitious program of street improvements in San Antonio's history and asked the voters to approve its $3.25 million price tag in a bond election in July. Such a large amount was unprecedented, and voters had almost routinely defeated much smaller proposals. In this case, however, voters endorsed Brown's plan by a margin of ten to one—in itself an unprecedented outcome.[127]

By focusing on streets Brown met the expectations of boosters, but not of reformers. He apparently had hoped that his devotion to physical improvements would divert attention from his campaign pledge to support commission government. If so, he had hoped in vain. His coalition's reformers gave him the time he needed to win approval for his priority, but within days of the bond election an unnamed citizen sent the council a petition to begin the process of adopting a new charter to establish a commission government.[128]

Brown and other boosters acted as if someone had dropped something very noisome on their victorious bond election. For the next seven months they engaged in a confusing series of delaying tactics to thwart their own campaign pledge. First they seized control of the charter reform process. The petition had requested the appointment of a citizens' committee to write a new charter. Alderman Steves introduced a council resolution authorizing Brown to appoint the committee, which he did by packing it with boosters. The committee went dormant for two months, only emerging in September to announce that it lacked authority to do anything, citing a new state law that gave city councils the right to amend a charter. Brown promptly asked the council to become a committee of the whole to write charter amendments, which caused another three months of inactivity that ended when Brown counter-marched in response to another reform petition and set a date to elect a public committee to write amendments in mid-January.[129]

In early January, however, the aldermen reclaimed their right to control the reform process and began writing an extensive set of amendments aimed at creating a commission government in form, but not in substance. The new government would have five departments: public affairs in general (assigned to the mayor); taxation; sanitation, parks, and public property; streets and public improvements; and fire and police. Despite a long local history of disliking boss politicians, the council created a strong mayor who could veto legislation, set the council's agenda, appoint all committees, and control the budget.

Tucked among the roughly seventy amendments was an important provision to regulate new subdivisions. Henceforth the city would only annex subdivisions after the property owners had laid out, curbed, and macadamized all their subdivision's streets. Although that stipulation ignored water and sewers services, it represented an important step in extending city control over subdivision development.[130]

Disappointed with Brown's maneuvers, the reformers established their own committee that solicited ideas from the public, wrote a series of amendments that they presented to the council, and watched as it rejected every proposal.[131]

With outrage growing over Brown's control of charter reform, he sought to allay suspicions about his motives. First he asked Thomas T. VanderHoeven, chairman of the Citizens' League, to comment on the council's amendments to the charter. He did so in a long rambling article that appeared on the front page of the *Light* a week before the election on the amendments. VanderHoeven rebuked the reformers, saying that "it was generally expected in this community that political agitation would cease" with the league's sweeping victory in May. But to his horror, agitation had indeed erupted. He considered that highly inappropriate because "the interest of the people . . . should not be jeopardized by having a change of government and the elections of new officers now." VanderHoeven did not explain the rather odd statement, moving on instead to issue a bizarre condemnation of the reformers, accusing them of plotting to replace the league's new administration with "designing politicians, grafters, and contractors" who would jeopardize the "best interests" of all San Antonians.[132]

VanderHoeven did not explain why the reformers wanted a return to alleged past corrupt practices, but his comments probably did not soothe the turbulent debate over competing versions of commission government. Brown therefore made his own attempt to defend the council's amendments. He began by accusing the reformers of seeking to replace the league's elected officials with "God knows who." Then he turned to one of the most contentious features of the council's amendments, the failure to include civil service requirements for city employees. He defended that omission by assuring his audience that the voters will elect good men as commissioners, and they "should be free to pick the men on whom they must rely." That was an odd statement coming from someone who had spent almost seven months manipulating the amendment process to avoid one of the reformers' fundamental goals.[133]

In the end, Brown had the votes to pass his version of commission government. On February 24, 1914, every amendment passed by a suspiciously similar vote. Indeed in eight of forty-nine precincts the vote was exactly the same; in thirteen others the vote varied only by a difference of two to four ballots. Overall the vote was ten to one in favor.[134]

With that election the boosters concluded a nearly twenty-year struggle to create their own political machine—although they would have strongly rejected that characterization. Their regime would last, technically at least, for thirty-eight years before another reform movement would dismantle commission government. Cooperation between professional politicians and boosters was a new approach to city-building in San Antonio, and the coalition would suffer from various strains over the years. The key question, though, would be whether the boosters could effectively utilize their political power to assist their ultimate goal of making San Antonio the state's dominant city.

SIX

Bronze, Not Gold

1900–1930

With the emergence of their political machine by 1914, the boosters had acquired a valuable tool for implementing an important part of their agenda. Boosterism, however, was more about economics and civic pride than politics. Controlling, or at least influencing, public policies gave them the ability to improve San Antonio's physical attractiveness, but an expanding economy that offered a variety of opportunities for employment and investment to people moving into Texas was essential to promoting growth. And growth was the key to achieving the boosters' goal of becoming the largest and most important city in Texas.

In 1899 Businessmen's Club members could not lead San Antonio toward that goal. They were a small group of activists floating in a sea of passivists opposed to organized boosterism. While Hicks and his successors led the Progressive reform coalition fight to overcome the political version of that opposition, the club's members needed to wage a simultaneous campaign to overcome the economic version that was so popular among local businessmen.

Transforming the club into an organization that would dominate economic development policies required its members to attend to some basic, even mundane, activities. They had to increase its membership to the point where the club's size would make its support for organized development credible. But increasing numbers was not sufficient if the club wanted to become truly influential. Its members also had to be willing to finance its initiatives and contribute their time to reaching its objectives.

A willingness to commit time and money to the club would draw the members into a shared experience of learning how to promote development. After fifty years of deliberately refusing to participate in organized boosterism, the business community lacked the ability to compete effectively with its rivals in Dallas and Houston, who had been learning how to foster development for several decades. Businessmen in both cities were much better prepared to sponsor local initiatives and to take advantage of opportunities that emerged from regional or national economic trends than San Antonians were.

Fortunately for the club, its struggle to develop into an effective organization coincided with the Progressives' control of local government from 1899 to 1905. For six years the club's members had valuable allies to help them learn the skills they needed to overcome their parlous situation. The Progressives had had to organize and lead their own citywide organization and to develop and implement a broad program that would encourage continuing commitments to improving the city. And they had had to convince voters to support specific proposals that supported that program.

Marshall Hicks in particular made sure that club members had opportunities to develop organizational skills through their participation in his campaigns that was not limited to attending party conventions and voting for his ticket. In April 1900 when the club was still hovering on the brink of dissolution, Hicks in essence conducted a case study in organizational skills when he presented his plans for a bond issue at a club meeting. Having educated them in the details, he asked the members to join the election campaign as canvassers who would spread out across the city to walk the precincts, meeting voters personally to present Hicks's case for the bonds. His presentation and invitation inspired 140 club members to work for the bond issue.[1]

Gaining practice at canvassing was invaluable to the club, which needed to launch its own efforts to build membership and solicit contributions for its projects. Since elections occurred every two years, club members had the opportunity to hone their skills on a regular basis before Callaghan's return to power in 1905. The results were encouraging. By 1902 membership had climbed back to what it had been in 1895, and by 1904 had increased to 671. That was not impressive given the size of the business community, but the fact that memberships were steadily increasing indicated that the club had learned how to recruit effectively. Membership continued to grow; by 1907 the club surpassed 1,000 members, increasing to 1,539 by 1909.[2]

Since there was an annual membership fee of $25, the club's canvassers obviously needed something attractive to offer potential members to convince them to join. A sales pitch based on the club's mission to attract wealthy investors who would develop the economy was too abstract to be an effective appeal, especially when so many San Antonians believed their city was so attractive that investors would flock to it without any inducements.

Needing something more concrete to demonstrate the club's value, President William H. Aubrey announced that it would sponsor a week-long carnival in April 1900. Aubrey and his board of directors had been trying to convince the Battle of Flowers Association to expand its celebration of San Jacinto Day into multiple days advertising San Antonio as a modern business-friendly city. The association, which represented the interests of the city's elite women, had rebuffed their idea. In 1900, however, the association failed to find a replacement for its president, who resigned in response to the club's forceful efforts to intrude on what she considered a purely patriotic civic event.[3]

Aubrey and his directors eagerly seized their opportunity to replace San Jacinto Day with a carnival. They scheduled it to coincide with the arrival of several conventions; hired a carnival company to run the event; organized a visitor's bureau to help tourists locate hotel and boardinghouse rooms; and arranged to close Commerce Street from Alamo to Main Plaza. Family-friendly events clustered in Alamo Plaza; male-friendly shows located in Main Plaza. The club even borrowed a key idea from New Orleans's Mardi Gras, adding a touch of royalty to the carnival with a king (and queen, which was not the New Orleans tradition).[4]

Carnivals were popular in cities at the time, and they were also opportunities to advertise a city's prosperity, attractions, and social sophistication. The club located the carnival's attractions on Alamo and Main Plazas because they had been transformed in the previous twenty years into San Antonio's most modern commercial spaces. Commerce Street provided a convenient link between them, especially when the club installed arches illuminated by electric lights (another symbol of modernity) along the street. The introduction of "royalty created an opportunity for visitors to socialize with the local elite in gatherings at the Opera House and Menger Hotel. Such social events gave wealthy San Antonians a natural setting to discuss the advantages of the city to potential investors."

Since the average conventioneer probably did not qualify for an invitation to an elite party during carnival, the city needed to offer appropriate entertainment for all its visitors. Scheduling friskier carnival shows at Main Plaza encouraged male tourists to amble across San Pedro Creek to peruse the saloons, gambling houses, and brothels of the vice district. As the *Light* not so primly observed, "People who attend conventions are out for a good time, and a very good time at that. They desire freedom from restraints of all kinds."[5] San Antonio needed to assure its tourists that all of the modern conveniences of metropolitan life were available, giving "West of the Creek" a secure role in advertising the city.

Although flagging attendance indicated that a week-long carnival was too ambitious, the idea proved popular enough to encourage the club to make it an annual event. Pairing conventions with a spring festival helped the club entice more conventions to town while simultaneously increasing the club's credibility within the business community. By making it an annual event, the club slowly built public support for a spring carnival as a standard tool in its campaign to increase tourism.

In 1904, however, the carnival's ability to generate income for its sponsor prompted the local chapter of the Daughters of the Texas Republic to challenge the club's control of over the event. The Daughters were searching for revenue to restore the Alamo, and a steady income from the spring festival would have served their needs well. In late February the city council received two petitions regarding the carnival that indicated that the Daughters had stolen a march on the Businessmen's Club. The Daughters asked the council to grant them exclusive use of Alamo, Main, and Military Plazas for one week to celebrate San Jacinto Day. Furthermore their petition asked the council to prohibit any other "street show or carnival" during that week. Adroitly undermining the club, the Daughters announced that they had already contracted with the railroads to bring "vast crowds of excursionists" to town to fulfill the festival's role in promoting tourism. Adding insult to injury, they also proposed that they should sponsor the San Jacinto Ball, "which has become a social function of statewide importance."

A second petition from a group of club members announced they had no intention of competing with the Daughters' plans, but they asked permission to plan a carnival during the same week. Implicitly acknowledging that the Daughters had outmaneuvered them, these petitioners asked to the right to locate their carnival at Military Plaza, Paschal Square, and Milam Park. In effect, the Daughters had thrown the club off its traditional carnival territory on the east side and relegated it to the west side of town. They had also changed the carnival's purpose from promoting San Antonio's image as a modern city to, once again, patriotism and a celebration of the past.

The competing petitions represented conflicting views about the purposes of civic celebrations, which in turn reflected differences among local Progressives about how to promote tourism. Confronted with a political conundrum, the aldermen sought refuge in compromise. They approved both petitions; then they appointed a council committee to iron out differences between the two groups.[6]

Surrendering control of spring carnival was not an option for the Businessmen's Club. It was the club's most effective advertisement of its effectiveness and its crucial tool for recruiting new members as well as conventions at this point in the club's development. Devoting prime public space that defined a modern city to celebrating patriotism and history was simply unacceptable. It was too late for an effective response in time for the 1904 spring carnival, but the club moved quickly to regain control. In January 1905 there was only one petition to the council for use of public space during carnival. And it was comprehensive in scope, asking for Alamo, Main, and Military Plazas as well as Milam Park, Washington Square, and Paschal Square. The council granted the petition without debate, and later that month the carnival's organizing committee announced plans to establish a permanent Spring Carnival Association with sponsors of the Battle of Flowers Parade and the Daughters of the Republic of Texas as members. The association, however, met in the Businessmen's Club headquarters and its members dominated the board of the new organization.[7]

Aside from establishing a more systematic approach to developing the spring carnival into an increasingly elaborate event, the association permitted the club to reclaim the carnival as a recruiting tool for conventions. Controlling the carnival meant that the club had a useful competitive advantage over rival cities within Texas in negotiating with the small- to medium-sized conventions that San Antonio could initially attract.

The convention business was itself in its infancy when the club turned to it as a development tool. A mere 170 conventions convened in the United States in 1899. Massive industrialization and urbanization in the late nineteenth century was spawning huge numbers of trade and professional organizations as well as fraternal and patriotic associations that would quickly develop an interest in convening to share ideas and information.

In 1900 the club had done well in attracting eight conventions to town for carnival: the Daughters of the Republic of Texas, the Confederate Veterans, the Grand Army of the Republic, the Knights Templar, the Nobles of the

Mystic Shrine, the Women's Relief Group, the State Undertakers and Embalmers Association, and the National Association of Sanitary Engineers.[8] In some respects, though, this list was less impressive that it appeared. The Grand Army of the Republic and the Knights Templar were huge national organizations with hierarchies of local, state, and national branches. San Antonio could not have hosted the entire national membership of either organization because it lacked the meeting facilities, hotel accommodations, and money to secure a contract with them. Instead the city hosted the Texas branches of each organization.

Considering the limitations of the infrastructure to support conventions, the club had done well to schedule those eight organizations during the first carnival. Four hotels graced the downtown. The Menger and the Maverick on Houston Street could accommodate about four hundred guests between them, but the Southern and the Central on Main Plaza had fewer rooms.[9] An unknown number of boardinghouses added to the city's guest rooms. Meeting space improved dramatically in 1900 with the completion of a new market house on West Commerce Street that had an auditorium on its second-floor seating up to four thousand. The city council was usually willing to make it available to assist the club with its recruiting efforts, but the lack of hotel rooms and the costs of large conventions severely constrained the club's ability to use the auditorium.

The club did venture into the economics of large conventions in 1907, when the site selection committee for the Confederate Veterans national conference met with club officials. The Confederate Veterans committee suggested that $10,000 might suffice to cover the entertainment costs of hosting the convention. Based on three years of attendance records, the committee members predicted between 25,000 and 40,000 people might visit San Antonio. After some debate, the club's board decided to bid for the 1909 convention and sent a delegation to Richmond, where the Confederate Veterans were currently meeting, to investigate how much that city had paid to secure the convention. The delegation reported that the site selection committee had committed to San Antonio for 1909 on the assumption that the club would raise $75,000 to cover entertainment costs. Since the club relied on public subscriptions to pay such costs, and it had never raised more than a couple of thousand dollars for that purpose, the topic of large conventions disappeared for club discussions.[10] Average attendance at conventions San Antonio did host varied from a few hundred to about two thousand.[11]

Despite that setback, the club's focus on tourism encouraged a flurry of hotel construction. Between 1908 and 1911 the city added eight hotels to its inventory.[12] Two hotels in particular, the Saint Anthony and the Gunter, symbolized the business community's growing commitment to the tourist industry. L. J. Hart, a longtime club member, created the San Antonio Hotel Company in 1908 to build the Gunter. He financed the project through a combination of public subscriptions and a $100,000 bank loan. Augustus Jones, a major financial backer of political reform and briefly mayor after Callaghan's death, was a wealthy cattleman who organized a syndicate to build the Saint Anthony. Both hotels opened in 1909 and quickly became major tourist attractions because of their opulent amenities.[13]

Luxury hotels were not built exclusively for conventioneers; their opulence was also intended to appeal to another kind of tourist, the "snow bird." These were the most prized tourists because they were the potential investors in San Antonio's economy. As such, they needed to be cultivated, and comfortable living quarters were a fundamental part of an increasingly organized campaign to attract wealthy people to stay for extended periods during the winter months.

Booster interest in a systematic campaign to attract wealthy investors was hardly new, dating back at least to the founding of the San Antonio Club in 1881. At the time, however, local businessmen made no attempt to supplement the advertising that the railroads distributed on behalf of the city. In the late 1880s promotional adverting was becoming increasingly common as western cities competed for new residents. Los Angeles and Denver were among the most successful at using this strategy prior to World War I. An awareness of those success stories convinced founders of the Businessmen's Club that they should use advertising as a major tool in their efforts to develop the city.

Creating a sustainable advertising campaign, however, posed two practical challenges for the club. It did not have the financial resources to cover the annual costs, which meant that its members had to solicit funds each year from the business community, which was typically not in a giving mood. In addition, soliciting was time-consuming; members had to be willing to commit time to the task, and that was also problematic.

Fortunately the railroads, persisting in their own advertising, had already established the basic idea of a winter season for tourism from October to March. This had evolved naturally from the fact that the heat of San Antonio's summers tended to undermine assertions that the city had a mild, attractive climate. The Businessmen's Club did need to modify the content of the railroads' advertising because they had sought to portray San Antonio as a historically and culturally interesting haven for consumptives. In addition to shifting the focus to healthy tourists after the revelations about the contagious nature of tuberculosis, the club needed to convince wealthy tourists that the city offered unlimited potential for investments, which meant shifting the emphasis in ads from a city with a fascinating past to one with a great future.

Achieving that shift took nearly a decade because of the practical problems the club encountered. It had had an advertising committee since its inception, but it appears not to have been very active until 1902, when the committee sought $1,490 in contributions to cover the costs of advertising materials "for the opening of the fall and winter season." There is no evidence they raised that amount, and the next year the committee depended on the railroads to distribute copies of a folder it designed. The committee supplemented that minimal effort with a written request to hotels and boardinghouses to ask their visitors to visit the club's headquarters to view exhibits about investment possibilities in San Antonio's hinterland as well as other business opportunities.[14]

In 1906 Judge William Kelso, chair of the advertising committee, tried to establish a better organized and funded campaign. He raised $5,000 toward its costs and negotiated a deal with the railroads that they would contribute $5 for every $1 raised by the club. Kelso, however, complained that in the past his committee's members had been too busy "with personal matters" to solicit contributions, and he wanted them to promise to commit their time to this effort. It is not clear that Kelso's arrangement depended on the club collecting more than $5,000 from the business community, but no more was heard of additional fundraising. The following year President Nat Washer complained that the club's income barely covered current expenses and noted that contributions "always fall short of urgent needs," which implied that efforts to raise money for advertising had not gone well yet again.[15]

This dismal state of affairs began to change due to other initiatives led by Washer in 1907. First the club announced a campaign to increase membership to a thousand. That took some time to achieve, but an infusion of members gradually increased the club's basic revenue stream and expanded its pool of volunteers to help with soliciting contributions for advertising. Second, planning for new hotels had reached the point that rumors about them were spreading beyond San Antonio. The advertising committee began receiving inquiries from travel agents about the prospect for a $1 million hotel that was changing their advice to clients. Prior to this news, the agents explained, they had been advising them against visiting San Antonio because it lacked proper accommodations for winter tourists. Now they were willing to recommend the city to their clients.[16]

Whether for that reason or due to other unexplained causes, tourism apparently expanded significantly in 1908. That well-timed increase combined with the surge in hotel construction to encourage a major change in the club's approach to advertising. In March 1909 Thomas Conroy, a longtime club member and a major civic leader, announced the creation of the Publicity League. Making no little plans or claims, Conroy said a well-funded advertising campaign would make San Antonio "a second Los Angeles." He set a goal of raising $25,000 and, for the first time, intended to conduct a truly national campaign by placing ads in three hundred newspapers and journals around the country. Defying previous disappointments, his canvassers reached their goal by July.[17]

Conroy also radically redesigned the city's approach to advertising. He arranged to publish booklets that divided tourism into four categories. There would be a separate sales pitch to short-term visitors (the average tourist interested in San Antonio's picturesque past and culture); the home seeker (people interested in moving permanently to the city or to its hinterland); the investor (the club's primary target); and the manufacturer (who would hopefully build factories). Conroy's approach provided tourists more complete information tailored to the interests of each category and shifted the traditional content of ads toward a greater focus on the attractions of the modern city.[18]

By 1911 the Publicity League's work led to a general belief that "San Antonio as a winter resort has passed the experimental stage."[19] In conjunction with Spring Carnival and conventions, tourism had emerged as the

Businessmen's Club most successful strategy for economic development. That in turn apparently provided the impetus for the club's most ambitious project since its inception. With tourism increasingly popular around the country, the industry had begun to develop specialists who offered their services to a national market. G. H. Genslinger was one such individual. He built athletic clubs that were more than elaborate gyms; they were temples to boosterism, and tourism in particular.

E. A. Peden, a member of the Businessmen's Club who lived in Houston, became familiar with Genslinger's work when he built an athletic club in Houston. He apparently convinced the club that Genslinger could do for San Antonio what he had done for Houston: build a headquarters for the city's booster community and a haven for a select group of winter tourists.[20]

When it was completed in November 1911, the seven-story Travis Club was one of the tallest buildings in the downtown. Located at Navarro and Martin Streets, it boasted all the amenities of an elite athletic club with first-class accommodations for wealthy tourists. They could socialize with boosters in the restaurant, in the gym, by the basement swimming pool, or in the rooftop garden where formal parties and dances occurred. Such pleasant surroundings would naturally encourage discussions about investment possibilities in San Antonio.

The number of dignitaries who attended the celebration of the club's opening indicated its importance to the Businessmen's Club. Governor Oscar Colquitt, Congressman James Slayden, Mayor Bryan Callaghan, and club president Nat Washer spoke to an audience of 150 businessmen about the significance of the new building. The Travis Club's Advisory Board included several Businessmen's Club loyalists, including Thomas Conroy and Augustus Jones, and it began operations with five hundred local members.[21]

In effect, the Travis Club symbolized the business community's belief that tourism was not simply their single most important tool for economic development; it also defined their destiny as a city. In spring 1911 Judge Webb, the booster reformers' mayoral candidate, had declared that "San Antonians have been trying to make of their city what nature meant it should become, the greatest resort for tourists on the continent."[22]

There were, however, problems with that vision. Promoting spring carnival and winter tourism had indeed proven popular enough to improve the

Businessmen's Club's membership and reputation. By 1911 it had become the city's largest organization dedicated to economic development. But its focus on tourism left the club unprepared to deal with important development opportunities that emerged simultaneously with tourism because of dramatic changes in South Texas.

San Antonio had long claimed South Texas as part of its hinterland, a claim reinforced by its crucial role in financing and supplying the cattle trade after the Civil War. Local businessmen had long-standing relationships with ranchers that assured the city's control over a vast, if undeveloped, territory until the early twentieth century. At that point, however, the cattle business began to encounter a variety of problems that fundamentally altered the trade. Many cattle barons decided to sell their land and move to cities where their wealth gave them opportunities to invest in local development. Augustus Jones, a partner in constructing the Saint Anthony Hotel who had served briefly as mayor after Callaghan's death, was one of several such men who moved to San Antonio.[23]

They sold their land to speculators who promptly began to recruit settlers who would transform undeveloped land into Texas's Winter Garden between 1900 and 1930. Eventually thousands of Midwesterners and Northerners would migrate to South Texas where they had to develop a marketing and labor system for their crops, and arrange credit to build homes, towns, irrigation, and roads.

Theoretically San Antonio's long involvement with South Texas should have given it an advantage in helping those settlers achieve their goals. But in fact the opposite was true. The cattle barons were gone, as were all the relationships that San Antonians had had with them. None of the new settlers knew anyone in San Antonio (or anywhere else for that matter); they had no loyalties to, or loans or contracts with, anyone. All such personal and business relationships had to be created anew. A large piece of San Antonio's historic hinterland was now available to whomever was willing to make the initial contacts to provide these settlers with whatever they needed.

King Ranch owner Robert Kleberg, who led one of the speculator groups working in South Texas, asked the Southern Pacific Railroad to build rail lines from San Antonio to Brownsville in 1900. Southern Pacific executives briefly explored Kleberg's request, even petitioning the city council for permission to use some additional city streets as a route. The petition was apparently withdrawn before the council could reply when those executives decided not to accept Kleberg's invitation.[24]

That decision by a national corporation with no particular loyalty to San Antonio cost the city its best opportunity to be the first to offer vital services before any of its rivals could do so. Kleberg and his investment partners financed their own railroad company to charter the Saint Louis, Brownsville, and Mexico Railroad in 1903. By 1904 the railroad had reached Corpus Christi; in December 1907 it reached Houston. That same year five hundred carloads of farm produce from the Valley reached Houston, stimulating a massive land rush. As the only railroad serving the area, it became the principal migration route into South Texas and the sole avenue for Valley products to reach market. That enabled Houston businessmen to establish lucrative connections to the new arrivals before anyone in San Antonio had an inkling of the threat that advantage posed to their own interests.

Concern about San Antonio's interests in South Texas emerged only as Kleberg's railroad finished laying track to Houston. In May 1907 the Jobbers and Manufacturers League alerted the Businessmen's Club of the "recent expansion of the Houston and Dallas businessmen into their territory." The club's initial response revealed their lack of experience in dealing with threats to the city's hinterland. Some club members met in July with Uriah Lott, who had constructed Kleberg's railroad, but nothing came of the discussions. A year later the club prepared a pamphlet for a contingent of businessmen traveling to Brownsville that "will be productive of much good in establishing closer personal and business relations between San Antonio and her sister cities."[25] Without concrete proposals to build a railroad to connect Brownsville to San Antonio, however, a visit accompanied by a pamphlet was not an adequate response to the challenges facing the club.

Nor was the club's first venture into promoting an actual railroad. In September 1908 the club decided to sign a contract with a Mr. Hogue of Dallas to construct a line to Pleasanton, Texas. Hogue had won the club's support by offering the cheapest bid for the contract, but within days of the agreement federal agents arrested Hogue for violations of lottery laws and fraud (the money for another railroad he had agreed to build in northern Texas had apparently disappeared). Again revealing its inexperience, the club admitted it had not vetted Hogue's financial situation to determine whether he could fulfill his obligations.[26]

In the absence of a united effort to deal with Houston's invasion of San Antonio's hinterland, a small group of individuals who had been attracted to the city because of investment possibilities in South Texas organized their own response. Thomas Coleman, Joseph Edwards, James and Charles Fowler, and Charles Hammond, among others, bought large tracts of land in counties south and west of San Antonio. They founded towns and recruited settlers to develop their land, and they shared the problem that they had no rail link to the coast. They solved that problem by chartering the San Antonio, Uvalde, and Gulf Railroad in 1909.[27] Five years later this line reached Corpus Christi, greatly increasing the value of farmland in the western region of the Winter Garden. That achievement was critical to preserving a portion of South Texas as part of San Antonio's sphere of influence, but Houston and Dallas dominated the eastern area.

Ironically the development of the Winter Garden did increase San Antonio's population. Harvesting the crops was a labor-intensive task that required cheap labor, and San Antonio had supplied the service to farmers since at least 1867. Mushrooming demand for labor made the city the second-largest migrant labor center, behind only El Paso. Hundreds and eventually thousands of Mexican immigrants clustered in San Antonio's Second Ward and traveled to the Winter Garden area during harvest times. Desperately poor, they packed into slum housing in the "corral district" that lacked basic city services. By the 1920s the district had become one of the unhealthiest slums in the nation.[28]

Impoverished Mexicans were not the only new arrivals by 1910. Dramatic population growth between 1900 and 1910 seemed to validate the Businessmen's Club's emphasis on advertising San Antonio as a modern city, but a nascent preservationist movement was beginning to challenge that focus. Businessmen were working hard to expand retail services and office space in the downtown by replacing old buildings with new ones. Travel writers still extolled the charm of the downtown's narrow, crooked streets, but work crews were busy widening and straightening them. Modernization finally came to Commerce Street in 1913 with a massive project that eliminated its seven different widths to create a straight, wide twentieth-century vista. And in 1911 a group of businessmen sponsored an engineering study to eliminate the Great Bend in the river, the greatest obstacle to a rationally planned, traffic-friendly, and larger downtown.[29]

All these changes, and the threat to the longest river bend, prompted a debate over the virtues of modernization. Newspaper editors succinctly captured the essence of an important emerging divide. The booster-friendly *Light* argued that "the old and obsolete must give way for the march of progress," while the *Express* countered with an appeal for preservation: "No longer let us be careless of the goose that lays our golden egg. The tourist comes because he has heard of San Antonio's fame as a picturesque, historically interesting city."[30]

Preservationists were at this point outnumbered. Adina De Zavala was engaged in a long, complicated struggle to preserve the Alamo and various groups inspired by the City Beautiful Movement were working to increase the number and attractiveness of public parks and streets, but they had not had much political power prior to 1911. The threat to the river bend created an opportunity to organize in defense of a very popular landmark. The river held a special place in the hearts of many San Antonians, who tended to ignore its stench from inadequate water flow in favor of idealizing it as a physical feature that made the city a special place. Because of that sentiment, politicians were wary of tampering with the river, and they quickly quashed the idea of eliminating the Great Bend. The fledgling preservationist movement organized the San Antonio River Improvement Association, which would become a critical asset in their battle to reestablish picturesque San Antonio as a major tourist draw.[31]

Unsuccessful efforts to recover San Antonio's influence in the Winter Garden and coping with the challenge of the preservationists would continue for several years, but in the meantime the Businessmen's Club unexpectedly fractured. In March 1910 the Bexar County Medical Association issued a critical report on the "inexcusable sanitary conditions" in the city that had caused the loss of San Antonio's "wealthiest visitors on account of the filthy condition" of its streets "in the very heart of the city and the strangers say they will not again visit San Antonio unless there are assurances the nuisance will be eliminated." The doctors warned, "Unless we do something now we will awake one fine day to find our elegant hotels empty and the guests gone to California . . . where cleanliness is the drawing card."[32]

Although the doctors disclaimed any political intent in their report, it clearly indicted Callaghan's approach to public improvements. Not indirectly, they were accusing the mayor of a policy that undermined tourism, the heart and soul of the Businessmen's Club's campaign to grow San Antonio. It was therefore perhaps not quite a mere coincidence that Thomas Conroy chose to organize the meeting that created the Commission Government League one week after the doctors' public warning.[33]

Initially Conroy's timing, and no doubt prior planning, worked well to launch the league. Callaghan failed to mount effective opposition to Conroy's plan for a city charter based on commission government, which the legislature approved late in the summer. By fall 1910 Callaghan had recovered enough to organize opposition to the league by naming a citizen's committee that would issue a report attacking Conroy's plan.

That committee revealed a deep split within the Businessmen's Club. Six of the twelve members of that committee were important members of the club: A .W. Houston, J. H. Kirkpatrick, H. E. Hildebrand, F. W. Cook, L. J. Hart, and August Briam.[34] None of these men ever explained their support for Callaghan, but club members had a history of working with professional politicians and the club itself had never taken an official position for or against any political ticket in the city's nonpartisan elections.

It may well have been their familiarity with, and ability to work within, the existing political system that encouraged boosters like Kirkpatrick and Hart to support Callaghan. Within the club's booster-reform coalition, boosters tended to be focused on economic development, and Callaghan, after all, did have his own version of boosterism. Reformers, who also supported boosterism, had more expansive interests in broad civic issues. Conroy, for instance, had solid booster credentials as the founder and leader of the Publicity League, but he was also active in several civic improvement organizations besides the commission government campaign.

Whether the doctors had been correct in their assessment of the connection between sanitary conditions as the flight of wealthy tourists quickly became a moot point. The Publicity League, which had assumed control over the club's most critical activity, suddenly found itself bankrupt. As the *Light* noted, "political divisions caused a lack of harmony among the business interests" in 1910, resulting in a collapse of fundraising for the league's annual advertising campaign. The intensity of the battle between the Citizens' Ticket aldermen and Callaghan after the spring 1911 elections reinforced the disharmony, causing cancellation of the league's 1912 campaign as well.[35]

Disunity apparently prompted the Businessmen's Club, which the press now referred to as the Chamber of Commerce, to make a desperate attempt at unity. It invited several independent organizations like the Jobbers and Manufacturers Association to become members. The chamber became an umbrella organization in which the presidents of each of the other groups formed the chamber's board of directors while superficially increasing membership in the club/chamber to three thousand.[36]

Mayor Clinton Brown's election and subsequent campaign to integrate professional politicians into his booster coalition within the framework of commission government ended the chamber's feeble attempt at unity. By 1915 its membership had collapsed to 250, an extraordinary low reminiscent of the harrowing days of the late 1890s, when the club had nearly voted to disband.[37]

That collapse had important consequences for local boosters trying to conduct a campaign to defeat San Antonio's rivals to become the state's largest city. Politicians had a critical role in that campaign, but economic growth was the responsibility of the business community, which had just eviscerated its capacity for organized development.

Fortunately Brown's victory in the 1913 mayoral race masked the chamber's ongoing collapse by providing an example of booster effectiveness. State policy on funding street improvement had recently changed, allowing cities to charge residents two-thirds of the cost of improvements. In exchange, residents gained considerable control over decisions about when to pave their streets and with what materials. Brown won voter approval for a $3,500,000 bond issue for street improvements in July 1913 and planned a citywide initiative to deal with six hundred miles of unpaved streets in the city. Fourth Ward alderman John W. Warren proposed, and the council adopted, an elaborate formula for distributing money to the wards based on miles of streets, population, and taxable property values. Oddly enough, the formula allocated his ward the largest improvement budget. On the other hand, the formula discriminated against East Side working-class Sixth and Seventh Wards and the impoverished Second Ward on the West Side.[38]

Over the next three years the boosters significantly increased the number of miles of paved streets, but they failed to create a thoroughly modern, integrated street system. A majority of residents on a city block had to submit a petition for paving; the council had to hold public hearings to authorize a contract, but the residents held the authority to decide on the type of paving. They had a choice of four pavements, including dirt for residents who did not sign the petition. Contractors would not pave the street in front of their homes, and such "skips" became quite common. The type and durability of paving could vary from street to street and neighborhood to neighborhood, an arrangement that foreshadowed major maintenance costs over time.[39]

Brown easily won reelection in 1915, but the voters dealt his improvement program an unexpected blow when they defeated a bond proposal in 1916 that would have expanded it. That interrupted the booster campaign to increase San Antonio's attractiveness, and it apparently discouraged Brown so much that he announced he would not campaign for reelection in 1917.[40]

With no obvious candidate to succeed Brown, the booster-politician coalition found itself in an awkward situation. Boosters had in effect been the senior partners in the coalition, and a resurgence of public interest in civil service reform, which had been an issue contributing to the defeat of the bond proposal, meant that nominating a ward politician to lead the booster coalition would be impolitic.[41]

The coalition solved this problem by turning to Sam Bell, a highly respected businessman and member of San Antonio's socioeconomic elite with close ties to the Steves and Terrell families.[42] Bell had no political experience, but he did have a useful brother-in-law, John W. Tobin, one of the most astute and influential politicians in the booster coalition. With the support of the coalition, Bell did not need to offer a detailed program to the voters; he campaigned as someone who "has the best interests of San Antonio at heart" and won easily because he had no opponent.[43]

While the politicians dealt with Brown's departure, the Chamber of Commerce worked on recovery. The board of directors reduced the number of committees to six to adjust for the loss of members. Fiesta remained the most important activity, attracting fifty thousand tourists in 1913 according to railroad passenger records. Conventions fared less well, adding perhaps another eight thousand visitors attending twenty-three meetings. Advertising suffered from the Publicity League's financial problems, which hurt efforts to attract snow birds and factories.[44]

The directors needed an attractive cause that would help them rebuild membership, and events in Europe were about to give them one: the military. Fort Sam Houston had never achieved the economic importance that the army's freighting contracts prior to 1877 had, but it had served the army's needs well since its founding. Between 1890 and 1910 the fort had proved useful to the army's need to consolidate commands in a few major installations around the country, and it had become increasingly important as a training center, which meant a significant number of the nation's small army lived at the fort. Congressmen James Slayden, who became a member of the House Military Affairs Committee in those years, quietly worked to expand the fort's physical size and troop strength. By 1905 three thousand soldiers were serving at the fort, and their monthly payroll added $50,000 a month to San Antonio's economy.[45]

Slayden's devotion to the fort was not matched by the Businessmen's Club, which ignored the army because of its limited economic potential at the time. The chamber initially continued that policy, but the army's importance to San Antonio began to change in 1909, the year Slayden asked the chief of the army's signal corps to introduce him to Lt. Benjamin Foulois.[46]

Foulois was one of the army's first pilots, and Slayden wanted him assigned to Fort Sam Houston where the climate and flat geography offered plenty of flight time and places to land (a significant issue given the dangers of flying at the time). The army's interest in airplanes arose from their potential for gathering reconnaissance, which was the responsibility of its signals division.

The novelty of airplanes guaranteed an audience for Foulois, and it also added to Spring Carnival's attractions in 1910 when a four-day aviation meet coincided with the usual festivities.[47] Slayden, though, regarded aviation as a potentially valuable way to expand Fort Sam Houston's mission, which in turn would justify its continued growth. In 1912 he gained a major ally when Texas senator Morris Sheppard joined the Senate Military Affairs Committee. They coordinated the creation of an aviation center attached to Fort Sam Houston in early 1913.[48]

At this point some members of the Jobbers and Manufacturers Association prodded the chamber into taking its first tentative steps toward forging ties with the military. The Jobbers, whose members had an interest in construction work, told chamber secretary John Carrington that secretary of war Lindley Garrison and army chief of staff Gen. Leonard Wood were in town with a contingent of officers to investigate a major project at the post.

How such distinguished visitors had managed to escape Carrington's attention remains unexplained, but he quickly notified the president, William Tuttle, and the board of this opportunity. The board duly appointed Tuttle to meet with the delegation to discuss their project. Although the secretary later decided against the project, this initial contact marked the beginning of a major shift in the chamber's development.[49]

The turmoil in Europe that would soon erupt into World War I halted the chamber's decline and gave it a new mission that would complement tourism as a major asset for promoting growth. For the next five years the military gave local boosters a lucrative lesson of its potential to spur economic development. The lesson would end abruptly and badly in 1919, but the experience of those years convinced San Antonians that close relations with the military had to be an essential part of their strategy for growth. In that regard, the city was ahead of the times. Neither the Congress nor a majority of Americans supported a large military, and only tolerated the idea for the sake of winning the war once the United States became a combatant.

The problems of being a pioneer in the development of the military-industrial complex lay in the future in 1913. In the meantime the chamber's board of directors immersed themselves in the immediate benefits of working with the military, adjusting its organization and budget to take advantage of federal largesse.

Since this was a new venture, the chamber's officers needed some time to develop relationships with and knowledge about local army officers and the bureaucracy in Washington that supported them. The directors spent most of 1914 working on Fort Sam Houston's expansion plans, especially the new aviation center that became Dodd Field in 1915. That work led to founding the Aero Club of Texas in June 1915, a cooperative venture in which army pilots offered flying lessons to civilians. Next the chamber created an annual banquet for the military, which created opportunities for informal discussions and expressions of mutual admiration. Finally, in May 1916, the chamber made a major change in its structure, organizing the Military Affairs Committee to coordinate its growing engagement with the army.[50]

Establishing productive relations with the fort's officers was easy compared to the challenges of cultivating Congress and army bureaucrats in Washington. San Antonio was in competition with many cities around the country who also sought the benefits of President Woodrow Wilson's preparations for war. Lobbying distant decision-makers was therefore essential, but it was also something local businessmen had to learn. Slayden and Sheppard were critical allies in the learning process; they alerted the chamber about forthcoming legislation as well as about threats from competitors, often inviting them to Washington for discussions.

But organizing an actual lobbying campaign required practice, and a hurricane that struck Galveston in August 1915 gave the directors their first opportunity to apply what they had learned to an actual opportunity. The Nineteenth Infantry regiment was stationed at Travis City, which was close enough to Galveston to suffer considerable damage. Its contingent of 1,000 men and officers would make a useful addition to the fort, and President Luther B. Clegg decided to make a pitch for transferring the regiment to a safer location. Clegg organized an impressive lobbying campaign. He contacted Slayden, who agreed to help because Houston businessmen had the same idea and Slayden was a loyal San Antonian. Clegg also telegraphed the secretary of war and the army chief of staff about the chamber's request and then led a delegation to Washington to meet with key congressmen to inform them that "the businessmen of San Antonio are aroused and anxious to use every possible influence to secure the troops." It worked; the regiment moved to Fort Sam Houston. This victory was not only impressive in its display of lobbying skills; it was also noteworthy for its speed. Clegg organized this campaign and accomplished his goal within one week of the day the hurricane hit Galveston.[51]

Clegg's effectiveness in organizing this lobbying effort was only one of many contributions he would make to the chamber's evolving relationship with the army. He and William B. Tuttle became the two most effective members of the chamber's Military Affairs Committee. Clegg was a North Carolinian by birth who migrated to Texas in 1895. He joined the Businessmen's Club that year and worked in the printing business. By 1906 he was president of the San Antonio Printing Company. Tuttle, an Ohioan by birth, graduated from the University of Virginia with a degree in mechanical engineering. After working in New Jersey, he arrived in San Antonio in 1906 to serve as vice president and general manager of San Antonio Gas, Electric, and Traction. Both men served terms as president of the chamber, but their real passion was the Military Affairs Committee. They served as members for decades and usually alternated as its chair for most of that time. Both were crucial to the success of the committee's evolving relationship with the military, especially in establishing new bases such as Kelly Air Force Base, Brooks Air Field, and Camp Normyle.[52]

And the chamber's role in priming the pump of federal largesse gave San Antonio a major, if brief, economic boost. By the end of 1917 San Antonio had ten military bases, five times as many as any other Texas city. Such a large concentration of bases attracted between 15,000 and 25,000 residents, perhaps 25,000 military family members, and around 20,000 tourists. The military population varied during that year from 45,000 to 80,000. Base construction work employed approximately 10,000 people, a quarter of whom were skilled workers. Demand for unskilled labor doubled the size of the Mexican and Mexican American population.[53]

This spectacular boost to the economy ended abruptly. Congress wasted no time reasserting its traditional minimalist approach to national defense, ordering the army to reduce its force of 2.6 million (as of January 1918) to 130,000 men and officers by January 1, 1920. That order had immediate local effects as the army halted the transfer of 25,000 recruits to Kelly Field and canceled all contract work at the base on November 14, 1918. By February 1919 Kelly's garrison fell to 4,500 on its way to 1,500 by May. Similar reductions at all other installations reduced the flow of federal funds into the local economy to a trickle in 1919.[54]

Such a dramatic reversal of national policy disrupted the city's economy and threatened the chamber's reputation as an effective organization. The directors could have searched for an alternative way to supplement tourism to promote growth, but the experience of the war proved too powerful. Determined to regain at least some of the benefits of federal largesse, the directors did something unprecedented in the chamber's history. They announced a long-term strategy for preserving the city's military bases. Declaring that an adequate air force was necessary to the army's mission, they set a goal of convincing Congress to make the air force an independent branch of the armed forces. However quixotic that idea was in a political environment of rigid frugality regarding the military, it had the virtue of creating a strong focus for lobbying. Other cities with the same problems had reached a similar conclusion and were maneuvering to save their bases. By 1922 the Military Affairs Committee had not only managed to save Kelly Field from closure, it had also lobbied successfully for Kelly to become the

Air Corps Advanced Flying School. San Antonio's congressional delegation also managed to arrange small troop transfers to Fort Sam Houston as well as a much-reduced flow of contract work for the bases.[55]

The boosters did not initially encounter any serious problems with their control of local politics with the war's end, primarily because the spring election cycle was over before the effects of Congress's abrupt approach to demobilization became apparent. Bell won reelection with the enthusiastic support of the business and political communities. Attorney Reagan Houston expressed the political coalition's general satisfaction with Bell and his fellow candidates, describing them as "the safest and most capable force for continuing the city's growth and prosperity.... We are toilers, workers, planners for San Antonio. We are the men who want to build here and we love San Antonio and we want to see her prosper."[56]

Reagan's enthusiasm did have some basis in fact. The commissioners were in fact rather accomplished men. Parks commissioner Ray Lambert, for instance, began his career as a saloon keeper and ward politician in the Callaghan era and had become an adroit politician who clearly understood his department's role in creating an attractive city. He was in the process of transforming Brackenridge Park into a haven for tourists and residents alike. Between 1915 and 1922 he installed roads and walking paths, a public golf course, the Japanese Tea Garden, the Texas Star Garden, and a Mexican village that served as a restaurant and crafts center. Lambert also built the city's largest municipal swimming pool, complete with changing facilities, and Lambert Beach. Recognizing the growing importance of the automobile for tourism he constructed a camp in the park with a hundred tent sites, parking spaces, concession stands, running water, lights, cooking and comfort stations, and showers.[57]

Voters respected Lambert's work as well as that of fire and police commissioner Phil Wright, who had earned widespread support from the business community for improving the city's physical safety. Such support led to the approval of a $3.9 million bond issue in July 1919 that was especially significant because it included provisions for an unprecedented expansion of city government into tourism. Although streets and sewers received the largest amount of funding, Lambert received funding separate from his department budget to acquire and improve parks. The bond money also allowed the city to take over a failed private effort to build an auditorium that could accommodate larger conventions and to fund a new round of river beautification as well as flood control projects.[58]

Postwar economic problems and social issues soured public support for the booster coalition by the end of 1919. The Chamber of Commerce participated in a national Open Shop Association campaign against unions which angered local workers; prohibitionists finally won their long battle to national abstinence, much to the consternation of ethnic voters; women won the right to vote, creating uncertainties about how to deal with a new electorate; and a new anti-Catholic, anti-Semitic, super patriotic Ku Klux Klan gained wide popularity and San Antonio became the headquarters for one of its "provinces."[59]

Some of these issues roiled local politics in the 1921 elections. Bell defended his relatively weak record as mayor by saying he had made "honest mistakes," which did not elicit sympathy among many voters. His campaign managers added to his problems when they decided to make anti-unionism a major issue. Local politicians had never campaigned so overtly against workers, which cooled enthusiasm for the boosters in the East Side working-class wards. Taxation commissioner Andres Coy, one of the city's most effective behind-the-scenes politicians, confounded audiences during the campaign by refusing to speak on any issue at any time. A colleague defended him at one rally by saying that Coy "has never made a political speech," but the voters were not impressed. In a close election, Orlando Black, another political neophyte, who promised frugality in government, narrowly defeated Bell. Voters rewarded Coy's silence with the worst drubbing of anyone on the booster ticket, and the boosters lost control of city government.[60]

Black proved to have the political acumen of a newt. He antagonized Lambert and Wright, the surviving booster commissioners, by cutting their budgets. Next he insulted local bankers and deprived them of lucrative contracts with the city by transferring $2 million in city funds to Houston banks. Then he lectured businessmen on the need for "rigid economy" in government, which resurrected Bryan Callaghan's policies that had neglected public improvements. Black did announce his support for the municipal auditorium, but he otherwise showed no interest in the booster agenda.[61]

On September 9, 1921, the worst flood since 1819 covered the downtown with two to twelve feet of water and swept away dozens of West Side homes.

City officials estimated that 51 people had died, but stories of families and individuals whose bodies were never recovered indicated a higher toll.[62]

While the Red Cross and numerous volunteers tried to help West Side residents deal with the flood's aftermath, Black and the commissioners concentrated on repairing damage downtown. But he used the crisis to further his goal of rigid economy by slashing the commissioners' operating budgets to pay for repairs to twenty-nine streets. He also appointed a citizens' committee to consider how to control flooding, but it received so many demands for an inexpensive solution from residents that it failed to recommend a solution.[63]

Black quickly managed to undermine whatever credibility he had earned with this prompt and effective response to the flood by creating a political crisis over jitneys. The Traction Company's streetcars had been losing customers to jitneys, the forerunners of taxicabs, and Black personally negotiated a deal with the company to charge a reasonable rate for its riders in exchange for which the commissioners would rescind all jitney licenses. Jitney drivers, many of whom were Mexican Americans, organized a recall campaign against Black that lasted for several bitter months. That, and several other controversies that raged into 1923, led to the understated judgment that Black's first term had "not been a success."[64]

Neither Black nor his colleagues bothered to file for reelection, setting the stage for the return of the booster-politician coalition in 1923. There was, however, a major shift in the balance of power within the coalition. John W. Tobin decided to run for mayor, and all of the commissioner candidates were professional politicians. Business and professional members of the coalition ceased serving as mayors or commissioners. Tobin's San Antonio ancestry traced back to the pre–Civil War era, qualifying him as a member of the city's social elite. That, combined with a political career dating from the 1890s, made him acceptable to both sides in the coalition, allowing professional politicians to recover their dominance in local government.

Relations within the coalition remained quite cordial. The Chamber of Commerce elected Tobin to its board of directors and routinely endorsed Tobin and his successors as men who "stand squarely for the proper planning of a beautiful city, looking far into the future."[65]

Indeed the politicians would prove to be loyal boosters who ensured the coalition's dominance until 1930 and routinely financed its program. Tobin began that dominance by winning 70 percent of the vote in 1923; in 1925 his entire ticket ran unopposed; token opposition in 1927 reduced Tobin's victory margin to 83 percent. Charles H. Chambers succeeded Tobin upon his death in 1927 and faced two opponents in 1929 whose combined 400 votes failed to overcome his tally of 13,289.[66]

Financing the boosters' program came from a series of bond elections that produced $13 million for civic improvements. Street improvements continued throughout the downtown and in selected neighborhoods. Tobin devoted nearly $3 million to flood control projects that included the Olmos Dam and work on West Side creeks. He also completed the municipal auditorium and converted the privately owned water company into a public utility funded by its own bonded debt.[67]

The politicians also ventured into uncharted territory to supplement or remedy problems with promoting the city. Preservationists had become much better organized and more politically influential after World War I and could claim to control 5,000 votes. Although that was not enough votes to defeat the booster coalition in general elections, the preservationists had the potential to disrupt bond elections, where voter turnout was traditionally low. From the coalition's perspective, there was no point in jeopardizing the flow of funding for improvements by alienating them.

Preservation was also a growing movement. The City Federation of Women's Clubs, sympathetic to preservation efforts for some time, acquired an invaluable ally in 1924. Emily Edwards and Rena Maverick Green founded the Conservation Society in reaction to Mayor Tobin's plan to widen Market Street, which threatened the 1859 market house. Although they lost that fight, they proved to be strategically and politically astute in the longer battle over the uses of the downtown in promoting tourism, as they demonstrated by naming Ray Lambert as the Society's honorary president in 1924.[68]

Lambert was not the only potential ally in city government. Tobin did insist on razing the old market house, but he was partial to river beautification to promote tourism, describing the river as "one of San Antonio's real assets, and we are to develop plans that will make it a thing of real beauty and something visitors will remember . . . long after they leave the city." Taxation commissioner Frank Bushick, first elected in 1923, also sympathized with some preservationist goals, attacking the "desire for novelty or mistaken devotion to a trite modernism" that prevailed in renaming many of the city's historic streets.[69] In the right circumstances, the preservationists had the potential to lobby a majority of these elected officials to their side.

They demonstrated that potential with two victories in 1928. In February the city completed a study of another proposal from the business community to fill in the Great Bend to create more space to develop the downtown. Alarmed preservationists inundated the commissioners with complaints, and they quickly dismissed the proposal. Then Tobin created a precedent for the city to fund historical treasures by agreeing to include a proposal to use bond funds to buy and restore the Spanish Governor's Palace. Whether he expected the proposal to pass or not, the preservationists used the occasion to demonstrate their growing political clout by campaigning successfully for it.[70] Defeating the business community's efforts to eliminate the Great Bend and gaining public support for restoration of the palace greatly enhanced the preservationists' slowly growing success in changing the boosters' preference for selling San Antonio as a modern city to refocusing on the city's history and culture.

Finally the commissioners rescued the Chamber of Commerce from its own ineptitude. The chamber's ability to fund its advertising campaign, which had always been the boosters' principal tool for promoting growth, declined steadily through the 1920s. Year after year the larger business community remained remarkably indifferent to its own best interests in developing the city. Since the boosters in their coalition were increasingly ineffective, the commissioners stepped in to help. In January 1929 they created a special advertising fund, created a three cent ad valorem tax to support it, and gave the mayor authority to manage this fund. The commissioners justified this tax by saying that they were promoting "the general welfare and . . . the good of the trade and commerce of the City of San Antonio."[71]

The boosters' inability to raise advertising money reflected the continuing indifference within the wider business community toward organized effort to develop San Antonio. In the 1920s superficial success probably reinforced that indifference. San Antonio had retained its title as the state's largest city in 1920. Many businessmen, reflecting on the fact that the city had now claimed and retained that title for the third time, probably assumed that San Antonio now had a permanent right to it. Furthermore, the city certainly looked more prosperous and impressive with new skyscrapers like the Frost National Bank (1922), the Medical Arts Building (1926), the Milam Building (1928), and the Smith-Young Tower (1929) looming over the downtown. Those symbols of urban progress combined with large numbers of new residents working in the construction and home and office furnishing businesses to create a general sense of prosperity. Mimicking a national trend, San Antonians found automobiles so essential that downtown traffic congestion—another symbol of metropolitan status—mushroomed into a major problem by the middle of the decade.[72]

Problems lurked beneath all the apparent prosperity. The boosters, for instance, continued to have difficulties protecting the city's stake in the Winter Garden. In January 1920 a delegation of farmers from the Valley asked the chamber's directors to build a railroad to improve their access to markets. In a pointed conversation, one of the delegates told the directors that "we have all the encouragement in the world from Houston, but very little from here." The directors appointed a committee to investigate this request, and it reported that San Antonio was losing a "large amount of business" because of its inadequate rail connections to the Valley. A second Valley delegation, which visited the chamber in April, displayed considerable annoyance with the chamber's slow response to their request, telling the directors that San Antonio was "a cattle town and has devoted itself chiefly to cattle loans. On the other hand, the Houston banks have backed the farmers of the Valley and loaned them money." Shifting to a more positive note, the delegates offered the city their business in exchange for a railroad.[73]

Considering that the farmers had bluntly described how Houston had been more supportive of their needs than San Antonio, the chamber's response was decidedly tepid. The directors appointed a committee to supervise construction of a railroad, but it apportioned the cost of the project among the Valley towns. Winter Garden farmers would have to raise the money to pay for the railroad because San Antonio was not pledging any financial help. Oddly enough, the project failed. Experiences like this eventually created hostility among Valley residents toward the city. In 1930 the chamber's president suggested organizing a goodwill tour to the Winter Garden because "there seemed to be some prejudice among the Valley towns against San Antonio."[74] He apparently could not imagine why that would be so.

The strategy of relying on tourists to grow the city was also encountering problems. Boosters were ignoring the changing character of tourism in the 1920s. With mass ownership of automobiles Americans were taking to the road in large numbers to see the country. They were a prime audience for the preservationist approach to tourism, and their needs for inexpensive accommodations, car parks, and family entertainment required attention of the sort that Ray Lambert was providing in Brackenridge Park. But the boosters continued their focus on wealthy tourists. They failed, however, to sustain the Travis Club, which went bankrupt in 1919. Major hotels provided space for snowbirds to socialize with local businessmen, and the Canopus Club, founded in the early 1920s, arranged an elaborate social season of parties, dances, golf tournaments, and other diversions to convince these elite tourists to move to town.[75]

The boosters claimed that these efforts convinced about 5 percent of the snowbirds to become permanent residents every year. Even if that estimate were true for the entire decade, snowbirds would account for a population increase of fewer than 40,000 people during the 1920s.[76] In the meantime Dallas was adding 100,000 residents and Houston's population would soar by 154,000. San Antonio needed to supplement its basic growth strategy with additional initiatives.

Diversifying the local economy by enticing more factories to locate in San Antonio had long been one of the more neglected ideas among boosters. As the nation recovered from a serious postwar recession, the San Antonio Manufacturers Association and the chamber launched separate campaigns to attract businesses in 1925. Chamber president Nat Goldsmith announced that the chamber would focus on industries that "are in the class which we now can support," which meant food and clothing factories. Even that relatively modest goal became problematic when the directors failed to raise the $250,000 they calculated was necessary for this campaign.[77]

The results were mixed. New York's legislature had passed legislation to protect women and children in factories, prompting several textile manufacturers to move to other states, including Texas. By 1929 those firms and some local entrepreneurs had established thirty-one garment factories employing approximately five thousand women. Food processing businesses essentially meant pecan shelling, which employed between eight and twelve thousand women and children. The size of its workforce made pecan shelling the single largest employer in San Antonio.[78]

Pay scales tempered the effects of these factories. Industrial growth typically contributed to urban development by increasing the total amount of money circulating in the local economy, which in turn created a richer internal market for those workers who could afford more goods and services. And the largest employer usually had the biggest payroll. Pecan shelling inverted those patterns. It was the largest employer, but with average wages of five cents an hour its total payroll was near the bottom among local businesses. In effect the campaign to increase industrial activity had created a larger, poorly paid workforce that did not include enough skilled workers to help raise the city's living standards.

Income from the military bases did compensate for this situation to some extent. Payrolls contributed perhaps $3 million a year to the local economy, but congressional penury severely restricted contract work. Military construction projects at Fort Sam Houston, for instance, totaled an uninspiring $42,000 in 1924 and a tepid $170,000 in 1926. Congress relented only once, when army officers finally convinced it to expand the nation's pilot training capacity. Gen. Frank Lahm notified the chamber in 1926 that there would be a new base and assured the directors that the army wanted it built in San Antonio.

Lahm also warned the directors that Congress expected the city to provide free land for the base. Despite repeated reminders, the directors assumed that Lahm could not possibly be serious about free land and ignored him for a year. Finally, in December 1927, the chamber sent a delegation to Washington to demand that Congress appropriate the money to buy the land. They received a blistering rebuke and hurried home to report that Congress really did mean it. Furthermore, the chairman of the Armed Services Committee informed them that San Antonio had three weeks to raise the money or the base would go elsewhere. William Tuttle and Luther Clegg led a frantic but ultimately successful effort to secure Randolph Air Force Base. Contract work for the new base brought a fairly steady stream of income into town for several years, but the military's overall contributions to the local economy could not compensate for weaknesses in the boosters' development program.[79]

Railroad advertising and freight rates provided an early warning about those weaknesses. In January 1926 the chamber's directors discovered that the Southern Pacific had begun advertising San Antonio as the third largest city in Texas. They immediately demanded that the railroad replace their "unofficial estimates" with the 1920 census report on San Antonio's size, which the Southern Pacific refused to do. A year later San Antonians learned the consequences of failing to protect their hinterland when the Missouri, Kansas and Texas Railroad lowered the freight rates it charged Dallas and Houston businessmen to transport goods from the Winter Garden. San Antonians had to pay higher rates that, as the directors complained to no avail, created "a serious handicap on San Antonio's business institutions in their efforts to compete with Dallas and Houston for business geographically located in San Antonio's legitimate trade territory."[80]

These hints that San Antonio's claim to metropolitan dominance might be problematic prompted chamber director Morris Stern to propose that "if San Antonio desired to hold her prestige as the largest city in Texas, the city limits should be extended to incorporate all suburbs of the city."[81]

Stern's idea suffered from a fundamental mathematical flaw. The North Side communities of Alamo Heights, Olmos Park, Los Angeles Heights, and Terrell Hills were the only "suburbs" north of the official boundary at Hildebrand Avenue. Alamo Heights became an independent city in 1922, but the others were unincorporated. Their combined populations did not exceed 20,000, which did not bode well as a solution to the boosters' problem.

Mayor Chambers enthusiastically embraced the idea, initiating a two-year campaign in January 1928 to annex all those suburbs. State law only dealt with annexation of incorporated cities of five thousand or more, leaving unclear the city's legal authority to absorb unincorporated territory without a petition from its residents. The commissioners dealt with that issue in December by obtaining approval for a charter amendment giving them authority to alter the city's limits and to annex territory "with or without the consent of the territory and inhabitants annexed" simply by passing an ordinance.[82]

Chambers dropped Alamo Heights from his plan after a dispute with its mayor, but the commissioners passed an ordinance in September 1929 that expanded the city limits a mile and a half in every direction, creating an eighty-one square mile "footprint" that absorbed the other unincorporated areas.[83]

It was all for naught. The chamber followed the early returns of the census takers closely and noticed the returns were disappointing. Its Ad Hoc Census Committee decided to help, submitting a list of 25,000 residents it said the census workers had missed; it also demanded that all military personnel be counted as permanent residents. The Census Bureau rejected both ploys, and when the committee met to consider demanding a recount of Mexican American residents, committee chair E. H. Kifer pointed out that many of those residents were migrant workers who were now leaving town, which would likely reduce the population count even more. With that the chamber admitted defeat. San Antonio had dropped to third place in the state's urban hierarchy.

After thirty years of sincere but checkered effort, the boosters had failed. Census data revealed the stark contrasts in San Antonio's performance compared to its rivals:

TABLE 4 Improvements in Manufacturing Performance in the 1920s

	Dallas		*Houston*		*San Antonio*	
	1920	*1930*	*1920*	*1930*	*1920*	*1930*
Number of Factories	457	535	383	475	318	390
Wage Earners	7,913	12,828	9,860	22,131	6,614	8,692
Wages	$7.9M	$13.6M	$10.4M	$28.0M	$5.8M	$8.3M
Value of Product	$98.7M	$142.5M	$86.9M	$285.2M	$35.5M	$56.4M

Source: U.S. Census of Manufactures, 1920, 1930.

San Antonio did retain one title. Its average wages were lower than either Dallas or Houston even though neither of them paid their workers particularly well.

None of these cities could claim to be an important manufacturing center in 1930. In fact, their major economic functions remained firmly rooted in exporting raw materials to the rest of the nation. San Antonio's boosters had long touted the size and wealth of their city's hinterland, but its failure to thwart its competitors' incursions into the Winter Garden seriously affected San Antonio's status as a major wholesale center.

TABLE 5 Performance as a Wholesale Distribution Center, 1930

	Dallas	*Houston*	*San Antonio*
Total Employment	5,416	6,770	3,342
Salaries and Wages	$9,823,000	$12,961,000	$5,237,000
Net Sales	$364,899,000	$413,163,000	$74,037,000
Number of Firms	326	409	239

Source: U.S. Census, Wholesale Distribution, 1930.

The Census Bureau's data did not reveal the reasons for San Antonio's inability to defeat its rivals to become Texas's largest city. Like success, failure has multiple origins. City-building is a learned, collective activity that requires years of experience to develop useful habits such as organizing, investing in, and inventing uses for its resources so that they are prepared to take advantage of opportunities as they arise. Merchants in Dallas and Houston developed those habits over several decades. Dallas entrepreneurs courted railroads aggressively, convinced farmers to feed their livestock cotton oil cakes and to buy insurance, and sold them agricultural equipment. Houston's businessmen poured money into railroads to control East Texas cotton, timber, and oil fields; and fought a long, hard battle with Galveston to become the state's major port.

San Antonio's businessmen, with the support of a significant number of voters, persistently refused to learn the lessons of city-building. Boosters, always a minority in any city, could not consistently overcome the basic cultural bias against organized development. It would take several more decades to change that bias, and in the meantime San Antonians had to deal with the effects of the Great Depression and World War II on their city.

BOOSTERS AND SLUMS IN THE 1930s

Tumbling to third place in Texas's urban hierarchy was a blow to the boosters' pride that enhanced their normal disinterest in the grave problems of San Antonio's poor. Slums and poverty were not useful symbols of urban progress, and the boosters had naturally ignored them in their efforts to grow the city. Such behavior was normal among boosters throughout America, as was their strong tendency to deny such problems existed. In the 1930s, however, the boosters' traditional reliance on San Antonio's supposed reputation for healthfulness inadvertently created a self-imposed wound that fatally undermined that claim as a city-building tool.

In early 1935 the Chamber of Commerce asked the United States Health Service to survey the city's health conditions to support a new advertising campaign. Much to the chamber's consternation, the service found that San Antonio was a pest hole of infectious diseases that were killing hundreds of its residents, most particularly in the West Side Mexican American slums. The chamber immediately attempted to suppress the bad news (a standard booster tactic with a long history), but the report became public anyway.

Serious health problems had been common in poor neighborhoods since at least the late 1840s, when a cholera epidemic killed several hundred people. But the massive influx of Mexican immigrants after 1910 created densely populated West Side slums. Landlords, many of whom were slum residents themselves, had little incentive—and often few resources—to install sewers or water services on their properties. With increased density came increased disease, and San Antonio briefly became notorious for its high rates of death from such diseases as tuberculosis and infant diarrhea.

Thousands of San Antonians lived in appalling physical conditions into the 1960s. Eventually the Good Government League would undertake a decade-long effort to ameliorate the health conditions by providing basic water and sewer services to the West Side. Its campaign, which coincided with the campaign for HemisFair, was part of the GGL's effort to rejuvenate the boosters' initiative to establish an image of San Antonio as an attractive city to live and work in.

The poor living conditions endured by the 1930s pecan shellers, a major constituency of the West Side slums, was documented in the 1940 Works Progress Administration pamphlet *The Pecan Shellers of San Antonio,* which referred to the area as the Mexican Quarter. These images, of a woman doing laundry with a child standing by and the close proximity of the shack housing in 1939, demonstrate the crowded quarters. These spaces were referred to as "corrals." The 1940s brought little improvement as overcrowded housing and unplumbed toilet facilities remained commonplace.

While most of San Antonio was readying itself for the 1968 World's Fair, which touted the inclusive theme "Confluence of Civilizations in the Americas," the promises of modern conveniences and amenities continued to bypass certain populations.

These 1960s San Antonio Development Agency photos, featuring two boys sitting on a concrete slab outside toilet facilities at a West Side housing complex and the communal faucet and trough, show how little had changed since the health scandal of the 1930s.

SEVEN

Frugality Restored

1930–1951

In June 1925 a City Water Board customer complained about the feeble water supply to his home during the evening peak usage hours. After listening to his complaint in a closed meeting, board chairman Arthur Seeligson announced an agreement: the board would not install a larger water pipe to serve the customer's neighborhood. In return, the customer would negotiate with his sixteen neighbors to solve the supply problem by allocating times when each of them would have exclusive use of their common water supply. Seeligson proudly concluded that "we... patched the matter up to the entire satisfaction of the petitioner."[1]

Seeligson neglected to explain how this agreement could possibly satisfy his customer. He did not, after all, receive improved service, and he now had to negotiate a plan to manage his neighborhood's water shortage. But this agreement did reflect the assumptions of private citizens and public officials concerning city services in a growing city. San Antonians had been proud of their city's constant growth, but they had also never been eager to pay the costs involved in providing basic services to sustain that growth. Self-help had been the preferred solution to obtaining services, and homeowners had organized improvement districts to finance their own neighborhood's services, or they relied on private utility companies to provide them. Either option was, however, available only to those residents who could afford them; other San Antonians simply had to do without such services.[2]

That tradition was the basis for Seeligson's agreement with his anonymous customer. Seeligson acknowledged the voluntary nature of the relationship between homeowners and city service agencies by offering him two options: convince his neighbors to pay the board $600 to cover the cost of a larger water main or negotiate a private agreement with them to regulate water use. He chose the less expensive option.

Boosters who wanted to build an attractive city that included modern services found this tradition of voluntarism challenging. Clinton Brown had tried to manage it by using the booster's political machine to win bond elections while leaving the decision to accept city services to individual property owners. That policy, however, was not without its costs. Large numbers of "skips" and diverse street paving choices detracted from booster efforts to create a more appealing urban landscape for prospective residents and investors. And West Side property owners' refusal to install adequate water and sewer lines in their rental houses contributed to the rapid evolution of a fetid slum on the West Side. The demand for frugality also limited funding for booster projects. Voters were quick to suspect "waste," "extravagance," and "corruption" whenever they decided that city budgets or bond issues had become too large. To avoid provoking such suspicions, Brown and his successors avoided frequent or large bond issues. As a result, they never had enough funding to implement their ambitious goals.

Despite this abundance of caution, the boosters eventually failed to manage the demand for frugality. Warning signs that voter patience was growing thin first appeared in November 1923, when the chairman of the Taxpayers' Protective Association asked the council to appoint poll watchers representing his organization for a bond election.[3] The commissioners ignored his petition, but from 1923 to 1929 the amount of unpaid property taxes quadrupled, signaling growing voter discontent.[4] Then the *San Antonio Light*, normally a bastion of boosterism, unexpectedly committed heresy in October 1929. Struggling to contain its virtuous indignation, the newspaper attacked flood control, a major booster project, charging that the river had developed a "ravenous appetite for money. . . . Into the maw of the river $3,000,000 has been poured by the taxpayers of this city since 1924." Chambers indignantly responded that "we are not going to run wild on any bond issues," but shortly thereafter he capitulated to rising discontent, announcing that the river was now safe and he was "not going to pour any more gold" into it.[5]

These tremors of discontent finally coalesced into organized outrage because the boosters' preoccupation with retaining the title as Texas's largest city blinded them to the rising tide of discontent, causing them to make a fatal error that would destroy their coalition. That error was the 1928 charter amendment that permitted the city council to annex territory with or without the consent of its residents.

In choosing to annex by administrative fiat, the commissioners expanded the power of local government by violating the custom that the residents of subdivisions decided when—or if—to petition the council for annexation. They then compounded that felony by scheduling a large bond election in May 1930 to install city services in those subdivisions, which enraged voters within the original city limits who objected to the expense as well as the tax increase that would be necessary to pay for the bonds.[6]

Annexation thus triggered a political revolt led by Maury Maverick and Walter W. McAllister. They made rather an odd pair of collaborators. Maverick was a World War I decorated combat veteran and a lawyer with a growing reputation for his fierce social liberalism; McAllister, who could match Maverick's deep family roots in San Antonio, was a successful and deeply conservative businessman. They did, however, share commitments to the traditions of low cost, efficient government and voluntarism in the delivery of city services or annexation, issues that would dominate local politics through the Depression and World War II.[7]

Their campaign to derail the bond issue began in January 1930 and culminated with the creation of a Citizens' League in early April. Unlike its namesake, this league had no interest in boosterism. Indeed the league opposed public improvements as a threat to frugal, limited government. Its leaders attacked Chambers's administration for its inability "to economically administer the funds they are asking for"[8] and characterized commission government as a "crooked political machine" that "should be destroyed" and replaced with city manager government.[9] The days when prominent boosters such as Reagan Houston could praise a ward boss like Ray Lambert were over.

Confronted with a fundamental threat to their plans, the boosters rallied their own resources for what turned into a Pyrrhic victory. In a record turnout, voters approved all seven bond issues, but only by a whisker-thin average of 261 votes for each proposal. Voters in the newly annexed areas, deeply upset at the prospect of life as city residents, predictably voted against the bonds, but West Side precincts provided enough votes to provide the boosters' margin of victory. Disaster, though, lurked in the results from the North

Side. Voters there had consistently supported booster ambitions, but they now split over the costs of annexation, and they would generally oppose public improvements for the next twenty years. Without their united support boosterism collapsed within the business community.[10]

With the boosters' demise, the city entered an era of growth without any organized effort to develop the city. Ironically the commissioners and mayor would struggle to continue the now defunct booster coalition's agenda. The Depression and their own internal problems would however thwart that effort. In the meantime various elements of the now defunct coalition abandoned public improvements as a development tool. Some groups sought to enhance tourism or attract businesses to town, but most civic activists devoted themselves to limiting the cost and authority of local government.

In these circumstances, any new booster coalition would (once again) need to reconcile the tension between using local government to promote systematic urban development and those traditional concerns. The political environment for attempting such a reconciliation did not exist in the 1930s and would only emerge as civic leaders struggled to cope with the impact of World War II on San Antonio.

In the meantime the Citizens' League led the attack on the remnants of the boosters' development program. Having lost the 1930 bond election only because it had failed to combine its powerful appeal to frugality and clean government with equally effective precinct organizations, its leaders simultaneously worked on that problem and turned to the courts to invalidate Chambers's hard-won victory. League member Albert Maverick Jr. filed a legal challenge to the election results and won a stunning victory in July. Judge George C. Calhoun ruled—wrongly—that the election had been technically illegal because the council had failed to file a required thirty-day notice of an election.[11] Calhoun then launched a gratuitous attack on the annexation effort that endorsed traditional political values. He accused the council of not giving voters "either inside or outside the city limits a voice in the matter"; declared that even if annexation was legal, "it is unreasonable"; and concluded this highly personal legal opinion with an attack on boosterism itself, saying that "in my opinion, the annexation was not justified nor is it necessary to the growth of the city."[12] Since the rationale for annexation—to inflate the city's population for the census—had become a moot point, Chambers declined to appeal Calhoun's decision.

League supporters celebrated their victory by announcing their intention to clean the Augean Stables at city hall and the county courthouse.[13] With a slate of candidates that included Maury Maverick for tax commissioner and his father, Albert Jr., for commissioner, the league won control of county government by promising honest, low-cost government.[14]

Having cleansed one stable by replacing a large number of the county machine's patronage employees with their own friends,[15] the league planned to sweep the second in the city elections in May 1931. The city machine, though, would prove to be a tougher challenge. Chambers led a well-organized coalition of veteran politicians who still had large personal followings, worked well together, and controlled the appointment of 2,100 city employees. In addition, the machine had good relations with the city's major banks and many contractors and merchants who earned steady incomes by providing supplies and services to the city.[16]

Chambers also inherited a certain amount of residual goodwill from groups that had benefited from the machine's alliance with the boosters. He enjoyed good relations with politically influential women working on historic preservation because he had authorized the use of bond money to buy and restore the Spanish Governor's Palace (which opened with much fanfare in March 1931) and had donated $75,000 from the city to help launch the Daughters of the Republic of Texas campaign to buy the land around the Alamo to create a public park. He also supported river beautification, contributing to his good repute among the city's club women. Many members of the Chamber of Commerce also supported the machine because it used tax money to improve the city's athletic facilities for winter tourists and to advertise San Antonio to potential investors and residents.[17]

Finally the Depression at this point enhanced the machine's electoral prospects. During the bond election campaign overall unemployment in the city had increased from 11 percent in February to 16 percent in March and had risen to 65 percent in the building trades. By 1931 city officials had managed to hire about a thousand men who, as Commissioner Paul Steffler explained, "don't want soup lines, but honest work." Those workers were also probably willing to vote for the administration in gratitude for that help.[18]

With the ward politicians still controlling considerable political capital, the Citizens' League needed a well-organized campaign to compete effectively with them. That proved to be a problem. League members did themselves no favors by engaging in an unseemly fight about distributing the spoils of offices at their nominating convention. The timing of this debate, before the campaign had even begun, and its subject—so reminiscent of old-fashioned ward politics—tended to compromise the league's reform credentials.[19]

Mixed campaign messages also may have created problems for the league. Walter McAllister spoke at several rallies, complaining that taxes on private homes worth more than $5,000 were too high. While most voters opposed high taxes, it is doubtful that they could muster much outrage over a problem that only affected a tiny minority of taxpayers.[20] Nor would they have known what to make of mayoral candidate Guy McFarland's promise to establish city manager government. The league had done nothing to educate voters about its presumed advantages, making it difficult for most voters to appreciate its significance.[21]

These missteps led to the league's defeat.[22] Chambers and the commissioners celebrated by issuing an unprecedented resolution thanking "religious and civic bodies and organizations . . . the multitude of business interests . . . the womanhood of the city," and the local newspapers that had defended "the fair name of our city against slander and abuse." The mayor invited San Antonians to join him in a "Forward San Antonio movement" (an allusion to Atlanta's successful booster campaign in the 1920s).[23]

Although the resolution had an obvious self-serving quality, the commissioners may well have believed their own rhetoric. Phil Wright, commissioner of fire and police, had been in office since 1918. Frank Bushick, commissioner of taxation, and Paul Steffler, commissioner of streets and sanitation, had joined the city council in 1923. Jake Rubiola, commissioner of parks, and Chambers had assumed their offices in 1927. Given their surprisingly easy victory, they had no practical need to issue their resolution of thanks; but they had spent many years implementing the boosters' agenda for developing the city and intended to continue those efforts.[24]

Their ultimately unsuccessful struggles to preserve the city's budget demonstrated their commitment to Chambers's Forward San Antonio program. Property tax revenues would decline nearly 60 percent from 1931 to 1934 as tax resistance grew in response to worsening economic conditions. City budgets, on the other hand, would decline only 37 percent because Chambers turned to the banks for help. In the 1931 fiscal year bank loans provided more than 40 percent of the city's budget to compensate for deficits in tax collections, a practice that persisted through the decade.[25]

Bank loans helped Chambers with operating expenses but not with public improvements. To fund those, Chambers became inventive indeed. In early August 1931 city employees assisted residents in several neighborhoods in petitioning the city council for a bond issue to relieve unemployment.[26] Chambers had no intention of sponsoring another bond election, but those petitions gave him a reason to reconsider the 1930 bond election. First, in a bow to frugality, the commissioners reduced the total amount of those bonds by almost 50 percent, retaining the original amounts only for new police and fire stations and an addition for the Robert B. Green Hospital. Those were important booster projects that contributed to improving health facilities and to protecting fire insurance rates for property owners.[27]

Next the commissioners recounted the votes of only those precincts within the city and announced those voters had approved the bonds. Judge Calhoun had of course declared that election, and therefore the bonds, invalid. The Citizens' League immediately sued to prevent implementation of Chambers's legerdemain, placing itself in the slightly awkward position of opposing projects than could employ a lot of people in the midst of a Depression. Calhoun did not, however, preside in this suit; a different jurist approved Chambers's deft maneuvers, giving him money for public projects that would employ some three thousand men.[28]

Those bond monies would of course not last forever, but a national political revolution fortuitously provided a new funding source for local projects. Franklin Roosevelt's New Deal sought, among other things, to transform the South's economy through federal laws, regulations, and, above all, money. Texas in particular would receive a massive amount of federal funding during the Depression and World War II.[29] Mayor Charles Quin, who succeeded Chambers when he died in 1933, seized the opportunity for federal assistance, submitting a request for $3.7 million to the Public Works Administration in June 1933. The federal government never fully funded any of the city's requests, but it did provide a steady source of money for public works. By January 1936 there were thirty-three projects employing 4,140 men.[30] The city could not hire all those needing work, but the mayor and commissioners were able to continue a modest version of their improvement program (with its attendant patronage benefits) for the duration of the Depression.

In the meantime the league floundered. It owed its early successes to an eruption of public outrage over the costs of annexation, but it lacked a core group of experienced and well-organized leaders who could sustain a political campaign for reform by winning elections. And a bitter internal controversy between factions within the league unexpectedly undermined its ability to develop that leadership.

In 1930 the league's candidates for county offices had pledged to serve only two terms. That unprecedented promise certainly set them apart from the typical office holder and may have helped them win reelection in 1932. In 1934, however, some league members rejected their pledge.[31] League president Charles Dickson attacked those renegades, announcing that it "would bar from [league] membership all of the old members who were elected to political office."[32]

Dickson's faction controlled the executive committee at this crucial point, but their purity created a practical problem for the league's survival: they had now expelled their most successful members, whom they needed to sustain the organization. They compounded this error by seizing control over all aspects of the league's 1935 campaign. Dickson's purists selected candidates who pledged fealty to term limits and then wrote a party platform without consulting them.[33] Riley Wyatt, the league's candidate for mayor, discovered he had health problems and withdrew from the race, causing the league's campaign to collapse.[34]

Although the league staggered on for two more years, this debacle essentially destroyed it. Dickson's faction had failed to solve the challenge of developing a systematic way to replace professional politicians with well-organized amateurs capable of winning elections, a problem that would plague advocates for city manager government for many more years.

Taxpayers' leagues now assumed the dominant role in efforts to restrain governmental activism. Six of these organizations had appeared between 1931 and 1933. Attorney and former state senator John L. Browne, who lived in the Fourth Ward, founded the largest of them, the San Antonio Taxpayers' Association, in 1932. Its members accused fellow San Antonians of wanting too many public services. At their first meeting, bank president John K. Barretta complained that citizens who were "demanding more and more improvements to be paid for with bond issues" were the root cause for profligate spending, implying that the demand for services had to stop.[35]

Eschewing electoral politics, the association worked with neighborhood improvement associations, civic clubs, school boards, and the Chamber of Commerce to lobby county and city government to lower taxes for all city services regardless of potential worth. Barretta, for instance, said that he favored education, but posed the question "can we afford it?" He argued that schools could function effectively on half of their current budgets because teachers' salaries were too high, and they taught too many unnecessary courses. Although he offered no evidence for his argument, the association convinced the county commissioners to slash school budgets and teachers' salaries by 40 percent, a reduction that lasted for the remainder of the decade.[36]

Demands to lower city tax assessments on property also had some success. The largest decline in assessments (18 percent) during the 1930s occurred in 1933. In addition the league's campaign against taxes apparently encouraged resistance to paying them. Tax receipts dropped 45 percent from 1932 to 1933.[37] Such a dramatic decline not only deprived the city of revenue, it also affected the administration's ability to issue bonds for public projects by undermining San Antonio's national credit rating.

The city's credibility as an attractive place to live also suffered a major—albeit inadvertent—setback. In spring 1935 the Chamber of Commerce decided to document the city's progress "during the past ten years in protecting its citizens against disease" as part of an effort to promote the city.[38] It asked the United States Health Service to conduct a survey, which turned out to be a huge mistake.

According to the survey, San Antonio led the nation in deaths from infant diarrhea and enteritis, and tuberculosis. Only three other cities had more deaths from pneumonia. Inadequate city services created the environment for these diseases to thrive. One quarter of the city's homes had only surface privies; running water was notably absent in the slums; and the city's sewage disposal plant was so overloaded that it routinely dumped raw sewage into Lake Mitchell on the South Side.[39]

Such a disastrous report created a major problem for the chamber. Its directors had just announced that "with the exceptional resources and attractions of San Antonio, we have an insurmountable advantage over every other community in the entire Southwest." To make good on that boast, the directors had completely reorganized the chamber in May and launched a fundraising campaign to support their plan to reclaim the title of the state's largest city by 1940.[40]

Since the health survey's conclusions were hardly conducive to encouraging larger numbers of tourists, new residents, or manufacturers to flock to town, the chamber tried to suppress it. But Quin, a member of the chamber's board of directors, arranged to make the report public. Why he did so is a mystery. He apparently failed to notice that the survey's author not only blamed environmental problems for the appalling death rates but also complained that incompetent health inspectors interfered with the city's ability to deal with the problems of disease. The health department, which reported to Quin, was indeed riddled with malfeasance, but its inspectors' incompetence was not the fundamental reason for the city's health problems. Blaming them, however, was certainly the path of least resistance for the chamber in dealing with this embarrassing report. Local physicians, who also regarded the inspectors as a major obstacle to coping with rampant disease, joined the chamber's campaign to depoliticize the department.[41]

Quin defiantly rebuffed those demands as an infringement on his authority, which transformed the city's health problems into a major political issue. The Bexar County Medical Society's members turned to their state and federal connections to apply political pressure on Quin to reform the board. Doctors also were a potent lobby within the chamber, and important officers like Walter McAllister and Albert Steves III decided they could not ignore the physicians because this dispute attracted national publicity that threatened their efforts to portray San Antonio as an attractive (and safe) city. In a symbolic but nevertheless important move, the chamber's members voted not to reelect Quin to its board of directors. More substantively, it also sponsored additional studies on the city's health issues that fueled growing disenchantment with him and the machine over the next four years.[42]

In the meantime the fundamental problems with disease persisted. The city's largest slum occupied four square miles of mostly concentrated misery south of West Commerce Street. Never a particularly attractive area, it had become home to refugees from the Mexican Revolution and Mexican Americans in South Texas who moved there in large numbers after World War I. Pitiful wages gave these new arrivals few housing options, and landlords had built "corrals" of several single-story two room shacks facing each other around a dirt yard served by one community privy and, sometimes, a single cold-water faucet.[43]

Ironically these shacks were built in strict compliance with the city's corral ordinance, which boosters passed in 1915. The ordinance adhered to then popular ideas about using building codes to protect public health, but it also bowed to local practices concerning public services by leaving the decision whether to install water lines, lighting, paved streets, and sewers to the property owners.[44]

By 1939 there were 488 corral landowners, some of whom fit the classic stereotype of absentee landlords who exploited the poor. Eighty-four landlords, for instance, lived in Mexico City.[45] Local absentee landlords included First Ward alderman J. R. Lambert; Fourth Ward funeral director Henry Guerra; and Mrs. F. Rubiola, widow of Joseph Rubiola, a successful grocer and dry goods merchant in the Fifth Ward. Many landlords, though, lived in or near the slums, including José Gomez, owner of the Gomez Pecan Factory; Pedro Lozano, owner of the Pedro Lozano Pecan Factory; Victoriano Valdez, restaurant owner; and Auralia Valdez, a watchman.[46]

Landlords who lived in the slums hinted at the complexities of the Second Ward. Its residents faced extraordinary obstacles to a decent life, but there were also opportunities to overcome those obstacles as well. Gomez, Lozano, and Valdez were small businessmen who invested in slum properties to improve their own economic prospects. There were other opportunities to gain a step or two up the ladder of success. West Commerce Street was the city's wholesale business district anchored by the city market house. Processing all of the produce shipments arriving daily provided many jobs to locals, and some of them managed to open modest restaurants, pharmacies, grocery stores, laundries, theaters, and other small businesses that relied on the district's large working population for their success. Those opportunities gave rise to a small but important group of Mexican American proprietors whose members lived in Prospect Hill, the Second Ward's middle-class neighborhood.[47]

Despite that complexity, though, the reality of so much poverty concentrated in such a small area created one of the worst slums in the country in the 1930s. Most San Antonians ignored or denied its existence. In 1931 J. Frank Davis flatly declared that "there are no slums in San Antonio" in an article for the *Ladies Home Journal*.[48]

A few people did attempt to deal with the human tragedy the health survey had exposed. Father Carmine Tranchese, the city's most outspoken advocate for the poor, launched a campaign to improve their housing. With the help of the Junior Chamber of Commerce, Congressman Maury Maverick, the archdiocese, and others, Tranchese obtained federal funding for three public housing projects (Alazán-Apache, Victoria, and Wheatley Courts). It was a bitter campaign. Henry Guerra and N. A. Quintanilla organized a committee to demand inflated prices for their land. Its intransigence nearly undermined all three projects and forced a reduction in the number of apartments (and therefore tenants) in the Alazán-Apache Courts. Despite the difficulties, decent, affordable housing for some, but hardly all, of the poor appeared in the slums for the first time.[49]

Elsewhere in the city, advocates for other causes also made some progress. The Depression had temporarily halted efforts to modernize the downtown by replacing older, frequently historic structures with new buildings. Seizing their opportunity, the Conservation Society, the Daughters of the Republic of Texas, and even a few businessmen worked to improve or create five major tourist attractions during the 1930s.[50] By the end of the decade they had managed to refocus tourism on the city's history and culture, undermining the boosters' emphasis on tourism as a tool for attracting residents and investors.

The Conservation Society's members were committed to adapting the city's Spanish and Mexican past to modern times. When city health officials banned the food stands of chili queens as a health hazard in 1936, society members fought to restore them to the plazas. In a classic example of adapting the old to the new, they succeeded by helping these vendors develop more sanitary procedures for operating their stands. That victory represented, in miniature, the Society's determination to enhance the value of the city's socially diverse heritage to the tourism industry.[51]

Mission San José, on the city's South Side, became the Conservation Society's signature contribution to the campaign to enhance tourism. The society launched its campaign to save this mission in the early 1920s. Proceeding methodically, society members gradually bought private land around the mission while negotiating with the archdiocese to support their plans. In the 1930s the society turned to sympathetic supporters like Congressman Maverick to obtain federal funding to restore the mission. By 1938 the society had transformed San José into one of the most completely restored Spanish missions in the Southwest. The society sponsored cultural events such as Los Pastores and an Indian harvest festival to promote tourism.[52]

Restoration projects in the downtown were, with one exception, necessarily more limited in scope. With city hall dominating Military Plaza, the Conservation Society had little opportunity to create an appropriate setting for the Spanish Governor's Palace, but the members convinced the city to use bond money to buy the building and pay for its restoration. While not as successful as Mission San José, the palace reflected the society's belief that preserving the old enriched the new urban environment; it also provided another venue for the society's events.[53]

The Daughters of the Texas Republic members faced an even more difficult problem about space in dealing with the Alamo. By the 1920s interest in the nation's history supported large restoration projects such as Williamsburg, Virginia, and the French Quarter in New Orleans, as well as new monuments like the Lincoln and Jefferson Memorials in Washington, D.C. As custodian of the city's only iconic symbol of American culture, the Daughters faced the challenging task of creating a suitable setting for a national monument in the middle of the city's most prestigious commercial area.

It resolved those difficulties by conducting an intense lobbying campaign for city and state help in acquiring land behind the church and by adopting a historical interpretation that made it the crucial site of the battle. Subsequent research would challenge that interpretation, but it accurately represented the beliefs of many people at the time. It also eliminated any need to restore the mission's entire compound to its original size and condition, an area filled with paved streets and commercial buildings. With the church as the climactic site of the battle, the mission's missing walls and decapitated convento paled into relative insignificance, allowing the Daughters to make maximum use of a limited space to create an urban oasis for this cultural icon when it opened to the public officially in March 1938.[54]

As the Daughters completed work on the Alamo, Jack White, who managed the Plaza Hotel on the river, was searching for a competitive advantage over his rivals. He had noticed that the 1936 Fiesta river parade celebrating the Texas centennial had attracted more than ten thousand people. In January 1938 White organized a small group of river property owners to turn the river into a major tourist attraction. They hired Robert Hugman, who had created an imaginative plan to beautify the river in the late 1920s that Chambers had endorsed but never implemented. While Hugman made modifications to his plan, White solved the financing problem by obtaining city permission to create an improvement district that could issue bonds that qualified the district for federal assistance. Construction on what became a strikingly beautiful River Walk began on March 29, 1939, and concluded two years later.[55]

While crews from the Works Progress Administration constructed the River Walk, mayor Maury Maverick added La Villita to the growing list of downtown tourist attractions. In 1939 La Villita was a small slum neighborhood to the south of the Alamo dating to the early nineteenth century. The Conservation Society had expressed interest in restoring it as early as 1935, but Maverick, who liked grand ideas, conceived of La Villita as a center for promoting world peace and Latin American culture. He used his mayoral authority and national connections to acquire the land and secured federal and philanthropic money to cover all the costs.[56]

The Conservation Society decided to transfer its administrative operations from Mission San José to La Villita when restoration work ended in 1941. It transformed its fall Indian harvest festival into a riverside event and later made it a springtime festival. In 1947 the society moved the event to La Villita and renamed it A Night in Old San Antonio, bringing its long campaign to integrate its vision of a multiethnic city into the local tourism industry to a successful conclusion.[57]

Despite progress in developing such attractions, tourism still had work to do, especially with conventions. An enormous number of business, professional, fraternal, religious, and special interest groups annually sought interesting sites for their meetings, but the chamber only resumed efforts to recruit conventions to town in 1934, when it created a Convention Bureau. Considering general economic conditions, the bureau managed to do fairly well, with the number of conventions increasing from 143 in 1934 to 245 in 1939.[58] But average attendance grew less impressively, from 313 to 350. Such a small average revealed the city's fundamental problem with conventions: it did not have particularly good facilities to offer. Municipal Auditorium could accommodate five thousand, making it difficult (but not always impossible) to meet the needs of large state and national organizations. Inadequate facilities would in time become a major complaint among hotel and restaurant owners who were important groups within the chamber.

The chamber, however, remained focused on attracting winter tourists who would hopefully move to town permanently.[59] Since wealthy snowbirds often stayed for several months, they needed a variety of leisure activities commensurate with their social status. Prior to 1930 the chamber had wooed them with golf, hunting, fishing, elaborate dinners, and ballroom dancing. Those activities continued through the 1930s, but the Depression created financial strains on public sport facilities. In response to that problem, the chamber lobbied the city administration to maintain them and expand the polo grounds (presumably a favorite sport of wealthy tourists).[60] Seeking to increase entertainment options, some chamber members also devoted time to promoting opera and symphonic music concerts that coincided with the winter tourist season.[61]

Since the chamber did not systematically collect information on how many well-off snowbirds became permanent residents, it is unclear how effective these efforts were. Nor did it recognize the growing importance of middle-class vacationers and conventioneers who were more interested in history and culture than in opera and polo.

The chamber would eventually need to help develop ways to accommodate the needs of short-term visitors to justify its commitment to tourism. In the 1930s tourism ranked only sixth among the ten largest employers in town. Wholesalers and retailers ranked first, employing 30 percent of the working population. Government was second, followed by personal services, manufacturing, and professional services. There were more domestic servants than tourism workers in San Antonio.[62]

Government would have been a minor work opportunity without the military bases. Fort Sam Houston employed about 7,300 civilians annually during the decade, and the other bases accounted for another 2,000, which meant more than 80 percent of all government workers were federal employees. Although a parsimonious Congress kept military expenditures low until the late 1930s, the bases were still among the largest employers in town, adding approximately $19 million to the local economy each year, primarily through military pay and civilian salaries.[63]

Local businessmen welcomed this federal subsidy to the city's economy, but they joined their southern compatriots in bitterly opposing federal efforts to undermine their cherished belief that low wages was their crucial competitive advantage over other regions in their quest to attract industries. President Roosevelt and his New Deal advisers, however, believed that low wages impeded economic recovery by restricting the purchasing power of ordinary Americans, especially in the South.[64] They had some success implementing their ideas with the Wagner Labor Relations Act (1935), which recognized workers' right to organize, and the Fair Labor Standards Act (1938), which established minimum wages for the first time.

Both laws affected workers in San Antonio. Congress of Industrial Organizations members attempted to organize unskilled and semiskilled workers whom the local American Federation of Labor had always ignored. Pecan shellers and textile workers (who were predominately women) organized several strikes for higher wages between 1934 and 1938. With the support of Quin, police chief Owen Kilday aggressively suppressed these strikes with a combination of tear gas, beatings, and arrests of CIO pickets. His tactics reflected police behavior toward CIO members across the country and were equally effective.[65]

Kilday could not, however, thwart the implementation of the Fair Labor Standards Act's minimum wage. Owners of pecan shelling companies like Julius Seligmann vehemently protested that raising wages to twenty-five cents an hour would force them to fire most of their workers and mechanize production. New Dealers understood that many unskilled workers would lose their jobs, but they believed that mechanizing outdated manufacturing plants would eventually create other, better jobs. Seligmann lost the argument, closed his business to install machinery and train workers, and reopened with a greatly reduced workforce. Local federal relief agencies assisted the transition by allowing the city to hire many of the newly unemployed for work on the River Walk.[66]

While businessmen fought implementation of federal laws, machine politicians struggled with a threat to their control of local politics. Ironically Quin was the source of that threat. In March 1936 he announced that "I am going to run this machine or break it." He fired all of the machine's precinct captains and assumed personal control over appointing their replacements.[67] Three days later he again arbitrarily expanded his personal power by assigning sole authority to suppress gambling to a special investigator in his office, a task normally among Phil Wright's responsibilities as commissioner of fire and police.[68]

Quin's rather startling behavior threatened fundamental customs that regulated relationships within the machine. Local elections had been nonpartisan since the end of Reconstruction, which meant that the official Republican and Democratic parties did not fund candidates' campaigns for city offices. Candidates had to assemble campaign volunteers as well as contributors into a personal following. Men who wanted a political career obviously had to maintain, and sustain, their following with concrete benefits such as patronage appointments and city contracts. Cooperating with like-minded colleagues enhanced their reelection chances since they could combine their personal followers into a citywide "machine." The shift to commission government in 1914 had reduced the number of office holders without changing this fundamental emphasis on personalities and cooperation.

Quin wanted to replace that traditional system by becoming the machine's undisputed boss. His coup initially succeeded because he created unchartered territory where decades-old political customs no longer governed collegial relationships. His colleagues needed time to ponder their options, so they greeted his initiatives with "frigid silence" while simultaneously assuring reporters that harmony still prevailed between them and the mayor.[69]

Quin apparently had more success gaining control over precinct workers than campaign funding. Moving the suppression of gambling into his own office was likely less about eliminating gamblers than about transferring their campaign contributions from Wright to himself. Gamblers and politicians in San Antonio, as in most large American cities, had had good relations for decades. Illegal slot machines, for instance, stood ready to serve golfers in the city-owned Brackenridge Park Club House, and betting on horse races was readily available. "Red" Berry, the city's most popular gambler, operated a large casino on the East Side and managed to parlay his popularity into a career as a state legislator.

Phil Wright had no effective way to block Quin's move to control campaign contributions, but the mayor's attempt to seize control of tax commissioner Frank Bushick's funding sources failed spectacularly. Bushick's political employees had either introduced or continued (it is unclear which) the practice of soliciting campaign contributions from businessmen, especially in the downtown area, in exchange for reductions in their tax assessments. Such arrangements were of course illegal, but no one complained about paying for lower taxes. Quin had an obligation as a public official to report illegal activities, but he instead began a quiet campaign in 1937 aimed at Bushick's "arrangements."

That campaign ended badly when Quin forced Bushick to fire an employee who apparently coordinated his fundraising, which caused the victim in this power struggle to leak details to the press in August 1938. A grand jury used the revelations to indict several of Bushick's employees, and he resigned as commissioner in November.[70] Seeking to quell public outrage over Bushick's corrupt practices, Quin replaced him with Theo Plummer, an influential and straitlaced businessman who had no patience with the machine's customary political practices. The mayor's quest for dominance had cost the machine an experienced colleague and valuable campaign funds, severely damaged its public image, and introduced a thoroughly uncooperative new colleague into the machine's clubhouse.

Quin had in the meantime found other ways to expand his authority. He increased his own budget at the expense of his colleagues' needs and refused to cooperate with important power brokers like police chief Owen Kilday and Martin Wright, brother of Commissioner Wright. He also insisted on a 30 percent increase in the property tax rate in 1937, prompting a major tax revolt whose lingering bitterness carried over into the 1939 election. By September 1938, a reporter noticed that "the desire for the elimination of C. K. is quite a luxuriant and malignant growth at city hall."[71]

The commissioners finally rebelled in February 1939, demanding that Quin step aside as mayor and agree not to seek reelection. When he refused, they abolished four of his departments to rebalance the budget in their favor and deprive him of patronage appointees.[72] In preparation for the May election they patched together a slate with no candidates for mayor and tax commissioner, essentially fighting to save themselves and their personal organizations.

With the collapse of the citywide machine a bumper crop of parties and candidates proliferated. Three other "tickets" challenged the commissioners: Quin's Peoples Party, Leroy Jeffries's Better Government Party, and Maury Maverick's Fusion Party. Counting independents, thirty-two candidates competed for five offices.

Businessmen divided their support between Quin, Jeffries, and Maverick. Bankers Joe Frost and Walter Napier backed Quin, while Walter McAllister and Chester Slimp (who was active in tax leagues) helped finance the

Better Government Party.[73] Maverick had a decisive advantage over his opponents, who had to build their campaign organizations quickly, because he had built a personal following in his successful campaigns for county tax assessor and Congress. His supporters included prominent former Citizens' Leaguers and longtime boosters like Ira Kirscheville, Reagan Houston, and A. B. Weakley. Interestingly Maverick also enjoyed the support of Andres Coy, whose political career dated back to the West Side Tobin-Rubiola-Coy machine in the World War I era.[74]

With so many candidates, none of whom was able to muster citywide support, success depended on whose organization could turn out the most voters. Maverick won the mayoralty with only 41 percent of the vote. Quin placed second with 34 percent when his supporters failed to rally enough voters to him in the traditionally reliable East Side black precincts.[75]

Fewer than 500 votes (out of 45,000) decided three of the four commissioner races. Jacob Rubiola and Phil Wright fell victim to Quin's determination to run the machine, leaving Paul Steffler as the sole survivor. Maverick's success was not, however, the culmination of a decade of reform agitation. His Fusion ticket had ousted "the machine," but the political system that had sustained professional politicians for almost seventy years remained in place. And Maverick was not interested in changing that.

San Antonio's most famous, and famously controversial, citizen had now become its political leader. His passionate dedication to free speech, organized labor, minimum wages, and economic opportunities for white as well as black Americans aroused dismay and sometimes outright hatred among many San Antonians. Indeed his beliefs earned Maverick fame because he was so out of step with the beliefs of southern conservatives.[76] He had joined a small group of southern liberals in the Congress from 1934 to 1938, where his support for the New Deal and for changing the South won him a wide audience within the Roosevelt administration and among northern reporters.

Maverick loved the attention and found it impossible to ignore opportunities to embellish his national liberal credentials, but he also wanted to use his fame and connections to improve San Antonio. In March 1940 he presented his vision for doing that to the commissioners and the public in a prepared lecture. Sounding very much like a booster, Maverick began by saying that San Antonio needed to become a more attractive city. He endorsed tourism as a key industry, but he devoted most of his lecture to arguing that every city in America had become "a part of the federal system or nation as a whole," which changed the rules for urban development because every city would now be competing for federal largesse to promote their own growth. He believed that "our greatest industry is the Army of the United States" and the city needed to protect that industry from competitors with intensive lobbying in Washington.[77] In effect, he had become a champion for an emerging "military-industrial" complex.[78]

When Maverick delivered his lecture, Congress had already taken the first steps in enhancing that complex. Abandoning its traditional hostility to large defense budgets, it approved President Roosevelt's request in 1939 to fund a massive expansion of the air force. Simultaneously the Defense Department began implementing a strategic plan to subsidize the relocation and construction of aircraft manufacturing plants around the country. And Maverick, as he rather immodestly but accurately explained in his lecture, had access not only to key congressmen through his service on the House Armed Services Committee but also to Roosevelt.

The chamber, of course, had its own long-standing political connections with the Defense Department. And some of its members had again (as in World War I) begun to express interest in aircraft factories. In June 1940 President D. A. Powell obtained his board's approval to ask the Commercial Aviation Committee to investigate ways to attract them to town.[79]

All the portents seemed favorable for a dramatic opportunity to transform San Antonio's economy by acquiring aircraft factories that would bring large numbers of skilled, well-paid workers to town. The federal government would not only subsidize construction of any factories; it would also pay to train the new workers. And Congress's approval of Roosevelt's plans for massive increases in airplanes guaranteed lucrative government contracts for every new factory. Maverick decided to capitalize on those portents. He invited H. M. Van Auken, the chamber's general manager, to accompany him to Wichita, Kansas, in February 1941 to interview aircraft manufacturers about relocating to San Antonio.[80]

It was not to be. Van Auken returned from the Wichita visit and reported to the chamber that "in his judgment it would be extremely difficult to move any of these factories, or others of a similar nature, to San Antonio, largely on account of this being a great military reservation and in the Army's 'theater of operation.'"[81] Although his logic is obtuse, Van Auken apparently concluded that San Antonio should not add military manufacturing to its economy because that would interfere with the military's existing operations. His chamber colleagues apparently agreed with his odd assessment; they would not even attempt to acquire aircraft factories.

Dallas boosters, on the other hand, did not hesitate to do so. Their chamber began cultivating airplane manufacturers in March 1940. When Roosevelt announced a plan to build fifty thousand planes a year in May, banker Robert Thornton led a delegation to California where they convinced North American Aviation to construct a plant in Dallas. Others would follow, and wartime aircraft manufacturing employed eighty-five thousand workers. Thornton and his colleagues had created the foundations for their city's development into a national center for aviation and electronics after 1945.[82]

San Antonio's businessmen were incapable of such aggressive behavior. Most believed that tourism, the military, and low-wage factories were the keys to future growth. That model guided the chamber's leadership, policies, and initiatives. Moreover chamber members typically belonged to specialized trade groups, such as the restaurant and hotel associations, that sought to protect and expand their own interests. There was little fallow ground for new ideas to germinate, and few men to nurture them. As a national reporter noticed, "Certain elements in San Antonio are strongly opposed to the coming of big industry to their town. With it will come fuller unionization of labor, which they feel will jack up wages in existing enterprises."[83] Local businessmen were so successful in keeping wages low that San Antonio's median wage ranked last among American cities of its size in 1938.[84] Despite that success, new factories did not flock to town.

The military as an industry did not challenge this emphasis on low-wage, unskilled labor. With the possible exception of pilots, who were not numerous yet, most military personnel had modest incomes. Local merchants and contractors, though, had benefited from the army quartermaster's need for food, supplies, and an occasional new building.

San Antonio's business leaders in effect chose not to change their traditional approach to development to take advantage of the single most important economic opportunity of their generation.[85] That contrasted starkly with Dallas and Houston, whose leaders aggressively pursued federal funding to expand their manufacturing sectors throughout the war. By 1945

Dallas's aviation and electrical plants and Houston's chemical manufacturers employed large numbers of skilled workers and white-collar managers who earned comfortable incomes. With greater diversification of economic opportunities, Dallas and Houston were much more attractive cities than San Antonio to potential residents and investors by 1945.

Nevertheless the war solved the problem of stagnant population growth. Ironically Maverick had pointed out in his public lecture that "great masses of people will not come to San Antonio unless there is some definite economic reason." War provided that reason. By 1944, 97,000 residents had crowded into town, and another 53,000 would arrive by 1950.[86] Overall the population increased 60 percent in the 1940s.

Military demand for civilian workers drove most of that increase. Kelly Air Force Base, for example, increased its civilian workforce when it became a logistical center from 1,163 in 1939 to 17,837 in 1943; Duncan Field had 1,116 workers in 1939 and 19,000 in 1942. By December 1943 all the bases employed a total of 48,742 civilians.[87]

The number of military personnel in town also increased dramatically. In September 1940 Maverick announced that 75,000 army regulars and 40,000 draftees would be joining the 20,000 officers and men living at local bases. After that initial burst, the military population declined slightly, but in 1943 it was still an impressive 90,000 personnel.[88]

Such sudden, massive increases greatly expanded the military's effects on the local economy. The army's needs for housing, food, and even office supplies skyrocketed, creating a massive market for local businesses. By the end of 1940 it had become $100 million business; by 1945 the military's annual contributions to the economy had transformed it into the city's most important industry.[89]

So many young military personnel provided a short-term boost to tourism, but they also offered a priceless opportunity to promote postwar tourism if they could recall pleasant memories of their time in San Antonio. The Chamber of Commerce produced a tour guide especially designed to cultivate such memories for servicemen.[90]

The war also introduced a small amount of social change in San Antonio. With so many men serving in the armed forces, the bases became (relative) bastions of opportunities for well-paying jobs for women and minorities.

Women temporarily benefited the most, finding employment not only in offices but also in Kelly's machine and inspection shops and as pilots. Their numbers declined dramatically after 1945, but they remained an important part of the local federal workforce. Kelly Air Force Base became especially important for minorities because the base commander deviated from normal discriminatory practices at other bases around the nation. He enforced Presidential and Fair Employment Practice Commission regulations on wages and equal treatment for about 5,000 Mexican Americans and 1,700 blacks during the war. As a result, minorities at Kelly earned incomes that exceeded average annual wages in local manufacturing. That made Kelly a magnet for minorities, especially Mexican Americans; by 1962 they were 43 percent of the base's workers, making it the largest employer of minorities in San Antonio.[91]

Despite all the advantages of an overheated wartime economy, massive population growth aggravated prewar environmental problems, challenging traditional ideas about providing city services and limiting governmental authority. In 1940 nearly half of the city's houses and apartments had no running water or toilets. By 1945 housing had nearly doubled, but the percentage of those without water and toilets remained the same. In effect, the number of people without access to basic sanitation facilities had vastly increased, creating a massive public health problem.[92] Unincorporated areas were experiencing the same difficulty. In Harlandale, south of the city limits, overflowing cesspools adjacent to its business center served a population of forty thousand residents. State health inspectors declared the cesspools a health hazard in 1944 and threatened to close all the stores until a sewer line could be constructed.[93]

Harlandale's business center was obnoxious not only for its stench but also for its threat to downtown merchants. Many of the thousands of people flocking to town seeking work on the military bases settled in San Antonio's suburban ring of unincorporated subdivisions, where their desire for convenient access to routine services such as grocery stores, doctors, dentists, gas stations, and cleaners encouraged the emergence of small business centers like Harlandale's. New subdivisions within the city limits created the same opportunities for commercial development. National chain stores like Red & White, which had seventy-five stores in San Antonio as early as 1930, and

Sears, which built a major branch just north of the downtown in the 1940s, attracted many of the newcomers who increasingly found it unnecessary to travel downtown.[94]

The dispersal of homes and businesses had been under way for several decades in most American cities. Decentralization, though, threatened the livelihoods of merchants who had relied on the custom of shopping downtown since the late nineteenth century. By 1941 many San Antonians believed that the city's "major problem is the trend of business away from the downtown district." They wanted to "halt any decentralization before it goes too far," a sentiment that was becoming increasingly common, and strident, around the country.[95]

Solving these problems would require political leadership and community consensus. Neither would be easy to create, particularly considering the potential for conflict over priorities and resources between advocates for halting decentralization and those who wanted to reverse the high death rates from preventable diseases.

Both problems would eventually become the bedrock issues for a new political coalition. After the collapse of the booster coalition in 1930, civic activists devoted their time to a wide variety of important, specific issues such as education, property taxes, public health, and tourism. But they lacked the ability to build a citywide organization that could combine their disparate interests and experiences into a coordinated campaign to promote San Antonio's development.[96] Their focus on narrower issues, however, introduced them to the practical problems of implementing change and contributed to the development of new leadership. By the late 1930s there were a number of people with enough experience promoting various causes to provide a basis for a new booster effort. Mrs. George Biering and Mrs. A. Y. Troutman, for instance, had spent several years promoting educational reform and organizing parent-teacher associations into effective precinct organizations that succeeded in gaining control of some local school boards in 1938.[97] Both were beginning to expand their interests into public health reform, illustrating the potential for applying skills learned in dealing with one problem to another.

All they needed was some sort of catalyst that would encourage them to unite in a common cause. Quin unintentionally but helpfully provided that with his ham-fisted efforts to dominate the commissioners. Civic leaders suddenly had a major opportunity to change the structure of city government and its political system. Don Politico, a political gossip column in the *Light*, "detected" a trend in 1939, "call it a reform movement if you will," that "was resulting from a combination of non-political factions which have during the past 18 months dabbled in politics." It predicted that "if all these elements become properly coordinated with the taxpayers group . . . it will be a combination C. K. [Quin] and his friends might well fear."[98]

Maverick's victory in 1939, though, thwarted political reform. On his first day in office he fired all current employees and personally appointed their replacements. He justified this Quin-like behavior by explaining that "like all political organizations we are attempting to select our political friends for these jobs," but he assured skeptics that "we are not attempting to build up a political machine." He offered his version of reform by having the commissioners approve his plan for a complete reorganization of city departments, which, he said, fulfilled his campaign pledge to establish efficient, economical, honest government. Finally he promised to submit a proposal for city manager government to the voters, but he strongly hinted that there was no need to do so since "we have already installed some of the best features of the council manager form of government."[99]

The skeptics found Maverick's reassurances unconvincing and created a new organization to advocate for reform. Paul Adams, Walter McAllister, Theo Plummer, and Joseph Sheldon, with help from another twenty-five civic leaders, established the Taxpayers' Defense League in January 1940. The name symbolized their commitment to frugality and minimal government, and the initial board of directors assembled some of the most accomplished civic leaders who had emerged in the 1930s: McAllister and Sheldon (from the Citizens' League), P. I. Nixon (the city's most prominent physician), and Mrs. Biering and Mrs. Troutman (school reformers). The Taxpayers' Defense League also offered membership to businesses, not just individuals. Adams, a highly respected realtor, became its first president. Russell Hill, president of Maverick-Clarke Printing, chaired its Civic Research Committee, whose first assignment was to study city manager government.[100]

In the 1940s the Taxpayers' Defense League would provide the leadership for many other civic and political committees that worked on solutions to the city's problems, making it the most important reform organization in the city.[101]

Despite its impressive pedigree, the league did not enjoy instant success. It persuaded Maverick to call an election to create city manager government in late 1940, but confusing charter amendments and Maverick's refusal to campaign for them undermined its efforts. Maverick paid a price for his disinterest when he lost a close election to a resurgent Charles Quin in May 1941.[102]

Quin's return to the mayor's office reflected the personalized nature of a now chaotic political system. Maverick had neglected to manage his administration, preferring to spend considerable time out of town lecturing and lobbying. While he cultivated his liberal image elsewhere, his commissioners reasserted their formal powers to administer their own offices. Sanitation commissioner Henry Hein led the way, replacing several Maverick appointees with his own supporters as he began building a personal following.[103] Relapsing to the traditional approach to politics helped Hein and tax commissioner C. Ray Davis win reelection, which meant Quin had little control over his new administration, a point the commissioners made clear to him when they replaced his first budget proposal with their own version in July 1941.[104]

They did, however, cooperate with Quin's determination to reverse all of Maverick's major initiatives. By the end of 1942 they had overturned his police and Board of Health reforms and dismantled his reorganization of city government.[105] Quin also made one important contribution to the city's development when he thwarted the Guadalupe-Blanco River Authority's attempt to buy the privately owned San Antonio Public Service Company, which provided the city's gas and electricity. Despite fierce opposition from the Taxpayers' Defense League, which complained that Quin was paying too much for the utility, the commissioners approved revenue bonds to buy it.[106] Then, showing an astute awareness of his prospects for reelection in 1943, he maneuvered himself into an appointment as a state judge and resigned from office in January 1943.[107]

Within days of Quin's resignation the commissioners elected Gus Mauermann to replace him. Mauermann was a successful businessman with an ancient lineage in San Antonio. He had never held political office, but his rumored interest in running for commissioner of police and fire, currently Paul Anderson's job, apparently convinced Anderson that Mauermann ought to be mayor, and he persuaded his colleagues to agree with him.[108]

Mauermann quickly discovered that he had inherited serious problems. Four days after assuming office, he chaired his first Board of Health meeting where he listened to the former director of the U.S. Public Health Service describe an "acute" health problem that required immediately expanding the sewer system into all areas of the city, enlarging the city's sewage disposal plants, and improving garbage disposal.[109]

The director was describing the effects of wartime population growth on a city that had neglected public service improvements for more than a decade. Lax regulations for creating subdivisions contributed significantly to the deterioration of public health. Developers typically "paved" streets with gravel and honored the tradition that homeowners should decide whether and when to petition the city council and City Water Board for water and sewer service.[110]

As a result, many of the subdivisions proliferating within and outside of the city had no access to adequate sanitation. Lower-class Mexican Americans faced especially severe problems. Developers like C. S. Fenstermaker, Waldo Lewis, and Aubrey Milner were developing a large area north of West Commerce Street beyond the city limits in response to demand for new inexpensive housing. That area would evolve into a major extension of the West Side's slums where water and sewer connections were practically nonexistent.[111] Middle-class subdivisions like Harlandale relied on cesspools and private water companies (which only served some residents) for their needs. When household garbage far exceeded the capacity of the city's small incinerators, sanitation commissioner Hein simply ordered his men to dump the increasingly large overflow wherever they could in city neighborhoods, or failing that, in the unincorporated areas.[112]

Mauermann would devote most of his time as mayor to struggling with the challenges of sanitation and disease in a rapidly growing city. The enormity of that task prompted him to take *Light* publisher William McIntosh's advice to create a postwar planning committee in March 1943. The committee, though, initially ignored public health issues to focus on solutions to traffic congestion in the city's center, demonstrating the business community believed that decentralization was a more important issue than public health.[113] The Taxpayers' Defense League had reinforced that point in 1941 when it unsuccessfully sued the city to prevent construction of a tuberculosis hospital after voters had approved bonds for it. League president Joe Sheldon justified the lawsuit by saying that 97 percent of the league's members had voted against the hospital even though San Antonio had recovered its distinction of having the highest death rate in the nation from TB in 1940.[114]

With important organizations like the Taxpayers' Defense League and his own Planning Board either indifferent or opposed to health reform, Mauermann needed a political strategy to make public health an important issue for them. That took some time to emerge, but in December 1943 he made some progress when he asked Alex Thomas to chair his Post-War Planning Board. As general manager of Alamo Lumber since 1930, Thomas was a successful businessman with solid connections to the influential San Antonio Builders Exchange and a long history of civic service as president of the Kiwanis Club, where he devoted considerable attention to the problems of underprivileged children. He had also held important positions in the Community Chest and the War Finance Committee (which sold war bonds), where he had worked with community leaders like Albert Steves, William Clegg, Nat Goldsmith, J. H. Frost, and others. He had not, however, been active in the Citizens' League and did not belong to the Taxpayers' Defense League.[115]

In short, Thomas was a well-respected businessman with considerable experience in civic affairs who was just beginning a distinguished career in public service that would rival the accomplishments of Walter McAllister and Joe Sheldon in the 1940s. He began that career by helping Mauermann develop a strategy for making health reform acceptable, even necessary, to businessmen working to create a new booster coalition.

Their strategy became public when Harlandale's businessmen decided to seek incorporation as a separate city in March 1944. Mauermann immediately submitted an ambitious ordinance to the commissioners that would annex subdivisions containing 125,000 people, explaining that the city needed to extend its limits to include all areas "which have presented sanitation problems to the city." The commissioners, though, were wary of annexation by fiat rather than the traditional practice of voluntary annexation by petition and delayed consideration of the ordinance.[116]

Mauermann had obviously expected opposition and had been campaigning for annexation by linking health issues to the city's economic development. At this point he had already convinced such long-term opponents of annexation as realtor Thurman Barrett to change their minds. Mauermann also received the Chamber of Commerce's endorsement, and won support from suburban residents like Cecil Llewellyn who wrote that "we as citizens of Bexar County want to help our City regain the standing that it has lost to Dallas and Houston" by becoming residents of San Antonio.[117] And the same day the council delayed action on his ordinance, he and Thomas began a publicity campaign for annexation, speaking to the city's Social Workers Association, where Thomas explained that "we cannot have a decent city unless we have a healthful city."[118]

A majority of the council, however, remained opposed to annexation. Mauermann solved that problem by arranging for Charles W. Carroll, a Pennsylvania capitalist who was a San Antonio booster, to speak to the commissioners. With Thomas and members of his Planning Board playing a supporting role, Carroll harangued tax commissioner Alfred Callaghan, the principal opponent of annexation. He asserted that the city had unlimited possibilities for manufacturing, but asked, "Do you think I would ask the president of one of my companies to move his industry to San Antonio when such a lack of interest is shown by so many alleged leaders here?"[119]

Despite Carroll's vehemence, Callaghan remained unconvinced. Commissioner Paul Anderson, however, announced his support for abandoning the tradition of voluntary annexation. Admitting that annexation by administrative fiat "may be filled with political dynamite," he justified his conversion as necessary "for the good of our whole community's health."[120] In doing so he articulated a principle that was slowly attracting attention among San Antonians who were struggling with the tension between their commitment to limited government and their realization that only the government had the potential authority to remedy the massive collapse of essential services. He was in effect admitting that community needs should on occasion trump individual rights for the sake of the whole city. With Anderson's vote Mauermann now had a majority for annexation on the council, and the final ordinances adding twenty square miles of densely settled suburbs passed in October 1944.[121]

As the ordinance wound its way toward final passage Mauermann turned to the challenge of providing those new areas with services. His hopes to extend that system, however, required support from the City Water Board, and that proved impossible to obtain from an institution philosophically committed to traditional voluntarism.

The City Water Board was a privately run city service. In 1925 voters had approved the creation of a small, self-perpetuating governing board with money from revenue bonds to maintain and expand the water system. The board's members, though, believed that their fiduciary responsibility to the owners of those revenue bonds trumped the need to keep pace with the city's growth by providing service to new customers. It therefore adopted rules that severely restricted its ability to expand water service. Rather than using all the revenue bond money for improvements, which had been the intention of Mayor Tobin at the time, the board set aside only 25 percent of that capital to pay for new water mains and connections to homes. But even that limited amount of money was not necessarily available to install new water connections. The board invested it in securities and adopted the rule that the profit from providing new connections had to at least equal the profit from those securities before it would approve a petition for service. Furthermore the petitioner(s) had to agree to pay for the costs of water mains and home connections in their neighborhoods.[122]

While the board's policies conformed admirably to traditional ideas about city services, they presented a major obstacle to solving its health problems. Mauermann needed water to improve sanitation, both in poor neighborhoods, whose residents could not afford to pay for water and sewers, and in recently annexed areas.[123] But the board adamantly refused to change its policies. After contentious debates with the board, the council finally passed an ordinance ordering it to expand water service to the entire city—and the board ignored it.[124] In December 1944 there were about forty thousand homes without water service, but the board had approved only 825 new customers during the year.[125]

The board would remain a major obstacle to health reform until 1955, when its charter expired with the retirement of its revenue bonds. In the meantime Mauermann's concern about health problems was slowly winning broader business support. In July 1945, for example, the Chamber of Commerce announced that San Antonio was "in a splendid position to attract new postwar industry" but conceded that the TB rate "looms forbiddingly on the debit side" and organized a campaign to control the disease. In a symbolic gesture that illustrated growing awareness of the relationship between health problems and development, the Taxpayers' Defense League's Joe Sheldon co-chaired this campaign.[126]

Mauermann, though, had also created some debits of his own with the league. Shortly after he became mayor the league tried to make city manager government a major issue in the 1943 spring elections. He won its enmity by denouncing their proposal and then handily winning the election.[127] Mauermann may also have aggravated his relations with the league over postwar planning. Walter McAllister chaired the Chamber of Commerce's City-County Planning Board, and he and Theo Plummer served on Alex Thomas's Post-War Planning Board. In May 1945 McAllister's board issued a $13.9 million city-county plan for public improvements. But in August Thomas's board submitted a $7.1 million plan to the city council that duplicated most of McAllister's projects while trimming their costs. Thomas's board also eliminated some of McAllister's proposals, including $4 million for sewers. McAllister had listed sewers as a county, not a city project, which the commissioners probably resented as an attempt to undermine their control of a vital city service.

As a result of this dispute, only 4 percent of this bond issue that was supposed to launch a postwar era of improvements went to health problems, specifically garbage collection. Nearly three quarters of the bonds were for major development projects (an interregional highway, street improvements, and airport construction), and the remainder sought to improve tourism (river and parks beautification).[128] Tourism also benefited from the proposed highway. Mauermann, McAllister, Thomas, and others worked with state engineers to plan a new highway system to ensure that "San Antonio's historic face will not be changed, and that most of the winding streets which help create her color will be left intact.... Indeed it was to preserve those winding streets and at the same time clear them of extreme congestion that the plan was completed."[129] Tourism, not residential shopping habits, was beginning to influence policies affecting the downtown's future development.

Voters barely approved the bonds in late September, but the election prompted county politicians Sam Bennett and Robert Uhr to resurrect the Taxpayers' Protective Association with the help of Jake Rubiola, Joseph Frost, and Alfred Callaghan, who ordered his employees to distribute literature about the association to voters.[130] Callaghan had bitterly opposed annexation as an invasion of the "personal rights" of subdivision residents. He believed that the council should immediately divide the newly annexed areas into improvement districts whose residents should tax themselves to pay for services in order to avoid tax increases on all property owners.[131]

Callaghan and the Taxpayers' Protective Association represented the average tax payer's beliefs regarding city services, and their leadership turned those beliefs into a significant political challenge to the Taxpayers' Defense League, which represented major business and civic organizations, for control of San Antonio's development. Since San Antonio was infertile ground for economic or political liberalism, this would be a fight between conservatives over how to perpetuate low taxes and define the role of government in an era of rapid population growth.

Hostilities commenced in the city council in February 1946. During a discussion about possible bond issues, Callaghan reiterated his belief that property owners should pay for their own improvements and declared that "there is no need to bring more people here." Mauermann immediately shot back with a booster retort that "something should be done to bring people here and keep them here."[132]

A few days later the city engineer reported that replacing the entire sewer system and improving the sewage disposal plant had become a "dire necessity," prompting the council to authorize a bond issue in May over Callaghan's objections.[133] The day after the Taxpayers' Protective Association and Callaghan demonstrated the tenaciousness of traditional political beliefs by organizing the defeat of that bond issue, representatives from the Taxpayers' Defense League, the chamber, the Real Estate Board, and the City Planning Board attended a council meeting to discuss the ways to respond to deal with that loss. Mauermann and a majority of the council, with the full support of those representatives, agreed to raise property assessments 20 percent as an emergency measure to provide funds for improvements. They also ordered Callaghan to complete a reassessment of property that would properly fund that increase.[134]

Citing city charter provisions that defined his authority as tax commissioner, Callaghan refused to obey the ordinance and spent the remainder of Mauermann's term blocking any attempts to deal with the effects of population growth on city services.[135] Callaghan and the Taxpayers' Protective Association had in effect won the initial skirmishes over the definitions of low taxes and minimal government.

Taxpayers' Defense League conservatives had few options for dealing with this political deadlock. Having opposed bond issues for so many years, they had no effective way to distinguish their version of frugality from Callaghan's at this point. And they had not yet adjusted their long, fitful campaign for political reform to the realities of massive population growth. Their most recent attempt at reform in 1943 had simply reiterated their standard request for a referendum on council manager government without any effort to relate it to the practical needs of the city.[136] Political reform had the potential to distinguish the league and its allies from Callaghan and the Taxpayers' Protective Association, but they needed to define it as a way to maintain traditional commitments to low taxes and minimal government that simultaneously would solve the city's problems.

Jack White became the first advocate for city manager government to make that attempt. Although not a Taxpayers' Defense League member, he was serving on the City Planning Board when it created the San Antonio Citizens' Committee to promote civic projects in summer 1946. White became the committee's president and quickly discovered that the members were strongly in favor of city manager government. He convinced the committee to survey public opinion about that reform, which he described as necessary because San Antonio's inadequate sewers were costing lives and promoting disease and "the city is losing industries because we have advertised our inadequate sewer disposal and they select some other Texas city as a location."[137]

White also attempted to create a political ticket for the 1947 elections, which represented a major change in the reformers' previous reliance on petitions for a referendum on reform. His colleagues, however, were not yet interested in seeking office to achieve change, and they ignored his foray into practical politics.[138]

Despite Callaghan's meteoric rise to political dominance, the 1947 election did not turn into the sort of triumph he may have expected. The presence of three tickets and twenty-eight candidates contrasted sharply with the 1945 election, which was notable for the absence of any organized opposition to incumbents and the lightest turnout in the city's history.[139] In these circumstances, candidates with the strongest organizations supposedly had a decisive advantage, and Callaghan's Economy Ticket featured Henry Hein, Paul Steffler, and Paul Anderson, all of whom commanded experienced campaign staffs.[140] But the voters, apparently divided over a solution to the city's problems, failed to deliver a decisive mandate to anyone, forcing runoffs in all five races. Callaghan managed a narrow victory over Maury Maverick, but his ticket emerged from the fray with only two of the four commissioner positions. Anderson (perhaps because of his support for annexation) did not even qualify for the runoffs, and Paul Steffler, Callaghan's most important ally and the last surviving member of the old machine, lost to James Knight, a political neophyte on Maury Maverick's Harmony Ticket. C. Ray Davis, another Harmony candidate and no friend of Callaghan, captured the tax commissioner post.[141]

Divided government, bad luck, and worse judgment turned Callaghan's victory into a personal disaster. The state legislature had recently passed an unfunded mandate requiring all Texas cities to give raises to their firemen and policemen that forced the council to increase property assessments to pay for them. C. Ray Davis maneuvered Callaghan into introducing the ordinance and ordered his employees to tell unhappy taxpayers to blame Callaghan, seriously undermining his image as defender of the average home owner.[142] Burned by one radioactive issue, Callaghan blundered into another one when Dr. Dudley Reckie, director of the Board of Health, resigned in high dudgeon because Callaghan refused to increase his budget. That provoked a nasty fight with the Chamber of Commerce and medical community, who inaccurately accused Callaghan of trying to repoliticize the health department.[143]

Callaghan contributed to his woes by inexplicably proposing a bond issue for sewers in early December. East and West side residents who suffered most from the absence of sanitation ensured its passage, but its $6 million price tag made a mockery of his carefully cultivated image as a budget hawk. He then compounded that felony by ordering his campaign workers to turn out a large majority for charter amendment to allow the city to build, own, and operate parking lots (his solution to the problem of downtown traffic congestion). That election in late December closed out a disastrous six months in office with a major embarrassment when his supporters deserted him in droves, causing the proposal to fail.[144]

As Callaghan's reputation imploded, political reformers became better organized and focused. Walter McAllister had become president of the City Planning Board in February 1948, and he used that position to coordinate a campaign for city manager government for the first time. McAllister had two key allies in that effort: Edward Conroy and Jack White. Conroy, an advocate of city manager government since 1940, became director of the board's new Government Research Bureau. McAllister and White founded the Council Manger Association, which replaced the Citizens' Council. Conroy wrote reports which argued that the administration of city services would be more efficient (i.e., less costly) under city manager government. White conducted a citywide recruitment campaign for the Citizens' Association and scheduled public lectures on city manager government.[145]

White's council, probably with McAllister and Conroy's help, sponsored an effort to write a draft charter for city manager government that revealed some stunningly muddled thinking. It divided the city into four geographical districts, each with one councilman, and added three councilmen elected at large. Some members of the drafting committee apparently realized that districts would invite a return to the ward-style politics they abhorred, and they attempted to gerrymander the district boundaries to decrease the influence of minority voters. Other committee members opposed gerrymandering, and the dispute deadlocked efforts to complete a draft.[146]

The reformers were equally muddled about the city elections. Despite their inability to write a draft of a new city charter, they insisted on supporting commissioners Davis and South for reelection because they had publicly endorsed a referendum on city manager government (Hein was also rumored to favor it). That placed the reformers in the awkward position of supporting professional politicians in the belief that they would support a proposal that would destroy their careers. If the commissioners temporarily held the reformers in thrall, Callaghan did not. They detested him, but their loathing was insufficient to overcome their extreme aversion to running for public office. Consequently when Callaghan and all of the commissioners announced their joint campaign for reelection in early February, there was no organized opposition.[147]

While Callaghan's ticket campaigned unopposed for the next two months, the reformers dithered. Enjoying their disarray, Callaghan challenged either McAllister or White to enter the race, but both hastily declined his invitation. Charles Carroll, the Pennsylvania capitalist, then turned his vehemence on White and convinced him to resign as president of the Chamber of Commerce to run for mayor (White neglected to explain how Carroll persuaded him).[148]

White's decision seemed quixotic at best. Barely five weeks remained before the election and he had no platform, no campaign organization, and no money—and Carroll left town for a vacation. White added to his woes by refusing to campaign for city manager government despite having become one of its leading advocates.[149]

By mid-April White had managed to assemble a semblance of a campaign staff and issue a platform promising low taxes, efficient government, and a fair reassessment of property values. Both sides in the battle between competing versions of conservative government endorsed the first two bromides, but that last idea had become a crucial belief among reformers who believed that a long overdue reassessment of property would increase city revenues for public improvements while simultaneously justifying a reduction in the tax rate.[150]

Although White's candidacy did not impress Callaghan or local reporters, it did have an impact on the voters. On May 8 White defeated him by thirty thousand votes, the largest victory margin in the history of local elections. Callaghan had been whistling past the graveyard of his own ambitions after his disastrous first six months in office, and the vote for White was an "anyone but Callaghan" rejection of his personal leadership.[151]

White's victory secured a political beachhead in city government for an emerging booster coalition of business and professional people who had finally decided that government needed to help solve the problems of population growth. Their growing activism heralded the return of the North Side as a political force in local politics. As in the days of Clinton Brown's coalition, a majority of boosters lived in a northern band of the city that stretched from Woodlawn Lake on the west side eastward through the neighborhoods of Laurel Heights and Monte Vista to Broadway. But North Side now also meant suburbs such as Olmos Park and Terrell Hills, both of which contained significant numbers of boosters who could not vote in city elections, but who belonged to various business associations and civic boards with headquarters in the city that would support this new coalition.[152]

Like boosters in practically every American city after 1945, these San Antonians wanted to deal with downtown congestion, urban blight, and other impediments to continuing growth. Arthur Biard, a major realtor, defined their approach to urban development in February 1946 at a council meeting considering a zoning change. Echoing former commissioner Anderson, he argued for rezoning a neighborhood close to the downtown from residential to industrial use because such a change "was important to the growth and progress of the city as a whole."[153]

Biard's argument raises the important question of how he knew that rezoning this particular neighborhood would contribute to the development of the city as a whole. This was a critical issue because the emerging booster coalition would eventually base their entire agenda for San Antonio's development on the belief that some projects benefited the whole city while others did not. Making that distinction apparently evolved from the participation of key businessmen boosters in various planning activities that in effect educated them to become boosters. Biard referred to his service on a Chamber of Commerce urban planning committee in the rezoning hearing, and he was also a member of the Postwar Planning Committee, as were McAllister, Alex Thomas, and others. That committee's plan for postwar development included an interregional highway to relieve downtown congestion and create new space for industrial expansion. Biard and other boosters who participated in such planning activities would have naturally assumed that their work defined projects that benefited the city as a whole.

These nascent boosters, ignoring the actual history of commission government, also assumed that the commissioners would thwart their agenda and therefore rejected the idea of cooperating with professional politicians. From their perspective, as McAllister noted, professional politicians only spent money "on individual projects instead of for the good of the whole city."[154] Their dim view of professional politicians had contributed to the collapse of the Citizens' League in the 1930s and persisted through the 1940s as they refused to run for office and condemned colleagues (like Maverick and Mauermann) who did. Such a firm commitment to principle, however, suffered from a crucial flaw: the reformers had to gain control of the existing political system to change it. Even petitioning for a referendum on council manager government (which was their favorite tactic) could only succeed if they created an organization that could win the referendum. And until the late 1940s no such organization existed.

Jack White's victory over Callaghan was a major breakthrough, but it did not mean the inevitable triumph of political reform. When White created a Peoples Charter Committee in July 1949, its members continued to fight among themselves over the still vexing problem of minority representation in a new government. In the meantime politicians and businessmen opposed to reform founded the Charter Revision Committee to offer counterproposals. The commissioners compounded the chaos by passing an ordinance that indiscriminately included all the proposals from both committees without identifying which committee had written which proposal. Understandably confused by all the machinations, voters rejected all the proposals in May 1950.[155]

While pondering the reasons for their defeat the reformers dealt more successfully with another major issue. In February 1950 the San Antonio Housing Authority began working on an application to the federal government for funds to construct more public housing under provisions of the Housing Act of 1949.[156] This law would provide federal grants to civic leaders across the nation who believed that they could revitalize their downtowns by eliminating inner-city slums and blighted neighborhoods.

Conservative reformers intensely disliked public housing in principle and distrusted the housing authority board as a haven for liberals like William Sinkin, its president. They opposed additional public housing projects, but they also recognized the 1949 act's potential for supporting urban redevelopment in San Antonio. As McAllister pointed out, "we'd be saps not to take the money if it were made available."[157]

Mayor White was sympathetic to the reformers' concerns and created the Slum Clearance and Urban Redevelopment Committee in June 1950 to assume control of the city's applications for grants. He appointed Albert Steves III as chair, and key members included Paul Adams, Joe Sheldon, Alex Thomas, and W. W. McAllister.[158] Under Steves's leadership the committee quickly restricted the housing authority's hopes for a major increase in public housing and convinced the city council to authorize a master plan for the city that would give reformers control of federal funding which would help keep local taxes low at a time when the city needed substantial amounts of money for redevelopment.[159]

Despite their success in gaining control of federal redevelopment funding, conservative reformers had not yet translated their dominance of the city's planning processes into real political power because they did not control the city council. Their naïve faith in the commissioners' support for reform had turned their latest attempt at charter reform into a fiasco, but the 1951 elections would give them an opportunity to benefit from that tutorial in the art of politics.

Opponents as well as proponents of reform had apparently recognized that a high turnout for the May 1950 charter election indicated considerable voter interest in city manager government. The commissioners responded to that interest in various ways. James Knight decided not to seek reelection as street commissioner, but his colleagues recruited John Zeller, a well-known realtor who showed a lukewarm interest in reform, to head their ticket. They also created another complicated charter ballot that required voters to decide whether to approve changing the charter and then to select members for a fifteen member charter revision committee.[160]

Reformers entered the campaign season better prepared than they ever had been to deal with artful political ploys because of the efforts of two key leaders. Jack White personally persuaded four businessmen, including Sam Bell Steves, to run as a complete ticket against his erstwhile colleagues. He also recruited Alex Thomas to serve as his campaign chair and Robert Sawtelle, a lawyer with considerable experience in local politics, to be his campaign manager. McAllister had in the meantime reorganized the Council Manager Association with the help of Charles Carroll and Thomas and proposed a complete slate of fifteen candidates for the charter revision committee, less than a week after the commissioners announced the charter election. McAllister's slate included two Mexican American businessmen and three women who were former presidents of the Federation of Women's Clubs and the San Antonio PTA. Like White, McAllister acknowledged the need for practical politics in announcing that all of his candidates would actively campaign for votes.[161]

The commissioners ran highly personalized campaigns that undermined effective cooperation between their staffs and Zeller, a neophyte campaigner, did not prove to be an inspired choice to lead their ticket. White, on the other hand, ran an aggressive, old-fashioned political campaign. The manager of the Texas Tiny Frocks company, for instance, wrote to tell White that "I . . . have been talking to all of the 133 employees in my factory to vote for you." J. M. Frost and several other individuals worked precincts across the city to turn out voters for him.[162]

Voters rewarded White's hard work with a sweeping, decisive victory. Indeed the results mirrored the victory margins of the old commissioner "machine" in its heyday, except that in this case four neophytes defeated four professional politicians (and a smattering of independent candidates). White won 60 percent of the vote for mayor and his colleagues posted even larger margins in all but the race for police and fire commissioner. Voters also granted permission for charter reform and elected McAllister's entire slate.[163]

With a referendum on a new charter set for October, the reformers still had two important, but not insurmountable obstacles to overcome. Their internal dispute over minority representation in a council manager government continued within the new Charter Revision Committee. Alex Thomas, who had "specialized in keeping all manager elements together," apparently negotiated a private agreement between conservatives and liberals to finally resolve that dispute in the late summer. Sam Bell Steves hinted at that bargain when he commented that "minorities as well as majorities can be helped without favoritism" by council manger government.[164] Whatever its details, that agreement allowed the committee to complete its work by September, in time for an October referendum on its work.

The Taxpayers' Protective Association created the other obstacle to reform by announcing its opposition to city manager government.[165] With the stage set for a direct confrontation between competing versions of conservative government, White assumed the role of chief advocate for city manager government by presenting an explanation and defense of reform to the voters in a series of radio speeches. He did not, however, rely on rhetorical persuasion alone. Having built his own organization in his mayoral campaigns, he turned to Alex Thomas and Robert Sawtelle once again to organize voter turnout. His personal prestige was also an important asset with such men as Dan Genard, a tire dealer, who wrote White that he did not think there was any need for reform, but "I pledge myself and my Westside organization to support" the cause of reform. Genard also promised to lobby the Downtown Improvement Association on his behalf.[166]

White's leadership and political resources ensured the Taxpayers' Protective Association's defeat. Sixty-five percent of the voters in a modest turnout approved the new charter, with victory margins of nine to one on the North Side and in Highland Park (a stronghold of the Citizens' League).

All that remained before the new government assumed office in January 1952 was an agenda for inexpensive redevelopment, and Steves's Redevelopment Committee provided that when it submitted the new master plan to the city council in December. The plan recommended nineteen projects, including relocating city hall, the county courthouse, and the city health department to a new civic center east of the Alamo; moving all black San Antonians into a single East Side neighborhood (an idea that did raise some eyebrows); creating new industrial areas; improving recreation facilities;

and eliminating several black and Mexican American slum areas. In a bow to the Conservation Society, the plan also recommended river beautification, preservation of the old King William German neighborhood, and similar projects.[167]

All this looked potentially expensive, but the boosters expected the federal government to bear most of the cost. Indeed the 1949 Housing Act required cities to prepare such plans in order to apply for federal funds. By relying on federal subsidies for their redevelopment projects the boosters expected to preserve their traditional commitment to low taxes.

But something fundamental died with their triumph. Voluntary participation in urban services ended (with the exception of the City Water Board, whose lease on life would end in 1955), and planning, a concept alien to the entire history of San Antonio's development, became a basic government function. The council could now use federal guidelines to declare whole neighborhoods blighted and subject to redevelopment. It could also plan and contract for the installation of services like streets (paving "skips" finally ended), sewers, and (eventually) water, and levy liens on property to require owners to pay the taxes for those services.[168]

By greatly expanding the authority of government in the interests of their conservative approach to urban development the reformers had wrought a revolution in local public affairs. But they had not yet solved the challenge that had undermined the Citizens' League in 1935: how to create a political system that could replace professional politicians with well-organized amateurs who could consistently win elections—and successfully run a government. Their revolution would be incomplete without an answer to that challenge.

EIGHT

The Political Economy of Military City

1951–1971

San Antonio's victorious reformers faced two unexpected challenges in the transition to city manager government in 1951: Jack White and Charles A. Harrell. White, a major advocate for reform, did not understand the reformers' expectations for city manager government; Harrell, the first city manager, did not understand San Antonio. Their misunderstandings would unintentionally provoke the creation of the Good Government League, a political regime dedicated to governing without politicians.

White's political leadership had been crucial to the campaign for city manager government. He had crushed Alfred Callaghan in the 1949 mayoral election and had then organized his supporters to defeat the remaining boss commissioners in 1951, clearing the way for a referendum on a new charter. Although he had become a local hero among reformers, he had also become a skillful politician accustomed to exercising power. His council colleagues, on the other hand, were political neophytes who lacked practical experience in governing. Charles Harrell was an experienced and widely respected city manager. In the 1920s he had worked in city planning in Cincinnati and had served as its manager before moving on to manage several other cities. When White and his colleagues recruited him in 1951 he had been the city manager for Norfolk, Virginia, since 1946. The Norfolk city council passed a resolution of fulsome praise commending Harrell's "honesty and character... sound judgment [and] foresight and skillful planning."[1] San Antonio's reformers had no practical knowledge of how city manager government actually worked, but they had hired an expert who knew how to do his job and had no qualms about exercising authority.

Reformers may not have had a good grasp of the details of city manager government, but they did believe that it was efficient; it eliminated politics from governing; and it enabled elected officials to concentrate on policies and projects that benefited the entire city. White and Harrell, in their separate ways, would educate the reformers about the need to clarify the precise meanings of those benefits.

Harrell began work in an extremely volatile political environment. Disagreements among councilmembers erupted early in 1952 and persisted into late spring 1953. Competing ideas about Harrell's authority and his proposals combined with a dispute over annexing suburbs to create bitter divisions among councilmembers. For his part, Harrell assumed that the reformers approved of his approach to managing a city—they had, after all, hired him.

San Antonio did not lack for serious problems requiring attention, and Harrell adopted an aggressive approach to solving them. Believing that he needed more resources to solve those problems, he launched a vigorous hiring campaign that added nearly six hundred employees to the tax rolls in a year. He also asked his department heads to submit budget estimates "outlining what is really needed for a respectable city operation." He combined those estimates into a proposal for the largest budget in the city's history, along with a request for a twenty-five-cent increase in the tax rate.[2]

Harrell also believed in preserving the city's tax base through aggressive annexation. The new city charter authorized the council to annex any unincorporated area by a majority vote. In March 1952 he supported a proposal to annex 120 square miles of suburban development and provided guidelines to councilmembers to defend their decision.[3]

The annexation proposal transformed White's political fortunes. Since the council elected the mayor under the new form of government, he had no independent power to support his assumption that council-manager government needed a strong mayor. Frustrated by his colleagues' pointed rebuttals of his efforts to control Harrell and key appointments, White resigned as mayor in late February. The council elected Sam Bell Steves to succeed him.[4] But the annexation proposal provoked a massive political crisis that threatened to undermine council-manager government. Former city attorney Jack Davis organized a recall petition against the five councilmembers who were Harrell's supporters. Davis attacked the new government directly, saying, "It's a theory based on the arrogant and false premise that the people are too dumb and ignorant to know or care about what is best for them."[5]

The recall petition gained momentum when Al Jergins and Morris Kallison, wealthy businessmen who lived in the area the council wanted to annex, announced that they would finance the effort. White in the meantime continued his attacks on Harrell, finally provoking councilman Harold Keller to accuse him of wanting to "get back to the old political haphazard way of conducting city affairs."[6] The council tried to stop the recall movement by reducing the annexed area to eighty square miles in September, when they finally passed the formal annexation ordinance, but that did nothing to quell the political crisis. White had by then joined the recall movement, prompting Steves to call him a "puppet" who had joined "with Morris Kallison and with all the others who have fought tooth and nail against council-manager government."[7]

Technical problems in signing petitions undermined the recall movement in December, prompting Kallison to create the San Antonians, a political ticket that would oppose the Citizens' Committee in the April 1953 elections. Kallison suggested that the San Antonians would offer voters an opportunity to return to the commissioner system "if they want it."[8]

Alex Thomas, who chaired the committee's reelection campaign, had considerable trouble convincing the incumbents to agree to another term. Harrell did not help Thomas's efforts when he presented a summary of his work for the past year in January, pointing to his budget and annexation as his proudest accomplishments. In doing so, Harrell revealed a remarkable indifference to the major controversies that those accomplishments had aroused. His management of the city in his first year indicated that he defined government efficiency as having the staff and money to provide adequate services to a growing city. Local reformers, however, defined efficiency as small staffs and small budgets, reflecting the century-old belief in frugality as the handmaiden of good government. John Hope, president of the Taxpayers' League, announced its opposition to Harrell's proposed tax increase for 1953, saying he looked forward to cutting the city budget and leaving the tax rate unchanged.[9] Since the league was a major advocate for council-manager government, and Walter McAllister, the architect of the new charter, served on the league's board of directors, this was not good news for Harrell.

Harrell had made himself and his policies the central issues of the spring elections. When the San Antonians' ticket won complete control of the new council, he and his department heads resigned.[10] Al Jergins and Morris Kallison emerged as the new powers in local politics, with White as their principal ally on the new council.

Reinstated as mayor by the new council, White wasted little time implementing his agenda, which included repealing the 1952 annexation ordinance, reducing the city bureaucracy, cutting the budget, and eviscerating the city manager's authority over appointments. The new city manager, Ralph Winton, prepared a major purge of city employees in late July, and the council passed a de-annexation ordinance in mid-August to advance White's agenda.[11] The mayor also introduced secret meetings in private homes or hotel rooms where he, the councilmembers, and Winton discussed city business. Kallison and Jergins attended these meetings to ensure that their ideas about policies and appointments received a proper hearing. This was obviously not the model the supporters of council-manager government had in mind when they wrote the 1952 charter.

All was not well among the victors, however. Winton had been Jergins's, not White's, choice for manager, which he resented as an imposition on his mayoral authority. He would retaliate for that slight by eventually barring both Kallison and Jergins from the private meetings in August 1953. At the same time, the council refused to approve Kallison's appointees for city jobs.[12] Those acts ruptured the San Antonians' coalition, threatening their ability to govern.

In October the Municipal Planning Committee met with the council to explain its proposal for a $15 million bond issue for municipal improvements. White offered only tepid support, saying, "It is not a question of what the city needs, but how much the people want and will go for." The mayor then decided to resurrect the politics of distribution, in which various groups representing neighborhoods around the city jockeyed for their pieces of the bond projects.[13] That violated the reformers' belief that council-manager government did not focus on neighborhood needs.

White withdrew from the negotiations over bond projects when he suffered a stroke in November, but the battle over their distribution only became more intense in his absence.[14] In the meantime Mary Green, president of the Conservation Society, created yet another controversy. The council had rejected her request for a public referendum on the question of constructing an underground parking garage beneath Travis Park, a project the council had attempted to conceal from public scrutiny. The society's members took a dim view of any attempt to undermine San Antonio's historic places. At the end of October the society announced a recall petition directed against all nine councilmembers. That was only the beginning of what turned into a four-year battle that eventually involved the Texas Supreme Court before the society prevailed.[15]

As the new year began, the form and substance of council-manager government was dissolving before its supporters' eyes. White was still recovering from his stroke and would eventually resign as mayor, allowing Jergins and Kallison to resume their participation in the council's private meetings on January 1, 1954. Their presence only added to the council's woes. Both men criticized its reassessment of property values, which the council intended to use to reduce the tax rate, and the impending bond issue, which was designed to start a long-delayed process of dealing with the city's infrastructure problems. Two-thirds of the $18 million bond issue was for highway construction, with the remaining money divided among sewage, street, and flood control projects. Despite the urgency of the city's needs, the council did not have the money to underwrite the campaign for the bond election that was scheduled for January 25. A suggestion that someone needed to finance the election apparently left Jergins and Kallison speechless because they made no offer to help.[16]

By the end of the meeting the men who had created the San Antonians political ticket undermined their minions' plans to improve the city. The Taxpayers' League helped by announcing its opposition. Opposing factions were now uniting to attack their own creations. Not surprisingly, voters rejected the entire bond issue.[17]

City Manager Ralph Winton contributed to the growing political dysfunction with public attacks on his critics, and by debating John Hoyo on the bond issue. Shortly thereafter he and the council parted ways over his friendship with Jergins and his refusal to make several appointments the council favored.[18] As with Harrell, the proper role (and behavior) of the manager continued to befuddle reformers who thought they had eliminated politics—and personalities—from government.

By fall 1954 the council was collapsing. Although it had managed to win approval for $12 million in highway bonds (thereby recovering the city's eligibility for $60 million in state and federal subsidies), its opponents had begun a new recall petition. Several councilmembers resigned; the council fired Ralph Winton, replacing him with an acting manager who had no background for the job; and the Citizens' Committee that had originally led the reform campaign had revived in preparation for the 1955 spring election.[19]

By this point there was broad agreement among San Antonio's leading citizens that something had to be done to save council-manager government. Tom Powell, president of the Chamber of Commerce, called a meeting at the Plaza Hotel on December 7. Of the roughly sixty people who attended, thirty-six were presidents of major civic organizations that represented the civic, religious, business, and professional elite who lived overwhelmingly on the city's North Side.

Powell apparently came prepared with a proposal to, as it were, reform the reform because the group quickly created the Good Government League, whose very name was a rebuke of the events of the past three years. The GGL was to create "stability and integrity in city government" by devoting itself to "community progress with efficient nonpartisan administration, and end to factionalism, sectionalism, patronage politics, and maneuvering for special selfish interests."[20]

Having condemned the historical practice of American urban politics, this group clearly had no interest in creating a political machine. But, ironically, that is what they did to solve the problem of operating a city government with amateur rather than professional politicians. Amateurs could not be expected to understand the complexities of policies for urban development, but the behavior of Harrell and Winton had taught the reformers that councilmembers should not rely on city managers to educate them. Jack White had taught the reformers that normal political behavior could in fact be injected into council-manager government even when councilmembers were elected in at-large elections rather than by wards. The GGL needed a way to develop policies that the council could adopt, and the city manager would dutifully implement.

Solving these problems required control over the process of governing. To achieve that goal, the GGL privatized local government by creating a board of directors who would develop public policies. By virtue of their race, occupations, educations, places of residence and outlook on life, the GGL's members were a special interest group that reflected one—important—aspect of urban life. Their shared vision of how to govern gave them common ground for determining those policies.

Residents of San Antonio who did not share that vision, who lived in other areas of the city, who came from different ethnic or racial, occupational, and educational backgrounds had their own ideas about development, but the

GGL ignored their ideas. Governing by balancing competing needs and ideas was anathema to the GGL. Its members believed in governing for the "city as a whole."

Excluding those voices was therefore essential. To achieve that goal, the GGL created a nominating committee that worked in secret prior to elections to select candidates for the council as a united slate. The committee first chose a mayoral candidate—even though the council was supposed to elect the mayor after an election. That candidate then had a veto over any one being considered for nomination. In selecting candidates, the committee sought people who had no interest in a political career, who had enough income to serve with virtually no pay, who had a record of civic engagement, and who believed in governing for the "city as a whole."[21]

Another GGL committee financed its slate of candidates, which made competing against them extremely difficult. Individuals who wanted to serve without the GGL's blessing were normally not financially capable of waging a citywide campaign and they also lacked the public recognition that attached to those running on a common ticket. The election results convey the best evidence of the GGL machine's effectiveness. Between 1955 and 1971 the GGL won 95 percent of the elections for city council, a record even Chicago's boss Richard J. Daley could not match.[22]

Having solved the problem of relying on amateurs to serve on the council, the GGL swept the city elections in spring 1955, except for Henry B. Gonzalez, a well-established Mexican American with high name recognition. Now all it needed to do was govern.

The near meltdown of council-manager government had deflected attention from the city's serious infrastructure problems. Although growth slowed somewhat in the 1950s, the decade ended with a more than respectable 44 percent increase in population. Subdivisions continued to proliferate on the North Side and near the military bases on the South Side as well as Randolph Air Force Base northeast of town. Providing services to all those subdivisions was a major challenge. In addition, the city's reputation was not faring well in the national press. *Look* magazine published an extremely unflattering article in 1951 excoriating the city for its slum conditions; it was not the sort of publicity that local boosters wanted circulating in the national press.[23]

Infrastructure improvements therefore became the GGL's primary concern. There was, however, one major constraint. For the GGL, frugality was the fundamental virtue in governing the city. Property taxes provided most of the funds for services, but the GGL's supporters expected low assessments and low rates, which in turn produced small budgets.[24] Bond issues could supplement the budget, but they had to be infrequent and carefully managed. State and federal assistance would also become a source for some additional funding, especially with the passage of the Housing Act of 1949 and the Highway Act of 1956, but local government bore most of the responsibility for routine infrastructure development during the GGL's reign.

Ironically the GGL's approach to infrastructure improvements therefore echoed Jack White's comment in 1953: "It is not a question of what the city needs, but how much the people want and will go for." The caveat to White's comment, though, is that the GGL, not the people, would define need in order to contain costs.

The GGL differed from previous reform and booster movements that had also preached frugality and the good of the whole city in its approach to governing. Previously reformers had allied themselves with professional politicians to strengthen their appeal to voters. Now the city's civic and economic leaders struck out on their own, intent on eliminating professional politicians. And they managed to do so for sixteen years, time enough to implement a rather extensive list of infrastructure improvements. By 1967 Mayor Walter McAllister could list improvements to 1,800 miles of streets; 1,681 miles of new sewer lines; 500 miles of new water lines and four new pumping stations; 121 miles of new storm drainage channels; and a new civic center under construction among the GGL's achievements.[25]

All those miles of improvements did make a significant contribution to the city's once disgraceful health issues. Local doctors had worked to alleviate the absurdly high death rates for tuberculosis and infant diarrhea on the West Side since the 1930s; improved employment opportunities during World War II and at the bases after 1945 had given many West Side residents access to better housing; and the introduction of antibiotics in the early 1950s had improved health care as well. But in 1950 indoor plumbing was available to only 48 percent of Mexican Americans as opposed to 84 percent of whites. After a convoluted struggle with the city's water board, the GGL managed to install enough sewer and water lines to provide indoor plumbing to 84 percent of West Side residents by 1960, and 97 percent by 1970. In the late 1960s infant diarrhea mortality among Mexican Americans still remained higher than among whites, but their overall health had greatly improved.[26]

This impressive list of accomplishments was essential to the city's efforts to rectify the massive infrastructure woes of the 1940s. But it was not sufficient to create an attractive city for investors and new residents. In fact, San Antonio's growth rate plummeted in the 1960s to 11 percent, down from 44 percent in the 1950s. Dallas also experienced a decline, but managed a 24 percent increase; Houston did even better with 31 percent. Neither city would rank high for physical attractiveness in a national competition, but the sun was not shinning as brightly on San Antonio as on its rivals in the emerging Sunbelt.

The massive migration of Americans into the Sunbelt after 1945 was the most obvious consequence of World War II's profound effects on the nation's economy. The war made the federal government a major, if not the major, influence in the economy, primarily—although not exclusively—due to national defense requirements. Military needs spurred new kinds of manufacturing products that scientists and inventors developed in universities and specialized research centers. President Dwight Eisenhower coined the term "military-industrial complex" to describe the economic transformation that would affect other, seemingly unrelated "industries" such as higher education and medicine. Southern governors, exploiting their region's long cultural affinity with the military, would seek to direct as much of this economic transformation as possible to their states with varying degrees of success.[27]

In Texas, Dallas and Houston were better prepared than San Antonio to benefit from the new economy. Both now had the ability to meet the needs of that economy because their business leaders had made decisions during the war that vastly expanded their manufacturing capabilities. Instead of emulating them, San Antonio's Chamber of Commerce had chosen to ignore the opportunity to acquire aircraft manufacturing plants. Although making the city more physically attractive remained a standard strategy by the 1950s, the economy remained rooted in wholesaling, tourism, and the military bases. As a result, San Antonio's boosters had no history of successful economic diversification from which to draw lessons in adapting to economic changes after 1945.

World War II had of course transformed the military into San Antonio's most important economic asset. It was, however, an asset that inhibited rather than stimulated economic diversification because the bases did not need technological innovations from San Antonians, they only needed services. Specifically, they needed civilian employees and contractors.

The bases became the city's most important employers. In 1940 they employed only 9 percent of San Antonio's workers; by 1950 that figure had grown to 20 percent, and ten years later military payrolls for civilians and non-civilians accounted for 46 percent of all local wages and salaries.

Military contracts were even more important. In 1954, admittedly a boom year for base construction, 56 percent of all construction under way in the city occurred on the bases. Purchasing contracts for supplies, though, had perhaps the greatest impact on the economy. In 1960 the San Antonio Air Material Area (SAAMA) at Kelly Air Force Base had become the largest "industry" in the entire Southwest, awarding more than $10 million that year in contracts to local businessmen for supplies. And that was just one base. By 1967 the combined flow of federal money exceeded $1 billion from wages, salaries, and construction and purchasing contracts. An estimated 52,342 San Antonians who were not employed at the bases owed their livelihoods to them, as did more than nine hundred retail business.[28]

The military had become San Antonio's overwhelmingly dominant "industry." For all of its benefits for the city, this was not good news for anyone interested in diversifying the economy. A large group of businessmen who thrived on government contracts had no need to support diversification. Their disinterest weakened the Chamber of Commerce as an organization by undermining support for initiatives to bring new industries to town. As in other southern cities that were too dependent on the military, San Antonio would discover that military bases, as opposed to defense-related factories, impeded industrial development.[29]

A few San Antonians did understand that World War II had created opportunities for economic development, but they usually had a limited understanding of what the city needed to do to benefit from them. Laurence Wingerter, chair of the chamber's Industrial Development Committee, observed hopefully in December 1948 that "technological and scientific developments during the war have opened up brand new industrial applications which old established concerns desire to put into production in a new location." He believed that San Antonio could attract industries by simply providing them with space: "We find it necessary to provide new construction to meet the needs of our industrial expansion."[30]

Subsequent committee chairs refined Wingerter's idea by creating industrial parks on the east and northeast sides of town.[31] That raised the possibility that firms with similar interests could cluster together, but this focus on the space needs of new industries ignored the basic issue of how to attract them in the first place.

Wingerter and his successors did not understand that firms in high-tech defense industries needed more than a new building; they also needed skilled workers, access to university graduate programs in engineering and science, a critical mass of similar firms conveniently close to them, and an urban environment that appealed to the lifestyles of their skilled, well-paid employees. In 1948 none of those additional locational requirements existed in San Antonio.

In addition to that problem, the chamber did not have an effective strategy for recruiting high technology manufacturing. Its Industrial Development Committee did not have a systematic approach to the task of identifying new industries to recruit. Rather than adopting a proactive approach to recruitment, the chamber asked individual businessmen to cultivate prospects through their own networks. If they identified a prospect, they would contact the chamber with the information so that it could then attempt to offer to assist the prospect. Businessmen, however, had no connections to high-tech firms, which meant the chamber was asking its members to replicate already existing businesses in San Antonio. Chamber vice president Harry Kruz, for instance, traveled to Saint Louis in 1953 to talk with several prospects in the needlework industry, which was already well represented in San Antonio.[32]

Retired Maj. Gen. Clements McMullen, who became chair of the Industrial Development Committee in 1954, and his vice chair Dr. Harold Vagtborg, tried to improve recruiting by reorganizing the committee. They created several subcommittees that included one devoted to research and another to facilities.[33]

As president of Southwest Research Institute, Vagtborg was uniquely qualified to deal with the issues of high-tech firms. In 1941 oilman Tom Slick had founded the Foundation for Applied Research (which became the Southwest Foundation for Biomedical Research) and the Southwest Research Institute to conduct scientific and industrial research for industry and government.[34] Slick used his private fortune to give San Antonio the capacity to conduct innovative research, but this was a gift that needed time and additional effort from likeminded people to succeed. Vagtborg was one of those people. He had developed the Southwest Research Institute into a successful institution whose talented engineers had won grants totaling $4.5 million in 1956, primarily to work on defense projects.[35]

As committee vice chair, Vagtborg attempted to expand the potential of Slick's research centers to promote economic diversification by tapping into that federal largesse. San Antonio did not, however, have a research university, which would have been a valuable asset to his plans. He decided to create a research park that could attract high-tech companies who would hire scientists and engineers, in effect creating his own cluster of talent tuned to the needs of the new national economy. In 1956 Vagtborg announced plans to build a $50 million "Science City" on the far northwest side of town on Highway 13 (later known as Loop 410). He moved the Southwest Research Institute and the Southwest Foundation for Research and Education to that location to have enough land to create a magnet attracting national companies engaged in high-tech electronics research and manufacturing. Science City would have forty research laboratories and 1,600 residences for employees to entice them to town. To promote his idea, Vagtborg sent a presentation to 250 companies, three of which were already negotiating with him to move to San Antonio.[36]

Vagtborg's ideas for Science City reflected the kind of entrepreneurial daring that San Antonio sorely lacked. But the city also did not have the kinds of amenities that skilled workers in technology intensive industries desired in choosing where to live. In the absence of those amenities and other businessmen who understood the significance of his ideas, Vagtborg could not accomplish his goal.

He may have inspired General McMullen to propose his own idea for a more aggressive approach to diversification. Believing that San Antonio needed an attractive package of enticements to offer prospects, he proposed an industrial foundation within the chamber, an idea first broached by the Finance Subcommittee in July 1954.[37] A year later he recommended raising a $500,000 fund for this foundation to support construction of buildings and assist new manufacturers with their initial production issues. Interestingly he did not propose tax incentives, which probably would have raised the ire of the Taxpayers' Association. At this point, however, the chamber had never raised $500,000 for any project, which made McMullen's idea moot for the next eleven years.[38]

With his more ambitious idea in limbo, McMullen reverted to what he knew best. Prior to his retirement he had been commander of the San Antonio Air Material Area at Kelly, which made him intimately familiar with businessmen who contracted with the base for its supplies. In January 1956 he asked them to distribute a new mailer to their suppliers. He reasoned that those businessmen "have more effective leverage" with such firms, increasing the chances that they would be interested in San Antonio as a site for a new plant or branch office. In other words, he was redirecting the Industrial Development Committee to reinforce the existing array of local businesses.[39]

This return to normalcy did bear some fruit. In 1962 Walter Beran, chair of the chamber's Industrial Development Committee, noted that "more San Antonio firms are *beginning* to capitalize on the millions of dollars in contract work let annually by the San Antonio Air Material Area at Kelly AFB." Apparently those firms had been slow learners since the air material area had been letting those contracts since the 1940s. Shortly thereafter the chamber confirmed Beran's impression with an announcement that fourteen "new industries have moved to take advantage of government contract opportunities." The statement advertised the air material area as "the largest industrial enterprise in San Antonio and indeed in the entire Southwest. Its procurement activities run into hundreds of millions of dollars."[40]

Describing the air material area as the "largest industrial enterprise" in the city revealed an interesting vagueness in the boosters' thinking about manufacturing. None of the bases manufactured the products their suppliers provided; they represented a large market for food, clerical and other supplies, and services. Firms that made those products were moving to town, reinforcing both the military's dominance in the economy and the lack of manufacturing diversity. That vagueness affected the chamber's thinking when it finally created the Industrial Foundation in 1965. All the money that it raised for the foundation went to an unsuccessful effort to locate the headquarters of the Army and Air Force Exchange Services in San Antonio.[41] For these boosters, industrial development did not mean diversification despite their rhetoric; it meant reinforcing existing, generally small, low-wage enterprises that reinforced the city's overdependence on the military.

Efforts to expand manufacturing therefore yielded unimpressive results. In 1947 industrial employment totaled 19,000 workers; in 1970 the total stood at 35,300, for an average annual increase of 708 employees over twenty-three years. Dallas, by comparison, added 7,000 manufacturing jobs every year during the 1960s, an achievement made possible by its transformation into an aircraft manufacturing center in the early 1940s.[42]

Mishandling the Industrial Foundation reflected a fundamental flaw in the chamber's approach to urban development. Dallas and Houston were led by core groups of businessmen who spent decades building economic, social, and political relationships that gave them resources for seizing opportunities when national or regional economic changes created them. They were not amateurs in the craft of city-building. San Antonio lacked such a core group, and its chamber was not organized to assume the primary role in development. Like all such organizations, it depended on volunteers to serve as directors, committee chairs, and presidents. Everyone served for only a year, which prevented individuals from developing expertise and the ability to pursue long-term projects to completion. However competent they might be as businessmen, they were amateurs at the business of development.

That had, however, begun to change as a result of a long campaign to acquire a medical center. Lessons from that experience would create support for the idea of making longer term commitments to projects that could promote growth.[43] San Antonio's challenging history with infectious diseases became a test of that approach. During World War II the University of Texas Regents invited proposals to establish a new medical school. For a medical community that was desperately short of trained physicians, nurses, hospitals to cope with the health crisis, the prospect of convincing the regents to choose San Antonio for the school seemed a heaven-sent opportunity.

Accordingly, a large delegation of doctors, reformers, and city, county, and state officials arranged a presentation to the regents in September 1944. Speaking for the group, Dr. Conn L. Milburn argued that the "abundance of clinical material and indigent people with frequent need of medical care" combined with the fact that "there is more of that class in San Antonio than any other city in the state" made it the obvious location for a new medical school.[44] Whatever the regents may have thought of Milburn's blunt, and truthful, presentation, choosing the medical school's location was not a matter of need; it was a political issue. The legislature had to authorize the center, which meant state representatives from rival cities would have a role in the decision.

After misjudging the political environment in the state capital by introducing a legislative resolution to move the Galveston medical school to San Antonio—which oddly enough aroused the ire of not only Galveston's representatives but also Dallas's, the Chamber of Commerce decided to organize a medical foundation to lead the campaign for a new medical branch.

In creating the San Antonio Medical Foundation, the chamber broke at least four major traditions. Ad hoc committees with specific responsibilities for dealing with a short-term problem or opportunity were common enough; committee members had some expertise or knowledge about the issue; these committees worked within and for the chamber; and they dissolved once they made a report. Ignoring those traditions, the chamber used Houston's Medical Foundation as a model. It established the foundation in 1947 as an independent nonprofit organization without a single physician on its board of directors.

The appointment of prominent community leaders to the first board indicated that chamber members who had an interest in a broad approach to the role of medicine in San Antonio's development had shaped the discussion and decisions about the foundation. Its charter combined practical issues, such as promoting medical, dental, and nursing education and hospitalization and treatment of the sick, with "research in the field of health and in the science of medicine and dentistry." Tom Slick, who had already demonstrated his interest in research as an urban development tool, joined the board as vice chair, indicating that he may have had an important role in shaping the foundation's mission.[45] Whatever the origins of its charter, the chamber designed the foundation to promote a much broader vision of medicine's role in the city than dealing with its serious, immediate public health problems.

Dallas's ambitions, combined with help from Austin and Houston, undermined San Antonio's campaign for a medical center. In 1949 the legislature created a review process that gave Dallas the opportunity to establish

Southwestern Medical Center. The San Antonio Medical Foundation suspended operations for the next seven years.

It revived when suburban expansion and the city's need for hospitals coalesced to create another opportunity to seek a medical center. San Antonio in the early 1950s had a serious shortage of hospital beds for a city of its size, prompting the chamber to create a Hospital Committee in March 1954 to work with the Bexar County Medical Association on that problem. In the fall both groups lobbied delegates at a meeting of the Southwest Texas Conference of the Methodist Church to build a new hospital in San Antonio. The Methodists agreed to do so in January 1955 with the proviso that the city would assist them in seeking federal funds and provide a free twenty-five acre site for the hospital.[46]

Although the chamber's directors quickly agreed to the Methodists' terms, they made one significant change in their request for assistance from city officials. Instead of asking them to help identify twenty-five acres, they requested a site of between one hundred and two hundred acres for the hospital and a medical center.[47] Their request indicated that the directors had ambitious ideas about using the Methodist hospital for a much larger project.

Using the Methodist hospital as "seed corn" for a medical center obviously created a much larger challenge for the chamber's directors. Land would prove to be an easier puzzle to solve than organizing a political campaign to convince the legislature to approve a new center. They turned to Vagtborg to solve the land problem, appointing him chair of the Hospital Committee in September 1955.

By September the city's director of planning had surveyed land near the Robert B. Green and Santa Rosa hospitals on the west side of downtown. His survey included an examination of land costs, concluding that obtaining property there would cost about $10 million and would require lengthy condemnation proceedings to convince landowners to sell. Finding that much public funding at a point when the GGL, with its dedication to frugality, had just assumed power was not politically feasible, and the prospect of the chamber trying to raise such a sum privately would probably have increased the incidence of cardiac arrest in the business community.

Vagtborg had a solution to the funding problem: land in nearby suburbia. His Hospital Committee looked for land in Olmos Basin, located between the elite suburbs of Olmos Park and Alamo Heights. The city attorney quashed this idea, pointing out that the land in question was located behind Olmos Dam and served as a reservoir for floodwater; in addition, it was legally a park and the Conservation Society was considering legal action to save it.[48]

A group of real estate dealers known as the Five Oaks offered another solution in early January 1956: move farther out. They offered to donate two hundred acres (and reserved another 160 acres for future use) to the San Antonio Medical Foundation (not the Hospital Committee) if it would agree to locate a medical center on the land. Simultaneously another developer with land adjacent to the Southwest Research Institute's new location offered two hundred to three hundred acres.[49]

Both offers reflected San Antonio's version of massive national suburbanization in the postwar era. The air force base locations on the fringes of the city acted as magnets for subdivisions because of their role as major employment centers. But the city's population more than doubled between 1940 and 1960, creating an unprecedented demand for housing. With so much vacant land available within the city's original thirty-six-square-mile footprint, developers initially built most of their subdivisions within Loop 13 (Loop 410), then a modest two-lane highway encircling the city. By the 1950s they were building beyond the loop on the North Side, where they needed help promoting their subdivisions.

North Side developers did not have any bases to act as magnets, but the Southwest Research Institute's move to Culebra Road just inside northwest Loop 13 offered some help, and they had already created the Oak Hills Country Club north of the loop about four miles from the institute as an attraction for future subdivision growth in that area.[50] The Five Oaks offer was conveniently close to the club, on the land of a former dairy farm. The second offer of land adjacent to the institute, on the other hand, offered the potential for cooperation between its staff and the researchers who would work at the medical center. Since the Hospital Committee had failed to find a site in or close to downtown, and the North Side developers wanted to work with the San Antonio Medical Foundation, the chamber's directors decided to reactivate it and to provide staff support for its work.[51]

The campaign to obtain agreement on a site, and support for the complex political process for approval of a medical school, began in April 1956, with the chamber formally recommending the two sites to the San Antonio Medical Foundation. Its trustees promptly arranged a tour of the sites for delegations from the medical and business communities. A meeting immediately after the tour did not go well.

Representatives of the Downtown Merchants and Property Owners Association objected strongly to a North Side site.[52] Their objections were simultaneously practical and parochial. Since alleviating the acute health problems of the West Side slums had been an important goal in pursuing a medical center, and since the Robert B. Green Hospital was within walking distance of those slums, it made eminent sense to locate the new Methodist Hospital and the proposed medical center near the Green. In addition, such a medical complex would no doubt strengthen the downtown's importance within San Antonio, which was a major goal of the association.

That, however, was a parochial view of the role that medicine might play in urban development. It restricted the focus of the proposed center to solving the clinical challenge of the West Side's admittedly still appalling health problems. And it did not solve the problem of finding the money to pay for some of the most expensive real estate in town to expand a medical center, which had prompted the Hospital Committee to look outside the downtown in the first place.

With their focus on clinical care and the economic health of the downtown, the association failed to appreciate the medical center's potential as a source of urban development. Research was the key to that potential. The 1947 charter for the San Antonio Medical Foundation had included research as an important element of a center's services to the community. And medical and defense research were critical components in transforming the nation's economy after 1945.[53] Skilled, well-paid researchers were crucial to innovations in health care as well as in medical technology that could encourage dynamic development.

Ordinarily doctors and entrepreneurs like Slick and Vagtborg who understood the importance of research would not have been sufficiently numerous to influence economic development decisions in the chamber during the 1950s. But the medical foundation, which they controlled, gave them the means to pursue their vision of a medical center. As an independent organization, it controlled site selection, and the choice of site determined the kind of medical center San Antonio would have. In May 1956 foundation trustees voted to accept the Oak Hills site.[54]

Coincidence would also play an important role in the politics of establishing the center. Its advocates had to negotiate with three layers of state bureaucracy: the University of Texas Regents, the Texas Commission on Higher Education, and the legislature. All three had to agree to San Antonio's plans for a center. Gaining their approval required not just a good argument backed by evidence; it also required influence within each organization. Fortuitously, Dr. Merton Minter was a member of the regents, and Hal Dewer was on the commission. Both San Antonians would provide essential assistance to the campaign to obtain authorization for a center.[55]

Dr. James Hollers, president of the Chamber of Commerce and chair of the Medical Foundation, coordinated the multiyear political campaign. He assembled a group of doctors, lawyers, and former legislators to help him with strategy, and they decided to start with the Texas Commission on Higher Education. With Dewer's help, they arranged a presentation in April 1957 that persuaded the commission to arrange a site visit, which was a requirement of the approval process. Three teams of outside experts and physicians visited San Antonio to inspect the proposed site. With their approval of the site, the commission recommended that the foundation apply for planning authority for a center from the 1959 legislative session.[56]

The legislature granted planning authority, but approval came with an amendment that required the foundation to build a teaching hospital for the medical center and San Antonio's voters to approve funding for it. The city's voters apparently had a statewide reputation for stinginess because the amendment's sponsor, a state senator from Dallas, believed they would not approve bonds for the hospital, which would kill the city's bid for a medical center.[57]

While the foundation pondered that challenge, its local opponents managed to convince the regents to have another visiting team of experts examine the Robert B. Green area as well as the Oak Hills site. That team, however, recommended the North Side site and the regents formally approved the medical center in October.[58]

Despite that defeat, the Downtown Merchants Association persisted in opposing the project's site, creating a political crisis. The legislature had only granted planning authority, which meant the Medical Foundation had to seek funding in the 1961 legislative session. If a community was badly divided over a project that required state funding, the legislature usually refused to approve it. Recognizing the gravity of the situation, Hollers attempted to restore unity in December 1959 by appointing a special community committee, with representatives from the Downtown Merchants Association, the Medical Foundation, and a group of uncommitted business and professional people to review the site issue once again. The committee met in January and voted to ask another outside expert to visit the sites and make a recommendation. He chose the Oak Hills site, which the committee accepted.

Still not convinced, Walter McAllister, now mayor and president of the Downtown Merchants Association, organized a delegation of its members to lobby the 1961 legislature to transfer the medical center to the Bexar County Hospital District and locate it at the Robert B. Green. That effort failed when Rep. Adrian Spears refused to amend his bill to fund the center because it would jeopardize its passage. Spears's bill then passed, funding the University of Texas Health Science Center (UTHSC).[59]

The foundation's work was not done, however. It helped organize a successful campaign to approve bonds for the teaching hospital in January 1961 and then spent seven years raising money to buy more land around the center, eventually expanding the site to six hundred acres.[60] The Methodists opened their hospital at the site in 1963, and the UTHSC opened for its first classes in 1968.

It had been a long battle that had significant consequences for San Antonio. The medical center came to town through the efforts of the foundation in close cooperation with the chamber. It was the first organized, sustained booster effort in San Antonio's history that added a genuinely new asset for promoting growth to the city's economy. But that success caused a split between the North Side and downtown business communities. The medical center was also the first, and in many ways the most important, magnet for North Side development. Beginning in the 1960s the North Side exploded with residential and commercial growth that reinforced the initial rupture, which would become a major reason for the disintegration of the GGL by the early 1970s.

The quest for a public university consumed less time, but it also exacerbated divisions within the business and political communities. Unlike the campaign for the UTHSC, this effort lacked a core group of supporters who knew what they wanted and worked to get it. It succeeded only because Governor John Connally and his political allies made it happen.

World War II and Korean veterans created a problem that launched this campaign. Generous benefits encouraged a national demand for a college education among veterans. Most states, including Texas, were not prepared to deal with that demand; their colleges and universities simply did not have the space to accommodate this massive surge in students. San Antonio, for example, had four small, expensive private colleges and the San Antonio Junior College, a two-year institution with a limited enrollment. The city's rapidly growing population in the 1950s included an increasing number of veterans who applied to the college. Facing a major problem of a gap between demand and classroom capacity, the school's president appealed to the legislature for more funding in 1955, provoking harsh criticism from conservative legislators adamantly opposed to large enrollments. They doubled tuition in the belief that the higher cost would stop rising enrollments.[61]

Demand for access to colleges increased across Texas in the late 1950s despite the legislature's efforts, and as the only public college in town, the Junior College bore the brunt of local demand. College presidents throughout the state faced the same problem, which would create rising pressure on the legislature to solve this problem. In the meantime James Hollers, Chamber of Commerce president, had created the Greater San Antonio Development Committee in 1956. A year later this committee decided to focus on recruiting aircraft, plastics, and chemical plants to town, all of which required skilled workers. The presidents of Trinity and Saint Mary's Universities, as members of the chamber, pledged that their institutions would create graduate programs to support that initiative.[62] Since their offer involved graduate, not undergraduate, training, their initiative was not related to the Junior College's challenges with undergraduate enrollment. In fact neither Trinity nor Saint Mary's had immediate plans to increase the number of undergraduates.[63]

Wayland Moody, president of the Junior College, developed an ingenious solution to his own enrollment problems and the need for training more skilled workers. He offered to donate his campus to the state if the legislature would convert it into a four-year institution that focused on scientific and technology training in the junior and senior years. Several other Texas community and teacher colleges had been converted into four-year universities, which made the idea seem reasonable. Rep. Rudy Esquivel, with the unanimous support of the other Bexar County representatives, introduced a bill to implement Moody's idea in January 1961. Esquivel, however, had not first consulted the Texas Commission on Higher Education, as required by law. The legislature took a dim view of his faux pas and referred it to the commission, which said it would provide its opinion to the 1963 legislative session.[64]

At this point fate intervened in the form of John Connally, who was serving as secretary of the navy in John F. Kennedy's administration. Connally's duties included oversight of naval contracts awarded to universities to conduct research on defense issues. Federal investment in that research had spiked considerably after the Soviets launched Sputnik in 1957, and Connally noticed not only the large amount of money involved but also that Texas was not among the states benefiting from this money.

In fact Texas had a rather troubling record in higher education. The state ranked thirty-first in the median years of schooling; thirtieth in the production of doctorates; and forty-sixth in faculty salaries. Adding insult to injury, 90 percent of honors graduates from Texas universities left the state for better employment prospects elsewhere.[65] There were no large clusters of scientists in Texas, and Connally concluded that "a concentration of brain power spelled the difference" between haves and have-nots in the competition to win large defense contracts.[66]

Connally met with a close circle of advisers in December 1961 to plan a campaign for governor. The group included Frank Erwin, an Austin lawyer with extensive political and business connections; Ben Barnes, a legislator and future speaker of the Texas House; Lloyd Bentsen, soon to become a U.S. senator; and John Peace, a San Antonio lawyer, longtime member of the State Democratic Party executive committee, and Connally's former college roommate.[67] With their help Connally won the governorship in November 1962 on a platform that stressed the need to reform higher education.

During the campaign season the Chamber of Commerce revisited the issue of graduate education. Esquivel's failed bill had focused on expanding undergraduate training in the sciences and technology, perhaps because of Trinity and Saint Mary's announced intentions to improve graduate education in those fields.

In August 1962 the chamber learned that its attempt to secure the Manned Spacecraft Center had failed because San Antonio did not have science and engineering graduate programs. The chamber decided to consult with professional engineers about a solution to that problem, probably because neither Trinity nor Saint Mary's had made much progress on their plans.[68] Business leaders were continuing to focus on graduate training while a significant part of its legislative delegation had, with Esquivel's bill, shown more interest in undergraduate education. The two were not incompatible, but there was a serious lack of knowledge about the practicalities of graduate education that created the possibility for confusion as the chamber and the legislative delegation turned to consider what Connally had in mind.

Connally's inaugural address to the legislators in January 1963 drew mixed reactions. Several state senators, for instance, tried to pass a constitutional amendment that would require a two-thirds vote of both houses and approval by a statewide referendum to create a new senior college. Their opposition reflected conservative beliefs that universities were expensive, and superfluous to the state's needs. Seeking room to maneuver, Connally proposed to study educational needs with a Committee on Higher Education beyond the High School. San Antonio's senator Franklin Spears guided that proposal into law.[69]

Connally appointed H. B. Zachry as committee chair, with instructions to have a report ready for the 1965 legislative session. Zachry was San Antonio's most successful businessman, having founded a construction company that was a world-class business by the 1950s. A deeply conservative man, he strongly supported the city's private colleges, believed that large universities encouraged mediocrity, and wanted a cost-conscious approach to Connally's desire to improve higher education.[70]

Spears also created some momentum for a public university in San Antonio. Testifying before the Texas Commission on Higher Education in January 1963, he suggested that San Antonio should have a new four-year state school because that could help relieve some of the problems that the University of Texas at Austin had in dealing with growing enrollment. Perhaps by prearrangement, President Moody had withdrawn his proposal to transform the Junior College into a four-year institution. Spears thus became the first San Antonian to suggest a new, comprehensive public university for the city.[71]

Spears, however, did not speak for a united San Antonio community. Liberal Democrats, energized by their contributions to electing John F. Kennedy as president, were becoming increasingly vocal within the party. They controlled the House delegation, and Esquivel's abortive 1961 bill had been their first attempt at creating a public university. Instinctively suspicious of Connally's conservative views, they would have their own ideas about what kind of university San Antonio needed.

Rep. Jake Johnson made that clear in February 1964 with an announcement that he would "go all out" in the 1965 session to obtain a four-year public university. But he made two stunning statements about that goal. He wanted the university to focus on Latin America, and he wanted it located at HemisFair.[72] Both were politically explosive ideas. Johnson's proposals deliberately attacked the core goals of the chamber and the GGL at this point. Focusing on Latin America contradicted the chamber's interest in science and technology as key tools for future development. And HemisFair was regarded as sacred ground for burnishing the city's national reputation and transforming the tourist industry. Interfering with either goal was tantamount to blasphemy.

Political conflict exacerbated Johnson's inflammatory announcement. Competing Democratic factions fought for control of the city's delegation to the state legislature and the national convention that would nominate Lyndon B. Johnson. John Peace led the Connally faction, and Albert Peña Jr. the liberals. The bitter conflict resulted in Peña's faction winning control of the local convention, prompting Peace and his faction to walk out. Peace appealed to Frank Erwin to overrule the outcome of the imbroglio, which he promptly did.[73]

Amid the bitter infighting nearly all the Democratic candidates did endorse Spears's idea for a new university.[74] But their political disagreements boded ill for the liberal-dominated state delegation's ability to work with the business community, which was itself split by Representative Johnson's proposals. The local political environment was thus rather poisonous when Zachry's committee issued its final report in August 1964.

Zachry's views on frugality and efficiency dominated the committee report. As Connally had expected, it recommended creating a Coordinating Board for Higher Education tasked with oversight of all the state's universities. Connally had wanted such a board to reassure his deeply conservative opponents that there would be a state agency responsible for ensuring economy and efficiency in higher education. Zachry applied those goals to his own solution to San Antonio's need to expand access to higher education.

The report recommended that the city should have a two-year technical school, not a new public university. Zachry was in a good position to implement his plan since he was chairman of the board for HemisFair. In October he offered the city's liberal Democrats a deal: he would use his political influence with Connally to raise money for the technical school, which he would locate at HemisFair.[75]

Speaking for the liberals, Johnson declined Zachry's offer, saying that he would introduce legislation to create a four-year university in the 1965 session. Unable to achieve his own goal, and perhaps with the cooperation of Peace, Zachry apparently talked with Connally about thwarting the liberals. In January 1965 Connally declared that San Antonio should have a four-year university dedicated to science and technology.[76]

The legislature had no intention of approving any new institutions at this point. In March it approved creating the Coordinating Board, which it charged with developing a master plan for higher education in time for the 1967 legislative session. Senator Spears did convince his colleague to adopt a resolution asking the board to consider Connally's desire for a university in San Antonio, but that did not commit the board to agreeing with the governor.[77]

The leaders of San Antonio's private colleges were unenthusiastic about Connally's proposal. Saint Mary's University was planning to build a center for mathematics and engineering, and Trinity had plans for a life sciences building. An inexpensive public university specializing in science and technology would not be a welcome addition for them. Since they presided over the chamber's education committee, they delayed endorsing Connally's proposal. Then, in March 1966, the committee did endorse a public university, but it pointedly ignored science and technology as part of the new institution's mission.[78]

Ignoring Connally's vision for the new university cost the private colleges their leadership roles on the chamber's education committee. In June 1966 Herbert Kelleher became its chair. Although a relative newcomer to San Antonio with no background in higher education issues, Kelleher was a member of Peace's law firm and had worked in Connally's gubernatorial campaign. Kelleher worked conscientiously with all the factions now swirling around the effort to obtain a university, but the fact remained that Peace now had a member of his team in charge of a key chamber committee.[79]

Connally then elevated Peace's importance to the campaign for a university by appointing him to the Board of Regents in 1967.

The Coordinating Board managed to delay any changes in Texas higher education by deciding that it would make no recommendations until 1969, when its staff had finished a master plan.[80] Frank Lombardino, who had been elected to the House in November 1966, now inadvertently created a firestorm in the business and political communities. The majority of the city's legislative representatives supported a university; Lombardino differed from them only in making the idea his campaign's central pledge. Perhaps anticipating that the 1969 legislative session would agree to a university for San Antonio, Lombardino decided to lead an effort to settle on a location for the university before the legislature authorized it.

In October 1967 Lombardino urged the city council to locate the university at HemisFair. He explained that doing so would be economical because the new Convention Center and other fair facilities could be converted into college buildings. Since representatives of the tourism industry had spent the last fifty years arguing for a modern facility to host large conventions, councilmembers struggled to find words to respond to his suggestion.[81]

Initially the council simply tried to ignore Lombardino's idea. Liberal Democrats, on the other hand, seized on it. Relying on their control of the Commissioners Court to support Lombardino, they met with the city's legislative delegation to investigate possible sites that ranged from vacant land at Fort Sam Houston to Camp Bullis (an interesting choice since it was an artillery firing range far north of town) to HemisFair. That provoked the city council to ask its HemisFair Reuse Committee to study the issue. It delegated that task to Douglas Harlan, director of the city's department of education and human resources. Harlan, a conservative with an unwavering commitment to frugality, concluded that HemisFair was indeed the best site.[82]

Harlan's report created the impression that the city had now made an official decision in favor of HemisFair. That attracted the favorable attention of Downtowners, Inc., which had been working to stop the erosion of retail shopping in the city's center due to the malls that developers had built along Loop 410. For downtown retailers a university at HemisFair implied a permanent increase in potential customers. The Hotel Owners' Association, on the other hand, was appalled by Harlan's recommendation. With help from chamber president John Steen, it conducted a poll that revealed a majority of the chamber's members opposed placing a university at HemisFair.[83]

Lombardino's suggestion had now provoked a major dispute over the future development of the downtown between two powerful factions within the chamber. Seeking to preserve peace, City Manager Jerry Henckle proposed limiting a university to thirty-two acres on the south side of HemisFair. Since the entire site consisted of only 142 acres, Henckle seemed to be making a fairly generous offer. Unidentified "people who would open and operate the college" called his offer "excessively optimistic," saying a university would need at least two hundred acres.[84]

Peace tried to restore calm by arranging a meeting between UT officials and the city's legislative delegation. The group toured various sites in town, after which Otis Singletary, vice chancellor for academic affairs, told the gathering that San Antonians needed to think big when considering a site by which, an unidentified source explained, he meant a minimum of three hundred and possibly six hundred acres.[85]

Downtowners, Inc. was not listening. In early January, as the 1969 legislative session was about to begin, Ed Harlee, its executive director, announced that Lombardino would include the HemisFair site in his bill to create a university. A UT System official promptly informed the delegation that including the site in the bill would kill it, and the Hotel Owners' Association announced it would only support the bill if a site was not specified. The level of discord among businessmen and the disconnect between the city council and the city's delegation prompted a summit meeting of system officials, regents, the city council, and the legislative delegation to inspect HemisFair again, after which Representative Johnson joined Vice Chancellor Singletary to announce that the legislators were not empowered to specify a site, as authority rested with the regents.[86]

Frank Erwin, chair of the Board of Regents, and Ben Barnes, now lieutenant governor, assumed leadership of the legislative process to approve several branch campuses for the UT System. Erwin worked quietly to ensure passage of the bill that Lombardino introduced with promises to spread the system's largesse among cities across the state seeking a branch campus. Barnes had the more difficult task because a small group of senators led by W. T. Moore of Bryan, Texas, adamantly opposed to the bill. Moore, who chaired the Senate Education Committee, deployed every parliamentary tactic available to thwart it. When Moore and a colleague launched a filibuster late in the session, Barnes refused to adjourn the Senate, forcing them to speak continuously until they literally dropped. Barnes then used Senate rules to transfer the bill from Moore's committee to another, much more amenable committee. With only days left in the session, the Senate finally agreed with the House, creating the largest expansion of universities in the state's history.[87]

It had not been a pretty campaign because liberal Democrats had chosen to use the city's need for a public university to attack the conservative business and political communities' vision of San Antonio. The chamber needed help attracting high technology firms that relied on research and technical training in their businesses; Johnson essentially proposed a liberal arts university. Hotel and restaurant owners wanted help promoting tourism, and GGL had obliged with support for HemisFair. Had it succeeded, the liberals' attempt to locate a university at HemisFair would have undermined its core mission. Neither faction had reckoned with the Coordinating Board, which had announced its basic approach to developing branch campuses in the UT System in 1968. The board wanted to limit enrollments and restrict the degree programs to bachelor's and master's degrees. It would pursue those policies after 1969 despite the legislature's clear language that the University of Texas San Antonio would be a "university of the first class."[88]

Political infighting continued over the selection of a site for the new university. Peace had been involved in the campaign to bring the UTHSC to town, and he supported Connally's desire to increase the state's scientific and technological capabilities. Peace therefore regarded the new university as another asset for economic development that should be located close to the UTHSC. County commissioner A. J. Ploch led the opposition to that idea, proposing instead a site on the southeast side of town that he believed would offer better access to higher education for the city's minorities. Peace used his role as a UT regent to win that battle, but the Coordinating Board intervened to impose its limitations on UTSA (and for that matter, all the other branch campuses). With a limited ability to provide the degree programs and training that boosters needed, UTSA became an underdeveloped asset for economic diversification for the next thirty years.[89]

Boosters had better luck stimulating the economy during the GGL's reign by diversifying tourism, their most traditional development tool. With the emergence of mass consumption, tourism was developing into one of the nation's largest businesses. Conventioneers and vacationers, though, had different interests and needs that created challenges for attracting them. Vacationers sought entertainment, the central theme of late twentieth-century tourism. Conventioneers needed space for meetings. Both groups needed hotels, restaurants, music, and alcohol. And both preferred these things to be conveniently located in aesthetically pleasing settings.[90]

Locally tourism stagnated after 1945 because it had not yet adapted to emerging national trends. The Conservation Society had succeeded in reworking the Alamo into a national monument and restoring Mission San José prior to World War II. In 1947 it established A Night in Old San Antonio, which became a major festival, and in the early 1950s the society worked to revive La Villita, Maury Maverick's now rather neglected restoration project on the Great Bend of the San Antonio River.[91] Although the society's efforts attracted a steady flow of tourists, its efforts had not dramatically increased their numbers. Conventions were also not providing much stimulus to the economy. In 1953 convention attendance averaged 521 people; in 1963 the average was 421. The typical conventioneer spent a miserly $71 during his visit in 1953, and $109 in 1963.[92] Inadequate space for large conventions and the lack of hotel rooms combined to limit the impact of conventions on San Antonio's economy.

Two businessmen independently suggested solutions to the challenges of improving San Antonio's appeal to tourists. Jerome K. Harris, a member of the chamber's World Affairs Committee, observed that better air connections to other American cities were enticing Mexican tourists away from San Antonio. He wanted to reassert the city's dominance in that trade by holding a "Hemis-Fair" every two to four years, an idea that prompted the chamber's president to create a Hemis-Fair Exploration Committee in 1958. His idea for frequent mini-fairs did not attract much support at the time, but it was an idea that others would soon refine.[93]

Other chamber members were mulling over the problem of attracting more visitors in the late 1950s, and in March 1958 the Summer Festival and River Development Committee met for the first time. Its members showed more interest in festivals than the river, which was perhaps understandable. The river had been the location for Conservation Society and other parades during spring and fall fiestas, but after the war it had gone into decline. The blank back walls of businesses loomed over its banks, and it lacked sports facilities and other entertainment that drew the public to more conveniently located parks around the city. Maintenance suffered after the war, and the military ruled it off limits in 1945 because of crime problems. By the late 1950s it was a major eyesore.[94]

A casual dinner party conversation in late 1959 lamenting the river's condition ignited a campaign to transform the river. David Straus, president of his family-owned wholesale appliance business, seized on a comment that the river needed more shops like Casa Rio, its sole restaurant. Straus convinced the chamber's president that a committee should adopt a master plan "whereby the downtown river banks might be lined with curio shops, handcraft shops, eating places, etc."[95] The details may have sounded trivial (or, later, mere common sense), but at the time Straus's idea was profound. Like Robert Hugman, the original architect of the River Walk, Straus conceived of the river as a unified space that should be aesthetically pleasing and simultaneously practical. Moreover it was centrally located and had enough vacant space to create a major, permanent magnet for tourists.

The campaigns for HemisFair and the River Walk would adopt the San Antonio Medical Foundation's model for dealing with long-term projects by organizing separate organizations to deal with the complex issues they faced. HemisFair, though, was unusual in having a deadline that had the effect of concentrating attention on it.

In November 1961 Henry B. Gonzales won a special election to Congress. A fiery-tempered liberal who had begun his political career as a San Antonio councilman, Gonzales already had a reputation as an effective advocate for civil rights, and he was also fiercely proud of his city's Mexican heritage. San Antonio would be 250 years old in 1968, and Gonzales wanted to mark the occasion with a major celebration, but he also wanted to promote trade with Mexico (an idea similar to Jerome Harris's). Coincidentally Seattle would open its Century 21 World's Fair in 1962, which may have been his inspiration for proposing a HemisFair. In January 1962 he contacted William Sinkin, a longtime supporter and successful businessman, to ask for help with his idea.[96]

Also coincidentally, the Good Government League had been working with the Urban Renewal Program to build a convention complex. Sinkin approached McAllister, who had little use for liberals, about a cooperative effort to boost San Antonio's national reputation by staging HemisFair.[97] McAllister agreed to cooperate with Gonzales, probably because an event of that magnitude would be a wonderful way to advertise the city's new convention facilities.

Staging the fair would become the most complex challenge in the business community's history. It would require successfully negotiating with the state and federal governments for approvals and funding as well as obtaining permission from the International Bureau of Expositions. Locally the idea of a fair was perhaps even more challenging because the business community had no experience in dealing with such a large project due to its long history of indifference to organized urban development.

The tightly knit social world of San Antonio's elite citizens created a solution to those challenges. A relatively small group of men owned most of the banks and largest businesses in town. Leadership within this group gravitated to individuals with reputations for especially successful business practices, civic mindedness, and commitment to conservative principles in politics. In 1962 McAllister was probably the single most powerful individual within this elite because of his accomplishments, although Zachry and banker Thomas Frost Sr. could give him stiff competition for that distinction. If any or all of their leaders endorsed an idea, the other members of the elite were likely to support it.

McAllister, Zachry, and Frost attended an organizational meeting chaired by Sinkin in February 1962 that included most of the city's bankers.[98] The attendees agreed to support a fair, and Sinkin spent the rest of the year cultivating public support with, by his count, more than two hundred speeches at any and every event he could find. Gonzales lobbied the Department of Commerce to create federal support for the project. In late December these preliminary activities led to the creation of San Antonio Fair Inc., a private corporation that would fund, build, and operate the fair. Sinkin became the fair's president, Zachry was chairman of its board, and McAllister and James Gaines, Chamber of Commerce president, were among the board members.[99]

The conservative elite assumed control over the fair. With its potential to draw national attention to San Antonio, it was a project that piqued their civic pride. It also bolstered their decades-long belief in tourism as a panacea for development. Conservative enthusiasm for the fair provided the social and political connections that fundraising required and that liberals like Gonzales and Sinkin did not have. Marshall Steves, scion of one of San Antonio's most successful families, assumed responsibility for raising several million dollars from local businesses to underwrite the fair. This was an essential task because the city council could not authorize a bond issue to support the fair without underwriters. Whether they were boosters or not, local businessmen had never raised even $500,000 for a development project, and Steves started with a goal of $3 million. He began cajoling contributions in June 1963 and quickly discovered the elite's enthusiasm for HemisFair, raising nearly $8 million by the early fall.[100]

Other relationships proved crucial to a thorny problem with industrial exhibits. The International Bureau of Expositions required a world's fair to have a minimum of twenty such exhibits. Branch offices of Southwestern Bell, General Electric, and IBM quickly agreed to sponsor exhibits, but San Antonio's leaders lacked the connections to attract another seventeen. Red McCombs, a successful car dealer, former chamber president and a member of the fair's executive committee, discovered that major national corporations "thought of San Antonio as being something maybe like Laredo or maybe like Abilene, Texas," when he tried to convince Lee Iacocca to build a Ford pavilion. After an angry phone conversation with Iacocca, McCombs decided to call Governor Connally to explain his problem with Iacocca. Connally said he would call Lyndon Johnson to ask him to call Henry Ford, Iacocca's boss. Johnson did; Ford Motor Company built a pavilion. Recognizing that obtaining commitments for additional pavilions was beyond San Antonio's capabilities, Connally and Johnson conducted their own successful campaign to convince national corporations to build pavilions.[101]

McAllister also made major contributions to the fair. He routinely attended fair board meetings to monitor progress and help solve problems, and he lent his prestige to securing bond issues with radio addresses to explain their importance and urge their approval. McAllister also worked hard at protecting and promoting the city's reputation for hospitality. He conceived the idea of a Visitors' Services Bureau for the fair that would help visitors obtain hotel reservations, parking, exhibit information and other matters that would cultivate good feelings toward the fair and the city. To achieve that goal, he presided over meetings to convince hotel owners to support a budget for the bureau and arranged to receive regular reports about complaints that he dealt with personally. His concern to protect the city's reputation extended to persuading hotel and restaurant owners to relent on their policies of refusing to serve minorities, a long-standing practice that could have had negative effects at a time of intense battles over civil rights.[102]

Despite their best efforts, though, the board created controversies that were probably inevitable. The fair was a private corporation in charge of a public event. Its directors were capable, but they also tended to be insensitive to public perceptions of conflicts of interest. When accused of holding secret meetings, they explained that such meetings were merely private—a distinction without a difference for most of the public. When accused of foregoing public bids for contracts to construct buildings or run concessions, they explained that they had carefully investigated the successful contractors to ensure their ability to perform work.[103] When they awarded a contract in 1966 to build the Tower of the Americas, the fair's iconic structure, to someone who happened to be a member of their board, they expressed confusion as to why anyone would object.

The tower contract precipitated a political crisis when Gonzales demanded that McAllister, who served on the board building it, either resign from the board or resign as mayor. He did neither, which did not help matters despite his spirited and angry radio address to defend himself. Sen. Ralph Yarborough, a liberal Democrat whom conservatives cordially hated, wrote restrictive amendments to the federal funding bill for the fair that nearly undermined it by requiring a reorganization of the fair and tower boards.[104]

Having survived that crisis, the board managed to complete almost all its work in time for opening day on April 6, 1968. Doing so created a tremendous, and justified, sense of achievement among HemisFair's supporters. The national press augmented that pride with favorable reviews that lauded its Confluence of the Americas theme and praised its architecture. Ada Louise Huxtable, architecture critic for the *New York Times,* noted that the fair had a "character that was tied to the city," a compliment to San Antonio's multicultural heritage.[105] Such favorable comments indicated that local boosters had finally lodged San Antonio in the nation's consciousness.

That achievement did not, though, translate into a financial success. National events were part of the problem. The year 1968 was a disastrous one, with the assassinations of Martin Luther King Jr. (just before the fair opened) and Bobby Kennedy, urban riots, and the catastrophic Democratic Party Convention in Chicago. The gloom such events created was not conducive to visiting distant places, and the lack of adequate air connections to major cities made traveling to the Alamo City difficult except by car.

Even accounting for that gloom, however, did not explain low attendance, a problem that surfaced quickly. In the first week, attendance was 40 percent below expectations. An analysis of attendance at the end of April revealed that only 25 percent of the fair's visitors lived in San Antonio or Bexar County, 36 percent lived outside of Texas, 31 percent lived in Texas, and 8 percent lived in foreign countries.[106]

In April 1963 fair president Sinkin had said that the fair's primary goal was to motivate "the population [of San Antonio] into unified activity."[107] Attendance figures indicated that local residents, particularly Mexican Americans, were not supporting the fair. Income problems explained part of this problem. Three-quarters of West Side workers did not earn a decent living in the late 1960s.[108] Many West Side families could not afford admission tickets selling at $2 per adult and $1 per child. But they were also less likely to attend because they were apathetic and resentful toward HemisFair, which they regarded as an event for wealthy San Antonians and tourists.[109]

Low attendance of course threatened financial disaster for the fair, and its supporters responded promptly. In May H. B. Zachry replaced Marshall Steves as president and James Gaines resigned as chief executive officer. Zachry reduced and reorganized the staff and sought ways to improve attendance. First he asked Governor Connally to address a meeting of more than five hundred local businessmen. Connally "scolded" them for failing "to take full advantage of HemisFair as the greatest educational and entertainment opportunity in the 250-year history of the city."[110] Zachry then arranged to sell them admission tickets for all their employees to boost attendance. Food and Beverage Day, for instance, attracted more than thirteen thousand of those workers to the fair.[111] Zachry also introduced lower prices for admission in the evenings, when West Side residents were more likely to have the time to attend the fair with such inducements. His timely, careful management rescued the fair from catastrophe, although it did not escape suffering a deficit. On closing day total attendance had recovered to only a 13 percent deficit (6.3 million visitors as opposed to 7.2 million) from projected numbers. Zachry then negotiated agreements with the city and other debtors using the underwriters' contributions to cover the final deficit.[112]

Despite all the difficulties, boosters generally believed that HemisFair had been a great success. And in many ways it had been. The city acquired a modern, large convention complex; the Institute of Texan Cultures; a new federal courthouse; two new hotels; and new business spinoffs such as La Quinta Motor Inns and Church's Fried Chicken. Inspired by the fair, Red McCombs launched a successful campaign to bring professional sports to town, eventually acquiring the Dallas Chaparrals in 1972, whom he renamed the Spurs.[113]

HemisFair also acquired legendary status among boosters because, they believe, it "set the stage for new growth in the... tourism and convention industry." If true, it took a long time to set the stage. The national economy suffered from inflation and growing unemployment in the 1970s, which probably accounts for the mixed record of tourism during the decade. Although the number of conventions grew by 71 percent (from 284 to 488), the average revenue each generated decreased from $73,943 to $69,877. Revenues remained in that range until 1986, when they jumped 81 percent, followed by a phenomenal increase of 126 percent by 1988 (when there were 897 conventions that averaged revenues of $311,259).[114] Attributing that rise solely to HemisFair twenty years after the event, however, strains credulity. It also ignores the complementary role of the River Walk in transforming San Antonio into a major tourist destination.

David Straus's campaign to revitalize the River Walk did not have the same cachet as HemisFair did. It never generated flamboyant rhetoric that combined promises of greatness with dire warnings of the consequences of failure. Chamber president James Gaines provided both when he asserted that HemisFair "will give San Antonio a glorious future," but added, "this is our chance. It may never come our way again. Unless we act, we will have lost our one great opportunity" to transform San Antonio.[115] Such energetic rhetoric created a sense of drama about HemisFair that nourished its supporters' sense of urgency but Gaines did not use the same sort of rhetoric to promote the River Walk.

That would have consequences for Straus's plans. Government support, for example, would be a far more limited than it was for HemisFair. The River Walk was located in the heart of a declining downtown, and urban renewal was the program of choice among cities trying to redevelop their downtowns. Yet the Good Government League, which controlled the local agency's board, would have no interest in using federal funding to help Straus. Likewise city bond issues that provided significant funding to HemisFair would offer only minimal help to Straus's project.

Straus therefore had to somehow inspire private property owners along the river's Great Bend to join him in transforming their frequently dilapidated buildings into tourist attractions. Aside from the costs involved in such upgrades, there was another problem. Shortly after his appointment as chair of the chamber's Tourist Attractions Development Committee, his secretary left him a telephone message: "Tax Problem Catalini... Relief for first few years—Prop owners afraid to invest & lease—tax increase—marginal deals anyhow."[116] Their fear of higher taxes initially undermined Straus's personal appeals to them: "And it was pretty futile, I mean, none of them were interested in doing anything with their properties."[117]

Temporarily stymied, Straus worked with his committee on ways to stimulate interest. Shortly after the committee began to meet, the members decided to seek city approval of their project and to create a plan for the Great Bend that would help property owners understand the Bend's potential for attracting tourists. The city manager and parks director endorsed their ideas, and in January 1961 the city council hired Macro Engineering, a Los Angeles firm that had planned Disneyland, to prepare a plan. Straus also visited Carmel, California, and the New Orleans French Quarter to gather ideas about city ordinances that established standards for attractive redevelopment of urban spaces because he "did not want the river to end up being a maze of flashing neon signs."[118]

Disneyland turned out not to be a model for San Antonio's river. Local architects were especially outraged by Macro Engineering's design ideas, and O'Neil Ford, a nationally important architect who had joined Straus's chamber committee, resigned in protest. Given his problems with the Great Bend's property owners, Straus could not afford a major battle over the plan, and he asked the local branch of the American Institute of Architecture to prepare an alternative. The AIA plan won enthusiastic acceptance at a public meeting at La Villita Assembly Hall in April 1963.[119]

Straus used the time waiting for the AIA plan to work on an organization to control development. Adapting what he had learned from his visits to

Carmel and New Orleans, he presented his draft ordinance to Mayor McAllister. With McAllister's support, the city council established the River Walk Commission in March 1962. The commission had no independent authority, but the department of buildings and inspections would not issue a permit for renovations or new buildings on the Great Bend unless the commission approved it first.[120] The commission would be crucial to Straus's goal of preserving the visual appeal of the original River Walk while simultaneously accommodating businesses that could attract visitors.

Mindful of the problem of overcoming property owners' resistance to his goals, Straus decided to lead by example and to deal with the tax issue. He bought three buildings with the assistance of investors whom he recruited to help him and renovated them into a well-designed complex named River Square. The Kangaroo Court, which would become an iconic River Walk restaurant, was one of the tenants recruited to show other property owners the potential for commercial development. He also apparently solved the tax problem by appealing to the Taxpayers' League of San Antonio. Paul Adams, the league director, asked the city manager "if he did not think that the down town properties should be reevaluated due to the many vacancies and hence loss of income."[121] Although Adams's language could have applied to many such downtown properties, his timing was suspiciously supportive of Straus's agenda.

These efforts did produce results. By summer 1962 the River Walk Commission had begun to receive inquiries from local businessmen seeking its help in locations for new shops and restaurants. Their requests provided evidence that there was growing interest in investing in the Great Bend, which was helpful in dealing with property owners reluctant to improve their buildings.[122]

Despite that progress, razing or renovating buildings, and reorienting them to open onto the river took time, forcing a leisurely pace to redevelopment. That slow pace became a problem when HemisFair's organizers began to generate considerable excitement over their project beginning in 1963, an excitement that the River Walk could not match—especially in terms of the fair's immediate economic impact from contracts for site preparation, large buildings, and entertainment concessions.

Straus tried to associate the River Walk with that enthusiasm, which could have enhanced public support for his work. In June 1963 he convinced several directors of the fair that the "River development should serve as the focal point of the HemisFair in the same manner as the Space Needle at Seattle."[123] Initially the agreement was quite a coup. The River Walk would have had an important role in the fair that would have generated useful publicity and access to funding for infrastructure improvements along the Great Bend.

Unfortunately Straus neglected to seal this deal with a written agreement. In fall 1963 he received a long list of physical improvements that the AIA plan envisioned for the Great Bend that required $3 million to complete. Straus submitted the list to the chamber's parks and recreation committee chaired by Red McCombs, which would make recommendations to the city council regarding the distribution of funds from a $30 million bond election scheduled for January 1964. Half of that money was for HemisFair, which should have given Straus some leverage if his agreement with the fair directors had any validity, particularly because McCombs was himself deeply involved with HemisFair. But McCombs's committee deleted the most expensive projects from Straus's list and recommended only $300,000 from the bond issue for the River Walk. Straus appealed the committee's decision to HemisFair president Sinkin and to mayor McAllister. Both declined to intervene, leaving Straus with insufficient funds to make significant progress on infrastructure improvements.[124]

This defeat hindered Straus's efforts, which was unfortunate. HemisFair's supporters fervently believed it would launch a new era in tourism, but it was a one-time event that would not give tourists a reason to linger in San Antonio once it closed. Most visitors did not stay as long as conventioneers did because they lacked a reason to do so. San Antonio attracted people interested in its history and culture, but that was not sufficient to make the city Texas's most important tourist destination. In fact, despite a lack of significant historical and cultural attractions, Dallas and Houston outranked San Antonio in attracting large numbers of tourists.[125] As one local businessman noted: "We have always been blessed with the Alamo. . . . But after the tourist saw that he left. There was nothing else to do."[126] Straus was trying to solve the "nothing else to do" problem by creating a major attraction that would permanently encourage tourists to extend their stays in town. By minimizing financial support for infrastructure improvements along the Great Bend, his fellow boosters were affecting Straus's efforts to attract more businesses there.

Despite this setback, Straus continued to work on strategic issues that could support long-term development. A Texas law, for instance, prohibited serving liquor by the drink in restaurants. Straus led a successful effort to change that law, which made restaurants more profitable.[127] His committee also convinced the air force to drop its prohibition against military personnel visiting the River Walk in the evenings to increase the number of available customers.[128] In March 1964 he established the Paseo Del Rio Association to give tenants and property owners an organization to promote the River Walk.[129] These initiatives, important in themselves, combined to provide a solid foundation for businessmen to invest in Straus's campaign to transform the Great Bend.

Some preparations for HemisFair did help Straus. The city lacked enough hotel rooms to handle anticipated demand, and this attracted the attention of H. B. Zachry and Patrick Kennedy. Kennedy converted what had been Saint Mary's Law School on the river into a new hotel, La Posada (later renamed La Mansion Del Rio); Zachry built the Hilton Palacio Del Rio across from HemisFair. Both hotels increased foot traffic along the River Walk, which helped create publicity and customers for its fledgling business community.[130]

All of these changes gradually encouraged more investment in renovating the Great Bend. In 1964 property sales reached $500,000, with another $1 million in building improvements under way. Six years later total investment amounted to $16 million and the number of businesses had grown to twenty-six.[131]

Considering the problems he had faced, Straus had made significant progress toward transforming the River Walk. The real test of his achievements, though, occurred in the 1970s with the nation's economic troubles. Within a year after HemisFair closed, tourism declined enough to cause stress on the River Walk's new businesses. The Paseo Del Rio Association worked hard to attract tourists and San Antonians to the river with a series of festivals; it also adopted a more inclusive approach to membership in the association, inviting hoteliers, restauranteurs, and other businesses involved in the tourist trade to join. That was an important step in improving cooperation within the tourism industry, but it did not immediately solve the problem of slow business along the River Walk. A nadir of sorts occurred in 1975, when mayor Lila Cockrell suggested that San Antonians should plan to spend their vacations at the River Walk, a strong indication that suburbanites were not patronizing downtown businesses.[132]

Aside from economic problems, hotel rooms remained an important issue. As early as 1971 Claire Regnier, executive director of the Paseo Del Rio Association, commented that San Antonio was unable to attract more visitors because it lacked a 1,000-room hotel that could serve large conventions. By the late 1970s organizers of several large conventions were threatening to cancel their reservations because of that problem.[133] Fortunately a solution coincidentally offered itself when Marriott announced plans for a forty-two-story hotel across from the Convention Center in 1977. It opened in 1979, the year Hyatt announced plans for a similar hotel located on the river across from the Alamo. By 1981 hotel space had significantly improved and tourism was once again on the rise.[134]

The Good Government League's era would end as it had begun, with the military dominating the city's economy. Some boosters, though, did tinker with ways to diversify the economy. The Southwest Research Institute and the UTHSC represented local efforts to introduce critical elements of the new national economy into San Antonio. And although HemisFair and the River Walk reflected the long-standing commitment to tourism, the boosters had for the first time raised their game to rejuvenate its ability to make important contributions to the economy. Participating in both projects created valuable lessons about the virtues of cooperation in urban development, denting the belief that good things come to those who wait. But before boosters could apply those to new initiatives, they would have to cope with the collapse of the social and political order that had ruled the city since the days of Samuel Maverick.

BOOSTERS AND SUBURBANIZATION

Suburbanization became a major issue for growing cities in the twentieth century because annexation involved cultural values, political power, and money. Suburban residents often resisted annexation because of their concerns about higher taxes and urban problems, while city residents resented the costs of annexation and subsidies that suburban developers sought from local government. Boosters, however, generally favored annexation as the best way to increase a city's tax revenues that could then fund improvements that made for an attractive city.

Annexation became increasingly difficult as state legislators usually responded to suburbanites' desire for independence with new restrictions on annexation, a trend that created large numbers of small municipalities surrounding major cities that, by midcentury, left them facing major problems in coping with declining downtowns and insufficient funds to deal with basic maintenance and services for their residents.

Texas legislators, however, were slow to join the national trends toward restrictions on annexation. Although important restrictions appeared in the early 1960s, they did not throttle local efforts to incorporate new subdivisions into places like Houston and San Antonio, whose official political boundaries grew impressively in the late twentieth century.

San Antonio's boosters nevertheless found annexation challenging. The local civil rights revolution of 1960s and 1970s added a new dimension to the usual opposition to annexation based on frugality. For the first time in San Antonio's history, minority residents had finally acquired the political power to demand adequate city services for inner-city neighborhoods.

Ironically they acquired that power just as North Side development beyond Loop 410 exploded. That explosion was due to the emergence of health services as a powerful component of the local economy. Medical centers around the country were potent engines of economic development, and the UTHSC was no exception. Such centers required land, not just for center facilities but also for the spinoff businesses that needed to cluster around them and large numbers of employees who would want to live close to their work. The regents' decision to locate the UTHSC on the North Side therefore made rapid growth practically inevitable.

Such growth was not in the best interests of inner-city neighborhoods whose residents naturally resented developers' success in using their political influence to obtain city subsidies for their subdivisions. That was a double-edged sword competing with the service demands of inner-city neighborhoods. The developers' subsidies diverted some funds from use elsewhere; even more importantly, annexing new subdivisions threatened the political power that San Antonio's inner-city minorities had just acquired.

The boosters were fortunate to have skilled political leadership from Lila Cockrell and Henry Cisneros when the political interests of the inner-city and the North Side collided. Cockrell and Cisneros managed, sometimes just barely, to negotiate a balance between those powerful competing interests that enabled San Antonio to incorporate much of its suburban population growth. Capturing its own suburban sprawl would bring its own problems, but at least San Antonio escaped the fate of declining budgets and declining services that plague many other major cities.

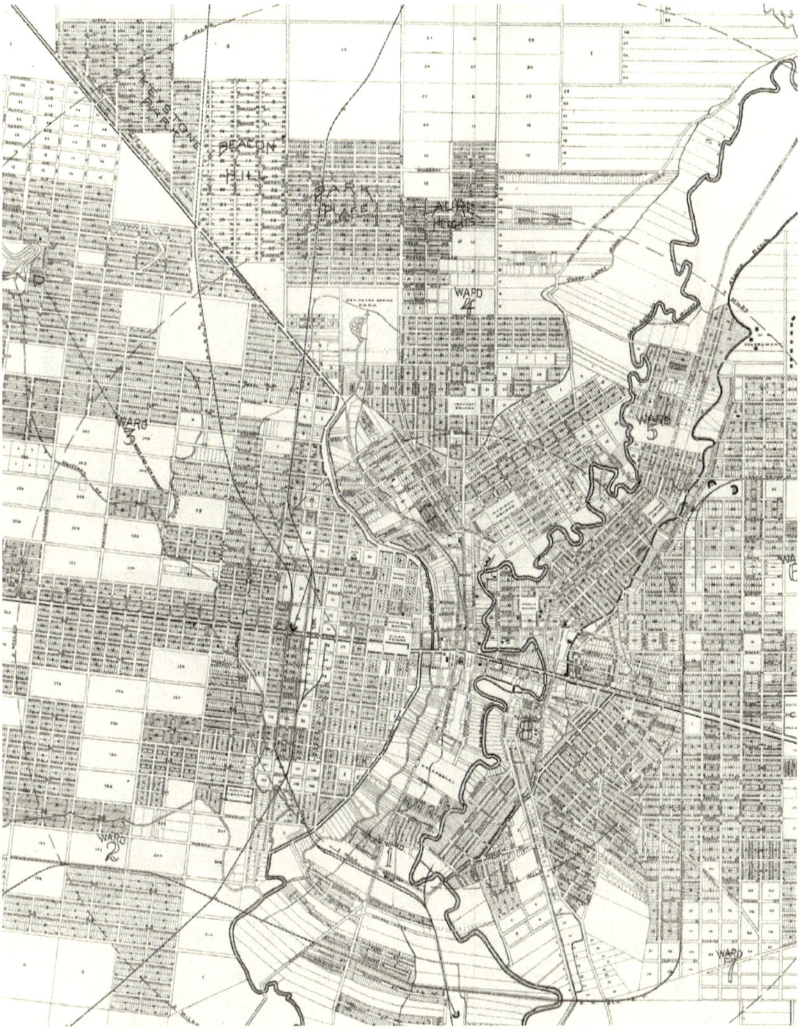

This 1889 map of San Antonio depicts the city petering out north of San Pedro Park.

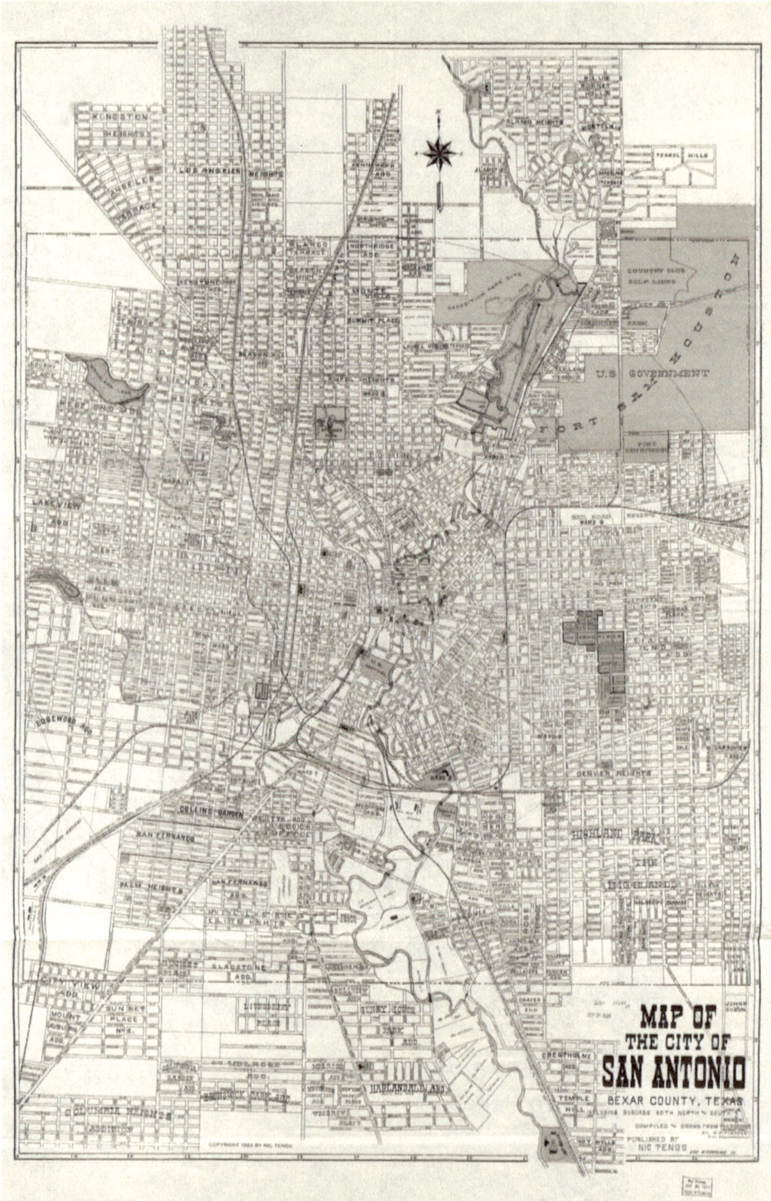

A 1909 map, just twenty years later, identifies solid growth through the northern edge of Hildebrand Avenue, which runs east to west and caps the city's growth at Incarnate Word.

One of San Antonio's first shopping complexes, Wonderland Mall, sat astride Loop 410, along with North Star Mall, in a rural environment, although this would quickly fill in.

The UTHSC was also originally an isolated outpost.

As projected, the area north of town filled in, with anchor corporations such as USAA and Valero building world headquarters there.

Today the north side of Loop 410 is fully developed.

NINE

Meltdown

1968–1974

In July 1950 journalist Charles Kilpatrick moved from Tyler, Texas, to San Antonio to accept a job at the *News.* San Antonio immediately impressed him as "a very attractive place to live." He also noticed, though, that the city "had a small-town outlook" and was not "as forward-looking as I'd expected." It was a city that "had its mind set in the past," which he attributed to "a conservative lifestyle where whole families … [are] inter-married, families that control the principle retail outlets, the department stores, the banks, almost anything that you could name." They "controlled the economy of the town. That's what gave them their power."[1]

Family-owned businesses that had benefited from San Antonio's growth between 1880 and 1930 created the core of that elite. Prestigious institutions like the Order of the Alamo (1909) and the Texas Cavaliers (1926) provided settings for socializing that defined their exclusivity and consolidated their social and economic power. Politics had been the one activity that the elite, with rare exceptions like Mayor John Tobin, had shunned. That changed dramatically with the adoption of council-manager government and the creation of the Good Government League. At-large elections essentially deprived minorities and working-class San Antonians of political influence, leaving the elite free to dominate public policies for urban development through its control of the GGL.

If San Antonio's oligarchs had been as creative as their cousins in Houston and Dallas, their focus on developing the city "as a whole" might have been more productive. They had, however, established an urban regime dedicated to the economic and social status quo.[2] With the exception of their campaign for the UTHSC (which they sought for public health, not economic reasons), they worked to reinforce the military and tourism as the basis of the economy, neither of which posed any threat to their control of San Antonio.

Dominance without creativity narrowed opportunities for businessmen who lacked connections to the elite. The city's family-owned firms might employ local men as managers, but as nonfamily employees they would not inherit such businesses. Ambitious individuals therefore had limited opportunities to test the talents and create their own wealth in such a closed business environment. They needed new avenues to personal success.

Massive population growth created those avenues. New residents needed housing, clothing, home furnishings, cars, and loans to help pay for all those possessions. Of all those services housing offered some of the best opportunities for enterprising individuals to become wealthy. Subdivision developers had been working in San Antonio since the late nineteenth century, but massive population growth created an unprecedentedly large market that encouraged local entrepreneurs to apply innovative approaches to home building. That market also attracted developers who lived elsewhere to town.

As "new men" seeking their fortunes, developers would eventually rebel against an oligarchy incapable of accommodating their approach to urban development. But the developers were not alone in their dislike of San Antonio's rulers. World War II also sparked a new era in civil rights. Better employment opportunities during the war combined with the service of thousands of African American and Mexican American veterans to transform civil rights into a major social and political issue in the United States. San Antonio would have its own version of a civil rights revolution culminating in the 1960s and 1970s with a revolt against the status quo. Despite the apparent calm that the GGL so carefully nurtured for nearly twenty years, the oligarchy's control of San Antonio was headed toward a meltdown.

Applying mass production techniques to building inexpensive houses was one of the many unexpected changes wrought by World War II. In New York, Abraham Levitt, together with his sons William and Alfred, used those techniques to build Levittown, Long Island, the most famous suburban project of the twentieth century.[3] The Levitts' techniques quickly found their way to San Antonio. James Burke Sr. and his son Elmo used them to build 500 houses in the Burkeshire subdivision adjacent to Kelly Air Force Base and 1,200 homes in Highland Hills, just north of Brooks Air Force Base, by the early 1950s. Ray Ellison, who worked as an aircraft mechanic and foreman at Kelly during the war, started building homes one at a time in 1949.

Adapting quickly to new production techniques, Ellison founded a business that built more than 50,000 houses over the next three decades.[4] Together, the Burkes and Ellison pioneered a new path to wealth and influence in San Antonio.

Developers could, in theory, use mass production techniques to build anywhere in San Antonio. But in practice, they much preferred building on unoccupied land at the edge of the city where land was cheaper. That had been true since at least the early twentieth century, as was another preference: building middle- and upper-class housing north of downtown and working-class housing south of it.[5] By the 1950s, however, the absence of a major employer in what was then the far north side threatened to curtail development. Civilian employment at Kelly, Brooks, and Randolph Air Force Bases had created demand for nearby housing, as the Burkes' first projects demonstrated. But Camp Bullis, an important training facility on the North Side, employed no civilians.

The emerging generation of developers needed to solve that problem. G. S. and S. E. McCreless, Edgar von Scheele, George W. Delavan Sr., and Carl Gaskin (otherwise known as the Five Oaks) would claim a special place in the pantheon of local developers when Leland Austin, a banker seeking land for the Methodist Hospital in 1956, asked them for help.[6] Although there was no guarantee then that the campaign for a medical center would succeed, they did not share the ruling elite's aversion to risk taking. Their decision to offer land for the hospital (and more if needed for a medical center) eventually accelerated San Antonio's northward march.

"Eventually" arrived in 1968, when the UTHSC welcomed its first class of students. From that point growth in and around the medical center area mushroomed. The UTHSC was a small but essential part of that growth, with 2,300 employees by 1977, but its location became a magnet for other medical and health facilities. Doctor's offices, hospitals, and research and testing laboratories flocked to the medical center, concentrating most of San Antonio's health workers in one large place. In 1965, 6,045 people had jobs in the medical and health fields; by 1980, 21,286 did.[7] No other segment of the city's economy was growing so fast, and most of its workers needed homes convenient to the center.

Although the center quickly became the single largest employer on the North Side, it was not alone in promoting rapid development. In 1968 Phil

Ray and Austin O. Roche left their jobs as engineers for General Dynamics to found Datapoint in San Antonio to produce their invention, desktop terminals (quickly improved into desktop computers). Datapoint enjoyed phenomenal growth, becoming a Fortune 500 company by the early 1980s. Ray and Roche located their headquarters on Interstate 10 just north of Loop 410. Simultaneously United Services Automobile Association (USAA) built a massive headquarters a mile farther north of Datapoint on I-10, a location that was also approximately a mile from the medical center. Originally founded as an insurance company for military officers, USAA would become the fourth largest insurer of homes and the fifth largest insurer of automobiles in the country.[8] Both corporations employed thousands of people who, like medical center employees, needed conveniently located homes and services.

Charles Becker built the foundation for those services in 1961. Becker had inherited the Handy Andy grocery chain from his father, who had moved to San Antonio in the 1920s. By the 1950s Becker's wealth and social connections had earned him membership in the ruling oligarchy. He was not, however, a devotee of the status quo, whose members he once described as "against progress and growth . . . because they've already got theirs, and now they don't want anybody else to get any."[9] Like the Five Oaks, he was a risk taker who spent a decade assembling enough retail tenants to justify building Wonderland, the city's first major mall, conveniently located at Loop 410 and I-10. Fredericksburg Road, which ran north from the loop past the future sites of the medical center and USAA, bounded Wonderland on its west side. It was a speculative venture built on Becker's faith in the North Side's rapid development, which made him a maverick within the oligarchy.[10]

Neither Wonderland nor the North Side location of the medical center initially threatened the oligarchy or the GGL's control of San Antonio. Their major effects lay in the future, and in the meantime the campaigns to create HemisFair and renew the River Walk diverted the attention and energies of downtown businessmen from their anger over the regents' insistence on building the center north of the loop. And Wonderland was an untested experiment in retailing that might fail in the absence of enough customers to support it in the early 1960s. HemisFair, after all, galvanized the oligarchy because its members thought that it would not only transform national attitudes toward San Antonio; it would also revitalize the downtown by turning it into a mecca for tourists.

Moreover the GGL favored development wherever it occurred because capturing suburban population through annexation increased the city's population and tax base. Annexation, though, became more complicated by the late 1950s. Suburban development was consuming large amounts of agricultural land around the state, and developers wanted to reduce their construction costs. Those concerns created a curious political coalition between farmers, who wanted to impede, if not halt, suburban development, and home builders, who wanted cities to provide utilities to subdivisions beyond their municipal boundaries. The legislature responded to their lobbying in 1963 by passing a complicated law that limited the amount of land cities could annex each year. Presumably that mollified the farm lobby. Then the law gave cities the authority to regulate subdivisions in unincorporated areas adjacent to them. By way of compensation to cities, the law prohibited the creation of new municipalities within a city's extraterritorial jurisdiction, in other words, within an area of unincorporated land adjacent to a city's legal boundaries. A formula for calculating extraterritorial jurisdictions for each major city gave San Antonio a jurisdiction extending five miles from its boundaries.[11]

Political compromises codified in law typically have unintended consequences, and the new annexation law was no exception. Jack Shelley, San Antonio's city manager, presented a proposal to the city council to annex nine narrow strips of land, each containing a major road, that stretched five-miles beyond the city's legal limits. That meant the city's extraterritorial jurisdiction extended in a five-mile radius in any direction from each "spoke," greatly expanding the actual territory within San Antonio's suburban hinterland. And because the 1963 law did not mandate that cities had to provide utilities in their extraterritorial jurisdictions, Shelley's proposal essentially gave the council control over a large undeveloped area at no cost. Not surprisingly the council quickly passed ordinances implementing his plan in 1964.[12]

With these arrangements in place, the GGL extended its benign support to developers at a time when North Side suburbanization was not a major political issue. The city's various agencies worked harmoniously with developers to approve their plans and compensate them for the cost of installing utilities and other basic improvements. In addition, the council practiced a laissez-faire attitude toward annexation. It waited for a developer to request annexation, reviving a policy that had been standard practice in the early twentieth century. Since developers paid only county taxes on their land and recovered their improvement costs, they were able to offer new houses at lower prices than home buyers paid in the city, enhancing the North Side's attractiveness for new residents.[13]

Tensions nevertheless percolated beneath the apparent harmony between businessmen who belonged to the oligarchy and those who did not. The "new men" were—ever so politely—excluded from the oligarchy's social circles; the banks frowned on lending money to them for projects outside the loop; the GGL ran a closed shop on decisions affecting public policies.[14] And there was a basic difference of opinion about how to develop the city. As one developer noted: "We don't have enough innovators here. This is not an imaginative community. For many years we had a group in control of things that simply was not tuned to change."[15]

An unwillingness to change was particularly perplexing to new arrivals like Glenn Biggs, who brought impressive credentials with him. A graduate of Baylor University, he first learned the intricacies of boosterism as director of the Abilene Industrial Foundation. With family connections to Sam Rayburn, Lyndon Johnson, and John Connally, Biggs quickly became involved in state politics, serving as administrative aide to Ben Barnes, speaker of the Texas House, in the mid-1960s. While in Austin he met many of the state's leading businessmen, including H. B. Zachry, who invited him to San Antonio in 1970 to lead the First National Bank, one of the city's most venerable institutions. His assessment of the local business community was not complimentary: "Nobody was really driven to excel. The main body of wealth was among people who were not forced to produce or achieve anything."[16]

Biggs introduced new ideas to local banking, including a call center to attract customers. That drew a reprimand from another bank, which accused him of calling its clients. Competition for business was not a gentlemanly thing to do. Biggs decided to move First National, which had been housed downtown in an elegant small building dating to 1886, to Travis Park and then to I-10 on the North Side because "the people that were moving out there were new to town and looking for relationships." It was a profitable move. First National's assets grew from $25 million to $225 million in a decade.[17] And

Biggs had identified the most important point about North Side growth: it had become the home territory of the "new men" and "new people" in town.

Having focused on "the whole city" for nearly twenty years, the GGL failed to consider that North Side developers might not treasure that policy as much as it did. Instead the mayor and city council blithely pursued their normal development policies because their political dominance seemed assured as the 1970s began, despite growing discontent with their policies among Mexican Americans.

Their confidence arose from an atypical surge in the GGL's interest in grassroots politics. For years the GGL had disdained cultivating voters in their precincts. The at-large election system instead relied on the GGL's financial support of candidates with citywide reputations. Election results justified this approach. Until 1967, the GGL did not lose a single council race. Then Pete Torres, a West Side lawyer, won a seat as independent, and the outcome of the 1969 elections proved even more disturbing. He proved to be a public thorn in the council's side, which made him popular enough to win reelection in 1969. The victory of Dr. D. Ford Nielson, another independent, perhaps created more alarm, because he was the son-in-law of G. S. McCreless, a charter member of the GGL in 1955. In a family-based oligarchy, the defection of a family member signaled trouble, as did the disastrous decline of West Side support for Mayor McAllister. In 1961 he had won 52 percent of that vote; in 1969 he managed only 20 percent.[18]

Shortly after the election GGL members met to discuss strategy for 1971. They decided to become a more traditional political machine, without, of course, admitting that that was what they were doing. Organizing meetings around the city and creating precinct organizations numbered among their more startling decisions.[19]

Jack Skipper, an executive with Charles Becker's Handy Andy grocery chain, served as executive director of the league (itself a new office). He became the league's principal spokesman, attending community meetings around the city as well as observing at, among others, meetings of the city council, the League of Women Voters, the Planning Commission, and the Taxpayers' League to enhance the GGL's public presence between elections. He would also serve as the league's campaign manager in 1971.

Amid all of this organizing the GGL suffered one huge setback: Walter McAllister retired as mayor. His departure created an insoluble leadership crisis that belied the formal structure of council-manager government, which was designed to rely on collective leadership from the entire council. The city charter made the mayor the weakest member of the government because he (it had never been a she) owed his position to the council, which elected him. With no independent electoral power base, the mayor in theory had no way to officially dictate or even persuade his colleagues how to vote on policies.

But McAllister had dominated city government for a decade. He did so because of his reputation. He had founded and built San Antonio Savings and Loan Association into one of San Antonio's largest companies. And he had led the council-manager reform movement that eliminated professional politicians from government. No one else matched that record, and it made him the dominant power in the GGL. When the GGL asked him to run for mayor in 1961, it in effect ceded its control of city government to him. The council duly elected him but then ignored that charter rule for the next ten years. For all practical purposes McAllister had become a political boss. Local columnist Paul Thompson opined that "as mayor he basically WAS the city council," while another reporter noted that "whatever Mayor McAllister wanted, he got, and quickly."[20]

McAllister was one of San Antonio's most effective mayors, but his dominating personal style and mastery of details left little room for disagreeing with him or allowing other councilmembers to develop into potential successors (with the exception of Lila Cockrell). Nor did it allow the council to develop its presumed role in deciding policy issues. McAllister's retirement created a leadership vacuum and a disempowered council, which in turn created the opportunity for a handshake to begin unraveling the GGL.

Seeking a reliable replacement for McAllister, the GGL turned to investment banker John Gatti, who had participated in the campaign for council-manager government and the creation of the GGL.[21] His community service included eight years on the city council. As was customary, Gatti recruited a slate of council candidates for the 1971 elections, but with its new focus on community organizations and precincts the GGL refined its selection process to counteract growing political unrest, especially on the West Side.

A Committee for Barrio Betterment had nominated four candidates to compete with the GGL. It responded by nominating three Mexican Americans who belonged to the League of United Latin American Citizens

(LULAC), an organization whose approach to civil rights issues conflicted with theirs.[22] Hoping to offset the legacy of McAllister's unpopularity on the West Side, the GGL's campaign committee also made a special effort to improve its appeal to African Americans on the East Side by nominating Robert Hilliard, a former Air Force flight surgeon and the OB/GYN chief at Lutheran General Hospital with excellent political connections within the African American community.[23]

The GGL's nominating strategy worked brilliantly. It swept the election. Gatti beat Torres to eliminate one irritant, and Nielson lost a runoff, removing the second. Voter turnout set a record, as did the vote for the GGL on the East Side.[24] Based on the results, the GGL was back, more powerful and popular than ever.

Except for that handshake. Becker seemed a safe choice for a council seat when Gatti recruited him. Becker had served on GGL recruitment committees and had otherwise been a loyal member. In his own words, he "was supposed to be an establishment person, and in a sense of the word I was" because he owned one of the city's largest businesses.[25] But he also believed the public had a right to attend meetings of city agencies, and he agreed to serve on the condition that Gatti implement open meetings: "We shook hands on it. And I thought that was all that was necessary." About a month after the election Gatti reneged on the deal. Becker turned to the Mexican American councilmen for help, and together they forced the council to agree to open meetings.[26]

That was not a trivial victory. Becker undermined a crucial GGL practice that probably originated in its governing model. The GGL members sincerely believed that running a city was exactly like running a business. Correct decisions on public policies depended on a chief executive officer who made final decisions after a thorough private review of issues. Opening that process to the public was tantamount to politicizing it. By the late 1960s that model was quickly losing credibility because the GGL's insistence on governing for the good of the whole city—as it defined that good—meant that the needs of neighborhoods remained unmet. In opening the boards to the public Becker made himself a hero in those neighborhoods and became a major political figure.

While Becker battled for open meetings, the GGL also found itself enmeshed in a complicated controversy over North Side development. In March 1970 a group of out-of-town developers with excellent state and federal political connections submitted a plan to build San Antonio Ranch to the Housing and Urban Development Department (HUD). They proposed a planned community over the Edwards Aquifer Recharge Zone that would grow to eighty-eight thousand residents over thirty years on a site twenty miles north of downtown San Antonio.[27]

Nothing of that size and complexity had ever been attempted by local developers, and the proposal created several problems. First the development might pollute the aquifer. Because it was the city's sole source of water, protecting it instantly became a permanent, controversial issue in San Antonio politics. Second, if approved, HUD would provide a multimillion-dollar grant for the project that would give it a major competitive advantage over local developers in pricing houses. They would not take kindly to the GGL endorsing the project. Finally the development's location created a serious challenge to the GGL's annexation policy because HUD might require the city to provide utilities without any compensating ability to annex it.[28]

The San Antonio Ranch project eventually failed. But until it did (after nearly three years), it roiled local politics and contributed to the GGL's demise. City Manager Gerry Henckel reacted to the initial proposal announcement by recommending a more aggressive approach in late 1970. He proposed annexing 156 square miles of land over the next eight years, effectively abandoning the informal policy of allowing developers to control annexation decisions. Aside from increasing the city's population, his proposal would expand its physical size, tax base, and extraterritorial jurisdiction, potentially giving the council more control over the San Antonio Ranch site.[29]

Further study and the 1971 elections delayed a decision on annexations, but in February 1972 HUD announced it would contribute $18 million to the proposal. Perhaps not coincidentally, Henckel proposed a modified annexation plan to the council in March. He stepped on a hornet's nest when he recommended that the annexations should be executed by May 25, which would place all the housing and businesses in the affected areas on the tax rolls immediately. Ray Ellison, among others, organized protests, but the developer community was split between those who insisted on retaining the informal annexation policy and those who were concerned about the San Antonio Ranch's impact on North Side development and supported a deal with the council.

Ralph Langley, a founding member of the GGL who had served as its vice chairman in the 1960s, testified before the council as the representative of those developers interested in a deal. He offered support for the annexations in exchange for a policy of subsidizing utility costs in subdivisions. The council accepted his proposal and approved the largest annexation in the city's recent history on October 25.[30]

Then, with an exquisite sense of bad timing, the council voted in March 1973, just before the city elections, to give the City Water Board extensive powers over utilities in unincorporated areas. The developers' fury was boundless because the council had withdrawn a competitive advantage that developers wanted as a hedge against the development's attractiveness. They also believed that increasing the board's authority interfered with their property rights.[31]

Divisive issues about annexation, development over the aquifer, and support (or not) of local developers combined with Becker's crusade for open meetings and rising opposition to the GGL on the West Side to create a toxic political stew. Mayor Gatti did not have the skills to deal with such a convoluted mess, particularly when he became a lame duck by announcing that he was moving to Houston.

Complicating matters further, Becker wanted to be mayor, and he demanded that the GGL nominate certain individuals whom he considered allies who would vote for him. In a clumsy attempt to get rid of him, the GGL Selection Committee first assigned Becker to run in place 3, traditionally designated as the mayor's slot. When he agreed, the committee recruited West Side attorney Roy Barrera to run for the same place, believing the prospect of a Mexican American becoming mayor would attract enough Mexican American votes to rid them of Becker.[32]

Becker countered that ploy by stealing Jack Skipper (who worked for him, after all) from the GGL to be his campaign manager; he also raised $300,000, half his own money, the rest from two developer friends, to fund his campaign.[33] That was an absurd amount at a time when GGL election costs, for example, normally amounted to around $50,000. Moreover the GGL's prospects were so dim that its own method for financing a campaign collapsed. Short of cash, it would end the election $70,000 in debt.[34]

The election turned into a comic opera. Although the GGL managed to assemble a complete ticket that Barrera led, only three candidates won outright: Lila Cockrell, the Rev. Claude Black, and Alvin Padilla. Among the six runoffs, the most important were those in which Becker beat Barrera; developer Cliff Morton, ironically, won as a GGL candidate; and Glenn Lacy defeated Milton Guess. Barrera's loss left open the question of who would become mayor. Lacy's victory left the pundits speechless. He was a South Side attorney with no political experience, no notoriety that made him a viable candidate, and no money of his own for the campaign. Guess was chairman of the GGL. Rumors circulated that Lacy had received anonymous donations of cash in unmarked envelopes to finance his campaign. At a time when campaign laws were not particularly strict about contributions, it is possible that the money came from the fourteen developers he numbered among his clients. Nevertheless Guess's defeat in an at-large runoff left the GGL in shambles.[35]

Selecting a mayor was the new council's first order of business. Dr. Jose San Martin and Lila Cockrell agreed privately that he should be mayor and she would become mayor pro tem (a permanent assignment at the time). They secured two more votes for their bargain, but needing one more made Reverend Black the key swing vote. As the council's only African American, Black thought it important to rotate the mayor pro tem positions among all the councilmembers, starting with himself to enhance the East Side's visibility in city government. When San Martin called to ask for his vote, Black interpreted his remarks to mean that he was, as a member of the GGL team, obligated to support the GGL, an impression San Martin reinforced by ignoring his proposal. Black found that offensive. Following that conversation, someone from Becker's faction called and declared Black's proposal acceptable. With the deal made, Black became the tiebreaker who made Becker mayor.[36]

The developers and their supporters celebrated their victory by asserting control over all the city agencies that dealt with North Side growth, including the City Water Board, where developer John Schaefer became chairman. In addition, the council tried to dismantle the at-large electoral system by proposing charter amendments to elect the mayor by popular vote and to create single-member council districts. Voters approved the first amendment but narrowly defeated the second in November 1974.[37]

Expanding their reform campaign to economic matters, the developers decided to create the North San Antonio Chamber of Commerce in August

1974, contributing to a trend toward fragmentation of the business community that reflected increasing dislike of the oligarchy's dominance of the San Antonio Chamber of Commerce. East Side businessmen had founded their Alamo Chamber of Commerce before World War II; in 1973 South Siders organized the South Bexar Chamber of Commerce; and the West San Antonio Chamber of Commerce appeared in August 1974.

The North San Antonio chamber became the most important of those regional chambers because of the North Side's growing importance to the city's development. Membership increased from 143 in 1974 to more than 2,000 by 1984, a rough measure of the area's rapidly expanding economy.[38]

Many San Antonians, however, were not pleased with the North Side developers' agenda. They cheered the GGL's defeat, but they also jeered the developers' preoccupation with the North Side. Inner-city residents had suffered through years of the GGL ignoring public improvement in their neighborhoods, and the developers' triumph did nothing to allay their anger about that neglect.[39] At-large elections had deprived them of the political power to rectify that neglect, but two national trends began the process of transforming minority neighborhoods into political powerhouses: the civil rights revolution and Lyndon Johnson's War on Poverty.

Segregation in San Antonio had always been de facto rather than de jure. Unlike most cities in the former Confederacy, San Antonio did not have an elaborate legal structure governing race and ethnic relations. That did not, however, mean San Antonio was an integrated city—far from it. Social attitudes reinforced by routine discrimination in employment proved effective in creating a segregated city. They had, for instance, begun to affect housing patterns as early as 1870, and by 1910 San Antonio's neighborhoods were thoroughly segregated along ethnic and racial lines.[40] In the early twentieth century the local press policed the color line with headlines like "Giant Negro Insults Two White Women." Stereotypes about Mexican Americans condemned them with casual comments such as, "If you paid the Mexicans more than 10 cents an hour they'd work only two or three days and then quit, because they would have enough money for beans and tortillas for a week."[41] These stereotypes reflected racial and ethnic prejudices that governed daily life.

Aggravating the indignities of everyday prejudice, an appallingly inadequate public-school system ensured that minorities who managed to graduate from high school lacked the qualifications for well-paying jobs. In 1960, when the official definition of poverty was an annual family income of less than $3,000, 46 percent of African American families and 42 percent of Mexican American families qualified as poor. Only 17 percent of white families were similarly impoverished.[42]

The oligarchy's control of the city ironically provided opportunities to improve the lives of its African American and Mexican American citizens in the decade after *Brown v. Board of Education*. Businessmen allied with the GGL believed that social controversies threatened economic development, creating a willingness to accommodate changes in race and ethnic relations, but only if civil rights advocates politely requested—and did not publicly demand—integration. In the late 1950s the city council passed ordinances desegregating parks, golf courses, tennis courts, and eventually swimming pools, using that strategy.[43]

Access to public facilities did not, however, lead to integration of private businesses that served the public. Retail shops, restaurants, hotels, and other businesses decided whom to serve and whom to hire. A department store executive, for instance, could complain that giving Mexican Americans and African Americans access to their restaurants would drive away white customers, undermining the store's bottom line. There were also legal issues to consider. A store served the public, but it was privately owned. Did the owner not have a right to decide whom he would serve on his property?

Employment was a particularly sore point, with employers insisting that they could rarely find qualified minorities to hire. By the late 1950s civil rights advocates were beginning to shift their attention to challenging the barriers erected by private businesses.

Unfortunately African Americans had to fight the initial battles to overcome those barriers by themselves. Mexican Americans harbored considerable prejudice against African Americans due to cultural differences and a belief that they were competing for jobs. Further complicating matters, only 7 percent of San Antonians were African Americans, which limited their political and economic power in the community.[44]

The solution evolved from yet another division, this time within the African American community. Some East Side leaders, such as the Rev. Samuel James, believed cooperating with the GGL offered the best hope for progress. Others, especially the Rev. Claude Black, believed in confrontation as the solution. The two factions did not cooperate with one another, but the East Side's campaign for civil rights proceeded as if they did. Black, with the cooperation of allies in the National Association for the Advancement of Colored People (NAACP), would organize protests that threatened the GGL's preference for private cooperation, which naturally turned its leaders toward working with Reverend James and his allies.

Events elsewhere initially set that arrangement in motion. In February 1960 four students in Greensboro, North Carolina, staged a sit-in at a lunch counter that inspired African Americans across the South to follow their example. San Antonio's branch of the NAACP had already announced plans to desegregate downtown restaurants, which prompted GGL member Rev. C. Don Baugh to arrange a meeting with the Chamber of Commerce president and major religious leaders to cope with this crisis.

Baugh did not invite NAACP representatives to this meeting because the oligarchy was assuming control of the effort to resolve a potentially violent confrontation. Tensions increased when the NAACP organized the largest civil rights rally in the city's history in March; more than 1,500 people enthusiastically endorsed a sit-in. Baugh responded to the rally by inviting help from four East Side leaders, including the Reverend James and two GGL members. Under pressure from the rally, the oligarchy's representatives negotiated a private agreement with store owners that made San Antonio the first southern city to integrate its lunch counters.

A month after this victory, religious and business leaders founded the San Antonio Interracial Committee to campaign for integration. The committee excluded the NAACP, instead inviting James and his faction to join. With the NAACP sidelined, the committee spent the next two years convincing a small number of business owners to integrate their stores and hotels.

Civil rights reemerged as an urgent issue with Congressman Henry B. Gonzalez's request to William Sinkin in January 1962 for help organizing HemisFair. Sinkin easily convinced McAllister to support Gonzalez, guaranteeing the oligarchy's participation. By the fall Sinkin was ready to establish the formal structure necessary to make HemisFair possible. Coincidentally, East Side leaders had become frustrated with the Interracial Committee's glacially slow work. In late October 1962 NAACP president Harry Burns asked McAllister to ban discrimination in public accommodations by ordinance.[45]

There were two "problems" with this request. First, it resurrected the NAACP, which the oligarchy viewed with distaste for its supposedly militant approach to civil rights. Second, Burns demanded that the council pass an ordinance prohibiting discrimination in February 1963. Doing so would undermine the business community's preference for voluntary integration. McAllister explained that belief as he and others struggled to undermine Burns's request. "I cannot conceive of my voting for an ordinance that forces a private owner of a business to do business with everyone who comes within his doors," he said. "Our program of voluntary integration, I think, can accomplish a lot of good. Coercion will not prove practical."[46]

Public opinion, however, was increasingly tilting toward coercion. Civil rights had become a major national issue by 1963. In August Martin Luther King Jr. would lead the March on Washington that galvanized support for integration. Locally the public mood was conflicted. Hotelier Harry Leffingwell wrote McAllister to say that he felt obligated to protect his customers from anything they regarded as objectionable. Furthermore he did not believe that it was "any part of my duties to try to convert them to the beauties of integration." On the other hand, KTSA Radio's management warned in an editorial that the council's refusal to deal with Burns's request "will continue to cause embarrassment, discontent, and spur controversy."[47]

Spring 1963 was not a good time for controversy. Not only was Sinkin busily organizing the HemisFair campaign, the city elections loomed ahead in April. Seeking a graceful delaying tactic, the council created a small committee composed entirely of liberals to study the problem of integration and make recommendations. It duly submitted its report in late May, when the GGL was once again securely reelected. The report called for an immediate end to discrimination, pointed out, among other things, that the controversy endangered the city's economic future, and recommended that the council oversee a campaign of voluntary desegregation.[48]

McAllister immediately organized the oligarchy into a highly effective campaign to implement the report. On June 5 the council established the Committee on Desegregation with James Gaines, a GGL member, as chair. Its members represented a Who's Who of San Antonio and included several African Americans who were amenable to voluntary desegregation. Establishment organizations such as the Chamber of Commerce and the local newspapers endorsed the committee, and more than fifty community leaders issued a public statement announcing that "desegregation of publicly used facilities is no longer a matter for debate."[49]

Marshall Steves began asking for contributions to fund HemisFair the same month that the Committee on Desegregation launched its campaign. The committee encountered more resistance than Steves did, but the enthusiasm for HemisFair bred an impatience with behavior—like racial and ethnic discrimination—that could undermine the elite's desire to showcase San Antonio to a national audience. And because the oligarchy controlled the city's social, economic, and political life so completely, few businessmen could afford to ignore its unsubtle demands for compliance. Within two months the committee had persuaded 95 percent of the business community to "voluntarily" comply with integration.[50]

It was an impressive achievement that preserved the elite's dominance, although the campaign made a mockery of its preference for private, genteel persuasion. That dominance faded within a year, when Lyndon Johnson made civil rights a cornerstone of his program to remake American society. In 1964 the Rev. Claude Black campaigned for an ordinance banning discrimination. McAllister opposed it, and the city attorney declared such an ordinance would be unconstitutional. Then Congress passed the Civil Rights Act in July.

Partly in response to the law, and partly to preserve its influence on the East Side, the GGL nominating committee decided to give African Americans a council seat for the first time in the 1965 elections, choosing the Rev. Samuel James as its candidate. James won, but he surprised the council by submitting an ordinance prohibiting discrimination. James's motion had the support of the League of Women Voters, who had studied the city's employment situation and reported to the council that the city lacked enforcement power to convince local employers to obey the Civil Rights Act's provisions. The council conceded the point that national law takes precedence over local preference in December 1965, explaining to San Antonians that "discrimination in places of public accommodation causes embarrassment and inconvenience to citizens and visitors to the city, creates breaches of the peace, and is otherwise detrimental to the welfare and economic growth of the city."[51]

Passage of the ordinance essentially ended the local campaign for African American civil rights. Considering their weak bargaining position, they had made some important progress.

San Antonio's Mexican American community would also become divided over the proper approach to combatting discrimination, but prior to 1960 LULAC and the American GI Forum were its undisputed advocates. Both represented a growing middle class whose ranks swelled as veterans used their benefits to earn college degrees and Mexican Americans found work as federal employees at the city's five military bases. Kelly Air Force Base was especially important in contributing to the expansion of the West Side's middle class. In 1962 Mexican Americans were 43 percent of its workforce.[52]

LULAC and the GI Forum worked to eliminate discrimination by promoting the importance of education, learning to speak English, and working within the existing political system.[53] Henry B. Gonzalez personified their philosophy and policies. His parents were refugees from the Mexican Revolution who moved to San Antonio, where he was born in 1916. After graduating from Jefferson High School in 1935, he attended San Antonio College and the University of Texas at Austin before earning a law degree from Saint Mary's University. After military service during World War II, he worked as a probation officer and rose through the ranks to become chief probation officer of the Bexar County juvenile court.

In 1953, with the new city charter in place, Gonzales won election to the city council, then won reelection as an independent candidate in the GGL's first campaign. He established a reputation as a staunch advocate for civil rights, proposing the ordinances that desegregated all city facilities in 1956. Turing his attention to state politics, he won election to the Senate in 1956, becoming the first Mexican American to serve there in more than a century. A year into his term he teamed with Abraham Kazan to launch the longest filibuster in the Senate's history, against ten laws designed to undermine *Brown v. Board of Education.* Their combined effort defeated eight of the ten, making Gonzalez the state's foremost champion of civil rights for both African Americans and Mexican Americans. When Paul Kilday vacated his Twentieth Congressional District seat in 1961, Gonzalez won the special election to replace him. He helped pass the Housing and Civil Rights Acts of 1964 as a congressman, demonstrating his staunch belief in integration for all minorities.[54]

Albert Peña was cut from the same middle-class cloth as Gonzalez, but he eventually fashioned a quite different pattern in his approach to civil rights issues. Born in 1918, he attended local schools, served in the navy during World War II, and earned a law degree in 1950. In the 1950s his career resembled Gonzalez's. He joined LULAC and the GI Forum, represented the plaintiffs in a suit to desegregate schools in Hondo, Texas, and won election to the Bexar County Commissioners Court in 1956, a position he held until 1972. Like Gonzalez, he was an often blunt (his opponents would say obnoxious) advocate for civil rights.[55]

Sharp differences in their approaches to fighting discrimination emerged rather abruptly in the early 1960s. Peña had gained national attention for his crucial role in organizing Viva Kennedy clubs in the 1960 presidential election, which John Kennedy won in part because he carried Texas with the help of Mexican American and African American voters. Peña capitalized on that success by organizing the Political Association of Spanish-Speaking Organizations, which became the original source of volunteers for his approach to civil rights. He also became a vocal, bitter critic of John Connally, who won the election for governor as a conservative Democrat in November 1962.[56]

Gonzalez was no fan of Connally's, but he believed that progress toward equality for minorities depended on working within the Democratic Party. Unfortunately conservatives with a dismal record on civil rights dominated the state's Democratic Party. Peña had at this point concluded that progress would only occur by creating an ethnic power base to challenge conservative control of the party.

He gained national attention with his first campaign to demonstrate the power of ethnic bloc voting. In 1963 he used volunteers from the Political Association of Spanish-Speaking Organizations and confrontational tactics to wrest political control of Crystal City, a small South Texas town, from conservative Anglos. It was a stunning symbolic victory that validated Peña's approach to campaigning for civil rights. When Crystal City's small Mexican American business community complained about his tactics, Peña dismissed their criticism by remarking that "we can do without the 'Tío Tomáses.'"[57]

Peña followed up that victory by provoking a bitter fight with John Peace, Connally's Bexar County coordinator, for control of the county delegation to the 1964 Democratic National Convention. With the help of liberal Democrats who detested Connally, he defeated Peace, who promptly walked out of the meeting with his supporters to create a contending delegation. Peace also appealed to his friend Frank Erwin for help. Erwin, as state chairman of the Democratic party, ruled that Peace's delegates should be seated at the national convention. The fierce battle, though, did increase Peña's influence with San Antonio's liberal Democratic legislative delegation for the remainder of the decade.[58]

Gonzalez and Peña thus defined, and would fight for, different approaches to civil rights in San Antonio just as Congress was preparing to pass the Civil Rights Act of 1964 and Lyndon Johnson was about to launch his War on Poverty. Federal funding would become a weapon in the struggle to decide which approach would triumph. It was a battle that had important implications for the GGL's hold on political power, a point its leaders understood as they made their own preparations to deal with a profusion of new federal programs.

Congress began the War on Poverty in August 1964 with the Economic Opportunity Act. The act inspired the creation of a large bureaucracy, all under the aegis of an Economic Opportunities Development Corporation (EODC) for each city that participated in the program. Each corporation supervised a standard set of initiatives, including the Community Action Program (CAP).

CAP embodied a core EODC belief that became so controversial that it helped destroy the War on Poverty: the people who would benefit from the war had a right to participate in it. Mayors across the country hated the CAP because it entitled poor and working-class citizens to serve on the oversight boards that supervised efforts to alleviate their poverty. They also objected that poor people did not have the training or experience to deal with complex initiatives to improve neighborhood infrastructure, social conditions, or employment opportunities. And they were concerned that people representing those neighborhoods might have different ideas about what to do and would have a vote in determining which programs to adopt. For mayors and other local officials, the War on Poverty was a war on their power to control and dispense federal funding according to their own priorities.

In addition, by giving minority residents in poor neighborhoods the opportunity to learn how public policies are created and funded, the CAPs introduced residents to the politics of governing. Theoretically an informed citizenry might be a good thing; in practice it created the potential for political upheaval.

And so it proved. San Antonio would be the first city to join the war, in December 1964. McAllister and the GGL immediately understood the challenges the program posed and spent the next two years trying to manipulate the selection of neighborhood residents to control it. That attempt drew the ire of Archbishop Robert Lucey, whose severe criticism would leave a lingering legacy of antagonism between Lucey and the EODC Board after Congressman Gonzalez finally intervened in February 1966 to overcome McAllister's opposition to CAP. The agreement with McAllister, however, left the GGL with considerable influence over the board.[59]

As that battle had dragged on, Gonzalez and Lucey used their personal relationships with Johnson to sidestep McAllister's opposition to jumpstart assistance to the poor. The archdiocese already had a Christian Youth Organization that Lucey and Gonzalez decided to expand. While the GGL fought to control the EODC, they prevailed on Johnson to create the San Antonio Neighborhood Youth Organization (SANYO) in May 1965 with money from the Department of Labor.[60]

Lucey appointed Father John Yanta, director of the archdiocesan youth program, to direct SANYO. Yanta harbored strong views about the sources of misery on the West Side: "The Good Government League and other institutions kept these [poor] areas disorganized and under oppression. It was only natural that churches, which were already leading in these areas, would lead the way in this situation."[61]

Yanta's comments confirmed that McAllister had cause for concern about the political implications of the War on Poverty, particularly because Gonzalez had found a way to enlist the Catholic Church in the war. West Side residents had an intense loyalty to their parish churches as the institution that created stability and distinct identities for their neighborhoods.[62] Their parish councils provided models for quickly introducing federal antipoverty programs into their neighborhoods. Yanta depended on that model to build SANYO into the city's most important antipoverty agency. He recruited residents from each parish to serve on local councils that brought SANYO's services into thirty neighborhoods at the height of its success. The archdiocese's parish priests usually had active roles in the councils, whose members also included women. SANYO also worked with East Side

Baptist churches to organize councils in accordance with the OEDC's official support for integration.

Considering his views on the GGL, it is not surprising that Yanta also encouraged political activism. SANYO sponsored civic action workshops to train councilmembers and other residents in the details of its programs, which gave them the ability to make informed decisions and to become accustomed to voting for their preferences. That training led to the creation of the Greater San Antonio Federation of Neighborhood Councils in 1967 which, while theoretically independent, served as SANYO's political lobby in funding low-income neighborhood programs.

SANYO and the War on Poverty aroused opposition across the political spectrum and from a variety of perspectives. McAllister, for instance, struggled to contain his ideological outrage over the use of government power to deal with social problems: "Every time we turn to government to assume a responsibility that is a personal one, we lose more than we gain. We lose independence and self-reliance.... [The] Great Society's War on Poverty is wasted effort and money."[63] Conservatives were not the only threat to SANYO, however, as political opposition also emerged within the Mexican American community.

In January 1966, as the GGL's battle to control the EODC was drawing to a close, Peña wrote to Sen. Ralph Yarborough. He complained that the War on Poverty had already collapsed because San Antonio's conservatives "don't want the poor to have equal representation" on the EODC board. Pondering a solution to that problem, Peña suggested that independent agencies should assume control of the war.[64] Establishing organizations that could compete effectively with federally funded agencies might appear quixotic at best, but Peña was a seasoned organizer who was quite capable of solving the challenges of identifying leaders, recruiting members, and raising money to support new enterprises.

He found the leadership among his supporters who were students at Saint Mary's University, a private Catholic institution that became the intellectual center of the Texas Chicano movement in the late 1960s. At a time when civil rights had become a powerful political issue that heightened minorities' sensitivities to injustice and discrimination, recruiting membership proved rather easy in Texas, as well as throughout the Southwest and California. The Ford Foundation, which had helped finance the Crystal

City campaign, provided the funding. On July 4, 1967, Saint Mary's students José Ángel Gutiérrez, Willie Velásquez, Mario Compean, Ignacio Pérez, and Juan Patlán announced the creation of the Mexican American Youth Organization (MAYO).[65]

MAYO's name challenged SANYO in two crucial ways. First, there were now two organizations claiming ownership of youth programs. Second, the name's focus on Mexican Americans declared a policy of a separate cultural identity as the basis for antipoverty programs. The Equal Opportunity Act had mandated integration as a basic policy in the War on Poverty. MAYO rejected that mandate, adopting a policy of ethnic exclusivity.[66]

The emergence of Mexican American militancy in San Antonio and elsewhere reflected a similar national trend among African Americans who supported Stokely Carmichael and the Black Power Movement in the late 1960s. Both challenged individuals and organizations that had spent decades struggling to integrate American society. In San Antonio the local LULAC branch moved leftward, attempting to retain its relevance to the civil rights campaign by demanding appointments of Mexican Americans to supervisory positions at Kelly Air Force Base and on the City Public Service board. That effort floundered in part because of GGL intransigence but also because Gonzalez refused to intervene. He castigated LULAC in May 1967 for supporting promotion based on ethnicity: "Let it be clear to you that I am not a professional Mexican. I have never presented myself as a power broker for what you call the Mexican American, but as a representative of all the people."[67]

MAYO sought to become the ethnic power broker that Gonzalez so emphatically rejected. Its militant advocacy was tailor-made to aggravate him, particularly because he was famously thin skinned, especially where his reputation as a major civil rights leader was concerned. And because of Peña's role in founding MAYO, his relationship with Gonzalez became increasingly bitter.

Both men now had organizations that represented serious divisions within San Antonio's Mexican American community. In effect SANYO and MAYO became the surrogates of their principal sponsors in what quickly turned into a political battle for control of the city's War on Poverty. Both organizations maneuvered throughout 1968 for control over programs that would enhance their funding and their political clout. Gonzalez, for instance, became deeply involved in the new Model Cities program. As a byproduct of his interest, SANYO members obtained five positions on the Model Cities board. Considering that Model Cities focused on infrastructure improvements for inner-city neighborhoods, and SANYO's writ involved summer recreation and employment programs, its involvement in Model Cities represented a strange expansion into uncharted waters. On the other hand, MAYO was busily creating rival youth programs in SANYO's "territory," which meant that becoming a major player in a new federal program helped increase its competitive edge over the militants.[68]

Tensions between Gonzalez and the militants reached a breaking point on April 10, 1969. MAYO called a press conference during which José Gutiérrez denounced gringos, by which he meant most Anglo Texans, as prejudiced against Mexican Americans. He made the mistake of referring to the possible need to eliminate gringos, which reporters found too injudicious to ignore. In response to a request to define elimination, he said there were various ways, but "you can certainly kill them." The rest of his answer, which focused on political solutions, got lost in a blizzard of headlines.[69]

Gutiérrez's rhetorical allusions to violence appealed to militants because they thought it created a sense of urgency regarding the need for immediate attention to their grievances. By the late 1960s, however, white Americans associated such rhetoric with the massive urban riots that had erupted across the country in the mid-1960s. Even rhetorical references to violence, especially in a city like San Antonio that had escaped such riots, aroused considerable anger instead.

Gonzalez moved quickly to take advantage of the uproar that followed the press conference. He spent the rest of April denouncing militants on the floor of the House of Representatives and helped insert provisions in the 1969 Tax Reform Act that curtailed the Ford Foundation's ability to fund MAYO and similar organizations.[70]

While Gonzalez attacked militants' funding, MAYO drove Archbishop Lucey out of San Antonio. Its campaign to undermine SANYO and convert the archdiocese into a funding source for its programs began with picketing Lucey's home in 1967. Young priests who sympathized with Peña's approach to civil rights advocacy began contacting him for support by January 1968; their numbers grew fairly rapidly and caused Lucey to retaliate by transferring several to parishes in small South Texas towns. In spring 1969 sixty-eight priests signed a petition to the Vatican asking for his removal.

In May Peña and several MAYO members attended a meeting to protest Lucey's transfers, asserting that lay Catholics had the right to be involved in such decisions. They also complained that "many have talked with Lucey for a piece of the action [i.e., funding] in the past, but have seen no results." The attendees organized a Concerned Chicano Catholic Committee to stage a mass protest against Lucey for June 8. Faced with mounting opposition to his policies, Lucey resigned on June 4.[71]

The internecine battle between SANYO and MAYO also gave conservatives on the EODC board an opportunity to play politics. On April 7, 1969, Walter H. Richter, director of the Southwest Region, Office of Economic Opportunity Development Corporation, sent the results of an investigation of San Antonio's antipoverty programs to the San Antonio EODC board. The origins of the investigation remain obscure, but the report focused primarily on SANYO, whose activities had concerned local conservatives since 1965. Richter's investigation had concluded that "the climate of hostility and ill will . . . permeates virtually every facet of the antipoverty operation . . . no real progress can be made in a community which has two or more solidly polarized camps often bitterly at odds with one another, largely devoid of goodwill toward one another, and apparently unable to communicate with any measure of effectiveness." As for where the fault lay for this situation, Richter blamed SANYO.[72]

Such an attack from the political right, especially at the outset of Richard Nixon's presidency, boded ill for antipoverty programs. Gonzalez responded with a sustained campaign to purge militants from those programs through summer 1969; MAYO lost wavering followers such as Willie Velásquez, and Peña tried to deal with funding problems by demanding aid from the new archbishop.[73]

Casualties continued to mount over the next two years, culminating with Yanta's resignation from SANYO in 1971 and Peña's loss to Albert Bustamante, a Gonzalez loyalist, in his 1972 reelection bid to the Commissioners Court. President Nixon contributed to the general disarray by reorganizing antipoverty agencies to eliminate citizen participation and political organizing and to restore the power of mayors and city councils in making decisions about which programs to fund.[74]

Nixon's policies revived the importance of traditional politics in improving inner-city neighborhoods. In San Antonio "traditional" meant the at-large political system that diluted the political importance of minority neighborhoods. Militants had capitalized on increasing discontent with the GGL to reduce its political strength on the West Side, but the at-large election system still diluted the political strength of minority neighborhoods. And it had shown its resilience by exploiting the militants' refusal to cooperate with African Americans to strengthen its influence on the East Side, which contributed to its impressive 1971 victory. Charles Becker's palace coup after the 1973 election had yet to occur. How, then, could militants continue their struggle?

The answer required blending militancy with tradition in two organizations: the Mexican American Legal Defense and Education Foundation (MALDEF) and Communities Organized for Public Service (COPS). Peña had founded MALDEF in 1968 with support from the Ford Foundation. Congressman Gonzalez had included it in his attacks on militants, forcing it to move from San Antonio to California, where it dealt with legal aid cases for the next three years. In spring 1971 Peña decided to use MALDEF in a systemic attack on the GGL. He met with representatives from the Center for Community Change and Common Cause, nonpartisan organizations that supported minority and working-class causes, to discuss a lawsuit "challenging the present methods of electing city councilmen in San Antonio." With a promise of funding from Common Cause, he recruited San Antonio attorney Phil Hardberger to assist MALDEF with the suit.[75]

Rectifying discrimination through lawsuits had been a traditional, long-term strategy that the NAACP had used for decades. And Peña, despite his role in promoting Chicano militancy, had African American friends and had retained his membership in LULAC.[76] Both LULAC and the NAACP's Legal Defense Fund supported the creation of MALDEF. Since the lawsuit would benefit African Americans and Mexican Americans, it in effect contributed to an integrated approach to minority politics in San Antonio. Convincing the federal courts that the at-large electoral system violated the rights of minority residents took five years. Ironically the GGL's large 1972 annexation of North Side subdivisions helped win the case in 1976. At that point the city council faced the choice of adopting single-member council districts or de-annexing those subdivisions.

Ernie Cortés created his own blend of militancy and tradition in founding COPS. His disillusionment with MAYO-style militancy led him to Saul Alinsky's Industrial Area Foundation in Chicago in the early 1970s.

MAYO's leaders had used Alinsky's rules and tactics to confront their opponents, but they had not traveled to Chicago to study at the foundation as Cortés did. That meant they lacked an understanding of some critical Alinsky ideas which, in their own way, were surprisingly conservative. Alinsky believed in well-informed citizens who identified practical issues that mattered to their neighborhoods and took the time to study them in detail. Community organizations also needed to be self-sustaining rather than relying on government or charitable funding. And last but not least, community organizations needed to build demonstrable nonpartisan political power. In sum, Alinsky's principles and tactics challenged the existing political system by training ordinary citizens to become active, effective participants in it.[77]

Alinsky's ideas provided useful tools for dealing with Anglo San Antonians who consistently ignored or misunderstood the dedication to family and neighborhood as well as the work ethic of inner-city residents. McAllister famously summarized those views in a nationally broadcast 1970 interview: "You have to bear in mind that there is a special temperament, a difference of temperament between the Anglos and our Americans of Mexican descent.... They are home living, they love beauty, they love flowers, they love music, they love dancing. Perhaps they're not quite, let's say, as ambitiously motivated as the Anglos to get ahead financially, but they get a lot out of life."

To the consternation of the oligarchy, COPS would become one of the ways that Mexican Americans and African Americans got "a lot out of life." Cortés returned to San Antonio in 1973 and began the hard work of building COPS. As with SANYO, the Catholic Church's parishes provided the recruiting ground for COPS. Cortés initially convinced priests like Edmundo Rodriquez and Albert Benavides to support him, which helped convince the archdiocese to provide startup funding. (COPS would become self-sufficient within three years.) Given Cortés's plan to focus on projects not causes, he did not recruit Chicano activists. Instead, in an innovative departure from Alinsky's guidelines, he worked with altar society presidents and Kelly Air Force Base employees who were the core members of the West Side's stable working class. And he recruited women for leadership positions. Andres Sarabia became COPS's first president, but all his successors were women.[78]

COPS relied on its members to identify and prioritize projects.[79] That was a significant departure from the kind of citizen participation that characterized federal CAP agencies, where residents worked on projects that had already been identified for them. Cortés's definition of participation created pride of ownership in projects, generated enthusiasm for the difficult task of convincing city leaders to fund their projects, and transformed COPS into a politically powerful force in local politics.

Fortunately for Cortés, he was building COPS into a major organization while Charles Becker was mayor. Becker insisted on hearing from the public at council meetings, a practice the GGL had frowned on. In August 1974 COPS members attended a meeting to protest the absence of effective flood drainage on the West Side. After Father Benavides, "looking like the prophet Jeremiah," gave a spirited denunciation of the GGL's indifference to that problem, Becker asked City Manager Sam Granata if Benavides was right. Assured that he was, Becker "ranted and raved about the evils of the Good Government League." The complementary jeremiads concluded with Becker ordering Granata to find a way to rectify the problem. Voters approved a $47 million bond issue for West Side drainage in November.[80]

In January 1975 Becker again displayed his unconventional approach to governing by holding a public meeting in which more than three hundred people debated how to distribute $16 million in federal funds. COPS members again came prepared; when the shouting stopped they walked away with $11 million for neighborhood redevelopment, sewers, and more drainage.[81] COPS's success in obtaining public funds for its projects made it a powerful new political force.

That same month Cortés attempted to expand COPS's influence by confronting the business community. Its November 1974 convention had adopted a $100 million program of improvements that it hoped the council would adopt in the next fiscal year, and Cortés needed its support. He organized a modern version of the sit-in to demand it. In January 1975 large delegations of COPS female members walked en masse into a department store and began trying on clothes for hours on end while Cortés met with the owner to demand that he support the budget proposal. Banker Tom Frost found his tellers counting rolls of pennies that customers politely asked to exchange for dollar bills before returning to the end of a long line to exchange the bills for coins. The tactics initially failed to sway owners to support the budget proposal, but television and press coverage of the protests convinced the Chamber of Commerce to bargain for peace. Its president met with Cortés to arrange a truce.[82]

Any agreement that the chamber made with COPS became a moot point after the 1975 city elections. John Steen, a longtime GGL member and respected businessman, declared that reports of the GGL's death had been premature. He announced that the GGL would discard its "country club" image and offer a full slate of younger, more diverse candidates. Becker surprised the pundits by refusing to run for reelection as mayor but also announced he would support the Independent Team, which was composed of mostly North Side residents and developers. In the absence of the old GGL's firm hand the election became rather chaotic. Only Henry Cisneros (GGL) and the Rev. Claude Black (Independent Team) won their contests outright. Everyone else ended up in runoffs. Lila Cockrell (GGL) won the mayoralty; but only one other GGL candidate won a seat on the council. The Independent Team won six council seats. Steen stubbornly refused to recognize the signs of mortality in the results, but the GGL was in fact dead at last.[83]

The Independent Team moved quickly to gain control of key positions that would promote their agenda for North Side development. Ed Harrington, president of the Greater San Antonio Builders Association, became chairman of the City Planning Commission, and John Schaefer, a major North Side developer, became chairman of the City Water Board.

Control of those two agencies was crucial for the developers' desire to use city resources to support North Side growth. It was rather awkward then that in early June Harrington received a preliminary "study" from the Planning and Community Development Department that recommended that future policies on growth should focus on the "promotion of development within the city."[84] That idea was diametrically opposed to the developers' preferences, prompting Harrington to ignore it until Charles Stromberg, the department's deputy director, published it in May 1976. After a private meeting between three Independent Team councilmen, Schaefer, and developer Cliff Morton, the council fired Stromberg.[85]

He became a casualty in what had turned into a fiasco. The Independent Team suffered from a curious inability to impose its will on public policies despite its technical majority. In September 1975 the team had to settle for a significantly smaller increase in water rates than it wanted for extending utilities to new subdivisions. Then in October the team managed to change zoning over the aquifer to permit construction of a huge mall, provoking a massive outpouring of rage from environmentalists in an alliance with COPS. Wavering in the face of such a heated response, the council scheduled a referendum to obtain public approval of the zoning change in January 1976. The voters rejected the ordinance. Although the courts later ruled the referendum illegal, the mall was never built.[86]

With COPS and the environmentalists in full pursuit, the team scurried from disaster into irrelevance. On July 9 the council voted to refuse funding for utility extensions to subdivisions outside the city's limits. Two months later the developers launched a recall petition against Mayor Cockrell and four councilmen. Becker supported the recall, explaining that the council was "knuckling under to COPS." Revealing the disarray within their own ranks, the developers included two of the Independent Team's councilmen in their recall.[87]

The recall failed and pressure from the U.S. Department of Justice forced the council to choose between de-annexation and creating a new political system. It developed a proposal for ten council districts with the mayor elected at large (an idea that had already won approval) and scheduled a referendum for January 1977. North Side voters had little interest in a new system, which depressed their willingness to vote. Turnout in fact would be extremely low (19 percent of registered voters), which enhanced the importance of organization in gaining approval of the proposal. COPS's superb voter organization delivered enough votes to approve the new political system.[88]

With that victory the meltdown of the oligarchy's political control of San Antonio was complete. Its party and the system that had sustained it had disappeared. In 1954 the advantages of taking control of city government had clearly seemed to outweigh the risks, but in replacing professional politicians with a strictly business model of governance, the reformers of the 1950s deprived themselves of the flexibility necessary to respond to social change. And even as a regime purportedly focused on promoting economic development, the GGL left a mixed record. The military's dominant role in the economy made business leaders complacent, which the absence of diversity only reinforced. The city needed new leadership and new ideas, and the collapse of the old order created the opportunity for it to emerge.

TEN

A Vulnerable Unity

1974–1991

Adopting a new political system was an essential first step in coping with the discontents that had undermined the GGL. The next, more important, step, would be to learn how to manage those discontents successfully so that promising economic development ideas could also succeed. Inner-city neighborhood advocates and North Side developers did not have much in common except that both groups needed the city's government to assist their very different goals. Their different interests naturally became a source of conflict over the council's decisions about the distribution of resources, which complicated the agenda of a new booster coalition. With conflict the new norm, it would require adept booster leadership to deal with the anger, and the power, of localized interests to implement their own goals for transforming San Antonio's economy.

In one of the more remarkable coincidences in San Antonio's history, Robert McDermott, Lila Cockrell, and Henry Cisneros would emerge as partners in an unprecedented effort to unite conflicting interests in a major effort to develop the city. There was nothing inevitable about their partnership, which evolved quickly as their different personal careers converged to produce a new economic and political order.

McDermott was born in Readville, Massachusetts, a close-knit community of about two hundred residents, in 1920. His father, Marlow, was a gifted professional musician who also worked as the village's milkman to help make ends meet.[1] Both jobs provided opportunities for his father to shape his son's character. McDermott helped him deliver milk in the early morning, and in the evenings often accompanied him on the long commute to Boston for concerts, which, in McDermott's words, created the opportunity for a "little bonding" between them. His father's example gave McDermott a strong work ethic, a strong desire to excel, and a lifelong love of music.[2]

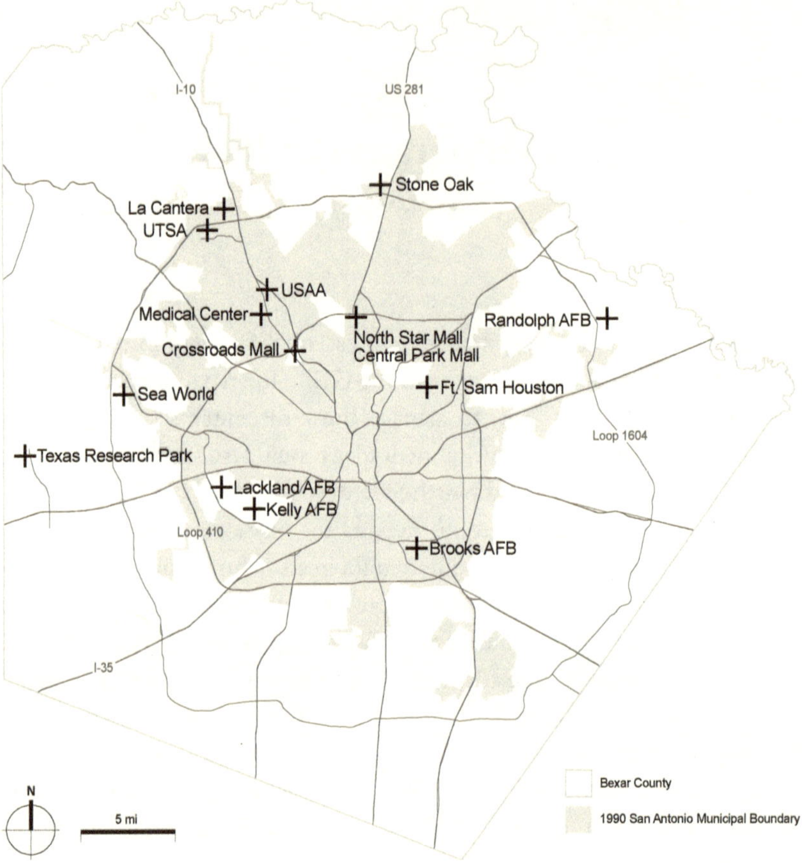

Religious and secular education also profoundly influenced him. His Catholic Sunday school teacher made him "very conscious throughout my life that I had an obligation to myself to develop [my] talents and then to help other people. Love your neighbor as yourself."[3] He excelled as a student at the Boston Latin School, one of the nation's best high schools, whose curriculum stressed the importance of the liberal arts. In addition to imbibing, among other subjects, four years of Latin, French, and German, he earned the school's music prize for his skill as a trombonist.[4]

His father, a Word War I veteran, guided McDermott into a military career.[5] While waiting for an appointment to West Point, McDermott attended

Norwich University, a military prep school, before entering the academy in 1939. At the time, the service academies followed rigid curriculum guidelines that forced McDermott to repeat all of his Norwich coursework. That did not sit well with him. He said, "I got angry at a system that made me repeat everything."[6]

His anger would later drive his determination to reform military education, but in the meantime he seized an opportunity to volunteer for flight school. Completing his training after graduating from the academy, he was assigned to the 474th Fighter Group of the U.S. Ninth Air Force. He flew sixty-one combat missions over Europe as a P-38 fighter-bomber pilot, earning the Bronze Star and the Air Medal with five oak leaf clusters, a record that probably enhanced his self-confidence for dealing with difficult situations.

When the war ended McDermott served briefly on Gen. Dwight Eisenhower's staff in occupied Germany and then at the Pentagon, where he developed relationships that would later prove useful to his work as an educational reformer.[7] He then earned an MBA from Harvard University in 1950, where he learned about the usefulness of early computers for data processing.[8]

McDermott then taught economics at West Point, where he wrote two books designed to educate military officers on the intricacies of personal finance and insurance. Promoted to colonel in 1954, he moved to the newly established Air Force Academy in Colorado Springs, where he soon found himself in a position to experiment with his ideas about military education.

He had become interested in the ways an education did, or did not, create leaders for the military. He believed that "leaders develop from a system where a man has many opportunities to solve problems, make decisions, and assume responsibility for the decisions he makes. He has to have time to think, time to sit, and time to reflect."[9] It followed that leaders needed choices, but at West Point "everybody was a civil engineer. It was stupid."[10]

McDermott's reforms included a new system for evaluating applicants to the Air Force Academy, an enrichment program that eventually offered thirty-eight majors, and innovative programs in computer science, international relations, and defense policy. He proved so successful that the army and navy adopted his ideas for their academies, earning him a national reputation as an educational reformer and a promotion to brigadier general.[11]

While pursuing ways to improve military education, McDermott also found time to engage in city-building activities in Colorado Springs. He had recruited highly qualified faculty who needed continuing education to stay current in their technical fields to encourage them to stay at the academy. McDermott used social connections he had developed with a former chancellor of the University of Colorado to arrange for a branch campus offering engineering courses in Colorado Springs, which helped his faculty and also made the city more attractive to tech companies in search of good business locations.[12]

Coincidence played a crucial role in his choice of a second career when he retired from the air force. John Cheever, who was president of both San Antonio's Broadway National Bank and USAA, a company founded by military officers at Fort Sam Houston in 1922 to provide insurance to their compatriots, had read McDermott's books of financial advice. He asked him to consider relocating to San Antonio to succeed him at USAA. McDermott had other offers as well, but he was impressed that San Antonio had staged HemisFair, which he thought meant the business community was organized enough to pursue urban development, a topic that interested him. With those thoughts in mind, he chose San Antonio.[13]

McDermott arrived in late summer 1968 as HemisFair was ending and local politics were heating up. Model Cities was only one of several programs contributing to the fierce intra-ethnic struggle for control of federal funding for inner-city improvements, but it was distinctive in having one unusual advocate who would eventually emerge as another city leader.

Councilwoman Lila Cockrell was an early and enthusiastic supporter of Model Cities.[14] McAllister had personally chosen her as the first woman to serve on the council, although he did not share her enthusiasm for Model Cities. Despite that, she lobbied her council colleagues so effectively that they voted to approve the program over his objections. That was not a politically healthy thing to do. Her victory would prove costly in the short run, but it established her as a major independent-minded political figure with the resources to become a critically important future mayor.

A variety of unusual circumstances contributed to Cockrell's development into an extraordinary politician. Born in Fort Worth in 1922 to Velma and Robert Banks, her father, a lawyer in San Antonio, died before she was two, and her mother moved back to Fort Worth to live with her parents, Julia and Andrew Campbell. Mr. Campbell, an administrator in the Internal Revenue Service, was assigned to New York City for several years and moved his extended family with him. When Lila Cockrell was in her early teens, her mother remarried in New York, but because her second husband was frequently ill, Lila spent a great deal of time with her grandparents. When Prohibition ended, Lila returned to Fort Worth with her grandparents and lived with them while attending high school, only staying with her mother during summer breaks.[15]

In those circumstances, Julia Campbell became the dominant influence in Lila's teenage years. A remarkable woman, Julia had divorced her first husband at a time when that was not the sort of thing respectable women did. She then converted the family home into a boardinghouse to support herself and her two children, saving enough money to buy an apartment building. While working toward financial independence, she became active in the Fort Worth Women's Christian Temperance Union, developing a reputation for effective public speaking and a strong interest in politics. Not surprisingly, Lila Cockrell would draw inspiration from her grandmother's example: "She had a lot of influence on my life because, first of all, she loved me very much, and she always instilled in me the idea that a woman could achieve."[16]

That influence became the basis for Cockrell's lifelong interest in community affairs. In high school she was drawn to debate, which she loved because "it helps you learn to marshal and organize facts to get the important 'meat' of the topic."[17] After graduating from Southern Methodist University with a degree in speech, she married Sid Cockrell, who was starting a career in nonprofit organizations in 1942. After wartime service, he became an administrator for the National Conference of Christians and Jews in Dallas, while she devoted herself to raising their two daughters and to the League of Women Voters, serving as its president from 1953 to 1955.

Cockrell's years with the Dallas league provided valuable training in understanding community issues. As a nonpartisan organization, the league is dedicated to offering voters accurate information on the backgrounds and qualifications of candidates as well as balanced analysis of campaign issues. The league also taught her an important technique for dealing with conflict: "Because of my background in the league, I've always been able to concentrate on issues, not personalities."[18]

Sid Cockrell's career eventually brought them to San Antonio in 1956, when he became the executive director of the Bexar County Medical Society. Lila Cockrell promptly resumed her interest in civic affairs, joining the San Antonio League of Women Voters and serving as its president from 1959 to 1963.

As president of a citywide, respected nonpartisan women's organization, Cockrell attracted the attention of the GGL. McAllister led the nominating committee that visited her at home to offer her a place on the GGL ballot. After receiving assurances that the GGL would never tell her how to vote, she accepted the offer.[19] Every candidate received that assurance because the nominating committee assumed that no one would ever disagree with the GGL's agenda.

Cockrell certainly believed in the "city as a whole" approach to governing. But she had her own interpretation of what that meant. Like McDermott, she found religion to be a source of inspiration for service. An active member in Presbyterian women's organizations, she believed that she was "here to try to serve the community." Community was a key idea for her because it encompassed everyone—not just businessmen—in the city. Debate had taught her the importance of assembling and analyzing evidence, and the league had trained her to think broadly about issues affecting the community. As a councilwoman, she made a habit of listening to people: "I tried to maintain very good communications with citizen organizations.... You can't always say yes. But at least you can listen and if you are not able to help, maybe you can think of a way that they can come away...with some type of encouragement or some road ahead that they can follow."[20]

Her interest in listening to other viewpoints led to some unusual behavior as a councilmember. Ordinarily the GGL arranged "meet the candidate" events during elections. All the candidates attended such events, but they did no separate campaigning because they did not need to—opposition was rare and ineffective. Cockrell recalled: "I went beyond that [GGL events] so I could have friends in all parts of town. I was invited to people's backyards or living rooms to meetings. I went out and tried to relate to people beyond the scope of the GGL."[21] She thought trying to understand what concerned voters was part of her job, which gave her a far better grasp of community needs than the GGL had and simultaneously created support for her that was independent of the GGL's electoral system. Midway through her second term on the council she had already developed a reputation as someone who "works for the best interests of the citizens."[22]

She also worked at mastering the details of city government: "I kept trying to grow and understand all of the new issues, to learn the parts of government that I did not know."[23] That gave her an understanding of the possibilities, as well as the limitations, of using governmental authority to solve problems. She initially focused on historic preservation, promoting the arts, and programs teaching the poor about nutrition, but the list grew to include upgrading the police department, and supporting urban renewal projects in the downtown, public housing, and, finally, Model Cities.[24]

Her support for Model Cities ruptured her relationship with the GGL. Although she appreciated its potential to solve inner-city infrastructure problems (such as flood control), she was most enthusiastic about its requirement that citizens participate in deciding which projects to adopt in their neighborhoods.[25] City Manager Gerald Henckel, on the other hand, harbored grave reservations about Model Cities, saying, "One of the things that scared us was the fact that the Board had to be comprised of citizens who lived within the area. This is contrary to good management.... You don't have the poor people running the banks."[26] McAllister shared Henckel's concerns, which meant that Cockrell had to overcome their opposition to win council approval of Model Cities by lobbying her council colleagues.

Her victory earned her the gratitude of Congressman Gonzalez, which was not a minor accomplishment considering his political influence among many Mexican American voters, but it also led to a failed attempt by several councilmembers to fire Henckel in October 1969 because of his attitude toward Model Cities. Cockrell's role in that effort is unclear, but "indications" began to circulate immediately after that fight that she would not remain on the council. She met with unidentified GGL officials in May 1970, where she probably learned that they would not be inviting her to join the 1971 GGL ticket because she announced her resignation from the council on May 31.[27]

She did not go quietly. Her remarks at her last council meeting amounted to a condemnation of the GGL's approach to governing: "The worst problem right now is simply the fact that citizens at the national level are irritated and frustrated with the state of the country's affairs. I think this mood of restlessness and discontent is present in San Antonio too. The greatest need is to find new goals to unify the people and move forward as a community.

Physical improvements are no longer sufficient goals alone.... Government must be able to have flexibility and try to lead, not react, to the problems."[28] Given her commitment to community service, her resignation speech amounted to a declaration of intent to return to government at the first opportunity.

While Cockrell was educating herself about city government, Henry Cisneros was becoming an academic expert on urban problems. He would be the youngest and least experienced member of what became the city's leadership group. Family connections gave him informal training in politics. His parents, George and Elvira Cisneros, lived in Prospect Hill, a West Side suburb founded in the late nineteenth century that had become home to a rising Mexican American middle class prior to World War II. George Cisneros was a federal civil servant and later an army colonel; Elvira was the daughter of Rómulo Munguía, a prominent Mexican journalist who fled Mexico in 1926 to escape the repressive regime of Porfirio Díaz. Elvira was deeply involved in community service, which would be an important influence in shaping her son's attitudes. Rómulo's brother Ruben was a printer and a leading member of the GGL's Westside Coalition. His nephew Henry, who was born in 1947, grew up listening to discussions about local politics in his uncle's print shop.[29]

Cisneros would combine that informal education in practical politics with impressive academic credentials. He enrolled at Texas A&M University in 1964, where he studied urban political and economic issues and won a fellowship to the university's urban and regional planning master's program. An assignment to give McAllister a campus tour resulted in a summer internship after Cisneros graduated in May 1968. He worked for the city manager on HemisFair issues and then in January 1969 accepted an invitation to serve as assistant director of the Model Cities program, which, he later said, taught him "everything I know about citizen participation and the mechanics of making government work.... I learned during those years that government is wise to put its money in physical projects... because only physical projects leave a lasting legacy."[30]

Cisneros then entered the doctoral program at George Washington University and moved to Washington, where he served a year as the assistant to the executive vice president of the National League of Cities, became a White House fellow, worked for Elliot Richardson, the secretary of health, education, and welfare, and won a Ford Foundation grant in 1972 to work on his dissertation.

Moving his family to Boston, which was the subject of his dissertation, Cisneros took advantage of Harvard University and MIT's preeminence as centers of urban studies. He earned a second master's degree, in public administration, from Harvard and worked in the MIT department of urban studies. Since he was also researching for his dissertation, he was able, as he noted, to consult "persons involved in urban affairs at the national level."[31]

Cisneros's dissertation argued that city government had a crucial role in promoting economic development. That was not a popular idea in San Antonio, where most businessmen and voters had traditionally opposed such a role. It was nevertheless a fundamental assumption that would guide his ambitions for his city and himself. He had already been elected to the city council when he wrote in the introduction to his dissertation, "I hope to be able to apply many of the lessons learned in the course of this analysis to the formulation of local economic policies."[32]

The dissertation also revealed Cisneros's unique blending of conservatism and populism. Boston was famous for its efforts to revive its downtown—a favorite goal for many cities struggling to deal with massive suburbanization after 1945. Cisneros rejected the idea that the emergence of a national service economy, which encouraged massive employment opportunities in suburbs (as the UTHSC was illustrating by the mid-1970s), doomed downtowns to obsolescence. Instead he argued that downtowns could become centers of finance, insurance, tourism, and government services.[33] His focus on the downtown would temper what little enthusiasm he had for North Side development.

But his practical, albeit brief, experience with citizen participation in San Antonio's Model Cities program had shown him the importance of neighborhood residents in urban redevelopment. He paid close attention to that issue in Boston, where Mayor Kevin White had "worked hard to improve traditional city services in the neighborhoods and to assure that they were made more responsive to citizens' needs."[34] Later reflecting on the situation in San Antonio, where the business elite had no interest in sharing the challenges of economic development with the city's neighborhoods, Cisneros concluded from his academic investigations that excluding "the working people, . . . the democratic polity of the city, . . . was at the heart of the problem" of improving San Antonio's development. He would enter public life convinced that the business elite's power "somehow had to be broken."[35]

The meltdown that had undermined the GGL did not create particularly favorable circumstances for the emergence of a new coalition dedicated to economic development. Boosterism required political stability, cooperation between politicians and businessmen, voter support, and respected leaders to succeed. None of that existed in the early 1970s. Initially working independent of one another and without the specific intent to birth a growth coalition, McDermott and Cockrell would reshape the city's private and public institutions to make that coalition possible.[36]

McDermott would do so by first transforming USAA, a project that would require twenty-five years of effort. His evident success as this project continued to evolve attracted the respect of San Antonio's business community, gradually transforming him into its most important leader. Drawing on his experience at the Air Force Academy, he began with a long-term strategic plan that emphasized customer service and employee loyalty. Applying what he had learned about computers to the challenges of customer service, he invested more than $130 million in technology to cultivate customer satisfaction. To promote employee loyalty, he developed innovative programs over time that introduced a four-day work week; built classrooms at USAA to encourage employees to enroll in educational programs that would qualify them for advancement; created an office to assist women and minorities within the company; and improved pay scales. By 1979 five thousand employees were enrolled in technical training classes annually, and an average of two thousand were taking management development courses. Those enrichment innovations reduced employee turnover from 43 percent in 1969 to 5 percent in 1993, when USAA became one of the top five companies to work for in America.[37]

USAA as a company also benefited from the plan. Customer satisfaction skyrocketed; USAA's assets grew from $207 million to $34 billion by 1993 (when McDermott retired); employees increased from 2,600 to 15,000; and USAA moved from sixteenth- to fifth-largest insurer in the country.[38] It was an extraordinary achievement that became the basis for his eventual status as one of San Antonio's indispensable boosters.

McDermott also developed formal and informal relationships between USAA and the community. He convinced his board of directors to increase the company's contributions to charitable organizations and expected his employees to engage in community service. He personally visited West Side schools, gave high school commencement addresses, and spoke to African American church congregations. His love of Mexican food made him a regular patron at Mi Tierra, a legendary restaurant that served as a meeting place for many West Side businessmen and politicians. Pete Cortez, Mi Tierra's owner, introduced him, among others, to Ruben Munguía.[39]

McDermott also sought an active role in the Chamber of Commerce because he wanted to apply his experience with economic development in Colorado Springs to San Antonio.[40] He joined the chamber's board of directors in December 1969, where he would spend the next five years dealing with its frustrating inertia before he invented a solution for its crippling limitations.

Those years convinced McDermott that the chamber lacked the ability to pursue long-term economic development because of the interests and limitations of small businessmen who dominated it. They regarded the chamber as their service organization, not as the city's champion for economic development. Its wealthiest members, who did own larger businesses, belonged to an oligarchy that was quite content with the status quo. There had always been a few individuals who had campaigned for economic diversification and less reliance on the military, but their victories—such as the medical center—had been rare.

McDermott was a strategic thinker who believed from his economics training that export industries that sold goods in regional and national markets created more dynamic urban economies.[41] San Antonio had few such businesses (USAA being one), and he wanted to attract more of them to town.

Several events coalesced to produce a solution to that problem. In January 1974 McDermott became president of the chamber, which enabled him to initiate changes as long as his directors agreed with his ideas. He met several times during the spring with Mayor Becker to discuss the city's contract with the chamber that funded its economic development program. Becker and his North Side allies informed McDermott that they intended to divert that money to advertising only the North Side. In the meantime developers were busily planning the North San Antonio Chamber of Commerce, which would split most of the business community into opposing camps.[42]

McDermott decided to take the city and the chamber out of economic development and simultaneously reunite the entire business community behind a privately financed, separate organization. Believing that unity was essential to growth, he denounced the current situation, which encouraged "fragmentation of the community's resources—leadership and dollars—[that] will only dilute the continued orderly economic development desired by all."[43] He convinced his board to discontinue the city's contract with the chamber and approve his plan for a "strong, new arm of the Chamber's economic development effort."[44] With the groundwork finished, McDermott announced the creation of the Economic Development Foundation (EDF) to a large meeting of the San Antonio Rotary Club on July 3, 1974.[45]

Although he asked his audience for their time and money for his project, he did not wait for their replies. Instead he took personal charge of recruiting a board of directors and raising money. Six weeks after the rotary meeting he had raised $600,000; by the end of the year he had reached his financial goal and had hired Ralph Thomas as the foundation's first president.[46]

McDermott wanted board members who understood the complexities of strategic, long-term economic development. He called on executives who had experience with and resources for such planning, which confined his recruiting efforts to large companies with substantial resources. He also established a high fee for participation that only they could afford. At a time when membership in the chamber cost $120 annually, the foundation's basic membership was $10,000.[47]

Thirty-nine downtown and North Side companies joined the original board, fulfilling McDermott's goal of uniting the business community. One-third of them qualified as exporters or national retail chains, which reflected McDermott's ideas for creating economic growth.[48]

McDermott created unity within a fraying business community by convincing the two most important factions to work together in the foundation. That achievement extended his influence beyond USAA to the most important businessmen in the city. Ralph Thomas observed that "there was so much respect for McDermott by the other... investors that if he elected a course of action, then that was fine with them. They held him in that much respect; I mean literally."[49]

Dominance within the business community was not, however, sufficient to establish McDermott as a major civic leader. He had founded the EDF as the GGL disintegrated. COPS had also emerged in 1974, and its agenda did not bode well for boosters who believed community unity was essential to growth. After three successful years of its own, COPS decided to challenge the EDF.

Low wages provided the spark that ignited a political conflagration. McDermott had hired the Fantus Company, "probably the best respected site location consulting firm and community development firm" in America, according to Ralph Thomas.[50] Its nearly two-hundred-page report analyzed San Antonio's strengths and weaknesses, including the fact that 55 percent of San Antonio's workforce was unskilled, noting that such workers could be trained and employed "at reasonable wage rates." The report also cautioned against attracting industries that would "upset the existing wage ladder," which was dismally low. In Texas in the 1970s average wages were 17 percent below those paid in the Midwest; in San Antonio they were 32 percent below.[51]

The EDF relied on the Fantus report to attract new industry to town for the next two years. Sometime in 1977 councilman Henry Cisneros, displaying his populist instincts, gave a copy of the report to COPS.[52] COPS ignored the report's broader context and complexity to focus on the justifiably emotional symbolism of low wages as a winning strategy for attacking the EDF.

McDermott believed that low wages played an important role in economic development, but he also wanted to attract companies that would offer better, higher-paying jobs. San Antonio, however, had a serious, systemic problem that affected the EDF's ability to attract such firms: public education for minorities was abysmal. Since McDermott had been an economics professor and was now managing USAA, he understood the connection between education and income, and he hoped to improve its quality to prepare people to work for those companies.[53] He had, after all, implemented such a program for his own employees at USAA.

COPS invited McDermott to what he thought would be a private meeting to discuss the Fantus report. He was quite surprised to walk into an auditorium filled with angry protestors. It was a brief encounter. Father Albert Benavides strenuously denounced his presumed cheap labor policy, the crowd drowned out McDermott's attempts at an explanation, and he stalked out.[54]

From a tactical perspective, COPS was doing what it did best; from a strategic perspective, it had wandered into uncharted territory where it had no practical experience. Its members had no knowledge of economics, and they had not prepared specific goals that could contribute to solving the problem of low wages beyond demanding termination of the "policy."

COPS's attack did, however, cause several firms to lose interest in moving to San Antonio, threatening the EDF's mission and therefore its existence. All of McDermott's work in unifying the business community and creating the basis for a sustainable campaign of diversifying the economy was now at risk.

The initial result was a long war of words in the local press.[55] COPS kept demanding another meeting; McDermott kept refusing. In the meantime work on economic development stopped. Finally, sometime in early 1978, Pete Cortez and Ruben Munguía invited McDermott and Ralph Thomas to lunch at Mi Tierra to offer their services as mediators.[56] Their covert intervention nudged both sides toward an agreement to meet in three private sessions attended by four representatives from each side beginning in February.[57]

Both sides agreed to abandon heated rhetoric in favor of calmer discussions in which McDermott sought to explain the challenges of economic development for San Antonio. COPS's representatives focused on expressing their frustration over the lack of decent employment opportunities for minorities.[58] The meetings in effect became a learning experience for both sides, as McDermott later admitted: "They understood my point of view or the business community's point of view, and I understood theirs. And I did understand that they wanted to be a part of the process" of diversifying the economy.[59]

That understanding was fundamentally important to the contentious evolution of San Antonio's new economic and political order. The business community had never conceded any role to the city's minorities in decisions affecting economic development. In 1978 McDermott was the only businessman who had the power to do that. After the initial meetings, two more months of detailed discussions produced a general settlement in which the two sides agreed to work together on economic development.[60]

On May 30 negotiations concluded, appropriately, with a public ceremony.[61] McDermott had succeeded in salvaging a permanent approach to systematically diversifying the economy when, coincidentally, Sunbelt cities were becoming increasingly attractive. During the 1970s major northern and midwestern cities lost large numbers of residents and companies that moved to the West and Southwest.[62] San Antonio would enjoy a 43 percent increase in its population between 1970 and 1990, a larger percent increase than either Dallas or Houston. In such circumstances, a pro-growth reputation served Sunbelt cities well, and with the settlement with COPS the EDF could return to cultivating migrating companies. It sent a copy of the agreement to the Fantus Company, which reinstated San Antonio on its list of recommended relocation sites. The EDF also sent news and copies of the agreement to companies interested in the city, and *Forbes* published a major article about the settlement, enhancing San Antonio's reputation as a pro-growth city.[63]

COPS also benefited by obtaining the right to participate in recruiting companies to San Antonio. McDermott had expanded the unity necessary for such a coalition beyond the business community to include the city's most powerful representative of its neighborhoods. It was a unity based on mutual convenience that left each party free to pursue its own version of development. Conflicts between those versions would continue but would do so now within a general framework of formal, although occasionally delicate, cooperation that usually constrained potential threats to the emerging new order.

In the meantime Lila Cockrell had returned to the city council in 1973—ironically as a GGL candidate—where she would work on reshaping city government into a partner in boosterism. Becker's behavior as mayor allowed her to quickly establish herself as an independent voice of reason on the council.

Initially Becker's impulsive dislike of the GGL had made him popular, but it also drove him into a political quagmire. He was a friend of Houston businessman Oscar Wyatt, who controlled Coastal States Gas Producing Company, which owned the network of pipelines serving most of South Texas, including Austin and San Antonio. In 1971 San Antonio's City Public Service utility became concerned about Coastal's ability to honor its contract, but Wyatt assured CPS in writing that his company had the necessary reserves.[64]

Events two years later indicated that Wyatt had lied. In May 1973 Coastal States reduced gas service to its customers, causing several local industrial plants to reduce or halt operations.[65] Inquiries into the reasons for the shortages soon revealed that Wyatt was selling Coastal's reserves to other customers on the "spot-market" for much higher prices. Wyatt tried to solve that problem by demanding that his customers replace their existing contract with one that gave them no guaranteed supply and allowed him to charge higher prices as he pleased. As a councilman Becker had argued in favor of that curious idea; as mayor he decided to settle the conflict with a televised public meeting in June 1974 where Wyatt explained to the uninitiated why the city should give him what he wanted. After that interesting presentation, Wilber Matthews, CPS's lawyer, grilled Wyatt, revealing a great deal about his business methods.[66] Matthews was a longtime associate of the GGL, prompting Becker to accuse him of a conflict of interest and to demand an investigation of his integrity.

The investigation exonerated Matthews and thanked him for his public service. In the meantime Becker's behavior had ignited widespread public indignation and a demand that CPS sue Coastal States. Becker opposed that idea, undermining his ability to run for reelection in 1975.

Cockrell, on the other hand, successfully urged the council to sue Coastal States over Becker's objections. During the ensuing legal battle she emerged as council's expert on energy issues, supporting the CPS policy of diversifying from gas to coal and nuclear power. The city finally won the suit in 1977. Wyatt lost San Antonio's business to Valero, a company created as part of the settlement, which would become one of the city's largest national corporations.[67]

That settlement occurred near the end of Cockrell's first term as mayor, and it reflected her basic approach to and interest in the use of political power. "The secret," she once remarked, "is to pick your issues."[68] And for her those issues had important implications for creating a booster coalition because she believed that city government should partner with private business to promote economic development.[69] In her 1975 campaign for mayor, she urged the Chamber of Commerce, the EDF, and the city council to form a "joint approach" to "bringing new industry to San Antonio" to attract better paying jobs because "San Antonio is a wonderful place to live, [but] it is not a wonderful place to make a living."[70]

Her mayoral platform also insisted on neighborhood participation in policy making, a point she had made in resigning from the council in 1970. She had become an advocate for development in all areas of the city without conceding political dominance to any one group, which was essential for a new booster coalition's evolution. Her ability to pursue her goals would be tested severely at times, but in the years from 1975 to 1981 she became the only politician who had the values, skills, and public support necessary to implement her ideas.

The 1975 election also created the opportunity for Cockrell, McDermott, and Cisneros to take the first tentative steps toward building their eventual partnership. McDermott was initially wary of a government role in development; Cisneros was inexperienced; but Cockrell's mayoral platform provided a basis for both men to work with her. McDermott did say her election as mayor was "an indication of progress" that would attract national attention, which the EDF ensured by announcing plans to highlight Cockrell in its promotional literature. Cisneros would soon find her helpful in establishing his own credibility among boosters like McDermott.[71]

In the meantime Cockrell worked on the ongoing political crisis occasioned by the GGL's collapse and Becker's self-destruction. An absence of appropriate institutional traditions complicated her task. The council had not routinely debated and adopted policies promoting San Antonio's development since 1954.[72] During the GGL's reign councilmembers passed ordinances that the mayor presented to them to implement policies that the GGL's board of directors had approved. There was no need to discuss, let alone debate, anything; there was no need to listen to citizens who might want to offer their opinions on policies, and no need to lobby or make deals with one's colleagues for their votes.

Cockrell relied on her experience as a debater and former president of the League of Women Voters to rectify that situation. Those experiences had instilled in her a respect for systematic, collaborative decision-making. As mayor, she took charge of council meetings by guiding discussions, summarizing points, asking questions, and making suggestions. She carefully explained her own opinions and shared information about her meetings with outside groups like COPS or the City Water Board. While she did not expect everyone to agree with her, she insisted on creating an open, orderly process.[73]

She did, of course, want progress on her own goals, and she found an ally in Henry Cisneros in working on ways to promote economic development and downtown revival. Their initial collaborations produced Centro 21, a citizens group charged with finding ways to promote revitalization. And despite causing alarm at the Chamber of Commerce, she and Cisneros established the Department of Economic and Educational Development, which helped attract new industry by greatly simplifying the process of obtaining approvals to operate a business.[74]

Unfortunately the developers on the Independent Team managed to convince the council to approve construction of a large shopping mall over the aquifer in October 1975. That provoked COPS, the Aquifer Protection Association, and several other civic groups to launch a successful petition drive to repeal that ordinance, which voters approved in January 1976. When a court overturned the referendum, the conflict morphed into a bitter symbolic and practical battle over the future of suburban development and the larger question of the city's policy toward growth in general.[75] It led to a council ban on subsidizing utility installations for subdivision development beyond the city limits in July, the firing of City Manager Sam Granata at the end of the summer, and the developers' recall petition against Cockrell, Cisneros, and two other councilmen in September.[76]

None of that was conducive to calm council discussions, and preparations for the April 1977 elections reflected the shifting sands of local politics that stalled Cockrell's campaign for orderly governing. With filing deadlines for those elections fast approaching, a group of diehard GGL supporters considered organizing a new coalition with North Side developers in November 1976 because, as one of the negotiators delicately phrased it, "we didn't work together before." Now, however, they had a common enemy in COPS, which they feared was maneuvering to take over the city.[77] Their discussions probably encouraged Cockrell to abandon the GGL because she filed for reelection as an independent.[78]

Further clouding murky political waters, the referendum to decide whether to adopt districts as the basis for council seats had been scheduled for January 1977. When voters narrowly approved the change, the last vestiges of organized tickets for city offices disappeared. Their absence created an odd situation in which candidates for office were now free to self-nominate and offer their personal solutions to the city's needs.[79]

That change initially created some chaos. Nine candidates filed for mayor and sixty-nine sought the ten council positions. Voters only gave four candidates, including Cisneros, clear victories, resulting in six runoffs for the other council seats. Cockrell also needed a runoff, which she won with 60 percent of the votes. She compiled landslide-level majorities in North Side districts, but she also won convincingly in two inner-city districts (Three and Seven). Even in District Five, the heart of COPS territory, she won a respectable 48 percent of the vote.[80]

Cockrell emerged as San Antonio's only politician supported by a citywide constituency, but that did not automatically transform her into the council's leader. For the first time since the early 1840s, a majority of councilmembers who hailed from inner-city minority districts had the votes to control public policy.

Except for Cisneros, the minority councilmen lacked practical experience in governing. Moreover they distrusted the professional staff, which deprived them of a major source of support in developing policies.[81] And most importantly they had not campaigned as a group advocating solutions to major issues. Instead, elected as independent agents with personal followings, they had little sense of group cohesion. As Cisneros noted: "It was a very rocky first two years, very rocky. We didn't know, frankly, how to use those six votes."[82]

They eventually found common ground in a united opposition to North Side development.[83] COPS and the Aquifer Protection Association had been demanding an outright ban on development over the aquifer since voters had rejected the ordinance authorizing a large North Side shopping mall in January 1976. The judicial rejection of that vote returned the issue of development to the council, which had temporized by directing the City Planning Commission to develop a master plan for growth. Less than a week before the April elections, the commission had finally sent the council a compromise draft plan that combined substantial inner-city development with continued North Side growth.[84]

Compromise was not what inner-city councilmen wanted. In June they imposed a temporary ban on all development over the aquifer. While their ban was a predictable reaction to the long history of neglecting the needs of inner-city neighborhoods, it also reflected a national debate over the consequences of massive suburbanization. Like many Sunbelt cities, San Antonio was attracting large numbers of new residents seeking economic opportunities. They needed homes and, in keeping with the cultural preferences that dominated post-1945 urban growth, they preferred to live in new housing that was most easily available in outlying areas.[85]

Massive suburbanization did have its critics, who urged policies to curb what they believed were the deleterious effects of urban sprawl.[86] Those effects included neglect of inner cities and environmental problems that, in San Antonio, allied the Aquifer Protection Association with West Side voters in a struggle to deal with North Side growth.

Unfortunately for its critics, North Side residents did not share the West Side's history of neglect or the Aquifer Protection Association's worries about the city's water supply. By implementing the ban on development, the council was creating a serious problem, not just for the pocketbooks of developers but for the future growth of the city. If San Antonians wanted to attract industries and residents, they needed housing options to support that desire, and the North Side offered the most convenient and attractive option at this point.

The ban did have the useful effect of declaring that city government would have to be an equal, not subservient partner, in suburban development. It did not, however, define the nature of that partnership because the council's majority did not initially have the inclination, knowledge, or experience to negotiate with the developers. When a judge granted an injunction against the ban and developers filed a $750 million lawsuit against the city, COPS defiantly called a public meeting in August, apparently assuming that a public display of support for their policy would overcome legal problems with the ban.[87]

Developing a more creative and practical solution to growth would take time. Cisneros had supported the ban, but he had abstained from the vote because he wanted the council to follow a more legally binding process. Cockrell asked city manager Thomas Huebner to draft an ordinance that began the process of educating the council about policies for dealing with growth. Huebner's ordinance gave the council firmer legal grounds for its policy, and the city hired a Chicago law firm that was familiar with environmental issues to recommend new zoning and subdivision regulations. That study took two years to complete. In the meantime the council majority maintained its intransigent attitude toward North Side growth, regularly extending the ban while the City Planning Commission worked on a master plan that favored development within the inner city and required developers to pay for municipal services in outlying subdivisions.[88] An actual solution to this fight would not occur, however, until voters elected a new council in April 1979.

Intransigence also marked another major debate over inequities in public policy. The whole city typically needed physical improvements but funding them was always challenging. President Nixon revised federal support for cities by introducing the Community Development Block Grant program in 1974, which gave cities wide discretion in using relatively modest amounts of money. Bond issues could raise greater sums, but they had to be retired with interest, and voters were normally wary of approving them too frequently. The memory of the GGL's policy of inequitable use of bond money gave COPS more than sufficient reason to demand disproportionate distributions of all improvement funds. To achieve that goal, COPS organized its own deliberative process for establishing priorities for neighborhood projects and secured commitments from councilmen to adopt its priorities. That process, however, created the possibility for a major confrontation between the council's minority members and Mayor Cockrell, which erupted in early 1978.

Although COPS's demands had prospered in Becker's term, Cockrell had introduced a more methodical approach in 1975 that resulted in a wider distribution of funds.[89] It was an approach that reflected her definition of equity: "We needed to be looking at issues . . . where you could see how each district's needs were met, but also how we could all work together on the needs of the whole city."[90]

Working together was critical to Cockrell's systematic approach to governing. When the council began discussing City Manager Huebner's proposal for a large bond issue in October 1977, she sought to manage tensions between various neighborhoods by insisting on a careful review of all their needs. She led the negotiations that concluded in early 1977 with a unanimous agreement for the distribution of bond funds.

She also conducted successful simultaneous negotiations for distributing block grant funds that differed from some neighborhood priorities. Prior to a final vote on that money, however, the council's minority members met secretly to amend allocations for the block grant agreement, presenting their revisions to their surprised colleagues as an accomplished fact. Their revisions included deleting a project for an inner loop to improve traffic flow in the downtown that was laden with symbolic and practical implications. As Cisneros explained it, "This doesn't have anything to do with the Inner Loop; it has to do with an inability to gain control."[91]

In effect, the council's majority sought to undermine the mayor's approach to governing. By deleting the inner loop project, they were dismissing the needs of the downtown business community, which, by implication, meant they might ignore the needs of other constituencies in their private meetings at any time it occurred to them to do so.

A great deal was now at stake. The council's majority was essentially claiming the sole right to distribute public resources without having to bother about due process and equal access to decision-making for other constituencies. That attitude violated a fundamental principle for Cockrell, which she explained to the council: "We [have] got to work together in good faith."[92]

Confident of her own popularity, she urged the voters to defeat the entire bond package, which had been scheduled before the disagreement over the block grant money occurred.[93] Ironically she now wanted the voters to reject an agreement that the council had agreed to because, she argued, minority members' maneuver on the block grant funds meant they could not be trusted to honor that agreement.

It was a risky accusation. The council's minority members were confident that they could defeat her, especially with COPS support. With only three weeks before the March 4 election, the campaign was short and furious, with accusations that COPS was attempting to become a "powerful political machine" reminiscent of the GGL.[94] Cockrell, however, insisted that the issue was whether voters would demand that "all members of this city council work together for the good of the whole city."[95] From her perspective, all of the city's neighborhoods and ethnic groups had to have a voice in government, but no single group had the right to dominate the council, as had been the case with the GGL.

COPS failed to turn out enough votes to overcome Cockrell's supporters, who rejected all seven bond proposals. In the final tally that mirrored the voting pattern for her mayoral victory, 59 percent of the voters said no.[96]

The victory marked a turning point in the evolution of the city's political system. Councilmembers had spent most of their time and energy on the needs of their own districts, virtually ignoring the council's role in governing the entire city. That focus had disturbed the mayor because she "felt very sincerely that my job . . . was to help these new council members understand . . . their roles and help them to see not only the needs of their own district, but to see the bigger picture of how their district related to the city."[97]

She used her appointive powers to further that goal. Cisneros, whose doctoral dissertation argued for a strong partnership between business and government, had aligned with his fellow minority councilmembers on such issues as the ban on development over the aquifer in 1977, which made him appear antibusiness. He had, however, worked with Cockrell to establish the Department of Economic and Educational Development, and in April 1978 he modified his populist commitment to inner-city needs by introducing a resolution announcing the council's support for economic development.

His timing was interesting. By April COPS discussions with McDermott about the EDF were heading toward a settlement. Cisneros's resolution, adopted overwhelmingly, expressed the council's intent to pursue "an aggressive program of incentives and aids that have never been available before in order to secure jobs via business expansions and plant relocations to our area."[98] For Cisneros, this amounted to a public declaration of his personal commitment to the city's overall development; for the council, it provided a well-timed (but conveniently unenforceable) acknowledgment of its need to do likewise.

Cockrell continued her work on educating councilmen about city issues beyond their district borders. She appointed Bernardo Eureste to oversee funding for cultural activities that the city funded, and he promoted subsidies to a greater variety of organizations, including what became the Guadalupe Cultural Center. Joe Webb, the council's only African American, became the council's representative to the Fiesta Commission, a bastion of the old oligarchy's social power. He began the process of increasing the number and diversity of participating organizations.[99]

Frank Wing, who represented District Four on the southwest side of town, made his own, apparently unprompted, contribution to more systematic governance by negotiating informal guidelines for dealing with the knotty problem of distributing public funds fairly. When COPS campaigned successfully to have the council, rather than the professional staff, control distribution of Community Development Block Grant funds,

Wing's negotiating skills became crucial to dividing that money among as many inner-city projects as possible.[100]

There was, however, more work needed on the council's ability to represent all the city's residents. Its long, bitter debate over a comprehensive master plan for growth and the continuing ban on development over the aquifer reflected the minority councilmen's hostility toward the North Side. In January 1979, with COPS accusing Cockrell of "racial polarization" in debates over the plan, they approved incentives for inner-city development and required developers to pay all costs for municipal services in outlying subdivisions. In the meantime the ban on North Side development remained in place until August, while the council awaited the report and recommendations of its outside experts.[101]

Then in the April 1979 city elections Bob Thompson replaced Rudy Ortiz in District Six. Although the council remained divided along ethnic and racial lines, the new Anglo majority created opportunities to incorporate some of the North Side's interests into policy decisions about the city's long-term development.

In June the outside experts submitted their report, which focused on protecting recharge zones that were essential to preserving the aquifer's role as the city's sole source of water. That focus not only left a great deal of North Side land available for development, it also created considerable room for debate over the precise ways to protect those zones. Attempting to deal with those ambiguities, the council passed ordinances to regulate subdivision construction. Then, after ordering revisions to the master plan's strictures on North Side development, the council lifted its ban.[102]

With those changes the council in effect recognized the North Side as one of its constituencies, bringing Cockrell's campaign to implement San Antonio's new political system to a successful conclusion. The GGL had adopted council-manager government to eliminate politicians and ward politics, creating a system that ignored the legitimate needs of the city's neighborhoods. In the 1960s Cockrell had been the only GGL councilmember who routinely campaigned among civic organizations in those neighborhoods, where she learned what concerned them. Beginning with her first term as mayor in 1975, she worked to make council-manager government more representative. Although the change to districts in 1977 created some major challenges, her superb political skills gave her the advantage she needed to succeed. As she later observed: "We had seen great growth in the ability of all the councilmembers now understanding the system, being part of the system, understanding how you work with the different neighborhoods, the different sectors of the city."[103]

There was nothing revolutionary to her solution, which in fact resembled the approach many cities used to deal with competing interests in local politics, but San Antonio had not had that kind of system for twenty years. With the collapse of the oligarchy's power, the city needed a skilled leader to make the new political system work, and Cockrell had the right combination of talents—and luck—to manage that.[104]

In the meantime McDermott had been working to transform that system into a booster alliance. In 1979 he had accepted Cockrell's advice to partner with Cisneros to unite political, business, and civic leaders in a voluntary organization to promote San Antonio.[105] After a year of meetings with local leaders, he announced the creation of United San Antonio in January 1980. USA would conduct a national advertising campaign to promote San Antonio; "act as a forum for widely divergent groups which, during the 1970s, represented images of divisiveness and controversy"; and coordinate business, government, and community ideas for developing the economy and improving the city's quality of life.[106]

USA served two important purposes. First, it cemented McDermott, Cisneros, and Cockrell's roles as leaders of a "growth machine" after Cockrell became USA's executive director in 1981.[107] Second, it coordinated the work of volunteers who were essential support to development initiatives.

This coalition benefited enormously from Cisneros's meteoric rise to national prominence after his election as mayor in April 1981.[108] Over the next three years practically every major news organization in the country interviewed him. He became a member of several prestigious organizations, including President Reagan's Council on Federalism, the National Council for Urban Economic Development, and the Texas Economic Development Commission. In 1984 Sen. Walter Mondale interviewed him for nomination as vice president on the Democratic Party's national ticket.[109]

All the attention made Cisneros a man with a promising future, someone whose youth, intelligence, and articulate passion created expectations that he was destined for higher, more powerful political offices. That became an important source of his personal power; it also made him welcome in practically any company boardroom in the country, an asset he could use to advance the goals of the new booster coalition.[110]

A variety of national and local issues provided several challenges that shaped those goals. Military City had been experiencing a fundamental reordering of its employment opportunities. With the end of the politically unpopular draft in 1973, the military faced the massive challenge of building a professional force that would dramatically reduce the number of personnel and support staff. By 1980 only 9 percent of San Antonio workers held federal jobs, while 20 percent worked in services. A decade later those figures were 8 and 27 percent respectively.[111] The boosters needed to create opportunities for employment as the city's job market continued to evolve.

It also needed, if possible, to consider where and how to direct the city's physical growth as total employment increased. During the 1980s the city gained 127,000 jobs and acquired 196,000 residents. Since major North Side businesses like the UTHSC and USAA were growing rapidly, most of those newcomers were destined to seek housing there. New residents, and the northward migration of middle-class African Americans and Mexican Americans out of their traditional East and West Side neighborhoods, added 200,000 more people to the North Side by 1990.[112] That growth had implications for attempting to mediate the political divide between the North Side and the inner city that had generated so much controversy in the 1970s.

McDermott's agreement with COPS provided a framework for dealing with that divide. COPS's commitment to neighborhood redevelopment would create challenges to that framework that Beatrice Cortez, its president, implied during the 1981 mayoral campaign when she told Cisneros, "We've looked over your record, and frankly we cannot believe what we see. . . . I think you've gone to the other side. We're going to give you a chance to prove us wrong."[113] The booster coalition needed to pay constant attention to such attitudes in negotiating and implementing development policies.

Downtown offered another challenge. By 1972 retail sales to San Antonio residents in the Central Business District had collapsed, and merchants located there had increasingly turned to tourism for support.[114] That collapse reflected national trends, and many cities in the 1970s were relying on tourism to revive their downtowns.[115] David Straus had convinced the

Chamber of Commerce to support attractions to supplement the River Walk and the Alamo, but convention facilities and hotel rooms remained inadequate. Those deficiencies curtailed the tourist trade. In 1979 San Antonio hosted 689 conventions with 216,000 attendees, but Houston, with only 465 conventions, attracted 666,700 visitors. Two years later Dallas ranked fifth among top cities for conventions; San Antonio ranked twentieth.[116]

Help was on the way in the form of two new, large hotels, and the booster coalition certainly supported tourism as an important industry. McDermott regarded it as an export industry because it brought money into the city's economy. Cisneros believed that it contributed to a healthy downtown, although he also believed that creating jobs there in government, finance, and other service industries was also necessary.[117] The boosters had a lot of work to do.

Last but perhaps not least, the boosters needed to cast a wary eye over the activities of their opponents, especially those voters devoted to frugality, whose views had dominated government spending and development policies since the 1850s. The GGL had been assiduous in paying obeisance to frugality, but that devotion had disappeared in the turmoil of the meltdown. Its decline, however, would prove only temporary, and "frugalists" would eventually reassert their objections to government support of development.

Planning as a tool for exercising political leadership would be essential to managing most of those issues. McDermott was a superb strategic planner who had already demonstrated his abilities by transforming USAA and founding the EDF, but he had not proposed a general plan for development when he established United San Antonio. Cisneros took on that task, beginning with his announcement of five development themes in his first mayoral campaign. Dealing with his sudden fame disrupted his ability to refine those ideas, but he returned to that task in September 1982, publishing *San Antonio's Place in the Technology Economy: A Review of Opportunities and a Blueprint for Action.*

Quickly dubbed the Orange Book for its cover's color, Cisneros's plan declared that technology had a critical role in solving San Antonio's most important problem, which he defined as "how to raise the income of our citizens and... how to assure a better quality of life" for all of its residents. He did not regard technology as a panacea, but he did argue that "unless it is at least a major part of our future, our citizens will continue to suffer the income disadvantages that arise from lagging behind the national economy and behind other more prosperous metropolitan areas." With typical booster optimism, he dismissed critics who said San Antonio was not equipped to participate in a technological economy "because such arguments shortchange our people and underestimate their capacities."[118]

Cisneros wanted to attract computer, electronic, biomedical engineering, aerospace, telecommunications, lasers, and robotics companies. And because technology required knowledgeable, skilled workers that San Antonio lacked, he and his coalition partners would devote a great deal of attention to improving high school and college educational opportunities.

The EDF had already had problems in attracting electronic and other high technology firms to town because the city lacked university-level civil, electrical, and mechanical engineering programs, a problem McDermott had already dealt with in Colorado Springs.[119] He sought to solve the EDF's problem by using USA to create the San Antonio Foundation for Engineering Education to provide student scholarships and organized the San Antonio Council on Engineering Education to prepare the case for engineering programs at UTSA to submit to the UT Coordinating Board in June 1981. Within the UT System, communities seeking to improve their branch campuses needed to demonstrate unity, but they also had to overcome the board's general opposition to such efforts. That required political persuasion, particularly after the board's staff unanimously rejected San Antonio's proposal. McDermott and Cisneros made the arguments against the staff's recommendation at the board's October meeting. Cisneros's speech was so convincing that it became a legendary example of his persuasive powers. The board overruled its staff—an exceedingly rare event at the time—and the city acquired valuable programs for long-term development.[120]

Winning that fight demonstrated USA's value as a booster organization, which Cisneros supported by creating the Coordinating Council for Economic Development to monitor progress. The council assembled the leaders of various development initiatives into a single committee to monitor and guide booster activities. By fall 1983 the council had twelve city, business, education, and civic organizations reporting on thirty-three initiatives. These arrangements distributed the coalition's work load and created opportunities and flexibility for the coalition's leaders to use their influence to support especially important projects or to pursue additional development possibilities.[121]

In March 1983, for example, Cisneros made two presentations to promote technology's role in diversifying the economy. In the first, he was responding to an unexpected external opportunity. Microelectronics Computer Corporation had announced a national search for a location for its newly organized consortium of major electronics firms. Cisneros and McDermott wrote separately to retired admiral Bobby Inman, who had been appointed chairman of the corporation, requesting an invitation to argue San Antonio's case to be that location. Cisneros traveled to Chicago to make the bid on March 18, but while corporation officials congratulated him on the quality of his argument, they chose Austin because San Antonio lacked a research university with graduate engineering programs.[122]

Cisneros's second March presentation was his own idea. He persuaded the San Antonio Medical Association to fund a feasibility study for a biomedical research park, demonstrating his ability to convince local organizations to lend their expertise to the booster coalition for special projects. The campaign to create the park also became a case study of the ways local attitudes toward development could disrupt booster effectiveness for promoting change.

The campaign turned first to experienced expertise. The foundation's executive director, William Peters, hired retired Maj. Gen. Gerald Cooke for the feasibility study. Cooke had commanded the Air Force's Institute of Technology and had also been involved in creating a research park in Ohio. Needing support staff to help with various issues, Cooke turned to Jim Dublin, a key member of the booster coalition who worked closely with McDermott and Cisneros, to assist him. Dublin assembled a team of experts on legal and land issues for Cooke (nicknamed the Tiger Team) and led a delegation to the North Carolina Research Triangle Park to gather information and to gain perspective (from another group of experts) regarding whether San Antonio's biomedical resources could support a research park.[123]

Cooke concluded that the park idea was feasible and made recommendations for creating an academic core and an administrative organization for the park.[124] The Institute of Biotechnology would soon become that core, and the boosters established the Texas Research and Technology Foundation in February 1984 to supervise land acquisition and park development. Although the park's 1,500-acre size and need to be near such institutions as the UTHSC required a North Side site, the boosters, as Jim Dublin explained, sought a new growth corridor that would benefit the West Side: "We knew that if we were going to be a biotech center there was no way we could locate that to the north, that [it] had to be in the west because a lot of people are still upset about where UTSA and the Medical Center are." COPS president Sonia Hernandez endorsed that decision, saying that the park would probably "attract some kind of industry to the [West Side's] Edgewood area and other parts of the city."[125]

At this point the campaign collided with local attitudes that sapped its momentum. Cooke assumed that the potential profit from land sales surrounding a research park would encourage developers to donate land for it.[126] But North Side developers had no interest in donating land in an area that had become so attractive to new residents, especially now that the boosters were touting the park as the anchor for a new growth corridor.

The first land offer reflected that attitude. In April 1984 Kyle Seale offered 1,500 acres to the foundation for $15 million. That was awkward because the foundation had no money. Martin Wender, a realtor who had an agreement with the foundation to locate the Institute of Biotechnology in his Westover Hills development, tried to solve that impasse by raising the asking price from contributions by other landowners in the area. They failed to see the logic in that idea, demonstrating that Seale was not alone in his opposition to the idea of a donation.[127]

McDermott finally resolved this impasse in December 1986 by convincing Tom Pawel, a former classmate of his from the Harvard MBA program whose company owned ranchland in the area, to donate the 1,500 acres. The two-year hiatus in developing the park nevertheless proved costly. Donations for the construction of the park's initial buildings slowed to a trickle, threatening to undermine the whole project. McDermott stepped in again, raising $5 million from the Houston Endowment, $15 million from Ross Perot, and $7 million from the city council. His success resuscitated the park, but it remained a problematic legacy of the boosters' development efforts.[128] The far West Side would in fact experience mushroom growth after 1990 without its help.

Disappointments and outright failures litter the history of boosterism, whose advocates often suffer from excessive optimism arising from over-confidence bred by success, as McDermott himself noted: "I think it's safe to say that we got exuberant too soon and fell victim to believing that it would be easy to put the park together."[129]

There were, though, other opportunities to improve the city's economy. Cisneros served on the search committee that recruited Dr. John Howe as president of the UTHSC in January 1985. Howe was a superb administrator who had an impressive talent for institution building that made him a crucial ally in the boosters' development campaign.[130] Coincidentally some of the researchers at the UTHSC had just begun exploring ways to share the results of their work with private businesses, which was the basis for Stanford University's role in creating Silicon Valley after World War II.[131] Howe would encourage and support that idea by lobbying the state and federal governments and the regents and Coordinating Board for increased funding and degree (including doctoral) programs as well as new research facilities. His leadership transformed the UTHSC into an important research center over the course of the next decade.[132]

The EDF also made progress recruiting companies to town. It assumed an indiscriminate approach to recruiting because its staff had no control over who contacted them. Small pharmaceutical companies moved to town as well as metal shops, electronics firms, shoe and jeans manufacturers, and a miscellany of other enterprises. Size also did not matter; firms with fewer than ten and more than four thousand employees were welcome.

As a new organization, the EDF needed time to earn a reputation that could attract the attention of footloose firms, a process that Cisneros's national repute helped. A breakthrough began in 1987. Of the fifty-two companies that became permanent residents in the first sixteen years of recruiting, half arrived between 1987 and 1991.[133]

The EDF did inadvertently create a trend in its recruiting efforts. San Antonio's long-term effort to diversify its energy sources had reduced electricity prices by the 1980s, giving the EDF a competitive advantage in recruiting call centers that used a large amount of power. Although these call centers paid low wages, they hired large numbers of employees, making them attractive to a city with so many unskilled residents. The first call center arrived in 1983; six more came between 1987 and 1991. Collectively they added 10,700 jobs to the economy, which was 56 percent of all jobs the EDF brought to town in the booster years.[134]

Their strong tendency to locate in the far northwest created a magnet for the growth corridor the boosters had expected the research park to create. Developers had opened thirteen business parks there by 1986 in anticipation of the park's impact on that corridor. Delays in its development probably made those speculators eager to find customers, creating attractive sites for the call centers that accelerated residential and commercial development in the area.[135]

That growth illustrated how booster decisions about the distribution of employment opportunities could influence San Antonio's physical growth. McDermott believed in a private company's right to choose its location, but Cisneros did not always agree. He had argued in his dissertation that creating job opportunities in the downtown was crucial to its revival, and he also believed that the same approach could revitalize impoverished inner-city neighborhoods. In those cases, location was a political as well as an economic decision.

COPS favored Cisneros's approach over McDermott's and used its status as a partner in economic development under the terms of the 1978 Treaty to steer companies to the West Side. But not just any company. It wanted high tech, high wage firms and began its campaign to attract them in 1979 when COPS representatives accompanied Cisneros to Minneapolis for a successful effort to convince Control Data, a computer firm, to locate 600 employees in Vista Verde South, an urban renewal project on the near West Side redevelopment project.[136]

Working on Vista Verde was an early example of COPS's growing sophistication and ambition. It had been the West Side's principal booster since its inception, and in 1981 it strengthened that role by forming the Edgewood Economic Development Committee to improve its effectiveness.[137] COPS had refused to join United San Antonio despite several invitations because it had little interest in McDermott's coalition, but it did attempt to use USA members to advance its own agenda in the new political environment.

COPS's approach to boosterism, though, would create stress on and eventually contribute to the demise of the larger coalition. Adopting a strategy of appealing to various partners in USA without working formally with it, COPS asked the city council to create a drainage district with taxing powers as well as a large bond issue devoted exclusively to drainage problems. While the West Side had the most severe problems with drainage, it was a citywide problem that required broad support. Probably for that reason, those business leaders told the organization to work with USA.[138]

Late in 1981 COPS finally requested a meeting with McDermott and Robert West, chairman of USA, to discuss its broad agenda for Edgewood. McDermott and West narrowed the scope of USA's role in West Side development to drainage instead of committing to support for that broader agenda. In March 1982 McDermott made a presentation to the city council supporting the drainage district, which the council approved.[139]

COPS persisted in attempting to gain USA's endorsement for its Edgewood improvements, but McDermott and West responded by asking it to join USA. In a July 1982 letter to COPS president Beatrice Cortez they pointed out that the West Side had become the location for sixteen of the nineteen manufacturing facilities that the EDF had attracted since 1975. That disproportionate share implied that the West Side had indeed been mysteriously fortunate since "the EDF staff does not have it in its power to direct industrial prospects to one segment of the city or another." Cisneros, in his role as a principal lobbyist to prospective companies, did have indirect power to do so, which would explain the imbalance in site selections that McDermott and West noted. They advised Cortez that "the larger job of addressing the community development problems of San Antonio—including all its neighborhoods and environs—is one that can best be handled under the auspices of United San Antonio, which was formed for that very purpose."[140]

COPS refused to move under USA's umbrella, continuing instead to work with Cisneros. He arranged meetings to work on West Side projects, pledging, among other things, to convene a meeting of developers and bankers to create an Edgewood Strategy Fund and to locate a major biomedical research facility in Edgewood instead of the Research Park.[141] COPS's disinterest in "the larger job" of USA therefore weakened McDermott's efforts to preserve the community unity that he regarded as essential to the boosters' success. His admonition to Cortez revealed that the seams binding together the private and public partnerships of his booster coalition were under constant stress.

Cisneros created a temporary solution to that stress by establishing Target '90. His Orange Book had codified USA's booster agenda more explicitly than McDermott's original statement of its purpose had, but the boosters still lacked an effective way to link neighborhood needs to its citywide development ambitions to inspire broad political support for their ambitions.

Facing barely token opposition in the 1983 election, Cisneros had time to plan a more explicitly inclusive booster agenda that he called San Antonio: Target '90, which included 148 goals for the city to reach in seven years. It was an impossibly large agenda that raised some eyebrows, but winning re-election with 92 percent of the vote quelled the doubters. The council made it an official city-sponsored project, which Cisneros launched in July with appropriate fanfare.[142]

McDermott and Cockrell served on Target '90's steering committee and the goals Cisneros had enumerated included not only most, if not all, of USA's specific projects, but also several initiatives to revive the downtown that were already under way. Cisneros added city services, transportation, utilities, and most significantly, "Southern Sector Development," which had become the common description for neighborhoods within Loop 410.[143]

This massive planning effort recruited more than five hundred people with different backgrounds and perspectives from around the city to make recommendations for implementing Cisneros's large agenda. It became a training ground for potential future community leaders by making them aware of the wide range of ways to promote urban development.[144] And it incorporated neighborhood concerns as well as the boosters' long-term initiatives into a single broad plan for the first time.

As Target '90 approached the deadline for its final report in spring 1984, the steering committee debated how to implement its recommendations. Since the final report would incorporate practically every USA project, McDermott supported continuing Target '90 as a voluntary organization with a small, full-time staff. After considerable discussion, the committee agreed that USA and Target '90 should merge, and the new organization would retain the Target '90 name.[145]

That decision left McDermott and Cockrell with no formal roles in the booster leadership coalition. McDermott remained its most powerful informal leader, working closely with Cisneros on long-range strategic projects such as the research park and doctoral degrees for the UTHSC and UTSA. Cockrell restricted her contributions to the City Public Service board, where she served as chairwoman and worked on the campaign to finish the South Texas Nuclear Project. Cisneros became the public face of the booster coalition, which made its fortunes dependent on his continued popularity and leadership skills.

His dominance initially proved effective, especially when he combined it with several Target '90 recommendations and assembled community representatives to decide some key issues, such as the distribution of bond funds. Advisory committees composed of representatives from the north and south sides of Loop 410, with Cisneros serving as referee, fought each other into agreements before the council scheduled an election. That arrangement was especially important for the April 1985 referendum, which required a tax increase for the first time and also set the date to coincide with his reelection campaign. Voters approved of him and the bonds, reinforcing his own confidence as an effective leader.[146] In his eight years as mayor he raised $277 million for drainage, street, police, fire, and library improvements in five bond elections based on Target '90 recommendations that significantly improved the city's basic infrastructure.[147]

His popular authority also proved vital in defeating a major challenge to boosterism in 1986. Frugality began to revive as a political force when Clauis Alden (C. A.) Stubbs organized the Homeowner Taxpayers Association to oppose the 1983 bond election. His efforts managed to dent but not deny victory for Cisneros, but the association gained confidence by defeating a referendum to fluoridate the city's water supply in late 1985. Encouraged by that victory, Stubbs launched a campaign to impose a cap on spending in 1986, arguing in the classic rhetoric of frugality that "adoption of the spending cap will signal a victory for the little man over the entrenched special interests.... The citizen will see the city's outrageous spending habits brought to a halt."[148] Although the popularity of the 1978 California Proposition 13 limit on property taxes probably contributed to the Homeowner Taxpayers Association's emergence, voter devotion to frugality had a long, successful history in San Antonio. Older voters who were the core constituents of the association would have remembered the GGL's frugal approach to governing that Stubbs's spending cap would presumably restore. In addition, limiting property taxes potentially transcended the otherwise firm divide between the city's northern and southern sectors as a popular political cause.[149]

Stubbs's "entrenched special interests" happened to be the booster coalition, which was at its height of popularity and cohesion. Having learned his lesson in neglecting to fight for fluoridation, Cisneros dedicated himself to defeating Stubbs's spending cap. He had a lot of eager help from the 170 organizations that had participated in Target '90, from North Side developers concerned about the cap's threat to government support for growth, from the Greater San Antonio Chamber of Commerce worried about the city earning a reputation for opposition to growth, from COPS, and even from the archbishop. Well-organized, well-funded, and committed to turning out anti-cap voters, the boosters defeated Stubbs by an almost two to one margin in August 1986.[150]

That victory suggested that the booster coalition had become an unstoppable tidal wave by 1986. It had been compiling an impressive set of accomplishments, including solving the problem of a site for the research park, regent approval for the Institute of Biotechnology, the acquisition of Sea World and a microchip manufacturing plant in the far northwest, progress on expanding the Convention Center and construction on Rivercenter Mall, and an impressive batch of new hotels with more on the way downtown.[151] Unfortunately, however, the wave hit a wall.

In April 1987 the city council voted 8–2 to authorize construction of La Cantera, a 1,600-acre USAA project that McDermott wanted at the northwest intersection of I-10 and Loop 1604. The project combined an upscale mall and a conference center (composed of a destination hotel and a golf course) that he had been considering since the early 1980s. He announced the project in February 1986 at a press conference where Cisneros praised it as a major asset for the city.[152]

A year later Cisneros voted against La Cantera, apparently because of pressure from COPS. It was an odd vote considering his previous endorsement of the project and the political situation in 1987. Since 1979, when the council's minority members lost control and a moratorium on North Side development ended, the booster coalition and the city council had been supportive of COPS's agenda for the West Side, which had needed more than drainage projects to recover from decades of neglect. However, the council also supported North Side developers who had resumed building subdivisions, including the exclusive Dominion on I-10 well beyond La Cantera's proposed location.[153] The council's support of COPS and the developers aligned with the basic principle that was Cockrell's legacy and Cisneros's policy of balancing the competing interest groups in the council's decisions.

COPS, though, occasionally took a different approach to politics that ignored informal rules of reciprocity that distributive politics relied on. Instead it insisted on preferential treatment for the West Side and remained opposed to North Side development.[154] Pressuring Cisneros to oppose a project that he had already endorsed was a classic case of ignoring the conventional understandings that sustained the city's political arrangements. In doing so COPS, with help from environmental groups, resurrected voter concerns about threats to the Edwards Aquifer, which remained the city's sole source of water. Although tests in 1983 by the Edwards Aquifer Research and Data Center had concluded that pollutant levels posed no threat to the public, those tests did not preclude the possibility of future damage, giving COPS reason to renew its opposition to North Side development yet again.[155]

Cisneros defended his vote by saying he had concerns about the effects of development on the city's water supply. North Side developers, who now included McDermott, erupted in astonished rage at Cisneros's unexpected no vote. They depended on the policy of balancing competing interests to provide a predictable environment for development, but it appeared that the city's most powerful politician was signaling an end to that policy.

Perhaps seeking a way to salvage the situation, Cisneros appointed a special committee to study possibilities for new aquifer zoning regulations. He also tried to signal moderation by refusing to appoint María Berriozábal, the council's most outspoken critic of the North Side, to that committee despite heated pressure from Ernie Cortés.[156] That may not have been particularly reassuring since there was a moratorium on development while the committee deliberated for six months, a situation fraught with uncertainty that was not conducive to calm relations between Cisneros and the developers. McDermott's reaction was particularly devastating. He "felt personally betrayed" and ended his relationship with Cisneros. COPS's successful pressure on Cisneros had wrecked a key relationship in the booster coalition that was likely unintended.

Although the breach between McDermott and Cisneros was not widely known at the time, their estrangement dissolved the booster coalition's highly effective informal coherence. Beginning with their partnership in founding USA, they had developed a close relationship based on frequent private discussions that created a unity of purpose and promoted concentrated effort that gave San Antonio a reputation as a city that welcomed change.[157] The coalition now had to adjust its tactics to the new reality that its leaders were no longer speaking to each other.

Progress on the booster agenda remained possible because McDermott and Cisneros had created networks that still had the ability to pursue development. McDermott, for instance, had good relationships with Hans Mark, who became chancellor of the UT System in late 1984, and Jack Blanton, who chaired the UT Board of Regents beginning in 1985. McDermott became acquainted with Mark, an MIT-trained physicist who had worked for NASA, when he was secretary of the air force; he initially met Blanton when he worked for the Houston Endowment, which had helped McDermott raise money for the EDF and the research park. Cisneros had developed his own relationships with both men through McDermott, which enabled them to continue working on new graduate programs at the UTHSC and UTSA.[158]

On projects where there was less overlap, McDermott and Cisneros relied on existing networks or created new ones. McDermott created partnerships for specific projects, such as Fiesta Texas in 1989. He also assembled a group of businessmen to buy the Spurs from Red McCombs in 1992 to keep the team in San Antonio.[159] Cisneros led a coalition of downtown businessmen in a long and complicated campaign from spring 1987 to January 1989 to win voter approval for the Alamodome.[160]

Cisneros's devotion to complicated long-term downtown projects like the Rivercenter Mall and the dome were particularly impressive considering that his domination of local politics was rapidly eroding. The tensions surrounding the special council committee's deliberations about more restrictions on North Side development simmered into fall 1987. Two events during the summer added to those tensions. In June his son was born with serious heart problems, creating emotional and financial stress for Cisneros's family. Then in August, while he was debating whether to run for governor, rumors began to percolate about an extramarital affair. In those circumstances, he decided not to seek the governorship, which raised questions about his political future.[161]

Then, as if he needed more problems, COPS unexpectedly, and stridently, denounced the Alamodome. With COPS having created two major challenges in a single year, Cisneros lost his temper and announced that he would no longer meet regularly with the organization to work on its agenda.[162]

Speculation mounted about his political future, and Cisneros finally announced in September 1988 that he would not seek reelection. His comment that "some of you may say, 'Why not?' And some of you no doubt will say, 'Thank goodness'" acknowledged the rapid decline in his political dominance without conceding anything to his critics.[163] He would, after all, stage his own last hurrah by winning the referendum on the dome five months later.

The booster coalition was not yet dead. Cockrell returned to the mayoralty in 1989, but a crisis in the savings and loan industry created a severe economic downturn that affected voter support for investment in urban development. Stubbs seized on voter discontent to pass a charter amendment imposing term limits on mayors and councilmembers in 1991, and Cockrell failed to win reelection that year, marking the official end of the coalition.[164]

Considering its ambitions, the coalition lost power prematurely. McDermott, Cockrell, and Cisneros did, however, demonstrate how productive cooperation between government and business could be for developing the city, and that lesson was not lost with the coalition's demise. Frugality did not disappear as a major influence, but it now had a rival to contend with. San Antonio was becoming a different city.

AFTERWORD

On Becoming a Creative City

1991–2017

C. A. Stubbs may have expected term limits to halt government support for booster programs, and his charter amendment certainly complicated that support, but he and his fellow frugalists failed to understand that McDermott's coalition had permanently altered San Antonio's approach to urban development. McDermott, Cockrell, and Cisneros had created a new vision for the city, set to work implementing it, and inspired others to continue pursuing that vision. In the next phase a more diffuse group of leaders pursued development in sometimes unexpected ways, but there was also a fundamental continuity that sustained steady progress toward that original vision.

Persistence was the key to continuity. John Howe, for example, continued building the UTHSC into a major research institution, although Cisneros and McDermott had had more limited success in developing UTSA into an important economic asset. They did, however, persuade the UT Board of Regents to hire more aggressive leadership with the appointment of Sam Kirkpatrick as president in 1989. His arrival coincided with successful legal challenges to discriminatory practices in public education that forced the state legislature to approve more funding for South Texas. Kirkpatrick began a major expansion of graduate degrees that prepared the groundwork for doctoral programs. Ricardo Romo succeeded him in 1999 and launched a successful effort to win Coordinating Board approval of doctoral degrees in fields crucial to the local economy, including those in civil, mechanical, and electrical engineering, as well as degrees in physics, chemistry, and environmental sciences.[1]

In the meantime the EDF continued its work to promote economic diversity. Between 1974 and 1991 it had recruited 52 firms to San Antonio; from 1992 to 2000 it enticed another 108—doubling its success rate and halving the time required to do so.[2] It was perhaps McDermott's most important and enduring legacy in terms of implementing his vision for the city.

Cisneros's most important legacy may have been his program to convince the rising generation of leaders to embrace boosterism. When he organized Target '90 he gave more than five hundred participants a tutorial on urban development. Borrowing from his professorial experience, he chose twelve focus areas and assigned each task force the role of developing specific recommendations. There was, of course, an immediate political benefit because Target '90 created enthusiasm for his goals. But 1990 was not supposed to define an end to all those goals. Several had no chance of completion by 1990, which is why the final report, in its chairman's words, was "a road map for San Antonio's future."[3] Nelson Wolff reinforced that tutorial after the publication of the report. He became chairman of Target '90 and developed Future San Antonio, a program that trained a hundred young professionals who became committed to implementing the report's longer-term goals.[4]

Wolff also became a major source of booster continuity after 1991. A former state representative, senator, and city councilmember, he succeeded Cockrell as mayor and served two terms. His policies on job training and environmental protection were important contributions to the boosters' program.[5] By the end of Wolff's second term, however, the inability of elected city officials to develop interest and expertise in long-term improvement projects because of Stubbs's victory was impeding city government's ability to be an effective partner for the boosters.[6] For the next several years government support for boosterism was unreliable.

On the other hand, a crisis in 1995 prevented that support from disappearing entirely. Congress shocked the business community by deciding to close Kelly Air Force Base. This was an unprecedented challenge for a city that had never had to deal with the loss of a major economic asset. The Chamber of Commerce and mayor William Thornton led a successful effort to convince Congress to extend the closing date to 2001, giving the city council time to redesign Kelly into a large industrial park. Military contracts for aircraft maintenance would continue, establishing a basis for a successful conversion, and the Greater Kelly Development Corporation eventually recruited eight companies to the park with the help of, among others, Wolff. Businessmen and politicians had rallied to convert a potential disaster into a more diversified asset, which contributed to the boosters' economic goals.[7]

As a solution to the closing of Kelly emerged, boosters unexpectedly acquired a new source of government assistance for their projects. In 1992 Cyndi Krier, who had served in the Texas Senate for a decade, became a county judge on the Commissioners Court. Traditionally the court and city council had not cooperated in development projects, but term limits did not apply to the judges, which gave them at least the opportunity to gain experience and expertise in booster projects. Krier improved the court professional staff's ability to deal with economic issues, enabling her to play a major role in building the AT&T Arena as a new home for the Spurs.[8]

Krier stepped down from the court in 2001 to join the UT Board of Regents, where she would have a vital role in developing UTSA. Wolff succeeded her and built on her work to make the Commissioners Court an essential source of government support for boosterism. That was opportune timing. By this point Cisneros had returned to San Antonio after serving as secretary of housing and urban development and launching a business career. Other veterans of the original booster coalition, such as Jim Dublin, were also available to help. The EDF once again had the political support it needed.

That became clear in 2002 when Toyota Motor Company announced San Antonio had become a finalist for its new manufacturing plant. This opportunity illustrated the value of long-term relationships that began, in this case, in the 1980s. Cisneros had established sister-city relationships with Japanese cities at a time when Japan had become a major expansionist economic power. Those connections gave San Antonio a critical advantage in the competition to secure the plant, and with the experienced leadership that Cisneros and Wolff could supply, the community rallied around this opportunity.

A broad coalition quickly emerged to work for many months on winning the plant. The EDF dealt with site location, but it also arranged a financing package at a crucial point in negotiations. Civic leaders and the Chamber of Commerce organized task forces to lobby state government for assistance, legal teams to work out contracts, and a public relations campaign to rally public support. One new plant, even one as large as Toyota's, did not translate into a booming manufacturing sector, especially at a time when the number of local factories was declining because of the North American Free Trade Agreement. The community's response, though, demonstrated that San Antonians were still willing to take risks and organize effectively to deal with opportunities. Winning that bidding war also enhanced San Antonio's national reputation as a city interested in development, which in turn supported the EDF's methodical campaign for diversification.[9]

The resurrection of strong government support for boosterism did not mean that the traditional reliance on the military and tourism became irrelevant. Indeed some aspects of that gospel remained quite strong. San Antonio lost Kelly and Brooks Air Force Bases, but the arrival of several thousand National Security Agency employees and the designation of Fort Sam Houston as the site for the new Medical Education and Training Campus in 2005 reinforced the federal contribution to the city's growth. The military, which had slipped to sixth place in importance in 2006, regained its position as the city's largest employer and contributor to the economy by 2011.[10]

San Antonio's tourism industry also remained important, strengthened by the explosive growth of the River Walk's popularity, increases in convention revenues, and efforts to restore the colonial era missions, which earned designation as a United Nations World Heritage Site.

Health care and biosciences, however, combined to claim second place in economic impact, and their need for more highly trained employees helped improve wages. A national survey of wage trends ranked San Antonio sixth among the nation's cities in creating high-wage job opportunities.[11] There was now a better balance between traditional and new sources of growth and development that had not existed prior to 1980.

While the core of the booster program remained focused on recruiting a diverse assortment of new firms to town, there were other initiatives that would support that work by making San Antonio a more attractive place to live. Arthur (Hap) Veltman had been an assistant to David Straus in the early phases of the River Walk's redevelopment and co-owned the Kangaroo Court, one of its more popular restaurants. In the 1980s Veltman was seeking tenants for some abandoned light industry properties that he had bought on the river just south of the downtown. He arranged to rent some space to UTSA's art department that became the Blue Star complex for artists who needed low rent apartments and exhibit space. Located adjacent to the King William neighborhood, which was itself undergoing revitalization, the Blue Star complex earned a national reputation for its exhibits and became the anchor for the success of many Mexican American artists. As an artist colony, Blue Star also became source of cheap labor that attracted restaurants to the area while the successful restoration of King William mansions spurred the rehabilitation of other historic homes in the surrounding area. Over the next twenty years San Antonio's first major experiment in gentrification earned the sobriquet South Town.[12]

In 2002 Kit Goldsbury bought the defunct Pearl Brewery property just north of the downtown, which was also on the river. His purchase coincided with a major effort by city and county government to extend the original River Walk to the north and south sides of town as spurs to development. As one of the city's wealthiest men, Goldsbury had the resources to create an ambitious redevelopment of the Brewery into a residential and commercial center. He convinced the Culinary Institute of America to establish a school at the Pearl, which quickly attracted a significant number of restaurants. And like Blue Star, the Pearl quickly spawned gentrification in the surrounding area.[13]

By bracketing the downtown, both complexes encouraged residential and commercial developments there as well. Residential tenants were generally young professionals who worked in high tech companies and other well-paying firms. And both contributed to the booster agenda by offering the kind of lifestyle that made San Antonio more attractive to those companies.

That balance was a testament to the success of McDermott, Cockrell, and Cisneros's coalition in changing the basic character of San Antonio. It is still a work much in progress; much, as always in the long history of America's cities, remains to be done. Progress, though, needs help. The business community had proved it could build a respectably large city by relying on the military, wholesaling, and tourism; the boosters proved they could build a better city by diversifying into more dynamic activities. In doing so, they created a much more diverse, more complex, and more attractive city.

APPENDIX

1850s Land Transactions

TABLE A.1 1852 Auction of City Public Lands

Purchaser	West Side Lots Purchased	East Side Lots Purchased	Total Lots Purchased
Alexander, D.	3	1	4
Brackett, O.	30	14	44
Callaghan, B.*	28	7	35
Casiano, J.	11	0	11
Childress, G.	0	3	3
Crawford, J.	8	0	8
Dashiell, J.	0	7	7
Devine, D.**	6	0	6
Devine, J.**	30	14	44
Devine, T.*	9	0	9
Dignowity, A.	24	12	36
Guilbeau, F.*	23	0	23
Houston, G.	0	5	5
Howard, G.**	39	6	45
Jackson, J.	0	5	5
James, J.*	6	5	11
Jones, E.*	12	0	12
Kampmann, J.	0	4	4
Lockwood, A.**	8	0	8
Maverick, S.*	19	6	25
McLeod, J.**	14	0	14

(continued)

TABLE A.1 1852 Auction of City Public Lands *(continued)*

Purchaser	*West Side Lots Purchased*	*East Side Lots Purchased*	*Total Lots Purchased*
Nette, A.	0	1	1
Paschal, F.**	4	0	4
Sappington, B.	12	0	12
Schleiser, G.	5	2	7
Smith, S.	7	4	11
Vance, W.	0	6	6
Total / Percent	298 / 74.5	102 / 25.5	400 / 100

Sources: 1849 Plat of the City Tract of San Antonio and 1852 Plat of the City Tract of San Antonio de Bexar, San Antonio City Archives.

*Original members of the San Antonio and Mexican Gulf Railroad Board of Directors.

**Relatives and associates of the original board members.

TABLE A.2 Land Transactions among Key Groups in Antebellum San Antonio

	22 SA&MG Charter Directors, 1848–1850	*8 Core Coalition Directors, 1850–1855*	*17 Former SA&MG Directors, 1848–1855*	*32 Know-Nothing Party Leaders, 1848–1855*
Transactions	274	278	232	272
Active Buyers	16	8	14	20
Nonparticipating	6	0	3	12
% Active Buyers	72	100	82.4	62.5
Average Number of Transactions per Buyer	18.4	34.6	44.4	13.6

Source: Office of the County Clerk, Bexar County, 1837–1863 Historical Records Online.
Notes: Sample size: 100 percent.

Column 1: Records land purchases of all the original directors prior to obtaining the SA&MB charter.

Column 2: Records land purchases of the core members of the booster coalition during the years when they worked to implement their program to develop San Antonio. The near doubling of their average number of transactions implies a high level of optimism for their program's success.

Column 3: Contrasts the land-purchasing activities of the core coalition members with that of those men who helped sponsor the SA&MG charter, but who failed to participate in the railroad project after 1850. This column may represent a split among land speculators in San Antonio based on different visions of how to utilize urban land to promote growth. Since their average number of transactions more than doubled those of the charter directors', they may have shared the core group's optimism while refraining from active support for the booster program. The absence of other evidence concerning possible conflicts over land use and attitudes toward that program among these speculators makes it impossible to prove either possibility.

Column 4: Represents the speculative activities of individuals later identified as Know-Nothings. Their lower participation rate and smaller number of transactions per participant during the period when the booster coalition was active indicate these men had fewer resources to invest in land.

TABLE A.3 Post-Coalition Land Speculation

	8 Core Directors, 1856–1861	*32 Know-Nothing Party Leaders*
Transactions	386	326
Active Buyers	8	19
Nonparticipants	0	13
% Active Buyers	100	59.4
Average Number of Transactions	48.3	17.2

Source: Office of the County Clerk, Bexar County, 1837–1861 Historical Records Online.
Notes: Sample size: 100 percent.
Although the average number of transactions among Know-Nothings increased by 27 percent, their speculative activities paled in comparison with those of the core members of the booster coalition. As a group, the Know-Nothings remained marginal in the race to control San Antonio's internal land market.

NOTES

CHAPTER ONE

1. Deed of Sale, Mar. 9, 1844, by James Dunn, Coroner, to Samuel A. Maverick, Maverick Family Papers, Business and Financial Papers: Samuel Augustus Maverick, 1842–1907, Dolph Briscoe Center for American History, University of Texas at Austin, Box 2F9.

2. On the theoretical elements required for successful city-building, see Mario Polèse, *The Wealth and Poverty of Regions: Why Cities Matter* (University of Chicago Press, 2009), 29–66.

3. Carl Abbott, *How Cities Won the West: Four Centuries of Urban Change in Western North America* (Albuquerque: University of New Mexico Press, 2008), 20–25 discusses the imperial context for town planning.

4. Gerald E. Poyo, "Immigrants and Integration to Late Eighteenth-Century Bexar," in *Tejano Origins in Eighteenth-Century San Antonio*, ed. Gerald E. Poyo and Gilberto M. Hinojosa (Austin: University of Texas Press, 1991), 96; and Jesus F. de la Teja, "Forgotten Founders: The Military Settlers of Eighteenth-Century San Antonio de Bexar," in *Tejano Origins*, 28–29. Entries for Los Adaes and La Bahía are in the *Handbook of Texas Online*, https://tshaonline.org.

5. For a discussion of the Spanish approach to Texas colonization, see: T. R. Fehrenbach, *Lone Star: A History of Texas and the Texans* (Toronto: Macmillan, 1969), 46, 50; and Jesus F. de la Teja, *San Antonio de Bexar: A Community on New Spain's Northern Frontier* (Albuquerque: University of New Mexico Press, 1995), 5–7.

6. De la Teja, *San Antonio de Bexar*, 7.

7. De la Teja, 9–10.

8. Gerald E. Poyo, "The Canary Islands Immigrants of San Antonio: From Ethnic Exclusivity to Community in Eighteenth-Century Bexar," in *Tejano Origins*, 42–46.

9. Fehrenbach, *Lone Star*, 76–77.

10. De la Teja, *San Antonio de Bexar*, 19–21.

11. Poyo, "Immigrants and Integration," 96–100.

12. Poyo, "Canary Islands Immigrants," 52–53; and Elizabeth A. H. John, "Independent Indians and the San Antonio Community," in *Tejano Origins*, 125–27.

13. Jesus F. de la Teja and John Wheat, "Bexar: Profile of a Tejano Community, 1820–1832," in *Tejano Origins*, 5–7, 17–24; and Raul A. Ramos, *Beyond the Alamo: Forging Mexican

Ethnicity in San Antonio, 1821–1861 (Chapel Hill: University of North Carolina Press, 2008), 27–41.

14. De la Teja and Wheat, "Bexar: Profile," 19.

15. De la Teja and Wheat, 19; Ramos, *Beyond the Alamo*, 86–93; and Fehrenbach, *Lone Star*, 137–38.

16. Fehrenbach, *Lone Star*, 143.

17. De la Teja and Wheat, "Bexar: Profile," 20.

18. Ramos, *Beyond the Alamo*, 39–47; and Andres Resendez, *Changing National Identities at the Frontier: Texas and New Mexico, 1800–1850* (New York: Cambridge University Press, 2005), 96, 98–100, 112.

19. Almonte's report quoted in John J. Linn, *Reminiscences of Fifty Years in Texas* (Austin: Steck, 1935; facsimile reproduction of 1883 edition), 98.

20. De la Teja and Wheat, "Bexar: Profile," 7.

21. De la Teja and Wheat, 5.

22. Poyo and Hinojosa, eds., *Tejano Origins*; Ramos, *Beyond the Alamo*; and Timothy M. Matovina, *Tejano Religion and Ethnicity: San Antonio, 1821–1860* (Austin: University of Texas Press, 1995) argue the case for this sense of distinctiveness.

23. Students of urban development will recognize here a version of the long debate over the importance, or insignificance, of local efforts to shape urban growth in the context of various forces that either inhibit or promote that growth. See, inter alia, Paul E. Peterson, *City Limits* (University of Chicago Press, 1981); John R. Logan and Harvey L. Molotch, *Urban Fortunes: The Political Economy of Place* (Berkeley: University of California Press, 1987); and Clarence N. Stone, *Regime Politics: Governing Atlanta* (Lawrence: University Press of Kansas, 1989). My point here is that San Antonio's leaders had little choice but to organize a local initiative to promote growth because the town ultimately found itself in an independent republic that had little capacity to defend itself, let alone any ability to help urban development beyond facilitating land sales to encourage immigration from the United States.

24. T. R. Fehrenbach et al., *The San Antonio Story* (Tulsa, Okla.: Continental Heritage, 1978), 21–23.

25. Fehrenbach et al., *San Antonio Story*, 27, 29; Poyo and Hinojosa, eds., *Tejano Origins*, 48–49; and Cecilia Steinfeldt, *San Antonio Was: Seen through a Magic Lantern* (San Antonio Museum Association, 1978), 32.

26. De la Teja and Wheat, "Bexar: Profile," 3; and Carland Elaine Crook, "San Antonio, Texas, 1846–1861" (master's thesis, Rice University, 1964), 151.

27. De la Teja and Wheat, "Bexar: Profile," 18.

28. Robert G. Albion, *The Rise of New York Port, 1815–1860* (Hamden, Conn.: Archon, 1961; reprint), 373–88; and John W. Reps, *The Making of Urban America: A History of City Planning in the United States* (Princeton University Press, 1965), 216–17.

29. Reps, *Making of Urban America*, 302–4, 314, 378.

30. Daniel J. Boorstin, *The Americans: The National Experience* (New York: Random House, 1965), 115–23, 161–68; Carl Abbott, *Boosters and Businessmen: Popular Economic*

Thought and Urban Growth in the Antebellum Middle West (Westport, Conn.: Greenwood Press, 1981); and William Cronon, *Nature's Metropolis: Chicago and the Great West* (New York: W. W. Norton, 1991), 53–54.

31. Wells A. Hutchins, "The Community Acequia: Its Origin and Development," *Southwestern Historical Quarterly* 31 (Jan. 1928): 261–63, 265, 271, 279–80.

32. Fehrenbach et al., *San Antonio Story*, 31.

33. An Act Incorporating the City of San Antonio and Other Towns Therein Named, in *The Laws of Texas, 1822–1897*, comp. H. P. N. Gammel (Austin: Gammel, 1898), I:1379–81; Matovina, *Tejano Religion*, 34; and Cecil Scanlan, "John W. Smith: G.T.T." (unpublished paper, 1984), 27, in author's possession.

34. John B. Pitts III, "Speculation in Head Right Grants in San Antonio from 1837 to 1842" (master's thesis, Trinity University, 1966), 2, 5–6, 10.

35. Pitts, 52–69.

36. Scanlan, "John W. Smith," passim.

37. L. W. Kemp, "Joseph Baker," *Handbook of Texas Online*, tshaonline.org.

38. Pitts, "Speculation in Head Rights Grants," 13–14.

39. "San Antonio Public Officials," compiled by the staff of the San Antonio Public Library, n.d., Vertical Files, Texana/Genealogy Department, Main Library.

40. Gammel, comp., *Laws of Texas*, II:704–7.

41. Arthur J. Mayer, "San Antonio: Frontier Entrepot" (Ph.D. dissertation, University of Texas at Austin, 1976), 207–9.

42. Pitts, "Speculation in Head Right Grants," 12.

43. Pitts, 41–42.

44. Pitts, 49; Mary Maverick quoted on p. 90.

45. Ray F. Broussard, "San Antonio during the Texas Republic: A City in Transition," *Southwestern Studies* 5, no. 2 (1967): 22, 33; and Ferdinand Roemer, *Texas; with particular reference to German immigration and the physical appearance of the country described through personal observation* (San Antonio: Standard Printing, 1935), 130–31.

46. Ramos, *Beyond the Alamo*, 81–82, 147, 151, 160–61, 173–77; and Matovina, *Tejano Religion*, 31–33.

47. Ramos, *Beyond the Alamo*, 133–65.

48. Bernardine Rice, "San Antonio: Its Early Beginnings and Its Development under the Republic" (master's thesis, University of Texas at Austin, 1941), 48. See also Ramos, *Beyond the Alamo*, 184.

49. Matovina, *Tejano*, 14–16, 39–48, 52–53, 56.

50. An eyewitness account of this confrontation appeared several decades later in the *San Antonio Express*, Mar. 15, 1890.

51. Rice, "San Antonio," 49; and Ramos, *Beyond the Alamo*, 185–86.

52. Steinfeldt, *San Antonio Was*, 154; and Betje Black Klier, "François Guilbeau Jr.," and "Cornelius Van Ness," *Handbook of Texas Online*, https://tshaonline.org.

53. Ramos, *Beyond the Alamo*, 186.

54. Ramos, 188–89.

55. Ramos, 188–91.

56. Thomas W. Cutrer, "Duncan Campbell Ogden," *Handbook of Texas Online*, https://tshaonline.org.

CHAPTER TWO

1. For background on the Mexican War and Texas annexation, see Robert W. Merry, *A Country of Vast Designs: James K. Polk, the Mexican War, and the Conquest of the American Continent* (New York: Simon & Schuster, 2009); and David A. Clary, *Eagles and Empire: The United States, Mexico, and the Struggle for a Continent* (New York: Bantam Books, 2009).

2. Arthur J. Mayer, "San Antonio: Frontier Entrepot" (Ph.D. diss., University of Texas at Austin, 1976), 330.

3. Clary, *Eagles and Empire*, 48–54, 57–61; and T. R. Fehrenbach, *The San Antonio Story* (San Antonio: Continental Heritage, 1978), 75–77.

4. This discussion of San Antonio's locational problems is adapted from the analysis of central place theory in Paul M. Hohenberg and Lynn Hollen Lees, *The Making of Urban Europe, 1000–1950* (Cambridge, Mass.: Harvard University Press, 1985), especially pp. 47–73, and William Cronon, *Nature's Metropolis: Chicago and the Great West* (New York: W. W. Norton, 1991), 38–39, 279–83.

5. San Antonio City Council Minutes (hereafter CCM), Feb. 20, 1846, San Antonio Municipal Archives.

6. United States Army, Corps of Engineers, *Reports of the Secretary of War, with Reconnaissances of Routes from San Antonio to El Paso* (Washington, D.C.: Union Office, 1850), 3; Brownson Malsch, *Indianola: The Mother of Western Texas* (Austin: State House Press, 1988), 46; and William H. Goetzmann, *Army Exploration in the American West* (New Haven, Conn.: Yale University Press, 1959), 211.

7. Mayer, "San Antonio," 217–20; and Bernice Strong, "John James," *Handbook of Texas Online*, tshaonline.org.

8. On the importance of entrepreneurship, see Joseph Schumpeter, "The Creative Response in Economic History," *Journal of Economic History* 7, no. 2 (November 1947).

9. On the importance of cooperation, see Clarence N. Stone, *Regime Politics: Governing Atlanta, 1946–1988* (Lawrence: University Press of Kansas, 1989), 8–9; see also John R. Logan and Harvey L. Molotch, *Urban Fortunes: The Political Economy of Place* (Berkeley: University of California Press, 1987).

10. Kenneth M. Wheeler, *To Wear a City's Crown: The Beginnings of Urban Growth in Texas, 1836–1865* (Cambridge, Mass.: Harvard University Press, 1968), 66, 96–103; Harry Williams Jr., "The Development of a Market Economy in Texas: The Establishment of the Railroad Network, 1836–1890" (Ph.D. diss., University of Texas at Austin, 1957), 115, 118–19, 124–25, 133.

11. Rupert N. Richardson, "Robert Simpson Neighbors," and Cornelia Marschall Smith and Otto W. Tetzlaff, "John O. Meusebach," *Handbook of Texas Online*, tshaonline.org.

12. See appendix.

13. Raul A. Ramos, *Beyond the Alamo: Forging Mexican Ethnicity in San Antonio, 1821–1861* (Chapel Hill: University of North Carolina Press, 2008), 195–96.

14. Cassiano's land transactions are recorded in 1837–1963 Historical Records of Bexar County, Bexar County Clerk's Office; and José A. Navarro to Enoch Jones, July 12, 1851 (recorded as Jan. 12, 1854), Historical Records of Bexar County, Bexar County Clerk's Office.

15. Logan and Molotch (*Urban Fortunes*, 57–62) argue that interest in a good business climate motivates local businessmen's involvement in growth machines. In San Antonio's situation in the 1850s, the army's contracts insulated freighters from the normal demands for a supportive, communitywide business climate.

16. Mayer, "San Antonio," 372–73.

17. *San Antonio Ledger* (hereafter *Ledger*), Dec. 30, 1852.

18. This discussion of the army's impact on local merchants is adapted from Mario Polèse, *The Wealth and Poverty of Regions: Why Cities Matter* (Chicago: University of Chicago Press, 2009), 18–23. Polèse characterizes similar situations in the modern era as the "Intrusive Rentier Syndrome."

19. Calculated by comparing the manuscript 1850 Census of U.S. Population for San Antonio with lists of businessmen in local newspapers.

20. Crook, "San Antonio, Texas," 47, 50.

21. While I prefer the term "influence," social scientists usually use "social capital" to describe the role of community leaders. See, for example, Jan Flora, Jeff Sharp, Cornelia Flora, and Bonnie Newton, "Entrepreneurial Social Infrastructure and Locally Initiated Economic Development in the Nonmetropolitan United States," *Sociological Quarterly* 38, no. 4 (1997): 623–45. I have found that those with "social capital" were often resistant or refused to use their influence to promote economic development in San Antonio, which casts doubt on the assumption that those with influence are willing to use it for such purposes. See also Guian McKee, "Are Urban Historians Bowling Along? Social Capital Theory and Urban History," *Journal of Urban History* 36, no. 5 (September 2010): 709–17.

22. Information on the biographies of these boosters was compiled from the *Handbook of Texas Online* and Crook, "San Antonio, Texas," 41–60. On boosters in general, see Carl Abbott, *Boosters and Businessmen: Popular Economic Thought and Urban Growth in the Antebellum Middle West* (Westport, Conn.: Greenwood Press, 1981); and Cronon, *Nature's Metropolis*, 32–33, 53–54.

23. Arthur M. Johnson and Barry E. Supple, *Boston Capitalists and Western Railroads: A Study in the Nineteenth-Century Railroad Investment Process* (Cambridge, Mass.: Harvard University Press, 1967), 34–37, 116.

24. Ferdinand Roemer, *Texas; with Particular Reference to German Immigration and the Physical Appearance of the Country Described through Personal Observation* (San Antonio: Standard Printing, 1967), 124, 133–34. On import replacement, see Jane Jacobs, *The Economy of Cities* (New York: Vintage Books, 1970), 146–50.

25. Walter L. Buenger, *Secession and the Union in Texas* (Austin: University of Texas Press, 1984), 91, notes that ethnic tensions did not reach the point of affecting local politics until the mid-1850s.

26. For examples of the greater complexity of other cities, see, for example, Robin L. Einhorn, *Property Rules: Political Economy in Chicago, 1833–1872* (Chicago: University of Chicago Press, 1991); and Philip J. Ethington, *The Public City: The Political Construction of Urban Life in San Francisco, 1850–1900* (New York: Cambridge University Press, 1994).

27. CCM, Jan. 3, Sept. 20, 1849; Mar. 25, Sept. 16, 1850; Oct. 13, 1851; Jan. 26, Nov. 8, 12, 15, 1852; and *Lewis and Others v. the City of San Antonio*, 7 Texas Reports, 288, *Reports of Cases Argued and Decided in the Supreme Court of the State of Texas* (Houston: N.p., 1877), VII:144–61.

28. A special committee of the council noted the altered sale terms in its report on the 1852 auction. CCM, July 13, 1853.

29. See appendix, table A.1.

30. CCM, Feb. 23, Apr. 20, Aug. 13, 1853; May 27, 1854.

31. CCM, June 7, July 13, 1853; Apr. 13, 1854; Jan. 31, 1856.

32. "An Act to Incorporate the San Antonio and Mexican Gulf Railroad Company," Sept. 5, 1850, in San Antonio and Mexican Gulf Railroad Papers, 1850–1853, Box 2G39, Dolph Briscoe Center for American History, University of Texas at Austin.

33. CCM, Dec. 4, 30, 1850.

34. CCM, Feb. 5, 24, 1851.

35. *Ledger*, June 12, 1851.

36. This conclusion is based on an analysis of board attendance patterns as recorded in San Antonio and Mexican Gulf Railroad Ledger Book (hereafter SA&MG Ledger), Oct. 6, 1851, University of Texas at San Antonio Archives, MS 287, Box OM1.

37. SA&MG Ledger, Oct. 6, 1851. Howard & Ogden was one of the oldest shipping firms in town, and Howard had filed the suit against Juan Seguín that led to the sale of his house in 1844. On Charles Riotte, see S. W. Pease, "They Came to San Antonio" (typescript, n.d.), 210, in the Texana Collection, San Antonio Public Library.

38. SA&MG Ledger, Sept. 22, 1852.

39. *Ledger*, June 19, 1851.

40. *San Antonio Western Texan* (hereafter *Western Texan*), June 3, 1852; and CCM, Feb. 24, Apr. 26, June 30, 1852.

41. CCM, Feb. 2, 1852.

42. *Western Texan*, June 3, 1852.

43. SA&MG Ledger, Feb. 11 and 18, May 7, June 6, Sept. 5, Dec. 23, 1853; and Report of the Committee to Investigate the Contract for Construction of the Road, in SA&MG Ledger, Oct. 3, 1853.

44. SA&MG Ledger, Sept. 9, Dec. 13 and 15, 1852; Malsch, *Indianola*, 78–79; and Frederick Law Olmsted, *A Journey through Texas; or, a Saddle-Trip on the Southwestern Frontier* (New York: Dix, Edwards & Co., 1857), 254.

45. SA&MG Ledger, Apr. 8, 1853.

46. SA&MG Ledger, Oct. 3, 1853.

47. Mayer, "San Antonio," 377, 569.

48. CCM, Feb. 10, Apr. 26, Nov. 27, 1852.

49. CCM, Nov. 26, 1853.

50. CCM, Nov. 30, 1853; Jan. 6, 12, 1854.

51. Crook, "San Antonio, Texas," 246–47.

52. C. A. Harper, letter to the editor, *Ledger*, Mar. 6, 1851.

53. Captain Beck, letter to the editor, *Western Texan*, Dec. 16, 1852; and A. A. Lockwood, letter to the editor, *Ledger*, June 19, 1851.

54. *Alamo Star*, June 3, 1854, quoted in Crook, "San Antonio, Texas," 7.

55. San Antonio's boosters had apparently reached the same conclusions as Brendan O'Flaherty, who, in *City Economics* (Cambridge, Mass.: Harvard University Press, 2005), 527–28, argues that enhancing city services is more likely to produce development benefits than any other strategy.

56. CCM, Nov. 23, 1853.

57. CCM, Nov. 23, 1853.

58. CCM, Jan. 6, 1854.

59. The entire platform of the German convention is reproduced in Rudolph T. Biesler, "The Texas State Convention of Germans in 1854," *Southwestern Historical Quarterly* 33 (April 1930): 297–61. For reactions to the platform's statement on slavery, see *Western Texan*, June 8, 1854; Kent Keeth, "Sankt Antonious: Germans in the Alamo City in the 1850s," *Southwestern Historical Quarterly* 76 (Oct. 1972): 198–99; Terry Jordan, *German Seed in Texas Soil: Immigrant Farmers in Nineteenth-Century Texas* (Austin: University of Texas Press, 1966), 181; Sister Paul of the Cross McGrath, "Political Nativism in Texas, 1825–1860" (Ph.D. diss., Catholic University, 1930), 92–95; and Buenger, *Secession and the Union*, 91–92.

60. Biesler, "Texas State Convention," 253–54.

61. Local reactions to the Catholicism of Devine and Guilbeau are conjectural. On the Paschals, see Claude Elliott, "The Constitutional Convention of 1866," *Handbook of Texas Online*, which describes Isaiah Paschal as "among the extreme Unionists," and Amelia W. Williams, "George Washington Paschal," in the *Handbook of Texas Online*, tshaonline.org.

62. CCM, Jan. 8, 1853.

63. *Ledger*, Oct. 6, 1853.

64. John D. McLeod to the Citizens of Bexar County, *Western Texan*, July 31, 1854.

65. *Western Texan*, Aug. 17, 1854.

66. SA&MG Ledger, Feb. 2, 1854.

67. This statement is based on an analysis of land purchases by boosters and Know-Nothings as recorded in the Bexar County Property Records.

68. Election results were recorded in CCM, Dec. 25, 1854.

69. CCM, Jan. 20 and 30, 1855.

70. CCM, Feb. 16, 1855.

71. CCM, Mar. 1, 1855.

72. For Menger's background, see Cecilia Steinfeldt, *San Antonio Was* (San Antonio: San Antonio Museum Association, 1978), 118, 120.

73. Crook, "San Antonio, Texas," 147–48; Jane L. Scarborough, "George W. Paschal: Texas Unionist and Scalawag Jurisprudent" (Ph.D. diss., Rice University, 1972), 40–41; Ramos, *Beyond the Alamo*, 209–15; *Ledger*, July 28, Nov. 24, Dec. 22, 1855; and *San Antonio Herald*, Dec. 26, 1855.

74. CCM, Jan. 28, Feb. 14, 1856.

75. "An Act to Incorporate the City of San Antonio," in *The Laws of Texas, 1822–1897*, comp. H. P. N. Gammel (Austin: Gammel, 1898), IV:550–67; and CCM, Feb. 14, 1856.

76. Wheeler, *Wear a City's Crown*, 126–29.

77. *Western Texan*, Oct. 19, 1854, lists thirty-five firms engaged in importing goods to San Antonio.

78. Crook, "San Antonio, Texas," 47, 122–33; Mayer, "San Antonio," 332–33, 356; and William F. Fleming, "San Antonio: The History of a Military City, 1865–1880" (Ph.D. diss., University of Pennsylvania, 1963), 347–48.

79. The values of military contracts in this paragraph are stated in 1850s terms and are not adjusted to modern equivalents due to inflation.

80. Mayer, "San Antonio," 372–73, 412–14.

81. *Western Texan*, Nov. 25, 1852.

82. "Mrs. Canterbury's Memoirs," *San Antonio Express*, Mar. 15, 1890; Robert Sturmberg, *A History of San Antonio and of the Early Days in Texas* (San Antonio: Standard Printing, 1920), 114–17; and Will C. Rogers, "A History of the Military Plaza to 1937" (master's thesis, Trinity University, 1968), 16.

83. Crook, "San Antonio, Texas," 7, 45; and Steinfeldt, *San Antonio Was*, 136.

84. Roger W. Lotchin, "Introduction: The Martial Metropolis," in *The Martial Metropolis: U.S. Cities in War and Peace*, ed. Roger W. Lotchin (New York: Praeger, 1984), x.

85. Mario Polèse, *Wealth and Poverty*, 28–29, provides the theoretical basis for this discussion.

86. "Samuel Augustus Maverick," *National Cyclopaedia of American Biography* (New York: J. T. White, 1892), VI:482, accessible at archive.org.

87. This behavior pattern among leading San Antonians was gleaned from biographical sketches in the *Handbook of Texas Online*. For a comparison to San Antonio's development at mid-century, see Cronon, *Nature's Metropolis*.

88. CCM, Feb. 26, 1851; and Crook, "San Antonio, Texas," 147–48.

89. For a discussion of the ways in which cultural beliefs shape economic development, see Joel Mokyr, *A Culture of Growth: The Origins of the Modern Economy* (Princeton, N.J.: Princeton University Press, 2017).

CHAPTER THREE

1. On San Antonio's position relative to its rivals, see Kenneth W. Wheeler, *To Wear a City's Crown: The Beginnings of Urban Growth in Texas, 1836–1865* (Cambridge, Mass.: Harvard University Press, 1968), 110–11.

2. Arthur J. Mayer, "San Antonio: Frontier Entrepot" (Ph.D. diss., University of Texas at Austin, 1976), 411–25, 445.

3. Mayer, "San Antonio," 490, 491–95; Wheeler, *Wear a City's Crown*, 155–56; and Marilyn McAdams Sibley, *George W. Brackenridge: Maverick Philanthropist* (Austin: University of Texas Press, 1973), 33–54.

4. Raul A. Ramos, *Beyond the Alamo: Forging Mexican Ethnicity in San Antonio, 1821–1861* (Chapel Hill: University of North Carolina Press, 2008), 207, 228–29. Tejanos had made up 48 percent of San Antonio's population in 1850 but declined to 35 percent by 1860.

5. Claude Elliott, "Union Sentiment in Texas," *Southwestern Historical Quarterly* 50 (April 1947): 450–77; Walter L. Buenger, *Secession and the Union in Texas* (Austin: University of Texas Press, 1984), 103–4; Cecilia Steinfeldt, *San Antonio Was* (San Antonio Museum Association, 1978), 90; and Terry G. Jordan, *German Seed in Texas Soil: Immigrant Farmers in Nineteenth-Century Texas* (Austin: University of Texas Press, 1975), 182–85.

6. Buenger, *Secession and the Union*, 67. On German voting on secession, see Jordan, *German Seed*, 184 (table 50).

7. Thomas A. Jennings, "San Antonio in the Confederacy" (master's thesis, Trinity University, 1957), 87–88; and Elliott, "Union Sentiment," 456–57.

8. Circular, Southern Defence [*sic*] Aid Society, San Antonio, July 16, 1861, in John Herndon James Papers, Daughters of the Republic of Texas Library, San Antonio, Texas.

9. Elliott, "Union Sentiment," 457–78.

10. Elliott, 458; and Alwyn Barr, ed., "Notes and Documents: Records of the Confederate Military Commission in San Antonio, July 2–Oct. 10, 1862," *Southwestern Historical Quarterly* 70 (July 1966): 93–94.

11. Alwyn Barr undertook to edit and publish the entire proceedings of this military commission in the *Southwestern Historical Quarterly*. In addition to his edited work cited in note 10, see "Notes and Documents: Records of the Confederate Military Commission in San Antonio, July 2–Oct. 10, 1862," *Southwestern Historical Quarterly* 70 (October 1966): 289–313; 71 (October 1967): 247–77; and 73 (October 1969): 243–74.

12. Elliott, "Union Sentiment," 465–66.

13. Barr, ed., "Notes and Documents," 243–52.

14. Elliott, "Union Sentiment," 458.

15. Constitution of the Southern Rights Association of Bexar County, May 18, 1865, copy in the Texana Collection, San Antonio Public Library.

16. Wheeler, *Wear a City's Crown*, 142–43; Steinfeldt, *San Antonio Was*, 177–96; Buenger, *Secession and the Union*, 82; and Carland Elaine Crook, "San Antonio, Texas, 1846–1861" (master's thesis, Rice University, 1964), 47.

17. On the connections between social structure and social capital in communities, see James Coleman, "Social Capital in the Creation of Human Capital," *American Journal of Sociology* 94 (1988): S98.

18. "An Act to Incorporate the San Antonio Commercial Club, Oct. 10, 1866," in *The Laws of Texas, 1822–1897*, comp. H. P. N. Gammel (Austin: Gammel, 1898), V:1322.

19. San Antonio City Council Minutes (hereafter CCM), Dec. 31, 1866, San Antonio Municipal Archives. Ethnic residential patterns are based on a sampling of the 1870 census. See David R. Johnson, "Frugal and Sparing: Interest Groups, Politics, and City Building in San Antonio, 1870–85," in *Urban Texas: Politics and Development*, ed. Char Miller and Heywood T. Sanders (College Station: Texas A&M University Press, 1990), 36 (table 2.1).

20. *San Antonio Herald* (hereafter *Herald*), Sept. 12 and 30, 1866.

21. CCM, Sept. 3, 1867.

22. Dale A. Somers, "James P. Newcomb: Texas Unionist and Radical Republican" (master's thesis, Trinity University, 1964), 11–15, 97–98, 124–25, 143; and Carl H. Moneyhon, *Republicanism in Reconstruction Texas* (College Station: Texas A&M University Press, 1980), 84–85. On Siemering, see "Siemering, August (1828–1883)," *Handbook of Texas Online*, tshaonline.org.

23. *San Antonio Express* (hereafter *Express*), Oct. 23, 1867.

24. *Express*, Oct. 23, 1867.

25. Char Miller and David R. Johnson, "The Rise of Urban Texas," in *Urban Texas: Politics and Development*, ed. Char Miller and Heywood T. Sanders (College Station: Texas A&M University Press, 1990), 11.

26. *Express*, Oct. 26, 1867.

27. Information on the careers of these men comes from their biographical sketches in the *Handbook of Texas Online*.

28. Kenneth Mason, "Paternal Continuity: African Americans and Race Relations in San Antonio, Texas, 1867–1937" (Ph.D. diss., University of Texas at Austin, 1994), 35 (table 6).

29. Mason, "Paternal Continuity," 123–26.

30. Mason, 122.

31. *Express*, Apr. 6, 1868; Jan. 23, Feb. 1, 1869; and Apr. 4, 1870.

32. Thielepape summarized the council's financial dilemmas in his "Mayor's Message to the City Council," reprinted in the *Express*, Jan. 8, 1870.

33. CCM, Jan. 21, May 25, 1867; Feb. 5, Oct. 27, Nov. 5, 1868; Oct. 11 and 14, Nov. 5, 1869; Aug. 8, 1871; and Aug. 26, 1872.

34. CCM, Feb. 22 and 23, 1868.

35. Thomas T. Smith, *The U.S. Army and the Texas Frontier Economy, 1845–1900* (College Station: Texas A&M University Press, 1999), 13 (table 3), 49 (table 4), 72 (table 6), 114 (table 9).

36. William F. Fleming, "San Antonio: The History of a Military City, 1865–1880" (Ph.D. diss., University of Pennsylvania, 1963), 37, 326, 338–39; Mayer, "San Antonio," 585–86; Bvt. Maj. Gen. E. S. Canby, Special Order No. 45, Feb. 24, 1869, and Bvt. Maj. Gen. J. A. Potter to Robert Eager, Feb. 24, 1869, in Riddle, Eager Business Records, Box 1, Aline B. Carter Family Papers, 1823–1997, University of Texas at San Antonio Archives.

37. *Express*, May 25, 1867; Mayer, "San Antonio," 560–68, 625; and Sibley, *George W. Brackenridge*, 89–90, 96.

38. Paul H. Carlson, "Sheep Ranching," *Handbook of Texas Online*, tshaonline.org.

39. Will C. Rogers, "A History of the Military Plaza to 1937" (master's thesis, Trinity University, 1968), 20, 40–41; and Steinfeldt, *San Antonio Was*, 38–46.

40. For background on Adams and Wickes, see Smith, *U.S. Army*, 55–56, 58. Data on their and other land speculators' real estate activities were compiled from the Historical Deed Records, Bexar County Clerk's Office.

41. *Express*, Mar. 2, 1868.

42. Fleming, "San Antonio," 365–73; and Bernice R. Strong, "Alamo Plaza: Cultural Crossroads of a City, 1724–1900" (master's thesis, University of Texas at San Antonio, 1987), 80.

43. *Express*, Jan. 31, Mar. 4, 1868. Sketch and handwritten note, signed and dated by Samuel A. Maverick, July 1, 1869, in Map Collection, San Antonio Municipal Archives.

44. *Express*, May 26, June 29, 1869; and Marilyn McAdams Sibley, *The Port of Houston: A History* (Austin: University of Texas Press, 1968), 58, 85, 97–98. On resignations and the petition drive, see Thielepape to Newcomb, Dec. 13, 1868, James P. Newcomb Papers, San Antonio Public Library; CCM, Aug. 3, Sept. 11, Nov. 16, 1868; Mar. 29, Aug. 2 and 16, Oct. 20, Dec. 18, 1869; for the state Republican Party's problems, see Moneyhon, *Republicanism in Reconstruction*, 104–28.

45. CCM, May 19, 1870; and Moneyhon, *Republicanism in Reconstruction*, 146.

46. CCM, Jan. 11, 1868; and Thielepape to Newcomb, July 13, 1870, Newcomb Papers.

47. "An Act to Incorporate the City of San Antonio," in *Laws of Texas, 1822–1897*, comp. Gammel, VI:762–803 (see Article II, section 43, for both the bonding and railroad provisions). In the absence of any contemporary explanations, my interpretation of Newcomb's motives or thinking is strictly conjectural.

48. CCM, Aug. 8, 1871; Aug. 26, 1872.

49. *Herald*, Sept. 16, 1870.

50. *Herald*, Sept. 18 and 20, 1870.

51. *Express*, Sept. 7, 1871.

52. CCM, Dec. 14, 17, 1870; and Mar. 21, Nov. 14, 1871.

53. CCM, May 22, 1871.

54. Fleming, "San Antonio," 293–97.

55. See, inter alia, A. W. Kempton to Newcomb, July 11 and Sept. 3; Stanley Welch to Newcomb, July 12; Malcolm Anderson to Newcomb, Aug. 4 and Sept. 11; James N. Fisk to Newcomb, Sept. [?], Oct. 27, 1871, Newcomb Papers. Ethnic political sensitivities emerged in Houston as well.

56. CCM, Sept. 2, 1871; Siemering to Newcomb, Sept. 12, 16, 1871, Newcomb Papers.

57. A. I. Lockwood to Newcomb, Feb. 24, and John C. Henson to Newcomb, Feb. 25, 1872, Newcomb Papers.

58. CCM, Jan. 23, 1872; Sibley, *George W. Brackenridge*, 128–32; and Charles R. Porter Jr., *Spanish Water, Anglo Water: Early Development in San Antonio* (College Station: Texas A&M University Press, 2009), 99–113.

59. Kampmann refers to Newcomb's offer in his response. Kampmann to Newcomb, Mar. 9, 1872, Newcomb Papers.

60. "An Act to Incorporate the San Antonio City Railroad Company," in *Laws of Texas*, comp. Gammel, V:1567–71; and *Express*, May 5, 1871.

61. *Express*, May 5, 1871. At this point, Siemering, not Newcomb, controlled the *Express*.

62. The range of Kampmann's business interests and civic activities were compiled from the *Express*, Oct. 4 and 17, 1867; Historical Deed Records, 1837–1964, Bexar County Clerk's Office; and Steinfeldt, *San Antonio Was*, 62, 90, 104, 120–21, 135, 146, 158, 163–64, 172. See also Raymond Boryczka, "'The Busiest Man in Town': John Hermann Kampmann and the Urbanization of San Antonio, Texas, 1848–1885," *Southwestern Historical Quarterly* 65, no. 4 (April 2012): 329–63; and Maggie Valentine, *John H. Kampmann: Master Builder; San Antonio's German Influence in the Nineteenth Century* (New York: Beaufort Books, 2014).

63. CCM, Mar. 21, 1872; and *Express*, Mar. 22, May 5, 1872.

64. San Antonio Commercial Club Dues Book, May 1871, Riddle, Eager Business Records, Box 1, Aline B. Carter Family Papers, 1823–1997. The Dues Book is the only known document surviving from the Commercial Club.

65. *Charter, Rules and By-Laws of the San Antonio Board of Trade* (San Antonio Daily Herald, 1872). Pamphlet, in Robert Eager Family Papers, Box 2, Daughters of the Republic of Texas Library, San Antonio, Texas.

66. *Herald*, Aug. 31, Sept. 8 and 10, Oct. 2, 10, 11, 15, 19, and 23, 1872; *Express*, Nov. 10, 1872; A. I. Lockwood to Newcomb, Nov. 10, 1872, Newcomb Papers; and CCM, Jan. 14, 1873.

67. *Herald*, Oct. 3, 1872; and Mayer, "San Antonio," 605, 608, 612.

68. Letter to the editor, signed "Observer," *Express*, Jan. 7, 1873.

69. M. Whilldin, comp., *A Description of Western Texas* (Galveston, Tex.: News Steam Book and Job Office, 1876), 68–69.

70. S. G. Reed, *A History of the Texas Railroads, and of Transportation Conditions under Spain and Mexico and the Republic and the State* (Houston: St. Clair Publishing, 1941), 195–96.

71. Mayer, "San Antonio," 612.

72. CCM, Nov. 18, 1872; and *Herald*, Apr. 29, 1873.

73. *Herald*, May 3, June 14, 1873; and Ira M. Dobbin to Newcomb, Apr. 30, 1873, Newcomb Papers.

74. *Express*, Jan. 15, 1873 (emphasis in original).

75. CCM, Jan. 21, July 12, 1873.

76. CCM, Apr. 29, May 23, June 18, and July 12, 1873.

77. CCM, Aug. 23, 1873, and June 4, 1874.

78. See for example, CCM, June 24 and July 22, 1873; Feb. 24, 1874. For a summary of financial practices and their consequences following the end of Republican control of city government, see Mayor James H. French, "Message on Financial Condition of the City," CCM, Apr. 6, 1875.

79. *Express*, Jan. 8, 1875 (emphasis in original). For the Democrats' perceptions, see *Herald*, Jan. 5, 6, and 7, 1875.

80. Details of French's life and connections come from his obituary in the *Express*, Sept. 9, 1893, and from *Encyclopedia of the New West*, 79–80; Circular, Southern Defence

[*sic*] Aid Society, San Antonio, July 16, 1861, in John Herndon James Papers; U.S. Census of Population for 1880; Kampmann to Newcomb, Mar. 9, 1872, Newcomb Papers; and *Express*, Nov. 11, 1872, Oct. 8, 1879, and Sept. 7, 1893. French had modest investments in land; from 1850 to 1890 he had only fifteen property transactions recorded in the Bexar County Deed Records.

81. *Express*, Dec. 19, 1876.

82. For details on French's reforms, see Johnson, "Frugal and Sparing," 48–51.

83. Documents on the tangled legal history of this struggle are in the Historical Files, Municipal Archives, City Clerk's Office.

84. Letter to the editor, signed "X," *Express*, Nov. 23, 1875.

85. J. H. Kampmann deed to Galveston, Harrisburg & San Antonio Railway Company, October 1874, in Historical Deed Records, 1837–1964, Bexar County Clerk's Office. For additional details on business indifference to the railroad, see Johnson, "Frugal and Sparing," 5.

Theoretical work on the dynamics of urban growth assumes that large property owners and businessmen support major initiatives that will increase land values and business prospects. Opposition to the railroad among ordinary voters and many businessmen may indicate how smaller cities that are dependent on a single major industry—such as the military—can become so dependent on it that they abandon common sense even when that industry supports change.

86. *Express*, Jan. 29 and 30, 1876.

87. Caroline M. Remy, "A Study of the Transition of San Antonio from a Frontier to an Urban Community, 1875–1900" (master's thesis, Trinity University, 1960), 20.

88. *Herald*, Feb. 10, 1876; and Mayer, "San Antonio," 605, 608, 612.

89. *Express*, Feb. 20, 1877.

90. *Express*, Feb. 20, 1877.

91. Calculated from Bexar County Clerk, Historical Deed Records, 1837–1964. On real estate transactions, see table 1 in this chapter.

92. James H. French, Annual Message, CCM, Jan. 31, 1877.

93. The physical conditions of San Antonio are described in *General Directory of the City of San Antonio for 1879* (Marshall, Texas: Jennings Bros., 1879), 55; for pictorial evidence, see Steinfeldt, *San Antonio Was*, 32–71.

94. An abundance of theoretical work debates the question of whether or not local government is relevant or useful in promoting economic development. French obviously assumed that it was and acted accordingly. From a theoretical perspective, the relevant issue may be how such efforts, in combination with national and regional "forces," succeed or fail to assist local development. That is a complex issue which has not received the attention it deserves, quite possibly because development is a cumulative process in which specific initiatives at specific times take years or even decades to take effect, making it impossible to trace the interrelationships between or among initiatives.

There are, though, defining moments in development for every city, and San Antonio's response to the railroad clearly belongs in that category. What the community, or any community, does in response to such moments is an important issue in addressing the larger question of whether "politics matters."

95. CCM, Apr. 3, 1877.

96. See CCM, Feb. 5, 1878, for Newcomb's booster agenda, which reflected French's earlier proposals.

97. CCM, Feb. 5 and Mar. 6, 1878.

98. *Herald*, Jan. 23, 1878; also see Feb. 6, 1878.

99. *Express*, Aug. 2, 1878.

100. *Express*, Aug. 7, 1878.

101. *Express*, Aug. 4, 1878.

102. *Express*, Nov. 27 and Dec. 3, 1878.

103. *Express*, Dec. 14 and 22, 1878; Jan. 9, 12, and 24, 1879; and Johnson, "Frugal and Sparing," 53.

104. *Express*, Apr. 10, 1879.

105. Their focus on using the river to power mills may have been due to concerns about a potential shortage of fuel sources for steam engines. John Kampmann had founded a planing mill driven by the city's first steam engine, but other applications of steam power were not yet common around the city.

106. *Express*, Apr. 10, 1879.

107. *Express*, June 15 and 18, 1879.

108. *Express*, Jan. 24, 1879; and *Charter and Revised Ordinances of the City of San Antonio* (San Antonio: M. M. Mooney, 1880), 6.

109. See Consolidated Returns of Elections held in the City of San Antonio, Texas, from Sept. 12, 1876, to Feb. 9, 1903, San Antonio City Archives.

110. On this point, see Robin L. Einhorn, *Property Rules: Political Economy in Chicago, 1833–1872* (University of Chicago Press, 1991), especially pp. 49–54, and Jon C. Teaford, *The Unheralded Triumph: City Government in America, 1870–1900* (Baltimore: Johns Hopkins University Press, 1984).

111. Augustus Koch, *Bird's Eye of the City of San Antonio, Bexar County, Texas, 1873*, Map Collection, San Antonio Museum Association (reproduction in author's possession). This discussion of the issue of urban size draws on Mario Polèse, *Wealth and Poverty of Regions: Why Cities Matter* (University of Chicago Press, 2009), 29–66.

112. Adapted from Mayer, "San Antonio," 664–65. Carl Abbott, *How Cities Won the West: Four Centuries of Urban Change in Western North America* (Albuquerque: University of New Mexico Press, 2008) briefly mentions the "urban twin" phenomenon; see p. 34.

CHAPTER FOUR

1. This statement is not intended as an endorsement of path dependency theory. As a historian, I am naturally inclined to believe that the past shapes the present and future by providing a context within which decisions are made. "Dependency" as such implies a too deterministic approach to the role of the past in development.

2. M. Whilldin, comp., *A Description of Western Texas* (Galveston, Tex.: News Steam Book and Job Office, 1876), 69–70; and Thomas T. Smith, *The U.S. Army and the Texas Frontier Economy, 1845–1900* (College Station: Texas A&M University Press, 1999), 49, table 4. Smith's figures are for the entire state, but since San Antonio was home to the quartermaster's depot, the transit hub of the army's distribution system, and the home of the largest transport company catering to the army's needs, I am assuming that the bulk of the transportation budget was spent in San Antonio.

3. Harry Williams Jr., "The Development of a Market Economy in Texas: The Establishment of the Railway Network, 1836–1890" (Ph.D. diss., University of Texas at Austin, 1957), 352.

4. This brief discussion of the issues facing San Antonians is based on various sources in the theoretical literature on city-building that debate whether or not local initiatives or external "forces" are more important to city growth. I favor the view that "partial autonomy" does exist with urban systems and does provide local communities opportunities to improve their own economies, but its existence is contingent on local leadership in business and politics understanding those opportunities and organizing effectively to make them actually happen. For a sampling of the literature, see Paul A. David, "Historical Economics of the Long Run: Some Implications of Path-Dependence," in *Historical Analysis in Economics*, ed. Graeme D. Snooks (London: Routledge, 1993), 38–39; Peter Hall, "Creative Cities and Economic Development," *Urban Studies* 37, no. 4 (2000): 639–49; John R. Logan and Harvey L. Molotch, *Urban Fortunes: The Political Economy of Place* (Berkeley: University of California Press, 1987); Paul E. Peterson, *City Limits* (University of Chicago Press, 1981); Clarence N. Stone, *Regime Politics: Governing Atlanta, 1846–1988* (Lawrence: University Press of Kansas, 1989); Paul E. Peterson, *City Limits* (University of Chicago Press, 1981); Stephen L. Elkin, *City and Regime in the American Republic* (University of Chicago Press, 1987); and Terry Nichols Clark and Edward G. Goetz, "The Antigrowth Machine: Can City Governments Control, Limit, or Manage Growth?" in *Urban Innovations: Creative Strategies for Turbulent Times*, ed. Terry Nichols Clark (Thousand Oaks: Sage, 1994), 105–45. On the theoretical issues of historical contingencies, see John Lewis Gaddis, *The Landscape of History: How Historians Map the Past* (New York: Oxford University Press, 2002).

5. See, inter alia, Whilldin, comp., *Description of Western Texas*; *San Antonio Herald* (hereafter *Herald*), Feb. 3, Mar. 5, May 19, 1878; William G. Kingsbury to James P Newcomb, London to San Antonio, May 20, 1878, James P. Newcomb Papers, San Antonio Public Library; *San Antonio Express* (hereafter *Express*), Sept. 23 and Nov. 14, 1878, and Feb. 18, 1879; Williams Jr., "Development of a Market Economy," 331–32; and Terry G. Jordan, "The German Settlement of Texas after 1865," *Southwestern Historical Quarterly* 72 (October 1969): 197–211.

6. Land transactions were calculated from the 1837–1964 Historical Records, Bexar County Clerk's Office, 1837–1964. San Antonio City Council Minutes (hereafter CCM), Nov. 20, 1877, San Antonio Municipal Archives.

7. *Herald*, May 24, 1878; and *Express*, Aug. 15 and 24, Oct. 4 and 5, 1878; Feb. 18, May 10, 1879.

8. *Express*, Nov. 18, 1878.

9. *Express*, Aug. 31, 1879 (emphasis added).

10. *Express*, Sept. 4, 1879.

11. *Express*, Oct. 7, 1879.

12. *Express*, Sept. 30 and Oct. 8, 1879.

13. Smith, *U.S. Army and the Texas Frontier Economy*, 13, 49, 72, 114. The Mexican American firms were primarily subcontractors hired by the Anglo companies that had bid successfully for the principal freighting contracts.

14. *Express*, Sept. 15, 1885; Smith, *Army and the Texas Frontier*, 98–99; Richard C. Batz, "The Development of Fort Sam Houston and Its Impact on San Antonio" (master's thesis, Trinity University, 1976), 43–44; and William F. Fleming, "San Antonio: The History of a Military City, 1865–1880" (Ph.D. diss., University of Pennsylvania, 1963), 424.

15. *Express*, Mar. 1, 1881; and Stephen Gould, "The Future Commercial Metropolis of Texas," in the *General Directory of the City of San Antonio for 1881–1882* (Washington, D.C.: Library of Congress, 1882), 12.

16. Gould, "Future Commercial Metropolis," 12–15.

17. U.S. Census of Population, 1880.

18. On Frost's career, see *Express*, Feb. 20, 1888.

19. *San Antonio Light* (hereafter *Light*), Jan. 11, 1882, and Mar. 14, 1884.

20. *Light*, Nov. 21, 1884.

21. On the importance of information for economic development, see Edward M. Bergman and Harvey A. Goldstein, "Dynamics, Structural Change, and Economic Development Paths," in *Local Economies in Transition: Policy Realities and Development Potentials*, ed. Edward M. Bergman (Durham, N.C.: Duke University Press, 1986); and Michael E. Porter, *The Competitive Advantage of Nations* (New York: Free Press, 1994), 157.

22. William Cronon provides an example of how important exchanges were in organizing hinterlands and developing expertise in urban development. See William Cronon, *Nature's Metropolis: Chicago and the Great West* (New York: W. W. Norton, 1991), 104–47.

23. *Herald*, Feb. 20, Mar. 10 and 26, Apr. 24, May 23, 1878; and *Express*, Nov. 14, 1878, and May 23, 1879.

24. *Herald*, May 19, 1878.

25. *Express*, Apr. 1, 1887. The club's founding in 1881 apparently received no coverage from the local press. A reporter provided its history and recruitment strategy only in this 1887 story.

26. *Express*, Apr. 1, 1887. Unfortunately the records of the San Antonio Club have not survived. Although the club began in 1881 with eighty-two members, this story does not indicate who the original members were, nor does it provide information on when the members in 1887 joined the club.

27. Some nonresident members may have founded businesses prior to 1887 (in which case they would have disappeared from the nonresident list), but the lack of records for this membership category prior to 1887 makes it impossible to confirm that. The statement that only two nonresident members had moved to San Antonio by 1892 is based on a comparison of the 1887 nonresident list published in the *Express*, Apr. 1, 1887, with the 1892 City Directory, which was consulted on the assumption that five years should have been sufficient time to convince a nonresident member to move to San Antonio.

28. The club apparently lacked an effective way to identify likely investors. Forty nonresident members, for instance, were army officers. Although the city's elite had made a habit of cultivating the military for decades, officers were unlikely to have access to the kind of funds needed to promote development in the late nineteenth century. The same could be said of many other nonresident members. Almost half of them lived either in San Antonio's hinterland or elsewhere in Texas, while only a fifth lived in eastern and midwestern cities where investment capital was plentiful (and none of them settled in San Antonio). The distribution of nonresident members was as follows: San Antonio's hinterland (residents of small towns in southern and central Texas): 53 (22.6 percent of total); Texas (outside of the hinterland): 59 (25.21 percent); South: 5 (2.13 percent); Midwest: 17 (7.26 percent); East: 35 (14.1 percent); Far West: 10 (4.27 percent); Mexico: 9 (3.8 percent); Canada: 1; U.S. Army Officers: 40 (17.09 percent); Unknown: 7 (2.9 percent).

29. On the rise in tourism, see Catherine Cocks, *Doing the Town: The Rise of Urban Tourism in the United States, 1850–1915* (Berkeley: University of California Press, 2001); A. K. Sandoval-Strausz, *Hotel: An American History* (New Haven, Conn: Yale University Press, 2007); and David M. Wrobel, *Promised Lands: Promotion, Memory, and the Creation of the American West* (Lawrence: University Press of Kansas, 2002). For urban competition based on tourism, see Carl Abbott, *How Cities Won the West: Four Centuries of Urban Change in Western North America* (Albuquerque: University of New Mexico Press, 2008), 115–31.

30. *Express*, Oct. 17, 1885.

31. *Express*, Nov. 28, 1884.

32. Galveston, Harrisburg, and San Antonio Railroad, *Western Texas as a Winter Resort* (Chicago: Rand, McNally, 1878), 3.

33. Shelia M. Rothman, *Living in the Shadow of Death: Tuberculosis and the Social Experience of Illness in American History* (Baltimore: Johns Hopkins University Press, 1995), 132, 141.

34. *Herald*, Apr. 21, 1878.

35. Cocks, *Doing the Town*, 107–8, 177; and Sandoval-Strausz, *Hotel*, 10–11. On cultural changes in general, see Michael Kammen, *The Mystic Chords of Memory: The Transformation of Tradition in American Culture* (New York: Vintage Books, 1993).

36. Whilldin, comp., *Description of Western Texas*, 62, 63; and Harriet P. Spofford, "San Antonio de Bexar," *Harper's New Monthly Magazine* 55 (November 1877): 836–37. Other examples of the appeal to different constituencies among tourists include *Express*, July 21, 1878, and Stephen Gould, *The Alamo City Guide, San Antonio, Texas. Being a Historical Sketch*

of the Ancient City of the Alamo and Business Review (New York: MacGowen & Slipper, 1882).

37. I calculated the size of San Antonio's footprint from Morrison & Fourmy's Revised Map of City of San Antonio, 1883; on the issues of land use and population distribution in the 1870s, see Galveston, Harrisburg, and San Antonio Railroad, *Western Texas as Winter Resort*, 11; Will C. Rogers, "A History of Military Plaza to 1937" (master's thesis, Trinity University, 1968), 23, 48; Arnold De Leon, *The Tejano Community, 1836–1900* (Albuquerque: University of New Mexico Press, 1982), 94–95; and Lewis F. Fisher, *San Antonio: Outpost of Empire* (San Antonio: Maverick Publishing, 1997), ix.

38. *Express*, June 3, 1879, reproduced in Donald E. Everett, *San Antonio: The Flavor of Its Past* (San Antonio: Trinity University Press, 1975), 32.

39. See, for example, Barbara Berglund, *Making San Francisco American: Cultural Frontiers in the Urban West, 1846–1906* (Lawrence: University Press of Kansas, 2007), 95–136.

40. On elite attitudes toward Tejano culture, see *Herald*, Feb. 20, 1878; and *Express*, Feb. 27, 1881. On parades, see Judith Berg Sobré, *San Antonio on Parade: Six Historic Festivals* (College Station: Texas A&M University Press, 2003). David Montejano, *Anglos and Mexicans in the Making of Texas, 1836–1986* (Austin: University of Texas Press, 1987) focuses on class as a key component of ethnic relations.

41. *Light*, Jan. 10, 1885. Ethnicity and race have not been studied extensively in San Antonio in the late nineteenth century. Important exceptions are Sobré, *San Antonio on Parade*, and Kenneth Mason, *African Americans and Race Relations in San Antonio, Texas, 1867–1937* (New York: Garland, 1998).

42. On efforts to suppress public expressions of minority cultural activities, see CCM, Nov. 18, 1873, June 26, 1874, and June 20 and Aug. 1, 1876.

43. This definition of the boundary between West and East Side San Antonio is based on the *social* distinctions between San Antonians beginning in the eighteenth century, when the elite Canary Islanders located on Main Plaza.

44. *Express*, Dec. 15, 1878, lists all the important businesses on Main Plaza; Cecilia Steinfeldt, *San Antonio Was* (San Antonio Museum Association, 1978), 36–42, provides a photographic depiction of the plaza's appearance.

45. *Express*, Dec. 15, 1878, lists every business on these streets and on Alamo Plaza; see Steinfeldt, *San Antonio Was*, 50–54, for photographs. For "Frog Pond" nickname, see www.tshaonline.org/handbook/online articles/WW/fwu6.html (accessed Mar. 23, 2010).

46. For early examples of this suburbanization, see *Herald*, Feb. 6 and 19, 1878; *Express*, Oct. 6, 1878; and *Light*, June 27, 1885.

47. *Herald*, Feb. 3, 1878, reproduced in Everett, *San Antonio*, 30. Flawed as it is, the manuscript census of population for San Antonio in 1870 reveals a relatively even distribution of social classes among the city's four wards. "Proprietors," which I interpret as owners of local businesses, were, according to a 10 percent random sample, 10 percent of the First Ward's population, 18 percent of the Second Ward's, 15.5 percent of the Third Ward's, and 12.5 percent of the Fourth Ward's. Unskilled workers were 40 percent of the First Ward's

population, 27.8 percent of the Second Ward's, 39. 6 percent of the Third Ward's, and 37.5 percent of the Fourth Ward's.

48. For construction and passenger traffic data, see *Herald*, May 10 and June 8, 1878; and *Express*, July 30, 1878.

49. *Express*, Feb. 7, 1887; and Andrew Morrison, *Historic San Antonio* (San Antonio: N.p., n.d. [ca. 1887]), 113–15. For an outstanding history of the streetcar system's evolution, see Maria Watson, "San Antonio on Track: The Suburban and Street Railway Complex through 1933" (master's research project, Trinity University, 1982).

50. *Herald*, Jan. 17, Feb. 9, May 8 and 10, 1878; *Express*, July 14, 1878, Feb. 27 and Mar. 2, 1879, and Feb. 7, 1887; and Arthur J. Mayer, "San Antonio: Frontier Entrepot" (Ph.D. diss., University of Texas at Austin, 1976), 284, 286.

51. *Herald*, Jan. 26, 1878; and Steinfeldt, *San Antonio Was*, 28.

52. Quoted in the *Express*, July 21, 1878; on the Alamo's attraction as a tourist site, see Thomas S. Bremer, *Blessed with Tourists: The Borderlands of Religion and Tourism in San Antonio* (Chapel Hill: University of North Carolina Press, 2004), 30–51.

53. *Express*, Feb. 2, 1878; and Bernice Strong, "Alamo Plaza: Cultural Crossroads of a City" (master's thesis, University of Texas at San Antonio, 1987).

54. *Express*, Nov. 14, 1878.

55. *Herald*, Apr. 24, 1878; and *Light*, Apr. 26, May 12, 1883, and Feb. 6, 1884 (Central Hotel renovated).

56. *Light*, Aug. 7, 1883; for the general frontier character and vice industry of San Antonio, see Ramsdell, *San Antonio*, 105; T. R. Fehrenbach et al., *The San Antonio Story* (Tulsa, Okla.: Continental Heritage, 1978), 109, 111–13; Terry T. Perrin, "Crime and Order in San Antonio during the Civil War and Reconstruction: Public Morals Crimes," in *South Texas Studies, 2003* (Victoria, TX.: Victoria College Press, 2003), 31–57; and David Browser, *West of the Creek: Murder, Mayhem, and Vice in Old San Antonio* (San Antonio: Maverick Publishing, 2003).

57. *Light*, July 12, 1882, Mar. 12, 1884, Apr. 8, 1886; *New York Times*, Mar. 13, 1884; Alice E. Geron, "The Fatal Corner," *San Antonio Magazine* (July 1982); Steinfeldt, *San Antonio Was*, 36–42; and Browser, *West of the Creek*, 5.

58. Cf. *General Directory of the City of San Antonio for 1879* (Marshall, Texas: Jennings Bros., 1879), 58; and *Express*, Feb. 20, 1888.

59. Economists prefer the terms "cluster" or "agglomeration" to describe concentrations of firms devoted to a similar economic activity. They typically apply these terms to industrial plants, but the idea that clustering promotes growth is, I think, equally useful for discussing the ways in which the emergence of purely commercial activities such as tourism also affect the social environment of the business community. For the principles involved, see, inter alia, Brendan O'Flaherty, *City Economics* (Cambridge, Mass.: Harvard University Press, 2005), 16–25; and Mario Polèse, *Wealth and Poverty of Regions: Why Cities Matter* (University of Chicago Press, 2009), 38–42. For a historical discussion of agglomeration as a basic principle of urban development, see Peter Hall, *Cities in Civilization* (New York: Random House, 1998), 311–42.

60. As a comparison, there were forty-seven manufacturing plants in San Antonio in 1888, ranging from flour mills to breweries to iron foundries. The argument here is not based on the total dollar value of the tourism industry, since there are no data available to calculate that amount in 1888. Rather, my point is that a concentration of tourist-oriented proprietors changed the social character of the business community. That in turn would shape attitudes and behavior among businessmen as they continued to make decisions regarding economic development.

61. *Herald*, May 29, 1878; *General Directory of the City of San Antonio for 1879*, 51; and Williams Jr., "Development of a Market Economy," 378.

62. Deed of sale, Sam Maverick, Reverna Vance, and John Vance to the Anheuser and Company Brewing Association, Mar. 25, 1879, Historical Deed Records, 1837–1963, Bexar County Clerk; and Mike Hennech, *Encyclopedia of Texas Breweries: Pre-Prohibition (1836–1918)* (Irving, Texas: Ale Publishing, 1990), 1215. There is no evidence that Busch actually visited San Antonio to make this purchase, so how he managed to identify an appropriate location and arrange to buy it remain a mystery.

63. *Light*, Aug. 7, 1883, and Nov. 28, 1884.

64. *Historical and Descriptive Review of the Industries of San Antonio, 1885* (San Antonio: Land & Thompson, 1885), 62–64, 103–4; Steinfeldt, *San Antonio Was*, 90; and Lewis F. Fisher, *Guenther & Son at 150 Years: The Legacy of a Texas Milling Pioneer* (San Antonio: Maverick Publishing, 2001).

65. On the importance of import replacement, see Jane Jacobs, *The Economy of Cities* (New York: Vintage Books, 1970), 21–22.

66. *Light*, Aug. 12, 1887.

67. Declines in real estate transactions were calculated from the Historical Deed Records, Bexar County Clerk. On the drought, see *General Directory of the City of San Antonio, 1885–1886* (Washington, D.C.: Library of Congress, 1886), 2; on problems with tourism, see *Express*, Feb. 20, 1888; and Robert M. Fogelson, *The Fragmented Metropolis: Los Angeles, 1850–1930* (Cambridge, Mass.: Harvard University Press, 1967), 63–70; and on cattle, see Jimmy M. Skaggs, *The Cattle-Trailing Industry: Between Supply and Demand, 1866–1890* (Lawrence: University Press of Kansas, 1973), 19–22.

68. *Express*, Feb. 20, 1888, describes the boundaries and characteristics of the hinterland; for the changes in Hill Country farming and ranching, see Terry G. Jordan, *German Seed in Texas Soil: Immigrant Farmers in Nineteenth-Century Texas* (Austin: University of Texas Press, 1966; paperback, 1975), 129, 147, 157.

69. For election results, see Consolidated Returns of Elections Held in the City of San Antonio, Texas, from Sept. 12, 1876, to Feb. 9, 1903, San Antonio City Archives. I deduced the importance of the Second Ward from the fact that French's margin of victory over Copeland was 454 votes in the overall balloting. The Second Ward gave French 314 of those votes, which amounted to 69 percent of his victory margin. For French's annual message see CCM, Jan. 30, 1883 (emphasis in original).

70. San Antonio City Council, *Charter and Revised Ordinances of the City of San Antonio, Comprising All Ordinances of a General Character in Force to June 1, 1884* (San

Antonio: San Antonio Light, 1884), 95, 101; Ordinance Book A (Aug. 25, 1884), 119–20, Office of the City Clerk, San Antonio Municipal Archives; CCM, Sept. 8, 1884.

71. *Express*, Aug. 7, 1878.

72. CCM, Mar. 3–Nov. 10, 1884. The full ordinance was published in San Antonio City Council, *Charter and Revised Ordinances of the City of San Antonio, Comprising All Ordinances of a General Character in Force May 1, 1886* (San Antonio: Times Job Printing House, 1886), 161–62.

73. O'Flaherty, *Urban Economics*, 531–40, reviews the modern debate over the effectiveness of tax abatements in promoting urban development and concludes that, on the whole, they are not particularly effective. In the 1880s city leaders lacked sophisticated statistical tools for analyzing their local economy, especially in San Antonio, where businessmen resolutely refused to collect data on economic performance. Hence I interpret the council's ordinance as a political tool for asserting its importance to development at a time when the Taxpayers' Association controlled the public agenda on that issue.

74. CCM, Apr. 14 and 22, May 26, 1884.

75. *Express*, May 10, 1884; quote from *Light*, May 20, 1884.

76. *Herald*, Feb. 6, 1878.

77. *Light*, Jan. 10, 1885; Gammel, comp., *Laws of Texas, 1822–1897*, IX:779 (emphasis added).

78. *Express*, Nov. 13, 1884.

79. On the Callaghan men's marital history, see Frederick C. Chabot, *With the Makers of San Antonio* (San Antonio: privately printed, 1937), 50, 264; on Bryan Jr.'s background, see J. Kaaz Doyle, "Bryan V. Callaghan Jr.," *Handbook of Texas Online*, tshaonline.org; John A. Booth and David R. Johnson, "Power and Progress in San Antonio Politics, 1836–1970," in *The Politics of San Antonio: Community, Progress, and Power*, ed. David R. Johnson, John A. Booth, and Richard J. Harris (Lincoln: University of Nebraska Press, 1983), 8–9.

80. For the emergence of these alliances, see *Express*, Jan. 11, 1881, Sept. 29, 1882; and *Light*, July 16 and Aug. 13, 1883.

81. *Light*, Jan. 8, 1885.

82. See *Express*, Jan. 13, 1885, for vote results. Callaghan's margin of victory was calculated from those returns. On Callaghan's ties to various Tejano individuals and organizations, see *Express*, Jan. 11, 1881; and Mason, *African Americans in San Antonio*, 173–75, 177.

83. CCM, Jan. 31, Mar. 9, 1885.

84. *Express*, Apr. 5, 1885.

85. *Express*, Sept. 7, 1886.

86. *Express*, May 6, 1887. Calculations of voter turnout were based on a comparison of election results in May with those for the mayoral election in February; see *Express*, Feb. 15, 1887.

87. *Express*, Sept. 9, 1887. Also see Mary B. Edelen, "Bryan Callaghan II: His Early Career, 1885–1899" (master's thesis, Trinity University, 1971), 29–36, for the convoluted debate over the city hall's location.

88. Edelen, "Bryan Callaghan II," 61–62; for the development of Military Plaza into a vice area, see Rogers, "History of Military Plaza," esp. 54–62; on the evolution of the West Side vice area, see Melissa Gohlke, "The Evolution of Vice Activity in San Antonio, 1885–1975" (honors thesis, University of Texas at San Antonio, 1997).

89. CCM, Dec. 19, 1883; and *Express*, Feb. 20, 1888.

90. Letter to the editor, *Express*, Mar. 21, 1879; and CCM, July 21, 1884.

91. *Express*, Feb. 11, 1887 (emphasis in original).

92. Apr. 20, 1889, bond election results in Consolidated Returns of Elections Held in the City of San Antonio, Texas, from Sept. 12, 1876, to Feb. 9, 1903, San Antonio City Archives. For Dallas and Galveston's bonded debt, see Gammel, comp., *Laws of Texas, 1822–1897*, IX:252, 1243.

93. *Express*, Dec. 20, 1889, quoted in Edelen, "Bryan Callaghan II," 64.

94. Sept. 30, 1890, bond election results in Consolidated Returns of Elections Held in the City of San Antonio, Texas.

95. Charles Dignowity, letter to the editor, *Express*, Aug. 11, 1887; and editorial, *Light*, Aug. 12, 1887.

96. *Express*, Aug. 10, 12, 22, 1887.

97. Citizen's Association Bylaws, published in the *Light*, Aug. 26, 1887.

98. Citizen's Association Bylaws, *Light*, Aug. 26, 1887.

99. Dr. S. T. Lowry, letter to the editor, *Express*, Sept. 18, 1887.

100. *Light*, Aug. 27, Sept. 5, and Nov. 19, 1887.

101. *Light*, Aug. 22, 1887, has the list of directors. Names on the list were compared to a city directory for 1887 to obtain occupational backgrounds; the *Express*, Feb. 20, 1888, conveniently listed all taxpayers with assessed worth of $10,000 or more.

102. *Light*, Aug. 26, 1887, notes the start of fundraising; the last mention of the association appeared in the *Light* on Mar. 8, 1890.

103. *Light*, Dec. 13, 20, 29, 1890, and Feb. 16, 1891; quote from Dec. 13.

104. *Light*, May 28, 1891, details the saga of the offer.

105. Apr. 6, 1892, bond election results in Consolidated Returns of Elections Held in the City of San Antonio, Texas.

106. For details on registered voters, see *General Directory of the City of San Antonio for 1879*, 3; and *Light*, Nov. 7, 1892. On Callaghan's career move, see Edelen, "Bryan Callaghan II," 73.

107. *Express*, Aug. 23, 1887, and Aug. 25, 1888.

108. CCM, Apr. 1, 1889.

109. CCM, June 20, 1892; and *Express*, Feb. 17, 18, 1891; Jan. 10, 1893; Jan. 10, 1894.

110. *Express*, Mar. 20, 1884, Nov. 11, 1885; and CCM, May 4, 11, 1885.

111. Mayor's Message, CCM, July 16, 1894; the "day off" was reported in the *Express*, Aug. 8, 1984.

112. For examples of the debate, see *Express*, July 18, 20, 22, 24, 25, 27, 30, and Aug. 1, 1894.

113. Analysis of the vote is based on results published in the *Express*, Aug. 8, 1894. Wards Four and Five were the north suburbanizing edge of the city that accounted for 56 percent of Paschal's margin of victory.

CHAPTER FIVE

1. *Jules A. Appler's General Directory of the City of San Antonio, 1895–96* (San Antonio: Jules Appler, 1895), 77.

2. *San Antonio Express* (hereafter *Express*), Jan. 14, 1895.

3. *Appler's General Directory*, 77.

4. For examples, see *Express*, Apr. 5, July 12, Dec. 22, 1878; Apr. 6, 1881; Apr. 20, 1887.

5. *Express*, Sept. 20, 1887.

6. Judith Berg Sobré, *San Antonio on Parade: Six Historic Festivals* (College Station: Texas A&M University Press, 2003), 155–74, 182–86, 189–91; and Laura Hernández-Ehrisman, *Inventing the Fiesta City: Heritage and Carnival in San Antonio* (Albuquerque: University of New Mexico Press, 2008), 18–43.

7. San Antonio City Council Minutes (hereafter CCM), Nov. 11, 1895; Dec. 16, 1895, San Antonio Municipal Archives.

8. On tuberculosis, see Shelia M. Rothman, *Living in the Shadow of Death: Tuberculosis and the Social Experience of Illness in American History* (New York: Basic Books, 1994); and Emily K. Abel, *Tuberculosis and the Politics of Exclusion: A History of Public Health and Migration to Los Angeles* (New Brunswick: Rutgers University Press, 2007).

9. CCM, Feb. 25, 1895.

10. Harvey K. Newman, *Southern Hospitality: Tourism and the Growth of Atlanta* (Tuscaloosa: University of Alabama Press, 1999), 52–55.

11. *Express*, Jan. 15, 1897.

12. *Express*, Jan. 15, 1897.

13. *San Antonio Light* (hereafter *Light*), Feb. 9, 1896; and CCM, Feb. 24, 28, 1896.

14. Martin V. Melosi, *The Sanitary City: Urban Infrastructure in America from Colonial Times to the Present* (Baltimore: Johns Hopkins University Press, 2000), 103, 149–74; and Stanley K. Schultz, *Constructing Urban Culture: American Cities and City Planning, 1800–1920* (Philadelphia: Temple University Press, 1989), 183–86. There is a vast literature on Progressivism; see, for example, Walter McGerr, *A Fierce Discontent: The Rise and Fall of the Progressive Movement in America, 1870–1920* (New York: Oxford University Press, 2005).

15. CCM, May 4, June 1 and 19, July 6, 1896.

16. *Express*, Jan. 1, 1897; and *Light*, Jan. 3, 1897.

17. *Light*, Jan. 10, 1897.

18. Calculations based on the delegate list in *Light*, Jan. 10, 1897.

19. *Light*, Feb. 8, 1914 (Cassiano obituary); and *Express*, Nov. 28, 1930 (Smith obituary). Examples of the cooperation among members of the Big Six can be found in *Light*, July 16, Aug. 13, 1883. Their frequent appearance together on various party tickets provides one way to trace their alliances. See, for example, *Express*, Sept. 29, 1882; *Light*, Oct. 23, 1898; and many city or county elections between those dates.

20. Dale Baum and Worth Robert Miller, "Ethnic Conflict and Machine Politics in San Antonio, 1892–1899," *Journal of Urban History* 19, no. 4 (Aug. 1993): 72.

21. Calculated from voter registration data in *Light*, Feb. 7, 1897.

22. *Express*, Jan. 1, 1897.

23. *Express*, Feb. 9, 1897; *Light*, Feb. 14, 1897, reported the detailed voting results by precinct.

24. *Light*, Jan. 24, 1897, details Callaghan's election platform.

25. Population figures for Mexican and Mexican American residents are approximate because the Census conflated both groups, either as native-born of foreign parents or as foreign-born with other ethnic groups. I calculated the percentages based on the continuing extreme segregation of Hispanics, who overwhelmingly lived on the West Side, and Germans, who lived overwhelmingly on the East Side.

26. On the declining ethnic vote, see Baum and Miller, "Ethnic Conflict and Machine Politics."

27. CCM, Oct. 26, 1903.

28. *Light*, May 17, 1894, Feb. 14, 1899; CCM, May 26, 1896; May 2 and 9, Sept. 19, 1898.

29. CCM, Jan. 3, 1898.

30. CCM, Jan. 13, 1896; Jan. 10, 15, Feb. 2, Mar. 7, 1898; June 26, 1899.

31. CCM, Mar. 22, 1897; Mar. 7, 1898.

32. CCM, Oct. 4, 1897; Feb. 28, Mar. 21, Apr. 18, May 2, 9, 1898.

33. CCM, Jan. 3, May 4, 1898; Jan. 16, 1899.

34. San Antonio Newspaper Artists Association, *Men of Affairs of San Antonio* (N.p., n.d. [ca. 1912]); Clarence R. Wharton, *Texas under Many Flags* (Chicago: American Historical Society, 1930), IV:17; and *Light*, July 31, 1898.

35. CCM, Feb. 10, 1899, contains the official list of candidates.

36. *Express*, Jan. 20, 1899.

37. *Express*, Jan. 20, 1899.

38. *Light*, Feb. 12, 1899.

39. *Light*, Jan. 26, 25, Feb. 13, 1899; and Randall L. Waller, "The Callaghan Machine and San Antonio Politics, 1885–1912" (master's thesis, Texas Tech University, 1973), 102–3.

40. Mayor's Annual Message, CCM, Feb. 22, 1899.

41. Charles Thomas Logan, "Quaint San Antonio: The 'Alamo City' of Texas Now Famous as a Health Resort," *Frank Leslie's Popular Monthly* 46, no. 1 (July 1898): 87, 95.

42. *Express*, Jan. 13, 17, 1899.

43. See, for example, Kenneth Fox, *Better City Government: Innovation in American Urban Politics, 1850–1937* (Philadelphia: Temple University Press, 1970); and Martin J. Schiesl, *The Politics of Efficiency: Municipal Administration and Reform in America, 1880–1920* (Berkeley: University of California Press, 1977).

44. CCM, Mar. 20, 1899.

45. CCM, May 22, June 5, 1899.

46. CCM, July 17, Dec. 11, 1899; Apr. 6, 1900; June 3, 1901.

47. CCM, Dec. 10, 18, 1899; and L. Waynne Cox, *The Spanish Acequias of San Antonio* (San Antonio: Maverick Publishing, 2005), 60–69.

48. On the evolution of refuse management, see Melosi, *Sanitary City*, 175–204.

49. Robert B. Fairbanks, *For the City as a Whole: Planning, Politics, and the Public Interest in Dallas, Texas, 1900–1965* (Columbus: Ohio State University Press, 1998), 18.

50. CCM, Mar. 26, 1900.

51. *Light*, Mar. 11, Apr. 3, 1900.

52. See CCM, Apr. 23, 1900, for the election returns.

53. CCM, May 7, July 14, Sept. 4, 1900.

54. CCM, May 14, 21, 1900.

55. CCM, Jan. 8, Feb. 26, Mar. 5, Aug. 20, 1900; Aug. 5, 26, Sept. 9, 1901; Marilyn McAdams Sibley, *George W. Brackenridge: Maverick Philanthropist* (Austin: University of Texas Press, 1973), 128–32; and Bobbie W. Morgan, "George W. Brackenridge and His Control of San Antonio's Water Supply, 1869–1905" (master's thesis, Trinity University, 1961).

56. CCM, Feb. 6, 1901; Consolidated Returns of Elections Held in the City of San Antonio, Texas, from Sept. 12, 1876, to Feb. 9, 1903, San Antonio City Archives.

57. CCM, Feb. 25, 1901; *Light*, Feb. 25, 1901.

58. *Light*, Feb. 18, 1901.

59. *Light*, Feb. 28, 1901.

60. *Light*, Aug. 21, 1901.

61. *Light*, Sept. 9, 1901 (for customer data); Feb. 26, 1900, May 27, 1901 (for contract cost).

62. *Light*, Nov. 4, 1901; Jan. 13, Feb. 10, Mar. 6, June 12, 1902; and Sibley, *George W. Brackenridge*, 158.

63. CCM, June 2, July 7, 1902.

64. CCM, Dec. 9, 1901, and Mar. 24, 1902.

65. CCM, July 7, 1902.

66. CCM, July 28, 1902; and J. C. F. Kerr, letter to the editor, *Light*, July 29, 1902.

67. Consolidated Returns of Elections Held in the City of San Antonio, Texas.

68. For Terrell, see entry in the *Handbook of Texas Online*, tshaonline.org; for Campbell, *Light*, Mar. 21, 1907 (obituary).

69. *Light*, Feb. 28, 1900.

70. Consolidated Returns of Elections Held in the City of San Antonio, Texas.

71. *Light*, Jan. 3, 1903.

72. *Light*, Jan. 26, 1903.

73. *Light*, Jan. 22, 1903; CCM, Mar. 4, 9, 11, 1903; *Charter of the City of San Antonio, adopted Jan. 22, 1903, Effective July 1, 1903* (San Antonio: Johnson Bros., 1903), 18.

74. CCM, June 1, 1903.

75. For examples of petitions to create these districts, see CCM, June 15, July 20, Oct. 12, 1903; Nov. 21, Dec. 5, 1904.

76. CCM, Nov. 10, 1903; Feb. 1, 1904.

77. CCM, Sept. 14, Oct. 13, 1903; Consolidated Returns of Elections Held in the City of San Antonio, Texas; and CCM, Nov. 14, 1905.

78. See for instance, Schiesl, *Politics of Efficiency*, 26, 74–94; and Fox, *Better City Government*, 77–78.

79. CCM, Oct. 5, Dec. 21, 1903; June 6, July 18, 1904.

80. CCM, Jan. 2, 1905.

81. *San Antonio Gazette* (hereafter *Gazette*), Jan. 25, 30, 1905.

82. *Gazette*, Feb. 13, 1905.

83. *Gazette*, Mar. 8, 1905.

84. On Brown's background, see *Light*, July 9, 1902; Stacey Lester, "Bryan Callaghan versus the Reformers, 1905–1912" (master's thesis, Trinity University, 1970), 6–8; on his platform, see *Light*, Apr. 23, 1905.

85. For studies of vice as a business, see David R. Johnson, *Policing the Urban Underworld* (Philadelphia: Temple University Press, 1979), 147–81; Timothy Gilfoyle, *City of Eros: New York City, Prostitution, and the Commercialization of Sex* (New York: W. W. Norton, 1994); and Melissa Gohlke, "The Evolution of Vice Activity in San Antonio, 1885–1975" (master's thesis, University of Texas at San Antonio, 1997).

86. See CCM, May 3, 1905, for election results.

87. J. C. F. Kerr, letter to the editor, *Light*, July 29, 1902.

88. For budgets, see CCM, June 25, 1906; Mar. 4, 1907; June 1, 1908; June 7, 1909; June 6, 1910; July 3, 1911; and July 12, 1912.

89. Petitions from Residents, 1906–1908, in City Council Proceedings, Box 8, Folder 2, San Antonio City Archives; CCM, Aug. 12, 1907; July 8, Aug. 2, Oct. 11, Nov. 15, 1909; and *Light*, Mar. 15, May 26, 1910.

90. CCM, June 5, 1905; May 14, 1906.

91. CCM, July 13, 1908.

92. CCM, Feb. 25, 1907; Sept. 14, 1908; Feb. 8, 1909; and *Light*, Feb. 3, May 23, 1911.

93. *Light*, Dec. 27, 1909.

94. Frank Putnam, "San Antonio: Our Gateway to Mexico," *New England Magazine* (July 1907): 595.

95. Schiesl, *Politics of Efficiency*, 2–3; William H. Wilson, *The City Beautiful Movement* (Baltimore: Johns Hopkins University Press, 1988), 73; Fox, *Better City Government*, 22; and Bradley R. Rice, *The Commission Government Movement in America* (Austin: University of Texas Press, 1977), 9, 17, 25–26.

96. Lester, "Bryan Callaghan versus," 36.

97. *Express*, Mar. 24, 1910.

98. *Light*, Apr. 25, May 2, 1910; CCM, May 2, 1910; and *Express*, May 3, 1910.

99. *Light*, May 5, 6, 1910.

100. *Light*, May 26, 30, 31, July 21, 1910; and CCM, July 11, 1910.

101. CCM, July 28, Aug. 16, 1910.

102. CCM, Oct. 24, 1910.

103. *Light*, Oct. 19, 1910.

104. CCM, Dec. 2, 1907, Dec. 7, 1908; and *Light*, June 4, 1908, Oct. 18, 1908; on Callaghan's health, see CCM, June through Sept. 1906, Mar. 4, 1907.

105. *Light*, Dec. 22, 1910.

106. CCM, Jan. 26, Feb. 2, 1911. For election results in the key precincts, see CCM, Feb. 6, 1911.

107. *Express*, Feb. 7, 1911. The *Express* reported the election results by precinct, but it relied on the city council's official revenue to report the total vote. When I calculated the precinct tallies, they showed the charter passed by a vote of 7,417 to 7,328.

108. *Light*, Feb. 6, 11, Mar. 28, 1911.

109. *Light*, Jan. 3, 1911.

110. *Light*, Mar. 31, Apr. 13, 1911.

111. *Light*, Feb. 24, 26, 1911.

112. *Light*, July 20, 1908, details the reorganization of the Big Six.

113. *Light*, Mar. 26, 28, 1911.

114. CCM, May 6, 1911.

115. For rule changes, see CCM, May 22, 1911; Callaghan's speech in recorded in CCM, June 5, 1911.

116. On the budget battles, see, inter alia, CCM, June 12, 19; July 3, 17; Aug. 7; Nov. 15, 20; and Dec. 4, 5, 6, 1911; on street widening, see CCM, July 3, 1911; on traffic, see CCM, Feb. 7, 1910.

117. CCM, May 27, 1912.

118. *Light*, May 23, 1912.

119. CCM, July 17, 1912; Lester, "Bryan Callaghan versus," 56.

120. CCM, Aug. 19, 1912.

121. For the origins and resolution of the attendance problem, see CCM, Aug. 23–Sept. 23, 1912.

122. CCM, Apr. 8, 1913.

123. *Light*, Apr. 11, 12, 23 (for quote), 1913.

124. *Light*, Apr. 13, 1913.

125. Francisco A. Chapa Family Papers, MS 405, Box 1, University of Texas at San Antonio Archives.

126. Analysis based on official returns, *Light*, May 14, 1913.

127. *Light*, May 26, 1913; CCM, May 30, July 7, 22 (election results), 1913.

128. *Light*, July 28, 1913.

129. *Light*, Sept. 2, Oct. 27, Nov. 10, Dec. 8, 1913.

130. *Light*, Jan. 15, 1914.

131. *Light*, Feb. 12, 1914; and *Express*, Feb. 14, 1914.

132. *Light*, Feb. 17, 1914.

133. *Light*, Feb. 22, 1914.

134. CCM, Mar. 3, 1914.

CHAPTER SIX

1. San Antonio City Council Minutes (hereafter CCM), Apr. 10, 1900, San Antonio Municipal Archives.

2. *San Antonio Light* (hereafter *Light*), July 2, 1902; *San Antonio Gazette* (hereafter *Gazette*), Mar. 26, 1907; and Charles Smith, "San Antonio Chamber of Commerce: A History of Its Organization for Community Development and Service, 1910–1960" (master's thesis, Trinity University, 1965), 12.

3. Judith Berg Sobré, *San Antonio on Parade: Six Historic Festivals* (College Station: Texas A&M University Press, 2003), 174–75, 178, 182–86, 189, 195.

4. Sobré, *San Antonio on Parade*, 195–97, 199.

5. *Light*, Mar. 22, 1907.

6. CCM, Feb. 29, 1904.

7. CCM, Jan. 9, 1905; *Gazette*, Jan. 30, 1905; and Laura Hernández-Ehrisman, *Inventing the Fiesta City: Heritage and Carnival in San Antonio* (Albuquerque: University of New Mexico Press, 2008), 48.

8. Sobré, *San Antonio on Parade*, 195.

9. Cecilia Steinfeldt, *San Antonio Was* (San Antonio Museum Association, 1979), 118–26; and Paula Allen, *San Antonio: Then and Now* (San Diego: Thunder Bay Press, 2005), 84.

10. *Gazette*, May 3, 17, June 11, 1907.

11. Attendance data is scarce in this period. For examples where it was mentioned, see *San Antonio Express* (hereafter *Express*), Apr. 30, 1908, Apr. 24, 1911; and *Light*, Mar. 28, Nov. 9, 1909.

12. *Light*, Dec. 17, 1911 (Real Estate section).

13. *Light*, Apr. 16, 1908, May 8, 1909, Apr. 8, 1913 (obituary of Augustus Jones); Gunter Hotel, *The Gunter Hotel in San Antonio's History* (San Antonio: Gunter Hotel, 1985); and Allen, *San Antonio*, 64–65.

14. *Light*, July 2, 1902; Jan. 4, 1903.

15. *Light*, Jan. 14, 1906; Oct. 2, 1907.

16. *Gazette*, Mar. 26, Apr. 15, 1907.

17. *Light*, Mar. 14, 19, 20, 24; May 19, June 3, 1909; July 9, 1911 (summary of Publicity League's history and achievements).

18. *Light*, Mar. 24, 1909.

19. *Light*, July 9, 1911.

20. *Light*, Nov. 12, 1911.

21. *Light*, Aug. 29, Sept. 3, Nov. 11, 12, Dec. 2, 31, 1911.

22. *Express*, Apr. 29, 1911.

23. Frank Putnam, "San Antonio, Our Gateway to Mexico," *New England Magazine* (July 1907): 595; and David Montejano, *Anglos and Mexicans in the Making of Texas, 1836–1985* (Austin: University of Texas Press, 1987), 103–5.

24. CCM, Apr. 4, 1900, notes receipt of the petition from the San Antonio and Brownsville Railroad Company; and Montejano, *Anglos and Mexicans*, 106–7.

25. *Gazette*, May 6, July 10, 19, 1907; June 26, 1908.

26. *Gazette*, Sept. 1, 2, 9, 1908.

27. Charles G. Norton, ed., *Men of Affairs of San Antonio* (San Antonio Newspaper Artists Association, ca. 1913), has biographical sketches of several businessmen who invested in the Winter Garden.

28. *San Antonio Herald* (hereafter *Herald*), Feb. 17, 1867, notes farmers searching for migrant labor in San Antonio; Minutes of the Board of Directors of the San Antonio Chamber of Commerce (hereafter MBD), June 28, 1912, San Antonio Chamber of Commerce archive; CCM, May 31, 1915; Montejano, *Anglos and Mexicans*, 164; and Emilio Zamora, *The World of the Mexican Worker in Texas* (College Station: Texas A&M University Press, 1993), 19, 24.

29. CCM, Jan. 6, 1913; Leo M. J. Dielmann, *Report of the Widening of Commerce Street* (San Antonio: Passing Show, 1915); Lewis F. Fisher, *Saving San Antonio: The Precarious Preservation of a Heritage* (Lubbock: Texas Tech University Press, 1996), 69–77; and Lewis F. Fisher, *River Walk: The Epic Story of San Antonio's River* (San Antonio: Maverick Publishing, 2007), 28–29.

30. *Light*, May 5, 1912; and *Express*, July 28, 1912.

31. Fisher, *River Walk*, 30.

32. *Light* and *Gazette*, Mar. 17, 1910.

33. *Express*, Mar. 24, 1910. See chapter 5 for a discussion of the broader context that also influenced Conroy's decision regarding the first meeting of the league.

34. *Express*, Dec. 31, 1910.

35. *Light*, July 9, 1911; and *Express*, Nov. 1, Dec. 8, 1911.

36. Smith, "San Antonio Chamber," 18–19.

37. Smith, 29.

38. CCM, July 7, 22, Sept. 29, Oct. 13, 1913; Jan. 12, 1914.

39. CCM, June 2, 1913; on "skips," see CCM, Mar. 20, 1916, and May 22, 1917.

40. CCM, July 24, Aug. 7, 21, 1916 (bond election results); and Brown's Letter to the Commissioners, CCM, Nov. 20, 1916.

41. On the issue of civil service reform, see *Light*, Mar. 30, 31, 1916.

42. On the social ties between these families, see *Light*, Jan. 1, and Feb. 2, 1917.

43. *Light*, Feb. 18, 22, 1917; and CCM, Apr. 24, 1917.

44. MBD, Jan. 13, 1914; and Smith, "San Antonio Chamber," 33.

45. Richard C. Batz, "The Development of Fort Sam Houston and Its Importance to San Antonio" (master's thesis: Trinity University, 1972), 43–44.

46. Barney M. Gils, "Early Military Aviation Activities in Texas," *Southwestern Historical Quarterly* 54 (October 1950): 144–45; and David R. Johnson, "The Failed Experiment: Military Aviation and Urban Development in San Antonio," in *The Martial Metropolis: U.S. Cities in War and Peace*, ed. Roger W. Lotchin (New York: Praeger, 1984), 90–94.

47. *Express*, Apr. 20, 1910.

48. Frances W. Isbell, "Military Aeronautics in San Antonio, 1910–1918" (master's thesis: Trinity University, 1962), 42–44.

49. MBD, July 13, 1913.

50. MBD, June 10, Nov. 23, 1915; May 9, 1916; and Isbell, "Military Aeronautics," 48–49, 68, 70.

51. MBD, Aug. 24, 1915.

52. *The Clegg Story: The Biography of a Business, 1901–1951* (San Antonio Printing, 1951); and *Express*, Sept. 10, 1954 (Tuttle obituary).

53. *Light*, Aug. 19, 1917; Jan. 1, 1918; Seth S. McKay and Odie Faulk, *Texas after Spindletop: The Saga of Texas, 1901–1965* (New York: Steck-Vaughn Co., 1965), 62–63; and Richard Garcia, *The Rise of the Mexican-American Middle Class: San Antonio, 1929–1941* (College Station: Texas A&M University Press, 1991), table I, p. 29.

54. *Kelly Field Eagle*, Nov. 14, 21, 1918; Feb. 20, May 22, 1919 (Kelly Air Force Base History Office Archives); and Russell F. Weigley, *History of the United States Army*, rev. ed. (Bloomington: Indiana University Press, 1984), 396.

55. MBD, Feb. 18, Nov. 12, 1919; Nov. 20, 1920; Jan. 28, May 25, June 29, 1921; Feb. 28, June 28, 1922; History of Kelly Field, 2 vols., typescript, v. 1:9–11 (Kelly Air Force Base History Office Archives).

56. *Light*, Apr. 15, 1919.

57. CCM, Aug. 3, 9, Sept. 20, Oct. 14, Nov. 1, 1915; *Light*, Feb. 2, 1919, Aug. 28, 1921; *Express*, Aug. 15, 1920, Nov. 19, 1922; and Brackenridge Park National Register of Historic Places, National Park Service No. 91449 (courtesy of Maria Pfeiffer).

58. CCM, July 30, 1919.

59. CCM, May 15, 1919; Harold A. Shapiro, "The Workers of San Antonio, 1900–1940" (Ph.D. diss., University of Texas at Austin, 1952), 295–99, 301–2, 304–5, 310, 330; and Norman D. Brown, *Hood, Bonnet, and Little Brown Jug: Texas Politics, 1921–1928* (College Station: Texas A&M University Press, 1984), 5, 6–8, 49, 51–52.

60. *Light*, Apr. 15, 28, 29, and May 3, 8, 1921; election returns for May 1921, in City of San Antonio Election Results, 1856–present, City of San Antonio Archives.

61. *Light*, June 1, 8, 1921.

62. Fisher, *River Walk*, 50–56.

63. Fisher, *River Walk*, 66; CCM, Sept. 19, Oct. 6, 1921; and *Light*, Dec. 25, 1921; Jan. 29, 1922.

64. CCM, Dec. 1, 5, 1921; and *Light*, Nov. 17, Dec. 6, 1921; Jan. 22, Feb. 22, 1922; Feb. 8, 1923.

65. *Light*, May 12, 1929.

66. City of San Antonio Election Results, May 1923, May 1925, May 1927, May 1929.

67. For bond elections, see City of San Antonio Election Results, Dec. 1923, May 1925, May 1927, May 1928, May 1929, May 1930. On improvements, see CCM, Nov. 19, 1923; Apr. 7 and 14, June 9, Aug. 25, 1924; Jan. 1 and 31, May 25, June 1, 1925; City of San Antonio, Annual Report for the 1929 Fiscal Year, June 1–May 31, 1930, no pagination, Municipal Archives and Records, City of San Antonio; and Fisher, *River Walk*, 63, 68–69.

68. Fisher, *Saving San Antonio*, 183.

69. Fisher, *Saving San Antonio*, 186–87; and CCM, Aug. 20, 1923.

70. *Light*, Apr. 2, 1928; July 6, 1930; Fisher, *Saving San Antonio*, 8; and Fisher, *River Walk*, 72.

71. CCM, Jan. 16, Aug. 19, Dec. 2, 1929 (quote). On the chamber's problems with fundraising, see MBD, June 29, 1923; Sept. 18, Oct. 23, 1924; Jan. 14 and 29, July 15, Sept. 18, Nov. 2, 1925; Jan. 20, Dec. 29, 1926; Feb. 9, 1928; Feb. 20, 1929; Mar. 30, 1930.

72. *Express*, June 7, 10, 11, 14, 1925; and Fisher, *Saving San Antonio*, 1.

73. MBD, Jan. 28, Apr. 16, 1920; and *Express*, Mar. 10, 1920.

74. MBD, June 16, 1930.

75. *Light*, Dec. 17, 1919; Feb. 16, 1928; and Bill Balthrope, *"On How to Do Nothing Well": A History of the San Antonio Canopus Club* (San Antonio: Naylor, 1975), 28, 32.

76. *Light*, Oct. 23, 1929, reported on this first attempt to analyze the impact of winter tourism. The study's author, T. C. Carrington, assumed that the city's tourist population in the winter season was seventy-five thousand but he gave no explanation for how he arrived at that number. He also did not explain his methodology in arriving at the 5 percent retention figure. Since there are no extant records of tourism statistics for this period, it is impossible to determine Carrington's accuracy. However, the city did not have enough first-class hotel rooms to accommodate seventy-five thousand wealthy tourists.

77. MBD, Sept. 5, Nov. 2, 1925.

78. *Light*, Mar. 10, 1929; Selden C. Meneffe and Orin C. Cassmore, *The Pecan Shellers of San Antonio: The Problem of Underpaid and Unemployed Mexican Labor* (Washington, D.C.: U.S. Government Printing Office, 1940), 8; Shapiro, "Workers of San Antonio," 38–41; and Julia Kirk Blackwelder, *Women of the Depression: Caste and Culture in San Antonio, 1919–1939* (College Station: Texas A&M University Press, 1984), 94, 96–99.

79. *Express*, Jan. 1, 1925; Hansford MacNider, Acting Secretary of War to Senator Morris Sheppard, May 17, 1927, Washington, D.C., TLS, in the William B. Tuttle Papers, Randolph Air Force Base Historical Office; William B. Tuttle, "The History of the 'West Point of the Air,'" *Southwestern Resources* 7, no. 4 (July 1930): 3–6, 39–44; and Johnson, "Failed Experiment," 99–101.

80. MBD, Jan. 20, 1926; Jan. 28, 1927.

81. MBD, May 26, 1927.

82. *Express*, Jan. 11, 12, Dec. 1, 1928; and *Light*, Dec. 2, 1928.

83. CCM, Aug. 5, 26, Sept. 30, 1929.

CHAPTER SEVEN

1. *San Antonio Express* (hereafter *Express*), June 13, 1925.

2. Heywood Sanders, "Building a New Urban Infrastructure: The Creation of Post-War San Antonio," in *Urban Texas: Politics and Development*, ed. Char Miller and Heywood Sanders (College Station: Texas A&M University Press, 1990): 154–55. See also chapter 4.

3. San Antonio City Council Minutes (hereafter CCM), Nov. 19, 27, 28, 1923, San Antonio Municipal Archives.

4. The history of back taxes owed is contained in City of San Antonio Annual Report for the 1936 Fiscal Year, June 1, 1935, to May 31, 1936, Finance Department Records, Annual Finance Report, Box 4, San Antonio City Archives.

5. *San Antonio Light* (hereafter *Light*), Oct. 3, 23, 1929.

6. CCM, Sept. 9, 1928, Sept. 30, 1929; and *Light,* May 15, Oct. 23, 1929.

7. On Maverick's career, see Richard B. Henderson, *Maury Maverick: A Political Biography* (Austin: University of Texas Press, 1970); McAllister has as yet had no biographer, but see Caroline Bass, "McAllister, Walter Williams, Sr.," *Handbook of Texas Online,* tshaonline.org, for a brief career summary.

8. *Light,* Apr. 8, 1930.

9. *Express,* May 7, 1930, quoted in Sanders, "New Urban Infrastructure," 158.

10. *Express,* May 8, 1930; the *Light,* May 8, 1930, did an extensive analysis of voting patterns that detailed the defections from the "machine" among Fourth Ward voters. The league also did extremely well in the Seventh Ward, the area that had been the stronghold for frugality since the mid-nineteenth century.

11. The *Light* published notice of the election of Mar. 13; the election occurred on May 7.

12. *Light,* July 10, 1930.

13. *Express,* May 10, 1930.

14. *Express,* July 6, 25, 1930; Henderson, *Maury Maverick,* 50–51.

15. *Express,* Jan. 2, 1931.

16. For the number of city employees, see Annual Report for the Fiscal Year Ending May 31, 1929, p. 5; Finance Department Records, Box 4, San Antonio City Archives. The relations with banks, merchants, and contractors are documented in the CCM, typically once a month when bills came due.

17. On recreation and advertising taxes, see *Express,* May 10, 1930; CCM, Nov. 29, 1930, June 29, 1931; for support of preservationist projects, see CCM, Nov. 10, 1930; and Lewis F. Fisher, *Saving San Antonio: The Precarious Preservation of a Heritage* (Lubbock: Texas Tech University Press, 1996), 103–8, 125.

18. *Express,* Apr. 9, 1930; May 10, 1931.

19. *Express,* Apr. 7, 1931.

20. *Light,* May 2; and *Express,* May 10, 1931.

21. *Express,* May 10, 1931.

22. *Express,* May 14, 1931. On average, the margin of victory for the machine was 58 percent to 42 percent.

23. *Express,* May 14, 1931; CCM, May 18, 1931.

24. Cf. Stephen L. Elkin, "State and Market in City Politics: Or, the 'Real' Dallas," in *The Politics of Urban Development,* ed. Clarence N. Stone and Heywood T. Sanders (Lawrence: University Press of Kansas, 1987), 26–27, 29.

25. Financial records for the city are extremely incomplete prior to the 1950s. The only extant reports cover the years from 1929 to 1937, which are the basis for this and other statements on budget matters. See the Annual Reports in Finance Department Records, Annual Finance Report, Box 4.

26. *Light,* Aug. 16, 24, 25, 1931.

27. CCM, Aug. 31, 1931.

28. CCM, Sept. 29, 1931; and *Light,* Oct. 25, 1931.

29. Bruce J. Schulman, *From Cotton Belt to Sunbelt: Federal Policy, Economic Development, and the Transformation of the South, 1938–1980* (New York: Oxford University Press), 46–47, 55–56, 58–61, 82–89.

30. Lyndon Gayle Knippa, "San Antonio II: The Early New Deal," in *Texas Cities and the Great Depression*, ed. Robert C. Cotner et al. (Austin: Texas Memorial Museum, 1973), 82–86.

31. *Light*, Jan. 1, 11, 1934.

32. *Light*, Feb. 6, 7, Apr. 8 (for quote), 1934.

33. *Light*, Feb. 28, Mar. 18, 27, 1935.

34. *Light*, Apr. 7, 12, 18, 1935.

35. *Light*, Apr. 28, 1932. For other leagues in this period see *Light*, Oct. 18, 1931; Feb. 7, Apr. 1, 1932; and May 4, Nov. 7, 1933.

36. *Light*, Apr. 25, Aug. 19 and 27, 1932.

37. Declines in assessments and taxes collected were calculated from the Annual Financial Reports.

38. *San Antonian*, April 1935, p. 19 (this was the official publication of the Chamber of Commerce).

39. K. E. Miller, *Abstract of U.S. Public Health Service Survey of Health Services, City of San Antonio* (San Antonio Chamber of Commerce, June 15, 1935), quoted in Diana L. Schiller, "The Fight to Clean Up San Antonio's Mexican Corrals," in Friends of the P. I. Nixon Medical Historical Library, *Annual Bulletin* 15 (Fall 1986): 2–5. For the best analysis of the public health threat and long-term efforts to deal with it, see Benjamin S. Bradshaw, Kenneth S. Blanchard, and George H. Thompson, "Postneonatal Diarrhea Mortality of Mexican American and Anglo American Infants: Trends and Results," *Population Research and Public Policy Review* 22 (June 1996): 1–18; and Bradshaw and David P. Smith, "The Decline of Tuberculosis Mortality in an Urban Mexican Origin Population, 1935–1984," *Social Biology* 44 (spring–summer 1997): 25–41.

40. *San Antonian*, Jan. 1935, pp. 4, 9; May 1935, p. 1; June 8, 1935, p. 5.

41. On the initial maneuvers in this controversy, see *Light*, Oct. 27, Nov. 12, 14, 24, 1935.

42. *Light*, Apr. 15, Dec. 19, 1937; see Schiller, "Fight to Clean Up," for the long struggle over the Board of Health; on national publicity, see Ralph Maitland, "San Antonio: The Shame of Texas," *Forum and Century* 102 (1939): 50–54.

43. Selden C. Meneffe and Orin C. Cassmore, *The Pecan Shellers of San Antonio: The Problem of Underpaid and Unemployed Mexican Labor* (Washington, D.C.: U.S. Government Printing Office, 1940), 24–52; Schiller, "Fight to Clean Up," 2; and Donald L. Zelman, "Alazán-Apache Courts: A New Deal Response to Mexican American Housing Conditions in San Antonio," *Southwestern Historical Quarterly* 87 (Oct. 1983): 123–50.

44. CCM, Aug. 5, 1914; June 7, 14, May 31, 1915; Ordinance Book F, pp. 28–38, San Antonio Municipal Archives; on compliance issues, see *Express*, June 26, 1925.

45. *Express*, Jan. 7, 1939.

46. There is no study of property owners in the slum area. I have compiled a list of such owners from CCM, Aug. 3, 9, 26, Sept. 23, Oct. 21, 1915; *Express*, Dec. 12, 1938; for

other information on landlords, see *Express*, Nov. 20, 1938. I identified the addresses and occupations of property owners using the city directors. This analysis is not definitive, but it does suggest some patterns for further investigation.

47. The social history of San Antonio's neighborhoods remains to be written. To construct this all too brief portrait of the city's worst slum, I relied on Gerald Suttles, *The Social Order of the Slum: Ethnicity and Territory in the Industrial City* (University of Chicago Press, 1968), for a theoretical framework, and on Ana Luisa Martinez, "Pablo Cruz and *El Regidor*: The Emergence of a Bicultural Identity in San Antonio," *Journal of the West* 15 (fall 2006): 23; Richard A. Garcia, *Rise of the Mexican American Middle Class: San Antonio, 1929–1941* (College Station: Texas A&M University Press, 1991); Charles Ramsdell, *San Antonio: A Historical and Pictorial Guide* (Austin: University of Texas Press, 1959), 163–73; Lionel Sosa, *Children of the Revolution: How the Mexican Revolution Changed America* (Austin: University of Texas Press, 2012), 49–50, 68; and Melissa Gohlke, "The Evolution of Vice Activity in San Antonio, 1885–1975" (master's thesis, University of Texas at San Antonio, 1997).

48. Quoted in Harold A. Shapiro, "The Workers of San Antonio, Texas, 1900–1940" (Ph.D. diss., University of Texas at Austin, 1952), 158.

49. *Express*, Dec. 12, 13, 1938; Green Payton, *San Antonio: City in the Sun* (New York: McGraw-Hill, 1946), 161–67; Schiller, "Fight to Clean Up"; and Zelman, "Alazán-Apache Courts."

50. Fisher, *Saving San Antonio*, 125, 146–47, 189.

51. Laura Hernández-Ehrisman, *Inventing the Fiesta City: Heritage and Carnival in San Antonio* (Albuquerque: University of New Mexico Press, 2008), 73, 93–94, 98.

52. Fisher, *Saving San Antonio*, 131–33, 148–69.

53. Fisher, 123–39.

54. On the campaign to redesign the area around the Alamo, see *Express*, Oct. 27, 1925; Aug. 9, 1931; Jan. 7, 1932; Nov. 22, Dec. 4, 1936; Feb. 26, Oct. 1, 1937; *Light*, Feb. 15, 1934; Dec. 5, 1936; Feb. 26, 1937; and Fisher, *Saving San Antonio*, 58–60, 103–8.

55. Lewis F. Fisher, *River Walk: The Epic Story of San Antonio's River* (San Antonio: Maverick Publishing, 2007), 87–90, 93–110.

56. For Maverick's views on La Villita, see CCM, Oct. 12, 1939; Mar. 14, 1940; also see Fisher, *Saving San Antonio*, 198–207.

57. Fisher, *Saving San Antonio*, 223–24; and Hernández-Ehrisman, *Inventing the Fiesta City*, 94–95.

58. *San Antonian*, Jan. 1935, p. 17; Feb. 16, 1940, pp. 3–7.

59. *San Antonian*, Jan. 1935, p. 12.

60. *Light*, Jan. 16, 26, 1940.

61. *Light*, Jan. 13, 20, 1935; Sept. 10, 1939; May 26, 1940; Sept. 18, 1940.

62. Calculated from the 1940 U.S. Census of Population, vol. 2, pt. 6, table D-42, p. 1058. Since tourism was not a separate category in 1940, I calculated tourism-related employment from eating and drinking places; hotel and lodging places; amusement, recreation, and related services.

63. Secretary of War George H. Dern to Congressman Maury Maverick, May 28, 1936, in *Congressional Record*, 74th Congress, Second Session, v. 80, pt. 8, p. 8245.

64. Schulman, *Cotton Belt to Sunbelt*, 21–22, 63, 65.

65. Julia Kirk Blackwelder, *Women of the Depression: Caste and Culture in San Antonio, 1929–1939* (College Station: Texas A&M University Press, 1984), 130–44.

66. Meneffe and Cassmore, *Pecan Shellers of San Antonio*, 8–9, 12–16, 18–22; and *Express*, Jan. 6, 1939.

67. *Light*, Mar. 3, 1936.

68. *Light*, Mar. 9, 1936.

69. *Light*, Mar. 3, 1936.

70. *Light*, Aug. 5, 7, 16, Oct. 11, 19, Nov. 26, 1938.

71. *Light*, Apr. 7, July 15, 1937; July 26, Aug. 21, Sept. 4, 1938 (for quote).

72. *Light*, Feb. 11, 1939; and *Express*, Feb. 7, 8, 12, 24, 1939.

73. *Light*, Feb. 11, 23, 1939.

74. *Express*, June 17, 1934, Apr. 26, 1939; *Light*, Apr. 24, 1917.

75. *Light*, May 10, 1939; *and Express*, May 11, 1939.

76. Maury Maverick, *A Maverick American* (New York: Covici Friede, 1937), 218, 222, 272; and Maury Maverick, "Let's Join the United States," *Virginia Quarterly Review* 15 (winter 1939): 64–77.

77. Maury Maverick, "San Antonio's Connection with the Federal Government and the Future of the City," in CCM, Mar. 14, 1940.

78. On the military-industrial complex, see Ann Markusen, Peter Hall, Scott Campbell, and Sabina Deitrick, *The Rise of the Gunbelt: The Military Remapping of Industrial America* (New York: Oxford University Press, 1991), and Roger Lotchin, *Fortress California, 1910–1961: From Warfare to Welfare* (New York: Oxford University Press, 1992).

79. Chamber of Commerce, Minutes of the Board of Directors (hereafter MBD), June 13, July 11, 1940, San Antonio Chamber of Commerce archive.

80. MBD, Feb. 11, 1941.

81. MBD, Feb. 25, 1941.

82. Fairbanks, *For the City as a Whole*, 139–40; and Markusen et al., *Rise of the Gunbelt*, 49.

83. George S. Perry, "The Cities of America—San Antonio," *Saturday Evening Post*, v. 218 (Nov. 24, 1945): 114.

84. Schulman, *Cotton Belt to Sunbelt*, 22–23; and Shapiro, "Workers of San Antonio, Texas," 234.

85. In the debate over how much, if any, autonomy cities have over their own economic development, the idea of "partial autonomy" is an attractive middle ground because it allows for some local initiative. In this instance, however, San Antonio businessmen chose not to seize that initiative. The ability to choose thus includes the possibility of not choosing, a point that theoretical literature typically ignores as an explanation for the different outcomes in the competition among cities seeking to grow.

86. Locality Digest, Jan. 30, 1944, p. 10, unpublished manuscript (typescript), in Mayor Gus Mauermann Papers, Box 1, Housing Authority File, City of San Antonio Archives.

87. Employment data derived from MBD, Jan. 28, 1941, July 14, 1942; History of the San Antonio Air Service Command from Inception to Feb. 1943, 2 vols.; v. 1: iii–vi, unpublished manuscript (typescript), Kelly Air Force Base History Office; and Locality Digest, Jan. 30, 1944, p. 10.

88. *Express*, Sept. 6, 1949; Locality Digest, p. 10; and Eldon Cagle Jr., *Fort Sam: The Story of Fort Sam Houston* (San Antonio: Maverick Publishing, 2003), 81.

89. Mary Oliva Handy, *History of Fort Sam Houston* (San Antonio: Naylor, 1951), 97.

90. Albert Curtis, *Military San Antonio* (San Antonio: Standard Printing, 1943).

91. Robert G. Landolt, *The Mexican-American Workers of San Antonio, Texas* (New York: Arno Press, 1976), 81–84; and Emilio Zamora, *Claiming Rights and Righting Wrongs in Texas: Mexican Workers and Job Politics during World War II* (College Station: Texas A&M University Press, 2009), 151–56.

92. Cf. Locality Digest, p. 10; and Greater San Antonio Housing Inventory Analysis, Dec. 31, 1945, pp. 3, 14, typescript ms., Box 2, Folder: Housing Reports, Mauermann Papers, City of San Antonio Archives.

93. *Light*, Nov. 1, 1944.

94. *Light*, Jan. 26, 1930; Aug. 7, 1941; Jan. 27, July 29, 1946.

95. *Light*, Feb. 7, 1941; on national concerns about decentralization, see Robert M. Fogelson, *Downtown: Its Rise and Fall, 1880–1950* (New Haven, Conn.: Yale University Press, 2001), 230–37; Jon Teaford, *The Metropolitan Revolution: The Rise of Post-Urban America* (New York: Columbia University Press, 2006), 40–54.

96. Neither the Citizens' League nor any of the taxpayers' leagues left any organizational records, or at least none have been found. To determine involvement in either type of league, I collected the names of individuals mentioned in the local press as serving as directors or participants in such organizations. Between 1930 and 1940, the press listed 124 such individuals. Of those 37 (30 percent) joined the Citizens' League; 38 (31 percent) joined a taxpayers' league. There was little overlap in membership between the two types of leagues; only 3 individuals belonged to both. With regard to city manager government, 13 (10 percent) of the 124 leaders devoted themselves entirely to that reform.

97. Don Politico column, *Light*, Jan. 22, 1939.

98. Don Politico column, *Light*, Jan. 22, 1939.

99. CCM, June 1, 1939.

100. *Light*, Jan. 17, Nov. 28, 1940. On Paul Adams, see *Light*, June 30, 1936; Feb. 7, 13, Aug. 2, 1939.

101. Between 1940 and 1950 the press identified 144 individual participants in tax leagues and various civic organizations devoted to solving the city's problems. Of those, 36 individuals (25 percent) served on multiple boards in leadership positions, and of those 36, 20 belonged to the Taxpayers' Defense League.

102. *Light*, Dec. 13, 18, 1949; and *Express*, May 28, 1941.

103. *Light*, Sept. 26, 1940.

104. CCM, July 3, 1941.

105. CCM, June 1, 5, 1941, Dec. 31, 1942.

106. CCM, June 8, Aug. 13, 1942; and *Light*, July 14, 1942.

107. *Light*, Jan. 7, 1943.

108. *Light*, Dec. 2, 1942, and Jan. 10, 1943 (Don Politico column).

109. *Light*, Jan. 13, 1943.

110. For examples of petitions for sewer connections from individual homeowners, see CCM, Mar. 16, 20, 30, Apr. 6, 13, 19, 1944.

111. CCM, July 22, 2943; and Robert J. Huff to Mayor Mauermann, Apr. 17, 1944, autograph letter signed, Mauermann Papers, Box 1, folder 2: Annexation Controversy.

112. *Light*, Sept. 26, 1943.

113. *Light*, Mar. 19, Sept. 5, 1943.

114. *Light*, Aug. 8, 1941.

115. *Light*, Oct. 12, 1930, Nov. 6, 1932, Feb. 12, 1933, June 30, 1936, Jan. 8, 1938, Sept. 14, 1941, Mar. 23, 1943, Dec. 15, 1943.

116. CCM, Mar. 16, 17, 1944.

117. Thomas Barrett to Mauermann, Mar. 16, 1944, typed letter signed; Chamber of Commerce General Manager H. M. Van Auken to Mauermann, Mar. 20, 1944, TLS; Cecil E. Llewellyn to Mauermann, Mar. 23, 1944, TLS, all in Box 1, Folder 1: Annexation Controversy, Mauermann Papers.

118. *Light*, Mar. 17, 1944.

119. *Light*, Mar. 19, 1944.

120. *Light*, Mar. 19, 1944.

121. CCM, Oct. 5, 12, 1944.

122. Extracts from Rules and Regulations of the City Water Board pamphlet, April 1934, Mayor Alfred Callaghan Papers, Box 1, Folder: City Water Board, San Antonio City Archives; City Water Board Manager W. D. Masterson to Mayor Mauermann, Aug. 16, 1944, TLS, in Mauermann Papers, Box 1, Folder: City Water Board; and City Water Board Chairman C. A. Goeth to Mayor Mauermann, Oct. 12, 1944, TLS, in Mauermann Papers, Box 1, Folder: City Water Board.

123. *Express*, Sept. 6, 1944.

124. CCM, Oct. 23, Nov. 30, Dec. 9, 14, 30, 1944.

125. For the total number of houses, see Greater San Antonio Housing Inventory Analysis, Dec. 31, 1945. *Express*, Oct. 15, 1944, reported 379 new connections completed and 446 more planned for completion by December. See also *San Antonian* 7 (Apr. 23, 1945), p. 3.

126. *Light*, July 16, 1945.

127. *Light*, Mar. 26, 31, Apr. 1, 7, 23, 1943; and *Express*, May 13, 1943.

128. Cf. *San Antonian* 7 (Apr. 23, 1945), p. 4; *Express*, May 21, 1945; Post-War Planning Board, Minutes of the Board of Directors, July 2, 1945, in Mauermann Papers, Box 2, Folder: Planning Board; CCM, Aug. 2, 1945; and *Light*, Sept. 30, 1945.

129. *Light*, Jan. 16, 1945.

130. *Light*, Sept. 21, Dec. 9, 1945.

131. CCM, May 11, 1944.

132. CCM, Feb. 14, 1946.

133. CCM, Feb. 20, 1946.

134. *Light*, May 28, 29, 30, 1946.

135. *Light*, May 30, 1946; and CCM, May 30, 1946.

136. *Light*, Mar. 31, 1943.

137. *Light*, Aug. 29, Sept. 26, 1946.

138. *Light*, Jan. 9, 1947.

139. *Light*, May 9, 1945.

140. *Light*, Mar. 11, Apr. 18, 1947.

141. *Light*, Feb. 17, 26, Mar. 11, May 14, 28, 1947.

142. CCM, June 2, 1947; and *Light*, June 8, 1947.

143. *Light*, June 27, 1947.

144. *Light*, Dec. 10, 14, 31, 1947.

145. *Light*, Feb. 24, 26, 29, Apr. 13, 1948; and CCM, Sept. 26, 1940.

146. *Light*, Mar. 20, 1949.

147. *Light*, Jan. 30, Feb. 2, 6, 1949.

148. *Light*, Mar. 27, 30, 1949.

149. *Light*, Apr. 10, 1949.

150. *Light*, Apr. 10, 1949.

151. *Light*, May 11, 12, 31, 1949.

152. The "suburban trend" in boosterism emerged from an analysis of civic leaders' residences. In the 1930s 9 percent of civic leaders lived in suburbs; by the 1940s that had risen to 22 percent.

153. CCM, Feb. 7, 1946; on reform trends elsewhere, see Abbott, *How Cities Won the West*, 187–88.

154. Transcript of taped interview with Mr. W. W. McAllister Sr., Apr. 7, 1977. In author's possession.

155. For the details of this convoluted campaign, see *Light*, July 14, Nov. 1, 3, 6, 7, 16, 20, 22 27, 29, Dec. 23, 28, 1949; Jan. 20, May 10, 1950.

156. *Light*, Feb. 19, 1950.

157. *Light*, June 8, 1950.

158. *Light*, June 15, 20, 1950.

159. *Light*, June 27, 28, July 10, Nov. 23, 24, 28, 1950; San Antonio's reformers' willingness to use federal funding to keep local taxes low reflected southern conservative attitudes in general: Schulman, *Cotton Belt to Sunbelt*, 120.

160. *Light*, Mar. 8, 18, 1951.

161. *Light*, Mar. 8, 14, 1951; White revealed his efforts in recruiting a slate in White to A. A. Meredith, City Manager of Borger, Texas, Oct. 26, 1951, TLC, Box 1, Folder: Charter Revisions, Jack White Papers, San Antonio City Archives.

162. Don Politico column, *Light*, May 9, 1950; and [illegible] to Jack White, Apr. 17, 1951; Theodore Minter to Jack White, May 10, 1951; Sam Biery to Judge Robert Sawtelle, May 15,

1951; Jack White to Manuel Ortega [Manger, San Antonio Charro Association], Apr. 28, 1951; White to J. H. Frost, May 4, 1951, all in Box 1, Folder: Elections, Jack White Papers.

163. *Light*, May 9, 1951.

164. *Light*, Aug. 31, Sept. 15, 1951.

165. *Light*, Sept. 23, 1951.

166. *Express*, Oct. 8, 1951, notes Thomas and Sawtelle's roles; transcripts of White's radio addresses are in Box 1, Folder: Charter Revisions, White Papers; Dan E. Genard to White, Oct. 5, 1951, in Box 1, White Papers.

167. *Light*, Dec. 12, 1951; and Walter H. Lilly and M. Winston Martin, Associate Planners, "San Antonio Takes Stock and Looks Ahead: A Comprehensive Master Plan for San Antonio, Texas, 1951," typed manuscript, pp. 318–71, 423–51, San Antonio City Archives.

168. See Charter and Amendments Copies, 1914–1951, 1951 Charter, Article I, section 3, Article VIII, section 91–92, Article IX (unpaginated), San Antonio City Archives.

CHAPTER EIGHT

1. The resolution is reproduced in San Antonio Board of Commissioners, Dec. 27, 1951.

2. *San Antonio Light* (hereafter *Light*), May 25, June 1, 1952; Jan. 25, 1953. For an assessment of Harrell's first year in office, see *Light*, Dec. 28, 1952; Jan. 1, 1953.

3. Arnold Fleischmann, "Sunbelt Boosterism: The Politics of Postwar Growth and Annexation in San Antonio," in *The Rise of the Sunbelt Cities*, ed. David C. Perry and Alfred J. Watkins (Beverly Hills: Sage, 1982), 156–57.

4. San Antonio City Council Minutes (hereafter CCM), Feb. 28, 1952, San Antonio Municipal Archives.

5. *Light*, May 9, 1953; and Fleischmann, "Sunbelt Boosterism," 157.

6. *Light*, May 30, 1952.

7. *Light*, Oct. 28, 1952.

8. *Light*, Dec. 18, 1952.

9. *Light*, Jan. 28, 1953.

10. CCM, Apr. 8, 1953; and *San Antonio Express* (hereafter *Express*), Apr. 23, 1953.

11. *Light*, July 26, Aug. 13, 1953.

12. *Light*, Aug. 16, 1953.

13. *Express*, Oct. 9, 17 (quote), 29, 31, 1953.

14. *Express*, Dec. 6, 24, 1953.

15. *Express*, Oct. 25, 28, 29, 1953; and Lewis F. Fisher, *Saving San Antonio: The Precarious Preservation of a Heritage* (Lubbock: Texas Tech University Press, 1996), 265–73.

16. *Express*, Jan. 1, 1954.

17. *Express*, Jan. 25, 1954.

18. *Express*, Jan. 12, 14, Feb. 14, 24, 1954.

19. *Light*, Oct. 2, 9, 10, 14, Nov. 5, 16, 1954.

20. *San Antonio Express*, Dec. 8, 9, 1954; and *In Search of Good Government* (San Antonio: Crumrine, 1972), 17, 19.

21. John A. Booth and David R. Johnson, "Community, Progress, and Power in San Antonio," in *The Politics of San Antonio: Community, Progress, and Power*, ed. David R. Johnson and John A. Booth (Lincoln: University of Nebraska Press, 1983), 23–24.

22. Booth and Johnson, 23.

23. *Look*, Mar. 27, 1951.

24. Heywood T. Sanders, "Building a New Urban Infrastructure: The Creation of Postwar San Antonio," in *Urban Texas: Politics and Development*, ed. Char Miller and Heywood T. Sanders (College Station: Texas A&M University Press, 1990), 167.

25. Testimony of Mayor Walter W. McAllister to support Transpacific Route Case, presented in Honolulu, Hawaii, Feb. 19, 1967, Box 5, Folder 1, Papers of Mayor Walter W. McAllister, 1961–1971, San Antonio Municipal Archives.

26. Benjamin S. Bradshaw, Kenneth S. Blanchard, and George H. Thompson, "Postneonatal Diarrhea of Mexican American and Anglo American Infants: Trends and Context," *Population Research and Policy Review* 5 (June 1996): 1–18; and Heywood T. Sanders, "Empty Taps, Missing Pipes: Water Policy and Politics," in *On the Border: An Environmental History of San Antonio*, ed. Char Miller (University of Pittsburgh Press, 2001), 141–68.

27. The federal government's impact on the national economy, cities, and the Sunbelt has generated a large literature. For some examples, see Roger Biles, *The Fate of Cities: Urban America and the Federal Government, 1945–2000* (Lawrence: University Press of Kansas, 2011); Roger W. Lotchin, *Fortress California, 1910–1961: From Warfare to Welfare* (New York: Oxford University Press, 1992); Bruce Schulman, *From Cotton Belt to Sunbelt: Federal Policy, Economic Development, and the Transformation of the South, 1938–1980* (New York: Oxford University Press, 1991); and Margaret Pugh O'Mara, *Cities of Knowledge: Cold War Science and the Search for the New Silicon Valley* (Princeton University Press, 2005).

28. Walter H. Lilly and M. Winston Martin, "San Antonio Takes Stock and Looks Ahead: A Comprehensive Master Plan for San Antonio, Texas, 1951," p. 24, typed MS, San Antonio City Archives; Chamber of Commerce, *San Antonian*, Oct. 6, 1954, and Feb. 2, July 20, 1961; *Light*, May 7, 1967; Howard W. Davis, "A Case Study of Industrial Location," *Land Economics* 45 (November 1969): 444–52; and Eugene Rodriguez Jr., "Henry B. Gonzales: A Political Profile" (master's thesis, St. Mary's University, 1965), 79.

29. Schulman, *Cotton Belt to Sunbelt*, 149–50; Thierry J. Noyelle and Thomas M. Stanback Jr., *The Economic Transformation of American Cities* (Totowa, N.J.: Rowman & Allanheld, 1984), 58; Nancy Ettlinger, "Development Theory and the Military Industrial Firm," in *The Pentagon and the Cities*, ed. Andrew Kirby (Newbury Park, Calif.: Sage, 1992), 24–25; and Markusen et al., *Rise of the Gunbelt*, 49.

30. Laurence Wingerter, "Opportunity Knocks," *San Antonian*, Apr. 10, 1948, pp. 1, 3.

31. *San Antonian*, Feb. 10, 1954.

32. *San Antonian*, Nov. 25, 1953. See also, *San Antonian*, Jan. 6, Feb. 24, 1954.

33. *San Antonian*, July 14, 1954.

34. For a brief history of these institutions, see *San Antonio Express-News*, Sept. 29, 2003.

35. *San Antonian*, Nov. 11, 1956.

36. Minutes of the Board of Directors meeting, San Antonio Chamber of Commerce (hereafter MBD), Jan. 24, Apr. 10, 1956, San Antonio Chamber of Commerce archive.

37. MBD, July 21, 1954.

38. MBD, Mar. 16, 1955.

39. MBD, Jan. 12, 1956.

40. MBD, July 5 (emphasis added), Sept. 13, 1962.

41. Minutes of the Executive Committee Meeting, Jan. 4, 1967, Board Minutes, v. 42 (June 2, 1966–May 24, 1967), Office of the Chamber of Commerce, San Antonio, Texas.

42. *San Antonian*, Mar. 5, 1947, Mar. 19, 1970; and Michael C. D. Macdonald, *America's Cities: A Report on the Myth of Urban Renaissance* (New York: Simon and Schuster, 1984), 113.

43. Cf. Clarence N. Stone, *Regime Politics: Governing Atlanta, 1946–1988* (Lawrence: University Press of Kansas, 1989), 179. I agree with Stone's point that relationships among what he terms "actors" in an urban regime are critical to their success. San Antonio boosters, though, had to not only create relationships among likeminded colleagues, but they also had to maintain relationships with businessmen convinced that doing nothing to promote growth made sense. The creation of committees dedicated to a particular goal appears to have been a tactic for encouraging some forms of development while conceding primacy to the dominant belief in laissez-faire growth.

44. *Light*, Sept. 29, 1944.

45. *San Antonian*, Feb. 15, 1947; and Wilbur Matthews, *History of the San Antonio Medical Foundation and South Texas Medical Center* (San Antonio: N.p., 1983), 1–6.

46. *San Antonian*, Jan. 5, 1955; and Matthews, *San Antonio Medical Foundation*, 8–9.

47. MBD, Jan. 11, 1955, v. 31 (Jan. 11–Dec. 27, 1955).

48. MBD, Sept. 13, 1955; Jan. 24, 1956, v. 32 (Jan. 24–Dec. 11, 1956).

49. MBD, Jan. 24, 1955.

50. *San Antonian*, Apr. 12, 1956, notes Oak Hills Country Club's proximity to the Five Oaks site.

51. MBD, Jan. 24, 1956.

52. Matthews, *San Antonio Medical Foundation*, 8–9.

53. O'Mara, *Cities of Knowledge*, 1, 18.

54. *San Antonian*, May 17, 1956.

55. Matthews, *San Antonio Medical Foundation*, 11.

56. Matthews, 11, 14–15; and *San Antonian*, Apr. 4, Oct. 22, 1957.

57. MBD, June 23, 1959; and Matthews, *San Antonio Medical Foundation*, 15.

58. Minutes of the Board of Regents of the University of Texas, Oct. 1, 1959, pp. 1–11, Office of the Board of Regents.

59. *San Antonian*, Dec. 17, 1959; Minutes of the South Texas Medical School Development Committee, Mar. 13, 1961, in folder titled "Historical Review of the Medical Center," San Antonio Medical Foundation Medical School History and Development, Library of the University of Texas Health Science Center; and Matthews, *San Antonio Medical Foundation*, 15–19.

60. Matthews, *San Antonio Medical Foundation*, 23–24.

61. *Express*, Jan. 1, Feb. 1, Mar. 2, 17, 18, May 10, 1955. This discussion of the campaign for a public university for San Antonio draws on David R. Johnson, "From Conception to Birth: The Origins of the University of Texas at San Antonio," 1955–1969 (unpublished manuscript, 2011).

62. Chamber of Commerce, Executive Committee Minutes, Aug. 20, Sept. 11, 1956; July 9, 1957, San Antonio Chamber of Commerce archive.

63. *San Antonio Express and News* (combined edition of *Express* and *News* published on weekends, hereafter *Express and News*), Jan. 24, 1960.

64. *Express*, Jan. 27, 1961; *Light*, Jan. 26, May 4, 1961.

65. Data from Deborah Day, "The Influence of Frank Erwin on Texas Higher Education" (Ph.D. diss., University of Texas at Austin, 1988), 14, 88, 99; and James Reston Jr., *The Lone Star: The Life of John Connally* (New York: Harper & Row, 1989), 290.

66. Quoted in Ann Fears Crawford and Jack Keever, *John B. Connally: Portrait in Power* (Austin: Jenkins Publishing, 1973), 96.

67. Crawford and Keever, 87n2.

68. *San Antonian*, Aug. 9, 1962.

69. *Light*, Jan. 13, 1963.

70. *Light*, Jan. 20, May 19, 21, 1963; and Amado Felipe Cavazos, *Zachry: The Man and His Company* (San Antonio: Metro Press, 1993), *passim*.

71. *Express and News*, Jan. 12, 13, 1963.

72. *Light*, Feb. 4, 1964.

73. *Light*, Mar. 23, 1964; *Express*, Mar. 12, Apr. 3, May 12, 1964; and *Express and News*, Feb. 1, Apr. 26, May 10, 1964.

74. *Light*, Apr. 26, 1964, reported the near unanimity among candidates regarding a university.

75. *Express*, Oct. 7, 1964.

76. *Express*, Nov. 11, 1964; *Dallas Morning News*, Jan. 24, 1965; *Light*, Jan. 27, 1965; and Sterlin Holmesly, interview with B. J. McCombs, May 27, 1994, pp. 8–9, Oral History Collection, Institute of Texan Cultures Archives. McCombs said that Connally "delivered" the creation of the University of Texas at San Antonio.

77. S.C.R. No. 95, 59th Legislature; *Express*, Mar. 5, 1965.

78. MBD, Nov. 9, 1965; *San Antonian*, Jan. 20, Apr. 29, July 21, 1966; *Express and News*, Mar. 26, 1966; and *Light*, Mar. 27, 1966.

79. *San Antonian*, Nov. 10, Dec. 22, 1966; and David R. Johnson, interview with Herbert D. Kelleher, Jan. 6, 2009.

80. Coordinating Board, Texas College and University System, "A Report to the 60th Legislature of the State of Texas on the Need and Feasibility of Establishing an Institution of Higher Education with Requisite State Support and Control in Bexar County, Texas," Feb. 21, 1967, p. 7, Office of the Texas Higher Education Coordinating Board.

81. CCM, Oct. 12, 1967.

82. *Express*, Dec. 15, 1967, July 24, 1968.

83. Chamber of Commerce, Minutes, Aug. 13, 1968, San Antonio Chamber of Commerce archive; *Express*, Aug. 19, 22, 1968.

84. Editorial, *Express*, July 24, 1968.

85. *Express*, Nov. 19, 21, 1968; and *Express and News*, Nov. 24, 1968.

86. *Express*, Jan. 9, 14, 1969; *Express and News*, Jan. 11, 12, 25, 1969; and *Light*, Jan. 14, 1969.

87. Day, "Influence of Frank Erwin," 198; *Express*, Mar. 6, May 6, 15, 16, 21, 22, 27, 28, 1969; and *Express and News*, Mar. 9, May 24, 1969.

88. *Express*, May 30, 1968; and *Express and News*, Sept. 15, 1968.

89. On local conservative expectations on research and job training, see *Express*, May 3, 1972 (Editorials); on the search for a site and Coordinating Board attitudes toward UTSA, see David R. Johnson, "UTSA@50: A History of the University of Texas at San Antonio," unpublished manuscript, in Special Collections, University of Texas at San Antonio Library, pp. 11–13.

90. Dean MacCannell, *The Tourist: A New Theory of the Leisure Class* (New York: Schocken Books, 1976), 39–40; Hal Rothman, *Devil's Bargain: Tourism in the Twentieth-Century West* (Lawrence: University Press of Kansas), 23–25; J. Mark Souther and Nicholas Dagen Bloom, eds., "Introduction," in *American Tourism: Constructing a National Tradition* (Chicago: Center for American Places at Columbia College, 2012), x–xi; and Thomas S. Bremer, *Blessed with Tourists: The Borderlands of Religion and Tourism in San Antonio* (Chapel Hill: University of North Carolina Press, 2004), 6.

91. Fisher, *Saving San Antonio*, 220–55; and Bremer, *Blessed with Tourists*, 77.

92. Calculations from data in *San Antonian*, Dec. 23, 1953, Jan. 2, 1964.

93. *San Antonian*, Feb. 6, June 26, 1958; and editorial, *San Antonio News* (hereafter *News*), July 25, 1967.

94. *San Antonian*, Feb. 6, Mar. 6, 13, 27, and June 26, 1958; Lewis F. Fisher, *Crown Jewel of Texas: The Story of San Antonio's River* (San Antonio: Maverick Publishing, 1997), 75.

95. MBD, Jan. 26, 1960.

96. Sterlin Holmesly, interview with William R. Sinkin, June 30, 1995, p. 9, Oral History Collection, Institute of Texan Cultures. *Express*, Apr. 2, 1968, discusses the early organizing efforts for HemisFair. Holmesly published excerpts from many of his interviews in *HemisFair'68 and the Transformation of San Antonio* (San Antonio: Maverick Publishing, 2003).

97. Holmesly, interview with Sinkin, June 30, 1995, p. 10.

98. Holmesly interview with Sinkin, p. 10.

99. Holmesly interview with Sinkin, pp. 10–11; *Light*, Dec. 4, 8, 1962; *Express*, Apr. 2, 1968; board members from Exhibit B, Executive Committee Meeting Minutes, Mar. 1963, in San Antonio Fair, Inc., Records, Series 01: Executive Officers, Special Collections, University of Texas at San Antonio.

100. *San Antonian*, June 20, July 18, Aug. 1, Sept. 19, Oct. 3, 1963; and Holmesly, interview with Sinkin, June 30, 1995, p. 11.

101. Sterling Holmesly, interview with Red McCombs, Aug. 7, 1997, Oral History Collection, Institute of Texan Cultures.

102. WOAI Radio Address, Nov. 29, 1966, Box 6, folder 10; Minutes of a Conference at HemisFair Headquarters, Oct. 11, 1967, Box 6, folder 23; List of frequent complaints filed with Visitor Services, Inc., Apr. 8, 1968, Box 6, folder 24, all in Papers of Walter W. McAllister, San Antonio Municipal Archives. The effort to integrate hotels and restaurants is noted in an interview with architect Allison Perry, who participated in the effort, in the *Express-News*, Dec. 18, 2005.

103. Minutes of the Executive Committee Meeting, May 31, 1966, in San Antonio Fair, Inc., Records, Series 01: Executive Officers, Special Collections, University of Texas at San Antonio.

104. Radio Address by Mayor McAllister, June 30, 1966, in Box 6, folder 10, McAllister Papers; *Texas Observer*, Sept. 30, 1966, pp. 1–7.

105. Ada Louise Huxtable, "HemisFair, Opening Tomorrow, Isn't Texas-Size but It's Fun," *New York Times*, Apr. 6, 1968.

106. Calculated from attendance data reported by the *Express* for the period from Apr. 6 to Apr. 24, 1968.

107. *Light*, Apr. 4, 1963.

108. "Economic Development and the West Side of San Antonio" (unpublished paper, n.d. [ca. 1973]), p. 4, in Albert Peña Papers, 1952–1977, Box 21, folder 25, University of Texas at San Antonio Libraries Special Collections.

109. *Express and News*, July 14, 1968.

110. *Express*, May 16, 1968.

111. *Express*, May 2, 15, 17, 1968; and *Express and News*, June 2, 1968.

112. *Express*, Oct. 7, 1968; and Cavazos, *Zachry*, 371–80.

113. Holmesly, interview with Sinkin, June 30, 1995, p. 20; Holmesly interview with McCombs, May 27, 1994, pp. 15–18; the founding of LaQuinta Motor Inns was noted in the *Express-News*, Apr. 6, 2008, in a review of HemisFair's legacy.

114. Calculated from San Antonio Convention and Visitor Bureau data reported in the *Express-News*, Mar. 28, 1993. Such data are notorious for their inaccuracies. The bureau, for instance, did attribute a specific amount of revenue to the convention business, but it did not explain how it arrived at those figures. In addition, this data set began with 1970, when the bureau was relatively small and its ability to collect data, let alone accurate data, was limited. The accuracy of these data may have grown over time as more staff were added, but that is an assumption that has yet to be tested with independent analysis. Despite such problems, the data as reported do serve as a rough estimate of the general trend in the growth of convention revenues.

115. Quoted in *Light*, Dec. 4, 1962.

116. Handwritten note, n.d. (ca. 1960) in David Straus Papers, Box 4, University of Texas at San Antonio Libraries Special Collections (hereafter Straus Papers).

117. Sterlin Holmesly, interview with David Straus, July 27, 1995, p. 4, Oral History Office, Institute of Texan Cultures.

118. Minutes of the TAD Committee, July 6, Aug. 17, 1960, Straus Papers; Dub Sanders to David Straus, Jan. 27, 1961, Box 5, Straus Papers; David Straus to A. F. Beyer, Feb. 2, 1961 (quote), Box 4, Straus Papers; and Fisher, *Crown Jewel of Texas*, 77–78.

119. Fisher, 80.

120. Memorandum, David Straus to Members of the River Bend Project Committee, Mar. 14, 1962, Box 1, Straus Papers; and Holmesly, interview with Straus, p. 6.

121. On the purchase of buildings, see Holmesly, interview with Straus, pp. 6–7; on quote, see Taxpayers League of San Antonio, July Bulletin [1962?], mimeograph, Box 5, Straus Papers. The bulletin is unfortunately undated, but its placement in Straus's correspondence indicates a date of either 1961 or 1962. There is no indication that the city manager agreed with Adams, but the league was a powerful political organization that worked closely with the GGL. The likelihood of the manager conceding Adams's point would have been high. Property tax rolls listing actual assessments for this period have not survived.

122. Minutes of the River Walk Commission, July 25, 1962, Box 1, Straus Papers.

123. David Straus to Walter Mathis, June 13, 1963, copy, Box 1, Straus Papers.

124. Cyrus H. Wagner to David Straus, Oct. 16, 1963, Box 4; Parks and Recreation Meeting Minutes, Dec. 19, 1963; David Straus and James L. Hayne to William R. Sinkin, Dec. 27, 1963; Straus and Hayne to Mayor W. W. McAllister, Dec. 31, 1963, Box 5, all in Straus Papers.

125. *Express and News*, Feb. 5, 1966.

126. Anonymous San Antonio businessman quoted in the *New Orleans Times-Picayune*, May 4, 1969.

127. C. S. Rogers to David Straus, May 8, 1963, Box 4, Straus Papers; and *Light*, Sept. 12, 1971.

128. River Walk Commission Minutes, May 17, 1963, Box 1, Straus Papers.

129. Paseo Del Rio Association Constitution, Mar. 11, 1964, Box 5, Straus Papers; and Fisher, *Crown Jewel of Texas*, 125.

130. *Express*, Dec. 22, 1966; River Walk Commission Minutes, Aug. 8, 1967, Box 1, Straus Papers; and Fisher, *Crown Jewel of Texas*, 127–28.

131. *Express*, Jan. 21, 1964; *Times-Picayune*, May 4, 1969; and River Walk Commission Minutes, Jan. 6, 1970, Box 1, Straus Papers.

132. See, inter alia, Jimmy Gause to Ed Fest, July 23, 1968; David Straus to Jimmy Gause, Dec. 26, 1968; Jimmy Gause to All Members of the Paseo Del Rio Association, Jan. 29, 1969; Jim Cullum Jr. to Claire Regnier, Mar. 10, 1971, all in Box 5, Straus Papers; *Light*, Sept. 12, 1971; *News*, July 16, 1975; and *Express and News*, July 19, 1975.

133. *Light*, Sept. 12, 1971; and Arthur Veltman, Centro 21 Commissioner Press Release, May 11, 1977, Box 4, Straus Papers.

134. Fisher, *Crown Jewel of Texas*, 135–36.

CHAPTER NINE

1. Sterlin Holmesly, interview with Charles O. Kirkpatrick, May 6, 1994, Oral History Collection, Institute of Texan Cultures.

2. Since the Good Government League controlled local politics for seventeen years, it qualifies as a "regime," but the oligarchy's devotion to the socioeconomic status quo created a booster environment resistant to innovation or diversification. The GGL as an

urban regime promoting growth thus differs considerably from Clarence Stone's analysis of Atlanta in *Regime Politics: Governing Atlanta, 1946–1988* (Lawrence: University Press of Kansas, 1989).

Land development also featured some complexities that affected boosterism. Members of the elite owned large amounts of North Side land where they built ranch houses as weekend retreats from the city prior to the 1960s. They were not interested in developing that land themselves, selling it instead to developers who did want to convert it to other uses. The developers, though, would have to confront the oligarchy's control of public policy before they could assume the role as major players in boosterism that John Logan and Harvey Molotch assign to them in *Urban Fortunes: The Political Economy of Place* (Berkeley: University of California Press, 1987).

3. For details on the revolution in construction techniques and Levittown, see Kenneth Jackson, *Crabgrass Frontier: The Suburbanization of the United States* (New York: Oxford University Press, 1985), 234–38.

4. Interview with Dorothy S. Hughes, Feb. 2, 2010, pp. 7–8, in author's possession. Mrs. Hughes was the widow of Mel Hughes, a business partner in Burke Enterprises. On Ellison, see obituary in *San Antonio Express-News* (hereafter *Express-News*), Aug. 25, 2015.

5. The history of San Antonio's suburban development, and the class composition of the subdivisions that evolved within that development, has yet to be written. My interpretation of these two trends is based on my analysis of subdivisions described by Maria Watson in "San Antonio on Track: The Suburban and Street Railway Complex through 1933" (master's research project, Trinity University, 1982).

6. Wilbur Matthews, *History of the San Antonio Medical Foundation and South Texas Medical Center* (San Antonio: N.p., 1983), 8–9.

7. Employment data calculated from the U.S. Census on County Business Patterns: Employees, Payroll and Establishments, by Industry, 1965–1975.

8. Lamont Wood, *Datapoint: The Lost Story of the Texans Who Invented the Personal Computer Revolution* (Engelwood, Colo.: Hugo House, 2010); and Paul T. Ringenbach, *USAA: A Tradition of Service, 1922–1997* (San Antonio: Donning, 1997).

9. *San Antonio News* (hereafter *News*), Feb. 26, 1975.

10. Sterlin Holmesly, interview with Charles Becker, July 18, 1994, pp. 23–24, Oral History Collection, Institute of Texan Cultures; and Nelson W. Wolff, *Mayor: An Inside View of San Antonio Politics, 1981–1995* (San Antonio Express-News, 1997), 3–7.

11. Arnold Fleischmann, "Sunbelt Boosterism: The Politics of Postwar Growth and Annexation in San Antonio," in *The Rise of the Sunbelt Cities*, ed. David C. Perry and Alfred J. Watkins (Beverly Hills: Sage, 1977), 159.

12. Fleischmann, 160.

13. Fleischmann, 160–61.

14. Wolff, *Mayor*, 6–7.

15. Kemper Diehl, "Power," *San Antonio Express* (hereafter *Express*), Feb. 18, 1974. For other critiques of San Antonio's oligarchy, see *San Antonio Express and News* (hereafter *Express and News*), Oct. 26, 1975; Sterlin Holmesly, interview with Charles Becker, July 18, 1994; Robert L. Linberry, *Equality and Urban Policy Distribution of Municipal Public Services*

(Beverly Hills: Sage, 1977), 17; and Sister Frances J. Woods, *The Model Cities Program in Perspective: The San Antonio, Texas, Experience*, Subcommittee on Housing and Community Development of the Committee on Banking, Finance and Urban Affairs, House of Representatives, 97th Congress, First Session (Washington, D.C.: Government Printing Office, 1982), 28.

16. Elizabeth Boyd, "Glenn Biggs believes in change," *Light*, Nov. 17, 1985. For Biggs's background and relationships, see *Light*, Dec. 14, 1975; and David R. Johnson, interview with Glenn Biggs, Jan. 31, 2006.

17. Boyd, "Glenn Biggs."

18. *Express and News*, Apr. 20, 1969, notes Nielsen's familial tie. Kemper Diehl and Jan Jarboe, *Cisneros: Portrait of a New American* (San Antonio: Corona, 1985), 40, reported McAllister's declining West Side support.

19. See Pete Torres, City Councilman's Newsletter, summer 1969, in Albert Peña Papers, Box 7, folder 7, University of Texas at San Antonio (UTSA) Special Collections. Also see Jack Skipper, "Where the Action Is," *Good Government League News*, Feb. 1970, p. 2. I am indebted to the family of Kurt Munier, a former chairman of the GGL, for providing me with a copy of this newsletter. Other records of the GGL have apparently disappeared.

20. Edwin L. Dickens, "The Political Role of Mexican-Americans in San Antonio, Texas" (Ph.D. diss., Texas Tech University, 1969), 217, quotes William Sinkin on McAllister's dominance of the GGL. For Thompson's comment see *Express-News*, Sept. 18, 1984 (emphasis in original); also "The Life and Legacy of Walter W. McAllister," *Light*, Sept. 14, 1984, and Kemper Diehl, "The Power Brokers," *Express and News*, Feb. 17, 1974.

21. *In Search of Good Government* (San Antonio: Crumrine), 42.

22. *In Search of Good Government*, 43. For backgrounds of GGL candidates, see *Light*, Mar. 21, 1971. The best account of the convoluted politics of West Side politics in the civil rights era is David Montejano, *Quixotes' Soldiers: A Local History of the Chicano Movement, 1966–1981* (Austin: University of Texas Press, 2010).

23. *Light*, Mar. 21, 1971.

24. For election results and commentary, see *Light*, Apr. 7, 1971.

25. Interview with Charles Becker, *Express-News*, Nov. 30, 1997.

26. Holmesly interview with Charles Becker, July 18, 1994, pp. 4–6.

27. Sidney Plotkin, "Democratic Change in the Urban Political Process: San Antonio's Edwards Aquifer Controversy," in *The Politics of San Antonio: Community, Progress, and Power*, ed. David R. Johnson, John A. Booth, and Richard J. Harris (Lincoln: University of Nebraska Press, 1983), 161.

28. Wayt T. and Roberta S. Watterson, *The Politics of New Communities: A Case Study of San Antonio Ranch* (New York: Praeger, 1975), 15.

29. Fleischmann, "Sunbelt Boosterism," 162.

30. Fleischmann, 163.

31. The developers' fury over the Water Board's new powers prompted a five-month political battle that ended temporarily in August when the council curtailed the board's powers. See *Express*, Aug. 24, 1973, *Express and News*, Aug. 26, 1973, and *News*, Aug. 30, 1973.

32. *Express*, Jan. 31, Feb. 2, 1973; and Holmesly interview with Becker, July 18, 1994, 7–8.

33. Jan Jarboe, "Who Pulls the Strings in San Antonio?" *SA Magazine* (Mar. 1977): 46.

34. On typical GGL campaign costs, see Mayor W. W. McAllister to Mayor Frank Taylor (San Marcos, Texas), Aug. 19, 1963, typed unsigned copy, Papers of Walter W. McAllister, 1961–1971, Box 1, folder 7, San Antonio Municipal Archives. On campaign debt, see *Express*, Nov. 28, 1973.

35. *News*, Apr. 4, 1973; and *Light*, May 6, 1973.

36. Holmesly interview with the Rev. Claude Black, May 26, 1994, pp. 19–20, Oral History Collection, Institute of Texan Cultures.

37. *Light*, Aug. 5, 1973; *Express*, Aug. 24, 1973; *Express and News*, Aug. 26, 1973; *News*, Aug. 30, 1973; *Light*, Sept. 16, Oct. 21, 1973; Jarboe, "Who Pulls the Strings," 48; and Tucker Gibson, "Mayoralty Politics in San Antonio, 1955–79," in *Politics of San Antonio*, ed. Johnson, Booth, and Harris, 116.

38. *Northside San Antonio Times*, Sept. 11, 1974, Aug. 23, 1984.

39. On the absence of public improvements, see Charles L. Cotrell, "Municipal Services Equalization in San Antonio, Texas: Explorations in 'Chinatown'" (San Antonio: St. Mary's University Department of Urban Studies, ca. 1975).

40. Hilton A. Córdoba, Rebecca Walter, and Nathan S. Foot, "The Residential Segregation of San Antonio, Texas in 1910: An Analysis of Ethno-Racial and Occupational Spatial Patterns with the Colocation Quotient," *Urban Geography* (Feb. 2018): 1–54; Rebecca Walter, Nathan S. Foote, Hilton A. Córdoba, and Corey A. Sparks, "Historic Roots of Modern Residential Segregation in a Southwestern Metropolis: San Antonio, Texas in 1910 and 2010," *Urban Science* 1 (2017): 1–19; and Hilton A. Córdoba and Rebecca Walter, "Measuring the Spatial Pattern of Ethnic Groups in San Antonio's Eastside: A Spatial Analysis Approach with the Colocation Quotient," *Papers in Applied Geography* (2016): 1–18.

41. *San Antonio Gazette*, Aug. 31, 1908; Audrey Granneberg, "Maury Maverick's San Antonio," *Survey Graphic* (July 1939): 422; see also Richard A. Garcia, *Rise of the Mexican American Middle Class: San Antonio, 1929–1941* (College Station: Texas A&M University Press, 1991), 24.

42. Robert G. Landolt, *The Mexican-American Workers of San Antonio, Texas* (New York: Arno Press, 1976), 69, 71.

43. The history of the African American civil rights movement in San Antonio has been neglected, with one exception: Robert A. Goldberg, "Racial Change on the Southern Periphery: The Case of San Antonio, Texas, 1960–1965," *Journal of Southern History* 49, no. 3 (Aug. 1983): 349–74. My account here relies on his work, although I differ with some of his interpretations, particularly in explaining the reasons that drove progress toward integration after 1962.

44. Goldberg, 362.

45. Goldberg, 365. Goldberg does not note the relationship of Burns's request to early work on HemisFair.

46. Mayor W. W. McAllister to John G. Goedike, June 4, 1963, Box 2, Folder 5, Papers of Walter W. McAllister, San Antonio Municipal Archives.

47. Harry L. Leffingwell to McAllister, Mar. 13, 1963, Box 1, Folder 12, and KTSA editorial broadcast, Mar. 18, 1963, Box 2, Folder 5, McAllister Papers.

48. Goldberg, "Racial Change in San Antonio," 367.

49. Goldberg, 367–68.

50. Goldberg, 369, notes the compliance rate.

51. League of Women Voters of San Antonio, Texas, "The Development of Human Resources: Evaluation of Policies and Programs in the United States to Provide for All Persons Equality of Opportunity for Education and Employment," September 1965, mimeograph copy, Albert Peña Papers, Box 2, Folder 5, UTSA Special Collections; *Light*, Oct. 29, 1965; and quote in *San Antonio Messenger*, Dec. 3, 1965, Peña Papers, Box 2, Folder 4.

52. Garcia, *Mexican American Middle Class*, 6–11; Peter Skerry, *Mexican Americans: The Ambivalent Minority* (New York: Free Press, 1993), 39; Benjamin Márquez, *Democratizing Texas Politics: Race, Identity, and Mexican American Empowerment, 1945–2002* (Austin: University of Texas Press, 2014), 13; Montejano, *Quixote's Soldiers*, 20; and Dickens, "Political Role of Mexican Americans," 83; for employment data, see Landolt, *Mexican-American Workers*, 56–57, 81–84.

53. Montejano, *Quixote's Soldiers*, 21–22.

54. "Henry B. Gonzales," *Handbook of Texas Online*, tshaonline.org; Eugene Rodriguez Jr., "Henry B. Gonzales: A Political Profile" (master's thesis, St. Mary's University, 1965), 23; and Márquez, *Democratizing Texas Politics*, 4.

55. Albert Peña Jr., "Obituary," *Express-News*, July 6, 2006; and Márquez, *Democratizing Texas Politics*, 8.

56. William S. Clayson, *Freedom Is Not Enough: The War on Poverty and the Civil Rights Movement in Texas* (Austin: University of Texas Press, 2010), 45; and Márquez, *Democratizing Texas Politics*, 39.

57. Márquez, *Democratizing Texas Politics*, 60, 67.

58. *Express*, Mar. 12, 23, Apr. 3, May 12, 1964; and *Express and News*, Feb. 1, May 10, 1964.

59. Clayson, *Freedom Is Not Enough*, 73–75.

60. "Brief History of EODC," typed manuscript, Box 5, Folder 10, McAllister Papers; James L. Turbon, "Glory Be to the Father: The History of the San Antonio Neighborhood Youth Organization" (master's project, Trinity University, 1988), 13–15; and Clayson, *Freedom Is Not Enough*, 69.

61. Quoted in Turbon, "Glory Be to the Father," 13–15.

62. Skerry, *Mexican Americans*, 35; and Montejano, *Quixote's Soldiers*, 27.

63. McAllister to Nancy Nowlin, Mar. 15, 1967, Box 2, Folder 45, McAllister Papers.

64. Albert Peña to Senator Ralph Yarborough, Jan. 3, 1966, unsigned copy, Peña Papers, Box 2, Folder 20, UTSA Special Collections.

65. Montejano, *Quixote's Soldiers*, 59.

66. Montejano, 59–60; and Clayson, *Freedom Is Not Enough*, 9, 84–85.

67. On the City Public Service Board, see Peter Torres Jr. to Leroy G. Denman, CPSB, O. W. Sommers, CPSB, and Mayor McAllister, Oct. 25, 1967, Box 4, Folder 24, McAllister

Papers; on the KAFB dispute and Gonzalez's reaction, see Gonzalezs to O. J. Valdez, EEO Chairman, LULAC Council No. 2, May 8, 1967, copy, Box 2, Folder 38, McAllister Papers.

68. For Gonzalez's involvement with Model Cities, see, for example, Gonzalez to Alfred V. Rodriguez, Administrator, City of San Antonio Model Cities Program, Sept. 18, 1968, Box 5, Folder 21, McAllister Papers; for SANYO appointments to Model Cities, see Federal Model Cities Inter-Agency Team Briefed in San Antonio, Mar. 11, 1968, News Release, Box 5, Folder 28, McAllister Papers.

69. Montejano, *Quixote's Soldiers*, 99–101, discusses the press conference in detail.

70. Montejano, 108.

71. Father William A. Killian and E. B. Duarte to Peña, Jan. 31, 1968, Box 4, Folder 13, Peña Papers; "Meeting at Los Archos Restaurant, May 13, 1969," typed minutes, Box 5, Folder 14, Peña Papers; and *News*, June 4, 1969.

72. Richter to M. C. Gonzales, Chairman, EODC of San Antonio and Bexar County, Apr. 7, 1969, Box 7, Folder 13, Peña Papers.

73. Montejano, *Quixote's Soldiers*, 115–16; handwritten notes for a meeting with Archbishop Furey, Sept. 4, 1969, in Box 5, Folder 14, Peña Papers, list requests for funding and for the church to fully commit to assist "M/A correct their own problems."

74. Clayson, *Freedom Is Not Enough*, 141.

75. Peña to Jerry Berman, Center for Community Change, May 31, 1971, and Hardberger to Ed Idar, Associate Counsel for MALDEF, Aug. 11, 1971, Box 10, Folders 1, 5, in Peña Papers.

76. Peña to the Gunter Hotel, attn. Mrg. Keystone Club, July 31, 1963, Box 1, Folder 17, Peña Papers; *Express-News*, July 6, 2006, obituary also notes Peña's friendships.

77. Mark R. Warren, *Dry Bones Rattling: Community Building to Revitalize American Democracy* (Princeton, N.J.: Princeton University Press, 2001), 30–33.

78. Joseph D. Sekul, "Communities Organized for Public Service: Citizen Power and Public Policy in San Antonio," in *Politics of San Antonio*, ed. Johnson, Booth, and Harris, 175–76; Warren, *Dry Bones Rattling*, 50–51; and Montejano, *Quixote's Soldiers*, 248–49.

79. Sekul, "Communities Organized for Public Service," 176.

80. This story is recounted in the *Express-News*, June 6, 2004.

81. Jan Jarboe, "Who Pulls the Strings," 45.

82. *Light*, Nov. 19, 1974, reported on the adoption of the budget proposal; on the protests, see Warren, *Dry Bones Rattling*, 40–41, and Sterlin Holmesly, interview with Tom Frost, Apr. 14, 1994, pp. 23–25, Oral History Collection, Institute of Texan Cultures; for chamber responses, see Minutes of the Executive Committee Meeting, Feb. 6, 27, 1975, Executive Committee Minutes, v. 51B (Jan. 1975–December 1975), San Antonio Chamber of Commerce.

83. For election results, see *Light*, Apr. 2, 16, 1975.

84. Planning and Community Development Department, SAMP 75: Alternative Growth Study, June 11, 1975, p. 9, San Antonio Municipal Archives.

85. Jarboe, "Who Pulls the Strings," 48–49.

86. Sidney Plotkin, "Democratic Change in the Urban Political Economy: San Antonio's Edwards Aquifer Controversy," in *Politics of San Antonio*, ed. Johnson, Booth, and Harris, 168–69.

87. *Express*, July 9, Sept. 3, 1976.

88. *Light*, Nov. 20, 1977; and Plotkin, "Democratic Change," 170.

CHAPTER TEN

1. Quote describing village: David R. Johnson, interview with Brig. Gen. (ret.) Robert McDermott, Mar. 2, 2001, p. 1, in author's possession.

2. Johnson, interview with McDermott, Mar. 2, 2001, pp. 4–8.

3. Johnson, interview with McDermott, Mar. 2, 2001, pp. 9–11.

4. Johnson, interview with McDermott, Mar. 2, 2001, p. 7; and John P. Lovell, *Neither Athens nor Sparta: The American Service Academies in Transition* (Bloomington: Indiana University Press, 1979), 71.

5. Johnson, interview with McDermott, Mar. 2, 2001, p. 12.

6. Johnson, interview with McDermott, Mar. 2, 2001, p. 15.

7. Johnson, interview with McDermott, Mar. 2, 2001, pp. 18–20.

8. Johnson, interview with McDermott, Mar. 2, 2001, p. 16.

9. Quoted in Lovell, *Neither Athens nor Sparta*, 74.

10. Johnson, interview with McDermott, Mar. 2, 2001, p. 14.

11. For details, see Paul T. Ringenbach, *Battling Tradition: Robert F. McDermott and Shaping the U.S. Air Force Academy* (Chicago: Imprint Publications, 2006).

12. Johnson, interview with McDermott, Mar. 2, 2001, pp. 25–27.

13. Sterlin Holmesly, interview with Robert McDermott, Dec. 5, 1994, Oral History Collection, Institute of Texan Cultures; and Paul T. Ringenbach, *USAA: A Tradition of Service, 1922–1997* (San Antonio: Donning, 1997), 225–26.

14. Sister Frances Jerome Woods, *The Model Cities Program in Perspective: The San Antonio, Texas, Experience*, Subcommittee on Housing and Community Development of the Committee on Banking, Finance and Urban Affairs, House of Representatives, 97th Congress, First Session (Washington, D.C.: Government Printing Office, 1982), p. 76.

15. Esther MacMillan, interview with Lila Cockrell, July 25, 1984, pp. 2–4, Oral History Collection, Institute of Texan Cultures.

16. MacMillan, interview with Cockrell, July 25, 1984, pp. 4–6.

17. MacMillan, interview with Cockrell, July 25, 1984, p. 38.

18. David R. Johnson, interview with Mrs. Lila Cockrell, Aug. 7, 2007, p. 9, in author's possession.

19. Sterlin Holmesly, interview with Mrs. Lila Cockrell, July 15, 1994, pp. 3–4, Oral History Collection, Institute of Texan Cultures.

20. MacMillan, interview with Cockrell, July 25, 1984, pp. 39–40.

21. Johnson, interview with Cockrell, Aug. 7, 2007, p. 12 (emphasis added).

22. Letter to the editor, *San Antonio Light* (hereafter *Light*), Aug. 16, 1966.

23. MacMillan, interview with Cockrell, July 25, 1984, p. 38.

24. Dick Balmos, "Beauty in the City: San Antonio Still Sets the Pace," *Nation's Cities* (July 1966): 26–27; *Light*, Jan. 12, May 2, 1969; and MacMillan, interview with Cockrell, p. 28.

25. Holmesly, interview with Cockrell, July 15, 1994, pp. 7–8.

26. Quoted in Woods, *Model Cities Program in Perspective*, 89.

27. For Gonzalez's praise of Cockrell, see *Light*, Nov. 2, 1973; on the Henkel fight and its consequences, see Woods, *Model Cities Program in Perspective*, 91n2; *San Antonio Express* (hereafter *Express*), May 20, 1970; *San Antonio Express and News* (hereafter *Express and News*), May 31, 1970.

28. *Express and News*, May 31, 1970.

29. Kemper Diehl and Jan Jarboe, *Cisneros: Portrait of a New American* (San Antonio: Corona, 1985), 27–31.

30. Quoted in Diehl and Jarboe, *Cisneros*, 41.

31. Henry Gabriel Cisneros, "City Government and Economic Development: A Study of Policy Formation and Administrative Implementation" (Ph.D. diss., George Washington University, 1975), x–xii; Diehl and Jarboe, *Cisneros*, vii–viii; and Holmesly interview with Cisneros, Aug. 12, 1997, pp. 4–5.

32. Cisneros, "City Government," xi–xii.

33. Cisneros, 37–38, 63–64.

34. Cisneros, 111, 116.

35. David R. Johnson, interview with Henry Cisneros, Dec. 8, 2001, p. 34, in author's possession.

36. The practical importance of booster coalitions in guiding development has been neglected in contemporary studies, which focus on the "creative" city. Cf., for example, Clarence N. Stone, *Regime Politics: Governing Atlanta, 1946–1988* (Lawrence: University Press of Kansas, 1989), and Richard Florida, *The Rise of the Creative Class and How It's Transforming Work, Leisure, Community, and Everyday Life* (New York: Basic Books, 2002).

37. Ringenbach, *USAA*, 257, 262, 320, 324; and Frederick F. Reichheld, *The Loyalty Effect: The Hidden Force behind Growth, Profits, and Lasting Value* (Boston: Bain, 1996), 284–86.

38. "McD: In His Own Words," Speech to the Board of Directors of USAA on the Occasion of His Retirement, July 22, 1993, in author's possession; *San Antonio Express-News* (hereafter *Express-News*), July 23, 1993; Ringenbach, *USAA*, 256–63; and Reichheld, *Loyalty Effect*, 29–30.

39. David R. Johnson, interview with Robert McDermott, Apr. 20, 2001, pp. 18, 19, in author's possession.

40. Sterlin Holmesly, interview with Robert McDermott, May 6, 1997, Oral History Collection, Institute of Texan Cultures, pp. 2–3.

41. David R. Johnson, interview with Robert McDermott, Mar. 9, 2001, pp. 18–20, author's collection. McDermott probably acquired his understanding of the importance of export industries to urban growth when he taught economics at West Point and the Air Force Academy. Its importance was widely accepted by economic theorists by the

1960s, although more recent studies have tended to portray exports as only one of many complicated and interrelated issues that contribute to urban growth. Cf. Wilbur Thompson, *A Preface to Urban Economics* (Baltimore: Johns Hopkins University Press, 1965), 27–33; Jane Jacobs, *The Economy of Cities* (New York: Vintage Books, 1969), 122–44; Mario Polèse, *The Wealth and Poverty of Regions* (University of Chicago Press, 2009), 29–66; and Brendan O'Flaherty, *City Economics* (Cambridge, Mass.: Harvard University Press, 2005), 517–68.

42. Johnson, interview with McDermott, Apr. 20, 2001, pp. 22–23; David R. Johnson, interview with James Dublin, Apr. 30, 1984, p. 23, in author's possession.

43. *Express and News*, June 15, 1974.

44. Minutes of the San Antonio Chamber of Commerce Board of Directors (hereafter MBD), June 25, 1974, San Antonio Chamber of Commerce archive; Statement by Robert F. McDermott, President, to the Board of Directors, June 28, 1974. The June 25 minutes are missing, but the result of that meeting is noted in MBD, July 9, 1974.

45. Robert F. McDermott, speech to the San Antonio Rotary Club, July 3, 1974, in author's possession.

46. MBD, Oct. 8, Dec. 10, 1974; and David R. Johnson, interview with Robert F. McDermott, Apr. 20, 2001, pp. 7–8.

47. By-Laws, San Antonio Economic Development Foundation, Inc., copy in author's possession. As the EDF added new members the basis fee declined to $1,500 by the 1980s.

48. Charter Members, San Antonio Economic Development Foundation, July 1974, Archives of the Economic Development Foundation at the Greater San Antonio Chamber of Commerce, copy in author's possession.

49. David R. Johnson, interview with Ralph Thomas (first director of EDF), Mar. 8, 2002, p. 24, in author's possession.

50. Johnson, interview with Thomas, Mar. 8, 2002, p. 11.

51. Fantus Company, "Economic Development Program for San Antonio, Texas," mimeographed typescript, August 1975, pp. 28–29, 50, Economic Development Foundation Archives. Wage averages from James Flanigan, "A Story of Our Times," *Forbes Magazine*, May 15, 1978, pp. 58–60.

52. Holmesly, interview with McDermott, May 6, 1997, p. 10.

53. Holmesly, interview with McDermott, May 6, 1997, pp. 9–10, 14–15.

54. *Express*, Oct. 27, 1977; Johnson, interview with Thomas, Mar. 8, 2002, pp. 15, 19–24. For McDermott's account of the meeting, see Holmesly, interview with Robert McDermott, Dec. 4, 1994, p. 10.

55. See, inter alia, *Light*, Nov. 20, Dec. 16, 1977; *Express and News*, Nov. 20, 1977; *Express*, Nov. 21 and Dec. 16, 1977, Jan. 27, 1978. See also David R. Johnson, interview with James Dublin, Apr. 30, 1984, pp. 31–38, for a thoughtful analysis of the entire confrontation.

56. Johnson, interview with Thomas, Mar. 8, 2002, pp. 25–27.

57. *Express*, Feb. 3, 10, 1978.

58. Details about the discussions have never been made public, but McDermott described his general approach to these meetings years later. See Holmesly, interview with McDermott, Dec. 5, 1994, pp. 11–13.

59. Holmesly, interview with McDermott, May 6, 1997, pp. 16–17; see also Johnson, interview with James Dublin, Apr. 30, 1984, p. 35; and Johnson, interview with Thomas, Mar. 8, 2002, p. 35.

60. *Light*, May 17, 1978; and Flannigan, "Story of Our Times," 58–60.

61. *Light*, May 31, 1978.

62. John H. Mollenkopf, *The Contested City* (Princeton, N.J.: Princeton University Press, 1983), 215–18; and Carl Abbott, *The New Urban America: Growth and Politics in Sunbelt Cities*, rev. ed. (Chapel Hill: University of North Carolina Press, 1987), 14–59.

63. *Light*, May 17, 1978.

64. Wilbur L. Matthews, *San Antonio Lawyer: Memoranda and Cases and Clients* (San Antonio: Corona, 1983), 182–85.

65. *News*, June 1, 1973; *Express*, June 1, 1973; and *Light*, June 5, 1973.

66. Matthews, *San Antonio Lawyer*, 186–87; *News*, June 18, 1974; *Express*, July 23, 1974.

67. For the progress of the lawsuit, Cockrell's role in it, and the outcome, see Matthews, *San Antonio Lawyer*, 189, 192–93; *Light*, July 20, 30, 1976, Feb. 18, June 14, 1978; *Express*, July 17, 1974; *Express and News*, Aug. 6, 1978; Holmesly, interview with Lila Cockrell, July 15, 1994, pp. 22–24, 26–30; and David R. Johnson, interview with Lila Cockrell, Aug. 25, 2006, pp. 117–18, in author's possession.

68. *Light*, July 7, 1974.

69. *Light*, Feb. 5, 1975.

70. *Light*, Mar. 8, 1975; and *Christian Science Monitor*, May 28, 1975.

71. On the initial connections to McDermott and the EDF, see *Light*, Apr. 23, 1975.

72. Although he focuses on a later period, former mayor Nelson W. Wolff makes this point in passing in *Mayor: An Inside View of San Antonio Politics, 1981–1995* (San Antonio Express-News, 1997), p. 4.

73. For a detailed description of Cockrell's techniques, see *Express and News*, June 15, 1975.

74. *Express*, Mar. 12, 26, Nov. 12, 1976.

75. Sidney Plotkin, "Democratic Change in the Urban Political Economy: San Antonio's Edwards Aquifer Controversy," in *The Politics of San Antonio: Community, Progress, and Growth*, ed. David R. Johnson, John A. Booth, and Richard J. Harris (Lincoln: University of Nebraska Press, 1983), 90–91; and Robert Brischetto, Charles L. Cotrell, and R. Michael Stevens, "Conflict and Change in the Political Culture of San Antonio," in *Politics of San Antonio*, ed. Johnson, Booth, and Harris, 91–92.

76. *Express*, Jan. 16, 23, July 9, Sept. 3, 1976.

77. *News*, Nov. 9 (for quote), 10, 1976.

78. *News*, Nov. 9, 1976.

79. David R. Johnson, interview with Henry Cisneros, Dec. 8, 2001, pp. 6–7, in author's possession.

80. See voting results in Ordinance 47842, Apr. 4, and Ordinance 47894, Apr. 18, 1977, in City of San Antonio Election Results, 1856–Present, City of San Antonio Archives; also, *Express and News*, Apr. 17, 1977.

81. Holmesley, interview with Cockrell, July 15, 1994, p. 15.

82. Holmesley, interview with Cisneros, Aug. 12, 1997, pp. 14–15.

83. On the issue of inequities, see Stone, *Regime Politics*, 205–6, which discusses the challenges of dealing with social inequities affecting minorities.

84. *Express*, Mar. 11, 25, 1977.

85. On the cultural preferences that drove suburbanization, see Tom Martinson, *American Dreamscape: The Pursuit of Happiness in Postwar Suburbia* (New York: Carroll & Graf, 2000). For Sunbelt suburban growth, see Carl Abbott, *How Cities Won the West: Four Centuries of Urban Change in Western North America* (Albuquerque: University of New Mexico Press, 2008), 219–36.

86. Robert Bruegmann, *Sprawl: A Compact History* (University of Chicago Press, 2005), is an important study of suburbanization's critics; see also Michael F. Logan, *Fighting Sprawl and City Hall: Resistance to Urban Growth in the Southwest* (Tucson: University of Arizona Press, 1995).

87. *Express*, June 17, July 5, 1977.

88. On this continuing battle, see *Express*, June 10, Sept. 9, Nov. 11, 1977, Mar. 30, Dec. 22, 1978, Jan. 12, 1979; and *Express and News*, Dec. 30, 1978.

89. See for example, *Express*, Jan. 14, 1977; *Express and News*, Jan. 23, 1977; and Heywood T. Sanders, "Communities Organized for Public Service and Neighborhood Revitalization in San Antonio," in *Public Policy and Community: Activism and Government in Texas*, ed. Robert H. Wilson (Austin: University of Texas Press, 1997), 41–50.

90. Holmesly, interview with Cockrell, July 15, 1994, p. 16.

91. Quoted in Sanders, "Communities Organized," p. 52.

92. Johnson, interview with Cockrell, June 22, 2001, pp. 20–21.

93. The council voted on Jan. 27 to call the bond election; the vote on the block grant funds occurred on Feb. 10. See *Express*, Jan. 27, Feb. 10, 1978.

94. *Express and News*, Feb. 26, 1978.

95. *Express and News*, Feb. 26, 1978.

96. Ordinance 49120, Mar. 4, 1978, San Antonio Municipal Archives.

97. Johnson, interview with Cockrell, Aug. 25, 2006, p. 9.

98. *Express*, Apr. 28, 1978.

99. *Express*, Apr. 28, 1978

100. On Wing's role on the council, see Sanders, "Communities Organized," 52–56.

101. On details of the plan, see *Express*, Mar. 30, 1978; for rejection of business concerns about the plan, see *Express*, Jan. 12, 26, 1979.

102. *Express*, June 8, July 20, Oct. 19, 1979.

103. Holmesly, interview with Cockrell, July 15, 1994, p. 17.

104. Mollenkopf, *Contested City*, 190–201, but see Stone, *Regime Politics*, 189, 206–7, 211, for a contrasting opinion. On Cockrell's achievement, see Rick Casey, "Lila exists at the height of power," *Express and News*, Apr. 5, 1981.

105. Sterlin Holmesly, interview with Jim Dublin, July 13, 1995, Oral History Collection, Institute of Texan Cultures, pp. 27–28.

106. Holmesly, interview with McDermott, May 6, 1997, pp. 18, 20, 31–32, 35; *Express*, Jan. 3, 1980; *Express and News*, Jan. 6, 1980; and Johnson, interview with Cockrell, Aug. 25, 2006, p. 21.

107. This new coalition makes an interesting case study for creativity as a major asset for successful cities. Richard Florida, *Rise of the Creative Class*, argues for the importance of an entire class of creative people as essential to economic development. But a small group of creative leaders may be a necessary precondition for establishing the environment that attracts such a class. Small groups are more likely to possess "the creative ethos" that Florida says "is built on discipline and focus, sweat and blood" (p. 33). Cf. Mancur Olson, *The Logic of Collective Action* (Cambridge, Mass.: Harvard University Press, 1977), 52–53, on the effectiveness of "relatively small groups" in making decisions.

108. Wolff, *Mayor*, 19.

109. *Express and News*, Apr. 17, 1982; *Light*, Jan. 25, 1984; *Express*, July 4, 1984; and Diehl and Jarboe, *Cisneros*, 1, 3, 12.

110. I am indebted to Jim Dublin, one of most astute members of the booster coalition, for the observation about the power of expectations. On Cisneros's access to boardrooms, see Holmesly, interview with Dublin, July 13, 1995, p. 34.

111. Calculated from Planning Commission, City of San Antonio, *San Antonio*, p. 14 (table 9: "Employment Trends by Major Industry").

112. For jobs and population data, see Planning Commission, City of San Antonio, *San Antonio: Report on Development and Planning Activities, 1980–1990* (City of San Antonio Planning Commission and Department of Planning, June 1991), pp. 13, 24 (table 14); for migration of minorities to the North Side, see the following articles by Richard C. Jones: "The Segregation of Ancestry Groups in San Antonio," *Social Science Journal* 40 (2003): 217–18; "Cultural Diversity in a Bi-Cultural City: Factors in the Location of Ancestry Groups in San Antonio," *Journal of Cultural Geography* (spring/summer 2006): 52; "The Ambiguous Roles of Suburbanization and Immigration in Ethnic Segregation: The Case of San Antonio," *Urban Geography* 29, no. 3: 204–5, 208.

113. *Express*, Feb. 20, 1981.

114. Payne Maxie Consultants and Blayney-Dyett, Urban and Regional Planners, *The Land Use and Urban Development Impacts of Beltways: Case Studies* (Washington, D.C.: Government Printing Office, 1980), S-17, S-23.

115. Dennis R. Judd and Susan S. Fainstein, eds., *The Tourism City* (New Haven, Conn.: Yale University Press, 199), 1–2, 4, 6–7.

116. "Tourism Industry Getting Help from Chamber," *San Antonian* (Apr. 8, 1975): 5; *Christian Science Monitor*, Oct. 1, 1980 (sixteen-page pullout, p. B6); and Dennis R. Judd, "Constructing the Tourist Bubble," in *Tourism City*, ed. Judd and Feinstein, p. 41, table I.

117. Johnson, interview with McDermott, Mar. 9, 2001, pp. 19–20; and Cisneros, "City Government," 37–38.

118. Henry G. Cisneros, "San Antonio's Place in the Technology Economy: A Review of Opportunities and a Blueprint for Action," pp. 1–2, in Papers of Mayor Henry G. Cisneros

(hereafter Cisneros Papers), Box 44, folder: San Antonio's Place in the Technology Economy, Municipal Archives of the City of San Antonio.

119. *News*, Feb. 14, 1980, reported an interview with McDermott about his experiences in Colorado Springs and his opinion that UTSA needed to have engineering programs.

120. "United San Antonio," unpublished manuscript, Box 1: History, 1984, Target 90/ Goals for San Antonio Collection, Special Collections, University of Texas at San Antonio; *Express*, June 24, 1981; *Express and News*, Oct. 31, 1981; *Light*, Sept. 8, Oct. 30, 1981; *Express*, Sept. 14, 1981; *News*, Oct. 14, 1981; Holmesly, interview with McDermott, May 6, 1997, pp. 8–9; Johnson, interview with Cisneros, Dec. 8, 2001, p. 26; and David R. Johnson, "UTSA@50" (unpublished manuscript, Special Collections, University of Texas at San Antonio), pp. 38–39.

121. Undated meeting notes (internal evidence indicates fall 1983), in Cisneros Papers, Box 35, folder: Coordinating Council for Economic Development.

122. Robert F. McDermott to Admiral Bobby Inman, Mar. 1, 1983, Box 35, Cisneros Papers; Expanded Outline of Remarks by Mayor, Mar. 18, 1983, Box 35, folder: Electronics, Cisneros Papers; and Holmesly, interview with Dublin, July 13, 1995, pp. 34–35.

123. On Cooke, see *Light*, Feb. 27, Mar. 13, 1983; on Dublin, see Johnson, interview with Dublin, Apr. 30, 1984, p. 48. *Light*, Oct. 23, 1983, discusses the forum.

124. Report to the Board of Trustees on a Study of a Research Park Concept for the Enhancement of San Antonio's Bio-Tech Economy, Dec. 31, 1983, p. 21, Box 3: Austin Corridor, 1983, in Target 90/Goals for San Antonio Collection, Special Collections, University of Texas at San Antonio.

125. Report to the Board of Trustees on a Study for a Research Park, Dec. 31, 1983, p. 15; Johnson, interview with Dublin, Apr. 30, 1984; *Light*, Mar. 11, 1984. On developers' projects on the far West Side, see *Express*, May 24, July 20, 26, 1984, May 31, 1985; *Express and News*, July 29, 1984, Mar. 24, 1985; and *Light*, Dec. 9, 1984.

126. Report to the Board of Trustees on a Study for a Research Park, p. 14.

127. See *Express-News*, July 19, 1985, for the history of the struggle over securing land for the park, although the only source I have located that discusses Wender's effort is the Texas Research and Technology Foundation, Texas Research Park Chronology, p. 2, in the uncatalogued papers of the TRP that I examined in the late 1980s. Copy in author's possession.

128. On the long search for a solution to the land problem, see *Express-News*, July 19, 1985; *Light*, Oct. 6, 1985, Mar. 12, 20, 1986; and Holmesly, interview with McDermott, May 6, 1997, p. 32 (tape 1); on McDermott's search for donations, see *Express-News*, Mar. 11, 12, 1987; *Light*, Mar. 15, 1989; Holmesly, interview with McDermott, May 6, 1997, pp. 3–5 (tape 2); and Holmesly, interview with Jim Dublin, July 9, 1995, p. 7 (tape 2).

129. *Light*, Feb. 2, 1986.

130. *Express-News*, Dec. 4, 1984; Sterlin Holmesly, interview with John Howe, Aug. 18, 1995, pp. 1, 2, 24, Oral History Collection, Institute of Texan Cultures; and Holmesly, interview with McDermott, May 6, 1997, p. 29.

131. Goodwin Steinberg with Susan Wolfe, *From the Ground Up: Building Silicon Valley* (Palo Alto, Calif.: Stanford University Press, 2002), 10–12; on UTHSC faculty interested in working with industry, see *Light*, Mar. 11, 1984.

132. *Light*, Feb. 9, Oct. 1, 1986; *Express-News*, Nov. 3, 1987, Mar. 4, Dec. 16, 1988; Mar. 26, Apr. 1, 7, 1989, Feb. 7, 1990.

133. Patterns in EDF recruiting are from an analysis of "Firms Located in San Antonio by the San Antonio Economic Development Foundation, 1975–2001," released by the EDF in June 2001. Copy in author's possession. This list underrepresents the number of companies that relocated because it does not include firms that either failed or left San Antonio. For instance, an earlier EDF list, "Progress Report, 1975–1980," has twenty companies, eight of which are not on the 2001 list. Considering the "wastage" implied by that discrepancy, the EDF actually had a problem with retaining companies over the long haul, but "lost" firms would have had some short-term effect on the economy that is impossible to calculate in the absence of any thorough analysis of the EDF's record.

134. See Catherine Nixon Cooke, *Powering a City: How Energy and Big Dreams Transformed San Antonio* (San Antonio: Trinity University Press, 2017) for an important study of San Antonio's energy diversification campaign.

135. *Light*, June 13, 1986.

136. *Express*, Dec. 7, 1979; and Diehl and Jarboe, *Cisneros*, 66.

137. *Express*, Sept. 14, 1983, discussed this committee's formation.

138. *Express and News*, May 31, 1981; and *Express*, June 19, 1981.

139. Robert McDermott to Beatrice Cortez, Nov. 13 and Dec. 18, 1981; COPS Meeting Minutes, Feb. 22, 1982; Robert McDermott, Statement before the City Council, Mar. 18, 1982, in Box 4: COPS, Target 90/Goals for San Antonio, Special Collections, University of Texas at San Antonio; Minutes, Executive Committee Meeting, Dec. 15, 1981, in Box 4: COPS, 1981–1982, Economic Development Foundation Archives, Greater San Antonio Chamber of Commerce.

140. Robert F. McDermott and Robert V. West Jr. to Beatrice Cortez, July 30, 1982, Box 4: COPS, 1981–1982, Economic Development Foundation Archives.

141. *Express*, Sept. 14, 1983; and *Express and News*, May 12, 1984.

142. A Possible Approach to Help Achieve Target '90 Goals, Mar. 17, 1983, typed memo, in Target '90/Goals for San Antonio, in Box 8, folder: Steering Committee, 1983–1984, Target '90 Collection; Wolff, *Mayor*, 25–26 argues for a different origin for Target '90 that does not take into account the context of USA's problems with COPS and neighborhoods that I find more compelling.

143. Minutes of Meeting of Target '90 Steering Committee, July 27, 1983, Box 4, folder: Steering Committee, Target '90 Papers; Table of Contents, *Target '90: Goals for San Antonio to Build a Greater City* (San Antonio: N.p., 1984), 6–7.

144. Wolff, *Mayor*, 28.

145. Minutes of Meeting of Target '90 Commission Steering Committee, Mar. 21, June 22, 1984.

146. Holmesly, interview with Cisneros, Aug. 12, 1997, p. 22; and Wolff, *Mayor*, 36.

147. Sanders, "Communities Organized," 58–59; Wolff, *Mayor*, 34–35, 88–91, 109–12. For the difficulties of the negotiations, see Holmesly, interview with Cisneros, Aug. 12, 1997, pp. 41–42.

148. *Light*, Aug. 7, 1986.

149. *Light*, July 22, 1986; for expressions of HTA ideas about government, taxation, and growth, see letters to the editor in *Light*, July 27, Aug. 4, 1986.

150. Holmesly, interview with Cisneros, Aug. 12, 1997, p. 26; and Wolff, *Mayor*, 38–42.

151. *Express*, Oct. 4, 1982; *Express and News*, Jan. 1, 1984; *Express-News*, Oct. 13, 1984; Jan. 10, 15, May 17, 1985; Dec. 15, 1986; and *Light*, Nov. 18, 1981; Jan. 29, 1986.

152. Ringenbach, *USAA*, 410–11; *Light*, Feb. 14, 1986; *Express-News*, Feb. 17, 1986; and Wolff, *Mayor*, 67.

153. *Express*, May 5, 19, 1983; and *Express-News*, May 14, 18, 25, 1985.

154. Peter Skerry, *Mexican Americans: The Ambivalent Minority* (New York: Free Press, 1993), p. 154.

155. *Express and News*, Dec. 25, 1983.

156. Wolff, *Mayor*, 65.

157. On the relationship between McDermott and Cisneros, see Johnson, interview with Cisneros, Dec. 8, 2001, pp. 3, 5, 8–9, 16–18.

158. *Light*, Apr. 12, 1987; Holmesley, interview with McDermott, May 6, 1997, pp. 8–11; Johnson, interview with Cisneros, Dec. 8, 2001, pp. 27–30, 33–34; and Johnson, "UTSA@50," 62–65.

159. *Express-News*, June 15, Oct. 13, 1989, Mar. 15, 1992; and Holmesly, interview with McDermott, May 6, 1997, tape 2, pp. 19–25.

160. *Express-News*, June 18, July 2, Aug. 25, 1987; Jan. 13, 29, Feb. 11, 16, 19, May 3, July 6, 21, Aug. 12, Sept. 4, 8, 22, Nov. 29, 30, Dec. 8, 19, 22, 29, 1988; Jan. 22, 1989; and Wolff, *Mayor*, 79–92.

161. Wolff, *Mayor*, 99–100.

162. Wolff, 84–85.

163. *Express-News*, Sept. 13, 1988.

164. Wolff, *Mayor*, 119–23, 144–49.

AFTERWORD

1. On the evolution of UTSA, see David R. Johnson, "UTSA@50," unpublished manuscript, Special Collections, University of Texas at San Antonio.

2. Calculated from Firms Located in San Antonio Assisted by the San Antonio Economic Development Foundation, June 2001. EDF Archives, Greater Chamber of Commerce of San Antonio.

3. Bob Marbut, Coordinating Chairman, Target '90 Commission, to Mayor Henry Cisneros, July 2, 1984, in *Target '90: Goals for San Antonio to Build a Greater City* (San Antonio: Van Steenburg Enterprises, 1984), 3.

4. Nelson W. Wolff, *Mayor: An Inside View of San Antonio Politics, 1981–1995* (San Antonio: San Antonio Express-News, 1997), 42.

5. Wolff, 152–54.

6. Nelson W. Wolff, *Transforming San Antonio: An Insider's View of the AT&T Center, Toyota, the PGA Village, and the River Walk Extension* (San Antonio: Trinity University Press, 2008), 4.

7. Wolff, *Mayor*, 326–39.

8. Wolff, *Transforming San Antonio*, 4–5, 9–49.

9. *San Antonio Express-News* (hereafter *Express-News*), Feb. 9, 10, 13, 15, 16, July 9, 2003.

10. *Express-News*, Feb. 2, 2006, June 29, Oct. 17, Nov. 9, 2017.

11. *Express-News*, June 29, 2017.

12. On artists, gentrification, and economic development, see Sharon Zukin, *The Culture of Cities* (Malden, Mass.: Blackwell, 1995), 109–86; Loretta Lees, Tom Slater, and Elvin Wyly, *Gentrification* (New York: Routledge, 2008), 118–20, 256–62; on Veltman and Blue Star, see Lewis F. Fisher, *River Walk: The Epic Story of San Antonio's River* (San Antonio: Maverick Publishing, 2007), p. 164n34; Johnson, "UTSA@50," 58–59.

13. Wolff, *Transforming San Antonio*, 146–47.

ACKNOWLEDGMENTS AND CREDITS

I have accumulated many debts to various people while working on San Antonio's history. John Booth, my colleague in political science in our early days at the University of Texas at San Antonio, shared my interest in the city, an interest that resulted in a coedited book that was an initial attempt to understand the city's development. Later I found allies in Heywood Sanders and Char Miller at Trinity University. Our mutual interests led to many hours of productive discussions and exploratory articles on various topics that greatly improved my own understanding of San Antonio. I was also enormously fortunate to discover a "civilian" enthusiast for San Antonio in Jim Dublin, who was, and is, intimately involved in the booster coalition that redirected the city's development. His own insightful observations about that coalition, and his willingness to grant me access to various records and to introduce me to Gen. Robert McDermott, gave me invaluable assistance in understanding the coalition's work and importance.

Bob Baron, professor of architecture at UTSA, and Rich Diem, dean of the UTSA Honors College, provided a different sort of inspiration by inviting me to participate in their study abroad program in Italy for many years. Having to learn enough to lecture semi-rationally about Italian city states afforded me the opportunity to study urban economic development from a different perspective that enriched my understanding of American urban history.

Ian Caine, director of the UTSA Center for Urban and Regional Planning Research, and Rebecca Walter, now an associate professor in the University of Washington's department of real estate, generously shared their work on San Antonio's urban sprawl and racial segregation. Ivan Ventura, research assistant at the Center for Urban and Regional Planning Research, worked at their direction to produce the map of modern San Antonio that appears in this book.

I would also like to thank the outside reviewers for their careful reading of the manuscript. They saved me from many factual errors and provided very useful critiques of my analysis of San Antonio's development. Marguerite Avery, senior acquisitions editor for Trinity University Press, patiently and effectively dealt with my many questions about the publishing process, and copyeditor Emily Jerman Schuster prevented many gaffes from seeing the light of day. Tom Shelton, who oversees an extraordinary photographic collection at UTSA's Special Collections Department, applied his amazing expertise to locating the photographs for this book. Carlos Castro, also in UTSA Special Collections Department, helped ease the process for acquiring those photographs.

And finally, but not least, I would like to thank my wife, Peggy, whose love has sustained me for more than four decades. Without her support this book would not have been possible.

IMAGE CREDITS

page 103, Dolph Briscoe Center for American History, University of Texas at Austin.

page 104, Gentlitz, Jore & Giraud, 1952 plat map, San Antonio Public Library Special Collections. Photo by Stephen Sumrall-Orsak.

page 105, Main Plaza, northwest corner, 1868. Photo by Ernst Raba. Image ITC 081-0518, UTSA Special Collections. Used with permission.

page 106, San Fernando Cathedral, Main Plaza, 1866. Photo by Ernst Raba. Image ITC L-0010-A, UTSA Special Collections. Used with permission.

page 107, ITC 2355-G, UTSA Special Collections. W. H. Parish Publishing Co. Used with permission.

page 108, Z-2126-K-4, UTSA Special Collections. Used with permission.

page 228, *Pecan Shellers of San Antonio*, U.S. Government Printing Office, 1940.

page 229, LC-USF34-032514-D, Library of Congress Prints and Photographs Division, Farm Security Administration/Office of War Information Black-and-White Negatives.

page 230, LC-USF34-032481-D, Library of Congress Prints and Photographs Division, Farm Security Administration/Office of War Information Black-and-White Negatives.

page 231, ITC-L-2322-C, San Antonio Express-News Collection. UTSA Special Collections. Used by permission of San Antonio Express-News/Zuma Press.

page 232, ITC-82-546, UTSA Special Collections. Used with permission.

page 233, ITC-82-548, UTSA Special Collections. Used with permission.

page 319, Rullman & Stappenbeck, 1890. Library of Congress Geography and Maps Division.

page 320, Map 06253. Courtesy of Texas State Library and Archives Commission.

page 321, UTSA E-0008-117-04, San Antonio Express-News Collection. UTSA Special Collections. Used with permission.

page 322, Author's collection.

page 323, Copyright © William Luther/San Antonio Express-News/Zuma Press. Used with permission.

page 324, Used by permission of Red Wing Aerial.

INDEX

DAVID R. JOHNSON is a professor emeritus of history at the University of Texas at San Antonio, where he taught for thirty-seven years, during twelve of which he served in various administrative positions, including as executive vice provost for academic affairs. His honors include the President's Distinguished Achievement Award for Teaching Excellence and the President's Distinguished Achievement Award for Service. His previous books on urban issues include *Policing the Urban Underworld*; *American Law Enforcement: A History*; *Illegal Tender: Counterfeiting and the Secret Service, 1863–1899*; and *The Politics of San Antonio: Community, Progress, and Power*, coedited with John Booth and Richard Harris. Johnson now resides in Durham, North Carolina.

www.ingramcontent.com/pod-product-compliance
Lightning Source LLC
LaVergne TN
LVHW100400050926
847404LV00017B/62/J
* 9 7 8 1 5 9 5 3 4 9 2 2 4 *